Thomas Ciardiello
#100523768
Univ. of Miami
Spring 1986
Dr. Dunham
Sociology Dept.

INTERPRETING DEVIANCE

INTERPRETING DEVIANCE

A Sociological Introduction

EDWIN M. SCHUR

New York University

HARPER & ROW, Publishers

New York   Hagerstown   Philadelphia   San Francisco   London

Sponsoring Editor: *Dale Tharp*
Project Editor: *Karla Billups Philip*
Production Supervisor: *Jeanie Berke*
Compositor: *Maryland Linotype Composition Co., Inc.*
Printer and Binder: *Halliday Lithograph Corporation*
Art Studio: *Allyn-Mason, Incorporated*

INTERPRETING DEVIANCE: *A Sociological Introduction*

Library of Congress Cataloging in Publication Data

Schur, Edwin M
   Interpreting deviance.
   Includes bibliographical references and indexes.
   1. Deviant behavior. 2. Social control. I. Title.
HM291.S368   301.6′2   79–15342
ISBN 0–06–045811–9

To my parents,
Samuel John Schur
and Johanna Bernhardt Schur

CONTENTS

VII

PREFACE

This textbook offers a systematic and comprehensive framework for sociologically interpreting deviance. Hopefully, many readers will agree that it is more than "just another text." There is no dearth of books marketed for use in deviance courses, but *Interpreting Deviance* is rather different from the usual fare. It provides both a systematic assessment of the field and a general interpretive scheme. It attempts a synthesis, not just a presentation of summaries; it stresses the development of key insights and multiple perspectives for studying deviance, rather than immersing the student in encyclopedic and typically narrow detail. A strong effort is made not to "talk down" to the student, but instead to describe and interpret major outlooks, concepts, and controversies (including some that are rather complex) in a lucid manner—and with many illustrative examples.

Of the other textbooks on deviance, there are, to my knowledge, none that combine a coherent theoretical outlook with the broad range of flexible classroom materials included in this text. Many existing texts are essentially "readers," usually with some accompanying interpretative commentary by the editors. Others lean toward the "succession of problems" format—describing in a series of chapters the "literature" on various "types" of deviance. While such an approach has its merits, it rarely leaves room for a full and adequate consideration of the most important issues and the most meaningful generalizations concerning deviance (although such books usually do make some attempts to provide a general discussion of this kind). In *Interpreting Deviance,* instead of having little blocks of the book devoted to specific problem areas (e.g., suicide, drug addiction, homosexuality, etc.), continuous references to such areas are used throughout to illustrate major theoretical points. This has the advantage of permitting a full and systematic elaboration of the general interpretive scheme, and it enables us to fully appreciate the central features that all deviance situations share. It may also help us to avoid the implication that the commonly discussed substantive behaviors somehow constitute the fixed, inevitable, or appropriate deviance categories. As the reader will see, virtually any behavior or condition is potentially susceptible, under certain circumstances, to being treated as "deviant." Since this is true, it is the common underlying defining-and-reacting process found in, and cutting across, all such situations—rather than the specifics of any one—that is most interesting and important sociologically.

The materials in this book can be used in a variety of ways, allowing instructors to vary the relative emphasis to be given its component parts. In addition to the comprehensive text, the book includes "Adaptations" integrated with the textual material in such a way as to underline and illustrate major ideas. "Projects" following the various chapters are designed to help make the key

XIII

themes and problems dealt with in the text "come alive" for the student. "News Spots," based on recent news accounts, illustrate the public and topical aspects of deviance issues. The "Review of Key Terms" briefly defines major concepts introduced in the chapters. A "Summary Overview of Five Major Orientations" summarizes the discussion in the first part of the book and provides a consolidated listing for review of major purposes, themes, shortcomings or problems, and lasting contributions of the most important "standard" deviance theories. A "Paradigm for Studying Deviance Situations," which organizes major focal points and research questions, serves dual functions as an overall review device for the student and a comprehensive guide for the deviance researcher. These materials not only allow considerable flexibility regarding specific classroom use, they also are quite easily adaptable for courses taught at different levels. Although this book is intended primarily as a basic undergraduate text, I have found (over the years and at several institutions) that the general formulations and specific content included here can work well in courses ranging up to and including the first graduate course on deviance.

Since this volume pulls together ideas and materials I have been developing over a long period, it simply is not possible to list all the colleagues and students whose ideas, comments, and critiques are no doubt reflected in it. At one time or another, the following persons have been particularly helpful in providing encouragement, reactions, and critical appraisals regarding my work on deviance. Howard S. Becker, Jack Gibbs, Walter Gove, David Greenberg, Edwin Lemert, Alfred Lindesmith, David Matza, Sheldon Messinger, and Alan Orenstein. In the present instance, I am especially grateful to Laud Humphreys, John Kitsuse, and Milton Mankoff for their careful reading of, and useful comments on, an earlier draft of this manuscript; however, responsibility for the content of this work is, of course, mine alone.

EDWIN M. SCHUR

INTERPRETING DEVIANCE

PART
1

PERSPECTIVES
ON
DEVIANCE

_____

PROLOGUE 1

What we must vigorously oppose is the view that one may be "scientifically" content with the conventional self-evidentness of very widely accepted value-judgements. The specific function of science, it seems to me, is just the opposite: namely, to ask questions about these things which convention makes self-evident.
    —Max Weber, *The Methodology of the Social Sciences*

Social research of any kind is advanced by ideas; it is only disciplined by fact.
    —C. Wright Mills, *The Sociological Imagination*

. . . it is important to keep in mind that the objectivity of the institutional world, however massive it may appear to the individual, is a humanly produced, constructed objectivity.
    —Peter Berger and Thomas Luckmann, *The Social Construction of Reality*

Interpreting deviance is an important task for the sociologist. As this book will emphasize, processes of defining and reacting to deviance are central to the workings of the social order. Each and every one of us needs to be able to make sense of these processes as we encounter them and "participate" in them continuously in our daily lives. We have to figure out how we should react to behavior that we or others define as problematic, how we should evaluate such reactions on the part of other people, and how we should govern our own lives in spheres where moral consensus is incomplete.

Social scientists cannot do all of this for us. They can provide us with much specific information that will influence our decisions. More important still, they can help us to develop interpretive skills and outlooks that will enable us to approach these situations with insight and good sense. Yet, in the last analysis, we must ourselves take some responsibility for the ways in which our social world develops. Although sociology teaches us how much we are influenced and constrained by social structures and forces, it also makes clear that we are, at the same time, in a way "producing" those structures and forces through our ongoing social interaction. In that sense, we are "interpreting deviance," even producing

3

it, all the time, whether or not we realize that we are doing so. If that is true, we would do well to become more fully aware of that process and to try to bring it under our conscious control.

This book offers the reader a range of ideas and perspectives that should be helpful in that regard. It seeks to develop a general way of thinking about deviance situations based on findings from careful research and concepts that have facilitated perceptive analysis. The approach adopted here recognizes and, hopefully, will help the student come to grips with the fact that in analyzing deviance we confront topics of both professional and public concern, areas in which the often tenuous relationship between "fact" and "value" comes to the fore. Most people feel strongly about deviance issues. As we will see, the field of deviance analysis has generated much recent excitement and professional controversy within the discipline of sociology. It is replete with social complexities and moral, as well as scientific, dilemmas.

INTRODUCTION: STUDYING DEVIANCE

AN ORIENTATION TO THE FIELD

The Elusive Meaning of Deviance

In trying to maintain a social life that is both stable and satisfying, human beings face many obstacles. Although we are sometimes unable or unwilling to admit it, the existence among individuals and groups of diverse needs, values, and interests necessarily implies that a conflict-free, smooth-running, and automatically self-regulating society is an impossibility. At least in complex, heterogeneous societies, and probably in all societies, collective life—much like individual life—is uncertain, fragile, and constantly undergoing change.

We know that a considerable amount of regularity and ongoing satisfaction of human and social needs is achieved, for if this were not the case, groups and societies could not exist at all. Basic elements of social organization, such as statuses and roles (that is, positions in the social structure and the rights and duties attached to them) and norms and sanctions (approved ways of behaving and rewards for same, or punishments for "violations") help to provide enough predictability and patterning that we can get on with the business of day-to-day living. Sometimes, however, laypersons and even sociologists may be inclined to assume the existence of more stability and consensus than actually emerge. Recent developments in the field of deviance analysis challenge such assumptions, whether held by the general public or by social science professionals.

As we will see, sociologists themselves are not in complete agreement regarding the scientific use of the term *deviance,* or the exact nature and scope of the subfield of sociology that is concerned with it. Further complicating this situation are the undoubted existence of various conceptions of deviance held by the general public and uncertainty as to the actual or desirable relation between the two realms. One of the greatest difficulties facing sociologists in this field has been the development of meaningful, workable, and widely acceptable definitions. As will become evident, this effort to scientifically define deviance highlights a number of perplexing theoretical and methodological dilemmas. These dilemmas will be concerning us throughout much of this book. In the present introductory overview, however, it should suffice to indicate more generally the nature of the field of deviance analysis, to suggest some of the major issues and trends in this area, and to convey a sense of the orientation and emphases of the present text.

What, then, is deviance all about? Perhaps one of the best ways to begin exploring this question is to think of the term primarily as a device for describing a common type of social situation. *Deviance situations,* in turn, are best seen as continuously evolving *outcomes.* They are the results of complex *interaction processes* through which particular *social meanings* come to be attached to categories of behavior or to individuals. We do not need to look very far in order to find examples of these situations. They are present in all human societies and groups, including those with which we are personally familiar. Ordinarily, they are built up around the following kind of individual or group *reaction.* Some people find other people or specific types of behavior offensive, threatening, troublesome, contemptible, disgusting, distasteful, or, on whatever ground, just plain unacceptable. When this happens, there are characteristic ways of reacting to the perceived "offenders." These frequently include efforts to punish them, to "treat" or "correct" them, to segregate or isolate them, to ridicule them, to avoid interacting with them, to deny them various social or legal opportunities, and overall to reduce their social standing in if not completely banish them from the community of "respectables."

The degree to which such efforts produce an outcome that the reactors find satisfactory will vary considerably, depending on various features of the specific situation. Foremost among those features is the **relative social power** of the reactors and the offenders. (See discussion in Thio, 1978, ch. 4.) But with any substantial degree of "success," this kind of reaction process results in a category of "outsiders" (see Becker, 1963), of individuals whose behavior and character have been disvalued (Sagarin, 1975). When this occurs, specific individuals placed in such a category will typically feel degraded and **stigmatized.** (Frequently, they will experience a sense of **depersonalization** to the extent that others treat them not as individuals, but simply as "instances" of the category.) These feelings, along with the limitations placed on their "legitimate" opportunities and contacts, may increasingly isolate and alienate them from, or even force them to actively oppose, the world of the respectables. Hence, the definition of them as offensive may gradually become self-fulfilling. Under pressure, they may more and more see themselves as, and act like, offenders.

Some Basic Propositions
Let us now begin to move beyond this rather abstract depiction of the nature of deviance situations. Taking it as a point of departure, we should be

in a position to formulate some basic propositions that can guide our analysis of deviance, and, in the process of doing this, we can also start to fill in the picture substantively by citing a few concrete examples. Among the most important points we can cull out of the discussion so far may be the following:

1. **Any kind of behavior or person potentially can provide the basis for a deviance situation.** There is a common tendency, even within sociology, to associate the concept of deviance with certain "standard" categories of behavior—crime and delinquency, drug addiction, homosexuality, and so on. Yet the only absolute prerequisite for the existence of deviance is that some (any) category of acts or people elicit appropriately negative reactions on the part of other persons who are prepared to try to "do something about it." Much of the material in Chapter 2 focuses on the relative nature of deviance. With respect to many if not most stigmatized categories of acts or individuals, we find important variations through time and from place to place. Even for our own society at the present time, we can see that any analysis of deviance-producing reaction processes must, at the outset, consider the issue of *who is reacting to whom or what*. Among nudists, it is the clothed person who is the outsider. In nonreligious social circles, it may be the devout believer who is seen as deviant. Persons who consider themselves sexually liberated may ridicule those (more commonly defined as conformists) who are committed to a conventionally heterosexual and monogamous marriage.

Now, there is little doubt that the behavior of nudists, atheists, and the sexually free tends to receive less *general* support in current American society than that of the clothed, the religious, and the sexually conventional. (Strong support for the former categories is likely to be found primarily in highly circumscribed situational contexts, such as the nudist camp.) This likelihood of low general support can, however, be interpreted in at least two ways. One interpretation focuses on "generally accepted" values and norms and asserts that such behaviors violate these values and norms. Because of this, and for no more complicated reason, they are deviant. The other interpretation attributes low support to inadequate social power. If atheists held more social power than did believers, then most likely (according to this view) the latter would be the deviants. Furthermore, as those adopting this outlook often insist, we can't really know which are the accepted values until we examine outcomes, that is, until we see which values gain a demonstrable ascendancy. Such outcomes reflect *real* or *operative values and norms* which tend to have more sociological importance than do values and norms that are merely stated.

Many of the uncertainties and disagreements surrounding deviance analysis center around the relation between these two kinds of interpretation. Just now the approach that emphasizes power differentials seems to hold a favored position among sociologists. At any rate, a growing recognition that there exist many diverse and competing judgments as to what is deviant and that, potentially, there is an almost unlimited number of them has forced a reappraisal of traditional sociological outlooks in this field. Above all, it has caused many sociologists to conclude that interaction processes and definitional aspects are the most sociologically significant features of deviance situations.

2. Deviance is a social construction or production. We create it by interacting and structuring our society in ways that give certain definitions of behavior socially sanctioned support. Sociologists of deviance increasingly emphasize *the distinction between the occurrence of behavior, on the one hand, and the characterization of behavior or of individuals, on the other.* Consider the example of one person hitting another. It may, of course, be of interest to know what "caused" the person to do the hitting. This type of explanation has been central in traditional approaches to analyzing deviance. But clearly such "causes" do not represent the whole story because they do not really tell us *what is made of the act socially.* Depending on the circumstances or, sometimes, on which of several alternative definitions prevails, the same sort of hitting might be seen as an athletic activity (as in a boxing match), a friendly scuffle, an assault, or an act of self-defense. To cite another kind of example, diabetics who are physiologically in need of insulin are just as fully "addicted" as heroin addicts. Yet we do not usually think of such persons, or react to them, as "insulin addicts." Whether a situation involves legitimate drug use or drug "abuse" cannot be fully explained in pharmacological or physiological terms or by studying the individual users. In many respects, it is the way the use of the chemicals is defined and reacted to that counts most. Types of behavior, specific individuals, and *patterns of meaning* are interwoven elements of deviance situations.

3. The sociologically significant feature common to all deviance situations is a particular quality of assigned meanings: deviantness. This quality of deviantness may incorporate in varying degrees a good many different substantive elements or components. We may attach deviantness to behaviors or individuals by seeing and treating them as being, among other things, wrongful, offensive, shameful, degraded, contemptible, decadent, or sometimes pitiable. Such meanings often provide a foundation for personal stigma and social, even legal, oppression. The attribution of deviantness cuts across the enormous substantive variability of deviance situations. The defining and reacting process through which this attribution occurs is always present regardless of the particular type of behavior involved and whatever individual causes may have precipitated specific instances of that behavior.

Unfortunately the connotations of traditional terminology make it difficult to adequately convey the importance of *process* and *meaning* in these situations. The terms *deviant* and, to a lesser extent, *deviance* seem inextricably linked to an emphasis on types of behavior and types of individuals. The term *deviantness* may help us to correct what has been a selective inattention to the meaning aspect. Although slightly awkward, a term such as **deviantizing**—the process through which deviantness is attached to behavior and individuals—might similarly help to bring out the processual side of the picture. Deviantness and deviantizing, and their consequences, are major concepts guiding the analysis in this book. A strong effort will be made to use the term *deviance* as little as possible; but sometimes it becomes very difficult to come up with adequate and readable substitutes. Where it is used, it should be read in the light of these comments about deviance situations, deviantness, and deviantizing. Above all, it should not be taken to imply in any way the intrinsic deviance of any kind of behavior or person.

4. **This focus on an underlying defining and reacting process implies a broad substantive and analytic scope for the field of deviance studies.** Clearly, how one conceives of deviance in the first place will help determine the substantive scope of the field. If we were to adopt the view that the deviantness or nondeviantness of particular kinds of behavior were intrinsic, or obvious, then presumably the parameters of the field would be neatly marked out for us. As we will see below, this is what some traditional perspectives have tended to imply; sociologists of deviance should study the behaviors "we all know" are deviant. On the other hand, if any and every behavior can potentially be treated as deviant, then it follows that types of behavior by themselves do not indicate the scope of deviance analysis. Any situations in which behaviors or individuals are defined and reacted to in deviantizing ways fall within the field.

As subsequent discussion will indicate more fully, changes in sociological thinking about deviance have been accompanied by an expansion in the scope of the field. Basically, this expansion has been along two lines: a widening of the range of substantive behaviors and conditions included within deviance analysis; and increased attention to various levels of social interaction at which deviance situations are seen to exist. As we have just seen, the first type of expansion follows directly from the recent focus on a common defining and reacting process. This focus has begun to lead deviance analysts well beyond the "standard categories" alluded to earlier. One major example of this has involved recognizing important similarities between situations involving "wrongdoing" and situations involving physical or mental disability. Typically, the person with such a disability is not—at least, openly—held blameworthy. Without doubt, this matter of blameworthiness and imputation of personal responsibility provides an important ground for distinguishing between the two types of situations. At the same time, however, very similar defining and reacting processes may be at work, often with highly similar consequences, in terms of personal and collective stigmatization. Blind persons, the mentally retarded, cripples, and dwarfs typically experience interpersonal rejection and social exclusion very much like that which affects more "intentional" deviators. Although the reactions of others are not exactly the same in the two instances, the basic process through which a category of outsiders is recognized is common to both. We must be very clear, though, as to just what this recent awareness of similarities does, and does not, imply. To include situations involving disabilities within the field of deviance analysis is most emphatically not to suggest that these conditions are "really" deviant and that sociologists are only just now beginning to realize this. (Indeed, as we have seen, recent approaches deny that any behavior is really deviant.) Rather, the point is no more and no less than to highlight the common element of stigmatizing definition and reaction. Often the same concepts and theories become relevant to, and similar findings emerge from, research and analysis in the two areas. In the chapters to come, we will be noting many studies that indicate more specifically these elements of similarity.

It may also be useful to carry this analogy still further by suggesting similarities between these several kinds of deviantizing and the stigmatization of members of acknowledged minority groups. Racial and ethnic minority-group members and, in our society, women and the aged (to cite just some of the major examples) share certain kinds of major life experiences with those persons more commonly viewed as deviant. Furthermore, as will be clear below, their organized efforts to change the ways they are defined and treated are beginning to serve as models for comparable efforts on the part of various categories of perceived deviators. It is true that those campaigning for such change invariably deny the legitimacy or validity of the stigmatizing labels and policies in question. At the same time, however, information circulated through such campaigns has forced other people in our society to recognize the existence of much systematic prejudice and discrimination. So the existence, as opposed to the legitimacy, of stigma and oppression has not been and should not be denied. The sociological study of past and present social definitions and reactions in no way implies any approval of them. Indeed, such studies, which can include consideration of alternative definitions and reactions, will often expose unjust treatment and provide evidence and arguments that will support the efforts to induce social change.

This discussion of minorities brings to mind a conception of deviance we have not considered as yet—one that may have a deceptive appeal. Some sociologists would define deviance as any behavior or condition that in a given group or society is numerically infrequent. In other words, they would focus on deviation from the statistical "norm." At first glance, such an approach seems to have the merit of taking into account the relative nature of deviance. It also seems to scrupulously avoid making moral judgments. Yet our discussion of similarities in minority and deviance situations should suggest the inadequacy of this conception. In both kinds of situations, it is not numerical frequency but rather the special quality of meanings imposed on acts and individuals that compels the sociologist's interest. A minority group or social category is not simply, or even necessarily, a group that is in the (numerical) minority. For example, we know of situations both in various African countries and in parts of the United States in which blacks have been a numerical majority yet nonetheless have been accorded, by more powerful whites, minority status. Similarly, women comprise a majority of our country's population, yet it is increasingly being recognized that their social subordination has placed them, sociologically, in a minority position. In other words, it is the process by which persons in such categories are collectively defined and reacted to that is the hallmark of minority status. (Various students of minorities have referred to *categorical discrimination* as their distinguishing feature.) Of course, the term *minority group* is often held to imply *unjust* treatment, whereas many people are inclined to feel that those they perceive as deviants get what they deserve. For this reason, persons commonly reacted to as deviators may, as we will see, sometimes organize collectively in an effort to gain public acceptance for themselves as a minority. Such acceptance can heighten public awareness both of systematic discrimination and of its unjust character.

In addition to these substantive aspects of the expansion of deviance analysis, there has also been widening of the field in terms of the *levels* of social interaction and organization with which it is concerned. As our discussion so far suggests, many deviance situations involve collectivities—social categories (of similarly situated individuals) if not actual social groups (persons displaying shared patterns and meanings who are also in direct interaction with one another). However, a focus on the basic deviantizing process implies ways of defining and reacting that may be found in small-scale, face-to-face interaction situations as well. Thus, we can at least conceive of a two-person situation in which one actor treats or tries to treat the other in deviantizing ways. As in more large-scale deviance situations—though perhaps even more clearly at this level of interpersonal interaction—it may be a moot point whether these reactions reflect pre-existing rules, which have been violated, or whether the reactions themselves in effect "create" the rules; that is, the reactions are all we have to go by in inferring what the rules really are.

At any rate, it may be useful as a complement to the subject-matter expansion of deviance studies to have in mind also a level of analysis that focuses on what we might call *interactional deviance*. When one person reacts directly to another in ways that embarrass, shame, scorn, or ridicule—or avoids contact, withholds favors, or imposes other "sanctions" because of perceived slights, hurts, or other offenses—this, too, may be interpreted as deviantness. The recent interest in *interpretive microsociology*—the intensive study of defining and interacting processes in small-scale situations of direct interpersonal contact (see, for example, Goffman, 1959; Scott and Lyman, 1968; Emerson and Messinger, 1977)—increasingly directs the attention of sociologists to such matters.

Of course, we must keep in mind that often there is no hard and fast line between the interpersonal and broader levels or domains in deviance analysis. In particular, it should be evident that what may be a large-scale and public-issue type of deviance situation (e.g., the heroin problem, white collar crime, or widespread cheating by college students) is at the same time, for the specific individuals involved, a matter of specific and crucial patterns of direct interaction. Individual drug addicts are concerned with how they personally are defined and reacted to by particular individuals. Corporate executives are preoccupied with their own situations. Students want to know what will happen to them. Characteristically though, the relation between the two domains runs in both directions. The publicly recognized situation or problem reflects innumerable small-scale interactions. At the same time, of course, the nature of such direct interactions is significantly shaped by broad social definitions and responses, which sometimes include formal public policies.

5. Deviantness is a matter of degree, not an all-or-nothing, present-or-absent "entity." In particular, there is no such thing as "a deviant." Many of the pitfalls of traditional deviance studies can be attributed to the sociologist's desire to be methodical—to classify and categorize, to count and compare. For certain research purposes such operations are highly desirable, even necessary. But as our discussion so far has begun to suggest, the defining and reacting processes in deviance situations do not readily lend themselves to complete quantification or clear-cut categorization. Neither the types of behavior involved nor the individuals can be neatly classified as falling into either of two mutually exclusive categories—the deviant and the nondeviant. Conventional researchers often have considered such a dichotomy essential to "causal" explanation. They have been preoccupied with isolating the deviants for purposes of research and analysis and comparing them with the supposed nondeviants. Obviously, it would be very convenient if we could do this; it is not, however, in any meaningful sense really possible. This kind of either-or thinking simply does not do justice to the complexities of deviance situations.

With respect to behavior that is sometimes imbued with deviantness, both the types of behavior and the specific instances elude this sort of neat classification. To consider just one example, how would we specify (for analytic purposes) whether adultery is deviant or nondeviant? What would we make of the fact that even within a given legal jurisdiction adultery might be proscribed by statute and subject to punishment, yet at the same time engaged in frequently and with apparently widespread social acceptance? Which of these aspects would we emphasize in seeking to classify the behavior as deviant or nondeviant? And how would we take account of the relative degrees of approval or disapproval attached to different kinds of behavior, even within one group and at a particular time? Does it make sense, for example, to classify, say, intentional murder and adultery as deviance (for comparison with nondeviance) when usually the former is so much more severely disapproved and more strongly reacted to than the latter?

Specific instances of adultery complicate our understanding of the category even more. The term *adultery* has special legal meanings in addition to its uses in common parlance. In a strictly legalistic sense, an instance of adultery cannot be said to have occurred until someone has been formally convicted of having violated a relevant (in our system, state or federal) statutory provision.

Even leaving aside this legal aspect, specific occurrences that might be called adulterous vary a great deal as to the social, let alone legal, characterizations that are in fact applied to them. We find the same kind of potential for variability here that we encountered in considering the example of one person hitting another. Within some social circles, adulterous behavior might conceivably be so common that it would be unlikely to elicit special negative reaction on anyone's part. Within more conventional circles, what is made socially of such acts will tend to vary considerably from case to case. In some instances, the adulterous partners may go undetected; in other instances, their behavior may come to the attention of other people, perhaps including concerned spouses, and this may happen by a variety of means and in a host of different kinds of circumstances. Once an incident is disclosed, a range of possible social and/or legal responses is likely to be available to the aggrieved or offended parties. What *they* decide to do will crucially affect the social consequences and social meaning of the act itself (Emerson and Messinger, 1977).

In the light of all this, we have to recognize that not all adulteries are equally deviant. (This is, of course, a sociological observation, not a moral one. We might well choose to view all the incidents as equally reprehensible; yet there is no getting around the sociological importance of the different ways in which they are *treated*.) On the contrary, it is more realistic and meaningful to think in terms of the degree of deviantness attached to the behaviors and individuals in particular situations. To think in terms of supposedly clear-cut categories of adultery and adulterers makes little sense for purposes of *social* analysis. Two adulterers, assuming agreement on how to define the act itself, may fall into the same *behavioral* category, but this does not enable us to take account of the actual ways in which their behavior is interpreted and the actual responses it elicits. Clearly, a greater degree of deviantness is likely to be attached to the detected adulterer than to the undetected one. (Could they report to us, adulterers discovered and killed by irate spouses would certainly state an appreciation of such distinctions!) But, again, the distinction is not an either-or one. There are indeed dominant public conceptions in our society imbuing the very idea of adultery with some deviantness. Many undetected adulterers will be affected to some degree by their knowledge of these general characterizations and of *potential* direct reactions to their own behavior.

The notion of degrees of deviantness applies with even greater force to specific individuals than to types of behavior. What does it mean to say that there is no such thing as a deviant? This extreme-sounding statement is but another reflection of the growing sociological disenchantment with the glib categorizing of individuals in the supposed interest of producing causal explanations of behavior. As we have seen, tracking down the factors that may have led individuals to engage in offending acts provides, at best, only a partial understanding of deviance situations. If we could get around the methodological difficulties involved in locating these individuals (a problem we will consider in more detail in the chapters to follow), we might be in a position to answer certain interesting research questions (e.g., how many acts of adultery occurred in place X during the Y–Z time period; what were the characteristics of the people engaging in those acts?). In other words, the focus on offending individuals could be useful in answering questions about the **occurrence of** specific **behaviors.** However, it would not greatly facilitate our understanding of the **characterization of the behaviors**—the assignment of meaning through social definition and reaction. It would tell us something about the act, but little about the deviantness as such.

For limited analytic purposes and with adequate control over methodological problems, we might conceivably find it useful to categorize certain individuals as adulterers, although even that usage seems to imply that they are nothing but adulterers—that they are locked into the category full time and for all time. But categorizing them more broadly as deviants—a step that would make sense only if our analysis were moving beyond adultery to seek generalizations about various deviance situations—would require our incorporating the deviantness element. Once we see that, we are again compelled to reject an either-or classification. The only sense in which the term *deviant* could have real sociological meaning would be as a way of referring to persons to whom deviantness has been attached. Yet even limited to this usage, deviantness can not be converted into an all-or-nothing attribute. As we are going to see, some students of deviance believe that once a person has been negatively defined and reacted to strongly "enough," he or she can hardly help but become deviant. There is considerable evidence to support this idea, and indeed some similar views are incorporated in the analysis developed in this book. However to fully appreciate the processual aspect of deviance situations we need to avoid the all-or-nothing trap. Without doubt there are crucial turning points in individual lives—some of which may well represent "points of no return." Some of these are largely self-generated (e.g., a homosexual "coming out of the closet," that is, openly revealing his or her sexual preference). Others are substantially imposed from without (e.g., a person being prosecuted and convicted of a serious criminal offense).

But deviance-defining processes and their impacts—the amounts of deviantness in particular situations—are fluid, changeable, unpredictable, and variably affected by a host of contingencies. Recently sociologists have emphasized that one crucial aspect of deviantizing is the treatment of the offending persons as though they were "nothing but" deviators. Although it is extremely difficult for people subjected to this "nothing but" treatment to fend it off, at the same time the sociologist recognizes that such persons in fact are much more than that for which they are rejected or condemned. The rejectors' perceptions and negative actions seek to deny the person a full humanness in all its complexity. While wanting to analyze the existence and considerable force of those perceptions and reactions, the sociologist does not want to enshrine them, even for research purposes. Avoiding the term *deviant* and thinking instead of degrees of deviantness that affect the life situations of particular individuals or categories of individuals helps us to tread the shaky line between analyzing and "accepting" deviantizing reactions. The degrees of deviantness approach enables us to study, yet not legitimate, elements of stigma. It also takes account of the fact that not even those who take on disapproved statuses and roles more or less "intentionally" (e.g., as a business) do *only* that with and in their lives. Thus the "professional thief" is not *just* a professional thief; he may also be a good family man, a contributor to local charities, a pursuer in his spare time of conventional and mild-manner recreations (see Sutherland, 1937, ch. 7). In short, since there is no meaningful way of drawing a hard and fast line between a deviant and a nondeviant that will do justice to varying and changeable involvements and commitments (and treatments by others), we are much better off avoiding that effort entirely.

6. **Deviance situations arise out of and reflect ongoing processes of social conflict and social change. Frequently, they involve running struggles over alternative characterizations of particular types of behavior.** It was suggested earlier that differential social power is a major factor shaping deviance outcomes. If that is so, and few sociologists today would deny it, then it follows that deviance analysis must centrally concern itself with the matter of social conflict. Efforts by various groups and individuals to achieve their particular goals, which may include symbolic and psychological goals as well as economic and political ones, comprise a major ingredient in any society's overall deviance picture. While shared values, education, and persuasion produce, even in complex societies, a certain amount of agreement on some deviance issues, more typically there is an uneasy accommodation of divergent and competing interests and outlooks. As a consequence, deviance situations are never static. The "outcomes" of previous processes that we may choose to study at any one point in time are actually only phases of a continuous stream of social change lifted out for purposes of analysis.

In subsequent chapters, we will encounter considerable evidence that this is so. For the moment, let us note just two examples from our own society— the long-term shift that has occurred with respect to the deviantness of being a divorced woman (it is not that long ago, after all, when divorcees were harshly stigmatized) and, to illustrate more short-term changes, the frequent fluctuations during the past decade in legal policies and rulings regarding abortion. Whether such temporal changes take the form of consistent long-run trends, sharp reversals and counterreversals, or an apparent cyclical sequence, it is important to realize that they do not just occur spontaneously or in some mysterious and unspecifiable way. Rather, there are at work empirically observable, describable, and analyzable sequences of events. In large part, these events reflect or consist of attempts people make to gain favored positions for their preferred "definition" of the situation (whatever the specific behavior or condition in question might be) or, to put it more bluntly, people's efforts to impose their rules on other people.

Typically, these are not one-sided efforts—notwithstanding the fact that one side may seem to win out, at least temporarily. On the contrary, there usually are competing forces, groups, and pressures involved. There is nothing reprehensible in people hoping that their favored definitions of these situations will prevail and doing everything they can to see that this happens. However, it would be a serious mistake for the sociologist to ignore these conflicting forces and to view the outcomes as some kind of static reflection of the society's values. Attitudes and policies toward marihuana use do not just pop up out of nowhere. They reflect active and organized efforts of promarihuana and antimarihuana groups, as well as more disinterested educational efforts by those concerned merely to disseminate what they believe to be accurate information on the topic. Sometimes cross-pressures of this sort remain hidden beneath the surface of events. At other times, as the brief discussion of minority groups suggested, deviance situations may become more openly **politicized**. (A good example would be the recent efforts of the gay liberation movement to advance the acceptability and legal rights of homosexuals.) More and more, sociologists are coming to realize that an important part of deviance analysis involves studying these conflicting forces that determine which definitions of deviantness take on the greatest social force. Sometimes a key individual exerts special influence in such a situation; at other times, organizations aiming to promote one or another policy may be active. Focus on these conflict processes sensitizes the observer to the frequently transitory nature of public judgments of deviantness. Behavior that some would define as offensive, others may see as a forerunner of desirable change. Not infrequently the latter type of forecast (by those who see themselves as being in some vanguard) may be vindicated by events, at least for a while. Today's perceived deviance may, then, become tomorrows' accepted pattern.

7. **Deviance interpretation must proceed on several different levels** (focusing on collective forces at the level of societies, on individuals, and on *people-processing organizations*). It must, furthermore, examine both sides of the deviance coin. We need to understand why certain behaviors and individuals are not imbued with deviantness, as well as why certain others are. No single unit of analysis will suffice if we want to develop a comprehensive understanding of deviance situations. Some early approaches to deviance focused exclusively on the motivation of deviating actors, without considering the social definitions of, and reactions to, their behavior. We now know that this narrow focus, while useful in a limited way, has definite shortcomings. But we are beginning to see that even the relevant definitions and reactions exist or occur on several levels. A brief suggestion of these levels of definition and reaction will be found in Table 3.1 on p. 161. The "Paradigm for Studying Deviance Situations" presented in the Appendix provides a more systematic outline of key focal points and questions to be used in studying deviance. (The reader may want to consult this Paradigm briefly now, in order to get an idea of the components of a really com-

prehensive look at deviance phenomena.) Our discussion to this point has provided some hints of this social and, hence, analytic complexity. We will be following up these hints and exploring many specific examples in the rest of this text.

Some of the questions we need to ask are the traditional ones—those that concern the initial determinants and social patterning of deviating acts. Others deal with the impact on the perceived deviator of a variety of social definitions and reactions. How does it feel to be stigmatized? When and how does it affect one's behavior or one's self-conceptions? What can one do to ward off or shed imputations of deviantness? Yet another level of analysis investigates collective aspects of deviance situations. How do collective conceptions regarding deviantness arise in the first place? How and why do they vary from place to place? How do they get translated into specific reactions and policies? Somewhere in between this very broad kind of (macrosociological) analysis and the more intensive small-scale (microsociological) focus on the social-psychological situation of the individual lies an important area of organizational analysis. In particular, we need to examine the role and impact of the so-called "social control" organizations that are set up to "deal with" perceived deviators. Increasingly sociologists of deviance are studying the impact of these people-processing organizations, the product of which is the "treated," "corrected," or otherwise "processed" deviator. As we shall see, this is part of a broader reevaluation of the relation between deviance and control. Some analysts are now emphasizing the *reciprocal* relation between the two. Control efforts have commonly been thought of as a response to offending behavior; yet, at times, such efforts may, inadvertently, promote or reinforce the deviation. Furthermore, the organization's processing activities often may reflect its own "needs" even more than those of its clients. At an extreme, social control organizations may develop strong vested economic interests in particular programs or policies; that is, their very existence may depend on perpetuating them. Thus, organizational analysis has become an increasingly important component of the field of deviance studies. The police, mental hospitals, rehabilitation agencies, criminal courts, juvenile treatment programs, and other kinds of control organizations are now commonly scrutinized for their diverse "contributions" to deviance situations.

A point that will be emphasized throughout this text, then, is that the field of deviance analysis does not revolve around a single, all-inclusive research question. There are many important questions we should be asking and trying to answer. There is, as the Paradigm highlights, a variety of different, albeit related, patterns and tendencies we should be trying to explain. Sociologists are not entirely clear as to whether there can be one all-encompassing theory, in the formal sense of a system of interrelated and testable propositions, that will incorporate these several dimensions of analysis and understanding. But whether or not we conclude that that is desirable or possible (we will be considering some claims and counterclaims about this later), one point does seem conclusive: To develop a full picture of what we are studying, a narrow focus on only one of these dimensions will prove inadequate.

The phenomenon of relative nondeviantness is another kind of dimension that we cannot afford to overlook. To ask how and why some behaviors come to be treated as deviant is at the same time to ask how and why others do not. Conformity-defining is the other side of the deviance-defining coin. Indeed, as we will see, some students of these matters argue, in effect, that we would not really know what constitutes conformity if we did not identify and react to deviation. By the same token, processes of conflict over deviance definitions have "winners" as well as "losers." From this standpoint, a *conformist* might be defined as a person who has managed to avoid being defined as a deviant. All too often, it is only the perceived deviator we feel we must "explain." Yet there may be important instances where analyzing the absence of deviantness reactions will tell us a great deal about the relevant social forces and processes. A major example would be the treatment in our society of white-collar crime (see Adaptation Two, p. 145) and other potential "offenses" of high-status persons—behavior widely viewed as improper, yet only occasionally reacted to with any real severity.

COMPLEXITY OF THE SUBJECT MATTER

The field of deviance studies is one of the most perplexing and, at the same time, one of the most exciting subfields within the discipline of sociology. To a large extent, both of these characteristics reflect the complex and controversial nature of the topics and issues the analyst must confront. Of course any study of human beings is bound to be complicated; we know that, in general, the lines marking off the social or behavioral sciences one from another can never be hard and fast ones. Few, if any, of the specific topics one might explore in the course of studying deviance-defining could be neatly and fully encapsulated within the bounds of any one discipline. Because we are biological, psychological, political, and moral beings—as well as social actors—it follows that perceived human and social "problems" are going to be viewed from multiple perspectives and analyzed by diverse specialists. Thus, a social psychiatrist, Martin Hoffman, has described homosexuality as "a problem the understanding of which requires a consideration of knowledge in all the disciplines concerned with human experience" (Hoffman, 1969, p. 3). Many of the deviance issues that recently have received wide public attention—drug use, governmental and corporate fraud, abortion, juvenile delinquency, alcoholism, cheating in schools and colleges, various types of violent crime—similarly call forth multidisciplinary and, sometimes, when the various practitioners can get together, interdisciplinary attention.

There is no simple way to combine or transcend all of these specialized approaches, and in this text no attempt is made to do so. The orientation adopted here is an avowedly sociological one. The aim is to show how sociological perspectives help us to understand deviance situations. Since such situations are inherently social in nature, no "general" understanding of them, that is, of what they have in common, would ever be possible if sociological outlooks were ignored. At the same time, it must be acknowledged that social analysis alone will not always tell us everything we always wanted to know about a specific behavior pattern or perceived problem. Although this text emphasizes sociological concepts and methods, it will be clear as we proceed that our very conception of sociological inquiry must be a broad and flexible one. In considering the stigmatizing and identity problems of the perceived offender, we will find that sociological and psychological aspects are inevitably intertwined. At yet a later point in the book, when we examine collective definition (societywide deviance-defining), we will see that historical and comparative perspectives become extremely important and, therefore, cannot be ignored by the sociologist. In these areas of cross-disciplinary concern it should not matter greatly to us which kind of specialist undertakes a particular study. What is much more important is that intelligent and cogent questions be asked and that efforts to answer them be pursued systematically and interpreted with insight.

Sociological analysis in the deviance field does not, then, supplant the work of other disciplines. Often it may actually point up important ways in which such work contributes to a comprehensive understanding of a specific topic or issue. At other times, it may enable us to integrate the concepts and findings used in other disciplines in new and illuminating ways. For example, in many places throughout this book we will be citing and evaluating the theoretical groundings and varied uses of psychiatric diagnosis. Placing such ideas and practices within a sociological framework allows us to explore meanings and, particularly, consequences that may not have been appreciated or intended by either the diagnosers or the diagnosed. More generally, this kind of cross-disciplinary insight enhancement may be found in connection with three broad areas of complexity that suffuse the field of deviance analysis—those involving medical, legal, and moral dimensions of deviance.

Medical Conceptions

Sociologists of deviance have had to take medical conceptions into account for a number of reasons. To begin with, there are influential strands of general sociological theory according to which illness itself constitutes a kind of deviance (see Parsons, 1951, pp. 428–447; also Freidson, 1971, pp. 205–301). The sick person departs from, and cannot meet, group expectations regarding ordinary behavior. As a consequence, there arises what Parsons has described as the "sick role." Sick people are relieved of certain responsibilities they might otherwise face—a circumstance that may even lead some individuals to want to "play" this role. At the same time, however, and precisely because of this perceived incapacity, the sick person's overall identity—as seen by others and also as incorporated in his or her self-conceptions—is likely to undergo change. Sick people are, to some extent at least, not often accorded the status of fully competent human beings. Clearly, there are similarities between this kind of situation and the defining-reacting processes involving deviantness that we considered earlier in this chapter.

However, if we place a special focus on the "negative" aspects of deviantizing—personal stigma, collective social discrimination, and so on—as we are going to be doing throughout this book, then most "ordinary" physical illness seems to involve relatively low degrees of deviantness. For that reason, we will not be as much concerned with such illnesses as with "mental" illness and physical "disabilities"—categories in connection with which one often finds strong social reactions and heavily stigmatizing identity transformations. In Chapter 4 when we consider the relation between deviance-defining and personal responsibility, we will return to the general question of illness as deviance. That discussion will highlight, once again, the importance of avoiding either-or thinking. Particular types of illness and disability are not neatly categorizable as being deviant or nondeviant. Rather the reactions they elicit produce or incorporate different degrees of deviantness for a variety of reasons and vary according to certain key circumstances.

The relevance of medical outlooks for deviance analysis has gone well beyond this question of illness as deviance. To a considerable extent, the recent focus on definitions of and reactions to deviance (on the social characterization of behavior) reflects a rejection of a "medical model" that characterized much earlier sociological work in this field. As we will see, analyses that were concerned only with "explaining" the behavior of offending individuals frequently tended to see such behavior merely as a symptom of some "pathology" that was to be located figuratively, if not literally, in the offenders themselves. Or, in more sociological versions of this model, the pathology was seen as social rather than personal. Conceptions of the possible "normality" of deviance, of the relativistic and socially constructed nature of deviantness—that deviance is a matter of definition—were not yet very influential. Current deviance theorists are little disposed to seeing the deviator's behavior as being determined by underlying pathology and are much more likely to emphasize the crucial role in deviance situations of social definition and reaction.

Paradoxically, accompanying this turn within sociology away from medical-type perspectives may be increased public willingness to view various perceived social problems in medical terms. In a recent exposé of glib diagnoses of "hyperactivity" in troublesome children and of "other means of child control," Peter Schrag and Diane Divoky allege the "dramatic growth of an ideology which sees almost all nonconfirmity as sickness" (Schrag and Divoky, 1976, p. 12). At various points throughout this text, we will be exploring the extent to which a "rehabilitative ideal," as some social and legal analysts have termed it, has influenced deviance-defining and deviance-processing in our society. Whether

Schrag and Divoky are correct in spotting a strong recent trend in that direction could only be determined by systematic research comparing attitudes and policies during different time periods. They do provide extensive documentation of a medical or, they would in effect argue, pseudomedical emphasis in recent approaches to the perceived problems of children (see also Schrag, 1978). In other areas such as abortion, marihuana use, and homosexuality, the recent political activity aimed at lessening restrictive legal policies (to which we will return in some detail) represents a trend in a slightly different direction—with decreased, rather than increased, emphasis on "sickness" elements.

Whichever trend may be the stronger at the present time, there is no doubt that medical analogies and extensions of the treatment reaction hold a strong appeal in modern American society. This appeal probably reflects conceptions of both laypersons and practitioners in the "helping" professions. (And, as we have just noted, it has at times influenced sociological thinking as well.) In a sense, the medical analogy is a modernized version of the oversimplified "good guys, bad guys" outlook so strongly emphasized in American popular culture. It enables us to maintain a belief in the basic "differentness" of deviators, while at the same time adopting what appears to be a less moralistic, more sympathetic stance. The treatment response to perceived problems fits well with the characteristic pragmatic optimism of Americans—our tendency to assume we can readily produce a pat solution to any difficulty.

Recent veneration of scientific expertise only serves to reinforce and strengthen this tendency with respect to deviantizing. In particular, the very high prestige of the medical profession, including the psychiatric and related specialties, encourages the belief in medical solutions. As a good deal of material presented below indicates, the extreme vagueness regarding the parameters of the category mental illness permits, perhaps even promotes, an enormous amount of diagnostic "flexibility." Often, the result is an overly casual disposition to diagnose individuals engaged in virtually any sort of troublesome, offending, or disturbing behavior—whether it be truancy, sexual "promiscuity," or right or left-wing political "extremism." Several important interpretations emphasize that the medical profession in general (see Freidson, 1971), and psychiatrists more specifically (Szasz, 1970), in effect, if unintentionally, derive benefit from the extension of medical interpretations and diagnoses. This is not to argue that such extensions represent some kind of conscious conspiracy on the part of doctors—a view toward which Szasz seems to lean. Rather, the main point is simply that medical prestige and medical livelihoods, both promote, and rest on, wide application of sickness labels.

In most instances, what the critic sees as overdiagnosis the psychiatric specialist sincerely believes, on the basis of theory, training, and clinical experience, to be enlightened and potentially curative medical practice. As we will see, sociologists emphasize the methodological limitations of making broad diagnostic-type generalizations about categories of behavior or classes of individuals on the basis of clinical "evidence" alone, that is, observations only of "patients"—who, by definition, are either disturbed or in trouble of some sort. Systematic research also suggests that rehabilitation schemes and programs, again, viewed from an overall standpoint and not simply in terms of individual cases, have not met with great success. The achievements simply do not justify the optimism underlying the efforts, and, in fact, as a consequence, that optimism is beginning to wane. Finally, recent deviance analysis has pointed up the ways in which well-intended and supposedly "therapeutic" treatment efforts can actually at times damage the individuals they are meant to benefit by stigmatizing them, lowering their self-esteem, restricting their future opportunities, and so on. A central theme of the analytic approach emphasized in this book and of the societal reaction or "labeling" perspective it incorporates and extends is that individuals may, in varying degrees, get "locked into" such diagnoses or other deviance designations. Identification of the "disorder" may trigger and almost exclusively determine the reactions of others, even the self-conceptions and behavior of the patient. And these consequences may prove highly resistant to change.

As we are going to see, the extension of rehabilitation-oriented thinking, and the occurrence of these kinds of unintended consequences, are found well beyond the domain of formal psychiatric diagnosis. For example, social-work professionals and specialists in various "correctional" fields often adopt very similar outlooks. Policy and practice for dealing with a wide variety of types of behavior reflect these views. Ironically, these ostensibly benevolent approaches frequently were first developed (as, for example, in the juvenile court movement discussed below) with an eye toward minimizing stigma and other damaging effects of official intervention in the lives of "troubled" individuals. Current sociological perspectives tend to suggest that such intervention often has unintended negative consequences, notwithstanding benevolent goals and benign terminology.

Legal Aspects

The relation between the social and legal aspects of deviance-defining is another significant feature of the field. As we have seen, the assignment or attachment of deviantness is a matter of degree. Likewise, the sanctions that these responses incorporate vary both as to severity and degree of formality. They can range all the way from personal ostracism to capital punishment. The existence of criminal law and a criminal justice system underlines the fact that deviance-defining very significantly involves societal-level processes and structures. It also suggests both the high degree of organizational elaboration that may develop around deviantizing reactions and the considerable severity that they may at times embody.

A good deal of the research and theorizing that has contributed to the development of modern deviance analysis has been concerned with statutorily defined crime and juvenile "delinquency." Necessarily, then, many of the studies and interpretations cited in this book deal with such matters. However, for our purposes in this text, we will be examining such materials primarily because of their contribution to our understanding of the more inclusive domain of deviance. We will be most interested in the elements of underlying process and likely consequence that criminal definitions and reactions display in common with other kinds of deviantizing. In one recent textbook (Sagarin, 1975, pp. 24–32), the author presents a lengthy discussion of the relation between deviance and crime—including a list of logically possible relations between the terms, several pages of illustrative diagrams, and a table purporting to show examples of specific types of behavior that fall into the two categories. From the standpoint adopted here, such an elaborate effort is unnecessary. Indeed, it may be misleading, to the extent it implies that certain behaviors are deviant (intrinsically? inevitably?) whereas others are criminal.

It is more realistic and meaningful simply to view the process of defining and reacting to crime as one version of the more general process of creating and dealing with deviance. Of course, it is a particularly severe version that has some distinctive determinants and characteristics. In an earlier work (Schur, 1965, pp. 5–7) the term *criminalization of deviance* was used to emphasize the heightened consequences of legislating against behaviors that otherwise might merely incur social disapproval and this usage may have inadvertently contributed to the idea of a sharp dichotomy. Certainly, it does matter a great deal to perceived offenders what form reactions to their behavior take and how punitive the reactions are. Likewise, there are "reasons" why in a given society some kinds of behaviors are "criminalized," others incur lesser degrees or other types of disapproving reaction, and still others, none of these reactions. Such variations are an important part of what we must study in analyzing deviance, but they remain variations on a basic underlying defining and reacting pattern. It is this pattern with which the field is centrally concerned.

When we view the relation between crime and deviance in this light, then it becomes apparent that most, if not all, of the basic propositions presented earlier in this chapter are relevant to the uses of law in the deviantizing process. We know that the substance of offending behavior does not, by itself, determine whether a law shall exist concerning it. Crime-defining, like deviance-defining in general, varies over time and from place to place. The one feature common to all criminal offenses is the characterization of the particular behaviors as criminal. This is what law professors have in mind when they sometimes tell beginning law students that, "The main cause of crime is law." (In the same sense that, after all, "the main cause of divorce is marriage.") Despite its apparent specificity, law too, then, must be seen as a kind of social construction or production. By virtue of some of its features—written legislation, trials attempting to determine whether particular statutory definitions or other legal rules "apply" to sets of facts (therein determined to exist), the crucial roles of the judge and jury, and so on—it is a special kind of social construction. We might, as the adultery example mentioned earlier may imply, speak of a "legal construction of reality." Both in its general formulations and in its uses in specific instances, law represents a distinctive version of or an overlay on the definitional and interaction processes through which social outcomes generally are produced.

Because the outcome of a criminal trial seems so definitive and, in the case of conviction, clearly does place the defendant in a new "category" or status, the notion that deviantness is a matter of degree might in this circumstance seem questionable. But as already mentioned, there are all kinds of gradations in criminal law rulings just as there are in other modes of defining deviance and attaching deviantness to specific individuals. Legally defined crimes vary greatly in the severity of the general reactions they incur, and within any one offense category there tends to be considerable variation among the "outcomes" of particular cases. However, even more noteworthy for our purposes, and illustrating again the need to avoid either-or categorization, is the fact that the general category criminal is a sociolegal construction. Strictly speaking, we can only describe an individual as a criminal if he or she has been determined to be such through the appropriate legal (defining-reacting) process. In our eagerness to view every perceived deviator as a basically different "type" of person, a point to be much emphasized below, we tend to be very glib about our use of the term *criminals*. Especially in the mass media—a major source of the aforementioned "good guys, bad guys," perception—reference to criminals often seems to imply a unique and identifiable "type," virtually a different species. Indeed, the word *animal* sometimes has been used to characterize especially condemnable suspects or offenders. This misleading kind of thinking has impeded efforts to shape sensible crime policies, just as it has at times adversely influenced theorizing about crime. In fact, with the possible exception of professional criminals, of whom there probably are not really very many in our society, a criminal is nothing more than a person held to have committed a crime.

The comments above, linking deviance outcomes to social conflict and social change, as well as those regarding multiple levels for analysis and the two sides of deviance determinations are most pertinent in considering the criminal law. Both the passage or nonpassage of criminal legislation and the patterns of its administration significantly reflect processes of conflict and change. As we have already seen, there frequently may be indications in the legal realm of ongoing struggles over alternative deviance definitions. The hotly contested, and recently fluctuating, legal policies on abortion represent but one of many examples that could be cited. In addition, each criminal trial itself represents an arena of conflict by virtue of the adversary system in which the prosecution (representing the state) and the defense present their typically clashing versions of what the "facts" are and what the outcome should be. At both levels (general legal rules and trends, and specific cases) instances of treating behavior as not criminal or less seriously criminal may also be extremely revealing.

The sociologist will want to explore why certain laws have *not* been passed and why certain individuals are *not* tried in the criminal courts or are "let off" at one or another stage in the criminal justice process. Relative social standing and power will usually account for many of these differentials. The strength of large corporations helps us to understand why strong laws against environmental pollution have not been rigidly enforced. The relatively high status and resources of well-to-do whites in our society help us to understand why they run less risk than do impoverished blacks of incurring harsh sanctions at various levels of criminal justice processing. As we already saw, outcomes of this sort reflect the other side of deviance-defining.

We must conclude then that various legal definitions, processes, and structures to some extent properly fall within the purview of deviance analysis. Although there is within sociology a subfield of sociology of law—which is concerned with the systematic study of all aspects of legal systems, including some that are of little concern to the student of deviance—the boundary between the two subfields cannot be rigidly drawn. Again, the technical designations and disciplinary credentials of fields and investigators should not be as important to us as the persuasiveness and perceptiveness of the interpretations themselves. Work by persons seeing themselves as sociologists of law can enrich our understanding of deviance-defining, while at the same time deviance analysis can strengthen our knowledge of legal systems.

Moral Issues

Deviance situations, as we have noted, involve behaviors or conditions about which certain people feel something "ought to be done." Yet, as we also saw, there is hardly ever a complete consensus regarding just *what* should be done or even that *anything* should be done. Thus the stage is set for disagreement or dispute. Since the responses that incorporate and impart deviantness imply strong personal feelings, often as to "right" and "wrong," deviance-defining invariably raises serious moral issues and dilemmas. Even with respect to behavior that is simply distressing or mildly threatening and, hence, not necessarily considered "wrongdoing," there may well be strong feelings regarding the rightness and wrongness of alternative reactions. One poses a moral question by asking, "What responses to and policies regarding the handicapped are fair, humane, and socially desirable?" just as one would by asking, "Are these people to be blamed for their condition?" In Chapter 7 we will return to the problem of relating judgments of the morality of particular behaviors to what we might call the "morality" of particular social and legal reactions. Much of the debate in the area of law and morality hinges on the rather tenuous relationship between these two kinds of determinations. As we will see, many legal and social interpreters of certain publicly disputed deviance situations such as drug addiction, prostitution, abortion, and homosexuality assert that even concluding a behavior is "immoral" is not always sufficient ground for passing a criminal law against it. If the consequences of passing such a law are perceived to increase rather than decrease the overall social harm associated with the behavior (see Schur, 1965), then the rightness or wrongness of the law may become an important moral issue in its own right.

Moral issues in the field of deviance analysis are heightened by the fact that often the major organized religions in our society have taken strong positions based on long-standing doctrines regarding one or another type of behavior they have viewed as problematic, offensive, or immoral. However we may personally feel about the moral value of particular pronouncements of this sort, it would be a big mistake to ignore their considerable social force. Despite the fact that ours is often called a secular society, many of its members do have strong religious beliefs that contribute to their views on controversial social issues. (For a recent example of how apparently sincere religious belief can enter into public efforts to deviantize, see "News Spot: Gay Rights in Miami," pp. 424–425.) Furthermore, we all know that the organized churches frequently declare public policy preferences and, at times, openly seek to influence legislation or other decisions that shape deviance outcomes. One of the clearest recent examples of this has been the various efforts by the Roman Catholic Church to affect decisions about policy on abortion. Critics of such activity may raise constitutional law objections, insisting on the traditional "separation of Church and State." They may argue that the Church should not try to influence laws and other general policies that affect the lives of nonmembers, that it should seek to instruct only those who voluntarily follow its guidance. Defenders of the Church's policy-related actions could assert the value of "a free market of ideas" (wide circulation of all kinds of conflicting views) on public issues. The critics might in turn at least insist that if the Church does enter the policy arena, it cannot claim any special immunity from public criticism for its statements. Again, whichever way one may feel about these matters, there is no disputing that such efforts in fact do represent a potent *social* influence, one that the deviance analyst must take into account.

Even if we accept the need to study such influences, we might ask just what, if anything, the sociologist can contribute to the *resolution* of deeply felt moral issues of this sort? Sometimes social analysis of a deviance situation may help to clarify or broaden our conception of just what the moral dispute ought to be about. (For example, in line with the earlier comment about the "morality" of laws, we might be impelled to ask: Which is the more important moral issue—the "morality of prostitution" or the "morality of alternative reactions and public policies concerning prostitution?") In the next section, we will be considering several additional kinds of contributions the sociologist can make to our understanding of and, presumably, our attitudes about deviance issues. Although these are important contributions (if they were not, there would be little justification for books and courses of this sort), it is necessary at this point to acknowledge that they are limited ones. *The sociologist cannot "prove" moral values, cannot tell us what we "ought to believe" or what public policy "ought to be."*

In a sense, conflicting moral judgments, if deeply enough felt, may actually never be fully resolvable. At the same time, public policies of one sort or another that affect our lives as well as the lives of others are continuously being made. So we deceive ourselves if we believe we can easily avoid taking a position with respect to these serious value clashes and contested policy issues. (As the social theorist Max Weber noted, nonaction is itself a kind of action; it, too, has social consequences.) How, then, are we to make judgments or reach decisions in these matters? All we can do is try to reach the best-informed judgments possible, given whatever relevant empirical ("factual") evidence is available and in the light of our own carefully considered *value priorities.* Just what does this mean? It means that no matter how much data sociologists or other researchers may collect, there will always remain a gap, a kind of "value leap," between this accumulated evidence and the making of a value judgment or policy decision. There is, in other words, a residue of values that no amount of empirical inquiry can fully eliminate.

For example, suppose we are trying to decide whether gambling or a particular policy toward gambling is "right" or "wrong." Sociologists, psychologists, economists, and perhaps others can study all there is to study about gambling—who does it, why, under what circumstances, with what consequences, in what ways affected by various policies, and so on. Although data of that sort are in a way morally "neutral," presumably the various bits of evidence might be arrayed in two columns—evidence that could be taken to support a conclusion of right and evidence seeming to support a judgment of wrong. Yet even if we could agree on how to place the data in these two columns, we would not be able to "know" conclusively, as a scientific matter, about the rightness or wrongness of gambling. The problem of conflicting value priorities would remain. Suppose we all agreed that much more evidence fell into the right column than into the wrong column. We would still have to confront the fact that people do not all agree as to how to weigh the various bits of evidence. For one person, the listing alone might be persuasive. For another, one particular item in the wrong column might be more significant than ten in the right column. There is simply no way for the social scientist to "disprove" that person's considered conclusion that gambling is wrong, for that person's judgment rests on his or her ordering of various values—the relative legitimacy or importance of which cannot be "established" scientifically. (All that those reaching an opposite conclusion could do would be to cite the evidence and arguments that seemed to them most pertinent and to try to convince others to agree with their assessment.) There are, of course, schools of moral philosophy, including doctrines of "natural law," according to which one might deem otherwise, but most empirical social scientists recognize such limits on knowing values. We would all like to be able to say that the moral judgments and value decisions we make are "true," but from a scientific standpoint such assertions will not hold up.

It should be clear by now that the analysis of deviance-defining inevitably brings us up against questions that are in part moral ones. Whether they be posed by organized religion, other organized groups, or simply by individuals, their persistence underlines the likely role of conflict in shaping deviance outcomes. Of course, there are some acts that are so horrendous we might all tend to agree on their immorality. (A classic example would be the systematic extermination policies of Nazi Germany.) But in deviance studies we confront an enormous range of behaviors and conditions that are often perceived as offending or distressing, yet about which no such clear consensus can be reached. What this rather extended discussion boils down to, then, is simply this: In the last analysis the sociologist *as* social scientist cannot tell us how to organize our society and our lives. As citizens in a democracy trying to shape our own destinies and, in the process, inevitably affecting those of other people as well, we should look to the social scientist for help in interpreting social situations and processes and in recognizing the likely consequences of the choices we make. However, the final moral and social responsibility for our decisions must be our own.

THE ROLE OF THE SOCIOLOGIST

If we conclude that the sociologist's role with respect to morally tinged topics and issues is limited, that is not to say, however, that it is negligible. As in so many spheres of human interaction, sociology can bring to bear in the area of deviance a considerable arsenal of informative research methods and revealing concepts. Diverse techniques, ranging from highly sophisticated statistical analyses to intensive observational studies, can help us uncover significant patterns and relationships that might otherwise elude attention. Presumably, too, sociological inquiry has special value because of the relatively distinterested stance of the investigator.

The term *relatively* is used here because of the controversial nature of this claim. One hears a great deal in introductory sociology courses about the goal of "value-free" sociology, about the efforts of the social scientist to maintain **ethical neutrality**—to research and analyze without letting his or her personal values affect the findings and interpretations. If this attempt is difficult generally (for example, because of the way in which the very choice of research topics may imply value priorities), it is even more so in the heavily value-laden area of deviance studies. At various points in this book, we are going to encounter arguments and interpretations relating to different aspects of this value-neutrality question. The difficulties presented when the analysis concerns topics on which there are active public policy disputes may already be apparent. However, the problem extends well beyond such instances, and it is one that complicates the methodological as well as the theoretical aspects of the sociologist's work.

Is it possible or even desirable to study deviance situations without taking "the point of view" of any of the participants? (As we shall see, a major recent emphasis has been on exploring such situations insofar as possible as they are experienced by the deviators themselves.) Does the sociologist sacrifice objectivity by adopting this standpoint? Or, is there really no alternative to adopting *some* participant's standpoint? Will different researches undertaken from different standpoints balance each other out and hence produce some kind of composite that is objective? Does the application of specialized sociological concepts itself constitute an imposition of the sociologist's own outlooks? Can the social investigator choose to study behaviors that have been deviantized without implicitly endorsing their deviantness? Are individual subjects in deviance studies treated as "fair game" for research (e.g., hospitalized mental patients or convicts in prison), or are they accorded the same rights and protections (to refuse to participate in the research, etc.) as other individuals? Does "disguised participant observation" in which the researcher "pretends" to be simply a participant and not a sociologist impair ethical neutrality? Is there any way in which the sociologist can define deviance in the first place without reflecting his or her own value priorities? If deviance is a social construction, isn't it really in large measure a social construction of and by the sociologists themselves? Indeed, one influential school of sociology argues that there is no real, objective social world out there apart from our study of it. Questions like these have challenged deviance analysts to consider carefully the moral implications of their own work. Yet it could be argued that this heightened sensitivity in itself strengthens the sociologist's ability to offer nonspecialists new and more meaningful insights into deviance situations. Some of the sociologist's major contributions are as follows:

Documentation and Description

Sociologists are sometimes chided for telling us in a complicated way "what we already know" about the world around us. Those who say this may very likely exaggerate the distribution of accurate understandings about social life. Yet, even to the extent this claim has merits, it overlooks the considerable value of systematic evidence substantiating points we might otherwise simply suspect to be true. A few examples of findings from deviance research that serve this documenting function would be the following: that full-fledged heroin addicts frequently commit money-producing crimes in order to support their illegal drug habit; that the customers of prostitutes are rarely prosecuted; that the social adaptation of mentally retarded persons may be greatly enhanced by the existence of helpful relatives or other "benefactors;" that unmarried persons are, as a statistical class, relatively more likely to commit suicide than married ones; and that inmates and custodians in correctional institutions sometimes strike "bargains" regarding formal rules and regulations.

Traditional social research, particularly, tended to produce masses of "facts and figures" and observational "findings" that provided much numerical and descriptive detail about deviance situations. Although growing methodological sophistication has led to the raising of many questions about the validity of some of the numerical data and related interpretations, it remains true—particularly where better sampling and other procedures can be adopted—that facts and figures can be extremely useful. We want to know who does what, when, where, how often, and what consequences most often ensue. Even if we are alert to the fact that "a correlation is not a cause"—that statistical association alone does not provide an explanation of such association—we wish to trace out as well as we can the relationships between variables, trends over time, and so on. Although this text does not emphasize the quantitative (facts and figures) side of studying deviance, we will be noting a great many specific findings of this sort that do contribute to a comprehensive understanding of deviance situations.

While quantitative techniques may enable us to organize and systematize large masses of data and also to disentangle complicated interconnections among them, nonstatistical approaches, heavily emphasized in recent deviance research, also have great usefulness. They may help us to get a sense of the "subjective understandings" of the participants in deviance situations—the meanings for them of the interaction they are immersed in. Close and thorough observations and individual case studies may in various ways provide an in-depth look at deviance-defining that could not be achieved through quantitative methods alone. As we will see, statistical analysis, numerical documentation, and intensive observation-description, all may have important parts to play in deviance analysis, notwithstanding some strong disputes among practitioners concerning their overall relative merits.

Demythologizing and Demystifying

Another extremely valuable function of sociological analysis is to dispel the misconceptions and the aura of mystery that often impede realistic and perceptive understanding of deviance issues. This is a field in which, perhaps even more than in other areas of social life, myths and misconceptions abound. There are at least several reasons why that is so. For one thing, we tend to imbue with deviantness behaviors and conditions, as well as people themselves, that are perceived as strange, different, upsetting, out-of-the-ordinary, or, by definition, then, relatively unfamiliar to us. At the same time, deviantness responses in part seem to reflect a desire not to know, or to know anything more, about these disturbing things. Such responses characteristically involve avoiding or segregating the people who offend. Thus we shut ourselves off from direct contact with patterns we consider offensive. It is hardly surprising if, under these circumstances, incomplete and misguided impressions and beliefs about these patterns become entrenched. Furthermore, as we have seen, deviance-defining tends to be grounded in or rationalized in terms of an assumption of the basic differentness of the offending individuals. One function of myths and misconceptions about deviance, that is, an objective consequence of their presence but not necessarily a consciously intended one, is to lend support to this differentness notion. If we can stay away from those people whose behavior disturbs us, we won't have to learn about the many respects in which they are really very much like ourselves.

Later on, when we examine more systematically the recent emphasis on societal reactions and deviance-defining processes, we are going to see that **stereotyping** (Simmons, 1969; Schur, 1971, pp. 38–52; and Goode, 1978, ch. 5) is a central ingredient of these processes. As already suggested, deviantizing responses usually involve viewing and treating specific individuals almost entirely in terms of their membership in some negatively evaluated category. For the reasons just mentioned, these preevaluations frequently, if not invariably, rest on inaccurate information, misleading conceptions, and glib generalizations. However, as our discussion also should suggest these widespread false beliefs—when acted upon—can become self-fulfilling in their impact. Throughout this book we will be citing numerous illustrations of how sociological analysis has disclosed, and at least partially corrected, misconceptions that have affected deviance-defining. Here are just a few examples of recently widespread but *false* beliefs that findings from systematic research and analysis now overwhelmingly contradict:

- that most persons defined as "mentally ill" have hereditary defects

- that abortion is always a dangerous operation (this was at least widely believed prior to the recent "legalization" rulings and the attendant spread of more accurate information; it probably still is the predominant belief in certain restricted social circles)

- that most "child molesters" are homosexual

- that people who smoke marihuana run a high risk of becoming heroin addicts

- that nudists are sex-obsessed voyeurs ("peepers")

- that all persons diagnosed as "legally blind" are totally unable to see

- that lesbians (female homosexuals) see themselves as really being, and display behavior patterns similar to those of, men

- that corporate "price-fixers" do not really understand that such behavior is against the law

- that early drinking is the main cause of alcoholism

- that prisons and mental hospitals nowadays are so "comfortable" they can no longer be "effective"

At various points below we will be examining substantive research findings or analyses that bear directly on most if not all of these misguided beliefs. As will become clear, there are several ways in which false beliefs of this kind circulate and get reinforced or amplified. To some extent, this occurs by word of mouth, and, given the characteristic avoidance-segregation pattern, the prospects for continuously amplified misconceptions are very high indeed. The mass media, particularly in their favored emphasis on highly sensationalistic accounts of news events and in other ways as well, may often disseminate misleading notions. However, it should be recognized that potentially they can serve a very important enlightening function as well. Sometimes groups or organizations with strong special interests (moral, economic, or whatever) in a particular "problem" will in their fervor spread exaggerated or even false ideas about it. Whatever the process of circulation and reinforcement, the strong susceptibility to misconception in the deviance area is evident. It follows that an important lesson for all of us is that we should very carefully think through and evaluate in terms of credibility of sources, persuasiveness of evidence, logic of argument, and common-sense plausibility any and all statements and claims about deviance.

Needless to say, these same cautions ought to be applied in assessing the claims and interpretations of sociologists and other specialists as well. Because of their attempts to investigate matters in a systematic and relatively objective manner, social scientists hopefully *should* be less inclined than other persons to exaggeration and falsehood. Yet they are human beings, too, and can easily get caught up in their enthusiasm about or even develop vested interests in their favored theories and contentions. We should apply to their output not only those technical (methodological, etc.) evaluative criteria of which we become aware, but also whatever resources of logic, good sense, and general judgment we have at our command. Here again, as in the moral realm, we cannot fully abdicate our responsibility for making choices. With respect to the varying and at times conflicting views and conclusions with which we are presented, even in the name of "science," we *ourselves* must be the ultimate arbiters.

Developing an Interpretive Understanding

Undoubtedly the major contribution of sociological deviance studies is to help us develop a coherent and meaningful way of thinking about processes and patterns found in deviance situations. Notwithstanding the many obstacles to total disinterestedness, most deviance analysts try to understand these matters in an objective way, whatever role their personal preferences and value orderings may play with respect to any public policy recommendations they might also make. As we might expect, most sociologists who specialize in and probably many of the students who are attracted to this field tend to have strong views about the relevant policy issues. Were this not the case, many vital topics might remain uninvestigated, unanalyzed, and, perhaps, professionally as well as publicly taboo. Nonetheless, this policy orientation, while extremely important and quite legitimate as part of the sociologist's role as citizen, ought to take a secondary place in the actual course of research and analysis.

One way we can maximize our chances of objectivity is to be systematic. We have to be on guard against the common tendency to generalize without an adequate basis. We cannot allow our conclusions to rest solely on those specific incidents or cases we have experienced or heard about, but rather we must attempt to develop a general knowledge base. How often we say, "Oh, everybody knows. . . ." when our only sources actually are our own parents, friends, acquaintances, and a few selective impressions from the mass media. If we really want to understand deviance or any other aspects of organized social life we have to get well beyond our limited personal experience. Our understanding must be *comprehensive;* it must help us to see how particular incidents and situations reflect or comprise broader patterns. The existence of shared, recurring, and structured elements in all human social behavior requires that we be analytic. To a large extent, this means that we must search out, document, and systematically interpret *patterns of similarity, difference, and interrelationship.*

Part of this effort often involves facts and figures—counting, measuring, comparing. Yet even more central to this enterprise may be the development of a *coherent and sensitive interpretive framework.* The approach to deviance situations that we have begun to consider in this chapter rests heavily on a belief in the crucial importance of this element. As we have seen, it aims at specifying and analyzing *the underlying defining-reacting processes* that cut across, and are the common elements in, all situations of this sort. This emphasis on a broadly **interpretive understanding,** as compared with a more prediction-oriented, statistical-comparison mode of analysis, reflects two major developments in the field. One is the recent general disenchantment of sociologists with what they conceive of as an earlier overreliance on "mere" quantification—what C. Wright Mills termed "abstracted empiricism" (Mills, 1959). As we shall see, this disenchantment has had a considerable direct influence on the course of the development of deviance theory.

The second development is the growing recognition that deviance situations themselves are essentially interpretive in nature; that is, they are (as we have started to see) "made up of" interpretations—some people's interpretations of other people's behavior or conditions—and the ways of reacting that those interpretations entail. It may well be that such interpretive processes (some sociologists insist that *all* social interaction is similarly interpretive) can only be adequately comprehended in interpretive terms. Just how such a conclusion limits our methodological options is not entirely clear, but, at the very least, it seems to suggest that the goal of insightful interpretation should receive extremely high priority in the field of deviance analysis. One major theme in this book is that deviance situations incorporate and illustrate some of the most significant basic processes that are at work more generally in all areas of our social lives. If that is so, then the development of a systematic and sensitive way of interpreting them has the potential to provide us with more than just knowledge of a restricted subject-matter area. It can make a major contribution to our overall ability to understand and cope with the social world, a world that is both around us and at the same time constructed by us through our ongoing interaction.

SOME COMMENTS ABOUT THIS BOOK

At this point, the perceptive reader most likely realizes that this text incorporates a distinctive and somewhat ambitious approach. It is taking us beyond the standard lists of theories and the typically uninspiring recital of myriad facts and figures about deviance. Students using this book are almost certainly going to come away from it considerably better informed (in the conventional sense) about deviance matters. But that mundane goal of increased information and the usual memorizing called for in association with it cannot by themselves point us in the most fruitful direction. Of infinitely greater value to the student of deviance will be a general interpretive framework of the kind just mentioned. This book presents such a framework. It offers the student a comprehensive approach that can be applied in analyzing *any* specific example of deviance-defining. To that end, a greater emphasis is placed on highlighting the major questions to be asked, then on providing what purport to be "the answers." Given the kinds of social and moral complexity we have considered in this chapter, to think in terms of learning the answers to deviance questions is to succumb to gross oversimplification. It would be highly misleading even to think of the many specific items of information and research findings cited throughout this book as answers. While students are most assuredly better off knowing about such findings than not knowing, they need above all to know how to ask the right questions.

In line with this book's focus on developing a general interpretive framework, the Paradigm referred to above presents a list of key questions to be pursued in studying deviance. Perhaps it should be reiterated that these questions cut across and, hence, can be posed in connection with any of the various substantive deviance "problems." Many of the questions included there are discussed in depth throughout this book, and their applicability to specific substantive areas is indicated. In the process of considering these several lines of analysis, students will learn a great deal about such topics as mental illness, drug addiction, crime and delinquency, stigmatized disabilities, drinking problems, sexual deviation, suicide, courts, police, psychiatry, treatment and correctional institutions and programs. However, no effort is made in the typical encyclopedic way to summarize "all there is to know" about any one of these matters. Numerous studies and analyses in each of these areas are cited at appropriate places in this book; such works are good sources for this kind of detailed information. The same is true of certain social problems texts that are organized partly in terms of a succession of specific problems—a chapter on suicide, a chapter on delinquency, and so on down the line (see for example, Merton and Nisbet, 1976; Turner, 1977).

By the same token, the alleged "schools" of deviance theory will be emphasized somewhat less than usual. We will be considering throughout this text the nature and influence, and the strong points and limitations, of a good number of specific theories and general perspectives used in analyzing deviance. Readers will learn what the major themes and claims of the influential approaches are and what significant criticisms have been leveled against them. But the book is not organized, as some are (see, for example, Davis, 1975) "around" the various schools and theories. Indeed, the suggestion is going to be made that perhaps there has been too much attention given to these supposedly "competing" schools of deviance theory.

Disagreement among the adherents to diverse orientations may have obscured the fact that there are many important propositions on which most deviance analysts would now agree. While the several major approaches do, without question, differ as to their emphases and, at times, suggest divergent lines of analysis, there are also (as we will see) significant points of convergence and complementarity. One aspect of the comprehensive approach adopted in this book is that it draws at various points on several different theories and orientations. Insofar as possible, we should make use of the best questions to raise, concepts to employ, and research methods that each major approach has to offer. Often, preoccupation with the goal of developing a single, all-inclusive theory of deviance has led sociologists to feel that they must "choose" between the several "leading" perspectives for once and for all. Considering the many different aspects of deviance situations that we may want to analyze, this goal of a single "explanation" that could cover them all may well be an unrealistic one. In fact, aspects of one approach may be most useful for one specific purpose, and aspects of another approach most useful for another purpose. It is nice to think that we might explain all aspects and levels of deviance-defining in one fell swoop, but that just may not be possible.

This is not to imply that we should or that this book does employ an indiscriminate eclecticism. On the contrary, we must be clear as to just when and why a given concept, hypothesis, or method is appropriate; and we should recognize that such use is for a specific and limited purpose. Furthermore, our recourse to different approaches should occur within the context of a general orienting perspective—such as that suggested in the early pages of this chapter and in part summarized through the "basic propositions" offered there. As we go on, there will be no doubt at all that throughout this text does adopt a clear orientation of this kind. In short, it is an opinionated book—hopefully, in the best sense of that term—that is, it adopts a distinct outlook, one that in the author's considered professional opinion incorporates the most useful and meaningful concepts and techniques for analyzing deviance. The so-called "labeling" approach to deviance, the perspective grounded (to greatly oversimplify for the moment) in the notion that "deviance is in the eye of the beholder," has been evaluated elsewhere (Schur, 1971) with considerable approval. As may already be apparent, the stance sketched out in this opening chapter and developed throughout this text represents to a large degree an outgrowth and an expanded version or interpretation of that labeling perspective.

Such an approach implies the basic propositions briefly mentioned above. If one wanted to succinctly characterize it, in the broadest way possible, one might say it is *relativistic, interpretive, and dynamic*. It insists on the need to view deviance situations in *sociocultural and situational context*, to examine just who is attaching the deviantness and to whom. It focuses attention on *characterization of behavior*, treating definition and reaction as *ongoing interactive processes* found at several levels of social life—interpersonal, organizational, societal. It highlights the dynamics of *conflict and change* through which deviance outcomes emerge. Such outcomes, in short, are treated as problematic in various important respects. They are *contingent upon the reciprocal or interactive relation between problem and response.* (Not only does perceived deviation lead to efforts at control, but at the same time control feeds back into the deviance situation—often with unintended effects.)

These then are some of the major themes emphasized in this book. Since both the vitality of and much of the current controversy in the field of deviance analysis involve a continuing debate about the merits of the so-called "labeling" approach, we are at numerous points going to be looking into one or another feature of that debate (Gove, ed., 1975; Hawkins and Tiedeman, 1975; Suchar, 1978). As we will then see, it has been suggested (e.g., by Becker, 1973; Goode, 1975; Kitsuse, 1975; and Schur, 1975) that critics of labeling analysis often have leveled misplaced charges against it and failed to appreciate its potential as a broad interpretive orientation. Actually, this potential may be easier to grasp when a more general-sounding term is used to designate the approach. (It is frequently called the "societal reaction" or "interactionist" perspective.) Probably the best way to describe the expanded version of the orientation developed here is to think of it as a "definitional-processual" approach. The appropriateness of that kind of designation will be made clearer as we continue.

Being aware of ongoing theoretical controversies in the field and, more particularly, scrutinizing the arguments posed therein can heighten our sensitivity to various dimensions of deviance analysis. At the same time, however, we should not allow these somewhat technical debates among professional specialists to obscure our overriding goal: to develop sensitive and comprehensive ways of interpreting deviance situations. For nonspecialists, including most students in courses on deviance, the relative current standing in the field of particular formal theories should be a matter of only secondary concern.

Uncertainties and complexities such as those outlined in this chapter— the very ones that inevitably present problems for the researcher and interpreter— at the same time help to make the field of deviance analysis a tremendously exciting one. In exploring deviance issues and situations, we confront a subject matter that is both complex and fascinating. Apart from the inherent fascination of some of the topics (inherent, really, in the sense that deviantness judgments themselves reflect a special kind of obsession with the behaviors in question), there is a sociological fascination in trying to work out a meaningful analysis. We must develop multileveled interpretations that take into account not only the many social aspects of these situations but also the moral, legal, and other facets noted earlier.

In addition, we are challenged to somehow make sense of matters that reflect an intriguing interplay between personal problems of specific individuals, general public attitudes and policies, and the researches and analyses pursued by sociologists themselves. Throughout this text, the juxtaposition of sociological and public-issue aspects is going to receive particular emphasis. Considerable attention will be paid to current public-policy questions and disputes. Studying deviance calls for a combination of interpretive skill, moral and humanistic sensitivity, and, in many instances, awareness of the interrelationships between perceived problems and adopted social policies. It is hoped that the ideas and materials presented in this book will increase the reader's ability to summon forth and put to good use these much-needed outlooks and skills.

REFERENCES

Becker, Howard S.
1963. *Outsiders.* New York: The Free Press.
1973. "Labelling Theory Reconsidered," in *Outsiders, rev. ed.*

Davis, Nanette J.
1975. *Sociological Constructions of Deviance.* Dubuque, Iowa: William C. Brown Company, Publishers.

Emerson, Robert M. and Sheldon L. Messinger
1977. "The Micro-Politics of Trouble," *Social Problems,* 25 (Dec.), 121–134.

Freidson, Eliot
1971. *Profession of Medicine.* New York: Dodd, Mead & Company.

Goffman, Erving
1959. *The Presentation of Self in Everyday Life.* Garden City, N.Y.: Doubleday & Company, Inc.

Goode, Erich
1975. "On Behalf of Labeling Theory," *Social Problems,* 22 (June), 570–583.
1978. *Deviant Behavior.* Englewood Cliffs, N.J.: Prentice-Hall.

Gove, Walter R., ed.
1976. *The Labelling of Deviance.* Beverly Hills, Calif.: Sage Publications, Inc.

Hawkins, Richard and Gary Tiedeman
1975. *The Creation of Deviance.* Columbus, Ohio: Charles E, Merrill Pub. Co.

Hoffman, Martin
1969. *The Gay World.* New York: Bantam Books, Inc.

Kitsuse, John I.
1975. "The 'New Conception of Deviance' and Its Critics," in Walter R. Gove, ed., *The Labelling of Deviance*. Beverly Hills, Calif.: Sage Publications, Inc. Pp. 273–284.

Merton, Robert K. and Robert Nisbet, eds.
1976. *Contemporary Social Problems, 4th ed.* New York: Harcourt Brace Jovanovich.

Mills, C. Wright
1959. *The Sociological Imagination.* New York: Oxford University Press.

Parsons, Talcott
1951. *The Social System.* New York: The Free Press.

Sargarin, Edward
1975. *Deviants and Deviance.* New York: Praeger Publishers, Inc.

Schrag, Peter
1978. *Mind Control.* New York: Pantheon Books.

Schrag, Peter and Diane Divoky
1976. *The Myth of the Hyperactive Child.* New York: Dell Publishing Company, Inc.

Schur, Edwin M.
1965. *Crimes Without Victims.* Englewood Cliffs, N.J.: Prentice-Hall, Inc.
1971. *Labeling Deviant Behavior.* New York: Harper & Row, Publishers.
1975. "Comments," in Gove, ed., *op. cit.*

Scott, Marvin B. and Stanford M. Lyman
1968. "Accounts," *American Sociological Review,* 33 (Feb.), 46–62.

Simmons, Jerry L.
1969. *Deviants.* San Francisco: The Glenessary Press.

Suchar, Charles S.
1978. *Social Deviance: Perspectives and Prospects.* New York: Holt, Rinehart, and Winston.

Sutherland, Edwin H.
1937. *The Professional Thief.* Chicago: University of Chicago Press.

Szasz, Thomas S.
1970. *Ideology and Insanity.* Garden City, N.Y.: Doubleday & Company, Inc.

Thio, Alex
1978. *Deviant Behavior.* Boston: Houghton Mifflin Co.

Turner, Jonathan H.
1977. *Social Problems in America.* New York: Harper & Row, Publishers.

REVIEW OF KEY TERMS

characterization(s) of behavior. What is made of an act socially; the meanings assigned to human actions and conditions; a concept of special importance in emerging outlooks on deviance to be distinguished from the ***occurrence of behavior*** (often the key focal point in traditional deviance research).

demythologizing. A major function of the sociology of deviance—helping to dispel the misconceptions and mystery that frequently surround deviance issues.

depersonalization. The feeling, often experienced by stigmatized and discriminated-against persons, of being treated as nonpersons, as but an "instance" of a preconceived category, rather than as a full and unique human being.

deviantizing. The interactive processes through which acts, conditions, or individuals come to be imbued with deviantness.

deviantness. The meaning qualities found in varying degrees in deviance situations—typically, characterizations of behavior as involving wrongdoing, social offensiveness, or incapacity and associated reactions to the acts, conditions, or individuals in terms of their wrongfulness, offensiveness, distastefulness, and so on. Where deviantness is "assigned," it often tends to overwhelm other persons' perceptions of the perceived deviator.

differential social power. Differential power of groups or individuals to achieve desired social outcomes, to influence the ways in which social situations are defined. It can be based on a variety of kinds of power resources (economic, political, symbolic, psychological, etc.) and implemented in different ways at several levels of the social order, ranging from personal snubs of "interactional" deviators in face-to-face situations to successful national lobbying for legislation concerning a public deviance issue.

ethical neutrality. The aim of the sociologist to engage in relatively objective, disinterested, research and analysis is never fully complete and is especially difficult in the field of deviance because of the centrality of moral and ethical issues and dilemmas, and the "residue" of value judgments and policy choices in decision-making that can never be eliminated by social sciences.

interpretive understanding. An in-depth understanding of social interaction and situations, particularly as they are directly experienced by the actors themselves, that is usually associated with qualitative (nonquantitative) research efforts such as intensive (often "participant") observation. It is particularly important in analyzing deviance because deviantizing processes are themselves so heavily "interpretive," and is a key focus (and goal) of the present text.

people-processing organizations. Organizations that have as their "product" the treated, corrected, rehabilitated, or otherwise processed, individual. A central aspect of the defining-reacting processes in many if not most deviance situations that is illustrated by the so-called "social control agencies," any one of which may itself be part of a more extensive organizational network (deviance-processing "system"). There has been special focus in recent deviance analysis on how, through "displacement of goals," the "needs" of such organizations affect the screening and processing of perceived deviators.

politicization (of deviance issues). Organized public efforts by or on behalf of deviantized persons to advance their collective interests. Typically, these have taken the form of "political" movements to reduce public discrimination, to advance legal rights, to redefine policies and attitudes in nonstigmatizing directions, and to gain increased general acceptance of behaviors, conditions, and individuals currently stigmatized (e.g., the gay liberation movement).

social construction. The social world viewed as an ongoing reality produced by the interactions and patternings of individuals who are, at the same time, shaped and constrained by that reality. In particular, "deviance as a social construction"—the product of a particular type of defining-reacting process, involving the attachment of deviantness to individuals, acts, or conditions.

stereotypes. False beliefs about types of behaviors, individuals, or situations which, when acted upon socially, can have potent real consequences, often self-fulfilling. These are extremely prevalent and, hence, important to recognize and analyze in the field of deviance.

stigmatization. The process of attaching to individuals "labels" and perceived qualities that permit or entail categorical discrimination and personal debasement. The imputation of and concomitant reactions based on, or producing, deviantness. It is roughly synonymous with *deviantizing* of individuals.

value priorities. One's ordering of personal and social goals; how strongly one feels about the relative desirability of particular outcomes and about the reliance on and maintenance or furtherance of particular principles or practices. Thus, they are an evaluative ranking of both ends and means—a continuous and inevitable source of problems and dilemmas for both social policy and social research in the deviance field.

PROJECT 1
Deviance-Defining in Literature

Introductory Comment

So far the reader has merely encountered a few of the central themes, tendencies, and problems posed in the modern sociology of deviance. We will be exploring each of these in greater depth below, and in that connection some student projects more directly relating to specific points will be suggested. For the moment, what should be helpful is an exercise enabling readers to pull together some of these preliminary but basic ideas and to begin to see how they are useful in analyzing specific deviance situations. Depictions of deviance-defining in literature provide an interesting opportunity to "try out" some of these concepts and perspectives. Deviance situations and deviantizing processes have intrigued writers just as they have intrigued people generally from time immemorial. The ways in which these situations and processes have been treated in literature, whether in the "classics" or in the "pulps," will often provide useful if rough indicators of more general understandings—or misunderstandings.

Assignment

Select a novel or play, or, if you prefer, a full-length movie or television film, in which the author depicts what seems to you on the basis of the ideas presented in this chapter to be a deviance situation or a deviantizing process or its consequences. Write a paper analyzing this depiction from two main viewpoints: (1) that of a sociologist interpreting the depiction (What kinds of understanding of the situation does the author seem to display? Do the concepts in this chapter find illustration in the depiction and/or help us to understand it?), and (2) that of a person hypothetically engaging in or exhibiting the "offending" behavior or condition (How might such a person feel about the author's depiction, and why? What kind of depiction might such a person prefer to have made, and why?).

General Suggestion

There are, of course, many novels, plays, and films specifically about one or another of the "standard," that is, currently deviantized, categories of behavior studied by sociologists of deviance. Thus, fictional works centering on crime and punishment, mental illness, drug use, suicide, illicit sexuality, and the like, offer myriad possibilities for this kind of project. They do have the advantage that treatment of the topic is likely to be extensive, affording more "data" for the

analysis. At the same time, depictions of deviantizing processes and their consequences are quite evident in a great many works that do not have any form of
deviance as their central concern. Adventurous students may wish to avoid the
obvious kind of choice, such as a TV crime-movie, for example, and to seek out
instead the latter kind of depiction. Although likely to be sketchier, it may also
be considerably less formula-ridden or of special interest as an exploration of
efforts to "deviantize" behavior or individuals in some nonstandard category.

Specific Guidelines

Whatever the source used and the behavior category involved, the analysis
and the paper may be enhanced by considering questions such as the following:

1. How is the "deviance" itself depicted—as an isolated incident or as a
continuing activity or persisting condition? Is it treated as intentional? accidental?
situational? beyond the individual's control?

2. To what extent does the author depict the deviance as self-evident;
to what extent as a matter of "definition" by others?

3. Does the depiction concern itself with "causes" of the perceived deviation, and, if so, what kinds of "causes" are suggested?

4. From whose standpoint does the author present the character or characters engaged in or exhibiting the deviation—a supposedly detached third party
or narrator's standpoint? the standpoint of other characters in the fiction? the
standpoint of the deviator(s)? multiple standpoints?

5. Does the depiction suggest, and, if so, in what ways, the roles of collective definition and direct interaction in the deviantizing process?

6. Do the reacting characters or the author appear to employ stereotypes
(insofar as your knowledge permits a guess) in characterizing the perceived deviation or deviator?

7. Is the characterization of the presumed deviator multidimensional, or
is the person treated *only* as a deviator?

8. What is the nature and apparent impact of whatever deviantizing activity occurs in the presentation?

9. Specifically, what stigmatizing, depersonalizing, or other effects on the
character defined as a deviator are shown or suggested? To what extent is the
person's general sense of self seriously affected?

10. To what extent and in what ways do the relative socioeconomic and
power positions of the various characters seem to influence the deviance-defining
and reacting processes? Has the author been perceptive and realistic in treating
this element?

11. What are the apparent responses of the defined deviator to any stigmatizing and rejecting efforts? Particularly, what resources and techniques are used to avoid, fend off, or lessen the negative impact of these efforts?

12. To what extent, if at all, is the deviance-defining presented as a moral issue? If so, how is that issue defined? How is it resolved?

13. How likely is it, overall, that hypothetical persons in roughly the same situation as the fictional deviator would view the presentation as a "fair" one? Are there specific aspects that would be especially likely to incur objections by such persons? Which aspects, and why the objections? Would the objections be on moral grounds, sociological grounds (accuracy, representativeness, etc.), political grounds, or other grounds?

Implications

This list of questions is meant merely to suggest various lines of analysis that may be fruitful. Not all of the questions will in every instance be pertinent or answerable. The student should keep in mind, too, that this is just *one* specific fictional presentation that is being analyzed. Without some kind of systematic "content analysis" ("sampling" of many cases, numerical tallies or categorizings of points uncovered, etc.), we could not hope to make sound generalizations regarding the nature of deviance-depiction in literature or even in this particular type of literature. (The possible *influence* on readers of such depictions would be yet another research question, the answers to which content analysis alone could never provide.) But this exercise is not meant to produce definitive "findings." Rather, it aims at developing familiarity with a general outlook—at nurturing a way of thinking, a mode of interpretation. It should encourage alertness to the underlying defining and reacting processes that shape deviance situations. As this chapter has emphasized, asking the right questions, in the light of a meaningful interpretative framework, is the key to analyzing deviance. This project provides a preliminary opportunity to learn and practice such an approach.

PROLOGUE 2

The mores come down to us from the past. Each individual is born into them as he is born into the atmosphere, and he does not reflect on them, or criticize them any more than a baby analyzes the atmosphere before he begins to breathe it. Each one is subjected to the influence of the mores, and formed by them, before he is capable of reasoning about them.
—William Graham Sumner, *Folkways*

The term social problem *indicates not merely an observed phenomenon but the state of mind of the observer as well. Value judgments define certain conditions of human life and certain kinds of behavior as social problems; there can be no social problem without a value judgment. . . .*
—Willard Waller, "Social Problems and the Mores"

To think sociologically is, in part, to examine and interpret the otherwise taken-for-granted features of our everyday experience. When we do this, we begin to recognize the specificity and limitations, and also the social determinants, of the situations and ideas with which we are personally familiar. To the extent we are able to transcend the very strong influence of the patterns to which we have been socialized, we can begin to appreciate the extremely diverse nature of human social life. In its concern to analyze patterns and develop generalizations about social behavior, sociology has always been preoccupied with the question of uniformities and variations, similarities and differences. The sociologist wishes to avoid *ethnocentrism* (judging other patterns from the standpoint of one's own accustomed values) and aims for as disinterested an analysis as possible. At the same time, there are important commonalities in social life that no sensible analyst can ignore. One way around the dilemma of unity-diversity is to make a distinction between basic functions and specific culture content. Repeatedly, and in diverse areas of social life (e.g., religion, the legal system, the stratification order), we find a combination of, on the one hand, basic structures or processes that seem present in ("needed" by?) all social systems and, on the other hand, an extremely variable and malleable "content" of the specific ways in which those basic functions are served. This kind of distinction appears useful in analyzing deviance, and it may help us to bridge alleged gaps between different approaches

44

and assumptions. Deviance-defining of some sort occurs in all social groups and societies. Yet "what is deviant" varies greatly from context to context. Although some recent deviance analysts have been criticized for succumbing to excessive relativism, they would no doubt counter with an assertion that more traditional approaches were unthinkingly absolutist in assuming it to be a foregone conclusion what is deviant. Much of the dialogue in recent deviance theory revolves around issues of this sort.

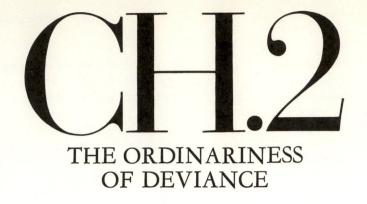

CH.2
THE ORDINARINESS
OF DEVIANCE

INTRODUCTION

Although the ideas sketched out in the last chapter are central to most modern conceptions of deviance, their ascendancy has not been easy. One of the major obstacles has been the persisting inclination to allow notions of basic individual differentness, specialness, and extraordinariness, to dominate our thinking in this field. We seem (some sociologists included) to cling tenaciously to the beliefs that deviators must be a special "type," that deviating acts are uncommon, that they demand causal "explanation" much more than does conforming behavior, and that somehow deviance and control phenomena are "outside of," or an unfortunate departure from, the ordinary workings of society. The development of modern deviance theory has involved a major turn away from these beliefs: a recognition that deviation and deviance-defining are not extraordinary, but ordinary.

How can we speak of the "ordinariness" of deviance? To do so, we must first of all keep in mind the recent emphasis on deviantness as a quality of meanings and the broadened conception of the deviance field referred to above. These developments both reflect and contribute to the thesis that deviance is ordinary. As we have seen, they involve rejecting the idea that it is a foregone conclusion or that "we all know" what or who is deviant. Deviance, then, is not simply a matter of acts that are almost universally condemned as atrocious or of behaviors and conditions widely viewed as exotic or eccentric. Such situations are part of what we must look at in analyzing deviance, but thinking only in those terms leads to a limiting and, in some senses, distorting conception of the deviance-defining process. Wherever and whenever deviantness meanings are in any degree imputed and applied—or this is attempted—to that extent, deviance-defining

is present. Sociologists of deviance increasingly examine the basic reaction processes that cut across, and represent the common underlying element in, instances
of deviance-defining that vary greatly as to substance, degree of consensus, and
"intensity."

From this standpoint, there are at least several different senses in which
deviance may be seen as ordinary. In this chapter, and elsewhere in the book,
there will be considerable development of this theme. At the outset, however, a
brief indication of these aspects of ordinariness may be useful.

1. Deviance is ordinary in the sense that the underlying defining-reaction
process of assigning deviantness is found in, and indeed central to, our everyday
interaction with one another.

2. At the same time, there is a broader, more structural kind of ordinariness involved, in that deviance-defining serves important objective though unintended "functions" for, and may even be necessary to, the groups and societies
within which it occurs. In other words, from the standpoint of social collectivities,
this process is a regular and, in fact, crucial part of (not some exception to, or
departure from) the social order.

3. Furthermore, all of the major social processes and factors found in
deviance situations are the ordinary ones studied by sociologists in any substantive
area: socialization, conflict, social definition, "self-fulfilling prophecies," transformations of identity, and so on.

4. In addition, perceived deviation is not always or completely a departure from even the dominant patterns and values in a given group or society.
On the contrary, the behavior that offends may nonetheless in certain ways reflect
these ordinary patterns. This tendency follows from the fact that deviance is
part of, not outside of, the social system; as such it reflects the structures and
preoccupations that shape the system more generally.

5. Deviation, even when viewed as departure from a specific set of more
or less established "norms," may be much more common and widespread than
we sometimes assume. In that sense, too, it may be no more extraordinary than
"acceptable" behavior.

6. Equally significant is the fact that universal consensus on norms is
rarely present in heterogenous and complex societies. Cultural diversity and
subcultural variation imply that behavior viewed and treated as offending from
one social vantage point may often be quite ordinary (at times, even required of
members) from another.

7. Individuals perceived from any one vantage point as deviators may
in fact be quite ordinary persons in other respects.

8. Overall, then, deviance-defining as an identification and reaction process is in many respects not an extra-ordinary social phenomenon. In fact, its stand-
ardness—rather than its specialness—is increasingly evident to the sociologist.

A number of interrelated trends and developments in the sociology of deviance and within the discipline of sociology have nurtured and encouraged this recognition of ordinariness. They include: the increased concern with meaning structures (characterizations of behavior as well as its mere occurrence); the associated focus on reactions and definitions; criticisms and reinterpretations of standard findings and theories about the distribution and causes of deviance; a renewed attention to diversity and conflict in social life generally, and deviance-defining more particularly; disenchantment with quantitative-comparison methods and renewed recourse to intensive observational techniques aimed at capturing the "subjective meanings of action;" and an associated skepticism regarding the "value-free" nature of sociological analysis.

In citing these newer or recently revived emphases that have affected the field of deviance analysis, a cautionary word should be added. Like other emerging conceptions in this field, the belief in the ordinariness of deviance is not *only* a reflection of recent and in many respects revolutionary challenges to conventional sociology. On the contrary, the list presented here (of senses in which we may view deviance as ordinary) includes some points emphasized in highly traditional sociological approaches (most notably, "functionalist" theory) as well drawing on some of the key tenets of "the new deviance sociology." The very fact that the ordinariness theme reflects these dual influences reinforces a belief that it may be wise to recognize that on some important points the several intellectual traditions and "schools" in deviance analysis converge or complement one another.

These trends, developments, and aspects of convergence will occupy our attention throughout this text. But before beginning to explore them further, it may be well to return to the note struck in the beginning of this chapter, where the not inconsiderable resistance to the new outlooks and, more specifically, to the "deviance as ordinary" concept was suggested. Among the reasons for such resistance are the following: the tendency (need?) people generally exhibit to believe in or assert the basic differentness of presumed deviators; the sociologist's urge to categorize and compare; the associated emphasis on explaining the causes and occurrence of behaviors—often in connection with the policy goal of identifying and treating "offenders;" the legacy of extreme biologically oriented "positivism," particularly in criminology; and the popular appeal of biological and psychological theories of deviance causation. In short, there has often been on the part of some sociologists as well as other persons a strong "urge to differentiate."

THE URGE TO DIFFERENTIATE

A Widespread Tendency

When we think of the kinds of feelings reflected and incorporated in deviance-defining, it is immediately apparent that the very concept implies an urge to differentiate, a desire to avoid and set apart. Because the behaviors or conditions people react to in this way are to them so dismaying and upsetting, the common tendency is to maintain one's distance in every possible way. Assumptions (frequently unwarranted) about the unusualness or the distinctiveness of the individuals involved are part of this pattern. Self-designated conformists often seem to need to convince themselves that "those people" are not at all like "us." Along with this belief or hope (corroboration of which, we might say, is often produced as a result of the very process of deviantizing) goes the assumption (again, in a way a need) that "those people" can be readily identified as such because they are so basically and thoroughly different.

An excellent indicator of this urge to set apart and render alien is the aforementioned and frequent reference to "animals" in popular accounts of particularly atrocious violent crimes. This usage, which has even been extended to descriptions of property looters in urban ghetto disorders, could, of course, be understood simply as figurative metaphor. Nobody really believes these perceived offenders *are* animals, it might be insisted; rather, the statements assert that the individuals were *behaving* like animals. Yet such modifying or qualifying words rarely appear in the heat of reaction, and the constant use of "hoodlums," "thugs," "scum," and even "vermin" in public discourse seems to reflect and, at the same time, very likely reinforces this urge to differentiate. More generally, and in a somewhat less extreme way, popular conceptions regarding criminals (alluded to earlier) illustrate this phenomenon. Criminals are thought of as a breed apart, doing something *to* society, enemies *of* society, to be combatted *by* society. We are unwilling to accept the fact that they are also members *of* our society, nurtured *in* it, *produced by* it (Schur, 1969, pp. 9–15).

There is, of course, no question but that certain acts of individual violence "deserve" a reaction of moral outrage and strong condemnation, though it is worth keeping in mind that such reaction is selective; thus, killing strangers ("the enemy") in wartime is not seen as "gratuitous" violence, but is condoned and even applauded. However, the alien-species thinking that often accompanies this outrage permits a glib evasion of significant elements of social reality. Furthermore, such reactions may sometimes and to some extent reflect general psychological or social-psychological needs of the *reactors*—dispositions to react that may be present regardless of the specific incidents that appear to trigger them. Thus, some psychoanalytic writers have argued that condemnation and punishment of offenders provide socially sanctioned outlets for the release of basic hostilities and aggressive impulses, and may also bolster the reactor's conscience (superego) in the face of his or her own supposedly rebellious (id) impulses (see, for example, Alexander and Staub, 1956).

To be sure, generalizations about such tendencies may well be subject to the same kinds of methodological limitations that sociologists find in most psychoanalytic formulations regarding the causes of deviation (see section on "Psychogenic Explanations"). Nonetheless, they are suggestive. In a somewhat more social-psychological vein, various analysts have pointed to the possible roles of free-floating resentments, generalized "moral indignation," and a possible link between various "authoritarian" responses and "status anxiety" as underlying and shaping the urge to punish (see Scheler, 1961; Ranulf, 1964; Lipset, 1963). The "functions" for the collectivity itself of identifying and reacting to offenders represent a third level of forces at work in this area. As we will see shortly, formulations about this level contribute importantly to our recognition of the central place of deviance-defining in social systems.

We must realize, too, that the urge to differentiate extends well beyond situations perceived as involving horrendous crime. Nor is its motivation limited to an actual desire to punish. In many areas a major component in such tendencies seems to be a sense of fear or threat, which may, of course, also be a factor in—and difficult to separate for analytic purposes from—the wish to punish. As we are going to see, current deviance theory emphasizes the role of a group's collectively experienced sense of threat in activating the mechanisms of deviance-defining. Fear and threat may be key features of deviantizing, whether we look at this process from the standpoint of individual reactions or collective ones.

One of the most frequently cited examples of this is *homophobia*—fear or dread of homosexuality. According to social psychiatrist Martin Hoffman, such dread, which is in large measure unconscious, is "a pervasive characteristic of contemporary Western culture." Along with many other analysts, Hoffman attributes much of the stigmatization and oppression of homosexuals, and many of their social and psychological difficulties, to such dread (Hoffman, 1969, ch. 11; see also, Weinberg, 1973, ch. 1). In addition, it may ultimately be the fear or dread that accounts for the commonly unidimensional stereotyped conception of homosexuals as being "all alike" (consistent, again, with the breed-apart way of thinking). In this connection, Hoffman comments that homosexuals "run the entire gamut from the swishy faggot who can be identified a block away, to the husband, son, or brother whom even the fairly sophisticated person would not suspect of any homosexual interest" (Hoffman, 1969, p. 33). Acknowledgment of such variability would, of course, undermine the general tendency to *classify*. As a recent writer on lesbianism puts it, "Something so alien as lesbianism is to our society must be explained away and dealt with by a class myth" (Simpson, 1977, p. 7). In his sociological research on public stereotypes of and reactions to various perceived deviations, J. L. Simmons found that, "women were significantly more intolerant [than men] of prostitutes and lesbians, and men were more intolerant of male homosexuals." Recognizing that his interpretation was speculative, Simmons suggested that "Women may find prostitutes and lesbians personally threatening, while men may be threatened by the male homosexual" (Simmons, 1969, pp. 33–34).

We find the setting-apart-as-a-distinct-type tendency operating as well in connection with various other conditions that have been deviantized in our society. A good example is mental deficiency or "retardation." As one important study of persons defined as mentally retarded has noted, retardation "is not a unitary disorder . . . the condition so named embraces several constellations of varied syndromes." Furthermore, even if we adopt the most widely used official diagnostic criteria and classifications (about which many questions could be raised), "Most persons who are defined as mental retardates are not profoundly [IQ range 0–24], severely [IQ range 25–39], or even moderately [IQ range 40–54] retarded. Quite the contrary, fully 85 percent of all mental retardates are only mildly [IQ range 55–69] retarded" (Edgerton, 1967, pp. 2, 5). Popular versions of such catchall designations as "idiots" and "morons" obscure the considerable variability that exists and enable people to ignore an important fact—that the problems experienced by many "retardates" are significantly shaped by social situation and the reactions of others.

In much the same way, the popular urge to delineate defined deviators as distinct and unitary "types" has inhibited public recognition of significant variability among those afflicted with blindness, that is, variability as to the degree of blindness itself, let alone the many other ways in which such persons vary. Noting that that most widely used diagnostic definition of blindness is to a considerable extent arbitrary as a way of distinguishing between blindness and severe vision impairment," sociologist Robert Scott (see Adaptation Ten, "Blindness Agencies," pp. 375–378) found that the blindness population actually is a quite heterogeneous one. Indeed, "The overwhelming majority of people who are classified as blind according to this definition can, in fact, [in some degree] see (Scott, 1969, p. 42). Scott's analysis of "the blindness role" (which will be discussed below) underlines a point suggested earlier in this section: the possibly self-confirming aspect of the tendency to differentiate. Public reactions geared to a supposed unitary rubric such as "the blind" can lead the people so designated, even when they vary greatly in degree of affliction, to all behave eventually in much the same way. They thus become a single and distinct type, even though under other definitions and conditions this might not have happened.

It should be clear, then, that the differentiating urge has as its objects many different types of offending or upsetting behaviors and conditions. Deviance-defining, quite simply, incorporates a tendency to construct "classes" of presumed deviators and to see all members of the class as being essentially alike in some special, distinguishing, way. How distinct a type can be constructed will presumably depend on the nature of the condition or behavior, including the extent to which it can be popularly and/or scientifically viewed as innate or "internal." But some version of differentiation is almost always present in deviantizing whether the category be "crazy people," nymphomaniacs," "murderers," "drunkards," "dope fiends," or "terrorists." As we will see below, this "typing" mechanism is central to deviance-defining in at least two major ways: The presumed deviator (as already noted) can be treated as "nothing but" an instance of the supposed type, and, at the same time, ancillary qualities can be imputed to and extraneous assumptions made about the typed individuals.

Biological Determinism

Those who seek scientific support for the urge to differentiate are quick to cite any and every "finding" that seems to suggest a link between deviating behavior and biological factors. Particularly in the areas of crime and delinquency, there is a long history of efforts to establish such links. (For an excellent critical review of same, see Vold, 1958, chs. 3–7.) Yet such efforts reflecting the scientist's urge to differentiate have produced extremely unimpressive results. Thus, as one leading criminologist has noted:

> The plain fact is that many years of biologic exploration of delinquency have not yielded any valid generalizations about biological factors in deviance. Almost without exception, the biological theories that have been advanced have been scientifically naive, while the research that has been conducted has been flawed in one way or another. Although it cannot unequivocally be claimed that there are no biogenic influences in delinquency, it is undeniably true that none have so far been shown to exist (Gibbons, 1970, p. 75).

Biologically oriented "explanations" of deviance can be traced back at least to the work of **Cesare Lombroso** (1835–1909), an Italian physician-psychiatrist, who is sometimes referred to as the "father of modern criminology." Lombroso's view of crime (often cited as the beginnings of **positivism** in this area) developed out of a reaction against the so-called "classical" and "neoclassical" formulations developed by Beccaria, Bentham, and others. The classical theorists, who were preoccupied with reforming the administration of criminal justice tended to emphasize the role of free will in motivating human behavior, including criminal acts. Lombroso believed that in order to study crime scientifically, the focus had to shift from the crime to the criminal. Criminal behavior was not freely chosen but determined and, in his early and best-known writings, Lombroso claimed that the major determinants were biological ones. Hence, his assertion that there was a "born criminal type."

On the basis of a loosely conducted comparison of less than 400 incarcerated Italian offenders with a group of Italian soldiers, Lombroso concluded that criminals displayed physical abnormalities and that crime was hereditary in nature. Examining and measuring the convicts, he "found" physical anomalies he termed "stigmata" ("deviation" in head size and shape, eye "defects and peculiarities," receding chin, "excessively" long arms, and the like) which were less often present among the soldiers. Such "stigmata," he argued, showed that criminals were *atavistic*—a kind of genetic throwback to an earlier form of animal life. Though he was sincerely dedicated to studying crime "scientifically," Lombroso's conception of research methodology was, by modern standards, quite rudimentary and inadequate. His claims were heavily discredited when an English research team headed by Charles Goring made careful measurement comparisons of about 3000 prisoners and large groups of nonprisoners, including undergraduates at Oxford and Cambridge. This much more systematic study revealed hardly any statistically significant patterns of physical difference between the two groups. The prisoners were found to be slightly shorter and, on the average, to weigh less than the nonprisoners. On the basis of their careful research, Goring and his associates concluded that, "there is no such thing as a physical type" (see Vold, 1958, pp. 50–58).

Nonetheless, the "legacy of Lombroso," as it is often termed, has continued to wield influence. In the 1930s an American physical anthropologist Ernest Hooton produced writings based on extensive "anthropometric research" in which he purported to show that criminals were "organically inferior," low-grade human types who would have to be systematically weeded out and kept from reproducing. Once again, careful evaluations of Hooton's work soon made clear the patent inadequacy of his methods. He assumed that prisoners constituted a representative sample of "criminals" (as we shall see below, a questionable belief); he compared them with a totally haphazard "control" group drawn with no systematic sampling and according to no discernible criteria from among assorted groups, including firemen, college students, hospital patients, and others); he emphasized only those findings that supported his views and ignored some that threw them into question; and nowhere did he indicate how his Lombrosolike "indicators" of criminality (e.g., low sloping foreheads, tatooing, compressed faces, narrow jaws) were determined to be "inferior." In short, the critics pointed out, Hooton's work was dominated by his predetermined conclusion that prisoners *must* be inferior or else they would not be in prison. (For further discussion and evaluation of Hooton's work, see Schur, 1969, pp. 57–58; Vold, 1958, pp. 59–65.)

A somewhat more influential effort to suggest innate crime tendencies has been the "constitutional psychology" analysis of body types grounded in the early ideas of the German psychiatrist Ernst Kretschmer and later developed and applied in the early 1940s by an American researcher William Sheldon. Through a system called **somatotyping** Sheldon would rate a person on each of three basic body-type components and then construct the person's composite score or overall profile. Associated with these types, he claimed, were characteristic temperamental and behavioral tendencies. George Vold has presented a succinct summary of this scheme, reproduced here as Table 2.1.

Using this scheme, Sheldon claimed that some 200 young males dealt with by a Boston welfare agency and whom he somewhat imprecisely defined as "delinquent" differed in dominant body types from other youths he had studied. Critics have noted that his data (often presented as impressionistic 'case" studies) did not really justify this conclusion, let alone his further interpretation (generally in line with Hooton's) that crime tendencies were inherited and that delinquents were constitutionally inferior. His overall approach commands some attention, however, largely because it was incorporated in the more recent and considerably more sophisticated delinquency research conducted by the criminologists Sheldon Glueck and Eleanor Glueck. In their large-scale correlational studies, they found (Glueck, 1956) that mesomorphy (the athletic, muscular body

Table 2.1 Sheldon's Basic Types

PHYSIQUE	TEMPERAMENT
1. *Endomorphic:* relatively great development of digestive viscera; tendency to put on fat; soft roundness through various regions of the body; short tapering limbs; small bones; soft, smooth, velvety skin.	1. *Visceratonic:* general relaxation of body; a comfortable person; loves soft luxury; a "softie" but still essentially an extrovert.
2. *Mesomorphic:* relative predominance of muscles, bone, and the motor-organs of the body; large trunk; heavy chest; large wrists and hands; if "lean," a hard rectangularity of outline; if "not lean," they fill out heavily.	2. *Somotonic:* active, dynamic, person; walks, talks, gestures assertively; behaves aggressively.
3. *Ectomorphic:* relative predominance of skin and its appendages which include the nervous system; lean, fragile, delicate body; small, delicate bones; droopy shoulders; small face, sharp nose, fine hair; relatively little body mass and relatively great surface area.	3. *Cerebrotonic:* an introvert; full of functional complaints, allergies, skin troubles, chronic fatigue, insomnia, sensitive to noise and distractions; shrinks from crowds.

Source: George B. Vold, *Theoretical Criminology.* New York: Oxford University Press, 1958, p. 71. Reproduced with permission.

type) was more predominant among institutionalized delinquents than among noninstitutionalized youths.

As various observers point out, such a finding (even if accurate) raises significant questions of interpretation and of the ordering of and interplay between several variables. A crucial point is that a statistical correlation by itself does not provide a causal explanation. For example, a "more basic" third factor might help to account for both mesomorphy and delinquency; or, perhaps, youths engaging in delinquent acts might gradually and increasingly develop signs of mesomorphy. Even assuming that the two factors are in some way associated, the inevitable role of social patterns and processes in delinquency would remain unconsidered. Social selection, for example, may imply "that recruits to delinquent conduct are drawn from the group of more agile, physically fit boys . . ." (Gibbons, 1970, p. 76). Finally, the body-type "explanation" is inadequate because it is based entirely on an institutionalized sample of officially adjudicated delinquents. As Hirschi and Selvin have pointed out, this implies neglect of an important "intervening variable"—the definitions and responses of the delinquency-processing system itself. "Judges may see in a muscular, broad-shouldered boy more of a threat to the community than they see in his pale and skinny counterpart. If this is so, the indifferences in the proportions of mesomorphs among delinquent and nondelinquent populations could well stem from this attitude on the part of the judge" (Hirschi and Selvin, 1967, pp. 96–97). What we might be getting, then, is really more a picture of the causes of institutionalization than one of the causes of delinquent acts.

More recently still, a great flurry of excitement surrounded claims that a specific genetic condition (an extra Y-chromosome in some men) might be associated with crimes of physical violence. (See the discussion in Taylor, Walton, and Young, 1974, pp. 44–47; and in Suchar, 1978, pp. 61–71). Initial research purporting to show an association between this XYY make-up and aggressive tendencies produced scattered and rather inconclusive findings for the most part based on relatively small samples of institutionalized convicts. When more large-scale and systematic studies have been done, the main finding seems to be that men with the XYY condition (often carrying with it lower intelligence) may be more frequently detected in or convicted of crimes. Furthermore, this recent research indicates that those crimes of which XYY men are convicted are no more likely to be violent in nature than those of XY ("normal") men (see Brody, 1976).

Even if these biological "theories" were to be conducted with great methodological scrupulousness so that the correlations they produced really held up, there would still be significant limitations as to just what they explained. If we were to discover an innate tendency toward "aggression," we would still be unclear as to how that tendency is socially influenced and channeled and how specific manifestations are evaluated and treated. We would not know why one aggressive person becomes a professional athlete or, say, a ruthless business tycoon and another commits a violent crime. We would not know how one person's barroom behavior comes to be designated 'horseplay" and the same behavior on another person's part is designated and reacted to as "assault." We would not know how to distinguish the aggressive violence of wartime killings from "genetic" violence, for it would never occur to us to characterize soldiers' violent acts in that way. In short, the biological formulations take no account of social patterning, situational contingencies, and defining-reacting patterns. They are concerned only with the occurrence of acts or, more vaguely still, with "tendencies" to act in certain ways, not at all with social meanings. They leave out, among other things, the crucial element of the attribution of deviantness.

This same glaring failure is apparent in similar efforts to apply biological formulations to other forms of perceived deviation besides that of crime and delinquency. As one sociological researcher notes, "The tendency to think in biological terms even when there is little or no evidence of organic pathology has been a particularly noticeable aspect of writing and thinking in the field of mental retardation" (Mercer, 1973, p. 10). This same writer's own studies (to be cited below) make clear that sociocultural variation in defining and reacting to retardates, especially social-class variation, vitally affects their situations and prospects. Thus her findings accord with the conclusion reached by Edgerton (just quoted on retardation "typing") that mild mental retardation "is a social phenomenon through and through" (Edgerton, 1967, p. 6). The entire area of mental testing and mental deficiency (in the early studies often labeled "feeble-mindedness") has long involved controversial and questionable claims regarding both the supposedly "innate" nature of intelligence and the relation between intelligence levels and offending behavior. (For an overview of early research, see Vold, 1958, chs. 5, 6.)

Recent developments in this area are exceedingly complex and seem generally to point in two rather different directions. There have been some startling revelations of error, bias, and possible fraud in some of the early research often relied on by those who stress the relative importance of "nature" over that of "nurture" (see, for example, Rensberger, 1976). Even apart from these charges, most sociologists today consider the available evidence on balance to clearly demonstrate the culture influencing and changeability of IQ, the absence of IQ measures that are free of cultural bias (i.e., in the content of their questions), and the relative insignificance of "hereditary intelligence" in shaping human behavior. On the other hand, the general popularity of various books on animal behavior (by Konrad Lorenz, Robert Ardrey, and others) along with the recent heralding of a new science of *sociobiology* (Wilson, 1975) testify to the continuing appeal of biological approaches. For our purposes here, however, it is important to note that the strong tendency among most sociologists is to reject the notion that biology and heredity directly cause deviance.

An area in which deviance-defining is common, and with respect to which we might especially anticipate an appeal to biological "explanations," is that of sexual behavior. Though we typically experience our own sexuality as highly compelling and may thus tend to think about it in "internal" terms, at the same time many aspects of sexual activity are patterned and learned through social processes and within specific cultural contexts. Writing of social "scripts" that shape and influence sexuality, specialists John Gagnon and William Simon note that, "Scripts are involved in learning the meaning of internal states, organizing the sequences of specifically sexual acts, decoding novel situations, setting the limits on sexual responses, and linking meanings from nonsexual aspects of life to specifically sexual experience" (Gagnon and Simon, 1973, p. 19).

While sexual impulses and even particular sexual inclinations may be partly attributable in the first instance to biological make-up, there are contributory social forces affecting their course of development. In particular, such forces help determine what we make of and do about our impulses and inclinations and what other people make of them. Thus, even if some adult homosexuals themselves find it convenient to assert and firmly believe or "feel" that they were "born that way," such glib notions almost invariably ignore the complex social-psychological processes of personality development influencing such preferences and their manifestation in adulthood (see Money, 1972; Schur, 1972). And whatever part of initial causation of such preference may be biological, an understanding of the extensive patternings and variations found in homosexuals' lives and situations would require other forms of explanation. The biggest explanatory gap would concern variations in defining and reacting to homosexuality in different settings and in the effects or concomitants of such variations.

The same thing is true with respect to biological theories about other kinds of sexual behavior that are imbued with deviantness. For example, we can see that it would be easy to casually explain various sexual offenses by claiming that the offenders (e.g., prostitutes, rapists, child-molesters, etc.) are "oversexed." Of course, it could be true that individual variability in strength or intensity of sexual drives is largely "innate." Yet that would tell us nothing about social and situational determinants of such acts, let alone about the processes through which the acts are defined and reacted to (in these instances, legal processes as well as social ones). It makes little sense to attribute to biological causes the complex outcomes of sociolegal processes. Actually, there is no evidence showing that people who engage in the behaviors mentioned have unusually strong sexual impulses (if anything, the available evidence may point in the other direction). But the overriding mistake is to jump from supposedly innate cause to outcome, without considering at all the contribution of the deviance-defining itself to the outcome, which consists, after all, not simply of an act, but an act *as we understand it and react to it*.

The point is clearer when we consider a less inflammatory and more commonplace example. How it is that a sexually active person can in one social context be considered "popular" or "liberated," whereas in another context the same behavior would be viewed as a sign of "promiscuity" or perhaps even "perversion?" Quite clearly, biology cannot tell us. These are not just acts in the abstract, as it were, but rather conclusions about acts (here, different possible conclusions about the same acts)—conclusions that shape reactions and that ultimately may affect the individuals so defined as well. Biological formulations, in other words, may provide some necessarily limited indication as to why given acts occur in the first place; however, they leave out entirely the extremely important meaning element in deviance situations.

This is so because, as British sociologists Taylor, Walton, and Young note, "Positivism as a doctrine is wedded to the position of taking social reaction for granted" (Taylor, Walton, and Young, 1974, p. 65). Ultimately, the urge to differentiate narrows our focus from the interrelated and changing network of elements that comprises a deviance situation to the perceived deviator—the meaning of whose actions are treated as self-evident. Further on in this chapter we will consider a good many examples pointing up the problematic and relative nature of deviance-defining. If the nature and even the existence of deviance, that is, the assignment of deviantness to the behaviors in question, is dependent upon social context as well as (in particular instances) specific situational contingencies, then biological explanations are patently inadequate. Thus when one focuses on the crucial defining-reacting processes, it becomes extremely difficult to accept Sagarin's recent claim that, "a biological basis for an understanding of deviance is not at all incompatible with a relativist view of crime and deviance" (Sagarin,

1975, p. 79). On the contrary, most recent deviance analysis treats biological theories as providing a highly limited and, as we have just seen, potentially distorting
contribution to our general understanding in this area.

The reason for devoting even this much space to such conceptions is not,
then, that they are professionally influential. Rather, the value of such discussion
lies in revealing the shortcomings and limitations of an approach that continues
to hold a considerable if deceptive popular appeal. Furthermore, we can through
looking at these formulations begin to recognize the nature and fallacies of the
more general effort to differentiate and to see in particular the methodological
problems attending research and analysis geared to such an effort. It is also worth
emphasizing that these misleadingly internal conceptions of deviance can generate or reinforce an ideology that supports particular kinds of political values
and policy decisions. As Taylor, Walton, and Young rightly assert in regard to
crime theories, biological determinism "removes any suggestion that crime may
be the result of social inequalities. It is something essential in the nature of the
criminal and not a malfunctioning of society. In addition, it achieves the utter
decimation of the possibility of alternative realities . . . (Taylor, Walton, and
Young, 1964, p. 40).

Psychogenic Explanations

A considerable amount of material in this book relates, directly or indirectly, to the meanings and applications of the concept "mental illness." Among
the pertinent points to be touched on are the following: cultural uniformities
and variations in identifying such conditions, subcultural variations in "symptoms" and their meanings (see, for example, Adaptation One, "Diagnosis Across
Cultures," pp. 75–80), processes of informal interaction leading up to defining
specific situations as involving mental illness (see Adaptation Three, "Normalizing
Erratic Behavior," pp. 162–171), the sociolegal processes involved in mental illness commitment proceedings, the stigma of being a "mental patient" and the
difficulty of removing such stigma (see Adaptation Seven, "Pseudopatients," pp.
280–283), the role of the psychiatrist as a "social control" agent, the nature and
consequences of institutionalization in mental hospitals, the wide-ranging uses
of mental illness concepts in explaining an enormous variety of quite diverse
behaviors that are subject to deviantizing definitions and reactions.

As this list should suggest, the key theme in the deviance sociologist's
approach to psychogenic (psychological causation) explanations is to place and
interpret both their content (meaning structures) and their uses (applications to
types of cases, situations, and in specific instances) in terms of sociocultural context and processes of social interaction. Thus, the crucial issue in connection
with analyzing deviance is not really (as one recent text seems to suggest) whether
or not mental illness is "real" (see Sagarin, 1975, pp. 180–201). It is true that
treating mental illness designation as a problematic social process at times seems
to come close to denying the reality of such a condition. As we shall see further,

this is part of what bothers some critics of the *labeling approach* to mental illness (e.g., Gove, 1970; but also see, contra, Scheff, 1974). Outside of sociology, this general stance has been pushed to an extreme by psychiatrist Thomas Szasz (see Szasz, 1961) and his British colleague R. D. Laing. Thus, we have Laing's not infrequent contention that those labeled as "insane" may in fact ("in the context of our present pervasive madness") be more sane than those we consider "normal": "The statesmen of the world who boast and threaten that they have Doomsday weapons are far more dangerous, and far more estranged from 'reality' than many of the people on whom the label 'psychotic' is affixed" (Laing, 1965, pp. 11, 12).

Yet nobody, not even Laing, would deny that many people do in fact experience serious psychological confusion and conflict, great personal unhappiness and discontent, or compulsions and obsessions that may stifle them or prevent them from living as they themselves want to live. The existence of deeply felt self-recognized personal problems of this sort is not the "target" of critical sociological analysis—although even at this level a comprehensive explanation will ordinarily call for some consideration of social structures, processes, and situations. But in analyzing deviance sociologically, there is much more to which one must attend. For personal problems (even self-perceived ones) to constitute "mental illness" that particular way of *designating* and *characterizing* the situation must be applied (by someone) to them; this aspect can *only* be understood by studying patterns of context and interaction. Furthermore, "mental illness" is a designation imbued with the meaning qualities of deviantness. As Theodore Sarbin succinctly states, "Persons who are labeled mentally ill are not regarded as merely sick, but are regarded as a special class of beings, to be feared or scorned, sometimes to be pitied, but nearly always to be degraded" (Sarbin, 1969, p. 20). As this suggests and as we will see further, being defined as mentally ill in many respects places the individual in a special social status and role that can greatly influence his or her life chances and overall sense of identity.

These comments should begin to indicate some of the substantive concerns underlying the emerging sociological view of psychiatric conceptions and of the ways in which they are used. Perhaps to an even greater extent, however, sociological analysis and evaluation in this area rest on considerations of methodology—assuming, for the moment, that it is possible to distinguish between the inevitably interwoven features of substance and method. Precisely because mental illness is a deviantizing characterization of personal problems and social behavior, on which characterizations there will frequently be less consensus than on those of "physical" illnesses or injuries, it is extremely difficult to define in a totally nonevaluative nonjudgmental way. As sociologist David Mechanic comments, "Attempts to define mental illness in some precise fashion have brought continuing disappointment. Although it is usually defined in terms of some deviation from normality, defining normality is not a simple matter" (Mechanic, 1969, p. 2).

It is particularly the apparent readiness to casually apply mental illness concepts to almost any and every kind of offending behavior that causes sociologists of deviance to emphasize the elusiveness of those concepts. When such applications are buttressed by or develop into specific psychodynamic explanations of particular categories of such behavior, the formulations commonly seem tainted by a kind of presupposition that mental illness *must* be present. This is not the result of a malevolent conspiracy on the part of psychiatrists or other students of the mind, but simply reflects their training and experience—both of which have been heavily limited to a focus on instances and signs of psychopathology. Confronted with a person who has attempted suicide, or who gambles and loses constantly, or who belongs to an exotic religious cult, the specialist in psychodynamics seems dangerous prone to assuming at the outset that such a person must be mentally ill. The "diagnostic" procedure then involves not so much establishing *whether* mental disorder is present, but rather *documenting* its (predetermined) presence. Thus we find a version of the general deviance-defining process of *retrospective interpretation* (see especially Chapter 4).

The specialist who in this way sets out to "find" the disease already seen to be present, implicitly takes for evidence the very symptoms that ought to be on an independent basis explained. One sociological commentator on disease theories of alcoholism states:

> If "loss of control" does constitute the essential foundation for the claim that "alcoholism is a disease," [citing an influential formulation of drinking specialist Mark Keller], and if, as is clearly the case, the existence of this "loss of control" cannot be independently determined but must be inferred on the basis of the failure of the chronic drunkard to comport himself in the manner of a prudent man, it seems to me that we cannot escape the conclusion that the disease formulation is a circular one. For . . . it is precisely the unreasonable character of the chronic drunkard's project that makes him problematic to common sense in the first place. The argument reduces to this: because no one who is "sound of mind and body" would conduct himself in the irrational manner of the chronic drunkard, anyone who does so conduct himself . . . must be diseased . . . (MacAndrew, 1969, pp. 497–498; see also Schneider, 1978).

A similar circularity and preordained certainty of diagnosis were noted by Alfred Lindesmith in his now-classic dissection of the thesis that the drug addict is a psychopath—a notoriously imprecise, catchall diagnostic category that often seems to be applied to any perceived deviator who does not neatly fit into one of the more standard categories. Commenting that there seemed to be an unspoken assumption "that any trait which distinguishes addicts from nonaddicts is *ipso facto* a criterion of abnormality," Lindesmith went on to observe:

> Addicts are said to become addicted because they have feelings of frustration, lack of self-confidence and need the drug to bolster themselves up. Lack of self-confidence is taken as a criterion of psychopathy or of weakness. But another person becomes addicted, it is said, because of "curiosity" and a "willingness to try anything once" and this too is called abnormal. Thus, self-confidence and the lack of self-confidence are both signs of abnormality. The addict is evidently judged in advance. He is damned if he is self-confident and he is damned if he is not (Lindesmith, 1940, p. 920).

Such factors as socioeconomic strain, general social alienation, neighborhood and subcultural traditions, opportunities to obtain and try drugs, availability of alternative opportunities, and the general learning processes that Lindesmith himself (in a theory cited below) claimed were the cause of addiction are just some of the factors these psychodynamic theories tend to overlook. This is not to say that there are never any sick drug users. At the same time, however, there are neighborhoods and groups in which practically everyone uses drugs; particularly, under such circumstances, psychodynamics as a *general* explanation becomes extremely questionable.

One of the most familiar and controversial extensions or applications of the mental illness concept has been in the area of homosexuality. Here again, the circularity objection is appropriate. Both psychoanalytic writings that stress the pathology of this orientation (see various articles in Ruitenbeek, 1963) and psychiatric research efforts claiming to document such pathology (Bieber, et al., 1962) are limited in perspective by the reliance on clinical "cases" and by the apparent presupposition of psychic disturbance. When psychologist Evelyn Hooker administered a battery of standard psychological tests to homosexuals drawn from the public at large, that is, persons who were *neither* in psychiatric treatment *nor* in trouble with the law, professionals who examined the results "blind" (unaware that the subjects were homosexual) found no greater indications of psychopathology than among Hooker's carefully selected nonhomosexual "control" subjects (Hooker, 1963). In the years since this landmark refutation of the thesis of invariable pathology, the gay liberation movement (see Chapter 7) and related currents of change in public attitudes have produced a further undermining of the illness conception of homosexuality.

There is a growing recognition of the variability in personality types and problems, as well as in other characteristics, within the homosexual population. (Bell and Weinberg, 1978.) As psychiatrist-author Martin Hoffman has aptly noted, if he had relied solely on his own clinical experience, he, too, would have concluded that all homosexuals are mentally ill. "What I have refused to do, however, is to assume that my patients were the only kind of homosexuals that there are" (Hoffman, 1969, p. 157). Hoffman concluded, actually, that homosexuals in our society may be more likely to experience psychological problems than are heterosexuals, but he attributes this to the stigma and oppression they confront and, ultimately, therefore, in large measure to the heterosexual's dread of homosexuality, referred to above (see also Weinberg, 1973). At the same time, under the collective impetus of gay liberation, homosexuals themselves are expressing increased unwillingness to accept illness designations. They are more and more insisting, as one writer puts it, that "homosexuals have, in effect, been *defined* into sickness by a mixture of moral, cultural, social, and theological value judgments, cloaked and camouflaged in the language of science" (Kameny, 1971, p. 61). In 1973 the American Psychiatric Association, after a heated and much-publicized controversy, removed homosexuality *as such* from its standard list of diagnostic categories, while noting that homosexuals *could* be disturbed in connection with their sexual orientation, just as heterosexuals might be in connection with theirs (see discussion in Spector and Kitsuse, 1977, pp. 17–20).

Yet another area of prevalent deviance-defining that has been heavily influenced by psychodynamic perspectives involves children judged to be troublesome. There are many long-standing as well as recent psychogenic explanations of delinquency—almost all of which are subject to the methodological objections we have noted thus far as well as to others we will be considering below. Neither "causal" research nor evaluation of treatment programs based on these theories provides impressive support for them (see Schur, 1973, pp. 29–78). Nor do these formulations take account of the extent to which delinquency is a social and legal construction involving outcomes and aspects produced through reactions to offending youths, including those built into the definitions and procedures of the juvenile justice system itself (see "Juvenile Justice" in Chapter 7). Many of the psychogenic approaches to delinquency are geared to unearthing presumed *tendencies* toward delinquency in order to head off trouble before it occurs. Thus, the frequent if delusive belief in an ability to discern some condition of **predelinquency** or latent delinquency.

Extreme notions of this sort lay behind the much-publicized 1969 "'Hutschnecker" proposal (by a former doctor of then President Nixon), urging that all children ages 6–8 be subjected to mass testing in order to detect those with "violent and homicidal tendencies," who could then be given various kinds of "corrective treatment" (see Schrag and Divoky, 1976, ch. 1). Quite apart from the obvious legal and moral objectives to "correcting" children for behavior they have not yet manifested, there is no meaningful evidence indicating the existence of such early crime tendencies or showing that scientists have the ability to spot them (Schur, 1973, pp. 46–61). Nonetheless, the goal of prediction, with an eye to "early identification and treatment," continues to have some influence among practitioners in certain juvenile justice programs. The same kind of impulse seems to be part of what is involved in the recent recourse to widespread screening of schoolchildren for alleged hyperactivity and related disturbances, which was mentioned earlier, and which one sociologist has termed a "medicalization of deviance" (see Conrad, 1975). As Schrag and Divoky document, the administration of psychotropic (mind-altering) drugs to control children found to be troublesome or *potentially* troublesome is now an extremely widespread practice in our society (Schrag and Divoky, 1976).

If we consider the array of diverse behaviors and conditions that have been strongly subject to deviantizing processes in our society during recent years, it is difficult to think of *any* for which psychogenic explanations have not sometimes been offered. The causes of prostitution, when approached from such a standpoint, reside in the supposed "personality" patterns or problems of the prostitute, whose "basic differentness" from all other women is simply assumed. There was a common (popular, and to a lesser extent, professional) tendency to view "hippies" of the 1950s and 1960s as psychologically "disturbed," though the actual evidence in support of such a proposition is quite inconclusive (Smith, 1969). Indeed, it was not all that many years ago when one specialist could describe most abortion-seeking women (he excepted those who had been raped or made pregnant through incest) as "sick" persons (Galdston, 1958, p. 119)—a proposition few would currently accept. The deviantizing of the elderly that persists in the United States today, where we "warehouse" many old people in mental institutions, is sometimes buttressed by psychogenic conceptions and "diagnoses." Psychiatrist Seymour Halleck, in an interesting book on "The Politics of Therapy," highlights the questionable nature of this extension of mental illness ideas:

> The psychiatrist who interprets the misery of the elderly as an illness helps to perpetuate a vicious form of oppression. It is commonly assumed that people will naturally become more depressed as they grow older. Failing strength, illness, and the fear of death . . . are indeed formidable stresses, but there is absolutely no evidence that these stresses inevitably cause depression. If the elderly person has an important place in society, he can live with grace and dignity. . . . if the psychiatrist treats the unhappiness of the older person as an illness, he may help to justify society's unwillingness to treat that person decently (Halleck, 1972, p. 131).

For the sociologist of deviance, then, it is the loosely expandable definitions on which the psychogenic approach is grounded, and the far-ranging uses to which they are put, that are of special interest. Whether or not these applications amount to "overdiagnosis" is, of course, a debatable question. What is not debatable is the fact that psychogenic formulations are widely resorted to in efforts to explain diverse behaviors or conditions that many people consider socially problematic. The overriding difficulty with such efforts (disentangling illness from social "objectionableness") arises because of the very nature of perceived social problems, which, as we have seen, inevitably rest on value judgments and social defining processes. In these varied guises, as well as in the enormous range of eccentricities, troublesomenesses, and unhappinesses that may be susceptible to psychogenic definition, designations of mental illness must be seen as encompassing more than just the extremes of troubled or bizarre behavior that laypersons often associate with "craziness."

There are certainly some disturbances so pronounced that few of us would doubt they involve severe psychological disturbance and pain. Even here, as in the clearly identifiable "psychoses," and notwithstanding the continuing easy appeal of internal explanations such as "chemical" or "hereditary" theories of schizophrenia, there is a wide range of developmental and situational factors that have to be looked into in explaining causes, let alone in explaining what is made socially of the disturbing behavior that results. (For a review of such factors, see Weakland, 1969.) But by far the largest proportion of diagnosed mental illness is not like this at all. As material presented below will indicate, in many situations consensus regarding the appropriateness of psychopathology designations will be incomplete, and thus the "outcomes" of the processes through which they may be applied have to be viewed as problematic.

Persisting Positivism

The "legacy of Lombroso" has exerted a continuing influence in the deviance area, even among sociologists who would be quick to repudiate biological or psychodynamic determinism. In Chapter 3, we will be considering some major trends and theories in the sociology of deviance. As we are going to see, the persisting influence of positivism lies not so much in the specific characteristics of deviators examined under different approaches; body types and even underlying psychopathology are quite far afield from the causal factors most sociologists investigate. Rather, the continuity (to the extent it exists) is a matter of underlying assumptions about human behavior generally, and deviation more specifically, and general methodological stance. In particular, three basic notions have continued to exert force in deviance analysis: **differentiation, constraint** (or determinism), and **pathology.**

These three ideas reflect the predecessors of and lingering resistance to the ordinariness theme in analyzing deviance sociologically. The "assumption of differentiation" represents a kind of technical sociological version or counterpart of the popular urge to differentiate that we have just been considering. Sociologist David Matza, who has played a major role in calling attention to the influence of all three of these assumptions, has described its impact in connection with sociological theories of crime and delinquency:

> The delinquent was fundamentally different from the law-abiding. . . . Differentiation is the favored method of positivist explanation. Each school of positive criminology has pursued its own theory of differentiation between conventional and criminal persons. Each in turn has regularly tended to exaggerate these differences. . . . A reliance on differentiation, whether constitutional, personal, or sociocultural, as the key explanation of delinquency has pushed the standard-bearers of diverse theories to posit what have almost always turned out to be empirically undemonstrable differences (Matza, 1964, pp. 11–12).

As we began to see in the introductory chapter, such differentiation reflects the basic methodological inclinations and preferences of many sociologists. In its attempt to produce generalizations about social life and its frequent reliance on classification and statistical comparison as means to that end, sociology has often produced in new guise theories of deviance that in varying degrees and forms carry on the "differentness" theme of the biological and psychological determinists. In the more extreme versions, the theorist adheres to the conception that the deviating individuals are *themselves* "basically" different. For example, they might be held to display distinctive personality traits even if the presence or development of those traits were recognized as being associated with social background factors or as having developed through social-psychological processes.

Such "kinds of people" theories, as Albert Cohen has aptly described them, remain at a psychological or, at best, a social-psychological level. Less extreme versions of differentiation make the difference between deviators and other people less internal and therefore somehow less basic. Thus, deviators may be distinguishable in terms of their *situations,* or there may be conjunctions of kinds of persons and kinds of situations that account for the varying frequencies of deviating behavior. (For a discussion of these approaches, seen as characteristic "research strategies," see Cohen, 1966, ch. 4.) At least to some extent, the more traditional of the theories to be reviewed in the next chapter all veer toward this basic logic of differentiating. Explaining patterns is seen to require systematic exploration of differences, and that, in turn (it is claimed), depends on the kind of either-or (deviance/nondeviance; deviant person/nondeviant person) classification which, as noted earlier, the newer outlooks insist we must repudiate.

Tied up with this logic is the frequent assumption of a high degree of constraint or determinism of the deviating individual's behavior. Setting aside the Lombrosian sorts of biological and hereditary determinism and the psychologist's frequent focus on early childhood experiences, the sociologist tends to emphasize the determining influence of the deviator's social environment. Neighborhood or subcultural traditions, socioeconomic strains, status pressures, and the like "push" individuals into deviation. As Matza has suggested, commenting on subculture theories, "Peers are for the sociologist what families are for the personality theorist. They represent the intimate setting within which delinquent impulses are transmitted and generated" (Matza, 1964, p. 19). Thus, the nature of the constraining and determining forces and pressures shifts and becomes more "sociological," but the assumption that some such forces and pressures account for deviation persists (see "Subculture Analysis" in Chapter 3). Even apart from the fact that this kind of explanation leaves the crucial attribution-of-deviantness element totally unexamined, it also produces a rather rigid and unvarying depiction of the causation of the acts so characterized. As we have already begun to note (and we will be much preoccupied with this matter throughout this book), the recently emphasized perspectives on deviance depict a much more *fluid, contingent,* and *unpredictable* process of human interaction, and they imply a less all-encompassing, more changeable "commitment" to behaviors and patterns, including those subject to deviance-defining.

A third strand in persisting sociological efforts to differentiate deviance is the assumption of pathology (see Matza, 1969, ch. 3). As already suggested, you don't have to be a physician to adopt a **medical model.** In its broadest version, the assumption of pathology inheres in the very assertion of nonordinariness, that is, in the belief that there is something so irregular about behaviors imbued with deviantness that we should want to explain them in some "special" way and that this is much more called for than a comparable effort to explain so-called "conforming" behavior. Thus, the effort to "understand" prostitutes, but not the customers of prostitutes; to develop special theories about the causation of homosexuality, but not of heterosexuality (or sexuality, generally); to be preoccupied with explaining the use of some drugs (heroin, marihuana, cocaine, etc.) while assuming the ordinariness of other perhaps equally dangerous patterns of drug use (tobacco, tranquilizers, alcohol) which seem only to concern us when we choose to find "alcoholism," and so on.

More specific versions of the pathology assumption can be found in particular sociological approaches to deviance. Perhaps the major example is the recourse to notions of *social disorganization* (see Chapter 3). Here what is posited is, in effect, a kind of social pathology rather than a personal one. As an early critical analysis of such ideas noted (Mills, 1943), some of the sociologists developing them, as a reflection of their own personal backgrounds, may have harbored a kind of "rural bias" according to which various conditions of complex urban living immediately appeared pathological ("disorganized"). Howard Becker has charged that **functionalist** approaches to deviance, which seem to assume we can know what is functional and what is dysfunctional for a group or society, likewise adhere to some version of a medical model (Becker, 1963, p. 7). As the discussion below will suggest, however, the functionalist tradition contains at least several interrelated strands of thinking about deviance. Some parts of the functionalist outlook, indeed, seem to strongly support the ordinariness thesis.

DECOMPARTMENTALIZING DEVIANCE

Up to this point, most of the discussion in this chapter has concerned factors promoting the tendency to differentiate. Yet, as we saw at the outset, the overall trend in the deviance field has been away from such a tendency and toward increased assertion (in a number of different senses) of deviance's ordinariness. One way of describing this trend would be to say that it involves a **decompartmentalizing of deviance.** Under the more traditional perspectives in sociology, both deviance and the sociology of deviance were, because of their "specialness," kept in special compartments. Not only did this imply a disconnected analysis of deviance, but it carried with it, too, a kind of second-class citizenry for sociologists specializing in the study of deviance. Deviance was seen as falling outside of, being a departure from, the ordinary workings of societies. And if that were so, then it followed that the analysis of deviance tended to draw one away from the mainstream of sociological work—the development of general theories about social life and social systems.

Recent outlooks on deviance and deviance-defining exhibit a shift in both these regards. Increasingly, sociologists treat deviance and social control as central facets of ordinary social life. Associated with this trend has been a more solid standing within the discipline of sociology for the subfield of deviance analysis. Such analysis is more likely now than before to be viewed as part of or as holding promise of contributions to general sociological theory. There are at least two aspects to this relatively recent development. One involves the increased attention being paid to microsociological studies intensely focused on processes of face-to-face interaction. The second involves recent efforts to draw on the venerable structural-functional perspective in sociological theory, in order to develop a kind of macrosociology (that is, analysis at the group or societal "system" level) of deviance-defining. At both these levels, the changing conceptions of deviance are similar to changes that have occurred with respect to the notion of "conflict" (see Coser, 1956); a previously neglected feature of social life (one viewed as uncommon, aberrational) has been recognized as an ordinary, indeed, central aspect of the social order (Scott, 1972).

A Basic Component of Interaction

The microsociological aspect of this "new look" for deviance has centered around a recognition that deviance-defining and "controlling" represent major ingredients of the processes we all engage in in everyday interaction with one another. There is an irony in the fact that this realization can in some sense be viewed as a new one, because most introductory sociology courses (and many of the studies typically cited in them) have long made this same point explicitly or implicitly. It has always been understood in basic sociological analysis that conformity to the "central tendency" in a particular behavior pattern and, likewise, to any "norm" or approved mode of behaving is never complete. So whatever a group's expectations or requirements of individuals, we know there is as a matter of course a good deal of variability or diversity in how particular group members behave.

In addition to this sense in which deviation has always been recognized as ordinary, we could cite all the standard studies in sociology that show how people develop and use informal norms and sanctions, even in situations supposedly governed by formal ones. Particularly in work situations, such as that observed in the famous "bank-wiring observation" room studies (see Broom and Selznick, 1977, pp. 145–147), we see how people are continuously engaged in what we would have to call deviance-defining: establishing informal norms regarding a "fair day's work," informally "punishing" those workers who do not adhere, and so on. What seems remarkable is that this kind of recognition of the centrality of deviance-defining was rarely carried over to what were perceived as "social problems" areas and situations. With respect to the standard social problems, deviation and its control remained special and required special causal theories. The recent work of ethnomethodologists who have been interested in both the general nature of everyday interaction and problems of deviance specifically may help to break down this kind of false dichotomy.

Ethnomethodology (see Garfinkel, 1967; Turner, ed., 1974) develops a radical version of the "social construction of reality" thesis referred to earlier in this text. It is grounded in the ideas developed by philosophers of the phenomenological school, who have called for in-depth understanding of "the phenomenon itself" through a "bracketing" of all preconceptions, including those of observers and interpreters. Challenging the empiricist's distinction between subject and object, ethnomethodology treats all social interaction as being highly problematic—in terms of the subjective meanings that may be attached to it. Accordingly, society is seen as an "accomplishment" of its members, and ethnomethodologists seek to explore what they describe as the not-readily-apparent "procedures" and "rules" through which people make sense of and "do" social interaction. To that end, ethnomethodology makes use of various modes of research and interpretation, including intensive observation, linguistic analysis, and efforts to reconstruct basic cognitive and perceptual processes.

Several of the important observation-based studies of deviance-processing that will be cited in subsequent chapters were undertaken by sociologists who view themselves as practitioners of ethnomethodology. These studies have usefully advanced our knowledge of deviance-defining in a number of specific substantive areas. However, our general understanding of deviance and control processes may have been even more greatly enhanced by a set of ethnomethodological projects that were not at the outset narrowly designed as studies of "deviance and control" at all. Believing that everyday patterns of social living are always in part governed by subtle and often unstated rules, Harold Garfinkel developed a series of ingenious field experiments aimed at illuminating these "background expectancies" (Garfinkel, 1964). By having his students radically depart from the expectations of others, and then interpret what happened as a result of this unexpected behavior, Garfinkel was able to show how dependent we usually are on the un-thought-about conformity that governs social interaction.

In one of these experiments, students were told to strike up a conversation with a friend or acquaintance and, whatever the other person said, to continuously seek further clarification. By repeatedly interjecting, "What do you mean?," or other similar responses in the wake of any and all comments by the friends, the student-investigators created conversational havoc and elicited predictably confused and antagonistic reactions. What they had done, Garfinkel suggested, was to violate the unstated rule barring endless requests for clarification. In another of the experiments, students were asked to act like boarders in their own homes, being polite but formal and only speaking when spoken to. As one might expect this procedure too provoked dismay and irritation. "Reports were filled with accounts of astonishment, bewilderment, shock, anxiety, embarrassment, and anger and charges by various family members that the student was mean, inconsiderate, selfish, nasty, or impolite" (Garfinkel, 1964, p. 232). What was being illustrated here, in a sense, was the unsettling nature of individual strangeness or differentness that also is found in reactions to virtually all standard categories of perceived deviance.

Another basic feature of deviance-defining—to which much emphasis is given in this text—was found to be present. Those subjected to the deviation tended to seek, by retrospectively looking at the individual's past actions and situations, a consistent explanation of the disturbing behavior. Thus, Garfinkel notes: "Explanations were sought in previous, understandable motives of the student: the student was working too hard in school; the student was ill; there had been 'another fight' with a fiancee. When offered explanations by family members went unacknowledged, there followed withdrawal by the offended member, attempted isolation of the culprit, retaliation, and denunciation" (Garfinkel, 1964, p. 232). In these and other similar field experiments, what Garfinkel did, in effect, was to use deviation as a research device that would help us appreciate the typically unrecognized controls that govern our ordinary activities. The very fact that he could do this testifies to the central and continuous role that a subtle kind of regulation of deviance plays in our everyday lives.

A Feature of Social Systems

If work such as Garfinkel's highlights deviance-defining as a key aspect of how we regularly interact with one another, other analyses that combine or cut across traditional and newer perspectives point up its significance from the standpoint of the social collectivities (groups and societies) within which it occurs. This is one of the major contributions to a sociology of deviance of the so-called "structural-functional" perspective that has focused on the complex interrelationships among elements that make up and sustain an ongoing, functioning, social system. Recent writers in this functionalist tradition have developed an important analysis of what might be called "the general functions of reacting to deviance," taking as a point of departure some well-known statements of the classic theorist Emile Durkheim (1858–1917).

In his *Rules of Sociological Method,* first published in 1895, Durkheim stated: "Crime is, then, necessary; it is bound up with the fundamental conditions of all social life, and by that very fact it is useful, because these conditions of which it is a part are themselves indispensable to the normal evolution of morality and law" (Durkheim, 1895, 1964, p. 70). As in so much of his work, Durkheim analyzed crime in terms of its relation to the development and sustaining of social cohesion and group solidarity. Our reaction to crime, he wrote elsewhere, "brings together upright consciences and concentrates them." The role of punishment, then, is not to be viewed simply in terms of what is done to deviators, but also in terms of its contribution to sustaining the social system. It is "above all designed to act upon upright people," for it helps to "heal the wounds made upon collective sentiments . . ." (Durkheim, 1893, 1947, pp. 102, 108). Similar themes have appeared in the writings of other major theorists, including Georg Simmel (1858–1918) and George H. Mead (1863–1931). (See Simmel, 1904, 1955; also, Coser, 1956; and Mead, 1928.)

Building on such ideas, contemporary analysts have elaborated on the functions of deviance, both in general theoretical terms (Coser, 1962; Erikson, 1962) and through observational studies of reactions to deviation in specific groups (e.g., the study of Quaker work camps in Dentler and Erikson, 1959). As already indicated, the emphasis in this body of functionalist writings is not on the substance of particular deviations, but rather on the *general* functions, for the system, of the process of deviance-defining and the social reactions it produces or incorporates. A major writer on these matters recently has been Kai Erikson. In his elaboration of the Durkheimian thesis, Erikson asserts that the deviating act:

> . . . creates a sense of mutuality among the people of a community by supplying a focus for group feeling. Like a war, a flood, or some other emergency, deviance makes people more alert to the interests they share in common and draws attention to those values which constitute the "collective conscience" of the community. Unless the rhythm of group life is punctuated by occasional moments of deviant behavior, presumably, social organization would be impossible (Erikson, 1966, p. 4).

By virtue of the reactions to it, then, deviance helps to hold a group or society together and indeed helps to establish the nature and parameters of conformity. Deviance-defining and conformity-defining are thus two sides of the same coin. It is, in a sense, only through the process of identifying deviators that we can say who the conformists are and what behaviors are conformist. As these analyses have brought out, a basic function of reacting to deviance is **boundary-maintenance** —marking off, through the identification of violators the domain and limits of proper behavior. Erikson expresses it this way: "The deviant is a person whose activities have moved outside the margins of the group, and when the community calls him to account for that vagrancy, it is making a statement about the nature and placement of its boundaries. It is declaring how much variability and diversity can be tolerated within the group before it begins to lose its distinctive shape, its unique identity" (Erikson, 1966, p. 11).

As we will see, Erikson has made many other important points about this boundary-maintaining process. For the moment, if we think about his general thesis in conjunction with the ideas of process, conflict, change, and outcome mentioned above, we can begin to realize that in many situations such boundary lines (social as opposed to geographical boundaries, of course) are neither clear-cut nor fixed. Whereas we do sometimes encounter boundary "markers" (such as laws, rules, etc.), even these are subject to change. In other instances it may actually be appropriate to speak of the boundaries being "created" in the very same process by which they are "maintained." Also, as Erikson further suggests (and, as we will see, other writers have picked up the point in interesting ways), the nature of the boundary-maintaining (social control) apparatus and the "placement" of the boundaries (or tolerance limits) help to determine *how much* deviance is present in a given society. (See Adaptation Four, "Producing Witchcraft," pp.

172–174.) Obviously, a narrow domain of conformity means there will be a large domain of potential deviance, and vice versa.

A Society Gets the Deviance It Deserves

In this sense, therefore, the defining-reacting process helps in a most intriguing way to determine at least the extent, if not the substance, of what is supposedly being reacted to. Erikson's sociohistorical analysis of "crime waves" in Puritan New England (Erikson, 1966) convinced him that the specific waves were, in effect, at least partly produced by fluctuations in public reaction and that they were not simply a direct reflection of actual fluctuations in overall deviation. Erikson's consequent suggestion that the "deployment" of social control resources helps to shape a society's deviance picture highlights one aspect of the self-fulfilling or self-confirming mechanisms that have been alluded to above (see also Fishman, 1978). Increased assignment of police to an area at least permits if not implies an increase in arrests. Increased investigation of graft implies an increase in "finding" cases of graft. Turning this point around, a shortage of beds in mental hospitals implies a limit on the number of hospitalized mental patients. A society, then, in a sense experiences the amount of deviance it seeks out and processes. It should already be clear that these points about boundary-maintaining, though derived from the system focus of functionalist theory, are quite compatible with and, indeed, constitute an important part of the social reactions-definitions framework that recently has become so influential in the field.

An additional comment of Erikson's to the effect that deviance reflects a community's fears, underlines the fact that social reaction also shapes the deviance picture in a more substantive way. As he states, "Men who fear witches soon find themselves surrounded by them; men who become jealous of private property soon encounter thieves" (Erikson, 1966, p. 22). Here, too, a possible link between a system perspective and a definitional-processual one is apparent. As already noted, the concept of "threat" is central to the latter approach. Threat activates deviance-defining, and a society's preoccupations will determine the kinds of threat likely to be experienced. Thus we might well expect that a society in which people are heavily preoccupied with sex will experience a high rate and many varieties of sexual deviance. Likewise, a society preoccupied with violence is particularly likely to experience violent forms of deviance. In short, a society not only gets the amount of deviance it processes; it also gets the kinds of deviance it fears.

It is not merely the dominant fears in a society, however, that affect the substance of deviance situations. There is a larger "mirroring" aspect in which it is true that "a society gets the deviance it deserves." The forms of deviance, far from being complete departures from the approved values and institutionalized patterns that dominate a society, in many ways reflect those very values and patterns. In an important summary (influenced by functionalism) of major themes in the analysis of social problems, Robert Merton and Robert Nisbet cited as their first two points the following:

1. The same social structure and culture that in the main make for conforming and organized behavior also generate tendencies toward distinctive kinds of deviant behavior and potentials of social disorganization. In this sense, the problems current in a society register the social costs of a particular organization of social life.

2. From this premise, it can be seen that the sociological orientation rejects as demonstrably inadequate the commonly held doctrine that "evil is the cause of evil" in society. Instead, it alerts us to search out the ways in which socially prized arrangements and values in society can produce socially condemned results (Merton and Nisbet, 1966, p. vii).

As Matza has aptly noted, a major contribution of the functionalist analysis of particular substantive deviance situations has been to bring out this irony—that good can produce perceived evil (Matza, 1969, ch. 4). By the same token, Matza suggests, such studies played an important role in purging deviance sociology of conceptions of individual pathology. Early analyses of prostitution, political bossism, and organized crime developed this type of functionalist deviance analysis.

In an essay first published in 1937 and then later revised, Kingsley Davis emphasized the extent to which prostitution (while often seen as pathological) actually shares common features (primarily the use of sex for nonsexual ends) with more-approved sexual arrangements in our society, including, at the other end of a continuum of essentially similar institutions, marriage. Noting the functional interrelationships among these various sexual institutions, Davis found that prostitution was in effect part of a system through which demands for sexual gratification were satisfied and, as such, met a genuine social demand. Though it might never be completely eliminated, its ties of mutual interdependence with approved sexual arrangements suggested a potential basis for change. As approved modes of gratification became more widely available, the demand for prostitution might decline. (At least until very recent years, this early prediction by Davis seemed to be coming true.) Davis also neatly turned around this point to see further implications of the linkages between prostitution and "respectable" sexuality:

If we reverse the proposition that increased sex freedom among women of all classes reduces the role of prostitution, we find ourselves admitting that increased prostitution may reduce the sexual irregularities of respectable women. This, in fact, has been the ancient justification for tolerated prostitution—that it "protected" the family and kept the wives and daughters of the respectable citizenry pure. . . . Such a view strikes us as paradoxical, because in popular discourse an evil such as prostitution cannot cause a good such as feminine virtue, or vice versa. Yet, as our analysis has implied throughout, there is a close connection between prostitution and the structure of the family (Davis, 1937, 1961, pp. 283–384).

A major concept through which functionalist writings such as this high-lighted the aforementioned irony (or, in the terms used here, suggested one type of "ordinariness of deviance") was that of **latent functions.** As Merton noted in an early formulation, analyzing these unintended consequences of social patterns helps us to interpret sociologically the "many social practices which persist even though their manifest purpose is clearly not achieved" (Merton, 1949, p. 64). Particularly in considering the persistence of blatantly unenforceable criminal laws, the concept of latent functions remains an extremely useful one for contemporary deviance analysis. Merton's own discussion of the political machine or boss system emphasized that such arrangements, often considered undesirable, persisted because they provided "an apparatus for satisfying otherwise unfulfilled needs of diverse groups in the population" (Merton, 1949, p. 73). Likewise, Daniel Bell, in a much-quoted essay on "Crime is an American Way of Life," noted a number of links between the urban "rackets" and dominant American values and structures. Gangsterism in a way mirrored the "jungle quality of the American business community, particularly at the turn of the century," and provided a means for achieving socioeconomic advancement and a kind of social acceptance to certain ethnic groups whose other opportunities for mobility were restricted (Bell, 1953). William F. Whyte, in his early work *Street Corner Society,* had also stressed the functions of the rackets. Those connected with gambling, particularly, met a perceived need in the community and, hence, received considerable community approval. Furthermore, in many respects the day-to-day operation of gambling rackets mirrored that of respectable business (Whyte, 1943).

Especially by pinpointing latent economic functions, these interpretations underlined important similarities between legitimate and illegitimate businesses. Both took the same basic form of "industrial and professional enterprises;" both provided "commodities" that some people wanted. As Merton pointed out, "in strictly economic terms, there is no relevant difference between the provision of licit and of illicit goods and services" (Merton, 1949, p. 78). We will be exploring this general matter of economic functions and linkages at various points throughout the text. As we will see, analysis of such linkages represents another element of convergence between, or common point of interest for, functionalist theory on the one hand, and both conflict theory (including Marxist and neo-Marxist versions) and social reactions perspectives (which, as noted, often find "vested interests" important to an understanding of deviance situations) on the other. Such convergence is facilitated when one keeps in mind Merton's warning regarding the need to specify the social unit from the standpoint of which a practice is viewed as functional, in other words, functional *for whom?* (See Merton, 1949, p. 51.) Provided that is done, this type of functional analysis accords well with dynamic and conflict perspectives and is not really open to the charges of conservative bias and "metaphysical assumptions" some critics have leveled against it. (See, for example, Davis, 1975, pp. 90–93.)

THE RELATIVITY OF DEVIANCE

A key theme in recent deviance sociology is that of relativity. As should be clear from the discussion so far, we cannot fully understand either acts of perceived deviation or instances of deviance-defining unless we take into account the specific sociocultural contexts within which they occur. Indeed, it follows directly from the recognition that defining-reacting mechanisms lie at the heart of deviance situations that we should expect deviance to vary—by place, over time, and from situation to situation. Concomitant with these ideas, as we have also seen, is an increased recognition of great diversity in the patternings of behavior and the attributions of meanings. The twin notions of relativity and diversity imply that often what we find in or underlying deviance situations is some kind of *culture conflict*. In a way, what is frequently happening in such a situation is that behavior which in one context is approved, tolerated, or at least common, is coming up against a contrary attribution of meaning that is dominant in another context. Whether the clash be between whole cultures, subcultures, groups, or social roles, some people are imposing or trying to impose their rules on other people— who either do not agree with, or cannot meet, such prescriptions.

This key aspect of what is often being studied in deviance sociology has great importance not only for a realistic specification and interpretation of the ingredients in deviance situations, but also for a proper understanding of the *social distribution* of deviance. The two points are interrelated, since many of the traditional theories of deviance causation were built up around, and attempted to explain, findings regarding that distribution. Much of the traditional research on deviance has been essentially *epidemiological* in nature, that is, aimed at discovering the amounts and distribution among social classes, other subcultures, geographical areas, etc., of deviating behavior. This approach, emphasizing the finding and interpreting of "rates" of deviation (asking in effect, "Who are the deviants?") did not always take adequate account of variations in meaning (deviantness) attributions in the associated patterns of reacting to deviance. Recognition of the importance of such variation, along with increased awareness of methodological flaws in many of the traditional interpretations, has contributed to the recognition that most instances of perceived deviance are from the standpoint of some other sociocultural vantage point likely to be "ordinary." Whereas criminologists early gave some lip service to the relativity of statutory criminal law, they often neglected this point as they proceeded with their causal analyses. In sociological studies of other types of perceived deviation, the significance of relativity usually received even less attention.

ADAPTATION ONE
Diagnosis Across Cultures*

During the course of a clinical psychology internship in a California state mental hospital, Donald P. Jewell had occasion to study at some length the case of a Navaho Indian who had been institutionalized for psychosis. Uncertain as to whether the patient's behavior and condition—viewed until then solely according to Anglo standards—justified the medical diagnosis that had been made, Jewell held many interviews with him, some with the aid of a Navaho interpreter. His study led to "an increased awareness that to call the patient psychotic was an arbitrary matter. When this Navaho is referred to as psychotic, then, it is merely because he carried such a diagnosis during his 18 months of hospitalization as a mental patient."

The Patient

The patient was a 26-year-old Navaho male. For purposes of anonymity, he will be referred to as Bill. He came to the writer's attention through a survey of Indian patients at the hospital. He was the only Navaho of 13 Indian patients scattered throughout the various wards and cottages, and of the 4000 general patient population.

The outlook for examination and therapy seemed at first quite discouraging. The patient was in a cottage ordinarily reserved for the most regressed patients. Unlike most of the others in this cottage, however, he was not there because of repeated failure of such routine therapies as shock treatment, occupational therapy, etc. It was unusual for a patient in his condition, who had been at the hospital for eight months, not to have received at least electric shock treatment.

A preliminary period was spent at the cottage, observing Bill's behavior. He was very withdrawn. Most of his day was spent in inactive sitting or sleeping. He would rouse himself only for eating or attending to other personal needs. He would assist with floor waxing, dish washing, or other activities the attendants might require of him, but in a perfunctory and apathetic manner. His behavior was not patently catatonic [*a variety of schizophrenia often characterized by extreme withdrawal*] but certainly suggestive of it.

Most of the attendants reported never having heard Bill speak. A few,

* *Source:* Excerpted from Donald P. Jewell, "A Case of a 'Psychotic' Navaho Indian Male," *Human Organization,* 11:1 (1952), 32–36. Excerpts reprinted by permission. (*Passages in italics are the present author's comments—not part of the original.*)

however, indicated that Bill would occasionally approach them and, in almost unintelligible English, ask if he could go home.

Shortly thereafter Bill was brought to the writer's office where he was greeted in Navaho. Bill responded in that language, glancing briefly at the writer before returning his gaze to the floor.

This closer inspection of Bill revealed occipital flattening, resulting from the cradle board as a child, and the pierced ear lobes of a conservative Navaho. During this first interview he complained about the close hair cuts he received at the hospital, further evidence that he belonged to the old-fashioned, "long-hair" conservatives of the reservation.

The interview proceeded very slowly, but gradually a system of communication began to evolve. By utilizing mutually understood Navaho and English words, by means of pantomime, and with the aid of penciled sketches, the system became increasingly refined during the following interviews.

Bill was seen three hours a week for three months. The writer then took an eight months' leave of absence from the hospital, during which time he spent several months in Bill's home area near Shiprock, New Mexico.

While in the Shiprock area, the writer endeavored to locate Bill's family to advise them of the patient's circumstances. Bill had previously drawn a map indicating the approximate location of his family's *hogans* (dwellings), but it proved impossible to find them. The *hogans* were located about 5 miles from the nearest road, and even if a horse and interpreter had been available the chances of locating the specific *hogans* were slight. The situation was complicated by the fact that the family did not have American names and the writer did not know their Navaho names. Missionaries and Bureau of Indian Affairs personnel were consequently given the problem of finding the family but several months elapsed before they were equipped with sufficient information to do so.

Although he could not communicate with Bill's family, the writer succeeded in talking with several Navahos who had known Bill, and in obtaining ecological and further case history material.

Shortly after the writer's return to the hospital a Navaho interpreter was brought in from the Sherman Institute, a large Indian school not far from the hospital. Interviews with the patient through the interpreter corroborated the case history material obtained, and further satisfied the writer in his clinical evaluation of the patient. Both of these areas are separately discussed in the following text.

Case History

. . . Bill was born in a part of the reservation noted for being both very conservative and poverty-stricken. Only 50 miles away is the markedly contrasting community of Shiprock, considered to be one of the most acculturated Navaho communities. It is also prospering from recently developed uranium operations in the region.

During his early years Bill saw very little of Shiprock, and was reared in the traditional Navaho way. He was born during an eclipse (it is not known whether of the sun or moon), and was thus destined to take part in a periodic ceremony identified to the writer as the "Breath of Life" sing. The first of this series of ceremonies was held while he was still an infant, the second about six years ago. During the ceremony he inhales the breath of a great deity, and is thus assured of continued good health in the respiratory and vocal organs.

Bill lived with his immediate family until he was 6 years of age. He had only one younger sister at that time, although the family was later to include seven living siblings. He did not become well acquainted with his family, however, as he was given to his grandfather when he was 6 years old. The grandfather, a widower, lived several miles deeper into the reservation and required Bill's assistance as a sheep herder.

Bill worked for his grandfather as a sheep herder until he was 17, except for one interruption when, at the age of 15, he spent 50 days at the Shiprock hospital with a back ailment. Bill reports that the old man never talked to him.

At his grandfather's death Bill went to work for the railroad in Colorado. This was cut short by an illness which confined him to the Navaho Medical Center in Fort Defiance, Arizona. The illness was diagnosed as tuberculosis, pulmonary, moderately advanced. He was in the hospital for eight months and was discharged in the summer of 1944.

Bill returned to railroad employment, and worked in Utah, Oregon, and Nebraska. He was always part of the Navaho crews and thus never exposed to acculturative influences. His father and a younger brother were also part of these crews.

Bill returned home for a brief visit in 1949, accompanied by his brother and father. He had saved $1,022. Subsequently, he went to Phoenix, Arizona, to pick cotton, a job that had been found for him by the employment agency in Shiprock. This was his first trip from home without a family member.

The employment at Phoenix did not last long and in December, 1949, on the advice of an Indian friend he went to Barstow, California, seeking railroad employment. At the section camp there his attempt to find work was unsuccessful, and after three days he started by bus back to Phoenix.

On this return trip he stopped for dinner at Colton. A white man he met there promised to obtain railroad employment for him. The stranger said that he required funds for this effort and in some way relieved Bill of his savings which had now dwindled to $725.

Bill returned home penniless, pawned some jewelry, borrowed some money, and returned to Colton to try to find the man who had taken his savings. He also looked for Navahos who might have information about employment. The many hours of waiting around the bus station searching for his man apparently caused suspicion, for he was arrested for vagrancy.

In jail he met some Navahos with whom he went to Barstow after release. But in Barstow he was still unable to find employment and after six days he was completely out of funds. He started walking toward Phoenix, and was picked up by a man driving a truck. This man gave Bill one day's employment which allowed funds for a return to Barstow and another attempt to find work.

He managed to raise a little money doing odd jobs about the section camp near Barstow, and then returned to San Bernardino on the first lap of his return to Phoenix and home. It occurred to him that if he could get to a hospital, the officials there would send him to a reservation hospital from whence he would be sent home. This was logical thinking: on the reservations, the hospital, schools, and trading posts are the major sources of assistance in all sorts of trouble.

As this idea occurred to Bill, he noticed a woman dressed in white whom he took to be a nurse. He approached her and endeavored to explain that he was sick, but his endeavors were misinterpreted and he was taken to jail.

At the county jail Bill was apparently mistaken for a Mexican since a Mexican interpreter had tried to interview him. When the interview failed he was transferred to the psychopathic ward. Interviewed by the medical examiner there, he reportedly demonstrated an anguished appearance and repeated, "me sick." He was diagnosed as Schizophrenia, Catatonic Type, and delivered to the state mental hospital.

Upon admission to the hospital, Bill was first taken to be a Filipino. The psychiatric admission note indicated that he was, ". . . confused, dull, and preoccupied. He has a look of anguish and appears to be hallucinating. . . . He repeats, " 'I don't know.' " He was diagnosed as Dementia Praecox, which was later specified as Hebephrenic Type.

Several months later the psychiatrist on Bill's cottage tested him for *cerea flexibilitas* (waxy flexibility) and, finding it to be present, altered the diagnosis to Catatonic Type.

Eight months after his admittance he was discovered by this writer.

Psychological Aspects

Concomitant with gathering the case history material presented above, endeavors were made to evaluate the patient's intelligence and personality. The lack of culturally unbiased examining techniques made this extremely difficult.

Bill's performance on the various tests that were administered led to a conclusion that his probable I.Q. was in the vicinity of 80. This had to take into consideration the patient's slowness. At best, a Navaho refuses to be put under pressure of time, and to what extent Bill's slowness was cultural rather than psychotically pathological was a question of primary concern.

Bill's apathetic and withdrawn behavior has already been described. For diagnostic purposes, however, this syndrome is confused by cultural factors. It is common for Navahos, with their morbid fear of hospitals, to demonstrate just such a withdrawal patterning. . . . It is not known whether or not this would reach a stage of *cerea flexibilitas* or how long this behavior will persist. Accordingly it was concluded that Bill's apparent catatonia should not be accepted as a symptom of schizophrenia until underlying signs of schizophrenic processes could be detected.

During the first interview Bill was given the Draw A Person Test. The figure he drew was indistinct and without facial features and clearly reflected his withdrawal.

On the seventh interview the test was again given. Compared with the earlier attempt, the second drawing clearly reflected an improvement. It probably indicated the therapeutic benefits derived from the extensive individual treatment the patient was receiving.

The second drawing filled the paper, the facial features were portrayed, the arms were extended, and the drawing generally implied those signs which are held to indicate good contact with reality.

Although Bill's second drawing seems to infer considerable personality change, no changes could be observed in his behavior. He continued to appear apathetic and withdrawn. On several occasions he indicated his reluctance to talk because, "me no good this place," pointing to his chest. This suggested the characteristic organ cathexes of schizophrenia. However, the patient's thinking behind this statement was made clear during the later interviews through an interpreter.

Bill was concerned about the fact that he had not completed the second series of the "Breath of Life" ceremony. This latter had gone too long unattended, and he assumed that he must conserve his vocal energies until they could be supplemented by the breath of the deity. He expressed a great need to return home to pursue the ceremony.

In continued endeavor to detect schizophrenic underlay of his apparent catatonia, Bill was given a series of tests, none of which revealed responses normally associated with schizophrenia.

During the early course of the interviews with Bill, although not satisfied that the patient was not psychotic, the writer recommended that the best therapeutic environment for him would be his own home. This recommendation was not acted upon, partly because no one knew where his home was, or how he could be supervised there, but chiefly because he continued to appear catatonic.

Later, as the writer became convinced that the catatonia—if such it could be termed—was not symptomatic of underlying schizophrenia, efforts were renewed to release the patient.

Outcome

As mentioned earlier, the final interviews with Bill were carried on with the aid of a Navaho interpreter. Bill conversed quite freely with the other Navahos and expressed gratitude at being able to talk to someone in his own language. The conversations . . . did offer an opportunity to inquire for the presence of hallucinations, delusions, and more subtle clues of schizophrenic thinking. Unless Bill's anxiety regarding the uncompleted "Breath of Life" ceremony could be considered bizarre, nothing of significance was elicited.

The interpreter's reactions to the interview represented their most significant outcome. He was a professional interpreter, with vast experience in interviewing Navaho youths in strange environments. He expressed a strong conviction that Bill's behavior and attitudes were not unusual under the circumstances.

The interpreter communicated his feelings to the superintendent of the Sherman Institute who took an immediate and active interest in the case. After several interviews with Bill, satisfied that he could observe nothing about Bill's behavior which could be considered atypical under the circumstances, the superintendent offered to accept him into the flexible program of the Sherman Institute.

Bill was accordingly released under custody of the superintendent and careful plans were made to assure his adjustment at the school. At first, he was quartered in the school hospital, but allowed to participate in the school's social and recreational activities. He was employed with the animal husbandry and gardening program.

The writer's last visit to the Sherman Institute disclosed that Bill's adjustment had been quite rapid. He had put on weight and after about two weeks announced that he "felt right at home, now."

It had been difficult at first, because in spite of all precautions the students had learned something of Bill's past hospitalization. To the Navahos the hospital symbolizes death, and death is particularly abhorrent to them as they have no clearly structured concepts of an afterlife. The students consequently shied away from Bill a little when he arrived, but he has since found acceptance.

He will go back to the reservation in the spring, at the close of the school year, and attend to the unfinished business of the "Breath of Life" ceremony.

> *With increased sensitivity to cultural variation, psychiatrists and psychologists are much less likely today than some may have been at the time of Jewell's study to make such blatantly culture-bound misdiagnoses. Nonetheless, his report underlines the fact that all assessments of "abnormality" necessarily rely on some yardstick (never completely culture-free) specifying the nature and limits of what it is that we consider normal. The fact that Bill was, with apparent confidence on the part of the diagnosers, repeatedly considered psychotic should alert us to the fact that ostensibly disinterested professional assessments, in this case psychiatric ones, may rather easily be "adulterated" by extra-scientific considerations. When the designators of deviance and the individuals they so designate come from different backgrounds or belong to different sociocultural groupings or categories (egs., white/blacks; middle class/working class; adults/youth; men/women), we must be especially alert to this possibility.*

Cross-Cultural Perspectives

If deviance-defining is a central process in human interaction and a key feature of social systems, then it is not surprising that we find deviance to be a "cultural universal." There is no known society in which deviance-defining has not existed, and it is extremely difficult to imagine how a deviance-free society might come about or what it might look like. Of course it is true that the amount of formal social control—criminal laws, police or comparable enforcers, etc.—

may vary considerably (see Malinowski, 1926, 1959; Hoebel, 1961; Schwartz, 1954; Schwartz and Miller, 1964). And as we have just seen, the extent and nature of such "enforcement" may affect the volume of perceived deviance in a society (paradoxically, in a way that runs counter to what we might expect or desire, since heightened enforcement will seem to produce more deviance rather than less). On the other hand, it does not at all follow that since deviance is a "matter of definition," a society can simply define away its existence, that is, decide not to have any deviance. Social policies, socialization of society members, and other factors may shape or limit deviance situations, but they can never fully eliminate the experiencing in some connections of troublesomeness, offensiveness, threat, and the like, that cause such situations to arise.

It is not the presence of some deviance-defining, but rather the specific forms deviance may take that are subject to variation from culture to culture. In line with the mirroring mechanisms we have just considered, the structures and values dominant in a given society will help to determine the substantive objects of deviance-defining (what behaviors or conditions are likely to be imbued with deviantness) and also the distribution within the society of specific instances of deviance-processing (the relative likelihoods of persons differentially "located" in the social order becoming or being treated as deviators). The phrase "relative likelihoods" is worth emphasizing, in both connections, because as we saw earlier we ought to try to avoid thinking in either-or terms about the often-assumed categories of deviant behavior and deviants. Furthermore, we should also keep in mind that even within the overall patterns of deviance-defining that a particular society seems to exhibit, the outcomes (applications of deviantness) in *specific* instances of possible, attempted, or actual deviance-processing are always unpredictable, shaped as they are by numerous situational contingencies. So, while we do find some context-bound patterns, none is completely fixed or self-evident.

Later on in this book, we will be noting some evidence from opinion surveys regarding expressed attitudes toward various sometimes-offending behaviors. These studies indicate a not inconsiderable amount of consensus regarding disapproval of various offenses—in one instance among respondents sampled in six different contemporary cultures (Newman, 1976). Such findings do make clear that there are *some* substantive areas of deviance-defining that tend to cut across cultures, rather than being totally relative to particular cultures. Apparent uniformities of this sort reflect the fact that certain general domains of human social behavior—such as interpersonal violence, sexual relations, acts relating to the distribution of key property resources—inevitably require some societal controls and hence can also be expected to give rise in various cultures to some kinds of offenses. (See, for example, the discussion of a "minimum content of natural law" in Hart, 1961, pp. 189–195.)

But if the substance of deviance-defining is not always or totally relative, neither is it ever totally uniform across cultures. There are three reasons why this is so. First of all, research findings that suggest apparent consensus usually report stated or *professed* attitudes or norms, and as we noted earlier these do not always coincide with *actual* or "operative" norms. In studying deviance situations sociologically, how people actually behave in real-life circumstances usually is of greater significance than what they say they believe or feel regarding hypothetical ones. Second, we should recall the extremely broad range of behaviors and conditions that *may* be subject to deviance-defining; theoretically, *any* behavior or condition carries the potential for being assigned some degree of deviantness. When we think of deviance in that way, as involving the highly varied "uses" of a common defining-reacting process, we can appreciate that there will be considerably more consensus regarding some types of deviance than as regards others. Thus, certain general types may appear in many societies, while other types do not. Probably the greater degrees of consensus will occur in connection with behavior in the key societal domains just mentioned and particularly where there could be perceived threat to the very survival of a society. The composite deviance-defining picture of different societies will, however, probably always vary. Finally, it should be noted that such consensus as does exist is general. A general agreement on relative approval or disapproval of a given kind of behavior leaves a great deal of room for cultural variation in at least three respects: the precise *degree* of approval/disapproval, the specific patterns of *response* that such attitudes generate (what exactly is "made socially" of the offending behavior), the *specificaiton of subtypes* within the general behavioral category (which subtypes may be reacted to in quite different ways). Perhaps the specification point is especially crucial in producing cultural variability. It is easy to see, for example, that different cultures may be likely to display in common the tendency to imbue with deviantness some kinds of violence and some kinds of sexual behavior, yet differ considerably as to just which types of violence or sexuality (and under *what circumstances*) will typically elicit such reactions.

Many examples that illustrate these conclusions regarding uniformities and variations can be found in the literature of cross-cultural research. One of the most frequently asserted universals, the incest taboo, does appear to be present in some form in virtually all societies. Yet, as Kingsley Davis has noted, characterizations of and responses to potentially problematic sexual behavior that does not directly threaten the stability of the nuclear family—such as premarital intercourse—exhibit much cross-cultural variability. Furthermore, Davis points out, "incest taboos outside the nuclear family vary from one society to another, because the number and kinds of external kinsmen who are socially important to the individual are different in different societies" (Davis, 1976, p. 226). With respect to another behavioral area we might think of as giving rise to cultural universals, anthropologist Paul Bohannan has stated:

In most African societies either today or in the recent past, some forms of homicide are positively sanctioned: this sort can be compared to execution. It is the duty—at least the right—of a person to kill some people in some situaitons. One such situation is the ritual of sacrifice. In some areas, such as nineteenth century Dahomey and Ashanti, human sacrifice was generally used as a means of executing criminals, although slaves might also be sacrificed. Many African peoples acknowledge—or in the recent past acknowledged—the necessity for human sacrifices in specific religious institutions. Occasionally newly institutionalized homicide, definitely extrasocietal, such as Mau Mau killings or the Diretlo murders of Basutoland, springs up in Africa even today. . . . They are branded criminal by the British-dominated law in all cases, and by "native law and custom" in many, but not in all (Bohannan, 1960, 1967, p. 232).

Similarly Robert Edgerton has noted that while excessive violence, or the wrong kinds of violence, are often penalized, there are also cultures in which too *little* violence may result in stigmatization. Citing a study of the Gros Ventre Plains Indians—a North American society in which warfare, fortitude, and bravery were highly prized and expected of women as well as men—he points to the plight of a woman named Coming Daylight: "She could not stand the sight of blood, would not mutilate herself, and detested violence of any sort. She was subjected to ridicule and coercion, but held her ground throughout her life, despite being regarded as a deviant" (Edgerton, 1976, p. 46). The same writer succinctly summarizes cross-cultural findings regarding another commonly deviantized form of behavior as follows: "Suicide is notable for the variation of its form, frequency, and motivation from culture to culture. In some folk societies it occurs rarely, perhaps never. In others, it occurs but is not considered to be deviant. In still others, it is a heinous offense" (Edgerton, 1976, p. 43).

As the analysis of the institutionalized Navaho (Adaptation One) suggests, cross-cultural variations in defining mental illness may be of special interest. A wide range of anthropological analyses suggests the strong influence of culture in determining the kinds of circumstances in which mental disorders will be seen to occur and the specific forms or content ("symptoms") such disorders will exhibit (see various discussions in Plog and Edgerton, 1969, pp. 73–284). Alternative interpretations of apparently culture-bound symptom patterns (e.g., "Artic hysteria") are possible. But whether they be seen as unique illnesses or as symptomatic variations on a (cross-culturally) common underlying psychological disorder, there seems little doubt that different cultures have their particular "socially approved ways of going crazy." Furthermore, we know that various specific conditions viewed as symptomatic of mental disorder in one culture context may in another society not only be condoned but sometimes required of some members, who may thereby achieve high social standing. Thus in certain American Indian traditions, self-mortification and the achievement of hallucinatory states of trance or "possession"—typically seen, in our society, as psychotic symptoms— often were defined in an approving way. The same, of course, has been true regarding the taking of various mind-altering drugs such as Peyote, a natural counter-part of mescaline and LSD.

Research by Edgerton on the identification and treatment of mental disturbance in four East African tribal societies (see Edgerton, 1969) presents interesting evidence on a related dimension of mental illness—certainty and uncertainty in identification or diagnosis. He found that in all four societies there was a widely known term for psychosis (or craziness) and considerable consensus, at least within each society, regarding its applications. In each of the societies, persons generally were able with relative ease to recognize as psychotic those individuals whose mental disorders were both severe and chronic (e.g., the man perpetually seen "driving" an imaginary bus along the main road). Yet, in these societies as in others, most of the cases of mental illness were not both severe and chronic. Where erratic behavior was more episodic or borderline, Edgerton found, consensus regarding diagnosis was diminished. When that happened, formal diagnostic procedures and specialists often came into the picture, and the outcome of the diagnosing process itself became not only uncertain but in some ways open to "negotiation"—a key factor in deviance situations generally, to which we will return below.

Evidence of cross-cultural variability in deviance-defining can be found in many additional substantive areas besides those discussed thus far. To cite just a few more examples, cultures vary considerably in how they define and treat marijuana use (see Rubin and Comitas, 1976), illegitimacy (Goode, 1976), and the drinking of alcoholic beverages (McCarthy, 1959; Pittman, 1967; Lemert, 1967, pp. 154–196). Of course, it is true that findings regarding cross-cultural variability can have only a limited pertinence to analyzing the perceived deviance within any one specified culture. Nonetheless, they remain extremely valuable as one antidote to the persisting notion that types of behavior are somehow intrinsically deviant. And, even more significantly, they point the way to a recognition of similar kinds of socioculturally shaped variability within, as well as among or between, cultures.

Subcultural Variations

Within our own society, no comprehensive understanding of deviance is possible unless we take into account some important elements of subcultural variation. As sociological studies repeatedly demonstrate, virtually every kind of social behavior displays systematically patterned variation—frequently along social-class, racial and ethnic, and geographical lines, and also by age and sex. In the deviance field, evidence indicating such variations has often influenced both lay conceptions and sociological theorizing. Findings of this sort have been taken to indicate who the so-called deviants are, and these conclusions have then led to or reinforced common public stereotypes, as well as generated a variety of purported causal explanations. Given the strong urge to differentiate that we have already noted, such stereotypes and purported explanations have usually reflected the general belief that offending individuals are clearly distinguishable from and different from nonoffending ones.

Recognizing elements of deviance situations that are relative to subcultures—value-norm systems existing within a broader culture—and to structured systems of social roles within a given society helps us to place these findings about patterned variations in more meaningful perspective. Here again, the distinction between the occurrence of behavior and its characterization (what is made of it socially) is basic. In this section, and further on in the book, we will be noting major methodological criticisms of many of the standard statistical-comparison findings regarding deviation. A major thrust of these criticisms has been to make clear that with respect to the actual occurrence of behaviors, statistical comparisons—at least those based on official statistics or relying on incarcerated and nonincarcerated "samples"—have not provided a valid picture of who the deviators really are. Above all, it now appears frequently to be the case that the actual distribution among the general population of acts that could potentially lead to deviance-processing is much wider than was previously thought to be the case. As this begins to suggest and as we have already seen, deviance situations always involve more than the mere occurrence of offending behavior. We need to incorporate into our explanations consideration of the patterning and applications of certain meanings, that is, the quality of deviantness.

When we adopt this broader outlook, three interrelated sources of possible variation are found to be important: (1) subcultural *diversity of value patterns* that affect the meanings assigned to sometimes-deviantized acts, (2) *differential distribution* among various subcultures *of forces or pressures* that may actually, or may simply be believed to, "push" people into certain acts of deviation, and (3) systematic *differences in formal reaction* patterns, depending on who the perceived deviators are. These three kinds of variation will be found in connection with almost any substantive deviance situation. Furthermore, it is likely that they will be reflected in official statistics whatever the comparisons that are made, for example, whether they be in terms of race, ethnicity, or social class. As this discussion will make clear, a standard fallacy has been to think that these sources of variation operate separately and therefore can be looked at separately for analytic purposes. In fact, they are so closely interrelated that it usually becomes very difficult to disentangle them one from another.

Looking at standard statistical comparisons with an eye to subcultural differences enables us to see that a given kind of behavior may be defined differently in different contexts within our society because of variations in value emphases, typical early socialization practices, characteristic life-style patterns, and the like. One commonly cited example of this has concerned the different outlooks on alcohol use characteristic of various ethnic (national- and religious-background) groups in the United States (see Trice, 1966, pp. 22–24). With respect to immigrant groups particularly, sociologists early noted relatively low alcoholism rates among Chinese-Americans and Italian-Americans and relatively high rates among Irish-Americans. Such differences seemed largely attributable to outlooks and drinking patterns carried over from the native country. Use of alcohol in connection with ceremonial festivals or routinely at mealtimes—along with strong traditional disapproval of drunkenness—not surprisingly contributed to the lower rates among some immigrant groups. By the same token, the high Irish-American rate was attributed to a quite different drinking "tradition"— drinking heavily for "effect" with less-strong traditional condemnation of drunkenness, unregulated introduction to alcohol outside the home, and so on.

Sociologists have shown special interest in the drinking patterns of Jewish-Americans, especially Orthodox Jews, among whom the alcoholism rate had tended to be negligible (see Snyder, 1958). Low Jewish alcoholism has been related to the association of alcohol with religious ritual, along with a traditional harsh condemnation of uncontrolled drinking. One discussion made the further point that, "What is probably the key to drinking by Jewish-Americans is that it *has tended to be relatively unimportant.* That is, drinking may take place in the course of a religious ritual, or on a special occasion, or as part of a social situation, but it is always as an accompaniment to something else—never for itself alone. Drinking is a way of taking note of an event, it doesn't become an event in itself" (Ullman, 1960, p. 38). As these early analyses noted and as the recent news item reproduced here makes clear, assimilation of immigrant or minority groups is likely to bring their drinking patterns more into accord with the dominant ones in the broader American culture.

However, as the news account also shows, subcultural variations in alcoholism reflect not only differing traditions that influence patterns of alcohol use,

---

NEWS SPOT
Recent Increase in Jewish Alcoholism

(January 1977). Concerned about a possible increase in alcoholism among Jews, the Federation of Jewish Philanthropies of New York City has established a special Task Force to explore this problem, to encourage general discussion of it in the Jewish community, and to sponsor relevant conferences and seminars at temples and synagogues in the New York metropolitan area. According to Rabbi Sheldon Zimmerman, one of the leaders in this activity, "For years we've been sweeping the problem under a rug." Finally, the Rabbi noted, "the Jewish community is beginning to do something about it." Recent assessments by various rabbis, doctors, and alcoholism specialists seem to indicate that the rate of alcoholism among Jews, which was traditionally low, may be approaching that of the general population—approximately one of 14 persons. The major reason cited is growing assimilation of Jews to the American cultural system generally and to the dominant drinking patterns more specifically. A special feature of the situation in the past has been the tendency among at least orthodox Jews to strongly deny their alcoholism even when they have had serious drinking problems. According to some specialists, doctors often tell Jewish alcoholics they are suffering from "depression" instead. One counselor-therapist was quoted as suggesting such persons "find it more comfortable and acceptable to be told they have a psychiatric problem."

Source: Based on news article in *The New York Times,* January 23, 1977, p. 32.

but also related differences in *defining* and *identifying* cases of problem-drinking. (Thus the Jewish reluctance to "find" alcoholism referred to in the news article has consequences for the official statistics on rates of Jewish alcoholism, which were thereby deflated, and also presumably for the statistics on mental illness among Jews, which may have been somewhat artificially inflated because of the disclosed "preference" for psychiatric designations. Here we have, then, a neat capsule demonstration of some of the ways in which alternative defining and identifying procedures help to determine recorded statistics on deviance.)

Another kind of behavior frequently subject to deviance-defining and with respect to which we find subcultural variations in emphasis and meaning is physical violence. Although the argument that there is some distinct "subculture of violence" involving certain segments of our population remains a rather controversial one, it is no doubt true that situations in which violence might arise are at times viewed differently depending on the sociocultural setting. Marvin Wolfgang, a major sociological proponent of the violent subculture thesis, has asserted, for example:

> . . . the significance of a jostle, a slightly derogatory remark, or the appearance of a weapon in the hands of an adversary are stimuli differentially perceived and interpreted by Negroes and whites, males and females. . . . A male is usually expected to defend the name and honor of his mother, the virtue of womanhood . . . and to accept no derogation about his race (even from a member of his own race), his age, or his masculinity. Quick resort to physical combat as a measure of daring, courage, or defense of status appears to be a cultural expectation, especially for lower socioeconomic class males of both races (Wolfgang, 1958, pp. 188–189).

Situations or comments that might in one context be treated as trivial can easily erupt into violence, then, when another set of cultural expectations applies. Wolfgang's interpretation emerged from his large-scale research on homicides. More recently, a somewhat different type of investigation—of physical aggression within families, that is, husband-wife and parent-child violence—produced some evidence further supporting the general cultural expectations thesis. This study found that "violence is the most common in families who have low education, low income, and low occupational status," and also that "violence, and violence towards family members in particular, is learned by experiencing violence while growing up in a family. Where an individual experiences violence as a child he is more likely to engage in violence as an adult" (Gelles, 1972, pp. 130, 181).

Reference in these interpretations to low socioeconomic status and related variables (we know that in our present society racial minority-group membership and low socioeconomic standing are highly correlated overall) suggests the likelihood that the second source of subcultural variation—differential subjection to social pressures that may generate deviating acts—is also reflected in these situations. One of the most frequently remarked findings in American crime statistics—the high recorded crime rates of blacks in relation to those of whites— must be seen at least partly in this light. We all know that blacks have long been subjected, systematically and to a much greater degree, to a wide range of socio-economic deprivations and social indignities that criminologists commonly identify as possible causes of crime, at least ordinary, "street" crime (see discussion in Schur, 1969, pp. 45–51). At the same time, the third source of variation—differential formal reaction—is also implicated in statistical comparisons of this sort. Although today the administration of justice is becoming, at least in certain locales, considerably more even-handed than it once was, blacks have routinely faced greater risks, all other things being equal, of receiving harsher treatment than whites at the various stages of the criminal justice process.

A central point in analyzing deviance, then, is to recognize that most officially recorded rate variations reflect *both* something about the culture and the social positions of the individuals involved *and* systematically patterned variations in definitions of their behavior and in associated formal reactions to it. The same complex interweaving of elements is apparent in another famous and still pertinent finding in the sociology of deviance—the social-class distribution of psychiatric patients unearthed in the classic research of August Hollingshead and Frederick Redlich. As Table 2.2 shows, Hollingshead and Redlich found among their sample of identified psychiatric patients in New Haven in 1950 a definite association between social class and type of mental disorder. At the higher levels of socioeconomic status (Class I being the highest in their scheme), neuroses predominated among the reported disorders; psychoses appeared to be concentrated at the lower levels of the social-class system. There are several different ways to interpret such findings. It is conceivable that the psychological disturbances were actually distributed in this way throughout the general population. (However, Hollingshead noted that the prevalence of schizophrenia in Class I of the sample was only one-fifth as great as would be expected if the disorder had been distributed in the same proportions as the overall class breakdown of the population; in Class V it was two and one-half times what one would have expected

Table 2.2 Distribution of Neuroses and Psychoses by Social Class

SOCIAL CLASS	NEUROSES		PSYCHOSES	
	NUMBER	PERCENT	NUMBER	PERCENT
I	10	52.6	9	47.4
II	88	67.2	43	32.8
III	115	44.2	145	55.8
IV	175	23.1	583	76.9
V	61	8.4	662	91.6
Total	449		1442	

Chi square = 296..45, *P* less than 0.001

Source: August B. Hollingshead and Frederick C. Redlich, "Social Stratification and Psychiatric Disorders," *American Sociological Review*, 18 (April 1953), 167. Reprinted with permission.

on that basis.) If this were the real social-class distribution of all neuroses and psychoses, then the thesis of differential forces and pressures might be applicable. Different pressures, it could be argued, generate different disorders, and the kinds of social-psychological pressures people experience tend to vary according to their socioeconomic positions.

But these deviance outcomes clearly reflected other factors as well. Hollingshead and Redlich were studying only persons who had been in psychiatric treatment, and, not surprisingly, perhaps, they found a social-class patterning in the kinds of treatment people received. "The percentage of persons who received no treatment care [i.e., mere custodial care in mental hospitals] was greatest in the lower classes. The same finding applies to organic treatment. Psychotherapy, on the other hand, was concentrated in the higher classes" (Hollingshead and Redlich, 1953, p. 168). Skeptical that these differences reflected the actual distribution of treatment needs and also unwilling to attribute them simply to the cost of certain kinds of treatment, the authors concluded that "the social distance between psychiatrist and patient may be more potent than economic considerations in determining the character of psychiatric intervention" (Hollingshead and Redlich, 1953, p. 168). In other words, how doctors reacted to potential patients and how hospitals channeled them influenced what treatment they would receive. Similarity in doctor-patient social backgrounds and, therefore, relative ease in doctor-patient communication probably was a major reason, for example, that psychoanalysis was found in this study to be limited to persons in Classes I and II.

Social-class variation in outcomes influenced by a combination of differences in applied meanings and formal reactions was similarly shown in Jane Mercer's findings on release from institutions of mentally retarded children (Mercer, 1965). Mercer's data, comparing a group of patients released to their families with a matched group of still-hospitalized patients, interestingly revealed a pattern that seemed in a way to run counter to that found by Hollingshead and Redlich. She found that lower-class retardates were more likely to be released to their families, while the higher-status patients were more likely to remain in the hospital. Questioning the parents in both groups, Mercer found that the lower-status ones, as compared with the higher-status ones, were more inclined to disagree with or be uncertain about the official definitions of retardation, more likely to deny that their children were "retarded," and more likely to be optimistic about improvement in their conditions. (All of these outlooks were, of course, conducive to accepting the child back on release from the hospital.) Higher-status parents whose children had the *same* levels of retardation were much less optimistic and much more likely to concur with official assessments. Asserting that "a person may be mentally retarded in one system and not . . . in another," Mercer found these particular deviance outcomes to be crucially shaped by variations in social definition, especially the class-patterned differences in agreement with the outlooks of the formal (hospital) agents of control.

Ecological Context

Attention to elements of relativity in deviance situations similarly helps us to interpret another large body of statistical findings—those relating to the geographical or ecological distribution of deviance. Human ecology, as understood by sociologists, focuses on the growth and development of social structures as they interrelate with aspects of the physical environment. As we will see in the next chapter, a very influential ecological school of sociological analysis has played a major role in the shaping of deviance theory, putting special emphasis on the study of area rate variations *within* particular cities. Both in that work and in more general efforts to analyze deviance, physical or ecological setting or location becomes important, primarily when it provides a basis for recognizing what is, in effect, a type of subcultural pattern.

Without too much difficulty, for example, we could specify some broad regional differences within the United States that might represent subcultural sources of variation shaping deviance situations. Thus, relevant specific points of variation might include the following: regional "traditions" regarding physical violence and the defense of personal honor, relative extent of secularization as against religious piety or fundamentalism, degree of receptiveness to "bohemian" or avant-garde experimentation, political liberalism or conservatism, general homogeneity versus diversity and other aspects of composition—including age distribution—of the region's population, and the region's recent history with respect to degrees of population mobility and general social and economic change. Particularly in official crime statistics, regional variations within the United States are repeatedly disclosed, and such variations are routinely attributed to the impact of what might be called "regional subculture." For instance, the President's Crime Commission cited the extremely high rates of recorded homicide and aggravated assault in the South, which it felt were "at least in part due to a tradition of resort to violence as a means of settling family arguments and personal disputes that had been carried over from frontier days and maintained, especially in the lower classes, because of the particular social and economic history of the region" (President's Commission on Law Enforcement and Administration of Justice, 1967, p. 31). However, it is significant, too, that the Commission also reported a trend toward reduction of the rate differentials between the southern states and other regions, which it attributed to increased general sociocultural similarity of the various regions.

Whether we are examining regional variations or other aspects of ecological distribution, the several interrelated elements of subcultural variation—differential pressures, variations in definitions, and differential reactions—can all be expected to play a role in determining recorded deviance outcomes. This is undoubtedly true as regards one of the most frequently cited disclosures in the official statistics—that of significant rural-urban differences in rates of recorded or processed deviance. Much higher urban rates—but, again, with a trend toward declining urban-rural differentials—are cited again and again in the deviance

Table 2.3 Current Use by Size of City of Residence
at Time of Interview (Percentages)

	TOTAL*	OUT-SIDE U.S.	1,000,000 OR MORE	100,000 PLUS	25,000 PLUS	2,500 PLUS	LESS THAN 2,500
	(2,510)	(36)	(146)	(631)	(575)	(757)	(352)
Cigarettes	60	64	57	61	58	59	62
Alcohol	92	97	92	93	93	91	88
Marihuana	38	36	53	44	42	32	28
Psychedelics	7	19	7	8	8	8	4
Stimulants	12	11	12	14	13	10	9
Sedatives	9	14	12	11	10	8	5
Heroin	2	6	4	3	1	1	1
Opiates	10	14	15	11	11	9	6
Cocaine	7	11	12	9	7	6	4

Source: John A. O'Donnell, et al., *Young Men and Drugs—A Nationwide Survey.* Rockville, Md.: National Institute on Drug Abuse, U. S. Dept. of Health, Education and Welfare, 1976, p. 39.
* Total includes 13 cases where size of city is unknown.

literature regardless of the specific types of behavior involved. Table 2.3, drawn from the recently published report of a nationwide representative sample of over 2500 men aged 20–30, illustrates such recurrent findings. Note that the use of cigarettes and alcohol exhibits relatively little variation, whereas for the more "deviantized" drugs there is a pronounced relationship between city size and self-reported drug use. Thus, 53 percent of the men living in cities of 1 million or more reported using marihuana, whereas the figure was only 28 percent for those residing in communities of less than 2500. Studies of suicide (see Labovitz, 1968), heavy drinking and alcoholism (Trice, 1966), mental illness (Plog and Edgerton, pp. 285–479), and crime—especially property offenses (President's Commission on Law Enforcement, 1967)—have tended to reveal higher rates for urban areas than for rural ones, but also with definite indications of a narrowing of these differentials (particularly pronounced in the case of suicide) as all areas in the United States have become increasingly "urbanized."

Urbanization can involve both increased migration of persons to the cities and an "exporting" of urban culture to the more rural locales—a process in which the mass media, especially television, have played a major role. Among those writers who place a heavy emphasis on urbanization as a key factor affecting deviance, the general nature and quality of urban living are key concerns. Drawing on the early essay by Louis Wirth, "Urbanism as a Way of Life" (Wirth, 1938), these analysts suggest that such characteristic features of city life as anonymity, mobility, and superficiality, along with density and heterogeneity of population, help to produce deviance situations. Thus Marshall Clinard has written that, "City living does not, of course, directly result in deviant behavior,

---

NEWS SPOT
Urban Mental Health

(May 1977). A leading specialist on the mental health of urban-dwellers now suggests that people living in cities may actually exhibit less mental disorder than those living in rural areas and, furthermore, that the mental health of city-dwellers may have been improving over the last few decades. In statements made at a national psychiatric conference and in a news interview, psychiatric sociologist Leo Srole, director of the much-publicized "Midtown Manhattan Study" conducted in the 1950s, which reported in 1962 that 23 percent of its New York City respondents were in need of psychiatric treatment, attributed exaggeration of urban psychological ills to an "anti-urban" bias. Srole noted that various studies had also shown high (at times higher) rates of mental disorder among rural and small-town residents. Efforts to follow up the sample from the Midtown Manhattan Study now indicate that the mental health of New Yorkers may have improved since that survey was done. Reinterviewing in 1974 of 695 of the original 1660 respondents and comparison of "mental health ratings" of those in their 40s now with those who were in their 40s 20 years ago disclosed that the percentage now needing psychiatric help has declined by half. (The same was true of now-and-then comparison groups in their 50s.) According to Srole, such apparent changes could reflect conditions and influences that affected respondents in their formative years as well as general socioeconomic changes both at those times and since then.

Source: Based on news article in *The New York Times,* May 4, 1977, pp. 1, B6.

---

but many of the conditions associated with city life are, to a preponderant degree, conducive to deviation" (Clinard, 1974, p. 49). If we are to be cautious in our appraisal, a phrase such as "conducive to deviation" must give us pause. It would be all too easy to uncritically conclude that urbanism or urbanization causes deviance in general, and thus to bypass the actual defining-reacting mechanisms that determine the character of specific deviance situations. Even studies such as the drug survey just cited, which avoid some of the pitfalls of official statistics by having respondents drawn from the general population report their own behavior, can only take us so far in analyzing deviance. We can see, for example, that urban living and marihuana use tend to be associated with one another. However, such a finding tells us nothing at all about why marihuana use is so much more heavily deviantized than, say, drinking alcohol. Then too, the nature and pressures of city living may help to "explain" the use of marihuana, but an element of differential opportunity (access to drugs) is probably also reflected in these statistics just as urban-rural differentials in property crime partly reflect the distribution of stealable property.

Interpretation of urban-rural variations is even more complicated when, as often has been the case, we are looking not at self-reports of behavior but rather at some type of official statistic. The point made earlier about official rate variations (that they reflect reaction as well as deviation) always must be taken into account. From this standpoint, all we can be certain about is that the statistics depict differentials found in the officially recorded or processed deviance. We need, then, to consider whether cases recorded and processed in the cities are ignored, tolerated, or dealt with more informally elsewhere. There is reason to believe this may often be so, notwithstanding the greater general visibility that any one instance of disturbing behavior may be likely to have in the less complex social setting. Thus behavior that in the small community is treated as amusing eccentricity may in the city become diagnosed mental illness. Similarly, the youthful troublemaker who in the rural setting is, say, informally chastised or allowed to make some kind of restitution for an offense may, in the urban context, instead be adjudicated a delinquent. As already mentioned, it is very hard to separate out these possibilities in evaluating official rates. Much early deviance analysis was based on methodologies in which the need to do so was scarcely recognized.

Variations Over Time

Analyzing deviance also requires taking into account the dimension of time. Temporal variations in deviance outcomes can mean a number of things. It is possible, of course, that changes in the factors that cause the deviating acts or conditions to occur are involved. It can also be the case, in changes over time as in variations among subcultures, that recorded deviance "trends" in part reflect trends in identifying and processing. Even more striking, however, are the changes that we know do take place in the meanings attached to particular behaviors or conditions, that is, in the attribution of deviantness. Again, this is not an all-or-nothing matter—behavior at one time being deviant, at another nondeviant—rather it is a matter of degree and, of course, continues to vary somewhat among different groups of reactors. But trends over time in the dominance of certain sets of meanings definitely do occur.

An interesting example—which, unlike many others we might think of, involves a recent *increase* in the attribution of deviantness—is that of cigarette smoking. Although this has not been one of the standard deviance categories, either in the public view or for purposes of sociological analysis, there is considerable evidence that in recent years smoking has become increasingly deviantized. Actually, as one systematic analysis has noted (Neuhring and Markle, 1974), there was an earlier period in American history (1895–1921) during which, as a result of pressure from fundamentalist and temperance groups, 14 states completely banned smoking. By the late 1920s, however, this anticigarette sentiment had receded (the laws were repealed) only to reemerge in a new form in the 1950s when medical evidence that linked smoking with lung cancer and heart disease began being publicized. Since then, as these same authors show, there has been a continuous struggle between procigarette forces (primarily lobbyists for the tobacco industry) and anticigarette forces, with the dominant outcomes now tending slightly to favor the latter. For our purposes, perhaps the most interesting development has been the recent increase in the deviantness people "read into" this widely prevalent behavior. Reviewing a number of national surveys conducted in the mid and late 1960s, Nuehring and Markle report:

> . . . both smokers and non-smokers attach a deviant label to the habit. Thus more than two-thirds of all non-smokers and about one-quarter of all current smokers, agree that "It's annoying to be near a person who is smoking." Further, about two-thirds of non-smokers, and one-half of smokers, thought that smoking is a "dirty habit." And from 1964 to 1966, a large number of people actually became convinced that "cigarettes are morally wrong": in 1964, 16 per cent of all male smokers and 13 per cent of all female smokers agreed with that statement; but by 1966, almost one-half of all men and women thought that there was something morally wrong with smoking (Neuhring and Markle, 1974, pp. 520–521).

To cite just one more example of possibly increasing deviantness, it will be interesting to see whether or to what extent public revelations connected with Watergate and other recent instances of governmental corruption effect a dramatic change in the meanings attached to what two sociologists have termed "official deviance" (Douglas and Johnson, 1977; Douglas and Johnson, eds., 1978; and Ermann and Lundman, eds., 1978).

Toward the end of this book, in considering recent public policy developments, we will be touching on a variety of examples involving changes over time that run in the direction of *decreased* deviantness. These are the familiar shifts that proponents tend to view as signs of liberalization, but that to critics imply excessive permissiveness or even decadence. At this point, it should suffice merely to note that in analyzing deviance, trends of this sort—indeed, any trends over time in whichever direction—will usually display or reflect both long and short-term patterns. One general area in which long-term trends seem to be having an apparent effect is that of sexuality, with a clear trend over time in the United States to lessen the stigmatizing meanings attached to a wide variety of behaviors and situations ranging from masturbation to abortion, from nudity to adultery, from premarital intercourse to adult homosexuality. In a similar and sometimes related way, a variety of changes in deviantness reflect broad shifts in the status of women in our society. As we will see shortly, such shifts have very great significance indeed in shaping the overall patterning of deviance-defining. A few "direct" examples of the impact of the changing status of women would be the gradual decline in the degree of deviantness attaching to being a divorcee, living as a single woman, premarital pregnancy, and having an abortion.

An especially intriguing case in point involves the decision of a married woman not to have children. As an interview study of "voluntary childless wives" has revealed, women making such a decision—at least until very recently—have routinely been subjected to direct and indirect pressures to have children as well as to characterizations that are typical of deviance-defining. "All of the wives interviewed feel that they are to some extent stigmatized . . . and that there exists an ubiquitous negative stereotype concerning the characteristics of a voluntarily childless woman, including such unfavorable traits as being abnormal, selfish, immoral, irresponsible, immature, unhappy, unfulfilled, and non-feminine" (Veevers, 1973, p. 505). Although this same researcher found that, as far as the social-psychological responses of these particular respondents were concerned, "existing social movements concerned with population or with feminism . . . provide relatively little intellectual or emotional support" (Veevers, 1973, p. 508), it does seem likely that increasingly active and organized opposition to "pronatalism" (pressure to bear children) will gradually lead overall to a decline in the deviantizing of this behavior.

Similarly, it will be interesting to observe in what ways the feminist movement, particularly its opposition to treating women as sex objects, may affect the stigmatizing meanings attached to another nonstandard type of deviance—obesity (see Clinard, 1974, pp. 237–239). One only has to consider the different consequences in our society of being excessively fat and excessively thin to recognize the deviantness assigned to obesity. Of course, this deviantizing has affected males as well as females, but it has been more consistently and rigorously applied to females, with minor fluctuations in various historical periods, depending on the dictates of fashion. Since this differential reaction to women and men and the excessive preoccupation in our culture with a narrowly defined ideal of physical beauty for the former are both abhorrent to the philosophy of the recent women's movement, we may anticipate that if it continues to exert influence this movement will produce some change in deviance-defining in this area. (We will return to the topic of obesity later in the course of considering certain group efforts aimed at avoiding, countering, and "removing" stigma.)

Along with, or sometimes within, long-term overall trends, such as those relating to sexuality and the status of women, we are likely to find more specific and shorter-term fluctuations in the attachment of deviantness to particular behavior patterns. This would be apparent were we to examine more closely any one of the specific behaviors just mentioned in connection with changing definitions of sexuality. Many examples in other areas of deviance-defining could be given. To cite just one, we can identify and analyze quite rapid short-term changes with respect to the apparent deviantness attached to marihuana use. These changes may, in turn, reflect or perhaps change or reinforce more general trends relating to decriminalization of borderline crimes, or to the relative strength in our society of general forces and values conducive to and discouraging of the use of various kinds of drugs. That the short-term indications of change can be quite dramatic is illustrated by a 1977 news account of "wider acceptance" of marihuana smoking in the American population: Citing recent national Gallup poll surveys, the article reported that the percentage of adult Americans who had tried marihuana doubled between 1973 and 1977 (from 12 to 24 percent) (Reinhold, 1977).

As these examples should suggest, an interwoven complex of elements—including individual behavior, individual and collectively held attitudes and values, changes in socialization and education, lobbying and legislation, the activity of organized social movements, and so on—will often be involved when deviance-defining, especially in its widespread and more public forms, changes over time. In Chapter 7 we will have some occasion to look into this interweaving a bit more in order to see what it can tell us about the general relation between deviance and social change. Even if it is extremely difficult to determine the causal relationships among these various factors (which influences which, which reflects which, etc.), the overall significance of changes over time in deviantness as well as in acts that may be so characterized seems undeniable. Perhaps the crucial point to keep in mind is this: Such changes do not just happen out of the blue, as it were. Yet they *do* happen frequently; they have important consequences and ramifications as well as causes; and they *need to be taken into account* in analyzing deviance.

Situational Deviance

The ordinariness or extraordinariness of deviance depends, in part, on the specific situation in which potentially problematic behavior occurs. There are at least two different senses in which deviance is relative to the situation. The first, which even theorists not much given to stressing the relativity of deviance often have noted, refers to highly distinctive situations that seem to generate behavior imbued elsewhere with deviantness. Undoubtedly the most frequently cited example is homosexual behavior in prisons (see Gagnon and Simon, 1973, ch. 8). Such acts are sometimes described as *situational deviance,* because the situation in which they occur is for most of the persons involved a temporary and extraordinary one and the behavior would to many of these participants themselves be objectionable outside this special situational context. For many deviance analysts, the citing of this example stems from their primary concern to explain the *occurrence* of the problematic behavior. Furthermore, the prison situation fits in well with the common constraint focus in traditional deviance analysis on social and psychological forces and pressures "pushing" people into deviation (in this instance, sexual deprivation, extreme loneliness, etc.). Yet it should be clear that this example also illustrates the importance of distinctive (related) characterizations of behavior that pertain in such situations. Indeed, in the prison setting we find something like a *situational subculture* which in some ways diverges from and in other respects mirrors the values dominant on the "outside." [Thus male and female homosexuality in prison tend to take somewhat different forms, with "lack of (other) emotionally satisfying relationships" apparently motivating the females more than sheer deprivation of sexual outlets (Gagnon and Simon, 1973, p. 254).]

Somewhat similar examples of situational deviance, which involve on the one hand less apparent constraint and on the other a less temporary situation, would be lesbian behavior among striptease performers and among prostitutes. In one interview study of strippers (McGaghy and Skipper, 1969), respondents gave high estimates (ranging from 15 to 100 percent, with most responses in the 50–75 percent range) of the extent of homosexual contacts within their occupation. McGaghy and Skipper found that contributing factors associated with their work situation included transciency, long and irregular working hours, consequent loneliness, disillusionment with men (they characterized many in their audiences as "degenerates"), a general "atmosphere of permissiveness toward sexual behavior" that surrounded their work, and a "cynicism regarding sexual mores" that such work engendered. As one respondent stated:

> Strippers go gay because they have little chance to meet nice guys. They come in contact with a lot of degenerate types. If they do meet a nice guy chances are he will ask them to stop stripping. If he doesn't he's likely to be a pimp. So the girls got to turn to a woman who understands them and their jobs. It is very easy for them to listen to the arguments of lesbians who will tell them basically that men are no good and women can give them better companionship (McGaghy and Skipper, 1969, p. 268).

A leading researcher on prostitution reports a study revealing 35.3 percent of the sample of prostitutes as having experienced at least one lesbian relationship, 7.4 percent reporting frequent homosexual activity, and 6.7 percent describing themselves as exclusively lesbian. Discounting claims that latent homosexuality may motivate women to become prostitutes, this analyst suggests to the contrary that, "homosexuality may be a result of being a prostitute" (James, 1977, p. 400). This is certainly quite plausible, since many of the situational factors cited in the stripper study are present in this occupational realm as well. Indeed, as Gagnon and Simon comment more generally, "the sharing of a special alienation and distance from the conventional society forces the prostitute back to other prostitutes for her social life" (Gagnon and Simon, 1973, p. 229). Again, in these two examples, we can see that there is an element of *subcultural differentiation* operating in such situations. In this connection, the fact that the occupational roles and, in the other case, the prisoner "role" are to begin with deviantized ones contributes significantly to such differentiation. These individuals presumably have "less to lose" than many persons might in taking up otherwise-problematic behavior. At the same time, the special patterns of behavior and meaning that emerge may partly represent a defensive adaptation to the stigma they have already encountered—an important general function of deviant subcultures, to which we will return in a later discussion.

There is a second, rather different sense in which *all* deviance is situational. In this view, emphasis is placed on the fluidity of defining-reacting processes and the fact that in *any* particular instance of deviance-defining, the *specific* outcome will always depend on numerous situational contingencies. Despite some patterning in reactions to possibly offending behavior, the way in which specific

Table 2.4 Suicide Rates per 100,000 Population by Marital Status,
Sex, and Age, Cook County, Illinois, 1959–1963

AGE GROUP	MALES			
	MARRIED	NEVER MARRIED	WIDOWED	DIVORCED
0–14	—	—	—	—
15–24	6.0	6.1	—	—
25–34	7.0	22.8	—	32.3
35–44	10.5	23.2	—	60.0
45–54	15.9	26.6	33.3	69.5
55–64	19.3	29.0	34.1	61.0
65–74	16.3	43.5	59.8	—
75 and over	36.2	67.3	63.5	—
Unknown	—	—	—	—
N	372	328	174	133
		1507		

Source: Ronald W. Maris, *Social Forces in Urban Suicide.* Homewood, Ill.: The Dorsey Press, 1969, p. 109. Reproduced with permission.

sequences of this sort will turn out is not fully predictable. (See a discussion of Cohen's formulation in Chapter 4.) Thus, even if there were, say, considerable overall consensus regarding a general attitude toward the degree of deviantness attaching to prostitution, every instance of behavior that might or might not be termed and treated as prostitution would nonetheless be situational in some very important respects. And indeed, in a sense, what prostitution "is" is nothing more or less than a composite of the outcomes in all such instances. Of course, to say this is to invoke the broad theme of deviance as a social construction mentioned earlier. For some writers (particularly those influenced by phenomenology) the thesis that ultimately all **morality** is situational or, as they often put it, **situated,** is in fact the touchstone of meaningful deviance studies (see Douglas, 1970).

Recent research by James Orcutt suggests that people sometimes do take situational context into account in attaching deviantness to certain kinds of behavior. In his study, respondents were asked to indicate how acceptable or unacceptable they considered marijuana or alcohol use to be under a variety of circumstances, ranging from a small party with friends to daily use before going to work. It should be recognized that what was being examined here was acceptability under certain hypothetical circumstances to the *respondents;* the issue was not situational variations in acceptability to the *participants* themselves. But to some extent the relativity thesis was supported by these data on the responses of "others," too. With respect to both behaviors, but more so for alcohol use ("where interpretations vary from almost unanimous acceptance to unanimous nonacceptance"), specifying the situation produced systematic and predictable

| | NEVER | | | | |
MARRIED	MARRIED	WIDOWED	DIVORCED	UNKNOWN	N
—	—	—	—	—	2
2.7	2.0	—	—	—	131
3.7	9.3	—	19.0	—	276
5.2	10.8	—	24.0	—	385
7.8	7.1	6.8	—	—	456
6.3	9.4	10.1	—	—	406
8.3	—	7.0	—	—	329
—	—	8.1	—	—	167
—	—	—	—	—	1
342	86	104	64	50	
		596			2153

FEMALES

variations in interpretations of acceptability. In short, the author noted, "what is non-deviant in some situations is deviant in others. These data generally lend empirical substance to relativistic discussions of deviance as a situated phenomenon" (Orcutt, 1975, p. 353). At the same time, certain findings (particularly, that marijuana use was more consistently disapproved in various contexts where alcohol use was not) seemed to caution against a "radical relativism which would deny interpretive significance to the nature of the act itself" (Orcutt, 1975, p. 354).

Deviance and Social Roles

Deviance-defining and deviance situations can be seen as relative to social roles and systems of social roles in at least five different ways.

1. **Roles that insulate from deviation.** Occupancy of certain roles may help to *insulate* persons from involvement in certain acts imbued with deviantness. A major example of this is seen in research findings that tend to confirm Emile Durkheim's classic thesis that from about 20 years of age on, marriage provided a "coefficient of preservation" against (a reduced likelihood to commit) suicide (see Durkheim, 1897, 1951, pp. 171–198). An illustration of such findings is seen in Table 2.4, drawn from a study of suicide rates in Chicago. Despite some variations between subcategories, the overall tendency of married persons, at least over a certain age, to have lower suicide rates conforms to a major theme in Durkheim's analysis; social ties that reduce feelings of isolation and enhance sentiments of solidarity will often be reflected in relatively low suicide rates.

2. Roles conducive to deviation. By the same token, analyzing social roles may sometimes help us to recognize some of the factors *conducive to* engaging in deviating acts. As we have just seen, certain occupational roles may provide encouragement of or permit behavior discouraged or condemned in other contexts or by other people. With respect to the suicide example, we might focus on the role of the unmarried as being conducive to suicide instead of on the married role as a suicide-inhibitor. For some purposes, it might be useful to think of being poor as constituting a social role—one that carries distinct implications regarding the likelihood of being pushed into some behaviors widely defined as deviation. Some of the patterned, age-based rate variations found in deviance statistics could be attributed to the roles of the various age groupings in the population. As both the age and occupation points suggest and whether one is thinking in terms of the deviance-conducive or inhibiting features of roles, there is an important element of opportunity associated with role occupancy. For example, typically one must either be a parent or occupy some other role involving child care in order to engage in child abuse. Presumably only a minor can be a delinquent. Only persons in certain occupations are able to commit certain crimes (e.g., embezzlement requires a position of financial trust); this example points up, too, the related influence of occupational structures on age rate variations (persons below a certain age are unlikely to hold such jobs).

3. Role conflict. This phenomenon is ofen cited in discussions of deviance. Usually such conflict is mentioned as a generator of strain and confusion that may produce deviation. An interpretation along those lines is, for example, part of the argument claiming that urbanization breeds deviance. The city-dweller, because of conflicting expectations and pressures, becomes confused, uncertain, and distressed (perhaps experiences feelings of "normlessness") and may therefore be driven to deviance of whatever sort. However, another version of the role conflict thesis seems to have even wider applicability. Illustrations of this version are seen in Figure 2.1. Earlier, it was suggested that any and every kind of behavior could be subject to deviance-defining. Figure 2.1 suggests that such a statement should perhaps be carried even further.

A complex society contains or consists of a multiplicity of often contradictory roles among which there are many points of intersection (through overlapping group memberships, overlapping activities of role occupants, etc.). As a consequence of these contradictions and intersections, it may well be the case that a great many behaviors deviate and conform *at the same time,* depending on which role expectations are taken as the basis of evaluation. Such situations may be especially blatant in totalitarian societies and, perhaps, in highly authoritarian organization settings, where the imposition of one set of role requirements involving behavior that implies deviation from another set may be stringently sanctioned. Albert Cohen cites analyses of the Soviet plant manager which indicate that extreme pressure to fill production quotas virtually *requires* deviation

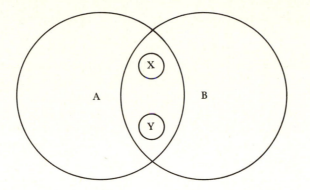

Example 1: Overlapping memberships and potentially conflicting roles

A = Youth's membership in "straight" family —dedicated to hard work, financial success, Puritan values, etc.
B = Same youth's membership in student or "hippie" subculture.
X = Extreme competitiveness aimed at "getting ahead" (financially)—in conformity with A, but involves possible deviation from norms of B.
Y = Casual work attitudes, or "easy" sexual behavior—approved in B, but represents deviation from norms of A.

Example 2: Potentially conflicting requirements of a dual role

A = Role requirements of pharmaceutical corporation as discoverer and disseminator of medicines for the public good.
B = Role requirements of same corporation as a "business," operated within capitalist system, with central norm of profit maximization.
X = Disinterested search for and marketing of "cheapest possible drug"—would represent conformity to A, but deviation in terms of B.
Y = Pricing policies or efforts to restrict competition in order to conform to B may involve deviation from A.

Figure 2.1 Deviation through contradictory role requirements.

from other norms—such as honest record keeping, maintenance of product quality, ordering and maintaining only necessary supplies and equipment, and the like (Cohen, 1966, pp. 82–83).

The examples presented in Figure 2.1 are not this extreme. Neither the youth who finds himself subjected to conflicting expectations from the "counterculture" and his "straight" family nor the pharmaceutical manufacturer who treads an uneasy line between "business" and disinterested "public service" aspects of his work faces the kind of severe pressure experienced by the Soviet manager. Nonetheless, in both cases full conformity to one set of expectations almost inevitably implies deviation from some aspect of the other set. Whether we describe such conflicts as arising through occupancy of separate and contradictory roles (Example 1) or occupancy of a single role with conflicting aspects (Example 2)—and the distinction is not always clear-cut—there seems little doubt that in complex and heterogeneous social systems situations like these are quite common. Thus understanding deviantness and ordinariness require, for a great many varieties of behavior, close attention to the structure of and relations between social roles.

4. **Appropriate and inappropriate deviance.** As these comments begin to suggest, there may be associated with conventional social roles ideas regarding what we might call *"appropriate and inappropriate deviance."* Not even all of the behaviors and conditions that throughout a given society are heavily imbued with deviantness will necessarily be seen as *equally* inconsistent with the expectations regarding a given conventional role. Again, thinking in these terms may help us to interpret certain kinds of reported deviance rate variations. Perhaps the best example in our own society involves statistical differentials according to sex and, in particular, the fact that, at least until very recently, American women have on the one hand displayed relatively high recorded rates of mental illness and, on the other hand, relatively low recorded rates of crime. There probably are several interrelated factors producing such results, but a large part of the explanation may well lie in the complex, confused, and now rapidly changing meanings and expectations commonly attached to the "woman's role."

Research on mental illness, including self-report studies, invariably discloses high rates of psychological disturbance among women—particularly those disorders diagnosed as "neurosis" and, among the more severe disturbances, "manic-depressive" psychosis (see Dohrenwend and Dohrenwend, 1976). There is some dispute among specialists as to whether these findings reflect real mental illness or, instead, are an "artifact" resulting both from women's greater willingness to admit psychological distress and from various aspects of the way in which mental illness research is conducted (content of questionnaire items, etc.) (see Gove and Tudor, 1973; Clancy and Gove, 1974; "Commentary and Debate" on Clancy and Gove, 1976; Dohrenwend and Dohrenwend, 1976). But despite this somewhat technical debate, there seems no gainsaying that in many ways the dominant definitions of "normal" behavior for women in our society encourage the identification by others of women as "mentally ill" and women's perceptions of themselves as being psychologically disturbed. A great deal of psychoanalytic and psychological theory has been grounded in and at the same time has reinforced extremely narrow and rigid conceptions regarding woman's "nature" (see discussion in Weisstein, 1972). According to such views, women are "supposed to be" warm, loving, nurturant, passive, noncompetitive, spontaneous, emotionally sensitive creatures. Though it is increasingly being recognized that such conceptions reflected and upheld the limited social roles into which women had been cast and for which they had been socialized much more than they reflected woman's "nature," they have unquestionably had a strong impact on perceptions of female mental illness. Because of their influence, any woman departing from such expectations—for example, by not seeming sufficiently warm and loving or by showing signs of "aggressiveness"—easily became subject to psychiatric diagnosis or was likely to view herself as "abnormal."

But by the same token, too close an *adherence* to the narrow "natural-ness" model could likewise easily produce psychological disturbance. Thus, to be as passive and self-preoccupied as the model often dictated was, almost by definition, to be "withdrawn" and "depressed." Similarly, to limit one's everyday activities largely to the housewife-mother role in the way the model implied was natural could readily produce boredom, "obsessive" behavior, extreme personal dissatisfaction, and the like. Psychologist Phyllis Chesler, exposer and challenger of this "mentally-ill-either-way" feature of women's situation, makes the point in a general and at the same time dramatic way: "What we consider 'madness' whether it appears in women or in men, is either the acting out of the devalued female role or the total or partial rejection of one's sex-role stereotype" (Chesler, 1972, p. 56).

The influence of dominant role expectations is also evident when we consider women's crime rates—though here their main impact has been to keep the recorded rates low. As the author of a leading criminology text notes: "Crime rates for males are always higher than for females, and that applies to all crimes except those that are by definition predominantly female, such as abortion and prostitution. Although males constitute roughly fifty precent of the population in the United States, they account for approximately ninety percent of the arrests for serious crimes" (Reid, 1976, p. 58). Once again, a combination of factors—including the differential socioeconomic pressures facing men and women in our society, the sex distribution of opportunities to commit various crimes (e.g., limitations on women's access to corporate jobs necessarily implies a low rate of white-collar crime), and possibly varying reactions of police, judges, and other crime-processors to woman suspects and defendants—influences such outcomes. But as the last of these factors indicates, the meanings attached to various kinds of behavior on the part of women have particular significance.

When students are asked to "picture in your mind's eye a typical criminal," they almost always conjure up the image of a man. Although this does "accurately" reflect male dominance in the official rates, it also highlights the importance of commonly held definitions and associations. There is, after all, nothing in women's physical or psychological make-up that precludes participation in robbery, burglary, assault, and most other "offenses." On the contrary, part of what is operating here is the dominant tendency not to associate crime with women. One early study suggested that even then, in 1950, women's actual crime involvement was very extensive but "hidden." Women's typical roles enabled them to commit crimes that were not easily detected (the author cited as an example wives poisoning husbands), and furthermore some of the most under-recorded offenses (e.g., abortion and prostitution) were female ones (Pollak, 1950). More recently, several commentators (Simon, 1975; Adler, 1975) have pointed to increases both in overall female crime rates and to an apparent broadening of the range of types of recorded female crime. In one or another way, these authors argue, such trends reflect the changing problems, opportunities, and situations of women in our society—including associated changes in the general conceptions regarding the qualities and activities considered "natural" for females.

Both the findings regarding mental illness rates and those regarding rates of criminality suggest the usefulness of the concept (advanced recently by Anthony Harris) of "functional typescripts" in deviance. In Harris's view, these typescripts consist of strong social expectations as to what kinds of people are to engage in which kinds of behavior. Thus, he states: "It is strongly type-scripted in American society that street crimes represent the preserve of blacks and the poor. From a somewhat different slant, it is (or was) scripted that it is nearly "impossible" for the highest officials in the land to act criminally. Similarly . . . it is (still) type-scripted that it is unlikely or "impossible" for women to attempt assassination, robbery or rape" (Harris, 1977, p. 12). Such typescripts, Harris argues, are functional in the sense that they represent part of a system of "stratification of behavior and identities" that upholds the dominance of certain persons within the society: "Male dominance in occupational, educational, political and legal institutions is not served by allowing the development of type-scripts which lead to putting women in jail. Rather, the prime structural mainstay of male institutional hegemony has been the continued assignment of females to the home and to the role of homemaker" (Harris, 1977, p. 13). At least to the extent women's mental illness is "ambulatory" (doesn't result in hospitalization or severe incapacity) this dominance theme in Harris's analysis would not be inconsistent with the high deviance rates in that area. And if we leave aside the issue of their precise function, there seems no question at all regarding the existence and influence of typescripting as regards both crime and mental illness. It is in the breakdown of excessively rigid and narrow typescripts (associated with a decline in male dominance?) that greater social equality for women may imply reduced deviance rate differentials between the sexes.

5. **Deviant roles.** Finally, we can note a rather different sense in which roles become important in analyzing deviance. A point strongly emphasized in recent deviance theory, and throughout this text, is that deviance-defining in varying degrees casts individuals into special kinds of roles that strongly affect their subsequent behavior and self-conceptions. As we will see, deviantized roles (e.g., being identified as "a drug addict," "a thief," "a corrupt politician," "a nut") threaten to engulf the individual. It is extremely difficult once one has been so branded to maintain any substantial "role distance" (to step back from the role into which one has been cast). Although some such roles may at times be voluntarily assumed (i.e., the behavioral side, if not the accompanying stigma) the implications and ramifications of occupying them are very significantly shaped by the responses of other people. When we think of the relation between deviance and social roles in this important sense, we are reversing the usual ordering of elements in the analysis. From this standpoint, it is not so much that standard

roles or role problems "lead to" deviance, but rather that deviance-defining itself constructs new roles, which in turn will often give rise to problems for their occupants. This also implies a twist on the typical role conflict analysis by a focusing less on such conflict causing deviance than on deviance-defining causing conflict—between a person's deviant role and his or her more conventional role commitments and requirements.

REFERENCES

Adler, Freda
1975. *Sisters in Crime*. New York: McGraw-Hill Book Company.

Alexander, Franz and Hugo Staub
1956. *The Criminal, the Judge, and the Public*. Glencoe, Ill.: The Free Press.

Becker, Howard S.
1963. *Outsiders*. New York: The Free Press.

Bell, Alan P. and Martin S. Weinberg
1978. *Homosexualities: A Study of Diversity Among Men and Women*. New York: Simon and Schuster.

Bell, Daniel
1953. "Crime as an American Way of Life," *Antioch Review*, 13(Summer), 131–154.

Bieber, Irving, et al.
1962. *Homosexuality: A Psychoanalytic Study*. New York: Basic Books, Inc.

Bohannan, Paul, ed.
1960, 1967. *African Homicide and Suicide*. New York: Atheneum Publishers.

Brody, Jane E.
1976. "A Chromosome Link to Crime is Doubted," *The New York Times*, September 12, 1976, p. 18.

Broom, Leonard and Philip Selznick
1977. *Sociology: A Text with Adapted Readings*, 6th ed. New York: Harper & Row, Publishers.

Chesler, Phyllis
1972. *Women and Madness*. New York: Avon Books.

Clancy, Kevin and Walter Gove
1974. "Sex Differences in Mental Illness: An Analysis of Response Bias in Self-Reports," *American Journal of Sociology,* 80(July), 205–216; and "Commentary and Debate" on same, *American Journal of Sociology,* 81(May), 1455–1472.

Clinard, Marshall B.
1974. *Sociology of Deviant Behavior, 4th ed.* New York: Holt, Rinehart and Winston, Inc.

Cohen, Albert K.
1966. *Deviance and Control*. Englewood Cliffs, N.J.: Prentice-Hall, Inc.

Conrad, Peter
1975. "The Discovery of Hyperkinesis: Notes on the Medicalization of Deviant Behavior," *Social Problems,* 23(October), 12–21.

Coser, Lewis A.
1956. *The Functions of Social Conflict.* New York: The Free Press.
1962. "Some Functions of Deviant Behavior and Normative Flexibility," *American Journal of Sociology,* 68(September 3), 171–181.

Davis, Kingsley
1937, 1961. "The Sociology of Prostitution," *American Sociological Review,* 2 (October), 746–755; as revised in Robert K. Merton and Robert Nisbet, eds., *Contemporary Social Problems.* New York: Harcourt Brace & World.
1976. "Sexual Behavior," in Merton and Nisbet, *Contemporary Social Problems, 4th ed.* New York: Harcourt Brace Jovanovich. Pp. 220–261.

Davis, Nanette J.
1975. *Sociological Constructions of Deviance.* Dubuque, Iowa: William C. Brown Company.

Dentler, Robert A. and Kai T. Erikson
1959. "The Functions of Deviance in Groups," *Social Problems,* 7 (Fall), 98–107.

Dohrenwend, Bruce P. and Barbara Snell Dohrenwend
1976. "Sex Differences and Psychiatric Disorders," *American Journal of Sociology,* 81 (May), 1447–1454.

Douglas, Jack D., ed.
1970. *Deviance and Respectability.* New York: Basic Books, Inc.

Douglas, Jack D. and John M. Johnson, eds.
1977. *Official Deviance.* Philadelphia: J. B. Lippincott Company.
1978. *Crime at the Top.* Philadelphia: J. B. Lippincott Company.

Durkheim, Emile
1893, 1947. *The Division of Labor in Society,* trans. Simpson. Glencoe, Ill.: The Free Press.
1895, 1964. *The Rules of Sociological Method, 8th ed.* trans. Solovay and Mueller. New York: The Free Press.
1897, 1951. *Suicide.* trans. Spaulding and Simpson. Glencoe, Ill.: The Free Press.

Edgerton, Robert B.
1967. *The Cloak of Competence.* Berkeley: University of California Press.
1969. "On the 'Recognition' of Mental Illness," in Stanley C. Plog and Robert B. Edgerton, eds., *Changing Perspectives in Mental Illness.* New York: Holt, Rinehart and Winston, Inc. Pp. 49–72.
1976. *Deviance: A Cross-Cultural Perspective.* Menlo Park, Calif.: Cummings Publishing Company.

Erikson, Kai. T
1962. "Notes on the Sociology of Deviance," *Social Problems,* 9(Spring), 307–314.
1966. *Wayward Puritans.* New York: John Wiley & Sons, Inc.

Ermann, M. David and R. J. Lundman, eds.
1978. *Corporate and Government Deviance.* New York: Oxford, University Press.

Fishman, Mark
1978. "Crime Waves as Ideology," *Social Problems,* 25(June), 531–543.

Gagnon, John H. and William Simon
1973. *Sexual Conduct.* Chicago: Aldine Publishing Company.

Galdston, Iago
1958. "Comments," in Mary S. Calderone, ed., *Abortion in the United States.* New York: Paul B. Hoeber, Inc.

Garfinkel, Harold
1964. "Studies of the Routine Grounds of Everyday Activities," *Social Problems,* 11 (Winter), 225–250.
1967. *Studies in Ethnomethodology.* Englewood Cliffs, N.J.: Prentice-Hall, Inc.

Gelles, Richard J.
1972. *The Violent Home.* Beverly Hills: Sage Publications, Inc.

Gibbons, Don C.
1970. *Delinquent Behavior.* Englewood Cliffs, N.J.: Prentice-Hall, Inc.

Glueck, Sheldon and Eleanor
1956. *Physique and Delinquency.* New York: Harper & Row, Publishers.

Goode, William J.
1976. "Family Disorganization," in Merton and Nisbet, *op. cit.,* pp. 513–554.

Gove, Walter R.
1970. "Societal Reaction as an Explanation of Mental Illness: an Evaluation," *American Sociological Review,* 35(October), 873–884.

Gove, Walter R. and Jeannette F. Tudor
1973. "Adult Sex Roles and Mental Illness," *American Journal of Sociology,* 78(January), 812–835.

Halleck, Seymour L.
1972. *The Politics of Therapy.* New York: Harper & Row, Publishers.

Harris, Anthony R.
1977. "Sex and Theories of Deviance: Toward a Functional Theory of Deviant Type-Scripts," *American Sociological Review,* 42(February), 3–16.

Hart, H. L. A.
1961. *The Concept of Law.* London: Oxford University Press.

Hirshi, Travis and Hanan C. Selvin
1967. *Delinquency Research: An Appraisal of Analytic Methods.* New York: The Free Press.

Hoebel, E. Adamson
1961. *The Law of Primitive Man.* Cambridge: Harvard University Press.

Hoffman, Martin
1969. *The Gay World.* New York: Bantam Books, Inc.

Hollingshead, August B. and Frederick C. Redlich
1953. "Social Stratification and Psychiatric Disorders," *American Sociological Review,* 18 (April), 163–169.

Hooker, Evelyn
1963. "The Adjustment of the Male Overt Homosexual," in Hendrik M. Ruitenbeek, ed., *The Problem of Homosexuality in Modern Society*. New York: E. P. Dutton & Co., Inc. Pp. 141–161.

James, Jennifer
1977. "Prostitutes and Prostitution," in Edward Sagarin and Fred Montanino, eds., *Deviants: Voluntary Actors in a Hostile World*. Morristown, N.J.: General Learning Corporation. Pp. 368–428.

Kameny, Franklin E.
1971. "Homosexuals as a Minority Group," in Edward Sagarin, ed., *The Other Minorities*. Waltham, Mass.: Ginn and Company. Pp. 50–65.

Labovitz, Sanford
1968. "Variation in Suicide Rates," in Jack P. Gibbs, ed., *Suicide*. New York: Harper & Row, Publishers. Pp. 57–73.

Laing, R. D.
1965. *The Divided Self*. Baltimore: Penguin Books, Inc.

Lemert, Edwin M.
1967. *Human Deviance, Social Problems, and Social Control*. Englewood Cliffs, N.J.: Prentice-Hall, Inc.

Lindesmith, Alfred R.
1940. "The Drug Addict as a Psychopath," *American Sociological Review*, 5(December), 914–920.

Lipset, Seymour Martin
1963. *Political Man*. Garden City, N.Y.: Doubleday & Company, Inc.

MacAndrew, Craig
1969. "On the Notion that Certain Persons Who are Given to Frequent Drunkenness Suffer from a Disease called Alcoholism," in Plog and Edgerton, eds., *op. cit.*, pp. 483–501.

Malinowski, Bronislaw
1926, 1959. Crime and Custom in Savage Society. Totowa, N.J.: Littlefield, Adams & Company.

Matza, David
1964. *Delinquency and Drift*. New York: John Wiley & Sons, Inc.
1969. *Becoming Deviant*. Englewood Cliffs, N.J.: Prentice-Hall, Inc.

McCarthy, Raymond G., ed.
1959. *Drinking and Intoxication*. New Haven: College and University Press.

McGaghy, Charles H. and James K. Skipper, Jr.
1969. "Lesbian Behavior as an Adaptation to the Occupation of Stripping," *Social Problems,* 17(Fall), 262–270.

Mead, George H.
1928. "The Psychology of Punitive Justice." *American Journal of Sociology,* 23(March), 557–562.

Mechanic, David
1969. *Mental Health and Social Policy*. Englewood Cliffs, N.J.: Prentice-Hall, Inc.

Mercer, Jane C.
1965. "Social System Perspective and Clinical Perspective: Frames of Reference for Understanding Career Patterns of Persons Labelled as Mentally Retarded," *Social Problems,* 13(Summer), 18–34.
1973. *Labeling the Mentally Retarded*. Berkeley, Calif.: University of California Press.

Merton, Robert K.
1949. *Social Theory and Social Structure*. Glencoe, Ill.: The Free Press.

Merton, Robert K. and Robert Nisbet, eds.
1966. *Contemporary Social Problems, 2nd ed*. New York: Harcourt Brace & World.

Mills, C. Wright
1943. "The Professional Ideology of Social Pathologists," *American Journal of Sociology*, 49(September), 165–180.

Money, John
1972. "Sexual Dimorphism and Homosexual Gender Identity," in National Institute of Mental Health, Task Force on Homosexuality, *Final Report and Background Papers*. Washington: U.S. Government Printing Office. Pp. 42–54.

Newman, Graeme
1976. *Comparative Deviance*. New York: American Elsevier Publishing Co., Inc.

Nuehring, Elane and Gerald E. Markle
1974. "Nicotene and Norms: The Re-Emergence of a Deviant Behavior," *Social Problems,* 21(April), 513–526.

Orcutt, James D.
1975. "Deviance as a Situated Phenomenon: Variations in the Social Interpretation of Marijuana and Alcohol Use," *Social Problems,* 22(February), 346–356.

Pittman, David J.
1967. "International Overview: Social and Cultural Factors in Drinking Patterns, Pathological and Nonpathological," in David J. Pittman, ed., *Alcoholism*. New York: Harper & Row, Publishers. Pp. 3–20.

Plog, Stanley C. and Robert B. Edgerton, eds.
1969. *Changing Perspectives in Mental Illness*. New York: Holt, Rinehart and Winston, Inc.

Pollak, Otto
1950. *The Criminality of Women*. Philadelphia: University of Pennsylvania Press.

President's Commission on Law Enforcement and Administration of Justice
1967. *Task Force Report: Crime and Its Impact—An Assessment*. Washington, D.C.: U.S. Government Printing Office.

Ranulf, Svend
1964. *Moral Indignation and Middle Class Psychology*. New York: Schocken Books, Inc.

Reid, Sue Titus
1976. *Crime and Criminology*. New York: Holt, Rinehart and Winston, Inc.

Reinhold, Robert
1977. "Smoking of Marijuana Wins Wider Acceptance," *The New York Times,* May 23, p. 29.

Rensberger, Boyce
1976. "Briton's Classic IQ Data Now Viewed as Fraudulent," *The New York Times,* November 28, p. 26.

Rubin, Vera and Lambros Comitas
1976. *Ganja in Jamaica: The Effects of Marijuana Use.* Garden City, N.Y.: Doubleday & Company, Inc.

Ruitenbeek, Hendrik, ed.
1963. *The Problem of Homosexuality in Modern Society.* New York: E. P. Dutton & Co., Inc.

Sagarin, Edward
1975. *Deviants and Deviance.* New York: Praeger Publishers, Inc.

Sarbin, Theodore R.
1969. "The Scientific Status of the Mental Illness Metaphor," in Plog and Edgerton, *op. cit.,* pp. 9–31.

Scheff, T. J.
1974. "The Labelling Theory of Mental Illness," *American Sociological Review,* 39(June), 444–452.

Scheler, Max
1961. *Ressentiment.* trans. Coser. New York: The Free Press.

Schneider, Joseph W.
1978. "Deviant Drinking as Disease: Alcoholism as a Social Accomplishment," *Social Problems,* 25(April), 361–372.

Schrag, Peter and Diane Divoky
1976. *The Myth of the Hyperactive Child.* New York: Dell Publishing Co., Inc.

Schur, Edwin M.
1969. *Our Criminal Society.* Englewood Cliffs, N.J.: Prentice-Hall, Inc.
1972. "Sociocultural Factors in Homosexual Behavior," in National Institute of Mental Health, Task Force on Homosexuality, *op. cit.,* pp. 30–41.
1973. *Radical Nonintervention: Rethinking the Delinquency Problem.* Englewood Cliffs, N.J.: Prentice-Hall, Inc.

Schwartz, Richard D.
1954. "Social Factors in the Development of Legal Control: A Case Study of Two Israeli Settlements," *Yale Law Journal,* 63(February), 471–491.

Schwartz, Richard D. and James C. Miller
1964. "Legal Evolution and Societal Complexity," *American Journal of Sociology,* 70(September), 159–169.

Scott, Robert A.
1969. *The Making of Blind Men.* New York: Russell Sage Foundation.
1972. "A Proposed Framework for Analyzing Deviance as a Property of Social Order," in

Robert A. Scott and Jack D. Douglas, eds., *Theoretical Perspectives on Deviance*. New York: Basic Books, Inc. Pp. 9–35.

Simmel, Georg
1904. 1955. *Conflict*. trans. Woolf. New York: The Free Press.

Simmons, J. L.
1969. *Deviants*. San Francisco: The Glendessary Press.

Simon, Rita James
1975. *Women and Crime*. Lexington, Mass.: D.C. Heath and Co.

Simpson, Ruth
1977. *From the Closet to the Courts*. New York: Penguin Books, Inc.

Smith, L. Douglas
1969. "The 'Beats' and Bohemia: Positive Social Deviance or a Problem in Collective Disturbance?" in Plog and Edgerton, eds., *op. cit.*, pp. 578–593.

Snyder, Charles
1958. *Alcohol and The Jews*. New York: The Free Press of Glencoe.

Spector, Malcolm and John I. Kitsuse
1977. *Constructing Social Problems*. Menlo Park, Calif.: Cummings Publishing Company.

Suchar, Charles S.
1978. *Social Deviance: Perspectives and Prospects*. New York: Rinehart and Winston.

Szasz, Thomas
1961. *The Myth of Mental Illness*. New York: Paul B. Hoeber, Inc.

Taylor, Ian, Paul Walton and Jock Young
1974. *The New Criminology: For a Social Theory of Deviance*. New York: Harper & Row, Publishers.

Trice, Harrison M.
1966. *Alcoholism in America*. New York: McGraw-Hill, Inc.

Turner, Roy, ed.
1974. *Ethnomethodology*. Baltimore: Penguin Books, Inc.

Ullman, Albert D.
1960. *To Know the Difference*. New York: St. Martin's Press, Inc.

Veevers, J. E.
1973. "Voluntary Childless Wives: An Exploratory Study," *Sociology and Social Research*, (April), 356–365.

Vold, George B.
1958. *Theoretical Criminology*. New York: Oxford University Press.

Weakland, John H.
1969. "Schizophrenia: Basic Problems in Sociocultural Investigation," in Plog and Edgerton, eds., *op. cit.*, pp. 672–701.

Weinberg, George
1973. *Society and the Healthy Homosexual*. Garden City, N.Y.: Doubleday & Company, Inc.

Weisstein, Naomi
1972. "Psychology Constructs the Female," in Vivian Gornick and Barbara K. Moran, eds., *Woman in Sexist Society*. New York: Signet Books, pp. 207–224.

Whyte, William Foote
1943. *Street Corner Society*. Chicago: University of Chicago Press.

Wilson, Edward O.
1975. *Sociobiology*. Cambridge: Harvard University Press.

Wirth, Louis
1938. "Urbanism as a Way of Life." *American Journal of Sociology*, 44(July), 1–24.

Wolfgang, Marvin D.
1958. *Patterns in Criminal Homicide*. Philadelphia: University of Pennsylvania Press.

REVIEW OF KEY TERMS

boundary-maintenance. The process of maintaining and affirming social "boundaries" of "conformity" and "deviance" by identifying and reacting to individuals and actions that exceed limits of acceptable variation. It is a major function (consequence) of deviance-defining.

constraint. The assumption that acts of deviation are "determined" by forces beyond the individual's control. It is a characteristic assumption in many sociological deviance theories as well as in biological and psychological ones.

decompartmentalizing (of deviance). The growing recognition that deviance situations and deviance-defining are central aspects of social life, with the associated increased standing of the subfield of deviance studies within the discipline of sociology.

differentiation. The assumption in many traditional sociological theories that "deviants" are basically different from "nondeviants" and that study of such differences will reveal the causes of deviance. This assumption is also quite widespread among the general public.

ecological context. The physical and locational setting of social interaction—in particular, the geographical distribution (regional, urban-rural, intracity, etc.) of factors that affect deviance-defining and deviance situations.

evil-causes-evil fallacy. The belief in early sociological approaches that problematic behavior was always and completely attributable to "bad" social conditions. It produced selective inattention to possible influences of prized social values and dominant arrangements.

functionalism. Analysis centered on the concept of society as a system of mutually interdependent parts. In deviance theory it has made varied contributions, including an emphasis on the links between deviance and socially approved values and behaviors, and on the analysis of systemic functions of reacting to deviance (e.g., boundary-maintenance).

latent functions. Unintended objective consequences of a behavior pattern or social arrangement. In deviance analysis, this concept is particularly useful in interpreting the persistence of patterns when stated purposes clearly are not met (as in "unworkable" criminal laws that remain "on the books").

Lombroso, Cesare. The Italian physician credited with founding the "positivist" school in criminology, which emphasized direct study of the criminal offender. He formulated the conception of the born criminal type, which has since been discredited.

Medical model. An approach to analyzing deviance in terms of "pathology," "abnormality," or "differentness," usually of the deviating individuals, that is roughly analogous to medical distinctions between sickness and health.

pathology. The lingering assumption of abnormality, of social conditions if not individuals, in social disorganization theories and other traditional explanations of deviance. See also *differentiation* and *medical model*.

positivism. The study of deviance through comparison of individual "offenders" with supposed "nonoffenders." Assumptions of *differentiation* and *constraint* are central to this orientation.

predelinquency. The supposed tendency to deviate that is claimed to be discernible in children prior to the actual occurrence of the offending acts. This concept reflects "early identification and treatment" goals associated with certain deviance theories as well as strong belief in the basic "differentness" of deviants." It is not much supported by available evidence.

psychopath. A catch-all diagnostic category, often described in terms of "antisocial" personality and absence of conscience or guilt, that has been applied in "explaining" a wide variety of types of offending behavior. It has been criticized for imprecision and misuse as a residual grab-bag accommodating any "offenses" that do not fit other psychiatric diagnoses.

situated morality. The idea that deviance and respectability are always relative to a particular situation because they are "social constructions of reality" that emerge only in the context of certain concrete situations and because the outcome in any particular instance of possible deviance-defining is influenced by numerous situational contingencies.

somatotyping. A scheme developed by Sheldon and following Kretschmer for rating individuals on body-type components which were believed to be associated with characteristic temperamental tendencies. It is an example of persisting biological determinism or extreme positivism.

PROJECT 2
Constructing Indicators of Deviance

Introductory Comment

Being clear as to just what it is one is about to study is an obvious prerequisite to meaningful research. Most sociologists would like, insofar as possible, to use precise and readily applicable definitions of the particular social phenomena they are going to investigate. Thus, the usual insistence that definitions should be "operational," that is, that one can convert them into specific research operations particularly by constructing workable "indicators" of whatever is being defined and studied. At the same time, as has been suggested in the first two chapters of this book, complex processes of social definition and reaction may not always be easy to pin down in this "operationalizing" way. Nonetheless, a great deal of the traditional research on deviance has attempted to do this as part of the "either-or" categorizing tendencies (deviance/nondeviance; deviant persons/nondeviant persons) previously mentioned. One of the best ways for students to assess such efforts may be to try out the operationalizing approach themselves. That is the aim of this rather modest exercise in constructing indicators.

Assignment

The following definition of "problem drinkers" is taken from an essay on alcohol use in a leading social problems textbook:

> . . . individuals who *repeatedly* use alcohol to an extent that exceeds customary dietary use or prevailing socially accepted customs or in amounts that, for them, cause problems of physical health, interfere with interpersonal relations, or disrupt the fulfillment of family, economic, or community expectations. (*Source:* Robert Straus, "Alcoholism and Problem Drinking," in Robert K. Merton and Robert Nisbet, *Contemporary Social Problems, 4th ed.,* New York: Harcourt Brace Jovanovich 1976. p. 193.)

Select *either* this definition *or* a definition (drawn from any textbook on deviance, social problems, introductory sociology, or psychology or from a more specialized source) of one of the following: neurosis, drug abuse, political extremism, sexual promiscuity, compulsive gambling.

Using the definition you select as a basis, try to construct specific research indicators of the particular behavior or condition, referred to as X in the discussion that follows. That is, make up specific questions that could be included in a questionnaire or asked during an interview concerning either the respondents' own behavior or direct experience, or their observations of other people they know, or items to be explored through your own observation, and responses to which would permit you to identify instances of or frequencies of X. In other words, the items should enable you to determine whether the people you question or observe have themselves engaged in X or know of people who do. Depending on your instructor's and the class's preference, you may either wish to try out these questions individually, as part of a small questionnaire or interview in which you could also ask various personal background and general attitude questions, seeking a small number of respondents at your school or in the local community, or the preparatory work of individual students in the class might be pooled to provide the basis for a somewhat larger group study dealing with several behaviors and conditions.

The most important part of the exercise, however, will be to *evaluate how well the indicators work* in specifying the presence or absence of X. This can be done partly on the basis of what happens when you actually try them out and also by asking yourself some of the questions listed below. NOTE: in constructing indicator items, you should neither present respondents with the definition itself (e.g., the statement on problem drinking quoted above), nor simply ask them whether they fit the given category (e.g., "Are you now or have you ever been a drug abuser?"). Even though self-report studies indicate that respondents will honestly answer questions about discreditable behavior, the latter approach would not only be "abusive," but it would also negate the point of the exercise—which is to see if the definition can be broken down into clear and readily answerable items that will then provide a basis for further study of the behavior, of those who engage in it, of its social correlates, and so on. Rather, you should try to develop specific indicators such as: How often do you drink alcohol? Under what circumstances? With what consequences? and the like (only you can be considerably more specific).

Evaluation

Evaluating your indicators will require examining them *in conjunction with* the original "definition," in order to see whether you are really able—with precision and likely agreement among different researchers who might want to use the indicators—to get at what is specified in the definition and, in turn, whether that enables you to get at the behavior or condition in question. In other words, to use the definition quoted here, are you able to "locate" instances of the condition Straus defines, and, if so, would you then be in a position to study (precisely and objectively) "problem drinking." In particular, you should ask yourself the following questions about the indicators singly and collectively:

1. Will respondents understand exactly what you are asking them, or will they require further specification? If so, what kinds of specification and how much?

2. Will the indicators work equally well (that is, tell you what you want to know) for respondents coming from different ethnic and religious backgrounds?

differing in socioeconomic status? having varying levels of education? living in different subareas of the community? If not, why not?

3. In particular, will respondents in these various categories all understand the items asked about in the same way? If not, could the items be modified so they would be appropriate for all categories?

4. Do the indicators permit you to take account of varying situations and circumstances that might be relevant to applying the definition you started with?

5. Do the indicators enable you to strictly specify the presence or absence of the behavior in question or, instead, the *degree* to which it is present or absent? Which kind of finding would be more appropriate, given what it is that is being defined and studied?

6. Can respondents answer all of the questions posed in a strictly objective way, that is, without having to *evaluate* their own or other people's behavior.

If you feel you have gotten over these potential hurdles, the next step might be to look at the definition you took as a point of departure. Presumably you now have worked out some devices for applying it. But to understand what such application entails, you might want to ask yourself the following additional questions:

1. If the various respondents were presented with this *definition,* would they all agree with it? If not, in what ways and to what extent would they disagree?

2. If all different kinds of sociologists were presented with this definition (you could "operationalize" this by asking all students in the class or by conjecturing about professional sociologists' views) would *they* agree with it? If not, in what ways and to what extent would they disagree?

3. If one would anticipate substantial disagreement in either of these two categories, then where does that leave us in regard to having a definition to operationalize? Are we justified in basing research on this definition when there is such disagreement?

Implications

Most likely you were able to deal with the first set of questions to your own satisfaction, but the second set is more difficult. The reason for this is quite simple, and in order to highlight it the exercise poses "loaded" examples. All of the categories of "behavior" suggested for study are really a good deal more than just behavioral. They imply moral judgments, and this is the problem one comes up against in reexamining the definitions. It is one thing to frame questions that will allow you to identify patterns of drug *use,* but it is quite another to try to identify through scientific operations drug *abuse.* We can readily measure amounts of sexual activity, but not *promiscuity*, because that is an evaluation or judgment, not a fact. We can find out who gambles and how much, but we will not all agree on when that behavior is *compulsive*. Of course, one can arbitrarily set up a criterion for any of these terms, but in the absence of consensus on same, we have to recognize that it remains just that—arbitrary. Of course, many sociologists do not fall into this kind of trap. They try to limit their studies to what is measurable, countable, and clearly categorizable, and leave out all of the evaluative "modifiers." Yet, as we have seen, it is these evaluative judgments that lie at the center of deviance situations. And all too often the judgments are taken for granted; the investigator proceeds as though drug abuse were a "thing," as though its presence or absence could be determined through sociological investigation. Working through this exercise should help one to recognize that the frequently relative, and varying definitions and reactions involved in deviance situations often make this effort at neat specification of the supposedly deviant behaviors and individuals a misguided one. Indeed, we could study those definitions and reactions directly and perhaps construct some kinds of indicators of them, but that would be a different enterprise altogether.

PROLOGUE 3

Sociological theory must advance on these interconnected planes: through special theories adequate to limited ranges of social data, and through the evolution of a more general conceptual scheme adequate to consolidate *groups of special theories.*
—Robert K. Merton, *Social Theory and Social Structure*

I will show how each viewpoint built on those of its predecessors and addressed itself to many of the same issues and dilemmas. Since the allegation of intellectual evolution or growth runs an especially high risk of forgery, the reader is forewarned. Except that the posited growth is slight, I would not seriously entertain so remote a possibility.
—David Matza, *Becoming Deviant*

The aim of sociology is to develop a systematic understanding of social interaction and social systems. Whatever specific orientation is adopted in sociological investigation, the development of theory (roughly defined as "generalizations about the facts") is almost always seen as one if not the major goal of the enterprise. Theories can, of course, be presented on varying levels of generality. Presumably we could have, on the one hand, a theory regarding "gambling activity in waterfront bars" and, at the other extreme, a theory of "the nature of human societies." Sociologists often seem torn between the two extremes in theorizing, much as they are torn methodologically between working "up" (inductively) from close investigation of the empirical world to theoretical propositions about it and working "down" (deductively) from large generalizations to lower-level testable propositions about the "facts." In actual social research, the two processes are usually intermixed; yet the two tendencies often are revealed in the overall work-style preferences of particular sociologists—according to which we might divide them into practitioners of what C. Wright Mills once called "abstracted empiricism" and "grand theory."

Theorizing in a subfield of sociology, such as that of deviance studies, often displays these general tendencies, but presumably the overall aim is to strike something of a middle ground between the extremes. Here, we are not primarily interested in a theory "about" a single narrow form of behavior, nor one about the "nature of society" in general. Instead, we seek to develop an understanding of one broad and significant patterned segment of social life, encompassing many specific forms of behavior and types of situations. Of course, even in connection with this intermediate-level task, there is always the hope that the great traditions of general theorizing will guide our efforts. And the concern for continuity and cumulation in theorizing—found in all of sociology—is in evidence here, too. To some extent each "new" theory represents a break with, an attempt to improve upon, its predecessors. (Yet even in the process of repudiation, we often show how we have been influenced by that which we repudiate.) Recently strong claims have been advanced in sociology of totally new ways of thinking about the social world. At the same time, as the Matza quotation suggests, basic issues and dilemmas persist, and each outlook that develops provides some of the basis for those that follow. Even if a single "definitive" theory does not show signs of emerging, neither is it the case that the course of development in deviance theorizing has been totally haphazard. A variety of important outlooks and concepts—admittedly no more than that, but quite significant in those terms—allows us to analyze many features of deviance situations with increased perceptiveness and clarity.

CH.3
TRADITIONS
AND TRENDS
IN DEVIANCE THEORY

INTRODUCTION

In the first two chapters of this book, we have already begun to note some of the shortcomings and a few persisting contributions of traditional outlooks on deviance. At the same time, by considering the potential usefulness of such concepts as "deviantness," "deviance-defining," and "deviance situation" (and by starting to use those terms in order to place the field's subject-matter within a broad and sociologically meaningful perspective), some indication of the general nature of recent "trends" in analyzing deviance has also been provided. However, with an eye to developing a comprehensive framework for studying deviance situations, additional discussion of these traditions and trends seems to be called for.

Therefore, we now turn to a consideration of certain major influences on the development of modern deviance theory with special attention, first, to key "traditions" not mentioned thus far. Some textbooks and deviance courses place a heavy emphasis on the so-called "schools" of deviance theory, but in this text we will be adopting a somewhat different tact. Although it is important for students to be familiar with the standard theories and perspectives, the stress on schools can have unfortunate consequences. In particular, it can lead to an exaggerated sense of discontinuity in the development of deviance theory—to the belief that the approaches are completely separate from, if not contradictory to, one another and that one must for *all* purposes "choose" between them.

Certainly it would be unwise to try to deny that there are some significant differences in underlying premises, theoretical emphases, favored methodologies, and the like. Many of these differences will be noted below. On the other hand, as we will also see, to some extent the various orientations may differ as much in terms of *what* they are trying to study and accomplish—the *objects* of analysis, the *kinds* of explanations sought, and so on—as in the specific *means* they have adopted in analyzing deviance. When that is true, rather than directly clashing, a number of approaches may actually point up alternative but complementary paths for analyzing different aspects of deviance situations. Thus, as already suggested, explaining the occurrence of behavior, on the one hand, and explaining the characterization of that behavior, on the other, may be two different though related tasks. It follows that they may require different modes of inquiry.

We should be on guard, then, against the common tendency to believe we must discard certain perspectives wholesale, while embracing others completely. Often, one may be particularly useful for some purpose (in answering certain kinds of questions about deviance), while another may be more helpful to us in pursuing other, related lines of inquiry. There may also be important research questions about deviance at which we can "arrive" from two or more points of departure. These are issues for analysis that reflect themes of interest common to, or elements of convergence between, several theoretical traditions. An example already cited (and to be explored further below) is the matter of boundary-maintenance—a concept highly consistent with both "functionalist" and "labeling" (societal reaction emphasis) approaches that one could easily be drawn to explore from either theoretical starting point.

This notion of complementarity among different perspectives through divergence and convergence is probably not the most popular among today's students of deviance. Partly this is because of the persisting quest for a single-all-encompassing theory that would explain all aspects of deviance situations. Given the enormous range of questions to be asked about deviance (see the Paradigm in the Appendix), it may well be that such a theory, at least in the technical sense of an empirically testable set of interrelated propositions, will never be forthcoming. When we attempt to deal with more and more of these questions in our explanation, what we come up with inevitably begins to look less and less like a formal theory and to take on instead the character of a general orientation or broad interpretive framework. The perspective developed in this book, with its focus on definitions and processes, illustrates the latter possibility. Although some social theorizers are disdainful of "mere" orientations, it would be a serious mistake to dismiss such formulations preemptorily. We do, of course, have to be on guard against excessive vagueness, but adopting the broadest possible outlooks on what we are studying can be extremely illuminating even when "untestable."

Testable propositions relating to *specific* questions about deviance may, of course, be possible, and some of these may be combinable into what Merton early called "theories of the middle range" (Merton, 1949, pp. 5–10). Unfortunately, some sociologists (perhaps, especially, younger ones) are impatient with such efforts and continue to yearn for a single grand scheme that will "pull it all together." At the same time, enthusiasm for favored outlooks and abrupt even contemptuous dismissal of opposing views have often produced an array of "sociological ideologues" endlessly contending with one another. In its narrower labeling theory form (see below), the definitional-processual approach emphasized throughout this text has become deeply embroiled in such contention. As will be clear shortly, critics and some avid proponents have exaggerated the unusualness of this orientation. It should be possible to develop and use such an interpretive framework and to make clear its characteristic emphasis and thrust without succumbing to ideological rigidity.

As this discussion suggests, being *au courant* in deviance theory does not require abandoning all of the ideas developed at earlier stages in the development of the field. The review of theoretical orientations that follows (one not intended to be encyclopedic of all of the multitudinous special theories of deviance, but rather to cull out the major lines of influence) is not, then, aimed at providing a basis for deciding which is the "right" theory. On the contrary, special emphasis is placed on the significant contributions of each approach to the general development of deviance theory and on concepts and methods that have persisting usefulness. Likewise, no one approach will be treated as a monolithic entity we must either accept or reject in its entirety. Instead, we should feel free ("unrigorous" as it may sound) to pick and choose among the key elements in a given perspective. Some ideas, techniques, and findings maintain their cogency in a contemporary and comprehensive analyzing of deviance; others do not.

TRADITIONAL ORIENTATIONS

Ecological Analysis

A major impetus for much of the contemporary work on deviance came from the extensive efforts of an influential group of sociologists located in Chicago in the 1920s and 1930s to treat the city as a "social laboratory"—an object of direct research and analysis. Even critics of the theories they generated recognize the significant contribution of these Chicago researchers. Thus, Nanette Davis, who disagrees with many of the assumptions and themes characteristically associated with these efforts, nonetheless comments: "Despite the reformist hangovers implicit in some of their work, the in-depth studies of groups, communities, mechanisms of communication, and processes of change begun at Chicago established a tradition of deviant studies that persist to this day" (Davis, 1975, p. 40). In several respects, the analyses of the Chicago sociologists (sometimes erroneously seen as representing somewhat old-fashioned outlooks) actually provided important paths of transition from the extreme positivism discussed in the last chapter to the rather fluid and relativistic conceptions that have come to the fore in recent years.

Central to their work were ideas about city life and structure developed by Robert Park and Ernest Burgess, who drew for many of their basic concepts on analogies from the biological sciences, especially plant ecology. (Hence, the new rubric, "human ecology.") (For a good overview and critical appraisal of this type of theory, see Morris, 1958.) Whatever one thinks of the specifically biological terminology and assumptions Park and Burgess adopted—their writings were heavily larded with references to "organisms," "symbiosis," 'biotic balance," and the like (see discussion in Taylor, Walton, and Young, 1974, pp. 110–125)—the direct focus on the impact of the city in structuring social life was a salutory one. In particular, it highlighted the continuous interplay between people's actions and the social structures that these actions produce and change as well as reflect. As Park stated, "The city, more than any other product of man's genius and labors, represents the effort of mankind to remake the world in accordance with its wishes, but the city, once made, compels man to conform to the structure and the purposes he himself has imposed upon it. If it is true that man made the city, it is quite as true that the city is now making man" (Park, 1923, 1961, p. xxiii).

In order to facilitate analyzing this interplay, Park and Burgess conceived of the city as consisting of a variety of "natural areas"—distinctive, spatially circumscribed communities, each having its characteristic population composition, life-styles, and social problems. Some of these areas were characterized by a concentration of institutionalized patterns that elsewhere would be viewed as deviation. Thus, Nels Anderson's study of Chicago's "hobohemia" noted:

> West Madison, being a port of homeless men, has its own characteristic institutions and professions. The bootlegger is at home here; the dope peddler hunts and finds here his victims; here the professional gambler plies his trade and the "jack roller," as he is commonly called, the man who robs his fellows, while they are drunk or asleep; these and others of their kind find in the anonymity of this changing population the freedom and security that only the crowded city offers (Anderson, 1923, 1961, p. 5).

These distinctive environmental settings helped to shape both behavior and people's general outlooks: "every community, through the very character of the environment which it imposes upon the individuals that compose it, tends to determine the personal traits as it does determine the language, the vocation, social values, and eventually, the personal opinions, of the individuals who compose it" (Park, 1923, 1961, p. xxv).

One of the major techniques used in studying the impact of "natural areas" was cartographic ("mapping") analysis. Burgess and his associates depicted Chicago in terms of a set of five "concentric zones," radiating out from the central business district to the commuters' zone in the suburbs. Using this method, Clifford Shaw and Henry McKay found a distinctive ecological patterning (concentration and spatial distribution) in cases of recorded juvenile delinquency. Figure 3.1, taken from one of their major works, illustrates this method and the characteristic pattern of findings it produced. Plotting the residences of iden-

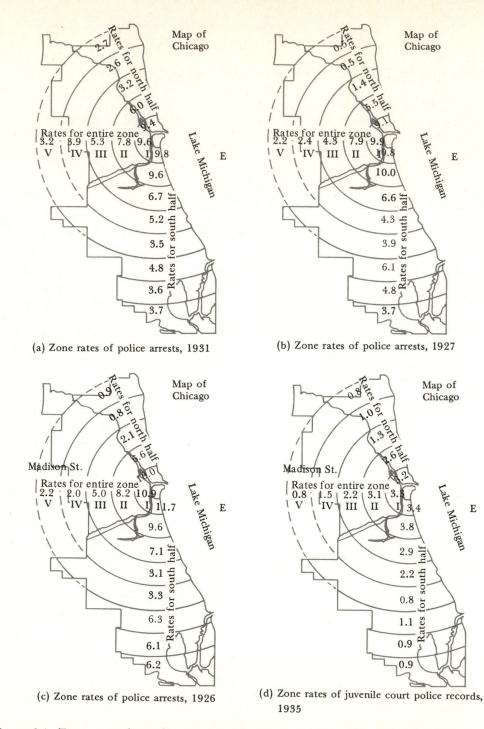

(a) Zone rates of police arrests, 1931

(b) Zone rates of police arrests, 1927

(c) Zone rates of police arrests, 1926

(d) Zone rates of juvenile court police records, 1935

Figure 3.1. Zone maps for police-arrests series. *Source:* Clifford R. Shaw and Henry D. McKay. *Juvenile Delinquency and Urban Areas, rev. ed.* Chicago: University of Chicago Press, 1972, p. 831; reproduced with permission.

tified delinquents, Shaw and McKay uncovered what they called a **gradient tendency,** with high concentrations in the center of the city (particularly the deteriorated "zone in transition" immediately surrounding the central business district) and rates declining progressively outward toward the suburban area. Shaw and his associates analyzed delinquency rates in other American cities and came up with similar results. At the same time, research in Chicago revealed similar patterns for other types of problematic behavior. Thus, Burgess, introducing a major report on the prior-residence distribution of mental illness cases that resulted in hospitalization, noted that although each of several different types of psychosis seemed to display a distinctive pattern, the overall tendency held true. "Cases of mental disorders, as plotted by residences of patients previous to admission to public and private hospitals, show a regular decrease from the center to the periphery of the city, a pattern of distribution previously shown for such other kinds of social and economic phenomena as poverty, unemployment, juvenile delinquency, adult crime, suicide, family desertion, infant mortality, communicable disease, and general mortality" (Burgess, 1939, 1965, pp. ix–x).

While sociologists today are unlikely to attempt ritualistic applications of the "concentric zone" theory as such, the more general social epidemiological approach, including mappings and chartings of distributions, has for some continued to hold appeal. There is now a considerable professional literature discussing various theoretical and methodological issues posed by such ecological analysis (see, for example, Gordon, 1967). A major criticism of the Chicago rate-variation studies was the reliance on official statistics in identifying "cases." As suggested earlier, when this is done, the possible influence on the patterning of rates of differential official reaction and processing (deployment of police, arrest activity, court processing—including influence of area of residence on judge's and others' decisions) cannot be taken into account. Likewise, such studies typically failed to consider the possible effect on the official rates of any systematic patterning of informal reactions—reprimands, referral to a private social agency, toleration of eccentric behavior (in the case of the mental illness studies), and so on. An area's low rates of officially processed deviation might sometimes reflect the availability and use of such informal alternatives.

Overall, the mapping technique has been one of the least influential features of the Chicago approach, at least in terms of contributions to deviance theory. Matza has made an exceedingly harsh assessment of work of this type, stating: "Ecology and epidemiology still exist in sociology, but as a source of ideas and commanding imagery, they have become almost mute. They tell us things but intellectually have nothing to say; they harbor knowledge but not wisdom" (Matza, 1969, p. 103). Yet even if tabulating and comparing area rate variations do not directly produce great insights, some consideration of the role of ecological setting remains relevant to contemporary deviance analysis. We know that specific conditions that encourage behaviors currently subject to deviance-defining continue to be concentrated in certain areas of our large cities. Thus, one rather sophisticated large-scale study of juvenile heroin use in New York City found that behavior to be heavily concentrated in certain neighborhoods:

> These are not a cross-section of the city's neighborhoods, but rather they are the ones which are economically and socially most deprived. Even within the relatively few census tracts in which we found the majority of the cases, the tracts of highest drug use can be distinguished from those with lower rates of juvenile drug use by a variety of social and economic indexes. The tracts with the greatest amount of drug use are those with the highest proportions of certain minority groups, the highest poverty rates, the most crowded dwelling units, the highest incidence of disrupted living arrangements, and so on, for a number of additional indexes (Chein, *et al.,* 1964, p. 78).

Notwithstanding the contemporary sociologist's reluctance to commit the "evil causes evil fallacy" previously noted, there can be no question but that the inner city slum remains an important focal point for researching *some* aspects (e.g., differential socioeconomic strain, differential definitions of certain behaviors, etc.) of *some* deviance situations (see Clinard, 1974, pp. 58–93; also, Schur, 1969, ch. 4; and Suttles, 1968). A good deal of attention to such matters is reflected in the various "delinquency subculture" theories, to which we will turn shortly.

Area concentrations in deviance have relevance in another sense as well. Although, for the most part, the Chicago researchers and the subculture theorists explored the influence of *residence* areas within the city, it may also sometimes be useful to think in terms of *activity* areas. Certain activities imbued with deviantness may be geographically concentrated, regardless of the areas of residence of the participants. As Daniel Glaser points out:

> Deviant selling is centered in the slums, though often financed and supervised from elsewhere, because this is the section of the city where such deviance is most tolerated. Certain types of illegal services, such as the numbers game and other cheap gambling, seem to have a unique clientele among the poor. The poor are more inclined to make small bets on long shots and to dream of sudden wealth than are the affluent, who can procure legal gambling services from stockbrokers. In addition, the market for drugs is centered in the slums, and users from elsewhere come there to purchase (Glaser, 1971, p. 29).

A similar kind of concentration, though not necessarily in the residential slum (for example, in New York it has been in the midtown Times Square and theatre district), now routinely occurs with respect to open prostitution and other sex-oriented businesses ("massage" parlors, pornographic movie houses, pornographic bookstores, etc.). In recent years, the concentration of such activities in Times Square has led to public protest demonstrations by area residents, actors and other theatre people, and even schoolchildren, as well as to controversial proposals (enacted in some other cities) for zoning regulations that would limit and regulate the number of sex-oriented establishments in various neighborhoods (see, for example, Carroll, 1976). As the references to toleration and anonymity in the statements by Glaser and Anderson (on Hobohemia) suggest, the line between activity areas and residence areas sometimes may be a hazy one. Particularly where the problematic behavior takes on continuing "life-style" aspects *and* requires participants to practice at least partial concealment, residences and activities may come to be concentrated together in restricted areas. Geographical concentration of homosexuals and homosexually oriented establishments (gay bars, etc.) in certain neighborhoods of large cities (to the extent this occurs) is perhaps the best illustration of this combined residence-activity, voluntary-defensive pattern (see Weinberg and Williams, 1975; Levine, 1977).

Other themes and aspects of the early Chicago research have a similarly mixed "record" of influence on contemporary deviance analysis. Many of the biologically based notions, some of which were mentioned above (other crucial concepts of this sort included "invasion," "dominance," and "succession"—terms used to describe the cyclical movement of different population groupings through the various areas of the city), have not had a lasting impact in the deviance field. The same is true of the idea of **social disorganization,** which was the key explanatory concept used in analyzing the findings of the various mapping studies. Particularly the zone surrounding the central business district (described as an "interstitial" one in the throes of constant change) was viewed as being in a state of continuous disorganization. It was thought that when an area displayed perpetual change and rapid mobility, stable institutions and mechanisms of social control broke down, and competing values—some of which encouraged deviation—emerged (see discussion in Kobrin, 1951). Furthermore, the general impact on human personality was seen to be devastating. Thus Faris and Dunham related area concentrations of severe mental disorder to the absence of "a consistent and fairly harmonious stream of primary social contacts," the disruption of crucial "paths of social communication," an inability to "derive sufficient mental nourishment from the normal social sources to achieve a satisfactorily conventional organization of their world" (Faris and Dunham, 1939, 1965, ch. X).

As Matza has cogently noted, the Chicago researchers never adequately resolved the tension between diversity and pathology. They recognized that the existence of diverse patterns was a social fact; yet they could not keep from branding some of the patterns as representing social if not individual pathology (Matza, 1969, pp. 45–53). On the one hand, the natural areas concept seemed to imply, indeed, with strange Darwinian biological overtones, the naturalness of all this diversity and change. On the other hand, there was a lingering resistance to the naturalness interpretation which manifested itself in the disorganization thesis. The major criticisms of this kind of analysis have been that it exhibits methodological confusion and is grounded in extrascientific and anti-urban value judgments. We have already seen the pitfalls of relying on official statistics. The likelihood of error was heightened through the disorganization concept because the Chicago researchers never really had any independent indicators of this alleged condition. There was no way of determining the existence of the supposedly causal disorganization other than by pointing to the very behaviors and conditions (delinquency, mental illness, suicide, etc.) that it was, in the first place, supposed to explain. These conditions were, in effect, then treated as both cause and effect. Or, as one writer has described this fallacy, "The independent variable (social disorganization) is being measured by a predicted outcome (social problems)."

Failure to realize the value assessment built into the conclusion that an area is disorganized was probably, the same commentator suggests, the main reason for falling into this methodological trap (Winslow, 1970, pp. 58–64). Gradually the concept of disorganization gave way to the considerably more viable one of "differential social organization." William Foote Whyte's "Street Corner Society" research on "cornerboy" culture (Whyte, 1943b) played a major role in effecting this shift. He found that racketeering (mentioned in the last chapter) was in fact highly organized and that the same thing was true regarding sexual activity:

> Respectable middle-class people have very definite standards of sex behavior. They are inclined to assume that behavior which does not conform to these standards is unorganized and subject to no set of ethics. It is my purpose to point out that, in one particular area commonly thought to be characterized by laxness of sex behavior, there is an elaborate and highly developed sex code (Whyte, 1943a, p. 24).

This gradually evolving conception, to the effect that one person's disorganization is another's organization, was a keystone in the development of the relativistic outlooks that now dominate the field. As we will see shortly, an explicit concept of "differential group organization" was also central to the influential formulations of criminologist Edwin Sutherland.

Related to the questionable disorganization thesis, but not as subject to criticism on methodological and value-bias grounds, was the Chicago analysts' depiction of a process that has come to be termed **cultural transmission.** For Park and Burgess and their associates, a given area of the city represented a "cultural matrix" that left its characteristic stamp on all those who lived in it. Shaw and McKay, referring to areas with high delinquency rates, noted:

> The maps representing distribution of delinquents at successive periods indicate that, year after year, decade after decade, the same areas have been characterized by these concentrations. This means that delinquent boys in these areas have contact not only with other delinquents who are their contemporaries but also with older offenders, who in turn had contact with delinquents preceding them, and so on back to the earliest history of the neighborhood. This contact means that the traditions of delinquency can be and are transmitted down through successive generations of boys, in much the same way that language and other social forms are transmitted (Shaw and McKay, 1942, 1969, p. 174).

This feature of community "traditions," the transmission of which might sustain persisting patterns of deviating behavior, came across particularly through an important research method by which the Chicago sociologists sought to complement their cartographic techniques—the case history or "personal document" method. Thus "Stanley," whose autobiography was edited and interpreted by Shaw, reported:

> Stealing in the neighborhood was a common practice among the children and approved by the parents. Whenever the boys got together they talked about robbing and made more plans for stealing. I hardly knew any boys who did not go robbing. The little fellows went in for petty stealing, breaking into freight cars, and stealing junk. The older guys did big jobs like stick-up, burglary, and stealing autos. The little fellow admired the "big shots" and longed for the day when they could get into the big racket. Fellows who had "done time" were big shots and looked up to and gave the little fellows tips on how to get by and pull off big jobs (Shaw, 1930, 1966, p. 54).

As will become clear below, the idea of cultural transmission has had persisting significance through later analyses of deviant subcultures and, more generally, has encouraged a focus on learning processes as a key factor in deviance situations.

On balance, despite many shortcomings, the Chicago researchers laid the groundwork for a good number of major advances in analyzing deviance. The ideas of differential organization and cultural transmission can be used in ways that are quite consistent with recently emphasized formulations, and the intensive case-study method was an important precursor of current close observation and "actors' own subjective viewpoints" approaches. Indeed, the entire notion of in-depth "field" research on deviance, as opposed to questionnaire studies and the like, is traceable to the Chicago experience. Furthermore, an associated body of theorizing centered in Chicago at that time—on which we have not yet touched —namely, the "symbolic interactionist" social psychology of George H. Mead, W. I. Thomas, and Charles Cooley, was, as we shall see, a direct forerunner of the labeling or interactionist perspective (sometimes even called the "neo-Chicagoan" approach) that recently has received so much attention. Indeed the notions of social reaction and group conflict that such a perspective emphasizes were at least implicit, and sometimes explicit, in even the ecologically oriented Chicago work. For example, in his study of youth gangs (he found over 1300 of them in Chicago at that time), Frederic Thrasher asserted that while their origins to some extent lay in spontaneous play groups, it was disapproval by and conflict with the forces of conventional society that gave rise to group consciousness and real gang identity (Thrasher, 1927).

These not inconsiderable contributions have to be kept in mind, then, in the face of the frequent criticisms made of the early Chicago studies. Besides the various critical points mentioned already, this body of work has been charged with adopting an unwarranted, albeit environmental, determinism (Matza, 1969), with exaggerating "the separation between deviant and conventional worlds" (Matza, 1969, p. 70), with failing to convey a sense "of men struggling against social arrangements as such" (Taylor, Walton and Young, 1974, p. 114), and with ignoring the key role of "political and economic elites" (Davis, 1975, p. 45). Even if these criticisms have some partial validity, it nonetheless remains true that almost all subsequent deviance analysts and researchers were in one way or another, directly or indirectly, influenced by the Chicago ideas and research example.

Differential Association

An important outgrowth of the Chicago tradition, but one that pushed deviance analysis in a somewhat different direction than had been emphasized in the ecological studies, was the "differential association" theory of Edwin Sutherland. In much of his work, Sutherland (1883–1950), who often is referred to as the "dean" of American criminologists, focused on the learned aspects of crime. Insisting that offending behaviors are learned through the same basic learning processes that underlie socially approved behaviors, Sutherland did a great deal to advance recognition of yet another underlying element of the ordinariness of deviance. This point came across most dramatically, perhaps, in his book *The Professional Thief* (Sutherland, 1937, 1956)—a thorough description of the profession of theft, produced through correspondence and interviews with a long-time professional thief, and then edited and interpreted by Sutherland himself. As "Chic Conwell," the author of this remarkable document, emphasized, not just anyone can be a professional thief. Much as in other more socially approved professions, one only becomes a "professional" by undergoing training in necessary skills, demonstrating ability, and eventually achieving acceptance among established professionals.

In other writings, Sutherland went beyond mere documentation and substantive description of "learned" criminal behavior to develop a general theoretical statement of the basic processes involved in all such learning. What Sutherland was trying to do in framing a general theory of crime was to provide an explanation that would cover the full range of criminal behaviors—one that would apply not only to professional theft, but also to white-collar crime (another one of his major research interests—see Adaptation Two, pp. 145–150) as well as to those types of criminality that commonly had been attributed to adverse social conditions or psychological states. He described this generalizing aim as follows:

> . . . hundreds of concrete conditions have something to do with criminal behavior, are associated with it in some way or other. But everyone of them had [been seen in past research to have] a relatively small degree of association. . . . Any concrete condition is sometimes associated with criminal behavior and sometimes not. Perhaps there is nothing that is so frequently associated with criminal behavior as being a male. But

it is obvious that maleness does not explain criminal behavior. I reached the general conclusion that a concrete condition cannot be a cause of crime, and that the only way to get a causal explanation of criminal behavior is by abstracting from the varying concrete conditions things that are universally associated with crime (Sutherland, 1942, 1973, p. 19).

Not surprisingly, since he sought the "things universally associated with" crime, his attention was drawn to process rather than to substance. Deviance situations (in his work, crime situations) that varied greatly in substance (e.g., "types" of behavior) might nonetheless display in common the operation of certain key social and social-psychological processes. Sutherland, who in this general theorizing effort was more directly concerned with initial causation than with societal reaction (deviance-defining), concluded that a common process of learning was the central causal ingredient in all crime situations. Furthermore, he insisted (as we have already seen) that this was the very same process of learning that determined or shaped noncrime situations as well. It involved "interaction with other persons in a process of communication;" the principal part occurred "within intimate personal groups;" and the learning included not only techniques, but also a "specific direction of motives, drives, rationalizations, and attitudes." Asserting that this specific direction of motives and drives is "learned from definitions of legal codes as favorable and unfavorable," Sutherland summed up his theory in the following statement: "A person becomes delinquent [i.e., criminal] because of an excess of definitions favorable to violation of law over definitions unfavorable to violation of law."

As he noted, this principle of **differential association** referred to the "counteracting forces" that produce both crime and noncrime outcomes. Furthermore, procrime and anticrime associations may vary in "frequency, duration, priority, and intensity." According to this formulation, then, it was the overall balance of these contradictory patterns of association and definition that would determine whether a person became criminal or law-abiding. At the same time, Sutherland claimed, one could account for overall variations in crime *rates* through the associated concept of **differential group (or social) organization.** Thus, he stated, "crime is rooted in the social organization and is an expression of that social organization. A group may be organized for criminal behavior or organized against criminal behavior. Most communities are organized for both criminal and anticriminal behavior, and in that sense the crime rate is an expression of the differential group organization." (All of the above summary is based on Sutherland, 1947, 1973.)

Over the years, Sutherland's thesis has been much discussed in the professional literature. Researchers have made efforts to "operationalize" it for testing purposes, with special attention to the problem of measuring the variations in "frequency, duration, priority, and intensity" to which Sutherland had referred (see Short, 1960). Some evidence to support Sutherland's argument has been found in self-report data regarding delinquents' perceptions of similar behavior among their close friends (Short, 1960) and in findings of similarity in actual delinquency among close friends (Reiss and Rhodes, 1964). Evidence from early parole prediction studies and from the Chicago cartographic research were also cited in support of the relation between "associations" and crime (Glaser, 1960). At the same time, some criminologists felt that Sutherland's theory was inapplicable to certain kinds of offenses (primarily nonsystematic, unrepeated, criminal acts) and that, as Sutherland himself recognized, it might have under-estimated the role of individual psychological make-up. Yet Donald Cressey, in a fascinating article, showed how Sutherland's general approach to motivation, when thought of in terms of role-theory, could even help to explain such sup-posedly compulsive behavior as "kleptomania." Noting that associations and identifications will influence a person's motives in performing various roles, Cressey argued:

> . . . a person might in some situations identify himself as a kleptomaniac, since that construct is now popular in our culture, and a full commitment to such an identi-fication includes the use of motives which, in turn, release the energy to perform a so-called compulsive act. The more positive the conviction that one is a kleptomaniac the more automatic his behavior will appear. The subject's behavior in particular situations, then, is organized by his identification of himself according to the linguistic construct "kleptomania" or its equivalent. . . . it is this kind of organization which makes the behavior recognizably recurrent in the life history of the person. The fact that the acts are recurrent does not mean that they are prompted from within but only that certain linguistic symbols have become usual for the person in question (Cressey, 1962, p. 460).

A similar broadening of the Sutherland thesis was evident in Daniel Glaser's suggestion that it should be reformulated in terms of **differential iden-tification** (Glaser, 1956). Glaser felt that the patterns of procrime and anticrime influence should be recognized to include not only direct personal contacts with other individuals but also more indirect identifications with groups and cultural patterns that were not experienced through direct social interaction.

It is in these broadened conceptions especially that we can see the be-ginnings of the profound and lasting influence Sutherland's work has had in the more general field of deviance theory. More important than the specific appli-cability of his formal statement have been the general focus he developed and the *type* of theory he presented. Even if his formulation is difficult to "prove," he very significantly pointed the way to the present-day emphasis on *process* and *social definition*. Clearly influenced by the ecological approach, he might be viewed as having succumbed to the spirit, if not the same letter, of its social deter-minism. Thus Matza suggests that Sutherland's notion of affiliation left actors no room for a "choice against being preordained" (Matza, 1969, p. 106); similarly Taylor, Walton, and Young tax him with depicting the actor as "a passive re-cipient of criminal and noncriminal motives" (Taylor, Walton and Young, 1974, p. 128). On the other hand, the concern for process, particularly at the social-psychological level, prefigures the interactionist focus that has become so important in recent deviance analysis. It provided a partial basis for some later discussions (to be cited below) of efforts by deviators to "neutralize" imposed definitions in order to maintain acceptable self-concepts. More generally, and as one can see in the quotation from Cressey on kleptomania, although Sutherland himself tended to concentrate on the influence of direct interpersonal associations, his work implicitly provided an impetus for examining the role of broader social definitions in affecting both people's self-conceptions and their behavior. Furthermore, the very type of explanation he was trying to develop—one that would not just be supported in probability terms, but that instead would hold true for *all* instances of what he was explaining (see discussion of the *analytic induction* method in Chapter 5—is very much in line with the notion of cause that seems to pervade much recent deviance sociology.

Merton's Anomie Theory

In the last chapter we considered two lines of deviance analysis traceable to the functionalist or structural-functional tradition in sociology—studies showing how specific patterns of deviance are related to approved values and arrangements and more general explorations of the functions for the group or society of identifying and reacting to instances of deviation (primarily the function of boundary-maintenance). A third strand of functionalist influence has had even greater impact on the field of deviance studies. It has involved formulations centering around the idea of "structured strain"—general forces and pressures in the social system that push individuals into deviation. The preeminent contribution to interpretation of this sort was made by Robert Merton in an essay entitled "Social Structure and Anomie" (Merton, 1938, 1949). Few, if any, sociological journal articles have been cited, quoted, and reprinted as often as this seminal statement.

Merton took as a point of departure the concept of **anomie** (or normlessness) developed by Durkheim in his analysis of the relationship between types and degrees of social cohesion and suicide rates (Durkheim, 1897, 1951). Durkheim had in part been drawn to this notion as a way of explaining the fact that suicide rates tended to be high not only in periods of economic depression, but also during periods of unusual prosperity. As Marshall Clinard has pointed out, Durkheim attributed both kinds of findings to a common type of disruptive impact. Both situations involved "large numbers of people suddenly being thrown out of adjustment with their typical ways of life, sudden economic prosperity being as disastrous as sudden loss. In both there is a sense of confusion and people become disoriented from their world. Under these conditions, most people no longer feel that they are 'getting anywhere' with reference to what they desire" (Clinard, 1964, p. 5). From this standpoint, sudden wealth could be a disruptive "crisis" in much the same sense as divorce was. Durkheim, again, attributed high suicide rates in both situations to the impact of anomic conditions. Furthermore, and this point particularly was taken over by Merton, norm-lessness often reflected a failure of social restraints on human ambition. According to Durkheim, "human activity naturally aspires beyond assignable limits and sets itself unattainable goals" (Durkheim, 1897, 1951, pp. 247–248).

In line with the general functionalist outlook noted earlier, Merton saw deviance as being generated by the social structures and cultural expectancies of the larger society within which it occurred. Rejecting internal explanations of deviance causation, he stated as his primary aim the discovery of how "some social structures exert a definite pressure upon certain persons in the society to engage in nonconformist rather than conformist conduct." (In a later essay, to be cited below, Merton actually drew a distinction between "nonconformity" and deviance. In the early article, however, the terms were used more or less interchangeably.) For Merton, these differentially structured pressures reflected the relationship between major cultural goals "held out as legitimate objectives for all or for diversely located members of the society" and the approved "institutionalized *means*" for achieving these goals. Attributing much deviance in American society to the dysjunction between the heavily stressed goal of monetary success and the distribution of legitimate opportunities for achieving it, Merton stated: "It is only when a system of cultural values extols, virtually above all else, certain *common* success-goals *for the population at large* while the social structure rigorously restricts or completely closes access to approved modes of reaching these goals *for a considerable part of the same population,* that deviant behavior ensues on a large scale" (Merton, 1938, 1949, p. 137).

Merton specified five **modes of individual adaptation,** which he believed were determined through the various possible combinations of a person's accepting or rejecting the dominant cultural goals and the available legitimate means. This famous "typology" is reproduced here as Table 3.1. Because he was primarily concerned with explaining deviance, Merton did not discuss at any length the first mode of adaptation—in which, presumably, the distributions of major culture goals

Table 3.1 Merton's Typology of Modes of Individual Adaptation

MODES OF ADAPTATION	CULTURE GOALS	INSTITUTIONALIZED MEANS
I. Conformity	+	+
II. Innovation	+	−
III. Ritualism	−	+
IV. Retreatism	−	−
V. Rebellion	±	±

Source: Robert K. Merton, *Social Theory and Structure.* Glencoe, Ill.: The Free Press, 1949, p. 133. Reprinted with permission.

Note: In this typology Merton used the symbol + to signify "acceptance," − to signify "rejection," and ± to signify "rejection of prevailing values and substitution of new values."

and legitimate means of achieving them are adequately coordinated. The second category, innovation, was intended to encompass most ordinary crime and delinquency—at least those offenses that produce direct monetary returns. It is mainly this adaptation that has led some commentators to call Merton's formulation an "illicit means theory," since, in this pattern, persons accept the dominant societal goals, but in the face of low access to legitimate means, adopt illegitimate ones to the same end. In Adaptation Three, ritualism, the individual scales down or abandons the goals of pecuniary success and rapid mobility, but compulsively adheres to institutionalized behavior norms. Here Merton viewed deviance quite broadly to encompass a variety of patterns in which individuals fall into a "rut," routinely "play it safe," and settle for little in the name of security. "It is the perspective of the frightened employee, the zealously conformist bureaucrat in the teller's cage of the private banking enterprise or in the front office of the public works enterprise." In the fourth category, "retreatism," Merton placed "some of the adaptive activities of psychotics, autists, pariahs, outcasts, vagrants, vagabonds, tramps, chronic drunkards and drug addicts." People who maladapt through this kind of private escape, are often especially maligned because they appear to have abandoned not only the approved behaviors but the major goals of the society as well. Although Merton originally stated that this adaptation was probably the least common, in fact, many of the behaviors most subject to deviantizing in our present-day society seem to fit this "type." (As we will see very shortly, however, his specific *interpretations* of the causes or social meanings of these behaviors has been questioned.) Rebellion, Merton's final adaptation, involves a general transfer of allegiance from the prevailing system to new groups actively organized to replace that system with a new one. To an extent, the recent "deviance liberation movements" to be considered later in this book (gay liberation, etc.) do involve a "substitution of new values," but most such movements fall considerably short of what Merton had in mind. By and large, they do not challenge and seek to overturn, for example, the broad economic structure and personal "success" emphasis that continue to heavily influence the lives of most Americans.

Merton's formulation has been subjected to frequent criticism on a number of different grounds. It has been charged with erroneously assuming a single common value system of "cultural goals" for the society as a whole, with neglecting psychological forces that may motivate deviation, with unwisely maintaining the constraint theme that leaves little room for elements of will or individual choice, with failing to consider the important role of societal reaction in shaping deviance situations, and with ignoring the fact that much perceived deviance involves collective rather than individual action. In making this last point, Lemert has commented that, "many forms of deviation, professional crime, prostitution, 'vagrancy,'' skid-row drinking, use of opiates, and marihuana smoking, even bureaucratic 'ritualism,' are collective acts in which group derived and group maintained values, as well as private values, are served" (Lemert, 1967, p. 14). Presumably this is part of what Davis more recently had in mind when she asserted that, "Because Merton and his followers pay so little attention to the social meanings held by participants or the existence of social situations that pattern behavior, they ignore the diversity of social motivation as well as the elements of differential learning and opportunity" (Davis, 1975, p. 113).

The largest body of criticism leveled against Merton's thesis focuses on his underlying assumption (based on official statistics) that deviation is disproportionately concentrated at the lower levels of the socioeconomic order. Although he explicitly cited early surveys showing high levels of unrecorded middle-class delinquency and crime and even commented in this connection that unlawful behavior "is in truth a very common phenomenon," such seemingly contradictory data apparently did not give him much pause in formulating his structured strain interpretation. Yet, as Lemert has noted (with the benefit of considerable research conducted *since* Merton's original statement), "extant research leaves serious doubts that deviant behavior is proportionately more common at lower than at other class levels of our society. The doubts increase as one proceeds away from crime rates, which are the starting point for Merton's formulation. . . . When attention is drawn to such forms of deviation as alcoholism, suicide, and drug addiction, there are no consistent data to show that these are more common adaptations of members of lower class society" (Lemert, 1967, p. 13). As several commentators have pointed out, if the pressures of lower-class life were as inexorably crime-producing as Merton seems to suggest, then we should actually be surprised that we have as little crime as we do have and that there are indeed some law-abiding members of the lower classes. By taking official crime statistics at face value, anomie theory, according to one recent assessment, "stands accused of predicting too little bourgeois criminality and too much proletarian criminality" (Taylor, Walton and Young, 1974, p. 107). Furthermore, if the official rates do in fact represent a distortion, and crime and other kinds of deviation are actually widespread throughout the entire population, then, as Lemert has cogently suggested, "conformity, which Merton makes no attempt to explain, becomes problematical as well as deviation" (Lemert, 1967, p. 5).

Recognition of distortions in official statistics and of the diversity of social meanings have both been involved in a more specific questioning of the applicability of at least one of Merton's adaptations—that of retreatism. Lindesmith and Gagnon, citing a variety of kinds of findings from drug addiction studies (including cross-cultural evidence, changes in drug use and attitudes over time, and findings that suggest the crucial impact of public policy in shaping drug problems) have denied that anomie can be the central explanation of drug use. In particular, they point to various categories of users with respect to whom the anomie thesis does not seem pertinent—especially addicted physicians: "Admitting that the available evidence does not permit secure conclusions about the differences between doctors who become addicted and those who do not, the simplest and most plausible explanation of the high rate of addiction in the profession is in terms of availability of drugs, not a high level of anomie" (Lindesmith and Gagnon, 1964, p. 171). Similarly, Snyder has questioned applying the retreatism concept to alcoholism: "Remembering, for example, that alcoholism in our culture typically involves fifteen to twenty years of excessive drinking for its full development, it is quite possible to argue that the evidence of deterioration of social relationships, isolation, and failure, among alcoholics—which might well be massed in support of a retreatist thesis—may only reflect the social consequences of the operation of biological processes . . ." (Snyder, 1964, pp. 203–204). As this quotation suggests, the problem of separating cause and effect is one that often has plagued efforts to test the anomie theory.

In a subsequent revision of his original paper, Merton acknowledged and responded to some of these lines of criticism and made the point that his theory had never purported to explain all forms of deviance or to suggest that "all those subject to these pressures respond by deviation" (Merton, 1957). Similarly, in his other and still more recent writings, he has indicated the need to take account of and relate his thesis to various contemporary developments in deviance theory (Merton, 1976). Undoubtedly, there will continue to be professional debate about the overall validity and range of applicability of Merton's formulation. Particularly the "political" implications of his thesis regularly generate diverse assessments. Building on groundwork provided through the earlier Chicago ecological studies, Merton significantly advanced deviance analysis beyond purely individualistic explanations, and, in particular, he underscored the role of the social-class system in producing deviance. At the same time, because his direct focus was on precipitating causes and modes of adaptation, he neglected to show how the impact of the stratification order was manifested in or mediated through the processes of social reaction and official deviance-defining. Thus, while he correctly saw that lack of economic opportunity, goal frustration, and social injustice might drive some persons to crime—and this claim continues to hold up well as a partial explanation of some deviating behaviors—he never really developed the complementary notion that injustice might also be directly built into the definitions of crime and the processing of crime. By the same token, the focus on individual "adaptations" has left some commentators unclear as to just how strongly Merton condemned the overall socioeconomic system within which such adaptations occurred.

While the structural-functional orientation to which he has been a major contributor dominated American social theorizing in the 1940s and 1950s, the two decades since have seen much criticism of functionalism on the grounds of conservative bias, that is, excessive emphasis on the equilibrium of social systems and inadequate attention to processes of conflict and social change. Furthermore, a new generation of sociologists who consider themselves more radical have asserted the need for deviance theories that emphasize in a more thoroughgoing way the widespread social oppression and basic contradictions that they find at the heart of our present socioeconomic arrangements. Yet even these theorists are hard put to dismiss the significance of Merton's work. Thus the militant

English writers Taylor, Walton, and Young acknowledge that, "Merton does take on the role of the rebel in the substantive analysis. He does stand outside the system and make criticisms, which, if taken to their logical conclusion, would necessitate radical social change. But he never follows the criticisms through to that point" (Taylor, Walton, and Young, 1974, p. 101). As this statement suggests, social policies that reflect the influence of Merton's analysis and of the associated subculture formulations, to which we will turn next, may tend toward the model of "liberal reform" (see Schur, 1973, pp. 81–114; also Table 7.4 on p. 468), rather than toward one of radical social reconstruction. Nonetheless, the line between the two is sometimes hazy, and Merton must be credited with raising the social consciousness of deviance analysts in a number of ways. Virtually all subsequent theorizing about deviance has built on, or had to take account of, his major formulations. Let us now turn to some other important theories directly influenced by his work.

Subculture Analysis

Albert K. Cohen, building in part on the foundation Merton had laid, similarly stressed the impact of the stratification order in his influential conception of the "delinquent subculture" (Cohen, 1955). While recognizing and discussing the extensive evidence of "hidden" middle-class delinquency, Cohen argued that very likely much working-class delinquency went similarly unrecorded; he concluded, along with Merton, that, "juvenile delinquency and the delinquent subculture in particular are overwhelmingly concentrated in the male, working-class sector of the juvenile population." He felt, however, that Merton's thesis was inadequate because of its failure to explain the specific substantive content of much juvenile misconduct. If delinquency involved using illicit means to achieve common success goals, why were so many delinquent acts "nonutilitarian, malicious, and negativistic?" Cohen believed that a theory of collective problem-solving would best explain how a distinctive delinquent subculture featuring these qualities of "short-run hedonism" and "versatility" had arisen. Delinquency, Cohen asserted, illustrated the more general conditions under which subcultures develop—namely, "the existence, in effective interaction with one another, of a number of actors with similar problems of adjustment."(Later in this text we will return to a variety of applications and possible implications of this general thesis, which is relevant to a wide range of deviance situations.)

Following Merton's lead in focusing on the common goal of financial success, Cohen defined a broader complex of middle-class values to which, he claimed, all children in our society were subjected, but in terms of which only middle-class children could realistically expect to succeed. Particularly in the schools, with their predominantly middle-class staff and orientations, the working-class boy is confronted with such middle-class virtues as rationality, specialization, gratification deferral, and control of aggression. Unprepared to meet the

standards of this "middle-class measuring rod" for which only middle-class children have been adequately socialized, he invariably finds himself at "the bottom
of the heap":

> . . . the working-class boy, particularly if his training and values be those we
> have here defined as working-class, is more likely than his middle-class peers to find him-
> self at the bottom of the status hierarchy whenever he moves in a middle-class world,
> whether it be of adults or of children. To the degree to which he values the good opinion
> of middle-class persons or because he has to some degree internalized middle-class stand-
> ards himself, he faces a problem of adjustment and is in the market for a "solution"
> (Cohen, 1955, p. 119).

In Cohen's view, the distinctive delinquent subculture represented a response and adaptation to this situation. It offered a solution to the working-class
youth's status problems by providing "criteria of status which these children *can*
meet." This came about, Cohen suggested, through a collective "reaction formation" to the middle-class values—in which they were completely repudiated and
replaced by an alternative value system that represented "their very antithesis."
Thus, "Group stealing, institutionalized in the delinquent subculture, is not just
a way of *getting* something. It is a means that is the antithesis of sober and dili-
gent 'labor in a calling.' It expresses contempt for a way of life making its opposite a criterion of status" (Cohen, 1955, pp. 121, 134). Recognizing that this
formulation did nothing to explain middle-class delinquency, Cohen developed
(though not as fully) a *separate* thesis about juvenile misconduct in that sector.
Drawing on functional theorist Talcott Parsons' earlier analysis of American
child socialization patterns, Cohen asserted that problems relating to masculine
identification might account for middle-class delinquency: "Since mother has
been the principal agent of indoctrination of 'good," respectable behavior, 'good-
ness' comes to symbolize femininity, and engaging in 'bad' behavior acquires the
function of denying his femininity and therefore asserting his masculinity"
(Cohen, 1955, p. 164). Though the difference in the two kinds of explanation
Cohen developed may seem startling, it highlights a possibility we should keep
in mind as we develop our more general outlooks on deviance analysis. It may
well be that sometimes and without necessary inconsistency a theory about the
precipitating causes of behavior subject to deviance-defining may have only limited applicability; to explain other categories of such behavior we may need
to adopt other formulations. This need not be viewed as untenable or self-
contradictory if we remind ourselves of the crucial distinction between explaining the occurrence of behavior and explaining the deviance-defining process itself.
It is the latter process of defining and reacting that all deviance situations have
in common. It is there that a unitary analysis and explanation become possible,
even necessary.

The concept of delinquent subculture was elaborated further by Richard
Cloward and Lloyd Ohlin in their book *Delinquency and Opportunity* (Cloward

and Ohlin, 1960). Focusing once again on the blocked avenues for achieving success goals that working-class youths often experience but with a heavier emphasis on economic striving than on a more general search for status, Cloward and Ohlin noted that illegitimate means as well as legitimate ones may be unavailable. The distribution or availability, for particular youths, of both types of opportunities could help to determine patterns of delinquency. Thus, depending on the social structure of the local neighborhood, one or another subtype of delinquent subculture might prevail—the criminal (rackets-oriented type), the conflict (or fighting-gang) type, or the retreatist (drug-oriented) type. Not all slum neighborhoods, Cloward and Ohlin pointed out, are sufficiently stable and well-integrated to provide an alternative avenue to success. In the more truly disorganized slum, where there is not only lack of access to legitimate opportunities but also no base for "stable criminal opportunity systems," the stage is well set for the violent behavior of the conflict pattern. The drug-oriented subculture, they went on to argue, may draw youths who are "double failures." For those youths who "have failed to find a place for themselves in criminal or conflict subcultures," the drug-oriented way of life may have a special appeal.

By focusing on variations in neighborhood structures and traditions, Cloward and Ohlin carried forward the cultural transmission theme originated in Chicago and developed by Sutherland, using it together with Merton's structured strain analysis in framing their own distinctive formulations. During the early 1960s, Cloward and Ohlin's work had a significant impact on public policy. Their book, which ended with a call for efforts "directed to the reorganization of slum communities," gave new impetus to the idea of confronting social problems by "treating" the community rather than the supposedly problematic individuals. It provided much of the basis for the varied programs of Mobilization for Youth on New York City's Lower East Side—built around the concepts of expanding opportunities and community involvement—which became a prototype for many of the federal "war on poverty" programs throughout the nation.

An interesting variant on the delinquent subculture idea was provided by anthropologist Walter Miller (Miller, 1958). In his view, urban lower-class life possesses a set of distinctive "focal concerns," some of which directly or indirectly promote violation of middle-class laws. These focal concerns are: *trouble*—in some situations "getting into trouble" may be acceptable as a means to a desired goal, and it may even confer prestige, *toughness*—an "almost obsessive" concern with masculinity, which Miller saw as a reaction to a predominantly female-based household, *smartness*—the capacity to outsmart others and not be "taken" oneself, *excitement*—adventure and the search for thrills, which may be counterbalanced, however, by periods of inactivity such as "hanging out", *fate*—belief that one's life is subject to forces beyond one's control, which may lead to a belief that rational goal-seeking is futile, and *autonomy*—overt resentment of external control, which may be coupled, however, with covert desire for nurturance and "authority". According to Miller, instead of constituting a reaction-formation against middle-class values, as in Cohen's theory, lower-class law violation is simply a direct reflection of these major "concerns" of lower-class culture. Although Miller apparently intended that this formulation would accord lower-class patterns a proper "integrity" of their own, his analysis remains extremely controversial. Sociologists are in considerable disagreement as to whether the concerns he mentions really do dominate working-class life. Nor is it clear that any such culture themes are distinctive to the lower-class community.

While the anomie and subculture theories discussed so far helped to move deviance analysis beyond conceptions of personal maladjustment—indeed, deviation came to be seen as a kind of adjustment, to problems posed by the socially generated strains and pressures of certain life situations—by the same token, they remained essentially deterministic. Youths, it seemed, often had "no choice but" to engage in misconduct. Delinquency had come to be seen as a kind of social maladie—extremely difficult to avoid and, apparently once "caught," almost impossible to shed—in certain neighborhoods, situations, or "subcultures." A major break with this outlook was made in David Matza's very important book, *Delinquency and Drift* (Matza, 1964). Adopting a processual orientation to deviance, Matza sought to depict a less constrained, more fluid and uncertain drift into and out of delinquency. Emphasizing the phenomenon of "maturing out" (i.e., that most juveniles who get in trouble do not go on to become adult offenders), he also asserted that conventional theories "predict too much delinquency even during the period of optimal involvement." As Matza noted, "Delinquency is a status and delinquents are incumbents who *intermittently* act out a role . . . The novice practitioner or researcher is frequently amazed at 'how like other kids' the delinquent can be when he is so inclined" (Matza, 1964, p. 26). In place of the deterministic and oppositional theories of the delinquent subculture, Matza proposed a concept of **drift,** which he believed would avoid "hard determinism" without assuming complete freedom of will or action:

> The image of the delinquent I wish to convey is one of drift; an actor neither compelled nor committed to deeds nor freely choosing them; neither different in any simple or fundamental sense from the law abiding, nor the same; conforming to certain traditions in American life while partially unreceptive to other more conventional traditions.
>
> . . .
>
> Drift stands midway between freedom and control. Its basis is an area of the social structure in which control has been loosened, coupled with the abortiveness of adolescent endeavor to organize an autonomous subculture, and thus an independent source of control, around illegal action. The delinquent *transiently* exists in a limbo between convention and crime, responding in turn to the demands of each, flirting now with one, now the other, but postponing commitment, evading decision. Thus, he drifts between criminal and conventional action (Matza, 1964, p. 28).

The image, then, is of a social context in which no youth *must* "become delinquent," but in which any *might* and many *do* (in varying degrees and for different lengths of time) get involved in problematic behavior. As is no doubt clear, a major thrust of Matza's approach was to challenge the notions of "basic differentness" that have pervaded so much deviance analysis. Furthermore, his formulation was quite consistent with the possibility that delinquency was much more evenly distributed throughout the society than official statistics might suggest.

Similar themes underline a related line of reaction to the traditional sociological perspectives—one reflected in formulations sometimes referred to as **control theory** (see Hirschi, 1969; also Schur, 1973, pp. 157–160). The central idea behind these formulations (there is a variety of such theories, each with its own special terminology) is that delinquent behavior is often to be expected. One should thus try to explain its absence as well as its presence. According to these theories, the persisting strength or the weakening in particular situations of bonds to conventional society makes the difference. For these theorists, differences in delinquency between social classes (recall this was Merton's starting point) may not be as interesting as those *within* any class. The control element (whether it is called "containment," "commitment," or "attachment"—the usages in several specific statements) is crucial, whatever the individual's position in the social order. Although these control theories might suggest a kind of reversion to earlier psychologically oriented efforts to compare deviators and nondeviators, the recent analysts do pose the central research question in an intriguingly new form: "The question 'Why do they do it' is simply not the question the theory is designed to answer. The question is 'Why don't we do it? There is much evidence that we would if we dared" (Hirschi, 1969, p. 34). In exploring "bonds to conventional society," control theorists replace the heavy focus on supposedly compelling subcultures with a look at youths' interaction with such institutions as the family, the school, and even religion. But the point of broad significance about this approach is that, as in Matza's work, the delinquency-generating process is seen as a relatively fluid one.

At first glance, the above discussion might seem a rather lengthy excursion into the specialized literature on juvenile delinquency. In fact, the significance of the developments traced there extends well beyond that particular topic. During the period in which there was a transition from deviance theories emphasizing individual differentiation to those stressing social definition and reaction processes, analysis of crime and delinquency dominated the field. Partly for that very reason, the formulations took on broader implications, even if they were not always specifically concerned with other types of offending behavior. As we have seen, this body of work raised many of the central issues that continue to preoccupy current deviance analysts and that were partly indicated in the opening chapters of this text. Even as the proponents of the several approaches "opposed" and criticized each other, they developed important new outlooks: on the question of deterministic versus more fluid and contingency-based explanations, on various aspects of the "ordinariness of deviance," on what to make of the official deviance statistics, and on collective, learned, and transmitted aspects of deviance situations.

In the strictest sense, they maintained the traditional focus on causation of deviating acts, but some of their formulations begin to move deviance analysis past that particular preoccupation. The notion of "subculture," for example, was introduced as an explanation of the causes of delinquency. Yet, as we will see in Part Two, it also becomes an extremely valuable orienting idea in analyzing patterns of collective adaptation to adverse societal reaction (deviance-defining). Especially when used in that way, the notion of deviant subculture takes on wide relevance in many substantive areas besides that of juvenile delinquency. Thus, examining "the gay community" or "the life" (as prostitutes sometimes call their special world), "the drug scene" or the "counterculture," remains an extremely important way of analyzing deviance. When sociologists today do this, they are less likely than before to be seeking the origins of the problematic behavior as such, but they are certainly applying, for somewhat different purposes, the basic focus developed by Cohen (on "a number of actors with similar problems of adjustment"). Matza's efforts to frame an explanation of deviance that did not rely on the assumptions of constraint and differentiation, which he, and now many others, have considered unwarranted, represented a major step in the direction of a more fluid and processual mode of analysis. As we will see shortly, his writings (which, more recently, have dealt with deviance in general and not just delinquency) significantly contributed to an overall outlook of "neoanti-determinism" that colors current work in the field.

OTHER MAJOR APPROACHES

Conflict Theory

It has become common in recent years for sociologists to distingush between "conflict" and "consensus" (or "order") perspectives (see Dahrendorf, 1958; Horton, 1966; Chambliss, 1976). This distinction may well become pertinent in considering certain contrasting *emphases* in the more traditional and newer outlooks on deviance. Aspects of contrasting (relative) attention or emphasis may at times include: assumption of a common system of values and norms in a society versus a focus on diverging and conflicting values and interests; seeing deviance as maladaptation (individual or social) rather than as meeting the needs of certain ruling elements; considering the lower classes as more deviance-prone (because of their socialization, situations, etc.) as opposed to viewing their high deviance rates as the result of systematic class oppression and arbitrary definition of "their" behavior as deviant; static acceptance of prevailing definitions of deviance as a "given," compared with recognition of the dynamic or, according to some statements, **dialectical, processes** of social conflict and change of which they are a part.

There is considerable value in keeping this set of potentially contrasting views in mind. However, as our discussion thus far should indicate, deviance theory has rapidly been moving past such a simplistic and essentially false dichotomy. The real issue, at least in contemporary deviance analysis, is not whether or not we should adopt a conflict approach, but rather *what kind of conflict approach we should employ*. As we have seen, several of the strands of traditional deviance theory (including the frequently maligned functionalism) contain at least elements of, or develop points that would also be germane to, a conflict analysis of some sort. Particularly in promoting study of latent economic functions of deviance, functionalism indeed came every close to one line of analysis suggested by Karl Marx himself, who wrote: "Crime takes off the labour market a portion of the excess population, diminishes competition among workers, and to a certain extent stops wages from falling below the minimum, while the war against crime absorbs another part of the same population. The criminal therefore appears as one of those natural 'equillibrating forces' which establish a just balance and open up a whole perspective of 'useful' occupations" (see Bottomore and Rubel, eds., 1956, pp. 158–159). When one goes beyond discussing functions in the abstract to ask, as most sophisticated functionalists do, "functional for whom?", the focus on "interests" that neo-Marxists and other radical sociologists now call for is invariably indicated.

As we have also seen, the Chicago analyses and Sutherland's theory (particularly with its component theme of the differential group organization of societies) contained the germs of, or can be found consistent with, a conflict orientation. If the conflict element was not made explicit or strongly emphasized in those bodies of analysis, it much more directly came to the fore in other important writings of Sutherland—those on white-collar criminality. Adaptation Two summarizes this work and suggests its lasting importance.

ADAPTATION TWO
White-Collar Crime*

Sutherland's Contribution

During the 1940s, Sutherland (whose more general theorizing we have examined above) published a number of research reports challenging the then conventional wisdom regarding crime and crime causation. These papers, and a subsequent book, introduced an important new term into the standard sociological vocabulary: white-collar crime. Sutherland's belief that criminal behavior was widespread among ostensibly "respectable" upper-class persons led him to reject causal theories that linked crime with poverty. He also was strongly skeptical of narrowly psychological explanations. In his view, it was the differential social reactions to upper-class and lower-class crime that produced the common impression that criminality is concentrated in the lower classes. He sought both to document the prevalence of hidden upper-class criminality and, as we have already seen, to develop a general crime theory that would apply equally to offenses of all sorts committed by persons variously situated in the socioeconomic order.

Sutherland defined white-collar crime as "a crime committed by a person of respectability and high social status in the course of his profession" and asserted that the financial loss from such behavior "is probably several times as great as the financial cost of all the crimes which are customarily regarded as 'the crime problem.'" But, as he went on to note, this enormous financial loss is even less important than "the damage to social relations. White collar crimes violate trust and therefore create distrust; this lowers social morale and produces social disorganization. Many of the white collar crimes attack the fundamental principles of the American institutions. Ordinary crimes, on the other hand, produce little effect on social institutions or social organization" (Sutherland, 1949, 1961, p. 13).

In his research, Sutherland carefully tabulated and analyzed the decisions of courts and administrative agencies against 70 of the largest manufacturing, mining, and mercantile organizations in the United States. He found that over the life careers of these corporations there had been 980 such decisions against them, or an average of 14 per corporation. Even when the decisions of administrative agencies were set aside and only the criminal court decisions looked at, 60 percent of the corporations were found to have received court convictions, with an average of approximately four convictions each. (In some states, Sutherland noted, individual persons convicted this many times would be labeled

* *Source:* A summary and interpretation of Edwin H. Sutherland, *White-Collar Crime.* New York: Holt, Rinehart and Winston, Inc., 1949, 1961; and other sources, as indicated in references noted below.

"habitual criminals.") Few of these convictions, however, led to an imposition of major criminal sanctions. Among the major patterns of criminality that Sutherland documented were the following: antitrust violations; illegal rebates; patent, trademark, and copyright violations; misrepresentation in advertising; unfair labor practices; financial manipulations (including embezzlement, "extortionate salaries and bonuses," and other misuses of corporate funds, along with security misrepresentation and frauds); and violations of special wartime regulations.

Sutherland also made a special study of the records of 15 of the largest power and light corporations. Such public utilities constituted a particularly interesting category for his investigation for at least two reasons: They were supposedly operating in the public interest, and there had been special efforts made to closely control their policies (by "regulatory" commissions such as the Federal Power Commission, the Federal Trade Commission, etc.). Here, again, he found that the corporations had violated various laws with "great frequency." Yet these violations (defrauding consumers, defrauding investors, restraint of trade and unfair competition, unfair labor practices) led to relatively few formal decisions against them on explicit criminal charges. Sutherland attributed this gap between violations and convictions to a number of factors: the ineffective procedures of the regulatory commissions, the strong lobbying by the utilities against really effective laws and regulations, the corporations' enormous propaganda efforts to gain public support, their largely successful fight against publicly owned power corporations, the outright use of "illegal methods of influencing elections and appointments," and the close ties the utilities had been able to maintain with the government agencies that were supposed to be regulating them (Sutherland, 1949, 1961, pp. 210–213).

Considered more broadly, the utilities example points up a major theme in Sutherland's analysis—namely, that the crucial difference between business crimes and other criminal violations lay in the ways in which they were reacted to publicly and officially. The corporation's behavior was itself no less "criminal," he insisted. The acts in question violated specific laws defining them as socially injurious and prescribing legal penalties for their occurrence. To Sutherland, the fact that the penalties imposed were rarely heavy and that administrative "sanctions" rather than criminal ones often were invoked did not mean that something other than "real crime" was involved. On the contrary, he concluded that a large class of criminals was being let off or at least was receiving preferential treatment because of their power and social positions. This argument, of course, raises complex issues regarding the sociological meaning and definition of crime and of deviance. Critics of Sutherland's position (see, for example, Tappan, 1947) emphasized two points: that "criminal" is essentially a legal term that should only be applied to a person after formal court conviction, and that the differential treatment and self-conceptions of white-collar "offenders" reflected an important distinction the general public would tend to draw between these and other kinds of offenses. In effect, these critics were arguing (partly along lines similar to those of the definitional/processual orientation emphasized in this book) that a person is only deviant or criminal to the extent he or she is treated as such. Yet recognizing the existence of these differences in reaction and treatment in no way tells us whether we should approve or disapprove of them. Indeed, Sutherland's analysis led him to conclude most emphatically that the preferential treatment was improper and unjust.

Even if one accepts the legalistic approach to defining crime, Sutherland's work would still have to be seen as indicating a major category of *potential* criminals. As such, it helps provide the basis for the kind of social critique the so-called "radical" sociologists now advance—the claim that we stigmatize and punish the "wrong" people, that we (and they would include sociologists in this) ignore the "real" criminals. With respect to explaining the causes of white-collar crime, Sutherland's approach again falls somewhere between the more conventional and the more radical perspectives. As we have seen, his theory of differential association accounted for individual involvement in these as in other types of offenses. Although this theory focused on individuals, it did stress the process of interaction that preceded law violation and that permitted one to rationalize engaging in such behavior. But Sutherland went well beyond that, because he also emphasized that social systems themselves are organized—in their dominant behavior patterns and values—so as to encourage or discourage particular kinds of law violations. Although his studies may seem relatively mild next to some of the more impassioned neo-Marxist critiques of current American society, nonetheless at the time his findings represented a considerable indictment of business-oriented values and of the moral and legal ramifications of having a business-dominated society. In many ways, he helped set the stage for the subsequent radical critiques.

The 1961 Price-Fixing Cases

By and large, it remains true today, as in Sutherland's time, that corporate crimes are less stringently penalized than other types of law violation. However, there have been occasional signs of more severe official reaction to corporate offenses. The most notable of these was the federal prosecution in 1961 of 29 corporations and 45 individual top-level executives in the electrical industry on charges of having conspired illegally to fix prices, rig bids, and divide markets on electrical equipment valued at $1.75 billion annually (see Smith, 1961; and Geis, in Clinard and Quinney, 1967). This was the biggest criminal case in the history of the Sherman Antitrust Act, and the penalties meted out were, for corporate offenders, unusually severe. Not only were fines totalling $1,924,500 imposed on the corporations, but 7 of the executives received 30-day jail sentences, and 27 others suspended jail sentences. Sending high-level executives to jail was perhaps the most startling outcome of the case, although these particular individuals insisted, and radical analysts might partly agree, that they were being treated as scapegoats for a well-entrenched "system" of business conduct.

The systematic nature of the law-violating behavior was clearly established by the extensive evidence in the case, as was the recognition by the individuals involved, of serious impropriety:

> The conspiracies had their own lingo and their own standard operating procedures. The attendance list was known as the "Christmas-card list," meetings as "choir practices." Companies had code numbers—G.E. 1, Westinghouse, 2, Allis-Chalmers, 3, Federal Pacific, 7—which were used in conjunction with first names when calling a conspirator at home for price information. ("This is Bob, what is 7's bid?"). At the hotel meeting it was S.O.P. not to list one's employer when registering and not to have breakfast with fellow conspirators in the dining room. The G.E. men observed two additional precautions: never to be the ones who kept the records and never to tell G.E.'s lawyers anything (Smith, 1961, p. 362).

Defendants claimed that they should not personally have been held liable, since price-fixing was already an established practice when they first entered their jobs. And while they acknowledged involvement in technical violations of the law, they did not really agree that that made them criminals. Thus, the following testimony by a Westinghouse executive, during hearings of the Senate Subcommittee on Antitrust and Monopoly:

Committee Attorney: Did you know that these meetings with competitors were illegal?

Witness: Illegal? Yes, but not criminal. I didn't find that out until I read the indictment. . . . I assumed that criminal action meant damaging someone, and we did not do that. . . . I thought that we were more or less working on a survival basis in order to try to make enough to keep our plant and our employees.

(Geis, in Clinard and Quinney, 1967, p. 144)

Similarly, an Ingersoll-Rand Corporation executive admitted, "It is against the law," but went on to state: "I do not know that it is against public welfare because I am not certain that the consumer was actually injured by this operation" (Geis, in Clinard and Quinney, 1967, p. 144).

Experts are disinclined to believe that the 1961 cases have had a major impact in deterring corporate crime, despite the relatively severe penalties they involved. Even the enormous fines that were levied (such as a $0.5-million fine against General Electric) need not have had much of an effect in restricting the freedom to act of such corporate giants. Financially more serious were the civil ("treble damage") suits brought by customers following the criminal prosecutions. According to one report: "A mid-1964 calculation showed that 90 per cent of some 1800 claims [against General Electric] had been settled for a total of $160 million," but as this same commentator noted, "General Electric could derive some solace from the fact that most of these payments would be tax-deductible" (Geis, 1967, p. 142). Although the heightened prospect of actually serving a jail sentence would seem likely to have some deterrent effect on individual corporate members, mixed reactions to the situation of the 1961 defendants may have undercut such impact. Thus, while General Electric dismissed employees involved in the offending practices, Westinghouse did not. The latter's action reflected its stated view that these persons had already been punished enough, that they hadn't acted for personal gain, and that they were basically moral and law-abiding citizens (see Geis, 1967, p. 146). It undoubtedly mirrored, too, a widespread awareness of and failure to condemn quasilegal and illegal practices in the business community. Public views on such matters, as well, were likely to remain ambivalent.

Continuing Criminality

At any rate, the continued emphasis in our society on the values of financial success and commercial aggressiveness, combined with the large corporation's position of special power and influence, virtually ensures the persistence of corporate crime. As one observer has noted, commenting on two recently publicized cases of corporate wrongdoing, the openly acknowledged scandals are "only the tip of an iceberg of industrial espionage, corporate conspiracy, law violation, and open contempt for the public interest" (Krisberg, 1975, p. 37). An important trend that has played a significant role in revealing corporate illegality has been the movement for consumer protection and protection of the natural environment. Public interest advocates in both areas are vigorously focusing attention on various kinds of corporate wrongdoing. Legal prosecutions that their investigations have generated are also revealing for what they tell us about the persisting rationalization of, and relative license for engaging in, corporate law violation. Referring to a set of indictments brought against major corporations for contaminating waterways through the dumping of mercury, two criminologists comment:

The responses of the spokesmen for the polluting corporations are most instructive. They all showed surprise and indignation, and tried to prove that they were concerned about the problem. The Penwalt Corporation issued the following statement: "At our Calvert City, Ky., plant, which uses mercury cells, we have been and are working on the subject of continuing compliance with the applicable state standards." Allied Chemical said in a statement that it had made substantial progress in eliminating mercury pollution and that it was continuing to work on the problem. The vice-president of the Olin Chemical Corporation said that the company was working on a "crash program."

Imagine how far a traditional offender, a murderer for example, would get if he argued, after committing his act, that he was working on his problem or that he was making considerable progress in finding ways to control his behavior. The violent offender has no right to show surprise that his conduct is being questioned. The criminal corporation seems to have this right (Clinard and Quinney, 1973, pp. 212–213).

As regards individual corporate executives convicted of crimes that reflect widespread business practice, recent experience seems to indicate that the likelihood of significant penalties remains low. Thus while Congress in 1974 increased the maximum punishment for price-fixing from one year in prison to three, "only a handful of antitrust violators had been sentenced to more than 60 days in jail when one-year prison terms were in force, and in the 1975–76 fiscal year, only two of 75 antitrust defendants were incarcerated at all. And so the authorized three-year antitrust penalty remains thus far an empty gesture" (Orland, 1976).

Critics of contemporary American capitalism insist that even such individual prosecutions as do occur represent a safety-valve kind of mechanism for deflecting public outrage and preserving the essential structure of corporate practice. For example, economist David Gordon argues that, if crimes committed by the wealthy "become so egregiously offensive that their victims may move to overthrow the system itself, . . . the State may punish individual members of the class in order to protect the entire class. Latent opposition to the practices of corporations may be forestalled, to pick several examples, by token public efforts to enact and enforce antitrust, truth-in-lending, antipollution, industrial safety, and auto safety legislation" (Gordon, 1971, in Chambliss and Mankoff, 1976, p. 204). Furthermore, as analyses of this sort make clear, corporate crime highlights the fact that to develop a comprehensive understanding of criminality or deviance, we need to examine a society's choice of behaviors to stigmatize and punish from two directions, not just one. Which patterns of behavior are *not* dealt with severely, and *why,* are just as important questions for research and analysis as those concerned with the behaviors that do receive strong negative sanctions. The relative public indifference to white-collar offenses is a significant indicator of the impact of dominant cultural values and economic arrangements on crime-defining in modern American society.

Since crime, by definition as a violation of the criminal law, so patently reflects the outcome of processes at work in the *political arena* (most notably, the legislative process and the administration of justice), it is particularly with respect to criminality that political conflict theories of deviance have been developed. Likewise, since so many behaviors treated as criminal represent economic offenses, it is readily understandable why the theme of conflicting *economic* interests has come to the fore in most of these explanations. An early formulation by the Dutch socialist writer Wilhelm Bonger attributed crime to the "egoistic tendencies" fostered by a capitalist economic system and implied that there would be much less criminality under more cooperative modes of living (Bonger, 1916). Similarly influenced by the ideas of Marxian socialism was an historical analysis, for many years ignored and now the object of renewed interest, of the relationship between fluctuations in penal policy, especially the use of imprisonment, and a variety of features of economic systems—such as dominant mode of production, state of the labor market, and the strength and nature of threats to the economic status quo (Rusche and Kirchheimer, 1939; see also Krisberg, 1975, pp. 135–166; and Taylor, Walton and Young, 1974, pp. 222–234).

An unpretentious but extremely cogent statement delineating the bases for a group conflict theory of crime was presented by criminologist George Vold, in his 1958 book *Theoretical Criminology*. Finding the seeds of such an approach not only in classic social theories (such as the writings of Georg Simmel, cited earlier) but also in the Chicago work of Park and Burgess and the writings of Sutherland, Vold asserted: "Many kinds of criminal acts must be recognized as representing primarily behavior on the front-line fringes of direct contact between groups struggling for the control of power in the political and cultural organization of society" (Vold, 1958, p. 214). In particular he noted that, "organized crime must be thought of as a natural growth, or as a developmental adjunct to our general system of private profit economy" (Vold, 1958, p. 240), and that white-collar criminality had to be viewed primarily as a problem not "of terminology or of proper legal definition, but rather one of deep and far-reaching divergencies in the political and economic ideology of different segments of the population" (Vold, 1958, p. 259).

More recently, influential conflict theories of crime have been offered by sociologists Richard Quinney and Austin Turk. Quinney, in his 1970 work *The Social Reality of Crime,* combined a focus on interest-group conflict with the "social construction of reality" ideas developed in the modern sociology of knowledge. Crime, he emphasized, is "created," it is a judgment some people make about the actions of others. Since crime definitions are created and enforced by "authorized agents in a politically organized society," crime situations are reflections of the structuring of political and economic interests. Indeed, "Criminal definitions describe behaviors that conflict with the interests of the segments of society that have the power to shape public policy" (Quinney, 1970, p. 16). Along rather similar lines and writing around the same time, Turk discussed criminality "as status rather than behavior" and stressed that "political power determines legality." A theory of "criminalization"—of some segments of a population—must, he indicated, be built on systematic differences in overall social power, factors influencing those in a position to enforce norms, and the nature and strength of patterned resistance to dominant norms (Turk, 1969, especially chs. 2 and 3). Similar outlooks on the legal system were adopted by William Chambliss and Robert Seidman in their book on sociology of law, entitled *Law, Order, and Power* (Chambliss and Seidman, 1971). Recent work by other professed radical criminologists has tried to depict the essentially political nature of criminal law, the interest-group dynamics of the legislative process, and the extent to which our present system of justice operates in the interest of a ruling elite and is built on oppression of the lower-class and racial minorities. (See, for example, Krisberg, 1975, and the various contributions in Chambliss and Mankoff, eds., 1976.)

Also helping to further interest in a conflict approach to deviance was an early body of "value-conflict" theory used in the sociological analysis of "social problems." These formulations (primarily by Willard Waller, Richard Fuller, and Richard Myers) emphasized that social problems have a "natural history," a characteristic sequence of stages, involving perceived threats to group values and interests and an associated mobilization of efforts to influence relevant public policies (Fuller and Myers, 1941; also see discussion in Rubington and Weinberg, 1971, pp. 81–87). Recently, Malcolm Spector and John Kitsuse have reformulated this general approach, perceptively treating social problem situations in terms of group efforts to press and sustain "claims" (Spector and Kitsuse, 1977; see also Kitsuse and Spector, 1975).

Unfortunately, the tendency to think of social problems and deviance as separate fields along with the strong individual differentiation theme that afflicted so much early deviance analysis often impeded recognition that deviance situations could all be conceptualized in group conflict terms. As the introductory chapter to this text should have made clear, the conflict theme certainly now is central to the outlooks that are being emphasized in most recent interpretations of deviance. Built around the ideas of deviance-defining as a response to threat, stigmatizing reactions as a device for subordinating and segregating, and differential power as the major determinant of "outcomes" in deviance situations, these emerging formulations inevitably view deviance in conflict terms. We will see this view further developed as we proceed to consider the so-called "labeling" approach, which is summarized in the next section and in a sense elaborated on throughout the rest of the book. Indeed, the author of one influential labeling-oriented analysis not only explores deviance in conflict terms, but actually defines it *as* conflict: "Deviance is the name of the conflict game in which individuals or loosely organized small groups with little power are strongly feared by a well-organized, sizable minority or majority who have a large amount of power" (Lofland, 1969, p. 14).

As these comments suggest, a conflict orientation of some sort is appropriate, indeed necessary, not only in analyzing crime but in considering any deviance situation. Of course, given the exceedingly broad conception of deviance adopted here, that is, that *any* kind of behavior can be subject to deviance-defining or imbued with deviantness, the "content" of the situation may in part determine what version of conflict theory we should employ and how we should put it to use. For example, if we recognize that, as suggested at the beginning of this book, interpersonal "slights"—inattention, ridicule, personal disloyalty, and the like—are potential objects of deviance-defining at the level of face-to-face interaction, we confront a domain in which applicability of a Marxian economic-conflict thesis would be extremely questionable if not patently absurd. But this example, which is about as far as one can get from the case of, say, specific legislation regarding property crimes—which one might easily interpret in Marxian terms—points up the fact that *some* element of *some* kind of conflict will always be present. Here the conflict may be implicit rather than explicit: It is interpersonal, not collective; it centers around personal dominance not the advancing of group interests. But just as in the broader, more clearly "political" cases, we cannot analyze situational outcomes if we do not take into account the distribution and uses of power. To effectively "cut" an offending acquaintance or to embarrass an opponent is, after all, an exercise of some kind of power; in the broadest and most subtle senses, a process of interpersonal conflict always underlies and determines the outcomes in such situations.

Power, then, has become a central focal point in most contemporary deviance theory. At whatever level of the social order and whatever the substantive "content" involved may be, exploring the distribution of power and the dynamics of conflict and change helps increase our understanding of both the general processes that are at work and specific outcomes that at any given time prevail. Basically, what is at stake in all deviance situations of varying content and complexity is the same: Who will be subject to deviance-defining and for what? When we have this central question in mind, we find, as much of the discussion so far has indicated, that a great deal of the available data about deviance reflect broad patterns of social dominance and subordination. (Recall Anthony Harris's provocative concept discussed in Chapter 2, in which he proposes that the function of deviance "typescripts" may be to maintain the dominance of certain segments or interests.) As Adaptation Two (pp. 145–150) makes quite clear, the dominant position of large corporations in the American economic and political system often has enabled these organizations and their key personnel to shield themselves from strong imputations of deviantness and particularly from official deviance-processing. Corporate lobbying and public relations efforts—set off against the activities of government antitrust forces and more recently citizen-protection public-accountability reform groups—show that the "conflict" in such a situation is not just potential or latent, but frequently quite overt.

The other side of this dominance-immunity pattern, of course, is that subordinate groups are likely to be especially vulnerable to deviance-defining and processing. Many of the "offenses" of women in our society can be seen in this light. One good example is the common use of sexual "promiscuity" as a ground for delinquency adjudication of young women, while such a charge is hardly ever leveled against male youths in trouble with the law (for an interesting historical discussion of this point, see Schlossman and Wallach, 1978). This difference openly reflects the double standard by which the sexual activities of males and females were, at least until recently, evaluated very differently; many people now are coming to recognize that the double standard itself rests heavily on and reinforces the general social subordination of women. Likewise, opponents of restrictive abortion laws have long noted that by and large these restrictions are imposed *by men* who heavily dominate legislatures *on women.* As Simone de Beauvoir commented in her now classic feminist work *The Second Sex,* "Men universally forbid abortion, but individually they accept it as a convenient solution of a problem; they are able to contradict themselves with careless cynicism. But woman feels these contradictions in her wounded flesh; she is as a rule too timid for open revolt against masculine bad faith; she regards herself as the victim of an injustice that makes her a criminal against her will, and at the same time she feels soiled and humiliated" (de Beauvoir, 1957, pp. 491–492). In the case of abortion laws, as we will see below, what for many years remained a latent conflict between those favoring legal limitations and those opposing them recently has erupted into a full-scale public political controversy.

Again, the administration of laws against prostitution mirror the relative power positions of men and women. According to one recent report, even under statutes that potentially subject the customer as well as the prostitute to criminal charges, "Unequal enforcement is prevalent throughout the country. For instance, although patronizing a prostitute is a crime in New York City, 1972 arrests for prostitution were more than one hundred times greater than were arrests for patronizing a prostitute . . . During the same year in Seattle, Washington, where the law is facially neutral, 620 women—and only 41 men—were arrested on prostitution charges" (James, *et al.,* 1975, p. 29). An observer of the New York courts even concluded that, "there's no clearer indication than prostitution that all women are a potential species of social or political prisoner. Prostitution is really the only crime in the penal law where two people are doing a thing mutually agreed upon and yet only one, the female partner, is subject to arrest" (Schneider, 1973, p. 146). Perhaps an especially extreme example of male-dominated deviance-defining has been the common tendency, now being vigorously and somewhat successfully opposed by feminists, of police and others to treat the female rape victim as though she were an "offender" of some kind by questioning her virtue, the adequacy of her resistance, and so on. That the person subjected to the offending act could in this way herself be branded with deviantness demonstrates the key influence of power on deviantizing—in an area of offense that Susan Brownmiller has recently suggested may, in the first place, have more to do with power and dominance than with sexuality (Brownmiller, 1976).

In the discussion that follows, we will be considering the matter of power and power resources quite a bit more. As we will see, in connection with dispute about the labeling approach, some writers have claimed that available evidence does not always support the dominance-immunity subordination-vulnerability thesis. Such claims, it will be suggested, may incorporate misunderstandings about the labeling argument, but we should recognize in any case that substantively different situations will vary as to what kinds of resources make for *relevant* power and *relative* immunity from deviantness. Thus the socioeconomic position of corporate executives has a direct bearing on the ease with which they can be branded "white-collar criminals;" it may have a reduced and more indirect influence in protecting them from imputations of deviantness connected with, say, homosexuality or alcoholism. At the same time, the bulk of the evidence regarding different kinds of deviance-defining does amply demonstrate the existence of systematic variations in the overall vulnerability of different segments of our population. All other things being equal, or notwithstanding inevitable variations in specific detail, the relative power positions of working-class and middle-class persons, of whites and blacks (along with other minorities), of men and women, and of young people and adults play a very important role one way or another in shaping a wide variety of deviance situations.

In all of the preceding discussion of conflict theory, the explicit or implicit and underlying premise has been that conflict as a general process is a basic feature of any social system and of all social interaction, just as we have seen deviance-defining itself to be. Before concluding this section, however, some reference should be made to a rather different (and to date considerably less influential) conception of conflict recently advanced by certain radical sociologists. This conception is more heavily influenced by the ideas of classical Marxism and of the school of "critical theory"—a philosophical socioeconomic outlook developed by an influential body of Marxist-oriented theorists centered in Frankfurt, Germany, beginning just before the second World War. When this approach is applied to deviance theory, the tendency is to deny the *inevitability* of conflict and deviance, to attribute them more directly to the specific "contradictions" of the *capitalist* system as such, and to envision a working-out of these contradictions through "dialectical" processes of change eventuating in a "true" socialist society. In this view, sociological analysis requires an active *critique of the existing social order*. The more traditional conflict theories are found to be inadequate because they underplay the themes of domination and exploitation; they are said to adopt a pluralistic rather than a ruling elite conception of the power structure. Rejecting a total separation of sociology and social action, this version of conflict theory insists, at a minimum, on an engaged or committed analysis: "The new criminology must therefore be a normative theory: it must hold out the possibilities of a resolution to the fundamental questions, and a social resolution" (Taylor, Walton, and Young, 1974, p. 28). In more extreme form, this merger of theory and practice now leads the influential criminologist Richard Quinney to the conclusion (hardly suggested in his earlier conflict-oriented writings on crime) that sociologists are or should be "engaged in socialist revolution" (Quinney, 1977, p. 165).

There is certainly no question but that a Marxian orientation can generate useful efforts at theorizing about deviance (see, for example, Spitzer, 1975). Furthermore, it is likely that many if not most sociologists will agree with much of the specific critique of crime control and of the vested interests in same that developed out of, but is *not* dependent on, such an orientation. (See, for example, Quinney, 1974; and Krisberg, 1975.) What is considerably less acceptable to a great many sociologists, however, is the assertion in some of these writings (see

Quinney, 1974; Taylor, Walton, and Young, 1974) that once a true socialist society is achieved, crime and deviance (and the sociology of crime and deviance!) will disappear. The experience of modern socialist societies (see, for example, Connor, 1972), including those to which these writers tend to point with special approval, such as China and Cuba (see Loney, 1973), provides little or no support for this line of argument. Some radical theorists counter that a "true" socialist society has yet to come into being, but their apparent belief that such a society would be able to *totally* do away with crime and deviance as opposed to simply altering types, distribution, and "solutions" can only be described as an article of faith. Such a projection seems, in fact, to run counter to the logic of virtually everything we know about deviance-defining as a process central to the workings of any society.

LABELING ANALYSIS

The themes emphasized in the introductory chapter—the relativity of deviance-definitions, their production and application through a process of imbuing (acts, conditions, individuals) with "deviantness," and the key roles of power and conflict—are all major ingredients of the now influential definitional-processual approach to interpreting deviance. More commonly, this approach is referred to as the **labeling orientation,** though, as we will see below, there are problems inherent in using that term, particularly when the approach is construed narrowly so as to refer only to the direct negative "labeling" of specific individuals. In the remaining chapters of this book, an effort is made to show where a more broadly construed version of this orientation leads us in interpreting deviance. Throughout that discussion, we will be examining at some length most of the major assertions made by labeling analysts as well as assessing various criticisms their work has evoked. This section, then, represents merely a brief overview of the approach and a preliminary indication of some of the controversy surrounding it.

To begin with, it should be noted that the labeling outlook has been built up over some time and reflects a variety of developments and influences (see Matza, 1969; Schur, 1971). In some ways it is a culmination of earlier work on deviance, incorporating certain ideas from the more traditional formulations just discussed and other ideas that have been generated through critiques of those formulations. It also reflects some important recent developments affecting the entire discipline of sociology which deserve at least brief mention at this point. One of these developments has been the renewed attention to the "symbolic interactionist" theories of George H. Mead, Charles Cooley, and others, stressing the "social self" developed through social interaction and incorporating or reflecting the actual and anticipated responses of other people. This general perspective (see Rose, ed., 1962; also Strauss, 1969; and Blumer, 1969) and the "self-fulfilling prophecy" concept closely associated with it (page 159) provided important groundings for the labeling and other societal reactions or definitional approaches to deviance (see Suchar, 1978, ch. 5). At the same time, the increased concern in recent sociology with the "subjective meanings of action"—a theme that had been emphasized not only by those theorists but by other classic social thinkers such as Max Weber—has given rise to a revival of interest in observational research, especially in-depth participant observation. Severyn Bruyn has suggested that this approach affords the researcher a unique manner of gaining knowledge: "By taking the role of his subjects he re-creates in his own imagination and experience the thoughts and feelings which are in the minds of those he studies. It is through a process of symbolic interpretation of the 'experienced culture' that the observer works with his data and discovers meanings in them" (Bruyn, 1966, p. 12).

As we saw above, direct and intensive field studies constituted one standard technique in the early Chicago research. Yet between the time of those efforts and the advent of the interest in labeling, such direct fieldwork had largely been eclipsed by the dominant emphasis within sociology generally on statistical comparisons of supposedly matched samples. Despite some sense of the shortcomings of using official statistics and studying officially processed individuals, deviance analysts, as Ned Polsky suggested in a pungent critique of conventional criminology, frequently were "trained out" of their capacity for direct observation, so that they could not "see people any more, except through punched cards and one-way mirrors." As Polsky went on to note, reflecting the renewed faith in the Chicago fieldwork approach that has now arisen among sociologists of varying orientations, it may in fact be much easier to study offenders in their "natural settings" than sociologists have often tended to assume (see Polsky, 1967, pp. 117–149). Many recent deviance analysts have adopted Polsky's suggestion, undertaking direct field studies that range across the full substantive spectrum of perceived deviation from abortion-seekers to drug addicts, from hippies to nudists, from delinquents to the disabled.

Along with the tendency to become more adventurous in basic research technique, there have developed (as we are going to see in the next chapter) new explanatory strategies appropriate to depicting deviance in interactionist terms and even some revised thinking about just what we mean by the notion of "cause." Then, too, all of these recent tendencies have been intensified and pushed still further through the work of phenomenologically oriented sociologists (ethnomethodologists, etc.) who believe they have developed not just a new approach to social research but, indeed, a more general and truly distinctive epistemology—a unique and comprehensive way of achieving, as they might put it, "doing" knowledge. This outlook, with its radical disbelief in any "social reality" other than that which we ourselves through our everyday interaction and our sociological studies "accomplish," has influenced and at the same time fits in well with the general course of development of recent work on deviance (see Douglas, ed., 1970a; Scott and Douglas, eds., 1972; Douglas, ed., 1970b; and Turner, ed., 1974; also discussion by Schur, 1971, pp. 115–136; and Suchar, 1978, pp. 232–237). We saw something of the intensive focus on interaction process that this approach can produce in considering Garfinkel's student experiments. We will return to some additional themes developed in connection with their critique of labeling analyses.

These recent developments (influenced also, one might note, by the important work of Berger and Luckmann, *The Social Construction of Reality,* 1966) have combined to create a strong interest on the part of many sociologists in what may be described as "interpretive approaches"—interpretation of the social world in general and of deviance more specifically. For phenomenologists, the idea of interpretation (documentary method) implies some specific assumptions and research orientations and, above all, specialized terminology that not all deviance sociologists would be prepared to adopt. But the broader conception of interpretation, sketched out in the opening section of this book and standing in contradistinction to quantitatively oriented techniques, seems to be one that now occupies a central place in the modern sociology of deviance. As noted in that section, an interpretive focus is particularly appropriate in studying deviance-defining if, as many are now convinced, the definitions and reactions that "constitute" it are themselves "interpretive" in nature. At least one writer has made the same kind of point more generally with respect to all social interaction, arguing the need for an interpretive focus in any sociological inquiry (see Wilson, 1970).

With these comments as background, let us now turn to a few of the statements and themes (many more will be presented later on) that are often cited as representative of the labeling outlook on deviance. In his landmark work, *Outsiders,* Howard S. Becker provided the gist of a definition of deviance as seen from that perspective:

> . . . *social groups create deviance by making the rules whose infraction constitutes deviance* and by applying these rules to particular people and labeling them as outsiders. From this point of view, deviance is *not* a quality of the act the person commits, but rather a consequence of the application by others of rules and sanctions to an "offender." The deviant is one to whom that label has successfully been applied; deviant behavior is behavior that people so label (Becker, 1963, p. 9).

In a very similar way and again stressing the focus on *characterizations* of behavior, Kai Erikson highlighted the fact that deviance becomes a kind of **ascribed status**—an attribution that occurs through the responses of other people. He also noted the implications of this process, in terms of a shifting focus of attention, for sociological research and analysis:

> Deviance is not a property *inherent* in certain forms of behavior; it is a property *conferred upon* these forms by the audiences which directly or indirectly witness

them. Sociologically, then, the critical variable is the social *audience* . . . since it is the audience which eventually decides whether or not any given action or actions will become a visible case of deviation (Erikson, 1962, p. 308).

As we can see from these statements, the labeling approach promotes or incorporates a "relativistic" stance and an "interactionist" perspective. Deviance is not simply a matter of the violation of fixed norms on which everyone is agreed beforehand. (Indeed, Becker's stress on a diversity of norms led him to note a second meaning of the term "outsiders": "The rule-breaker may feel his judges are *outsiders*.") On the contrary, deviance depends not only on the actions of so-called offenders but also on the reactions of other people to types and specific instances of behavior. In short, as we have noted earlier, deviance essentially reflects *what is made socially* of various acts or conditions. Deviance, then, is always (again, as emphasized in this text) an outcome—a culmination of processes of interaction. As Becker pointed out, such interaction processes are not well depicted through *static* (statistical comparison) types of explanation. Instead, a *sequential* model is needed: ". . . all causes do not operate at the same time, and we need a model which takes into account the fact that patterns of behavior *develop* in orderly sequence" (Becker, 1963, p. 23). We will return below to this question of static versus sequential models. At the heart of Becker's suggestion is a basic difference in the *kinds* of questions typically addressed by labeling analysts and more traditional deviance specialists. The labeling approach is much less interested in exploring *why* individuals engage in perceived deviation than it is in depicting *how*, through what social processes, deviance situations and outcomes emerge.

A central theme in this type of analysis (though, as we will see, *not* the only theme) has been the impact on a person's self-conceptions and subsequent behavior of being negatively labeled. The idea that reactions to perceived deviation might actually become a contributing cause of persisting deviance problems is one that is well grounded in traditional sociological formulations. This side of labeling analysis is, in effect, an application of the famous aphorism of W. I. Thomas, "if men define situations as real, they are real in their consequences," which Robert Merton later discussed as the **self-fulfilling prophecy** (Merton, 1949, pp. 179–195). An early illustration of the use of this idea in deviance analysis was provided by Frank Tannenbaum when he argued that early stigmatization generates delinquent and criminal careers:

> The process of making the criminal, therefore, is a process of tagging, defining, identifying, segregating, describing, emphasizing, making conscious and self-conscious; it becomes a way of stimulating, suggesting, emphasizing, evoking the very traits that are complained of. . . .
> The person becomes the thing he is described as being. Nor does it seem to matter whether the valuation is made by those who would punish or by those who would reform. . . . The harder they work to reform the evil, the greater the evil grows under

their hands. The persistent suggestion, with whatever good intentions, works mischief, because it leads to bringing out the bad behavior that it would suppress. The way out is through a refusal to dramatize the evil (Tannenbaum, 1938, pp. 19–20).

A more ambitious theoretical effort to systematize such ideas was made by Edwin Lemert in a 1951 book now recognized as a major contribution to the development of the labeling or societal reaction approach. Lemert pictured deviance-defining as one of the basic processes of social "differentiation," a process in which often "penalties and segregative reactions of society or the community are dynamic factors which increase, decrease, and condition the form which the initial differentiation or deviation takes" (Lemert, 1951, p. 22). Building on this idea, he developed the now-famous distinction between primary and **secondary deviation:** "When a person begins to employ his deviant behavior or a role based upon it as a means of defense, attack, or adjustment to the overt and covert problems created by the consequent societal reaction to him, his deviation is secondary" (Lemert, 1951, 76). We will be considering this matter of primary and secondary deviation at some length in the discussion that follows, noting in particular the dispute that has arisen regarding problems of separating these two aspects from one another for purposes of research and analysis.

In considering the social-psychological impact on the individual of being defined and treated as an offender, recent labeling analysis has placed heavy emphasis on the use of stereotyping, the characteristic occurrence of "retrospective interpretation" (once labeled a deviator, the individual is seen only and completely in that light), and the relation between power resources and the "negotiation" of labels. (We will return to a further exploration of these matters in Part Two, but it should be noted here that similar mechanisms, subprocesses of the overall labeling process, are present as well when we examine deviance-defining from an organization or societal vantage point.) Table 3.1, to which we will want to refer in connection with later discussion, provides a schematic indication of these processes as they appear at different levels of social interaction. These broader levels of analysis represent important aspects of a comprehensive labeling-oriented approach. The twin emphases in such an approach are on *definition* and *process* at all the levels that are involved in the production of deviance situations and outcomes. Thus, the perspective is concerned not only with what happens to specific individuals when they are branded with deviant-ness ("labeling," in the narrow sense) but also with the wider domains and processes of social definition and collective rule-making that frequently lie behind such concrete applications of negative labels. Becker highlighted this broader conception of labeling when he began his now-famous statement by noting that "social groups create deviance by making the rules. . . ."

Adaptations Three and Four provide an initial basis for exploring the varied dimensions and characteristic emphases of an interpretation of deviance grounded in the ideas of definition and process. One of these studies illustrates the intensive exploration of interaction process that characterizes a good deal

Table 3.1 Basic Processes and Key Levels of Analysis

BASIC RESPONSE PROCESSES	LEVELS OF ANALYSIS			OUTCOMES
	COLLECTIVE RULE-MAKING	INTERPERSONAL REACTIONS	ORGANIZATIONAL PROCESSING	
Stereotyping	*Public stereotypes of deviants*	*Reliance on observed or assumed cues (application of cultural stereotypes in interactions)*	*Typification in processing "normal cases" (classification partly according to stereotypes)*	*Individual role engulfment in deviant careers*
Retrospective interpretation	*Rule-making that imputes ancillary qualities to the deviator, as in employment policies toward homosexuals*	*Consideration of actor as having "been that way all along;" review of past for early "cues"*	*Use of "case record" or "case history"*	*Secondary expansion of deviance "problems" of society*
Negotiation	*Pressure-group conflict over legal and public definitions*	*Direct bargaining over labels, as in psychiatric diagnosis*	*Bargaining between client and organization, as in pleading in criminal court*	
Outcomes		*Individual role engulfment in deviant careers; secondary expansion of deviance "problems" of society*		

Source: Edwin M. Schur, *Labeling Deviant Behavior.* New York: Harper & Row, 1971, p. 39.

of labeling analysis and particularly points up the need to see deviance as an outcome of such interaction. The other, summarizing a much broader investigation, shows how deviance-defining and processing reflect social context and, indeed, may be "determined" by the nature of the prevailing social-control apparatus. The very fact that these studies differ from each other so greatly may be an indication of the potential richness of the definitional focus.

ADAPTATION THREE
Normalizing Erratic Behavior*

According to the definitional-processual perspective, a determination that deviance has occurred is always best viewed as the outcome of a complex sequence of social interaction. From such a standpoint, the ways in which other people view and react to an individual who might be seen as deviating are crucial to an understanding of the situation. How "offending" the behavior is, and, to express the same point another way, how "negative" the reactions are will often be unpredictable beforehand. These elements frequently undergo change in the course of the interaction sequence. Thus, ways of recognizing and defining deviance in such situations and the points at which changes in this process occur are of great interest to the sociologist. The research report that follows, from which several statistical tables in the original are here omitted, shows how the authors attempted to reconstruct through inerviews with the wives of men who had been hospitalized for mental illness the events and interpretations that preceded hospitalization. (The italicized passages below are included in the original article.)

This paper presents an analysis of cognitive and emotional problems encountered by the wife in coping with the mental illness of the husband. It is concerned with the factors which lead to the reorganization of the wife's perceptions of her husband from a *well* man to a man who is mentally sick or in need of hospitalization in a mental hospital. The process whereby the wife attempts to understand and interpret her husband's manifestations of mental illness is best communicated by considering first the concrete details of a single wife's experiences. The findings and interpretations based on the total sample [the sample consisted of the wives of twenty-three men hospitalized as "psychotic" and ten men hospitalized with a diagnosis of "psychoneurotic"—*Ed's. note*] are presented following the case analysis.

Illustrative Case

Robert F., a 35-year-old cab driver, was admitted to Saint Elizabeth's Hospital with a diagnosis of schizophrenia. How did Mr. F. get to the mental hospital? Here is a very condensed version of what his wife told an interviewer a few weeks later.

Mrs. F. related certain events, swift and dramatic, which led directly to

---

* *Source:* Adapted and abridged (footnotes and tables omitted) from Marian Radke Yarrow, Charlotte Green Schwartz, Harriet S. Murphy, and Leila Calhoun Deasy, "The Psychological Meaning of Mental Illness in the Family," *Journal of Social Issues,* 11:4 (1955), 12–24. Reprinted with permission; introductory comments are the present author's—not in the original.

the hospitalization. The day before admission, Mr. F. went shopping with his wife, which he had never done before, and expressed worry lest he lose her. This was in her words, "rather strange." (*His behavior is not in keeping with her expectations for him.*) Later that day, Mr. F. thought a TV program was about him and that the set was "after him." "Then I was getting worried." (*She recognizes the bizarre nature of his reactions. She becomes concerned.*)

That night, Mr. F. kept talking. He reproached himself for not working enough to give his wife surprises. Suddenly, he exclaimed he did have a surprise for her—he was going to kill her. "I was petrified and said to him, 'What do you mean?' Then, he began to cry and told me not to let him hurt me and to do for him what I would want him to do for me. I asked him what was wrong. He said he had cancer. . . . He began talking about his grandfather's mustache and said there was a worm growing out of it." She remembered his watching little worms in the fish bowl and thought his idea came from that. Mr. F. said he had killed his grandfather. He asked Mrs. F. to forgive him and wondered if she were his mother or God. She denied this. He vowed he was being punished for killing people during the war. "I thought maybe . . . worrying about the war so much . . . had gotten the best of him. (*She tries to understand his behavior. She stretches the range of normality to include it.*) I thought he should see a psychiatrist . . . I don't know how to explain it. He was shaking. I knew it was beyond what I could do . . . I was afraid of him . . . I thought he was losing his normal mental attitude and mentality, but I wouldn't say that he was insane or crazy, because he had always bossed me around before . . ." (*She shifts back and forth in thinking his problem is psychiatric and in feeling it is normal behavior that could be accounted for in terms of their own experience.*) Mr. F. talked on through the night. Sometime in the morning, he "seemed to straighten out" and drove his wife to work. (*This behavior tends to balance out the preceding disturbed activities. She quickly returns to a normal referent.*)

At noon, Mr. F. walked into a store where his wife worked as a clerk. "I couldn't make any sense of what he was saying. He kept getting angry because I wouldn't talk to him. . . . Finally, the boss' wife told me to go home." En route, Mr. F. said his male organs were blown up and little seeds covered him. Mrs. F. denied seeing them and announced she planned to call his mother. "He began crying and I had to promise not to. I said, . . . 'Don't you think you should go to a psychiatrist?' and he said, 'No, there is nothing wrong with me.' . . . Then we came home, and I went to pay a bill . . ." (*Again she considers, but is not fully committed to, the idea that psychiatric help is needed.*)

Back at their apartment, Mr. F. talked of repairing his cab while Mrs. F. thought of returning to work and getting someone to call a doctor. Suddenly, he started chasing her around the apartment and growling like a lion. Mrs. F. screamed, Mr. F. ran out of the apartment, and Mrs. F. slammed and locked the door. "When he started roaring and growling, then I thought he was crazy. That wasn't a human sound. You couldn't say a thing to him . . ." Later, Mrs. F. learned that her husband went to a nearby church, created a scene, and was taken to the hospital by the police. (*Thoroughly threatened, she defines problem as psychiatric.*)

What occurred before these events which precipitated the hospitalization? Going back to their early married life, approximately three years before hospitalization, Mrs. F. told of her husband's irregular work habits and long-standing complaints of severe headaches. "When we were first married, he didn't work much and I didn't worry as long as we could pay the bills." Mrs. F. figured they were just married and wanted to be together a lot. (*Personal norms and expectations are built up.*)

At Thanksgiving, six months after marriage, Mr. F. "got sick and stopped working." During the war he contracted malaria, he explained, which always recurred at that time of year. "He wouldn't get out of bed or eat. . . . He thought he was constipated, and he had nightmares. . . . What I noticed most was his perspiring so much. He was crabby. You couldn't get him to go to a doctor. . . . I noticed he was nervous. He's always been a nervous person. . . . Any little thing that would go wrong would upset him—if I didn't get a drawer closed right. . . . His friends are nervous, too. . . . I came to the conclusion that maybe I was happy-go-lucky and everyone else was a bundle of nerves. . . . For a cab driver, he worked hard—most cab drivers loaf. When he felt good, he worked hard. He didn't work so hard when he didn't. (*She adapts to his behavior. The atypical is normalized as his type of personality and appropriate to his subculture.*)

As the months and years went by, Mrs. F. changed jobs frequently, but she worked more regularly than did her husband. He continued to work sporadically, get sick intermittently, appear "nervous and tense" and refrain from seeking medical care. Mrs. F. "couldn't say what was wrong." She had first one idea, then another, about his behavior. "I knew it wasn't right for him to be acting sick like he did." Then, "I was beginning to think he was getting lazy because there wasn't anything I could see." During one period, Mrs. F. surmised he was carrying on with another woman. "I was right on the verge of going, but he explained it wasn't anyone else." (*There is a building up of deviant behavior to a point near her tolerance limits. Her interpretations shift repeatedly.*)

About two and a half years before admission, Mrs. F. began talking to friends about her husband's actions and her lack of success in getting him to a doctor. "I got disgusted and said if he didn't go to a doctor, I would leave him. I got Bill (the owner of Mr. F.'s cab) to talk to him. . . . I begged, threatened, fussed . . ." After that, Mr. F. went to a VA doctor for one visit, overslept for his second appointment and never returned. He said the doctor told him nothing was wrong.

When Mr. F. was well and working, Mrs. F. "never stopped to think about it." "You live from day to day . . . When something isn't nice, I don't think about it. If you stop to think about things, you can worry yourself sick . . . He said he wished he could live in my world. He'd never seem to be able to put his thinking off the way I do . . ." (*Her mode of operating permits her to tolerate his behavior.*)

Concurrently, other situations confronted Mrs. F. Off and on, Mr. F. talked of a coming revolution as a result of which Negroes and Jews would take over the world. If Mrs. F. argued that she didn't believe it, Mr. F. called her "dumb" and "stupid." The best thing to do was to change the subject." Eighteen months before admission, Mr. F. began awakening his wife to tell of nightmares about wartime experiences, but she "didn't think about it." Three months later, he decided he wanted to do something besides drive a cab. He worked on an invention but discovered it was patented. Then, he began to write a book about his wartime experiences and science. "If you saw what he wrote, you couldn't see anything wrong with it. . . . He just wasn't making any money." Mrs. F. did think it was "silly" when Mr. F. went to talk to Einstein about his ideas and couldn't understand why he didn't talk to someone in town. Nevertheless, she accompanied him on the trip. *(With the further accumulation of deviant behavior, she became less and less able to tolerate it. The perceived seriousness of his condition is attenuated so long as she is able to find something acceptable or understandable in his behavior.)*

Three days before admission, Mr. F. stopped taking baths and changing clothes. Two nights before admission, he awakened his wife to tell her he had just figured out that the book he was writing had nothing to do with science or the world, only with himself. "He said he had been worrying about things for ten years and that writing a book solved what had been worrying him for ten years." Mrs. F. told him to burn his writings if they had nothing to do with science. It was the following morning that Mrs. F. first noticed her husband's behavior as "rather strange."

In the long prelude to Mr. F.'s hospitalization, one can see many of the difficulties which arise for the wife as the husband's behavior no longer conforms and as it strains the limits of the wife's expectations for him. At some stage the wife defines the situation as one requiring help, eventually psychiatric help. Our analysis is concerned primarily with the process of the wife's getting to this stage in interpreting and responding to the husband's behavior. In the preceding case are many reactions which appear as general trends in the data group. These trends can be systematized in terms of the following focal aspects of the process:

1. The wife's threshold for initially discerning a problem depends on the accumulation of various kinds of behavior which are not readily understandable or acceptable to her.

2. This accumulation forces upon the wife the necessity for examining and adjusting expectations for herself and her husband which permit her to account for his behavior.

3. The wife is in an "overlapping" situation, of problem–not problem or of normal–not normal. Her interpretations shift back and forth.

4. Adaptations to the atypical behavior of the husband occur. There is testing and waiting for additional cues in coming to any given interpretation, as in most problem solving. The wife mobilizes strong defenses against the hus-

band's deviant behavior. These defenses take form in such reactions as denying, attenuating, balancing and normalizing the husband's problems.

5. Eventually there is a threshold point at which the perception breaks, when the wife comes to the relatively stable conclusion that the problem is a psychiatric one and/or that she cannot alone cope with the husband's behavior. . . .

The Beginnings of the Wife's Concern

. . . In retrospect, the wives usually cannot pinpoint the time the husband's problem emerged. Neither can they clearly carve it out from the contexts of the husband's personality and family expectations. The subjective beginnings are seldom localized in a single strange or disturbing reaction on the husband's part but rather in the piling up of behavior and feelings. We have seen this process for Mrs. F. There is a similar accumulation for the majority of wives, although the time periods and the kinds of reported behavior vary. Thus, Mrs. Q. verbalizes the impact of a concentration of changes which occur within a period of a few weeks. Her explicit recognition of a problem comes when she adds up this array: her husband stays out late, doesn't eat or sleep, has obscene thoughts, argues with her, hits her, talks continuously, "cannot appreciate the beautiful scene," and "cannot appreciate me or the baby."

The problem behaviors reported by the wives . . . have occurred many times before. This is especially true where alcoholism, physical complaints or personality "weaknesses" enter the picture. The wives indicate how, earlier, they had assimilated these characteristics into their own expectations in a variety of ways: the characteristics were congruent with their image of their husbands, they fitted their differential standards for men and women (men being less able to stand up to troubles), they had social or environmental justifications, etc.

When and how behavior becomes defined as problematic appears to be a highly individual matter. In some instances, it is when the wife can no longer manage her husband (he will no longer respond to her usual prods); in others, when his behavior destroys the status quo (when her goals and living routines are disorganized); and, in still others, when she cannot explain his behavior. One can speculate that her level of tolerance for his behavior is a function of her specific personality needs and vulnerabilities, her personal and family value system and the social supports and prohibitions regarding the husband's symptomatic behavior.

Initial Interpretation of the Husband's Problem

Once the behavior is organized as a problem, it tends also to be interpreted as some particular kind of problem. More often than not, however, the husband's difficulties are not seen initially as manifestations of mental illness or even as emotional problems. . . .

Early interpretations often tend to be organized around physical diffi-culties (18% of cases) or "character" problems (27%). To a very marked degree, these orientations grow out of the wives' long-standing appraisals of their hus-bands as weak and ineffective or physically sick men. These wives describe their husbands as spoiled, lacking will-power, exaggerating little complaints and acting like babies. This is especially marked where alcoholism complicates the husband's symptomatology. For example, Mrs. Y., whose husband was chronically alcoholic, aggressive and threatening to her, "raving," and who "chewed his nails until they almost bled," interprets his difficulty thus: "He was just spoiled rotten. He never outgrew it. He told me when he was a child he could get his own way if he in-sisted, and he is still that way." This quotation is the prototype of many of its kind.

Some wives, on the other hand, locate the problem in the environment. They expect the husband to change as the environmental crisis subsides. Sev-eral wives, while enumerating difficulties and concluding that there is a prob-lem, in the same breath say it is really nothing to be concerned about.

Where the wives interpret the husband's difficulty as emotional in nature, they tend to be inconsistently "judgmental" and "understanding." The psycho-neurotics are more often perceived initially by their wives as having emotional problems or as being mentally ill than are the psychotics. This is true even though many more clinical signs (bizarre, confused, delusional, aggressive and disoriented behavior) are reported by the wives of the psychotics. . . .

Initial interpretations, whatever their context, are seldom held with great confidence by the wives. Many recall their early reactions to their husbands' be-haviors as full of puzzling confusion and uncertainty. Something is wrong, they know, but, in general, they stop short of a firm explanation. Thus, Mrs. M. re-ports, "He was kind of worried. He was kind of worried before, not exactly worried . . ." She thought of his many physical complaints; she "racked" her "brain" and told her husband, "Of course, he didn't feel good." Finally, he stayed home from work with "no special complaints, just blah," and she "began to realize it was more deeply seated."

Changing Perceptions of the Husband's Problem

. . . three relatively distinct patterns of successive redefinitions of the husband's problems are apparent. One sequence (slightly less than half the cases) is characterized by a progressive intensification; interpretations are altered in a definite direction—toward seeing the problem as mental illness. Mrs. O. illus-trates this progression. Initially, she thought her husband was "unsure of him-self." "He was worried, too, about getting old." These ideas moved to: "He'd drink to forget. . . . He just didn't have the confidence. . . . He'd forget little things. . . . He'd wear a suit weeks on end if I didn't take it away from him. . . . He'd say nasty things." Then, when Mr. O. seemed "so confused," "to forget all kinds of things . . . where he'd come from . . . to go to work," and made "nasty, cutting remarks all the time," she began to think in terms of a serious personality disturbance. "I did think he knew that something was wrong . . . that he was sick. He was never any different this last while and I couldn't stand it any more. . . . You don't know what a relief it was . . ." (when he was hospitalized). The husband's drinking, his failure to be tidy, his nastiness, etc., lose significance in their own right. They move from emphasis to relief and are recast as signs of "something deeper," some thing that brought "it" on.

Some wives whose interpretations move in the direction of seeing their husbands as mentally ill hold conceptions of mental illness and of personality that do not permit assigning the husband all aspects of the sick role. Frequently, they use the interpretation of mental illness as an angry epithet or as a threatening prediction for the husband. This is exemplified in such references as: "I told him he should have his head examined," "I called him a half-wit," "I told him if he's not careful, he'll be a mental case." To many of these wives, the hospital is regarded as the "end of the road."

Other wives showing this pattern of change hold conceptions of emotional disturbance which more easily permit them to assign to their husbands the role of patient as the signs of illness become more apparent. They do not as often regard hospitalization in a mental hospital as the "last step." Nevertheless, their feelings toward their husbands may contain components equally as angry and rejecting as those of the wives with the less sophisticated ideas regarding mental illness.

A somewhat different pattern of sequential changes in interpreting the husband's difficulties (about one-fifth of the cases) is to be found among wives who appear to cast around for situationally and momentarily adequate explanations. As the situation changes or as the husband's behavior changes, these wives find reasons or excuses but lack an underlying or synthesizing theory. Successive interpretations tend to bear little relation to one another. Situational factors tend to lead them to seeing their husbands as mentally ill. Immediate, serious and direct physical threats or the influence of others may be the deciding factor. For example, a friend or employer may insist that the husband see a psychiatrist, and the wife goes along with the decision.

A third pattern of successive redefinitions (slightly less than one-third of the cases) revolves around an orientation outside the framework of emotional problems or mental illness. In these cases, the wife's specific explanations change but pivot around a denial that the husband is mentally ill.

A few wives seem not to change their interpretations about their husband's difficulties. They maintain the same explanation throughout the development of his illness, some within the psychiatric framework, others rigidly outside that framework.

Despite the characteristic shifting in interpretations, in the group as a whole, there tend to be persisting underlying themes in the individual wife's perceptions that remain essentially unaltered. These themes are a function of her systems of thinking about normality and abnormality and about valued and devalued behavior.

The Process of Recognizing the Husband's Problem as Mental Illness

In the total situation confronting the wife, there are a number of factors, apparent in our data, which make it difficult for the wife to recognize and accept the husband's behavior in a mental-emotional-psychiatric framework. Many crosscurrents seem to influence the process.

The husband's behavior itself is a fluctuating stimulus. He is not worried and complaining all of the time. His delusions and hallucinations may not persist. His hostility toward the wife may be followed by warm attentiveness. She has, then, the problem of deciding whether his "strange" behavior is significant. The greater saliency of one or the other of his responses at any moment of time depends in some degree upon the behavior sequence which has occurred most recently.

The relationship between husband and wife also supplies a variety of images and contexts which can justify varied conclusions about the husband's current behavior. The wife is likely to adapt to behavior which occurs in their day-to-day relationships. Therefore, symptomatic reactions which are intensifications of long-standing response patterns become part of the fabric of life and are not easily disentangled as "symptomatic."

Communications between husband and wife regarding the husband's difficulties act sometimes to impede and sometimes to further the process of seeing the difficulties within a psychiatric framework. We have seen both kinds of influences in our data. Mr. and Mrs. F. were quite unable to communicate effectively about Mr. F.'s problems. On the one hand, he counters his wife's urging that he see a doctor with denials that anything is wrong. On the other hand, in his own way through his symptoms, he tries to communicate his problems, but she responds only to his verbalized statements, taking them at face value.

Mr. and Mrs. K. participate together quite differently, examining Mr. K.'s fears that he is being followed by the F.B.I., that their house has been wired and that he is going to be fired. His wife tentatively shares his suspicions. At the same time, they discuss the possibility of paranoid reactions.

The larger social context contributes, too, in the wife's perceptual tug of war. Others with whom she can compare her husband provide contrasts to his deviance, but others (Mr. F.'s nervous friends) also provide parallels to his problems. The "outsiders," seeing less of her husband, often discount the wife's alarm when she presses them for opinions. In other instances, the friend or employer, less adapted to or defended against the husband's symptoms, helps her to define his problem as psychiatric.

. . . Thus far, we have ignored the personally threatening aspects of recognizing mental illness in one's spouse and the defenses which are mobilized to meet this threat. It is assumed that it is threatening to the wife not only to realize that the husband is mentally ill but further to consider her own possible role in the development of the disorder, to give up modes of relating to her husband that they may have had satisfactions for her and to see a future as the wife of a mental patient. . . . One or more of the following defenses are manifested in three-fourths of our cases.

The most obvious form of defense in the wife's response is the tendency to *normalize* the husband's neurotic and psychotic symptoms. His behavior is explained, justified or made acceptable by seeing it also in herself or by assuring herself that the particular behavior occurs again and again among persons who are not ill. Illustrative of this reaction is the wife who reports her husband's hallucinations and assures herself that this is normal because she herself heard voices when she was in the menopause. Another wife responds to her husband's physical complaints, fears, worries, nightmares, and delusions with "A lot of normal people think there's something wrong when there isn't. I think men are that way; his father is that way."

When behavior cannot be normalized, it can be made to seem less severe or less important in a total picture than an outsider might see it. By finding some grounds for the behavior or something explainable about it, the wife achieves at least momentary *attenuation* of the seriousness of it. Thus, Mrs. F. is able to discount partly the strangeness of her husband's descriptions of the worms growing out of his grandfather's mustache when she recalls his watching the worms in the fish bowl. There may be attenuation, too, by seeing the behavior as "momentary" ("You could talk him out of his ideas.") or by rethinking the problem and seeing it in a different light.

By *balancing* acceptable with unacceptable behavior or "strange" with "normal" behavior, some wives can conclude that the husband is not seriously disturbed. Thus, it is very important to Mrs. R. that her husband kissed her good-bye before he left for the hospital. This response cancels out his hostile feelings toward her and the possibility that he is mentally ill. Similarly, Mrs. V. reasons that her husband cannot be "out of his mind" for he had reminded her of things she must not forget to do when he went to the hospital.

Defense sometimes amounts to a thorough-going *denial*. This takes the form of denying that the behavior perceived can be interpreted in an emotional or psychiatric framework. In some instances, the wife reports vividly on such behavior as repeated thoughts of suicide, efforts to harm her and the like and sums it up with "I thought it was just a whim." Other wives bend their efforts toward providing the implausibility of mental illness.

After the husband is hospitalized, it might be expected that these denials would decrease to a negligible level. This is not wholly the case, however. A breakdown of the wives' interpretations just following the husband's admission to the hospital shows that roughly a fifth still interpret their husband's behavior in another framework than that of a serious emotional problem or mental illness. Another fifth ambivalently and sporadically interpret the behavior as an emotional or mental problem. The remainder hold relatively stable interpretations within this framework.

After the husband has been hospitalized for some time, many wives reflect on their earlier tendencies to avoid a definition of mental illness. Such reactions are almost identically described by these wives: "I put it out of my mind—I didn't want to face it—anything but a mental illness." "Maybe I was aware of it. But you know you push things away from you and keep hoping." "Now you think maybe you should have known about it. Maybe you should have done more than you did and that worries me."

ADAPTATION FOUR
Producing Witchcraft*

Since witchcraft is, in a sense, a kind of imaginary deviation, it provides an extreme example of the extent to which deviance situations may be "created" by social definition and response. Here we find that persons have been treated as deviant, in fact often executed, not only with the possibility of false accusation of them personally but also typically in the absence of a specific rule-violating act on anyone's part. Such a situation, then, forces us to recognize that an actual "offense" is not always required for the social mechanisms that produce deviance outcomes to be set in motion. Under such conditions the number, characteristics, and social distribution of the "deviants" will depend largely on the nature and extent of the "control" effort and apparatus. Sociologist Elliott Currie has provided an excellent illustration of this point by comparing witchcraft in continental Europe and in England during the Renaissance (roughly the fifteenth to the seventeenth century). His analysis shows that significant differences between European and English witchcraft strongly reflected and perhaps even "resulted from" the social-control systems found in the two locales.

In continental Europe, a witchcraft-processing system that typified what Currie calls "repressive control" took shape. Although it had its origins in the unparalleled ecclesiastical-legal powers of the Holy Inquisition, even the secular court version that later emerged was largely free from any institutional restraints on its capacity to prosecute witches. This was true in part because the ordinary criminal courts on the Continent followed the "inquisitorial" model, rather than the "accusatorial" one with which we in the United States are more directly familiar. As Currie notes, under the inquisitorial approach, "accusation, detection, prosecution and judgment are all in the hands of the official control system." The trial is not so much a confrontation between accuser and accused, as "an attack by the judge and his staff upon the suspect, who carried with him a heavy presumption of guilt." Special features gave European witchcraft trials a steamroller quality: They were usually held in secret; prisoners did not often have adequate information about the charges against them or active legal assistance, and acquittal was virtually impossible. There was a tremendous pressure for confession, with a corresponding regular use of torture to obtain it.

As Currie points out, confession not only justified the penalty of execution, but it involved the denunciation of accomplices, "which assured a steady flow of accused witches into the courts." Furthermore, since confessions were

* *Source:* A Summary and interpretation of Elliott P. Currie, "Crimes Without Criminals: Witchcraft and Its Control in Renaissance Europe," *Law and Society Review,* 3 (August 1968), pp. 7–32. Direct quotations reproduced with permission.

made public, this "reinforced the legitimacy of the trials themselves and recreated in the public mind the reality of witchcraft itself. If people *said* they flew by night to dance with the devil, then surely there was evil in the land, and the authorities were more than justified in their zeal to root it out." The incentive for the controllers to do so lay largely in the court's power to confiscate the accused's property even in the absence of confession. What emerged under this combination of unrestrained power to persecute and pecuniary motive to do so, Currie describes as a witchcraft "industry." Processing witches became a profitable business: "Watchmen, executioners, torturers and others, as well as priests and judges, were paid high wages and generally lived well." In order to maintain a high level of profits, expansion of the "problem" was necessary. The control agents, in other words, had a strong "vested interest" in a high rate of purported deviance, and their active efforts to ensure this had a self-fulfilling quality: "Several hundred thousand witches were burned in continental Europe during the main period of activity, creating a picture of the tremendous extent of witchcraft in Europe. The large number of witches frightened the population and legitimized ever more stringent suppression. Thus, a cycle developed in which rigorous control brought about the appearance of high rates of deviance, which were the basis for more extreme control, which in turn sent the rates even higher, and so on." The nature of the control system also determined the typical social characteristics of witches. Since a major motive behind the control effort was property confiscation, many of the continental witches were relatively well-to-do property owners. It is significant too that, as Currie notes, "when torture and/or confiscation became from time to time unlawful, the number of witches decreased drastically or disappeared altogether."

The corresponding situation in England was very different, indeed. There, the absence of an Inquisition and the legal tradition of accusatorial trials (public trial by jury, with separation of prosecution and judge, adequate confrontation of accusers, and right of appeal) lent the witchcraft-processing system a quality of "restrained control." Legal safeguards precluded the use of torture, and confessions were rare. Special ordeallike evidentiary techniques such as "pricking, swimming, and watching" were employed, but in contrast to the even more coercive European approach, the English witch trial remained "an unsystematic and inefficient process." Highly significant was the fact that in England the practice of confiscating the property of accused witches did not develop. As a result, the English officials "had no continuous vested interest in the discovery and conviction of witches . . . they had neither the power nor the motive for large-scale persecution."

Under this restrained control system, no large-scale witchcraft industry emerged. Rather, witchcraft-prosecuting became a kind of haphazard "racket," in which a variety of witch-spotting entrepreneurs participated. This was a risky enterprise, since while they might earn fees from the court, they were also themselves open to charges of fraud or even witchcraft. At any rate, theirs was a small-scale, small-profit, private operation. The regular English court, because of its tradition of fair trials and its tightly controlled procedures, "could not have processed masses of presumed witches even had it had the power to initiate such prosecutions; and because of the absence of authority to confiscate witches' property, it had no interest in doing so even had it been able to."

The extent and distribution of witchcraft mirrored the limited scope of witchcraft-processing. In England, rates of witchcraft accusation were considerably lower than in Europe, and only small numbers of presumed witches were executed. Furthermore, since accusation was not linked with confiscation of property, there was no motive for acting against well-to-do persons. We see this factor reflected in the social distribution of the witches in England. Most of them were relatively powerless women, "already in disfavor with their neighbors. Household servants, poor tenants, and others of lower status predominated. Women who worked as midwives were especially singled out, particularly when it became necessary to explain stillbirths." As Currie goes on to point out, even the decline of witchcraft in the two locales was tied to differences in the control systems. On the Continent the decline occurred only in the face of curbs imposed on the court procedures; in England it resulted largely from a growing disbelief in witchcraft itself, which led courts to begin to treat it as unlikely or at least unprovable.

In his cautious interpretation of these findings, Currie is quick to admit that witchcraft is an extreme case, because it is "an *invented* form of deviance, whose definition lacks roots in concrete behavior." How concrete and potentially visible the alleged act is helps to determine how much latitude the control system itself has in shaping the deviance situation. As Currie states, it is more difficult to create murderers, "and especially difficult to create more murderers than there are victims." But granted that particular forms of perceived deviance may vary "in the degree to which they can be creatively imputed to people," some generalizations about the impacts of different sorts of control systems may be possible. Repressive control systems tend to create relatively high officially recorded rates of deviance. This is because control agents develop a vested interest in processing deviators and because such a system is likely to generate a complex organizational structure for that purpose. Because more restrained control systems do not usually entail such vested interests and organization and do not set in motion the self-confirming cycle in which increased enforcement provides its own justification, they are likely to produce low rates of deviance. As Currie comments, "Restrained systems may, and generally do, process *less* deviance than actually exists; rarely, however, can they successfully or consistently process *more*."

Some brief comments about these two adaptations may help to suggest in a preliminary way how certain critics of the labeling approach may have defined it too narrowly or misunderstood its basic thrust. At this stage in our discussion, extensive analysis of the Currie witchcraft study would take us too far afield, but a few of its major implications should be noted. For our purposes now, the general point that it underlines most forcefully is the importance of including a societal-level focus in a comprehensive and broadly construed labeling, societal-reactions, or definitional-processual approach. Critics of labeling analysis often have construed it as being totally concerned with narrow studies of the direct negative labeling of individuals. To the extent labeling-oriented research has in fact been preoccupied with the stigmatizing impact on a person of being identified and reacted to as a deviator (see Chapters 4 and 5), this narrow characterization of the approach does have some validity. At least in terms of the kinds of research they have most often undertaken, it could indeed be charged that some labeling analysts have not really done what they claimed to do, that is, study social *reactions*, as such (see Gibbs, 1966). To do so would be to focus not only on the stigmatized individuals, but also on how different groups and societies vary in their definitions and processing of deviance.

But, as Currie's essay suggests, the overall logic of a labeling perspective does point the researcher in this complementary direction even if the full potential for relevant comparative and historical analysis may not yet have been met (though see the important work by Erikson, 1966). In this connection, the very term "labeling" has probably contributed to the misunderstanding. It has taken on strong connotations of direct stigmatizing of individuals, whereas alternative formulations of the approach in terms of "definitions" or "societal reactions" suggest more readily the different levels on which the analysis of deviance must proceed. Currie's work also bears on another point of objection sometimes raised by the critics of labeling. They have charged that in emphasizing the reaction process, labeling analysts tend to ignore the deviating *act* itself. Isn't that, they ask, where all the trouble came from in the first place? After all, doesn't the offending act cause the reaction rather than vice versa, as the labeling outlook seems to suggest. As we are going to see in much of the material that follows, this argument glosses over the very important distinction between the occurrence of acts and their social characterization. But as the Currie article further implies, in an admittedly unusual type of situation, deviantizing *can* occur even when there has really been no deviating act at all. Here we see, in extreme form, how definitions can create deviance! More generally, as will be clear below, the definitions and reactions that help constitute deviance situations often tend to maintain a partial independence and a momentum of their own.

The article by Yarrow and her associates points up rather different aspects of a labeling approach, and allows us in yet another way to begin to assess some standard criticisms of the perspective. Here we have, in a sense, a depiction par excellence of how at least one kind of interaction process may be involved in producing deviance outcomes. We begin to get a feel for the labeling analyst's insistence on the dynamism, fluidity, and contingent nature of deviance-defining. But there are very different ways of thinking about the findings in this study. There are some perplexing questions we can ask about them, questions that may help us to see basic differences in outlook between labeling analysts and their critics.

We might ask ourselves, for example: At what point in the sequence depicted by Yarrow, *et al.,* can we say that "mental illness" was first present? Perhaps an even trickier question: *How* are we to determine this? Were the husbands mentally ill all along, even though the wives were unable or unwilling to recognize it? (This would, no doubt, be the most common interpretation; and it is the one toward which the authors in their use of "denial" and "normalization" concepts clearly lean.) There is, however, an alternative interpretation through which we recognize that in a sense we can only identify the emergence of "mental illness" (which is, after all, a *designation*) *through* the shifting reactions of the wives. Suppose the wives had *continued* to normalize the erratic behavior; would the husbands *then* have been "mentally ill"? By posing such issues, we can see that, in terms of concrete outcomes as opposed to abstractly stated "norms," it is what other people "make of" eccentric behavior that in specific situations determines how the individuals exhibiting it are characterized and dealt with.

Interestingly, the Yarrow study has been cited both in support of a labeling approach (Schur, 1971) and by at least one major critic in alleged refutation of the labeling perspective (Gove, 1970; Gove, 1975). How can this be, and what does it mean? The main argument advanced by Gove has been to the effect that people treated as mentally ill really *are* mentally ill. Criticizing an influential labeling formulation by Thomas Scheff (Scheff, 1966) in which stereotyped and casual processing of mental patients had been highlighted, Gove points to the mechanisms of denial and normalization as evidence that mental illness determinations are not casual or arbitrary. Such labeling, in Gove's view, only occurs when it is really necessary; the wives took action, he insists, *only* when the husband's behavior "became impossible to deal with." What this reasoning overlooks, however, is that we only know that the behavior had become "impossible to deal with" because of the action the wives took! To revert to our hypothetical alternative again, if the wives were to take no action, that is, if they were to continue to deal with the behavior, to "normalize" it, then, by definition, the very same behavior would *not* be "impossible to deal with."

Gove's interpretation reflects the common preoccupation with what were referred to earlier as *why* questions. He argues, in effect, that the individuals in question were reacted to *because* of their erratic behavior. Yet seeing this as an exclusive explanation ignores the varying types and degrees of reaction to any given behavior that *can* occur and the fact that the reaction that *does* occur must be included in any explanation of *how* (through what process) mental illness outcomes emerge. Gove and the labeling analysts are, in part, at least, really interested in two different things. Indeed, both can be "right." Even if we were to say that these particular husbands acted in ways that initially caused their wives' reactions, it would be equally true that *without* some such reactions, either by the wives or by other persons, the situations would have been very different. The processes of action, response, and counterresponse would not have proceeded to the same kind of outcome. Leaving aside the possibility that the wives simply and completely created their husbands' deviance (in these cases, an unreasonable conclusion), we nonetheless have to recognize that wives as well as husbands significantly participated in the interaction. It is Gove's apparent conviction that deviance is caused by the basic differentness of deviants that brings him to slight the wives' "contribution."

Differences in outlook of the sort just discussed and apparent disagreement regarding the key questions to be answered by a deviance theory underlie many of the disputes about labeling. Some of the dilemmas posed by the Yarrow and Currie studies will come to mind below, particularly when (in Chapter 4) we consider the controversy over "primary" and "secondary" deviation. Critics of the labeling outlook frequently argue that it understates the significance of primary deviation, and cannot really substantiate its claim that much deviation is secondary. (This is one way of describing Gove's viewpoint: He is intent on analyzing primary deviation and its causes.) Here again, as we will see, there are uncertainties or misunderstandings as to just what labeling analysis sets out to do, with the critics often faulting its practitioners for not "proving" what *they* (the critics) are interested to prove.

We will also be encountering other criticisms of the labeling perspective, including the argument that it fails to acknowledge the supposedly substantial consensus on norms and the claim that it is wedded to a moderate liberal reform stance that inhibits radical social change. These claims, too, will be subject to varying assessments, depending on the meaning and scope we give to the approach. When the broadened definitional-processual framework we are considering here is used, these criticisms lose much of their force. Under that expanded conception, labeling ideas become a major grounding for a comprehensive interpretive framework for analyzing deviance.

REFERENCES

Anderson, Nels
1923, 1961. *The Hobo.* Chicago: University of Chicago Press.

Becker, Howard S.
1963. *Outsiders.* New York: The Free Press.

Berger, Peter L. and Thomas Luckmann
1966. *The Social Construction of Reality*. New York: Doubleday & Comany, Inc.

Blumer, Herbert
1969. *Symbolic Interactionism*. Englewood Cliffs, N.J.: Prentice-Hall, Inc.

Bonger, W. A.
1916. *Criminality and Economic Conditions*. trans. by Horton. Boston: Little, Brown and Company.

Bottomore, T. D. and M. Rubel, eds.
1956. *Karl Marx: Selected Writings in Sociology and Social Philosophy*. London: Watts and Co.

Brownmiller, Susan
1976. *Against Our Will: Men, Women and Rape*. New York: Bantam Books, Inc.

Bruyn, Severyn
1966. *The Human Perspective in Sociology*. Englewood Cliffs, N.J.: Prentice-Hall, Inc.

Burgess, Ernest W.
1939, 1965. "Introduction" to Robert E. L. Faris and H. Warren Dunham, *Mental Disorders in Urban Areas*. Chicago: University of Chicago Press.

Carroll, Maurice
1976. "Times Square Cleanup: Breach of Civil Liberties?" The New York *Times,* November 15, p. 35.

Chambliss, William
1976. "Functional and Conflict Theories of Crime," in William J. Chambliss and Milton Mankoff, eds., *Whose Law? What Order?* New York: John Wiley & Sons, Inc. Pp. 1–28.

Chambliss, William and Robert Seidman
1971. *Law, Order, and Power*. Reading, Mass.: Addison-Wesley Publishing Co., Inc.

Chein, Isidor, *et al.*
1964. *The Road to H: Narcotics, Delinquency, and Social Policy*. New York: Basic Books, Inc.

Clinard, Marshall B.
1964. "The Theoretical Implications of Anomie and Deviant Behavior," in Marshall B. Clinard, ed., *Anomie and Deviant Behavior*. New York: The Free Press. Pp. 1–56.
1974. *Sociology of Deviant Behavior, 4th ed.* New York: Holt, Rinehart and Winston, Inc.

Clinard, Marshall B. and Richard Quinney, eds.
1973. *Criminal Behavior Systems, 2d. ed.* New York: Holt, Rinehart and Winston, Inc.

Cloward, Richard A. and Lloyd E. Ohlin
1960. *Delinquency and Opportunity*. Glencoe, Ill.: The Free Press.

Cohen, Albert K.
1955. *Delinquent Boys: The Culture of the Gang*. Glencoe, Ill.: The Free Press.

Connor, Walter D.
1972. *Deviance in Soviet Society*. New York: Columbia University Press.

Cressey, Donald R.

1962. "Role Theory, Differential Association, and Compulsive Crimes," in Arnold M. Rose, ed., *Human Behavior and Social Processes: An Interactionist Approach.* Boston: Houghton Mifflin Company. Pp. 443–467.

Dahrendorf, Ralf

1958. "Out of Utopia: Toward a Reconstruction of Sociological Analysis," *American Journal of Sociology,* 67(September), 115–127.

Davis, Nanette J.

1975. *Sociological Constructions of Deviance.* Dubuque, Iowa: William C. Brown Company.

de Beauvoir, Simone

1957. *The Second Sex.* trans. by Parshley. New York: Alfred A. Knopf, Inc.

Douglas, Jack D., ed.

1970a. *Deviance and Respectability.* New York: Basic Books, Inc.
1970b. *Understanding Everyday Life.* Chicago: Aldine Publishing Company.

Durkheim, Emile

1897, 1951. *Suicide.* trans. by Spaulding and Simpson. Glencoe, Ill.: The Free Press.

Erikson, Kai T.

1962. "Notes on the Sociology of Deviance," *Social Problems,* 9(Spring), 307–314.
1966. *Wayward Puritans,* New York: John Wiley & Sons, Inc.

Faris, Robert E. L. and H. Warren Dunham

1939, 1965. *Mental Disorders in Urban Areas.* Chicago: University of Chicago Press.

Fuller, Richard C. and Richard R. Myers

1941. "The Natural History of a Social Problem," *American Sociological Review,* 6(June), 320–328.

Geis, Gilbert

1967. "White Collar Crime: The Heavy Electrical Equipment Antitrust Cases of 1961," in Marshall B. Clinard and Richard Quinney, eds., *Criminal Behavior Systems.* New York: Holt, Rinehart and Winston, Inc., Pp. 139–151.

Gibbs, Jack P.

1966. "Conceptions of Deviant Behavior: The Old and the New," *Pacific Sociological Review,* 9(Spring), 9–14.

Glaser, Daniel

1956. "Criminality Theories and Behavioral Images," *American Journal of Sociology,* 56 (March), 433–444.

1960. "Differential Association and Criminological Prediction," *Social Problems,* 8(Summer), 6–14.

1971. *Social Deviance.* Chicago: Markham Publishing Company.

Gordon, David M.

1971. "Class and the Economics of Crime," *The Review of Radical Political Economics,* 3(Summer), 51–72; reprinted in Chambliss and Mankoff, eds., *op. cit.,* pp. 193–214.

Gordon, Robert A.
1967. "Issues in the Ecological Study of Delinquency," *American Sociological Review,* 32 (December), 927–944.

Gove, Walter R.
1970. "Societal Reaction as an Explanation of Mental Illness: An Evaluation," *American Sociological Review,* 35(October), 873–884.

1975. "Labelling and Mental Illness," in Walter R. Gove, ed., *The Labelling of Deviance.* New York: John Wiley & Sons, Inc. Pp. 35–81.

Hirshi, Travis
1969. *Causes of Delinquency.* Berkeley: University of California Press.

Horton, John
1966. "Order and Conflict Theories of Social Problems as Competing Ideologies," *American Journal of Sociology,* 71(May), 701–713.

James, Jennifer, *et al.*
1975. *The Politics of Prostitution.* Seattle: Social Research Associates.

Kitsuse, John I. and Malcolm Spector
1975. "Social Problems and Deviance: Some Parallel Issues," *Social Problems,* 22(June), 584–594.

Kobrin, Solomon
1951. "The Conflict of Values in Delinquency Areas," *American Sociological Review,* 16 (October), 653–661.

Krisberg, Barry
1975. *Crime and Privilege.* Englewood Cliffs, N.J.: Prentice-Hall, Inc.

Lemert, Edwin M.
1951. *Social Pathology.* New York: McGraw-Hill Book Company.
1967. *Human Deviance, Social Problems, and Social Control.* Englewood Cliffs, N.J.: Prentice-Hall, Inc.

Levine, Martin P.
1977. "Gay Ghetto: Urban Residential Patterns of Male Homosexuals," unpublished paper presented at the annual meeting of the American Sociological Association, Chicago, Ill.

Lindesmith, Alfred R. and John H. Gagnon
1964. "Anomie and Drug Addiction," in Clinard, ed., *op. cit.,* pp. 158–188.

Lofland, John
1969. *Deviance and Identity.* Englewood Cliffs, N.J.: Prentice-Hall, Inc.

Loney, Martin
1973. "Social Control in Cuba," in Ian Taylor and Laurie Taylor, eds., *Politics and Deviance.* Baltimore: Penguin Books, Inc. Pp. 42–60.

Matza, David
1964. *Delinquency and Drift.* New York: John Wiley & Sons, Inc.
1969. *Becoming Deviant.* Englewood Cliffs, N.J.: Prentice-Hall, Inc.

Merton, Robert K.
1938, 1949. "Social Structure and Anomie," *American Sociological Review*, 3(October), 672–682; reprinted in Robert K. Merton, *Social Theory and Social Structure*. Glencoe, Ill.: The Free Press. Pp. 125–149.
1949. *Social Theory and Social Structure*. Glencoe, Ill.: The Free Press.
1957. "Continuities in the Theory of Social Structure and Anomie," in *Social Theory and Social Structures, rev. ed*. Glencoe, Ill.: The Free Press. Pp. 161–194.
1976. "The Sociology of Social Problems," in Merton and Robert Nisbet, eds., *Contemporary Social Problems, 4th ed*. New York: Harcourt Brace Jovanovich. Pp. 5–43.

Miller, Walter P.
1958. "Lower-Class Culture as a Generating Milieu of Gang Delinquency," *Journal of Social Issues,* 14(Summer), 5–19.

Morris, Terence
1958. *The Criminal Area*. London: Routledge and Kegan Paul.

Orland, Leonard
1976. "Jail for Corporate Price Fixers?" The New York *Times,* December 12, Sec. 3, p. 16.

Park, Robert E.
1923, 1961. Editor's "Preface" to Nels Anderson, *The Hobo*. Chicago: University of Chicago Press.

Polsky, Ned
1967. *Hustlers, Beats, and Others*. Chicago: Aldine Publishing Company.

Quinney, Richard
1970. *The Social Reality of Crime*. Boston: Little, Brown and Company.
1974. *Critique of Legal Order*. Boston: Little, Brown and Company.
1977. *Class, State and Crime*. New York: David McKay Co., Inc.

Reiss, Albert J., Jr. and A. Lewis Rhodes
1964. "An Empirical Test of Differential Association Theory," *Journal of Research in Crime and Delinquency,* 1(January), 5–18.

Rose, Arnold M., ed.
1962. *Human Behavior and Social Processes*. Boston: Houghton Mifflin Company.

Rubington, Earl and Martin S. Weinberg
1971. *The Study of Social Problems: Five Perspectives*. New York: Oxford University Press.

Rusche, Georg and Otto Kirchheimer
1939. *Punishment and Social Structure*. New York: Columbia University Press.

Scheff, Thomas J.
1966. *Being Mentally Ill*. Chicago: Aldine Publishing Company.

Schlossman, Steven, and Stephanie Wallach
1978. "The Crime of Precocious Sexuality: Female Juvenile Delinquency in the Progressive Era," *Harvard Educational Review,* 48(Feb.), pp. 65–94.

Schneider, Liz
1973. "Discussion," in Kate Millett, *The Prostitution Papers*. New York: Avon Books.

Schur, Edwin M.

1969. *Our Criminal Society*. Englewood Cliffs, N.J.: Prentice-Hall, Inc.

1971. *Labeling Deviant Behavior*. New York: Harper & Row, Publishers.

1973. *Radical Nonintervention: Rethinking the Delinquency Problem*. Englewood Cliffs, N.J.: Prentice-Hall, Inc.

Scott, Robert A. and Jack D. Douglas, eds.

1972. *Theoretical and Perspectives on Deviance*. New York: Basic Books, Inc.

Shaw, Clifford R.

1930, 1966. *The Jack Roller: A Delinquent Boy's Own Story*. Chicago: University of Chicago Press.

Shaw, Clifford R. and Henry D. McKay

1942, 1969. *Juvenile Delinquency and Urban Areas, rev. ed.* Chicago: University of Chicago Press.

Short, James F., Jr.

1960. "Differential Association as a Hypothesis: Problems of Empirical Testing," *Social Problems,* 8(Summer), 14–25.

Snyder, Charles R.

1964. "Inebriety, Alcoholism, and Anomie," in Clinard, ed., *op. cit.,* pp. 189–212.

Smith, Richard Austin

1961. "The Incredible Electrical Conspiracy," *Fortune,* April 1961; reprinted in Marvin Wolfgang, *et al.,* eds., *The Sociology of Crime and Delinquency, 2d. ed.* 1970. New York: John Wiley & Sons, Inc. Pp. 357–372.

Spector, Malcolm and John I. Kitsuse

1977. *Constructing Social Problems*. Menlo Park, Calif.: Cummings.

Spitzer, Steven

1975. "Toward a Marxian Theory of Deviance," *Social Problems,* 22(June), 638–651.

Strauss, Anselm L.

1969. *Mirrors and Masks*. San Francisco: The Sociology Press.

Suchar, Charles S.

1978. *Social Deviance: Perspectives and Prospects*. New York: Holt, Rinehart and Winston.

Sutherland, Edwin H.

1937, 1956. *The Professional Thief—By a Professional Thief.* ann. and ed. by Edwin H. Sutherland. Chicago: University of Chicago Press.

1942, 1973. "Development of the Theory," in Karl Schuessler, ed., *Edwin H. Sutherland on Analyzing Crime*. Chicago: University of Chicago Press. Pp. 13–29.

1947, 1973. "A Statement of the Theory," in Schuessler, *op. cit.,* pp. 7–12.

1949, 1961. *White Collar Crime*. New York: Holt, Rinehart and Winston, Inc.

Suttles, Gerald D.

1968. *The Social Order of the Slum*. Chicago: University of Chicago Press.

Tannenbaum, Frank

1938. *Crime and the Community*. Boston: Ginn & Company.

Tappan, Paul W.
1947. "Who is the Criminal?" *American Sociological Review,* 12(February), 96–102.

Taylor, Ian, Paul Walton, and Jock Young
1974. *The New Criminology: For a Social Theory of Deviance.* New York: Harper & Row, Publishers.

Thrasher, Frederic M.
1927. *The Gang.* Chicago: University of Chicago Press.

Turk, Austin T.
1969. *Criminality and Legal Order.* Chicago: Rand McNally & Company.

Turner, Roy, ed.
1974. *Ethnomethodology.* Baltimore: Penguin Books, Inc.

Vold, George B.
1958. *Theoretical Criminology.* New York: Oxford University Press.

Weinberg, Martin S. and Colin J. Williams
1975. *Male Homosexuals: Their Problems and Adaptations.* New York: Penguin Books, Inc.

Whyte, William Foote
1943a. "A Slum Sex Code," *American Journal of Sociology,* 49(July), 24–31.
1943b. *Street Corner Society.* Chicago: University of Chicago Press.

Wilson, Thomas P.
1970. "Conceptions of Interaction and Forms of Sociological Explanation," *American Sociological Review,* 35(June), 697–710.

Winslow, Robert W.
1970. *Society in Transition: A Social Approach to Deviancy.* New York: The Free Press.

REVIEW OF KEY TERMS

anomie. A term meaning "normlessness" that was used by Durkheim in his work *Suicide* and was later developed by Merton to describe the dysjunction between culturally prescribed (monetary-success) goals and "institutionalized means" of achieving same.

ascribed status. Traditionally a social position into which one is cast by birth and which is unchangeable, such as one's sex, race, and so on. In deviance theory ("labeling" and other societal-reactions approaches), it refers to the notion that persons defined as deviant are subject to characterizations, prescriptions, and limitations "beyond their control" or, in other words, that deviance is an imposed status and role that cannot easily be discarded or disavowed.

control theory. An approach to delinquency analysis that assumes delinquent behavior to be common and seeks to explain why some youth do *not* engage in it by focusing on bonds to conventional society.

cultural transmission. The concept of the passing along of a deviant "tradition" from one generation to another. A major theme in the Chicago ecological studies, it is an important grounding of subculture analysis and also was developed by Sutherland in his differential association theory.

dialectical processes. These are unfolding dynamic processes of change that involve contradiction of opposites and lead to the eventual resolution of same. A tradition in philosophical-historical analysis developed by Hegel and Marx (using concepts of thesis, antithesis, and synthesis), they have been emphasized in deviance writings of neo-Marxist and "critical" theorists, some of whom foresee eventual resolution of contradictions that produce deviance in capitalist societies.

differential association. Sutherland's thesis that a person becomes criminal because of an "excess of definitions" favorable to law-violation over those favorable to law-abidingness. It is a concept that was intended as a general statement of the learning process involved in all kinds of criminality and later broadened, beyond the focus on direct associations, by Glaser in terms of **differential identification.** According to the structural (societal vantage point) counterpart to Sutherland's processual thesis about definitions—**differential group (or social) organization**—groups and societies are seen to be "organized" around definitions favorable and/or unfavorable to crime, the imbalance of same being used to explain crime *rates*.

drift. Matza's concept, developed in his critique of delinquency subculture theories, of a less fixed and deterministic relation between youths and delinquency-encouraging patterns and forces. It stresses the partial and changing nature of commitment to deviant roles and activity.

gradient tendency. A general finding in Chicago ecological research of decreasing rates of officially-identified deviance as one went out from the center of the city. It is an outgrowth of the "concentric zone" theory.

labeling orientation. A perspective that treats deviance as emerging through processes of social definition and reaction. Its proponents usually place heavy emphasis on the ways in which direct negative labeling stigmatizes perceived offenders, but in its broader dimensions the approach also directs attention to the social groundings and creation (as well as application) of rules—including processes of collective definition at the societal level. Other terms used to characterize this general orientation have included: interactionist, societal reactions, social definitions, social constructionist, and processual.

modes of individual adaptation. In Merton's typology, these are the different ways in which individuals might adapt to the success goals-means dysjunction. Merton's "types" were: conformity, innovation, ritualism, retreatism, and rebellion. In later subculture formulations, especially that of Cohen, the focus shifted somewhat to modes of *collective* adaptation.

secondary deviation. In Lemert's writings, which were influential in the development of the "labeling orientation," those aspects of an individual's behavior and self-conceptions that can be attributed to the social reactions to the initial, primary rule-breaking. In a broadened societal reactions perspective, the notion can be used also to refer to additional nonindividual aspects of secondary expansion of deviance situations.

self-fulfilling prophecy. A process by which even false beliefs, if *acted* upon, can have self-confirming consequences. It is a concept developed by Merton (drawing on W. I.

Thomas) that is central to the reactions-definitions focus in deviance analysis, including the labeling approach.

social disorganization. A theme fostered by the Chicago studies which is now partly discredited or modified. Certain neighborhoods were viewed as "disorganized," with conflicting values that helped produce deviation. The theme was later reformulated (as in Sutherland's writings) in terms of "differential organization."

Summary Overview of Five Major Orientations

ORIENTATION	OBJECTS OF EXPLANATION	CENTRAL THEMES	MAJOR GROUNDS ON WHICH CRITICIZED	SIGNIFICANT CONTRIBUTIONS (INCLUDING METHODS)
1. The Chicago Ecological Studies	area rate variations; neighborhood traditions; lives of individuals (case studies, personal documents)	"natural areas"; cultural transmission; social disorganization	biological analogies; relied on official statistics; neglected patterns of social reaction; assumed "constraint"; adopted social version of "pathology"	employed direct field-work methods; instituted the use of personal documents (actors' subjective meanings); examined area concentrations of deviance; developed cultural transmission theme; link to intergroup conflict analysis; link to subculture theories
2. Differential Association	processes through which persons "learn" to deviate; categoric rate variations	"association" (interaction); "definitions"; differential group organization	difficult to operationalize; uneven applicability; assumed "constraint"	focused on processes and definitions; developed concept of differential group organization; link to role analysis
3. The Functionalist tradition				
a. General Functional Analysis	specific patterns of deviance functions (for the system) of identifying and reacting to deviance	latent functions; links to approved patterns and values; boundary-maintenance	pathology implications ("functional" and "dysfunctional"); tendency toward static and conservative bias	recognized "irony" of good producing bad; rejected individual pathology; boundary-maintenance (a link to societal reactions focus)
b. Anomie and Subculture Theory	categoric rate variations (lower-class concentration); content of deviant subcultures	dysjunction between goals and means; structured strain; status problems; modes of adaptation (individual and collective)	relied on official statistics (assumed lower-class concentration); neglected role of social reaction; assumed "constraint" even if social rather than biological	highlighted role of social class system in producing deviance; focused on collective adaptations; led to less narrowly positivistic conceptions

ORIENTATION	OBJECTS OF EXPLANATION	CENTRAL THEMES	MAJOR GROUNDS ON WHICH CRITICIZED	SIGNIFICANT CONTRIBUTIONS (INCLUDING METHODS)
4. Conflict Theory				
a. "Traditional" Conflict Theory	dominance of certain arrangements and ideas dynamics of conflict and change	interests (individual and collective) power and balance of power power resources negotiation social change	neglects elements of stability understates degree of "normative" consensus	highlighted historical/comparative/political aspects of deviance focused on interests (especially economic ones)
b. "Radical" Conflict Theory	same as above	exploitation dialectical processes contradictions eventual eradication of crime and deviance	unwarranted ("utopian") projections	renewed focus on systemic sources (dominant institutional groundings) of deviance questioned separation of theory and action
5. Labeling Analysis	who gets labeled "deviant" and how collective definitions of deviance consequences of deviance-defining (societal and individual) nature of defining-reacting processes	characterizations of behavior (and individuals) self-fulfilling prophecies stigma retrospective interpretation primary and secondary deviation	overly relativistic neglects role of "norms" inadequate concern with primary deviation difficult to operationalize weak supporting "evidence"	emphasizes reciprocal relation between "deviance" and "control" potential for multiple levels (and focal points) in deviance analysis highlights struggle over competing "definitions" (potentially) encourages both processual and structural analysis incorporates diversity, conflict, change, and "social construction" themes underlines distinction between studying occurrence of behavior and characterizations of behavior

PROJECT 3
Drawing on Diverse Traditions

Introductory Comment

There is a strong tendency to think of the various deviance theories in all-or-nothing terms. In this view, one wishes to determine which is the "right" theory, and, in addition, one anticipates that it will explain all types and aspects of deviance. Sociologists who approach deviance analysis in this way may be inclined, once they have settled on a theory, to dismiss out of hand the ideas and concepts developed in all the other theoretical traditions. This reflects a largely commendable desire to "advance" theorizing and to have and use one cohesive and exhaustive set of concepts that can be tested, retested, and, if validated, widely applied. Yet, as suggested above, different kinds of questions about deviance situations may call for different modes of inquiry and, hence, different orienting concepts. Furthermore, the usefulness of a particular concept does not always rest on the user's acceptance of the overall tradition of which it is a part. Thus, one does not have to commit oneself to an anomie theory in order to find the concept of "subculture" of value, or to wholeheartedly embrace labeling analysis in order to make some use of the notion of self-fulfilling prophecy.

It is important to recognize also that to the extent the concepts do prove applicable, they should help us understand nondeviance as well as deviance. Actually, as emphasized in this book, there are no clear-cut categories of deviance and nondeviance, only situations varying in degrees of deviantness, and those often depending on the point from which one views the behavior. But if all behaviors and individuals are potentially subject to deviantizing, we do know that, overall, some behaviors and conditions are treated much more often in this way than are others. Theories and concepts should help us to understand the degrees of deviantness that potentially problematic behaviors evoke, including the ways in which some situations with apparently strong "deviantness potential" do *not* develop much, if at all, in that direction.

Assignment

COLUMN A	COLUMN B
fraudulent advertising	(3) subculture
pornography	(4) economic interests
violating auto speed limits	(2) differential association
adultery	(4) domination
cheating in college	(1) cultural transmission
stuttering	(3) boundary-maintenance

male (homosexual) prostitution	(5) self-fulfilling prophecy
commercial spying	(3) latent functions
wife-beating	(2) differential group organization
cigarette smuggling	(5) secondary deviation

In column A are listed ten kinds of behavior that vary considerably in potential and actual (current, overall) deviantness in present-day American society. In column B are listed ten major concepts drawn from the various theoretical traditions preceded by numbers in parentheses which identify the traditions as presented in the Summary Overview of Five Major Orientations (preceding Project 3).

Select one topic from Column A. Go to the library and, insofar as possible (drawing on texts, specific studies, news and magazine articles, and any other relevant material you find), read up on the topic. Then, *select any three concepts from Column B* (drawn from *at least two* of the general traditions) that strike you as relevant to some aspects of that topic. State as fully as possible how each of these concepts might help you to understand some features of the problem situation you selected and also *indicate* in what *specific ways the concepts could be put to use* in the course of further research and analysis of the topic.

(NOTE: Once individual students have done the preliminary library research, the remainder of the exercise could be carried out in a number of different ways. Class discussion sessions could be organized around sets of student reports, with each meeting centering either around several different substantive applications of particular concepts, or around alternative concepts for analyzing a given deviance situation. If an out-of-class procedure is preferred, students could prepare written papers developing their own analyses.)

Guidelines

In thinking about ways in which the concepts you have selected will prove useful, it may help to have in mind the following general suggestions:

1. Allow yourself free reign to think in the broadest possible terms about the facets and dimensions of the behavior or situation you have chosen. For example, if you explore in a very broad way its interconnections with approved patterns and values or its economic aspects and ramifications, this may help you to recognize ways in which particular concepts help to advance your understanding of the problem (in these examples, perhaps such concepts as "latent functions" and "economic interests").

2. Do not allow your analysis to become hamstrung by a concern with the issue of which of the three concepts you have selected is the *most* useful. The purpose of the exercise is definitely not to compare concepts in terms of their relative explanatory power. Rather it is to determine whether each may

be helpful in its own ways in considering different aspects of the same problem or situation.

3. Accordingly, you should at least leave open the possibility that the concepts will work in complementary ways. It can happen, of course, that two of your concepts will seem to be leading your analysis in contradictory directions. If that happens, carefully think through whether the contradiction is inevitable and whether it is a complete or only a partial contradiction. If the contradiction does seem clear, think a bit about how one might try to reconcile it. For example, would you need to abandon one of the concepts completely or could you simply limit its use in a way that would render the contradiction less troublesome?

4. Keep in mind that you are considering the concepts as explanatory tools in their own right; you needn't, as noted earlier, adopt the entire theoretical framework or tradition with which any concept you use is typically associated. (This may help in removing possible contradictions, since it may be *other* aspects or assumptions in a given tradition that may be inconsistent with the analysis you are developing.)

5. It will be helpful, along with a very broad consideration of aspects and dimensions of the problem, to think a bit about how the concepts would be used more specifically in further research on the subject. What kinds of research methods (e.g., historical-comparative, attitude surveys, direct observation, etc.) would use of the concept lead you to in this instance? What general problems might you encounter in your efforts to "test" the relevance of the concept to the subject matter you are exploring?

6. Be sure to adopt a comprehensive and flexible outlook regarding what it is about the situation or problem that you want to use the concepts to explain. In particular, you should not consider yourself limited to "causes" of the behavior seen in any narrow sense. You may be interested in why the behavior occurs in the first place. But a concept may also be useful in helping you to understand the degree of deviantness typically attaching to it, specific patterns of social reaction to it or policy on it, what happens to the individuals reacted to in those ways, or other varied dimensions of the overall problem situation.

Implications

It should be apparent that *not* every concept will prove equally useful or even, necessarily, at all useful in the exploration of a given problem. To some extent, then, the success of the exercise will depend on your good sense in choosing potentially relevant concepts to work with. On the other hand, one of the main values of this project may indeed be to help one develop that kind of good sense in assessing concepts for possible use.

Overall, one should come away from this exercise with a respect for the potential usefulness of *diverse* theoretical traditions. The concepts provided for selection here all represent important ideas with some persisting relevance in interpreting deviance. Furthermore, each of them has a usefulness that is *general*, that is, a helpfulness in exploring a good many deviance problem situations; they are *not* problem-specific concepts, the relevance of which is closely tied to very limited domains of subject matter. Finally, they will usually work in either of two directions, helping us to see why some situations involve a lot of deviantness, while at the same time providing clues as to why other situations do not.

PART
2

THE MAKING
OF
"DEVIANTS"

PROLOGUE 4

*There tends to grow up about a status, in addition to its
specifically determining traits, a complex of auxiliary characteristics which come to be expected of its incumbents.*
　　—Everett C. Hughes, "Dilemmas and Contradictions
　　　　of Status"

*Self-criticism is essentially social criticism, and behavior
controlled by self-criticism is essentially behavior controlled
socially.*
　　—George H. Mead, *Mind, Self and Society*

The main concern will be with the moral *aspects of career
—that is, the regular sequence of changes that career entails in the person's self and in his framework of imagery
for judging himself and others.*
　　—Erving Goffman, *Asylums*

How we interpret and study socially problematic situations will inevitably reflect
our general perspectives on the social world. The modern sociology of deviance
has been strongly influenced by a variety of broad trends in social theory and
research methodology. Among the most powerful of these influences recently
have been the renewal of interest in an interactionist social psychology, the associated penchant for intense observational studies, and the popularity of theories
of knowledge and of science itself that have emphasized their problematic nature.
In deviance studies, such influences have been felt in a number of specific ways.
Deviance is now widely seen as problematic and not taken simply as "a given."
Accordingly, the focus in research has shifted from violations of abstract or stated
norms to the interaction processes through which such norms emerge and are
applied. Increasingly, researchers are drawn to direct observational studies "in
the field." As they evince a renewed attention to "the subjective meanings of
action," the situation of the perceived deviator becomes a central concern. More
and more sociologists are asking: What do deviance situations "look like" from
the standpoint of the people embroiled in them? What does deviance-defining
characteristically do to those people?

In exploring such issues, the importance of processual or sequential modes
of interpretation and analysis has come to the fore. This is why the concept of

"career" is so often used in contemporary writings on deviance. Although originally used in the sociology of occupations, which was initially centered around research and theorizing at the University of Chicago, the term has come to have a much broader meaning and application. When Goffman refers to the "moral career of the mental patient," obviously he does not have in mind what we usually think of as occupational "advancement." Rather, he sees "career" as referring to "such changes over time as are basic and common to the members of a social category." In Goffman's own work and in much recent interpretation of deviance, these changes are seen as heavily influenced by the reactions of others. Deviant "careers" are unpredictable precisely bcause we can never fully know in advance "what other people will do." This is what Goffman means when he states further that mental patients "distinctively suffer not from mental illness, but from contingencies."

Though individual outcomes are not fully predictable, there are characteristically at work in deviance-defining certain "basic and common" processes. (See especially Focal Point Two, Sec. B(1) in The Paradigm in the Appendix.) It is to these central mechanisms, the underlying processual core in deviance situations, that we now turn.

CH.4
ACQUIRING DEVIANTNESS

INTRODUCTION

The emergence of deviance outcomes can be examined on several levels: that of the individual who is treated as a deviator, that of deviance-processing organizations, and that of society at large. In actuality, the mechanisms at work on these different levels often are closely interrelated, sometimes simultaneous in their operation, and they produce cumulative or composite effects on the individuals caught up in them and on other facets of deviance situations. For purposes of convenience in organizing this book, we will examine the different levels separately. In this chapter and the next, we are going to explore these processes from the standpoint of the individuals who are subject to deviantizing definitions and reactions. Then, in subsequent chapters, we will turn to the broader dimensions of deviance situations.

A useful starting point is the distinction, emphasized earlier, between the occurrence of acts or displaying of conditions and their social characterization. This very important distinction is often glossed over in discussions of how people "get to be deviant." As we have seen, this happens because of the tendency to treat deviance as a given. Yet once we recognize that the term "deviance" in fact refers to a kind of meaning-attribution, a kind of "social construction" process, then it becomes clear that one can never "become a deviant" without certain kinds of definitions and reactions having at some point taken place. Acquiring deviantness, in other words, always *requires* that one's behavior or condition will have been viewed and treated in certain deviantizing ways. In that sense, at least some of the ongoing debate about the role of societal reaction arises from failure to see a crucial point: *All* the deviantness is "caused by" or "produced through" definition and reaction processes.

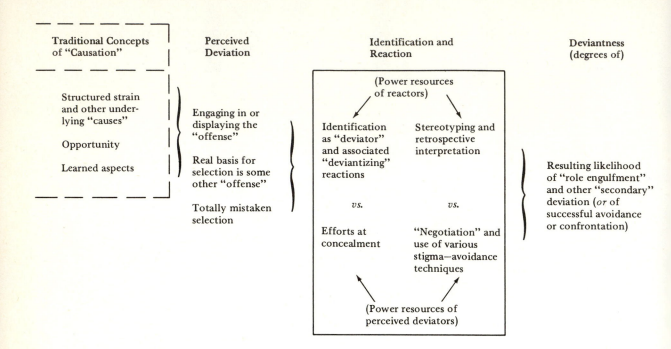

Figure 4.1. Acquiring deviantness.

Figure 4.1 roughly depicts the major components of the process through which individuals acquire deviantness. Note that the segment in the upper left-hand corner (set off in broken lines) represents the limited interests of most "traditional" approaches to the causes of deviance. In those approaches the distinction between acts or conditions, and the deviantness associated with them, is simply not made. Theorists using these approaches seek only to explain why individuals engage in the acts, and they do not see the attachment of deviantness to the acts or to the individuals as being in any way problematic. They are little, or not at all, concerned with the selection and reaction processes shown at the right of the broken lines, and, as the figure also shows, they tend to assume that those selected are in fact actual "offenders."

It should be realized that not all relevant processes and factors are represented in this chart. Readers should assume the frequent background operation of "collective definitions"—broad societal-level characterizations of *types* of behavior or conditions. Similarly, there is no direct depiction of "social control agencies," but it should be understood that in many situations they are crucially involved in the selection of and reaction to perceived deviators. In this chapter, our main focus will be on the likelihood that selection of and reaction to supposed offenders may have stigmatizing and deviance-amplifying consequences. We will primarily be considering the operation of mechanisms depicted in the top half of the "box" in the middle of the chart. But as the versus notations indicate, persons who are or could be reacted to as deviators usually try to combat or avoid those reactions in various ways. They try to keep from being labeled or to neutralize the stigmatizing impact of negative labeling. These stigma-avoidance efforts will be the chief focus in Chapter 5. Again, the reader should know that such separation is only for the sake of convenience. In fact, labeling efforts and avoidance efforts are not totally separable entities; rather, there is a continuous dynamic interplay between these opposing forces. As Figure 4.1 shows, the relative likelihood of acquiring deviantness (i.e., in what degree this occurs) will depend on the outcome of such a struggle. As will also become clear below, an important determinant of this outcome will be the relative power resources of the "reactors" and the perceived deviators.

DEVIATION

The Range of Perceived Deviations

It has been strongly emphasized in this text that any behavior or condition can be deviantized. As we have seen, the only real limitations on the "content" of what can be reacted to in this way have to do with the reactors' definitions, expectations, and moral "boundaries." Anything that is strongly felt to depart from the dominant expectations or to exceed the prevailing boundaries of acceptability can trigger the reaction processes through which deviantness is acquired. Furthermore, it is not always the case that we can state with assurance beforehand the precise substance of these expectations and boundaries. In a sense, we can only know which eccentric behavior exceeds the limits of acceptability and will be viewed as "disturbance," or which use of chemicals constitutes drug "abuse," by looking at the outcomes—by seeing what have been the actual objects of deviance-defining reactions. The boundaries, then, are "located" or at least reaffirmed in the very process of being "used." At first glance, this seems to be somewhat less true when we have established normative guides—as in the case of enacted criminal statutes, regarding some of which there is considerable public consensus. Yet, even here, we can only establish by studying "the law in action" (how these statutes are actually administered) what the "operative" boundaries really are.

If the potential objects of deviantizing are virtually unlimited, the substantive variability and range in *actual* deviance-defining, even within a given group or society, are themselves striking. Assignments of deviantness may be directed toward acts, omissions, acquired conditions, beliefs, even chosen and basic "life orientations." We are accustomed to thinking almost exclusively in terms of deviating acts, yet if we really wish to explore in a comprehensive way the acquiring of deviantness as a distinctive quality of meanings, it soon becomes clear that a broader focus is necessary. At least theoretically, as the witchcraft article showed, these defining-reacting processes may be set in motion without having been "preceded" by *any* special act *or* condition, though, as we will see below, presumably there must be some identifiable impetus that helps to account for such a development.

Failure to act may not be the most common basis for deviantizing, but quite a few examples do come to mind. In our system of criminal law, it is rather unusual for an omission to constitute an offense. There are, however, and perhaps increasingly, exceptions to this principle. Failure of manufacturers to meet safety or environmental protection standards, failure of an individual to relinquish a telephone "party line" in the event of an emergency, and failure of a soldier to obey a lawful order would all fall into this category of "offense by omission." Turning to a rather different area, quite a few of the grounds for diagnosing mental illness involve failure or perceived inability to act. Psychiatrists employ such a criterion when they speak of a person's "leaving the field;" lay usage incorporates recognition of it, too, as when we refer to someone being "out of it." Various obsessions, phobias, and depressions seem to involve this element of inaction, and, of course, at an extreme we find the immobility characteristic of certain diagnosed schizophrenics. In yet another substantive area, a good example of the deviantness potential in failing to act is one cited earlier: the likelihood that a female rape victim may herself be treated as the deviator if she is perceived as not having resisted adequately.

Deviance by omission is perhaps one way of interpreting at least some of the deviantness-imputation encountered by persons who are physically "disabled" or mentally "deficient." As the words in quotation marks suggest, the perception of these individuals by others is largely organized around their alleged incapacity to act—in "normal," fully acceptable ways. This point comes across most strongly in the case of the blind, whose "offense," after all, is simply "failure to see." The significance of that which the handicapped person does *not* or cannot have or do is further indicated in Fred Davis's depiction of the initial identity problems of the previously nonhandicapped child who contracts polio:

> His attempts, if any, to be accepted by "normals" as "normal," are doomed to failure and frustration: not only do most "normals" find it difficult to include the handicapped person fully in their own category of being, but he himself, in that he shares the "normal" standards of personal evaluation, will in a sense support their rejection of him. For the fact remains that, try as he may to hide or overdook it, he is at a distinct disadvantage with respect to several important values emphasized in our society: e.g., physical attractiveness; wholeness and symmetry of body parts; athletic prowess; and various physiognomic attributes felt to be prerequisite for a pleasant and engaging personality (Davis, 1963, p. 138).

Whatever specific hypothesis we choose to make about the basis for deviantness-imputations directed toward the physically disabled, there is little doubt that such imputations do exist and are deeply felt. Robert Scott's succinct statement regarding stigmatization of the blind points this up with force and clarity:

Blindness is also a condition that stigmatizes. The social identity of a man [or woman, of course], indeed his whole personality, is spoiled when he is blinded. That he is regarded as a different and lesser person than others is sharply brought home to him whenever he has dealings with the sighted. A major component in the experience of being a blind man is defending the self from imputations of moral, psychological, and social inferiority. For some this defense succeeds and for others it fails, but for all blind men it is another fact of life (Scott, 1969, p. 118).

In the next chapter we will be considering at some length this "defense" aspect—efforts by perceived deviators, including physically disabled persons, to avoid, divert, or reduce personal and social stigma. For present purposes, the point of importance is simply that physical conditions or "handicaps" represent one major type of perceived deviation.

This assertion raises an interesting issue that is often discussed in writings about deviance—the issue of "responsibility." Certain phenomenologically oriented sociologists have considered this element a key to the very defining of deviance. Jack Douglas, for example, has insisted that the fundamental problem in deviance studies is "that of determining the conditions of responsibility: under what conditions is an individual considered by members of our society to be (morally) responsible or (morally) unresponsible for a given event?" (Douglas, 1970, p. 12). Similarly, Peter McHugh has stated: "A deviant act is an act that members deem 'might not have been," or 'might have been otherwise;' second, it is an act the agent of which is deemed to 'know what he's doing' " (McHugh, 1970, p. 61). In this conception, blameworthiness becomes the essence of deviance. If a condition or act is unavoidable or beyond the actor's control, or occurs without real awareness and intent, then presumably it is not "deviant." Under such formulations, which seem again to adopt a present-or-absent approach to deviance rather than a degree of deviantness approach, physical and mental disabilities would appear to fall into the "nondeviance" category.

A more moderate and, to this writer, more meaningful formulation has been developed by Eliot Freidson, who acknowledges that responsibility is a "critical dimension" in deviance-defining but is unwilling to rest a definition of deviance on that dimension alone:

. . . the simple moral dichotomy of responsibility does not allow for the halo of moral evaluation that in fact surrounds many types of behavior for which, theoretically, people are not held responsible, but which in some way damage their identities. Some diseases, such as syphilis, leprosy, and even tuberculosis, are surrounded with loathing even though they are all "merely" infections. And many forms of organic dysfunction or maldevelopment for which the sufferer is not held responsible occasion responses of fear or disgust—epilepsy, dwarfism, and disfigurement, for example (Freidson, 1965, p. 76).

Going on to consider the possible combined bearing on outcomes of prognosis and imputed responsibility, Freidson presents a suggestive typology of deviance situations, reproduced here in Table 4.1. Even if this effort may involve some straining to categorize, it does help us to recognize the variability in "types" of deviance. If we were to go further and think in terms of "degrees of stigma" rather

Table 4.1 Types of Deviation, by Imputed Responsibility, Stigma, and Prognosis

IMPUTED PROGNOSIS	RESPONSIBLE		NOT RESPONSIBLE	
	NO STIGMA	STIGMA	NO STIGMA	STIGMA
Curable	Parking violation	Syphilis	Pneumonia	Leprosy
Improvable but not curable		Burglary	Hearing loss	Crippling
Incurable and unimprovable		Sex murder	Cancer	Dwarfism

Source: Eliot Freidson, "Disability as Social Deviance," in Marvin B. Sussman, ed., *Sociology and Rehabilitation*. Washington: American Sociological Association, 1965, p. 80; as slightly revised and reprinted in Eliot Freidson and Judith Lorber, eds., *Medical Men and their Work*. Chicago/New York: Aldine/Atherton, 1972, p. 337; reproduced by permission.

than its presence or absence, then we could recognize the existence of a still wider range of slightly varying deviance situations, some of which, as Freidson shows, would involve "involuntary" physical conditions. (That approach, however, would elude even this broad type of categorization procedure.)

There is no easy way to resolve the different sociological points of view about the role of imputed responsibility in deviance outcomes. On the one hand, it undoubtedly is true that when responsibility *is* imputed (when people are held morally accountable), deviantizing may take on a special tone, incorporating more negative feelings, imposing more stigma and harsher "penalties." Yet, as we have just seen, it is *also true* that various disabilities and conditions perceived as being beyond a person's control do evoke responses that basically are highly similar to those elicited by more "voluntary" offending acts. To complicate matters still further, the very process of designating a person "not responsible" may itself be stigmatizing in its impact. As we will see, studies of mental illness and juvenile delinquency court proceedings—in both cases built around ideas of diminished responsibility and originally intended as alternatives to stigmatizing—highlight this possibility. It is also apparent in the situations of those who have been defined as mentally retarded. Indeed, Robert Edgerton comments, regarding the formerly hospitalized retardates he studied, that "their lives are directed toward the fundamental purpose of denying that they are in fact mentally incompetent" (Edgerton, 1967, p. 145).

Nobody can say with absolute certainty which aspect is the more important one sociologically—the variation in reaction according to the type of perceived deviation (voluntary, involuntary, etc.) or the overall similarity in reaction that cuts across all the types. Several writers have attempted to find some middle ground between these two focal points, in effect arguing that reactions to disability display *some* features in common with other deviance-defining but that they nonetheless are not as central to the concerns of deviance sociology as are the more voluntary deviating acts. For example, Daniel Glaser refers to "deviant attributes," possession of which "may result in a person's being treated as objectionable in many communities, organizations, or other social systems," and he notes that racial minority-group membership could also be classified in this way. Yet he goes on to say that, "All of these are somewhat marginal to much use of the concept 'deviance,' since these are conditions rather than acts, and thus cannot be called 'deviant behavior,'" even though in terms of the "reaction they arouse" there is much similarity (Glaser, 1971, p. 21).

In some ways this statement begs a key issue for deviance analysis: *Has* the prevailing "use of the concept 'deviance,'" been a meaningful one? If not, should not the element Glaser terms the "reaction they arouse" perhaps be seen as the key to deviance phenomena. Edward Sagarin has also taken a middle-ground position, adopting the term "involuntary deviants" for those who are disabled or have other involuntary stigmatizing conditions (Sargarin, 1975, pp. 201–214; see also, Sagarin and Montanino, eds., 1977, pp. 3–5). Milton Mankoff, in a broad critique of the labeling approach to which we will return below, distinguishes between "ascribed" (involuntary) and "achieved" deviance and maintains that most deviance sociology is concerned with the latter (Mankoff, 1971). All of these formulations flounder somewhat because of the apparently felt need to establish clear-cut categories of behavior. Focusing instead on the common reaction process and emphasizing variability in kinds and intensities of attributed meanings (degrees of deviantness) better enables one to consider *both* the similarities *and* the differences in these situations. This text has obviously adopted this more inclusive approach, in which disabilities, too, can be treated as falling within the domain of deviation.

It should be noted, however, that even if one were to adopt the narrower interpretation, making personal responsibility a requirement for deviance, there are some stigmatizable conditions that would be very hard to classify on this dimension. The most striking example is poverty, at least some versions of which are currently imbued with much deviantness (see Beck, 1967; Horan and Austin, 1974; Matza and Miller, 1976). In his apt phrase "blaming the victim," William Ryan succinctly captured the strange mixture of responsibility/nonresponsibility themes through which dominant middle-class ideologies permit a public disvaluing of those who have already been undermined by socioeconomic deprivation. Even in allegedly humanitarian explanations, the locus of attention in discussions of poor health, criminality, low school performance, and the like, often remains on the individual—his or her cultural, if not biological, "deficiencies." The poverty itself is seen simply as the result, rarely as the cause. As Ryan states:

. . . the stigma, the defect, the fatal difference—though derived in the past from environmental forces—is still located *within* the victim, inside his skin. With such an elegant formulation, the humanitarian can have it both ways. He can, all at the same time, concentrate his charitable interest on the defects of the victim, condemn the vague social and environmental stresses that produced the defect (some time ago), and ignore the continuing effect of victimizing social forces (right now). It is a brilliant ideology for justifying a perverse form of social action designed to change, not society, as one might expect, but rather society's victim (Ryan, 1972, p. 7).

Rounding out the possible content of deviation are disvalued and stigmatized beliefs and personal orientations. As Glaser has observed, "Alleged adherence to particular ideas, usually on religion or politics, has been one of the most widespread yet variable bases for defining people as deviant" (Glaser, 1971, p. 15). The examples cited earlier, of atheism, "extremism," nudism, and sexual "liberation," all involve, in some degree, beliefs as well as acts. The same is true of membership in various religious "cults" (this term itself might be considered no more than a deviantizing label for religious groups of which the labeler disapproves) and adherence to any currently unorthodox political doctrines. During many periods of American history, governmental effort to control political dissidents and suspected subversives, has routinely established (in each case, temporarily) groups and categories of political deviators. It is, however, always "difficult to assess trends in political deviance because so much that is regarded as deviant one period becomes acceptable in a later period" (Glaser, 1971, p. 17). An especially intriguing wrinkle found in connection with antisubversion policies has been the frequent involvement of government agencies and officials in various purported "control" activities (illegal wiretapping and other covert surveillance, improper opening of mail, illegal entry of private premises, falsification of documents) that later themselves came to be widely viewed as constituting deviation. This tendency toward deviation in the name of rooting out deviation is nicely pointed up by the titles of two recent books: *The Lawless State—The Crimes of the U.S. Intelligence Agencies* (Halperin, *et al.,* 1976) and *Official Deviance—Readings in Malfeasance, Misfeasance, and Other Worms of Corruption* (Douglas and Johnson, eds., 1977).

In Chapter 7, when we examine the relation between deviance and social change and, in particular, the "politicization of deviance," we will be noting various organized efforts to expand public conceptions as to which types of "belief" and associated behavior should be perceived as being "political" rather than as constituting "deviation." Indeed, as previous discussion implies, the fact that elements of group conflict and power seem central to most deviance situations may provide some basis for claims that "all deviance is political." At any rate and notwithstanding the professed aversion in our political tradition and legal system to punishing people for their beliefs, there is no doubt that ideas as well as acts and personal conditions have at times been deviantized.

A final area of deviance-defining, in which acts, conditions, and beliefs seem at times to blur together, involves personal or life orientations. Perhaps the clearest example of this is sexual preference. Current homosexual-rights activists often seem uncertain or in disagreement as to whether to assert that homosexuality is an involuntary condition or that it is a freely "chosen" orientation, a "way of life," or even some kind of "belief system." But whatever one makes of these different conceptions, it is undeniably true that the social deviantizing of homosexuals goes well beyond their specific "acts," even though legal prohibitions are directed only against acts and cannot proscribe "being a homosexual." Whether they are seen or even see themselves as being "born homosexual," as gradually developing that preference, or as having freely chosen it, homosexuals invariably are categorized and stigmatized for *their general orientation* or what some writers have referred to as their "state of being."

Something like this mixture or confusion of bases for deviantizing is also apparent in the negative social reactions that have sometimes attended other, particularly bohemian, life-styles. Thus the imputations of deviantness directed not long ago toward "hippies" were evoked not only because of specific acts such as drug-taking, but because of a general orientation to life: attitudes, including those toward work; perceived lack of concern for or contemptuousness toward various proprieties, such as those regarding cleanliness; alleged "irresponsibility;" and the like. Here again, a complex mixture of acts, beliefs, and even appearance seems to have summoned forth the negative response (see Davis, 1970; also Yablonsky, 1968).

Conceptions of Cause

We have seen that traditional deviance sociology was almost exclusively preoccupied with determining the causes of deviating acts, as supposedly revealed in individual "differentiation." The deviantness of the acts usually was just assumed, and the possibility that conditions or beliefs might also constitute deviation was given little or no consideration. Among the most important developments in recent deviance analysis have been new ways of depicting causal processes, and new conceptions regarding the very notion of cause that ought be applied in studying and interpreting deviance. Central to these developing outlooks have been the interrelated themes of *sequential process, unpredictability and contingency,* and *reciprocal or interactive influence.*

In Chapter 3 we noted some groundings and manifestations of these recently emphasized perspectives. As we saw there, the labeling analysts have placed a heavy emphasis on exploring process, and this, in turn, is seen to require (in Becker's words) a "sequential" rather than a static model of causation. We also saw that Matza, in his critique of conventional subculture theories, posited a notion of causal drift, according to which deviation could be seen as one path an individual might take, but not a necessary or inevitable one. For Matza, the drift concept was a way of steering a middle-ground between assumptions of absolute "free will" and what he saw as a "hard-core determinism."

Traditional explanations tended to adopt a static or discontinuous approach to study cause. Basically, this involved establishing correlations between antecedent conditions or factors (socioeconomic status, residence area, minority-group membership, neighborhood association patterns, or whatever) and subsequent deviating behavior. What was entirely missing was a notion of the latter as an outcome of a process. There was no effort to depict "what went on in between" the assumed precipitants and the resulting acts. The assumption was simply that the latter were determined or caused by the former. As we have seen, these statistically oriented studies aimed at producing neat classifications (fourfold tables, and the like) presenting comparisons between alleged deviants and nondeviants. If we adopt, instead of this conception of cause, one grounded in the notion of interaction process, then such clearly categorizable but misleading results are not going to be forthcoming.

One of the best statements of an alternative causal model has been made by Albert Cohen, who suggests that a tree diagram (reproduced here as Figure 4.2) is needed to depict deviation in interaction terms. Such a diagram graphically shows how:

> . . . the deviant act develops over time through a series of stages. Some individual, in the pursuit of some interest or goal, and taking account of the situation, makes a move, possibly in a deviant direction, possibly with no thought of deviance in mind. However, his next move—the continuation of his course of action—is not fully determined by the state of affairs at the beginning. He may, at this juncture, choose among two or more possible directions. Which it will be will depend on the state of the actor and situation at *this* point in time, and either or both may, in the meantime, have undergone change. . . . The completed pathway A, AA, AAA—represented by solid lines—is the course of action that, according to the theory, culminates in deviance. The other pathways, represented by broken lines, are the other courses that action *could* have taken. Pathways are not predictable from initial states or initial acts alone; prediction is contingent on the state of affairs following each move (Cohen, 1966, pp. 44, 45).

From the standpoint of depicting the entire process of "acquiring deviantness," this statement remains an incomplete one. Thus, Cohen examines the processes leading to particular kinds of acts, but he treats the deviantness of particular paths, directions, and so on, as a given. Furthermore Cohen's diagram is intended primarily to show processes *leading up to* acts perceived as deviation; it does not fully enable us to consider how such reactions then affect the situation. Nevertheless, it is to Cohen's great credit that his general approach in this formulation is consistent with and even invites an exploration of such social reaction. In fact, some early reaction process is presumably part of what he has in mind in noting that "the actor and the situation" are likely at various points in the sequences to "have undergone change." In short, Cohen's thesis provides an excellent start-

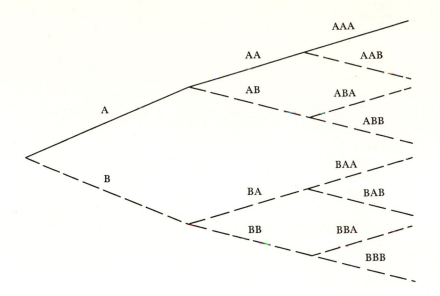

Figure 4.2. Interaction process and deviant outcomes. *Source:* **Albert K. Cohen. *Deviance and Control.* Englewood Cliffs, N.J.: Prentice-Hall, 1966, p. 43; reproduced with permission.**

ing point for recognizing that both deviation and deviantness are outcomes formed through processes of social interaction.

This conception of a fluid, contingent, unpredictable process was part of a broader shift in the explanatory aims and efforts of deviance sociologists. In recent years, they have become less and less concerned with studying and interpreting the underlying or precipitating causes of initial acts of rule-violating behavior, the mere occurrence of deviation. Many would now recognize that analyzing even this supposed "first stage" of deviance requires attention to social definitions and reactions, for, as we have observed, the existence of rule-violation is not always self-evident. In thinking about the components that were presented in Figure 4.1, it would not always be strictly correct to view the deviation as chronologically *preceding* the identifying-reacting processes. Sometimes, as the Yarrow study (Adaptation Three) suggests, the two may "occur" simultaneously in the sense that the deviation is "established" *through* the reacting process.

But the turn away from preoccupation with initial acts and their causes involved as yet an additional broadening of focus. Sociologists began to trace the processes out further, examining more closely than before what happened *along with and after* persons were identified and reacted to as deviators. They began to focus on **deviant careers**—*developing* sequences of change in behavior and self-conceptions—and to view these partly as outcomes of interaction between perceived rule-violators and those who defined them as deviators and who reacted to them in that way. Exploring this interaction coincided with and reinforced the new attention to elements of imputed meaning (referred to in this text as "deviantness") and also involved a new recognition of *reciprocal* rather than unidirectional influences in the deviance and social-control cycle.

A conviction grew that, as Lemert had emphasized earlier, the precipitating or underlying causes of the initial behavior were *less interesting or important sociologically* than these more fully elaborated ("later") deviance outcomes. Lemert referred to "the fallacy of confusing *original* causes with *effective* causes," and pointed out that the "original causes or antecedents of deviant behaviors are many and diversified" (Lemert, 1951, p. 75). This latter point becomes particularly relevant when the full range of behaviors and conditions that can be and are deviantized is taken into account. If, as we have seen, efforts to come up with a definitive, universally acceptable, systematic theory of the causes of, say, crime and delinquency have not fared well, then it is certainly unreasonable to expect that a single causal theory (in this traditional sense) will be able to cover the full range and varying substance of deviation, including numerous kinds of acts, omissions, conditions, beliefs, and life-styles.

Not only did the search for these alleged underlying causes end up taking one in various directions because of the extreme variability in what was being studied, but the sociological "payoff" from such efforts was bound to be a limited one. For example, how much would we really know about prostitution if we learned why some women and not others "became" prostitutes? When we include disabilities within the scope of deviation, the limits of this kind of knowledge become even more glaringly apparent. Sometimes the cause of such a condition is genetic; sometimes it is a result of subsequently acquired illness; or then, again, it may be caused by traumatic accident. Obviously why a person became blind, or crippled, or disfigured tells us little or nothing of sociological interest about such stigmatized conditions. As Lemert suggested, we have to get beyond these "original causes" in order to study the sociologically significant features of deviance situations:

> Whatever the original reasons for violating the norms of the community, they are important only for certain research purposes, such as assessing the extent of the "social problem" at a given time or determining the requirements of a rational program of social control. From a narrower sociological viewpoint the deviations are not significant until they are organized subjectively and transformed into active roles and become the social criteria for assigning status (Lemert, 1951, p. 75).

This was the starting point for Lemert's important ideas about primary and secondary deviation, to be discussed in a later section of this chapter. In developing such ideas, Lemert played a vital part in promoting sociological awareness of reciprocal or interactive influences in deviance and control processes. Although traditional studies had not really been much interested in social control as such (deviance was thought to be a completely separate entity), implicit in their logic was the notion that deviance "led to" control efforts. But once one starts thinking in terms of interaction processes, the likelihood of influences or effects in both directions becomes clear. Referring to the traditional conceptions, Lemert has written that he gradually came to feel that "the reverse idea, i.e., social control leads to social deviance, is equally tenable and the potentially richer premise for studying deviance in modern society" (Lemert, 1967, p. v). It was thinking of this sort that ushered in the central focus of the recent labeling analysts on the self-fulfilling aspects of deviance situations. Increased policing might "produce" more officially recorded crime. Formal and informal reactions to the prostitute might partly determine her behavior and self-conceptions, perhaps even driving her into increased involvement in or commitment to "the life." In a sense, what this shift in attention involved was a change from paramount interest in studying the background causes of isolated behaviors to one centering around the examining and interpreting of more broadly conceived "deviance situations."

Another way of describing the change in perspective on cause is in terms of a decreased inclination to ask "why" questions and also "who" questions. As the emphasis shifted from static comparisons to analyzing process, from differentiation to interpretation, from mere deviation to definitions and reactions, many sociologists lost interest in the standard issue of "why this person ['became' a rule-violator] and not that person." Instead, they started trying to explain *what* happened when people came to be perceived and treated as violators, what it was that *all* those instances had in *common*. Attention to shared process, as opposed to differentiating factors, implied really a new outlook on what deviance sociology was trying to explain and a new version of what "cause" itself meant. It began to seem that deviance did *not* "occur" *because* of the traditional causal factors, so much as it "emerged" *in and through* the process found in *every* deviance situation (i.e., deviantizing definitions-reactions). The new deviance analysis adopted, then, something like a "universalistic" approach to cause in place of the conventional "probabilistic" one, according to which statistical comparisons had been used to establish categorical differences in the likelihood of "becoming deviant." Sociologists began to find it more meaningful to *describe* the common underlying process, to explicate *how* it worked in all instances rather than to predict or explain *who* would be likely to be caught up in it in the first place.

This overall approach to the deviantizing process seems to display some of the features of a research method known as **analytic induction.** Originally attributed to the early social theorist Florian Znaniecki, this method has exerted influence on the deviance field through its use in a number of major studies. It rests on the assumption that a true causal explanation must apply to all instances of what is being explained. With this in mind, the researcher (on the basis of preliminary exploration) proposes an initial working hypothesis about cause in the broadest sense and then searches for cases that are not covered by that hypothesis. Each time such a negative case is encountered, the hypothesis is revised to take it into account, and this procedure is continued until an explanation is developed that covers every instance of the phenomenon to be explained. One of the best-known examples of this approach was Alfred Lindesmith's now classic theory of drug addiction. Based on interviews with opiate addicts and developed through this hypothesis-reworking technique, Lindesmith's final thesis was that, "the knowledge or ignorance of the meaning of withdrawal distress and the use of opiates thereafter determines whether or not the individual becomes addicted" (Lindesmith, 1947, p. 69). (This statement referred to a craving for the drug that reasserted itself after "withdrawal," and not simply the physical dependence on the drug which sufficient use invariably entailed.) The specific content of Lindesmith's formula has been challenged (McAuliffe and Gordon, 1974) on a variety of grounds, including the suggestion in some recent research findings that drug users often take drugs *not* primarily to avoid withdrawal distress but in order to experience positive euphoric effects. However, at least as an example of a *type* of deviance explanation, Lindesmith's treatment of the topic remains extremely useful.

The same basic approach was adopted by Donald Cressey in his early study of embezzlement, based on interviews with convicted embezzlers. Through his work, the following explanatory statement evolved: "Trusted persons become trust violators when they conceive of themselves as having a financial problem which is non-shareable, are aware that this problem can be secretly resolved by violation of the position of financial trust, and are able to apply to their own conduct in that situation verbalizations which enable them to adjust their conceptions of themselves as trusted persons with their conceptions of themselves as users of the entrusted funds or property" (Cressey, 1953, p. 30). The analytic induction approach to cause also exerted a considerable influence (by his own account) on Sutherland's formulation of the differential association thesis, and it provided the basic methodology adopted by Howard Becker in his well-known study of marihuana users (see Adaptation Five: "Becoming a Marihuana User," in the next section).

What this approach seems essentially to provide is a kind of retrospective description of a common process through which all instances of a given outcome are believed to have evolved. It is not geared to predicting who will and who will not become immersed in such a process in the first place. Rather, as one perceptive commentator notes, such a theory "defines a set of uniform relations existing in a 'closed' causal system, but does not take account of the inevitable external or 'intrusive' factor which 'activates a system'" (Turner, 1953, p. 609). While the studies just mentioned were concerned with processes leading up to deviating acts and did not focus very directly on subsequent societal reaction, nonetheless we can see that the basic orientation and logic of this approach, conforms well with more recently emphasized themes in deviance theory. It should be apparent, too, that these studies all developed what were essentially "learning" theories: It was a basic learning process that they found to be the key causal element.

(In the next section of this chapter, we will be noting a variety of more specific "learned" aspects of deviation.)

Whether these "newer" conceptions of cause can somehow be reconciled with the more traditional approaches is a central issue plaguing contemporary students of deviance. Albert Cohen has made an important effort in this direction by showing how elements emphasized in the anomie tradition (particularly "opportunity structures") may be *inter*related with social reaction processes in shaping deviance outcomes (Cohen, 1965). In the traditional approaches, anomie and opportunity structures were seen only as underlying cause, in other words, they helped drive people to deviation. But, as Cohen points out, deviation can, in a sense, through a kind of feedback process, also cause or shape opportunity structures: "The opportunity structure consists in or is the result of the actions of other people. These in turn are in part reactions to ego's [i.e., the deviator's] behavior and may undergo change in response to that behavior. . . . More specifically, alter's [i.e., reactor's] responses may open up, close off, or leave unaffected legitimate opportunities" (Cohen, 1965, p. 10).

Table 4.2, taken from Cohen's article, shows these possibilities. Possibility I is illustrated by special efforts to help offenders, such as providing "employment opportunities for delinquents and criminals." Possibility II is present when control agents actually facilitate deviation, perhaps by joining in "some sort of collusive illicit arrangement from which both profit." Possibility IV is what would usually be termed "effective" social control—as when social reaction curbs subsequent rule-violation by reducing the opportunity for same. It is Possibility III, however, that has been heavily emphasized by recent social reactions and labeling theorists. Here, the reaction process itself paradoxically increases the likelihood of subsequent deviation by shutting off still further the perceived offender's legitimate opportunities. As Cohen notes, when we conceive of the opportunity structure "as a dependent as well as an independent variable," that is, an effect as well as a cause, we begin to see that all of these developments (each involving a *reciprocal* relation between opportunities and deviation) are possible ways in which deviance outcomes may evolve.

When we turn, shortly, to the concept of primary and secondary deviation and especially to the major criticisms of that concept, we will find ourselves, again, confronting the problem posed by differing conceptions of cause. As we

Table 4.2 Responses of the Opportunity Structure to Ego's Deviance

	LEGITIMATE OPPORTUNITIES	ILLEGITIMATE OPPORTUNITIES
Open up	I	II
Close off	III	IV

Source: Albert K. Cohen, "The Sociology of the Deviant Act: Anomie Theory and Beyond," *American Sociological Review*, 30 (February 1965), 101; reproduced by permission.

will see, then, there is a common tendency to think that this problem must be solved quantitatively and to assume that it can be solved in that way: *How much* deviation is caused by the traditional kinds of explanatory variables and how much by labeling? But if, as we have now seen may indeed be the case, the newer approaches are built around a truly different notion of cause itself (i.e., cause as a process "through which," rather than cause as a "reason why"), then the different explanations may not really be at all comparable in that manner. They may be, instead, to repeat a point made earlier, complementary in at least some respects, in effect explaining different kinds of things. To try to force some kind of choice between them may then be a mistake.

Learned Aspects

There are several different senses in which deviation, and even deviant-ness, are learned. These include:

1. Learning that precedes and contributes to deviation.

2. Learning how to deal with—adjust to, lessen the impact of, reject, or combat—the undesired consequences of having one's behavior or condition imbued with deviantness. Presumably this involves learning, in the first place, that such imputations do exist and may be directly experienced. Coping with such knowledge is the main topic of Chapter 5. There, but also in the present chapter, we will be noting a variety of kinds of learning that this coping may entail. One way of conceptualizing many of these efforts is in terms of learning to play deviant roles. Sometimes this may involve a consciously dissembling kind of role playing. An example would be the blind beggar. As Scott has noted, this version of "the blindness role" permits both a venting of hostility toward the typically patronizing sighted and an exploitation of common definitions and emotional responses for personal gain (Scott, 1969, pp. 110–112). More frequently, perhaps, learning a deviant role is not as much a matter of "putting on" behavior, as it is one of learning how to get along. To cite how just one example, the author of a study of paraplegics (persons paralyzed below the waist) describes their efforts at adjustment as a process of "self-socialization into a devalued role." She notes that, "Paraplegics must learn the physical and social skills necessary to play the role with sufficient ease to prevent contamination of their identity as well as their performance of other roles" (Cogswell, 1968).

3. As we will also see, this second kind of learning is intermixed with a yet broader process of learning to think of oneself as being a certain kind of person. This is what labeling analysts have in mind when they depict the deviator's self-conceptions as often gradually incorporating the deviantizing responses of other people. The notion of secondary deviation (discussed below) is at least in part built around this possibility that deviantized persons may increasingly come to see themselves as others do.

It should be evident that the three kinds of learning are not neatly separable from one another, but rather may combine in producing, or cumulatively contribute to, various kinds of deviance outcomes. However, since later sections of the text will include much discussion of the second and third types, our concentration here will be mainly on the first category—aspects of learning that precede and contribute to initial deviation.

As a point of departure, we might recall from Chapter 3 Sutherland's specification of the elements learned through "differential association." These included not only "techniques," but also a "specific direction of motives, drives, rationalizations, and attitudes." Such a statement seems still to have great pertinence and also a wider substantive applicability than that which he had in mind (i.e., only to "crimes"). Both the methods and content of learning will, of course, vary a good deal depending on the specific features and "requirements" of the deviation. The learning of specific techniques will be especially apparent in connection with deviation one intends to carry on over a period of time, as opposed to isolated "acts," and particularly where the behavior in question constitutes a "skilled occupation." As Sutherland's study of the professional thief revealed, to succeed in such work requires learning many skills relating to "the planning and execution of crimes, the disposal of stolen goods, the fixing of cases in which arrests occur, and the control of other situations that may arise in the course of the occupation." Furthermore, he commented: "The division between professional and nonprofessional thieves . . . is relatively sharp. This is because these techniques [including wit, 'front,' and 'talking ability'—for use in the various fraudulent theft 'rackets'] are developed to a high point only by education, and the education can be secured only in association with professional thieves . . ." (Sutherland, 1937, pp. 197–198).

Even in relatively unskilled occupations, novices may undergo certain kinds of tutelage, even a formal period of apprenticeship. Based on his research interviews with call girls, James Bryan reported:

> . . . the structure of the apprenticeship period seems quite standard. The novice receives her training either from a pimp or from another more experienced call girl, more often the latter. She serves her initial two to eight months of work under the trainer's supervision and often serves this period in the trainer's apartment. The trainer assumes responsibility for arranging contacts and negotiating the type and place of the sexual encounter.
>
> The content of the training pertains both to a general philosophical stance and to some specifics (usually not sexual) of interpersonal behavior with customers and colleagues (Bryan, 1965, p. 294).

These apprentice-prostitutes were "taught" to have contempt for the "johns" and to exploit them as much as possible and also to view themselves as doing an honest, decent, even necessary job. More specific learning during the training period centered around telephoning and other negotiating techniques, personal hygiene, prohibitions on alcohol and drugs during work, and sexual preferences call girls could expect to encounter (see also, Heyl, 1977). As Bryan pointed out, being a prostitute does not, basically, require any highly specialized knowledge or technique. In large measure, it appeared to be "the secrecy rather than the complexity of the occupation" that led to an orienting and protecting apprenticeship period.

Sometimes the relevant occupational skills may be primarily self-taught. This is what Ned Polsky has reported regarding pool hustlers who play pool for a living and who deceive the opponents with whom they gamble as to their skill level. Becoming a pool hustler seems to happen "almost without thinking about it" among certain youths who spend a great deal of time around poolhalls and develop the requisite talent. To achieve as a hustler, it is not the pool-playing itself as much as it is a general way of interacting with potential opponents that must then be "learned." As Polsky states, "the hustler's cardinal rule is: don't show your real speed [skill level]." He must play accordingly, refraining from making certain very difficult shots, winning by only a small margin, and occasionally losing, and must also master the verbal skills needed to make the kind of game he wants (Polsky, 1967, pp. 41–116). This reference to "he" is, incidentally, intentional: As Polsky's further historical research showed, though poolrooms are now often open to women, they developed as "the exact center and veritable stronghold" of the "heterosexual but all-male subculture" in America.

Where a deviantized occupation involves virtually no special skill, learning may only amount to acquiring certain appropriate attitudes, or else it may be simply a kind of "negative" learning in which one realizes the advantages of the work in comparison with available alternatives. Skipper and McGaghy, in their study of stripteasers, discovered little or no apprenticeship, although they did report "evidence of congruence between the content of previous jobs and stripping." Over 70 percent of their respondents had "held jobs prior to stripping in which the display of their physical attributes was an integral part" (dancers, go-go girls, models, bar waitresses, etc.). Such past experience, these writers suggest, made it easier when opportunities to strip arose "to view stripping as an acceptable occupational alternative" (Skipper and McGaghy, 1970, p. 400). The main "learning" for these women, actually, concerned the relatively high financial benefits of this occupation. Of the 35 strippers interviewed in that study, the authors estimated that, "only one had the talent, training, or education to make more money at any other legal occupation than stripping" (Skipper and McGaghy, 1970, p. 398).

The above examples should not be taken to imply that only occupational deviation involves learning. Indeed, as Adaptation Five shows, what might be termed "recreational deviance" may also require training both in techniques and in relevant outlooks. One learns how to "become a marihuana user," though perhaps often without realizing one is engaged in a learning process.

ADAPTATION FIVE
Becoming a Marihuana User*

Today the smoking of marihuana is sufficiently common that, at least in many social circles, no complicated effort to explain it seems necessary. Some commentators, particularly psychiatrically oriented ones, may persist in claiming as causes of this phenomenon personal instabilities, efforts to escape from reality, and so on. Yet many other professional observers would now acknowledge that most "pot smokers" take up the practice simply because they find it pleasurable. From a sociological standpoint, however, an unanalyzed statement of this latter view—that marihuana use is "simply pleasurable"—can also prevent our appreciation of the interaction sequences and definitional processes involved in such a phenomenon. In his already classic study, "Becoming a Marihuana User," Howard S. Becker closely examined the elements of interaction and social meaning that shape the context within which marihuana is used.

Becker, a sociologist who also had been for some years a professional musician, studied marihuana use at a time (the late 1940s and early 1950s) when familiarity with this drug was much less common than it is now; at that time, too, both social disapproval and psychological theories of marihuana smoking were more likely to be encountered than at present. The music business, to which Becker had unique research access, was one social circle in which experience with marihuana was relatively common. His study, however, extended beyond that circle to include use of the drug by people in various walks of life. Becker was convinced that existing explanations, which tended to attribute marihuana smoking to supposedly predisposing or motivating traits of the individuals involved, could not adequately account for the practice. Such interpretations were at best incomplete because they ignored the social context within which drug use is experienced. Indeed, Becker suggested, "instead of the deviant motives leading to the deviant behavior, it is the other way around; the deviant behavior in time produces the deviant motivation. Vague impulses and desires—in this case, probably most frequently a curiosity about the kind of experience the drug will produce—are transformed into definite patterns of action through the social interpretation of a physical experience which is in itself ambiguous." Thus his research focused on "the individual's conception of marihuana and of the uses to which it can be put" and showed how this conception changes in the course of the individual's experience with the drug.

In analyzing the 50 interviews he conducted with marihuana users, Becker found the dominant pattern to be one of occasional and "recreational" use; in

* Source: A summary and interpretation of "Becoming a Marihuana User," in Howard S. Becker, Outsiders: Studies in the Sociology of Deviance. New York: The Free Press, 1963, pp. 41–58. Direct quotations reproduced with permission.

most instances, marihuana smoking was a "noncompulsive and casual" practice. As he perceptively noted, however, even such apparently casual behavior is socially patterned and contains elements that are socially learned. These patterned and learned elements fell into three major stages: learning the techniques of marihuana smoking, learning to perceive the drug's effects, and learning to enjoy those effects. At each of the three stages, Becker discovered, continued use of the drug was an outgrowth of the individual's interaction with other users. To begin with, as Becker's respondents made clear, a person does not usually "get high" the first time he or she smokes marihuana. The first prerequisite for achieving this sensation is learning the proper smoking technique. As one user put it:

The trouble with people like that [who are not able to get high] is that they're just not smoking it right. Either they're not holding it down long enough, or they're getting too much air and not enough smoke, or the other way around or something like that. A lot of people just don't smoke it right, so naturally nothing's gonna happen.

It is through participation in marihuana-using groups that the individual learns an effective smoking technique, either through direct teaching or more indirectly through observation and imitation. None of Becker's interviewees continued marihuana use for pleasure without learning such a technique. Only when this barrier had been passed, Becker concluded, "was it possible for a conception of the drug as an object which could be used for pleasure to emerge. Without such a conception marihuana use was considered meaningless and did not continue."

But more than technique is involved in "getting high." The user must still recognize the drug's special effects and connect them consciously with the smoking process. This does not occur automatically. Typically the novice must learn from other users to identify the major symptoms of being high. Thus, respondents sometimes referred to having been high during their early experiences with the drug, but not having realized they were. For example, one user told Becker:

[Did you get high the first time you turned on?] Yeah, sure. Although, come to think of it, I guess I really didn't. I mean, like that first time it was a more or less of a mild drunk. I was happy, I guess, you know what I mean. But I didn't really know I was high, you know what I mean. It was only after the second time I got high that I realized I was high the first time. Then I knew that something different was happening.

[How did you know that?] How did I know? If what happened to me that night would of happened to you, you would've known, believe me. We played the first tune for almost two hours—one tune! Imagine, man. We got on the stand and played this one tune, we started at nine o'clock. When we got finished I looked at my watch, it's a quarter to eleven. Almost two hours on one tune. And it didn't seem like anything.

I mean, you know, it does that to you. It's like you have much more time or something. Anyway, when I saw that, man, it was too much. I knew I must really be high or something if anything like that could happen. See, and then they explained to me that that's what it did to you, you had a different sense of time and everything. So I realized that that's what it was. I knew then. Like the first time, I probably felt that way, you know, but I didn't know what's happening.

As Becker pointed out, "With increasing experience the user develops a greater appreciation of the drug's effects; he continues to learn to get high. He examines succeeding experiences closely, looking for new effects, making sure the old ones are still there. Out of this there grows a stable set of categories for experiencing the drug's effects whose presence enables the user to get high with ease."

In addition to knowing how to recognize marihuana's effects, the user must learn to enjoy them. The various sensations that one is likely to experience (such as dizziness, thirstiness, disorientation with respect to time and distance) are not in themselves necessarily enjoyable. As Becker rightly noted, "The taste for such experience is a socially acquired one, not different in kind from acquired tastes for oysters or dry martinis." Often the first reactions are negative ones. If the novice is to continue marihuana use, the effects must be interpreted and, hence, experienced as pleasurable ones. If not, "getting high, while a real enough experience, will be an unpleasant one he would rather avoid." Through his interviews, Becker found that sensations that often were initially experienced as frightening or unpleasant gradually came to be seen as enjoyable through a redefinition process involving the individual's guidance and reassurance by other users. The important role played by the more experienced drug smoker is suggested in the following comments by one respondent:

Well, they get pretty high sometimes. The average person isn't ready for that, and it is a little frightening to them sometimes. I mean, they've been high on lush [alcohol], and they get higher that way than they've ever been before, and they don't know what's happening to them. Because they think they're going to keep going up, up, up, till they lose their minds or begin doing weird things or something. You have to like reassure them, explain to them that they're not really flipping or anything, that they're gonna be all right. You have to just talk them out of being afraid. Keep talking to them. reassuring, telling them it's all right. And come on with your own story, you know: "The same thing happened to me. You'll get to like that after awhile." Keep coming on like that; pretty soon you talk them out of being scared. And besides they see you doing it and nothing horrible is happening to you, so that gives them more confidence.

As in the other stages of the process leading to regular use, the extent and rapidity of the redefinition depends on the degree to which the person participates with other users. Becker's study had great significance in showing how a behavior pattern we might easily attribute to the particular traits of given individuals is in fact subtly shaped by social process. It is through such an interactive process that the mere act comes to be endowed with meaning.

In a companion paper entitled "Marihuana Use and Social Control", Becker supplemented this analysis by considering some of the ways in which social disapproval and illegality further affected the marihuana user's situation. Participation in groups through which "connections" with drug suppliers can be maintained, use in secrecy or at least in insulation from nonusers or serious disapprovers (including, of course, agents of the law), and justifications for using marihuana that permit one to discount claims as to its harmfulness—all these facets of the user's experience stem in part from actual or potential social reaction. Although Becker did not discuss them explicitly in quite the same terms, these aspects clearly imply the "secondary" expansion of problematic behavior situations under conditions of stigma and illegality that we will be noting repeatedly throughout this book.

_____

As Becker's analysis of learning to enjoy marihuana may suggest, an important learned aspect in many deviance situations involves coming to appreciate the personal benefits to be derived from deviation. Often, of course, this will be pretty obvious. The poverty-immersed ghetto-dweller, for example, requires no special training in order to understand the possible payoff from stealing. Where pressing need is not such a factor, a kind of learning process may occur, even with respect to recognizing economic benefits, frequently in an indirect way through unhappy or unsuccessful experiences pursuing alternative options. This was what happened to many of the stripteasers Skipper and McGaghy studied. They had made early unsuccessful starts at some other kind of show business career, then found that only less "respectable" work would be steadily open to them, and eventually realized that the relative financial rewards from stripping outweighed all the available alternatives. Something similar often seems to be involved in a woman's entry into prostitution, which current evidence suggests is only rarely a direct result of really pressing economic need (James, 1977, pp. 389–393). The authors of a feminist-oriented report on prostitution state:

> Whether a woman chooses prostitution at a dollar a minute or clerk-typist at two dollars an hour, feminists eventually recognize that our response to a woman's choice must be essentially the same. We can legitimately explain to a woman how we believe her situation is discriminatory. We can write, lobby for and pass laws which open better options for women and which make their current situation tolerable. But when a woman decides, "If you've ever been a clerk-typist, you'd rather be a prostitute," we cannot annul her choice. To do so would be paternalisitc and thus anti-feminist, repugnant in a movement dedicated to individual choices for women (James, *et al.,* 1975, p. 4).

These examples point up an element in deviation that is usually closely tied up with learning—that of opportunity. As we saw earlier, in the discussion of Cloward and Ohlin's writings, deviance studies need to take into account the nature and distribution of illegitimate opportunities as well as legitimate ones. (And although Merton did not focus on lack of illicit opportunity, his analysis had already begun to show us that it is the relation between the two types—the relative merits of available alternatives—that may be central in much deviation.)

Quite simply, in order to deviate, one must have an opportunity to do so; just as opportunity is a necessary condition with respect to any behavior—deviating or conforming. As in the case of being aware of the benefits to be gained by deviating, there are some offenses for which the necessary opportunities are readily available to all. Just about anyone can find people to be rude to, to punch in the chest, or, for that matter, to kill "for no good reason." Similarly, no highly distinctive opportunity factor need be present in order to shoplift or to commit suicide. For suicide one must, of course, find a method, but at least several means of self-destruction are easily available to most persons.

As types of deviation become more highly differentiated and complex and particularly when they require special devices, commodities, or the involvement of other persons, opportunity becomes more of an issue. To engage in armed robbery one must have a weapon or at least a convincing imitation. A person cannot be a drug user unless he or she obtains drugs. Nobody can engage in homosexual (or heterosexual) relations by themselves. It may be relatively easy to engage in sex for money, but it is nonetheless necessary to locate and contact "customers." By the same token, various counterpart forms of deviation may require that customers find illicit distributors or practitioners. In line with his reference to "deviant selling" patterns (cited above in the discussion of area concentrations in deviance), Glaser calls these counterparts "deviant consumption" (see Glaser, 1971, pp. 10–13). A major example is the illicit drug user's need to find a drug seller. As one recent depiction of the heroin world, presented as seen by its participants, put it: "There aren't any special rules for making connections. It is simply one of the most important things about dope use. Anybody who can't make good connections will never make it with dope. He just doesn't know how to take care of himself" (Gould, *et al.*, 1974, p. 40). Similarly, when abortion has been illegal, even relatively well-to-do and educated women, who have been at a considerable advantage in procuring competent, safe abortions, have had to seek out specific information and often follow up numerous unsuccessful leads in order to locate illegal operators (Lee, 1969, esp. ch. 5).

Several general points about learning to deviate now deserve emphasis. First of all, we should always keep in mind that, apart from "content," this learning is *basically no different* from learning how to engage in more approved types of behavior. Learning, of some kind, precedes and contributes to all human action. Whatever our conclusion regarding the validity of Sutherland's specific differential association thesis, something like the process he depicted (or, perhaps more accurately, Glaser's differential identification revision) has to occur in connection with most deviating acts. (Presumably, in the case of deviantized "conditions," most of the learning comes later—after being afflicted.) One learns to deviate by becoming familiar with general possibilities, by acquiring specific opportunities and skills, by developing attitudes that permit and support the deviating acts. This happens, just as any other learning does, through a variety of direct and indirect "transmissions" of knowledge, ranging from childhood and continuing socialization to formal preparation for and apprenticeship in a deviant role.

As some of the examples we have noted and, perhaps, particularly the Becker marihuana study indicate, these learning processes frequently bear close relation to the existence of a specialized subculture built around a given pattern of deviation. Initiation into and appreciation of a given activity, information about relevant opportunities, and training in any necessary skills or appropriate attitudes can all be facilitated or provided through such a subculture. Perhaps an even more important contribution of these subcultures, however, is to the "coping" or adjustment-related types of learning that mainly occur *after* entry into deviantized behavior patterns. In the next chapter, we are going to be considering such stigma-avoidance functions and implications of subcultures.

By looking at these facilitating and supportive functions as well as at the role that formal "trainers" play in certain patterns of deviation, we can see that often *a person may need help to deviate*. Sometimes what is needed is preliminary help; in other instances, one needs help on a continuing basis. Sometimes what is involved is the direct or indirect influence of a "role model." In other situations, very practical types of everyday assistance may be required. Particularly when we turn to the learning processes involved in adjusting to stigmatization, the deviator's need for assistance as well as social and psychological "support" will become especially clear. Such assistance, we can easily recognize, is of the utmost importance not only to persons who engage in deviating acts, but also—perhaps even more so—to persons who "have" deviantized conditions. How necessary such assistance will be will understandably depend upon the nature and extent of the disability. In Edgerton's study of 48 formerly hospitalized mental retardates, he found only 3 to be fully independent of special "benefactors" (usually spouses or lovers, landladies or neighbors, or employers). Seven he deemed largely or periodically independent; 17 heavily but not completely dependent; and 21 "for all practical purposes, completely dependent" (Edgerton, 1967, pp. 193–197). "It would not be an exaggeration to conclude," he noted, "that, in general, the ex-patient succeeds in his efforts to sustain a life in the community only as well as he succeeds in locating and holding a benefactor." Since much of the benefactors' activity was secretive (helping the retardate, for example, to carry out insofar as possible an effective public "denial" of the disability), they might even be thought of as engaging in a kind of "benevolent conspiracy (Edgerton, 1967, p. 204).

REACTING TO DEVIATION

By engaging in behavior or even by having a condition that is widely stigmatized, the individual *begins* to acquire deviantness or, at least, a potential for it. Provided the collective definitions that generate and convey these meanings are sufficiently strong, the very knowledge that by dominant standards you are deviating is bound to affect you in some degree. More typically, however, the process of acquiring deviantness does not stop there. To the extent one experiences, in addition to this potentially "incriminating" self-knowledge, direct negative reactions (official or unofficial) by other people, the deviantizing impact is likely to be heightened. *How much* deviantness you personally acquire will, then, depend upon many factors. As we will see, there are various ways of defending against (possibly even "rebutting") the negative impact of both the self-knowledge and the reactions of others. What personal or collective resources can be brought to this effort will make a big difference. Obviously, it will also make a difference just how much direct negative reaction one encounters, in what forms, and from what sources.

It is also important to remember that deviance outcomes always grow out of sequences of interaction and that, therefore, the lines of influence are *reciprocal*. Although recently deviance theorists have tended to stress how reactions influence the deviator (our major concern in this chapter), it is well to keep in mind that the reactors are also influenced *by* the deviators—not simply by their initially deviating acts, but also by their continuing responses to the reactors themselves and to whatever they do. One way of conceptualizing this (to which we will return below) is in terms of an interactive process in which relative degrees of power help to determine what deviance outcomes are "negotiated." But even leaving aside the power element, it is important to recognize that *the reaction itself develops and changes over time and through interaction*. Fred Davis, in discussing how family members reacted to children who had contracted polio, provides an excellent description of this process, which he terms one of "emergence," in contrast to "the more familiar sociological notion of inherence."

> . . . reactions displayed by the families were not in any strict sense "determined" by the objective events themselves; nor, on the other hand, can it be said that they issued mainly from any personality characteristics, attitudes, or interpersonal configurations pre-existent and latent in the makeup of each family. Instead, the reactions of the families can best be described in terms of an ongoing developmental process—an improvisatory "building up," as it were, in which each new event posed new problems that in turn generated a trial-and-error search for new interpretations and definitions of the situation. . . . the actual undergoing of the process sets its own conditions for further action. . . . (Davis, 1963, p. 10).

Davis' statement, as we can see, provides a nice substantive illustration of the kind of sequence depicted in some of Cohen's formulations (his tree diagram, etc.) cited earlier. How well-elaborated this "building up" process becomes will, of course, depend upon the nature and particularly the degree of continuousness of the relationship between deviators and those reacting to them. In this case, the permanence and intensity of the relation between the children and their families lent the process special importance.

Reactions to deviation, then, are not fixed or fully predictable, nor are they uniform. Nonetheless, it is apparent that in a very general sense we can identify some key determinants of patterned variations in this reacting (factors we will look at again when we explore the topic of collective definition in Chapter 7). In particular, as already suggested, reactions are likely to vary significantly depending on *who* is doing the reacting, to *whom* they are reacting, and to *what* particular behavior or condition they are reacting. One of the most convenient ways of thinking about such variations is in terms of **tolerance limits.** In our earlier discussion, the idea of tolerance limits has frequently been developed, even if this specific term was not used. We encountered it particularly in considering how to interpret the Yarrow findings about husband-wife interaction preceding mental hospitalization. It is, essentially, the same idea that Erikson was developing through his concept of "boundaries." Indeed, the overall conception that deviance situations arise out of feelings of perceived threat is itself heavily grounded in a notion of tolerance limits. When people decide that "something must be done" and act accordingly, we can say that their tolerance limits (as we will find below, Lemert used the similar term "tolerance quotient") have been exceeded.

Another concept of Erikson's mentioned earlier, that of the "audience of reactors," also suggests a focus on tolerance limits. The audience is, as he properly puts it, the crucial variable for research precisely because its tolerance limits determine the occasions for and the nature of deviance-defining. Actually, there are multiple audiences any of which may be involved in this defining-reacting process. Each individual who responds to a perceived deviator is, in a sense, an audience. Formal control agents or agencies are among the most crucial audiences directly encountered by some deviators. And at a yet broader and less direct level, we can think of the entire community or society as an audience of reactors. By the same token, we find tolerance limits operating at any or all of these levels and with respect to a variety of perceived deviations and deviators. We have already seen that collective tolerance limits for specific types of behavior are likely to vary from place to place and also over time. It may also sometimes be appropriate to consider the tolerance limits of particular individuals which contribute to the broader patterns of reaction and which in certain highly specific situations represent "what counts" to the participants. One especially important point about tolerance limits is that, whether individual or collective, they may vary depending on who the perceived deviators are. As material in the next section (on "identification" of deviators) and elsewhere in the book makes clear, the very same behavior or condition may elicit different reactions depending on the social characteristics of those identified as offenders.

One more introductory point about reacting to deviation should be mentioned. The reader should recall that, according to the perspective adopted here, a number of substantively *different kinds* of reactions as well as reactions of different intensities may be involved in deviantizing. Many of the examples we have taken up throughout the text (as, for example, in the section of this chapter on "The Range of Perceived Deviations") illustrate the various possibilities. Deviantizing outlooks and reactions may in some instances feature condemnation or outrage; in other instances, the underlying themes may be pity and condescension; sometimes the "gist" of the response cannot be pinned down to anything more than the quite apparent strong discomfort of the reactors themselves. But there is a core of common substance that cuts across these diverse reactions. As we have already begun to see, this core is an amalgam of rigid personal "typing," negation-avoidance, and denial of full human status.

Specifying this core response more rigorously for research purposes is difficult and in some ways questionable. The various kinds of reactions are not entirely comparable, and, furthermore, their occurrence is typically a matter of degree. However, a very rough approximation may be provided by the so-called social distance scale. In this survey or interview technique, respondents are asked to indicate how willing or unwilling they would be to accept designated kinds of persons in relationships to them of systematically varying degrees of intimacy (e.g., in your community, in your school or church, as a neighbor, a close friend, a marital partner, etc.) (see, for example, Phillips, 1963). While the results of such inquiries are only hypothetical, they may serve as a general indication of likely degrees of actual acceptance and rejection. In one pilot study, respondents showed a strong desire to maintain "social distance" between themselves and homosexuals, lesbians, prostitutes, and even marihuana smokers. (The data were gathered in 1965 and published in 1969.) Relatively little distance was desired with respect to gamblers, ex-convicts, atheists, former mental patients, and intellectuals. Falling into a middle range were political radicals, adulterers, alcoholics, and "beatniks" (Simmons, 1969, pp. 31–35). This kind of study would probably produce different results today, especially as regards marihuana smokers and perhaps also with respect to homosexuals and lesbians. Were this the case, it would only serve to confirm the point emphasized earlier: that deviance-defining or, we might say, any tolerance limit is subject to variation over time. We also should be aware that the main significance of findings from research of this sort may sometimes be to inform us about the tolerance limits and inclinations of particular types of respondents, rather than about the overall deviantness of particular behaviors and conditions. Indeed, one of Simmons' main conclusions from the study just cited was that certain people are especially prone to deviantize, regardless of the substance of the offending behavior. Finding some respondents to be consistently more rejecting and others to be consistently less rejecting, he suggested that, "the tendency to accept or to discriminate against those who differ seems to be a basic part of a person's way of looking at the world" (Simmons, 1969, p. 23).

Of course, individuals who are actually subject to deviance-defining are not too concerned about responses to hypothetical questions. They orient their behavior and outlooks in terms of what has happened, is happening, or may happen to them. As the social distance idea may suggest, substance and process meld together in actual deviantizing reactions. "Rejection" is a substantive attitude, but at the same time it is a process (one shows rejection *by rejecting*). It is through studies of the common process in deviance situations that the very meaning of deviance is being revealed. Let us now turn our attention more directly to some of the major features of that deviantizing process.

Identification or Selection

Before other people can react directly to a given instance of deviation, they must be aware of its existence. Therefore, how obvious deviations are will be extremely significant in determining what happens to individual deviators. Most sociologists now recognize the important role of **visibility** in shaping deviance outcomes of various sorts. [Actually, as Erving Goffman has perceptively noted, "evidentness" would be a more inclusive term than "visibility" since some deviations, such as stammering, are never really seen but only heard (Goffman, 1963, p. 48).] It is because of their blatant evidentness that disfigurement, crippling, and certain other physical disabilities or deformities carry an especially strong potential for immediate deviantizing reactions. At the same time, as one writer on disabilities recently pointed out, "Physiological impairments are not always immediately evident. Although hemophiliacs cannot participate in contact sports, they can carefully structure their social lives so that these impairments do not become widely known social facts" (Levitin, 1975, p. 550).

As we will see in Chapter 5, particularly when the deviation is more social than physical, individual deviators may go to some lengths to keep it from becoming apparent. Why they should choose to do so is quite obvious. Whether, when they succeed in this effort, the sociologist should nonetheless consider them to be "deviants" has become a matter for dispute among recent deviance analysts. In a much-discussed typology, reproduced here as Table 4.3, Becker delineated four possible deviance-related situations. Critics of Becker's labeling approach were not long in pointing out an apparent contradiction in the term **secret deviant** (see Gibbs, 1966). If Becker insisted that deviance is "behavior that people so label," how could he also maintain that a person who remained hidden and, therefore, unlabeled could be a deviant of any kind—"secret" or otherwise? This problem,

Table 4.3 Types of Deviant Behavior

	OBEDIENT BEHAVIOR	RULE-BREAKING BEHAVIOR
Perceived as deviant	Falsely accused	Pure deviant
Not perceived as deviant	Conforming	Secret deviant

Source: Howard S. Becker, *Outsiders*. New York: The Free Press, 1963, p. 20; reproduced by permission.

which Becker sought to deal with in a subsequent essay by referring to the "potential deviant" (Becker, 1973), results from the unfortunate use in this chart of either-or, presumably clear-cut categories. As we saw in our earlier discussion, the resulting dilemma is removed as soon as we recognize the distinction between the mere occurrence of behavior and what is made of it socially and when we think in terms of degrees of deviantness.

Recall the earlier depiction of adultery situations that would vary, in terms of what happened to the actual participants, in degrees of deviantness. In his critique of the term "secret deviant," Gibbs used precisely this example, arguing that it would be most strange to assert that, "if persons engage in adultery but their act is not discovered and reacted to in a certain way (by the members of the social unit), then it is not deviant!" (Gibbs, 1966, p. 13). Gibbs is indeed correct to note Becker's inconsistency in using the term "secret deviant," but the real reason why it is unwieldy is that the term "deviant" itself is misleading, as are all efforts to neatly categorize "deviants" and the "nondeviants" and "deviance" and "nondeviance." Indeed, the basic *idea* behind Becker's typology holds up perfectly well once we consider degrees of deviantness. All we need to say is that the hidden deviator experiences *less deviantness* than would be the case if he or she were identified. As we just noted, *some* deviantness will attach to the self-knowledge that one is deviating (we will return to this point shortly, in discussing so-called "self-labeling"), but the impact of this on the individual is unlikely to be as pronounced as that which would follow disclosure.

The very same kind of reasoning applies to criticism of Becker's "falsely accused" category. In Figure 4.1, we saw that the basis for identification as a deviator *could be* a mistaken perception regarding the individual's actual behavior. Again, people who get into this kind of situation (assuming no prompt "correction" of the mistake) are without question susceptible to *more* imputation of deviantness than are those who are perceived as totally conforming. The question of whether such a person is "a deviant" is not very meaningful sociologically. As Lemert commented many years ago, "A community may be entirely wrong in its estimation of a young woman's behavior, mistaking unconventionality for immorality. But yet the fact remains that however much its reaction is founded upon false premises, it is still the immediate social reality to which the woman must respond" (Lemert, 1951, p. 93). However, the precise impact of that reaction, he went on to note (and as we will see later), is subject to variation on a number of grounds. But the central point seems clear: People can experience deviantizing reactions regardless of whether they "really" deviated, just as actual rule-violators can sometimes avoid or be spared such reactions.

We have already explored quite a bit the enormous variety of substantive bases for reacting to people as deviators. It should be added that the kinds and sources of information that can activate identification and negative response are also numerous and diverse. A person can be identified as a deviator through direct observation, through hearsay and rumor, and, as the "false accusation" reference suggests, through "mistaken" perception or interpretation. Furthermore, the point of reference may be the individual's real or imagined present behavior or condition, past behavior or condition, or even anticipations of future deviation (recall, for example, the notion of "predelinquency"). Labeling and societal-reactions perspectives often place special emphasis on the persistence of stigma attached to past events; once you are labeled a violator, it long remains difficult to get people to react to you on any other basis. We will be touching on many examples of this as well as analyzing the processes through which such results are shaped. One particularly interesting test of the carry-over impact of deviantness imputations from the past was made in a field study of "legal stigma" conducted by Richard Schwartz and Jerome Skolnick. When prospective employers at resort hotels were shown employment dossiers on job applicants, that were prepared for purposes of the experiment and that were all similar except for systematically varied information about purported criminal records of different degrees, the results pointed up the impact on present opportunities of discrediting information from the past. Only 1 of 25 employers shown the "convict" folder expressed interest in the job applicant; an even more striking finding was that only 3 of 25 employers were prepared to offer jobs to the applicant who had been "tried and acquitted" (Schwartz and Skolnick, 1962).

An interesting twist to the possibility of being identified as a deviator on the basis of information about the past is found with respect to suicide. Although sometimes a suicidal act may be directly observed, more often it is through indirect information and interpretation that suicide is determined to have occurred. As part of his challenging critique of conventional suicide studies (particularly their reliance on officially recorded suicide statistics), Jack Douglas has emphasized the emergence of suicide outcomes (determinations) through an interactive and retrospective identification process. In the strictest sense, a suicide only occurs if and when the appropriate cause-of-death determination is reached:

. . . sociologists who have used the official statistics on suicide have erred in not recognizing that the imputation of the social category of "suicide" is problematic, not only for the theorists of suicide but for the individuals who must impute this category to concrete cases in fulfillment of their duties as officials. . . .

The imputation of the official category of the "cause of death" is very likely the outcome of a complex interaction process involving the physical scene, the sequence of events, the significant others of the deceased, various officials (such as doctors, police), the public, and the official who must impute the category (Douglas, 1967, pp. 189, 190).

Identification of and reaction to people on the basis of *anticipated* deviation is, not surprisingly, a significant aspect of the work of those control agencies that are concerned with treatment and particularly prevention. Some of the legal and moral objections to this kind of prior response have already been mentioned. Often posed against those objections are rationales or rationalizations in terms of treating conditions before they "get too bad," or "heading off" trouble before it can occur. But this kind of response is hardly limited to formal organizations. As we have seen, an element of threat is central to most deviance situations. Sometimes the threat is not directly perceived, but only anticipated. The News Spot summarized here ("The Buzzer System") shows how the desire to *avoid* threatening situations can trigger imputations of deviantness.

If operation of the "buzzer system" reveals that deviantness may be attached to people in advance of actual offense, of even greater importance may

---

NEWS SPOT
The Buzzer System

(February 1975). During recent years in New York City, it has become a widespread practice for shopkeepers to keep their stores locked, admitting prospective patrons "by buzzer." *Village Voice* writer Clark Whelton wanted to know how this system worked. In order to find out, he sought admittance to, and interviewed shopkeepers in stores located in various parts of the city. What determined, he wondered, who would be readily "buzzed in" and who not. Talking with store owners and managers, he discovered that the system required instant screening, that they did this by categorizing potential customers on the basis of preconceived notions as to likely risk, and that by and large they preferred to err on the side of avoiding trouble.

One woman told him that: "I have a sixth sense about these things and I just hope I'm right," but when he asked further about this, Whelton discovered "a set of fairly well-defined guidelines" on which she actually relied. She was least likely to admit black men to the store, and most likely to admit white women. Throughout the city, he found similar tendencies at work. Because decisions had to be made fast and necessarily on the basis of superficial clues ("glimpsed through glass"), such factors as sex, race, age, general appearance, and size of the group seeking admittance were heavily relied on. As Whelton noted, a store owner could not tell anything about the specific individuals involved by using these criteria, but they did "permit the merchant to place the person at his door into predetermined categories." Such categorizing depended on the owner's "image" of likely trouble, formed on whatever basis. Locked doors, Whelton pungently commented, "demand instant judgments based on prejudice or they're useless."

Among New York City shopkeepers a fairly common ordering of perceived risks seemed to be in evidence. Black men were the most likely to face exclusion. Teenagers were next. White women and Orientals were the least likely to be excluded. Somewhere in between came certain other set categories such as black women, Hispanics, and dog owners.

Whelton concluded that: "The trend toward locked stores—theoretically open to the public but in fact open only to a diminishing number of people approved by a merchant's 'sixth sense'—is another long step toward authoritarian government." As fear of crime grew, he hypothesized, and recourse to "private solutions" increased accordingly, respect for the law would be further eroded. The result could well be: "Government of the strongest, by the strongest, and for the strongest. All others can ring for admission."

Source: Based on Clark Whelton, "Shops and Robbers," *The Village Voice,* February 17, 1975, pp. 6–7.

be its illustration of the central place of *typing* or *categorizing* in the production of deviance outcomes. Most of the discussion in the rest of this chapter and a good deal of that in the next directly or indirectly concerns typing tendencies and mechanisms. The process of acquiring deviantness is, in large measure, that of being categorized and treated as belonging to a special deviantized type. This notion, central to all definitional and interactionist perspectives on deviance, is nicely summarized by Earl Rubington and Martin Weinberg:

> Because both typer and audience share a new understanding of the person, they act on that understanding when in his presence. The person who has been typed, in turn, becomes aware of the new definition that has been placed upon him by members of his group. He too, then, takes this new understanding of himself into account when dealing with them. Thus, the situation between typer, audience, and person singled out for typing undergoes a change. The situation for interaction has been redefined and all parties subscribe, willingly or otherwise, to this redefinition. When this happens, a social type has been ratified, and a person has been socially reconstituted (Rubington and Weinberg, 1973, p. 5).

As those authors point out, this is a depiction of what happens in "successful" (from the standpoint of the typers) typing; many factors will affect the degree of success—how far this "ratification" process goes (see further discussion in Rubington and Weinberg, 1978, pp. 5–7). But the idea of at least a partial redefinition of the situation has wide applicability. Once a significant typing effort enters the picture, it must be taken into account, one way or another.

Typing mechanisms seem to come into play especially in the identification and selection aspects of deviance-defining and processing. (As we are going to see very shortly, we should probably avoid the temptation to think of identification or selection as a separate and distinct "stage," for, in fact, it is inextricably intertwined with other aspects of the reaction process.) At whatever levels and in whatever specific contexts it occurs, the process of imputing deviantness invariably incorporates special beliefs or assumptions about, and corresponding reactions to, supposed types of people and types of behavior. As we have already seen, most of us carry around, regardless of whether we have had any direct contact or experience with the particular types, a variety of often misconceived mental associations relating to them. As Walter Lippmann commented, in his classic discussion of stereotypes:

> . . . we do not first see, then define, we define first and then see. . . . We are told about the world before we see it. We imagine most things before we experience them. And those preconceptions, unless education has made us acutely aware, govern deeply the whole process of perception. They mark out certain objects as familiar or strange, emphasizing the difference, so that the slightly familiar is seen as very familiar, and the somewhat strange as sharply alien (Lippmann, 1922, pp. 81, 90).

These "pictures in our minds," as Lippmann aptly described them, help to activate and at the same time are "brought into" deviantizing responses.

Adaptation Six (in the next section) shows, specifically with respect to imputations of homosexuality, how perceived deviators are, at the level of general social interaction, "reread" by other people in a way that conforms with and is heavily dominated by their conceptions regarding a given type, including the very notion that there is a distinct type. The significance of typing becomes even more glaringly apparent when one examines (as we will do two chapters hence) the work of organizations that process deviance. Here the term "selection" becomes especially appropriate because, as we will see, most control agencies and agents have considerable leeway to select out from among a much larger pool of potential "clients" those with reference to whom they will at any point take action—and who will, therefore, remain in the processing system. When these organizations and their personnel thus implement what Erikson has termed the "community screen," typing or **typification,** as it is sometimes also called, often plays a major role in the process.

A good example of this can be found in an often-cited study of police encounters with juveniles, by Irving Piliavin and Scott Briar. Stressing the officer's considerable discretion to choose among various actions and dispositions, they reported:

> . . . both the decision made in the field—whether or not to bring the boy in— and the decision made at the station—which disposition to invoke—were based largely on cues which emerged from the interaction between the officer and the youth, cues from which the officer inferred the youth's character. These cues included the youth's group affiliations, age, race, grooming, dress, and demeanor. Older juveniles, members of known delinquent gangs, Negroes, youths with well-oiled hair, black jackets, and soiled denims or jeans (the presumed uniform of "tough" boys), and boys who in their interactions with officers did not manifest what were considered to be appropriate signs of respect tended to receive the more severe dispositions (Piliavin and Briar, 1964, p. 210).

We should not take this report to indicate that all police everywhere systematically discriminate in this way. In fact, there is quite a bit of evidence from other studies suggesting that often their decisions will not be based on such superficial cues, but on sounder information and good professional judgment (see Reiss, 1971; also Black and Reiss, 1970). However, what seems incontrovertible is that, particularly where statutes and working conditions allow large amounts of discretion in taking action or not taking some kind of typing (accurate or inaccurate, arbitrary or consistently even-handed) will occur. Choices must be made; some categories of persons will be processed and others will not.

The strong tendency to place individuals and their behavior (inferred as well as observed) into standardized categories was also shown in David Sudnow's study of the work of a public defender's office. One of his most important findings (we will note some others later on) was that this work was facilitated by informally developed experience-based conceptions regarding typical offense situations, which Sudnow called "normal crimes," and typical offenders:

> In the course of routinely encountering persons charged with "petty theft," "burglary," "assault with a deadly weapon," "rape," "possession of marijuana," etc., the P.D.

[Public Defender] gains knowledge of the typical manner in which offenses of given classes are committed, the social characteristics of the persons who regularly commit them, the features of the settings in which they occur, the types of victims often involved, and the like. He learns to speak knowledgeably of "burglars," "petty thieves," "drunks," "rapists," "narcos," etc., and to attribute to them personal biographies, modes of usual criminal activity, criminal histories, psychological characteristics, and social backgrounds (Sudnow, 1965, p. 259).

As our analysis proceeds, we will be exploring various features and likely consequences of this standardizing, categorizing process.

Recall that we began this section by noting the significance of visibility or, more aptly, evidentness, when considered from the standpoint of the individual who has a potential for being reacted to as a deviator. By and large and other things being equal, the more widely evident deviation is or becomes, the greater the individual's likelihood of encountering deviantizing responses. The same factor has a broader public significance in determining how certain policy measures are implemented. Those types of law-violators whose activities necessarily bring them into full public view, for example, are more likely to receive attention from official reactors than are those whose behavior may be similar but who can pursue it in private. Thus, streetwalkers much more than residentially situated call girls, street addicts but not the equally drug-dependent physician-addicts (who rarely need to resort to street "connections" to obtain drug supplies) are likely to bear the brunt of law-enforcement activity. More generally still, it is now widely recognized that laws seeking to ban private consensual activities are (as we will see below) notoriously unenforceable (Schur, 1965).

People whose behavior or condition makes them subject to deviance-defining come to the attention of others, as we just saw, in a number of different ways. Concealment (see Chapter 5) can hardly ever be total, and even partial concealment of certain activities and conditions will often be difficult. Various personal resources (financial, educational, assistance from "benefactors," etc.) may make a difference in this, particularly through their bearing on the need to enter contexts in which the deviation will be widely evident. For example, the disabled person who is financially independent may be able to avoid many deviantizing situations, even if confronting them may sometimes be the long-run path to a satisfactory and active adjustment.

Before turning to an examination of "retrospective interpretation," one further point about identification might be worth mentioning. Sometimes, people do identify themselves as deviators by openly revealing their discreditable activity or condition. A good example of this would be a homosexual's "coming out of the closet" (although this term does not always imply public disclosure—at least one writer defines "coming out" in terms of the person's self-recognition of "being" homosexual) (see Dank, 1971). As we will see, there may be various ways of "neutralizing" some of the potentially self-damaging consequences that open disclosure might be expected to produce. For a variety of good reasons—

including self-respect, the desire to combat hypocrisy, insistence on one's full personal rights, solidarity with one's fellow-stigmatized, and the wish to remove the very considerable strains of attempting concealment—people (perhaps increasingly) publicly identify themselves as deviators of various kinds. However, such self-revelation will rarely occur without *some* "price" in terms of stigma-potential and restriction of opportunities being "paid" for it, even if the individual feels that the gains outweigh the losses. Finally, a point to which we will return in considering the issue of "self-labeling": When a person in this way openly reveals what others view as a deviation, they are most emphatically not avowing their deviantness. To unapologetically assert you are a homosexual, or a prostitute, a radical, or a pot smoker, is not at all to acknowledge that you are a deviant. On the contrary, all that is being avowed is that you do what you do or that you are what you are. Far from constituting an avowal of deviance, this will usually entail a repudiation of any such characterization.

Retrospective Interpretation

When individuals are identified as deviators, other people begin to see them "in a totally new light." Deviance imputations seem to have special influence on interpersonal perceptions. As we saw in the Introduction, it is common to see the deviator as nothing but a deviator. Becker, drawing on a classic essay by Everett Hughes, used the term "master status" to describe this influence. As he pointed out, perceived deviance tends to "override all other statuses and have a special priority." The identification of a person as a deviator, "proves to be more important than most others. One will be identified as a deviator first, before other identifications are made" (Becker, 1963, p. 33; see also Hughes, 1945).

We can easily recognize this tendency at work in everyday interaction by thinking about the labels we are likely to use as basic "identifiers" of other people. At least among those whose own conditions place them in the approved or socially dominant categories, deviantized identity tags take on a special centrality in characterizations of other people. Thus, in speaking to third parties, the sighted will quite often identify the object of discussion as "that blind woman," whereas it would be inconceivable that they would identify someone as "that person who can see." Political outlooks and activity come to be used in this way mainly when they are "radical" or "reactionary." Similarly, perceptions of a person may be crucially centered around the fact or belief that he or she is a homosexual. The fact that another person is a heterosexual remains unremarked, virtually unnoticed, insofar as basic ways of characterizing the person are concerned. (We should note, however, that to those in the gay community, hetero-sexuality—establishing the person, from that frame of reference, as an "outsider" —might indeed be noteworthy and serve as a key identifier.)

Now it could be argued that there is a certain element of convenience for the social majority in identifying people in less frequently encountered groups and categories through such tags. Yet, as our earlier discussion of minorities indicated, more than mere numerical frequencies are involved in shaping these situations. Women in our society actually constitute a slight numerical majority, yet in various contexts their womanhood is immediately remarked upon, whereas a man's gender would be considered, in the situation, irrelevant. If common perceptions of female doctors and female executives are dominated by an awareness of their womanness—implicit in the typical comments about how remarkable or exceptional such women must be—it is not simply because these categories occur infrequently, but also because women are still somewhat deviantized in such situations. When they come to be less deviantized as well as numerically more common, they will be viewed in those situations as doctors and executives first, *then* as women or, at least, equally as both. That maleness may be noteworthy in certain other situations only illustrates the same point. The maleness of a nurse is remarked upon because, in addition to not yet being numerically common, male nurse remains a partly deviantized status. Equalizing of social approval or acceptance as well as of frequencies can be expected to produce changed responses to both of these kinds of situations.

At any rate, when we turn to the more "standard" deviance categories, the overbearing effect of identification as a deviator on other people's perceptions is undeniable (for interesting experimental findings that document this tendency, see Snyder and Uranowitz, 1978). As emphasized earlier, the element of perceived threat is central to most deviance situations. We have also seen that the type of threat may vary considerably, and this is certainly true as regards the "nothing but" response to the deviator. Such response can grow out of little more than the personal discomfort of those encountering deviation; at other times, it may be based on strong feelings that people who engage in serious wrongdoing should be set apart and negated. Whatever the source of this response, the impact on the perceived deviator is usually more or less the same, and frequently it is quite devastating. The "nothing but" characterization incorporates ancillary assumptions about the supposed type and, by the same token, squelches recognition of the person's full individuality. As Leonard Kriegel, himself a polio victim, has perceptively commented:

The cripple is judged . . . by those for whom neither the cripple nor his family possess any meaningful reality. His "condition" is an abstraction; he himself is not quite real. Who is going to recognize *me?* asks the cripple. But society has already called into question the very existence of that *me* for it refuses to look at that which makes it uncomfortable. . . .

What the cripple must face is being pigeonholed by the smug. Once his behavior is assumed from the fact that he is a cripple, it doesn't matter whether he is viewed as holy or damned. Either assumption is made at the expense of his individuality, his ability to say "I" (Kriegel, 1969, 1971, pp. 175–176).

We have already seen that such stigma can persist over time, even when the deviation consists of a discrete past act rather than a continuing condition.

Some of this carry-over effect, as we saw in the Schwartz-Skolnick "employment applicant" study, involves restriction of specific opportunities. But, in addition (and as we will be going on to consider in greater depth), the overall character of the person is tainted in a way that is difficult to overcome. As one ex-prostitute has put it, "I don't feel that I'm a whore now, but the social stigma attached to prostitution is a very powerful thing. It makes a kind of total state out of prostitution so that the whore is always a whore. It's as if—you did it once, you become it" (Millett, 1973, p. 65). More generally, as Becker states, "To be labeled a criminal one need only commit a single criminal offense, and this is all the term formally refers to. Yet the word carries a number of connotations specifying auxiliary traits characteristic of anyone bearing the label" (Becker, 1963, p. 33).

The tendencies to see offending people "in a totally new light" and as "nothing but" deviators come together through the process usually referred to as **retrospective interpretation.** Perhaps the classic description of what is involved is that presented by Harold Garfinkel in his discussion of "status degradation ceremonies":

The work of the denunciation effects the recasting of the objective character of the perceived other: The other person becomes in the eyes of his condemners literally a different and *new* person. It is not that the new attributes are added to the old "nucleus." He is not changed, he is reconstituted. The former identity, at best, receives the accent of mere appearance . . . the former identity stands as accidental; the new identity is the "basic reality." What he is now is what, "after all," he was all along (Garfinkel, 1956, pp. 421–422).

This "rereading" of the deviator by others occurs perhaps most dramatically in the formally organized "ceremonies" with which Garfinkel was most concerned. Major examples would be the criminal trial and court proceedings for the commitment of the mentally ill. In such situations, the overall status of a person dramatically shifts. One day you are simply an ordinary citizen, the next in many people's eyes you are "a murderer," "a rapist," "a mental patient." As Adaptation Six shows, retrospective interpretation also occurs in informal ways in everyday interaction. It illustrates, too, that the "reconstituting" process Garfinkel describes is not limited to situations in which deviators are literally condemned and denounced; it is characteristic of other types of deviantizing as well.

ADAPTATION SIX
Imputed Homosexuality*

In an essay that is now considered to be a major early contribution to the newer (definitional, societal reaction) perspectives on deviance, sociologist John Kitsuse called for a shift in focus "from the forms of deviant behavior to the processes by which persons come to be defined as deviant by others." The behavior itself, he emphasized, is not deviant per se. Rather, it is the "processes of societal reaction which sociologically differentiate deviants from non-deviants." As part of a broader interview study that examined reactions to a variety of "forms" of perceived deviance, Kitsuse explored the processes through which individuals are identified and reacted to as "homosexual." His findings point up the way in which the reactions of others contribute to a redefinition of the social identity of the presumed deviator.

Evidence of Homosexuality

Responses to the question "When was the first time you noticed (found out) that this person was homosexual?" and the related probes suggest that an individual's sexual "normality" may be called into question with reference to two broad categories of evidence. (A) *Indirect evidence* in the form of a rumor, an acquaintance's experience with the individual in question subsequently communicated to the subject, or general reputational information concerning the individual's behavior, associates, and sexual predilections may be the occasion for suspecting him to be "different." Many subjects reported that they first "found out" or "knew" that the individuals in question were homosexuals through the reports of others or by "reputation." Such information was generally accepted by the subjects without independent verification. Indeed, the information provided a new perspective for their retrospective as well as prospective observations and interpretations of the individuals' behaviors. An example of how hearsay organizes observation and interpretation is the following statement by a 35-year-old male (a draftsman):

I: Then this lieutenant was a homosexual?

S: Yes.

I: How did you find out about it?

* *Source:* Excerpted from John I. Kitsuse, "Societal Reaction to Deviant Behavior: Problems of Theory and Method," *Social Problems,* 9:3 (Winter 1962), pp. 247–256. Excerpts reprinted with permission; introductory and concluding comments are the present author's—not in the original.

S: The guy he approached told me. After that I watched him. Our company was small and we had a bar for both enlisted men and officers. He would come in and try to be friendly with one or two of the guys.

I: Weren't the other officers friendly?

S: Sure, they would come in for an occasional drink; some of them had been with the company for three years and they would sometimes slap you on the back, but he tried to get over friendly.

I: What do you mean "over friendly?"

S: He had only been there a week. He would try to push himself on a couple of guys—he spent more time with the enlisted personnel than is expected from an officer.

(B) *Direct observation* by the subject of the individual's behavior may be the basis for calling the latter's sexual "normality" into question. The descriptions of behavior which subjects took to be indicative of homosexuality varied widely and were often vague. Most frequently the behaviors cited were those *"which everyone knows"* are indications of homosexuality. For example, a 20-year-old subject reports an encounter with a stranger at a bar:

I: What happened during your conversation?

S: He asked me if I went to college and I said I did. Then he asked me what I was studying. When I told him psychology he appeared very interested.

I: What do you mean "interested?"

S: Well, you know queers really go for this psychology stuff.

I: Then what happened?

S: Ah, let's see. I'm not exactly sure, but somehow we got into an argument about psychology and to prove my point I told him to pick an area of study. Well, he appeared to be very pensive and after a great deal of thought he said, "Okay, let's take homosexuality."

I: What did you make of that?

S: Well, by now I figured the guy was queer so I got the hell outta there.

The responses of other subjects suggest that an individual is particularly suspect when he is observed to behave in a manner which deviates from the *behaviors held in common* among members of the group to which he belongs. For example, a behavior which is presumed to be held in common among sailors in the U.S. Navy is intense and active sexual activity. When a sailor does not affirm, at least verbally, his interest in such activity, his competence as a "male" may be called into question. A 22-year-old engineer, recently discharged from the Navy, responds to the "how did you first know" question as follows:

All of a sudden you just get suspicious of something. I began to wonder about him. He didn't go in for leave activities that most sailors go for. You know, girls and high times. He just never was interested and when you have been out at sea for a month or two, you're interested. That just wasn't Navy, and he was a career man.

Although the responses of our subjects indicate there are many behavioral gestures which "everyone knows" are indicators of homosexuality in males, there are relatively few such gestures that lead persons to suspect females of homosexuality. Following is an excerpt from a 21-year-old college co-ed whose remarks illustrate this lack of definite indicators prior to her labeling of an acquaintance as a homosexual.

I: When was the first time you noticed she was a deviant?

S: I didn't notice it. I thought she had a masculine appearance when I first saw her anyway.

I: What do you mean?

S: Oh, her haircut, her heavy eyebrows.

I: Exactly when did you think she had a masculine appearance?

S: It was long after [the first meeting] that I found out that she was "one."

I: How do you define it?

S: Well, a lesbian. I don't know too much about them. It was _____ who told me about her.

I: Did you notice anything else about her [at the first meeting]?

S: No, because you really don't know unless you're looking for those things.

Unlike "effeminate" appearance and gestures in males, "masculine" appearance in females is apparently less likely to be immediately linked to the suspicion or imputation of homosexuality. The statements of the subject quoted above indicate that although "masculine appearance" is an important element in her conception of a lesbian, its significance did not become apparent to her until a third person told her the girl was homosexual. The remarks of other subjects in our sample who state they have "known" female homosexuals reveal a similar ambiguity in their interpretations of what they describe as indicators of sexual deviance.

A third form of evidence by direct observation is behaviors which the subjects interpreted to be *overt sexual propositions*. Descriptions of such propositions ranged from what the subjects considered to be unmistakable evidence of the person's sexual deviance to ambiguous gestures which they did not attempt to question in the situation. The following is an excerpt from an interview with a 24-year-old male schoolteacher who recounts an experience in a Korean Army barrack:

> I: What questions did he [the alleged homosexual] ask?
>
> S: "How long have you been in Korea?" I told him. "What do you think of these Korean girls?" which I answered, "Not too much because they are dirty." I thought he was probably homesick and wanted someone to talk to. I do not remember what he said then until he said, "How much do you have?" I answered him by saying, "I don't know, about average I guess." Then he said, "Can I feel it just once?" To this I responded with, "Get the hell out of here," and I gave him a shove when he reached for me as he asked the question.

In a number of interviews, the subjects' statements indicate that they interpreted the sequence of the alleged deviants' behavior as progressively inappropriate or peculiar in the course of their interaction with them. The link between such behavior and their judgment that a sexual proposition was being made was frequently established by the subjects' growing realization of its deviant character. A 21-year-old male subject recalls the following experience with his high school tennis coach who had invited him to dinner:

> S: Anyway, when I get there he served dinner, and as I think back on it—I didn't notice anything at the time—but I remember that he did act sort of effeminate. Finally he got up to change a record and picked up some of my English themes. Then he brought them over and sat down beside me. He began to explain some of my mistakes in my themes, and in the meantime he slipped his arm around me.
>
> I: Would you say that this was done in a friendly manner or with an intent of hugging you or something?
>
> S: Well, no, it was a friendly gesture of putting his arm around my shoulder. At that time, I didn't think anything of it, but as he continued to explain my mistakes, he started to rub my back. Then he asked me if I wanted a back rub. So I said, "No! I don't need one." At that time, I began thinking something was funny anyway. So I said that I had to go. . . .

The Imputation of Homosexuality

When a detailed description of the subject's evidence concerning the alleged homosexual was obtained, he was asked, "What did you make of that?" to elicit information about how he interpreted the person's observed or reported behavior. This line of questioning yielded data on the inferential process by which the subject linked his information about the individual to the deviant category "homosexual."

A general pattern revealed by the subjects' responses to this section of the interview schedule is that when an individual's sexual "normality" is called into question, by whatever form of evidence, the imputation of homosexuality is documented by *retrospective interpretations* of the deviant's behavior, a process by which the subject reinterprets the individual's past behavior in the light of the new information concerning his sexual deviance. This process is particularly evident in cases where the prior relationship between the subject and the alleged homosexual was more than a chance encounter or casual acquaintanceship. The subjects indicate that they reviewed their past interactions with the individuals in question, searching for subtle cues and nuances of behavior which might give further evidence of the alleged deviance. This retrospective reading generally provided the subjects with just such evidence to support the conclusion that "this is what was going on all the time."

Some of the subjects who were interviewed were themselves aware of their retrospective interpretations in defining individuals as sexually deviant. For example, a 23-year-old female graduate student states:

I: Will you tell me more about the situation?

S: Well, their relationship was a continuous one, although I think that it is a friendship now as I don't see them together as I used to; I don't think it is still homosexual. When I see them together, they don't seem to be displaying the affection openly as they did when I first realized the situation.

I: How do you mean "openly?"

S: Well, they would hold each other's hand in public places.

I: And what did you make of this?

S: Well, I really don't know, because I like to hold people's hands, too! I guess I actually didn't see this as directly connected with the situation. What I mean is that, if I hadn't seen that other incident [she had observed the two girls in bed together] I probably wouldn't have thought of it [i.e., hand-holding] very much. . . . Well, actually, there were a few things that I questioned later on that I hadn't thought really very much about. . . . I can remember her being quite affectionate towards me several times when we were in our room together, like putting her arm around my shoulder. Or I remember one time specifically when she asked me for a kiss. I was shocked at the time, but I laughed it off jokingly.

Exploring the processes of reaction further by asking his respondents, "What did you do then?", Kitsuse found that the interpersonal sanctions imposed on identified deviants varied greatly. While some persons had reacted with strong explicit disapproval and immediate withdrawal from contact, the modal reaction was "disapproval, implicitly rather than explicitly communicated, and a restriction of interaction through partial withdrawal and avoidance." This variation, he noted, underlines the necessity of studying the interpretation given to a behavior pattern in diverse situations and under varying circumstances. "A sociological theory of deviance must focus specifically upon the interactions which not only define behaviors as deviant but also organize and activate the application of sanctions by individuals, groups, or agencies."

The "master status" concept reflects a recognition that when people impute deviantness, they often draw on sets of beliefs, assumptions, or images that cluster around or comprise their conceptualization of a given behavior or condition. Part of the rereading process consists of connecting these varied and associated elements—including the "auxiliary traits" Becker refers to—with the specific individuals identified as deviators. This mechanism, in turn, seems largely attributable to the reactors' *need for consistency*. Such consistency helps reactors make sense of a deviance situation, and, particularly for formal control agents, it also constitutes a kind of *validation* of any direct action they have taken with respect to the deviator. Erving Goffman has sensitively portrayed how psychiatric case records and case histories may serve these validating and consistency-providing functions. Asserting that such records invariably seem to support the current diagnosis of the person as mentally ill, he comments that the dossier rarely includes notations of contrary evidence:

[It is not regularly used] to record occasions when the patient showed capacity to cope honorably and effectively with difficult life situations. Nor is the case record typically used to provide a rough average or sampling of his past conduct. One of its purposes is to show the ways in which the patient is sick and the reasons why it was right to commit him and is right currently to keep him committed, and this is done by extracting from his whole life course a list of those incidents that have or might have had "symptomatic" significance (Goffman, 1961, pp. 155–156).

Goffman's use of the term "purposes" here may be a bit strong, for his main point is not really that psychiatrists are conspiring against their patients in some ulterior way. Indeed, psychoanalytic theory and psychiatric practice would seem to require this kind of thoroughgoing scrutiny of a patient's past life. Yet, while most of the information in these dossiers may be true, it is probably also true, as Goffman indicates, "that almost anyone's life course could yield up enough denigrating facts to provide grounds for the record's justification of commitment" (Goffman, 1961, p. 159). Through the process of retrospective interpretation there emerges, in Goffman's words, "a new view of the patient's 'essential' character" (Goffman, 1961, p. 375).

John Lofland has argued that such "biographical reconstructions" reflect, "the social need of Others to render Actors as consistent objects . . . there must be a *special* history that *specially* explains current imputed identity. . . . Relative to deviance, the *present evil* of current character must be related to *past evil* that can be discovered in biography" (Lofland, 1966, p. 150). From that standpoint, such professionals as psychologists and psychiatrists may often serve as "specialists in biographical reconstruction" or, as Lofland puts it elsewhere, "consistency" or "imputational" specialists (Lofland, 1966, pp. 150, 155–158). He goes on to mention, as another illustration of this consistency-rendering process, the newspaper coverage accorded two widely publicized crimes: the murder of eight student nurses in Chicago in 1966, of which Richard Speck was convicted; and the case of Charles Whitman who, also in 1966, shot 14 people from a tower at the University of Texas. According to Lofland, in both instances the Detroit *Free Press,* in which he followed the story, kept its coverage restricted to the inside pages *until* continuing investigation of the cases had produced an appropriately "consistent" biography for the offender. This was particularly difficult in the case of Whitman, who had been an Eagle Scout in childhood, had served honorably in the Marines, and had earned good grades in college. Lofland found that in both situations it was only when "a biography supportive of a mad murderer identity" emerged—abetted in the Whitman case by allegation of a brain tumor—that the press coverage moved to the front page (Lofland, 1966, pp. 150–151). Even assuming that Lofland's specific thesis about differential news coverage might only pertain to certain instances, the general idea behind it remains a most suggestive one. We all know that imputations of deviance carry with them potential damage to the recipients. It is no doubt easier for us to foster such imputations when we can justify our responses and actions to others and also to ourselves. A consistent "picture" of offender and offense helps us do that.

This strain toward consistency is also evident in suicide determinations—with respect to which, of course, all interpretation *must* be retrospective. Douglas has noted that the inference processes linking possibly suicidal acts with alleged internal states work in both directions. People believe that severe depression and allied conditions can lead to suicide. By the same token, once they determine a suicide has occurred, they find it easy—at any rate, necessary—to "know" that such a condition was present. Referring to the much-publicized death of film star Marilyn Monroe, Douglas comments: "After most people had decided that her death was a suicide, there was still a need to *understand* (to impute plausible meaning to) her actions by imputing some form of 'deep unhappiness' or 'misery' seen to be *caused* by some situation" (Douglas, 1967, p. 218).

PRIMARY AND SECONDARY DEVIATION

The master status quality in deviance designations and the associated mechanism of retrospective interpretation underlie another major concept—that of **secondary deviation.** Lemert developed this term largely as a way of conceptualizing the impact of negative reaction on the individual deviator. He wanted to show how, in the fact of such response, initial devation came to be "organized subjectively and transformed into active roles" (Lemert, 1951, p. 75). From the standpoint of the individual rule-violator, these "secondary" aspects developed when the deviating behavior "or a role based upon it" came to be used as "a means of defense, attack, or adjustment" to the "differentiating and isolating" reactions of other people (Lemert, 1951, 76, 73). Lemert also suggested, as part of this early and now extremely influential statement, that there usually is "a progressive reciprocal relationship between the deviation of the individual and the societal reaction, with a compounding of the societal reaction out of the minute accretions in the deviant behavior, until a point is reached where in-grouping and outgrouping between society and the deviant is manifest" (Lemert, 1951, p. 76). In other words, deviance situations display a kind of snowballing quality, in which often the negation and isolation of the offending individuals will gradually be expanded and intensified. That this snowballing process may produce self-fulfilling consequences was indicated in Lemert's rough depiction of its likely stages:

> . . . (1) primary deviation; (2) social penalties; (3) further primary deviation; (4) stronger penalties and rejection; (5) further deviation, perhaps with hostilities and resentment beginning to focus upon those doing the penalizing; (6) crisis reached in the tolerance quotient, expressed in formal action by the community stigmatizing of the deviant; (7) strengthening of the deviant conduct as a reaction to the stigmatizing and penalties; (8) ultimate acceptance of deviant social status and efforts at adjustment on the basis of the associated role (Lemert, 1951, p. 77).

It should be emphasized, since the primary-secondary distinction has given rise to much controversy, that Lemert held this out *only* as a rough model of the *probable* sequence. If we think of it in that way—rather than as depicting an invariable and completely irreversible process—it remains a useful guide to the progressions we see at work in many actual deviance situations.

Role Engulfment

We can explore the nature and impact of such **amplification of deviance** (see Wilkins, 1964; Young, 1971) on at least two levels: either in terms of what it means for individual deviators or in terms of the expanding nature of the broader deviance situations or perceived "social problems" in which such individuals become immersed. Actually, the two levels are not easily separable. The social problem is really composed of the experience of many such individuals; at the same time, what happens to any single rule-violator closely reflects the overall dimensions and features of a broader problem.

At each of these levels or when both are seen in combination, to the extent stigmatizing and isolating-restricting responses become widespread, con-sistent, and powerful, the likelihood grows that their impact will be self-confirming and, hence, deviance-amplifying. From the standpoint of the individual toward whom the responses are directed, this tends to involve **role engulfment** (Schur, 1971, pp. 69–73). Both the self-concepts and the behavior of the individual come to be more and more centered around the "deviant role." Increasingly the deviator begins to see himself or herself as "nothing but" a thief, a homosexual, a cripple, a radical. More and more of his or her activities seem to grow out of or be associated with this developing "identity." And, as Lofland has pointed out with respect to this process, "other things being equal, the greater the *consistency, duration* and *intensity* with which a definition is promoted by Others about an Actor, the greater the likelihood that an Actor will embrace that definition as truly applicable to himself" (Lofland, 1966, p. 122).

Lemert has discussed an interesting extreme example of this process: stuttering, which he described as representing in many respects a "pure case" of secondary deviation. He made this claim, "because stuttering thus far has defied efforts at causative explanation. It appears to be exclusively a process-product in which . . . normal speech variations, or at most, minor abnormalities of speech (primary stuttering) can be fed into an interactional or evaluational process and come out as secondary stuttering" (Lemert, 1967, p. 56). As Lemert notes, early reactions to childhood speech difficulties—by family, peers, schoolteachers, and so on—may well be the major determinant of whether or not the difficulty persists and expands. Particularly significant, he suggests, may be the role of speech therapy, which could actually foster rather than impede the growth of secondary stuttering:

. . . we may safely say that going to a speech clinic in all cases confronts the individual with a clear-cut societal definition of the stuttering self. The association with other stutterers and with speech cases in the clinic situation has a clear implication for self and role, as well as the knowledge that other students or members of the community know the function of the clinic. One well-known clinic, at a middle western college, makes it more or less of a prerequisite for treatment of adult stutterers that they make frank avowals in speech and behavior that they are stutterers. This is done by having the stutterers practice blocks in front of mirrors, exaggerate them, copy one another's blocks, and have or fake blocks in public situations. While there are several objectives behind this procedure, one of its chief consequences is to instill an unequivocal self-definition in the stutterer as one who is different from others . . . (Lemert, 1951, p. 159).

One of the things crucially at stake in these self-reconstituting processes is the very basic and general social psychological need for *validation of statuses and identities*. Particularly through retrospective interpretation, the deviantizing process works to deny a person's former legitimate status and identity and to substitute a new and debased conception of the person's "essential character" (to recall Goffman's phrase). Although some people will have personal and social resources that can help them to maintain favorable self-conceptions in such a situation (see Chapter 5), it is never easy to withstand across-the-board redefining by those who, for one reason or another, "count." We always need appropriately confirming and sustaining responses from some reactors who count in order to see ourselves as we would wish to do. Peter Berger has succinctly commented on this point:

> One cannot be human all by oneself and, apparently one cannot hold on to any particular identity all by oneself. The self-image of the officer as an officer [citing an earlier example] can be maintained only in a social context in which others are willing to recognize him in this identity. If this recognition is suddenly withdrawn, it usually does not take very long before the self-image collapses (Berger, 1963, p. 100).

A key element in role engulfment is the sudden or gradual collapse of the supports that uphold and reinforce a person's conception of himself or herself as being socially acceptable. Despite the specially strong impact of "being caught and publicly labeled" (Becker, 1963, p. 61) and of being subjected to the aforementioned status-degradation "ceremonies," this process of engulfment is probably more often a gradual than a sudden one. The transition from acceptableness to deviantness is likely to occur by degree, because it is unlikely that *all* actual and potential supports will be removed or will disappear at once or, to state the same point in another way, because individuals are hardly ever totally lacking in *some* means of resisting such negation. For that reason it may often be misleading to think of secondary deviance as some distinct and absolute culmination of the amplifying process. (Lemert's "ultimate acceptance of deviant social status" does seem to imply such a culmination.) Here again, a reference to degrees of deviantness might be more appropriate.

One of the most insidious aspects of this self-altering process is the strong likelihood that deviators will begin to view themselves with contempt or even hatred. They will tend not only to see themselves as "nothing but"—whatever the specific behavioral category is—but also to incorporate in their self-conceptions the deviantness that has been attached to that category. This is the same social psychological process, in which stigmatization produces low self-esteem, that many observers have noted in connection with studies of racial minority-group membership. As the psychoanalysts Abram Kardiner and Lionel Ovesey stated in their classic exploration of the personality problems of blacks, "the Negro gets a poor reflection of himself in the behavior of whites, no matter what he does or what his merits are," and this leads to, "endless vicious circles and blind alleys that are set in motion by the frantic efforts to remove the causes of self-hatred . . ." (Kardiner and Ovesey, 1951, 1962, p. 297; see also Grier and Cobbs, 1968).

Martin Hoffman has attributed the frequently noted "promiscuity" of male homosexuals to this kind of self-hatred generated through social negation and stigmatization. Because of these social attitudes and forces, the gay individual develops "a sense that his homosexual behavior is morally wrong, and also that, therefore, his partner is bad." Under these circumstances, "The homosexual's own self-concept cannot easily commit him to being any more of a homosexual than is required by the sexual drive itself." According to Hoffman, this is (along with the practical wish to preserve anonymity) a major factor in the apparent appeal of temporary sexual encounters with strangers. It is also a major obstacle to forming long-term, intimate homosexual relationships. "The feelings of guilt —conscious or unconscious . . . serve to contaminate the relationship and prevent the possibility of its developing into one of warm intimacy" (Hoffman, 1969, pp. 175, 176). In a less psychoanalytic vein, homosexual activist Dennis Altman has noted the impact of guilt and self-hatred "in most overtly homosexual literature" and in "the hostility that many homosexuals have for any kind of homosexual movement," as well as in "the way in which homosexuals 'objectify' each other—through involvement in a "world that is organized around sexual barter and its dehumanizing effect" (Altman, 1973, pp. 62–63). Guilt and low self-esteem are, of course, also implicit in the extensive efforts of many homosexuals to conceal their sexual preference (Chapter 5). We know that many individuals do manage to overcome these problems, yet Altman, who poignantly describes his own coming to grips with his homosexuality and his eventual ability to openly acknowledge it, comments that, "even now there are times when I flinch from being identified as a homosexual, for one feels the contempt that the identification brings. It requires a self-assurance that very few, either gay or straight, possess, to be fully immune to the effect of social disapproval" (Altman, 1973, p. 64).

When the deviation, as in this case, involves such a central aspect of a person's life situation as sexual orientation, this self-hatred tendency is bound to be especially pronounced. But the same general process can be seen at work in substantively varied realms of deviantizing. It is particularly evident with respect to highly visible physical disabilities. As Erving Goffman states, of the person subject to this kind of stigma:

> . . . the standards he has incorporated from the wider society equip him to be ultimately alive to what others see as his failing, inevitably causing him, if only for moments, to agree that he does indeed fall short of what he really ought to be. Shame becomes a central possibility, arising from the individual's perception of one of his own attributes as being a defiling thing to possess, and one he can readily see himself as not possessing (Goffman, 1963, p. 7).

It is not surprising then, that a student of dwarfs finds that such persons often engage in "overcompensation"—bravado, boasting about sexual exploits, wearing elaborate attire or make-up—"centered around their concern with the normal-sized world's recognition of their status as *adult, fellow human beings*" (Truzzi, 1971, pp. 190–191). Or that Scott, in his perceptive study of blindness, emphasizes that its stigma "makes problematic the integrity of the blind man as an acceptable human being." Blind persons cannot ignore the imputation of inferiority, even though there may be possibilities for defending against it. "If, as sometimes occurs, the blind man shares the values of the sighted, the process becomes even more insidious; for when this is the case, a man's personal identity is open to attack from within as well as from without" (Scott, 1969, p. 25).

Closely related to the potentially emerging congruence of other people's conceptions of the deviator and his or her own conceptions are the somewhat more "objective" aspects of role-restriction. The person's available life opportunities as well as available self-concepts become more and more limited. And again, of course, there is a "feedback" from what one is able to do to how one is able to see oneself. Lemert used the concept of "role primacy" ["the degree to which a given role takes precedence over other roles" (Lemert, 1951, p. 90)] to describe this self-reinforcing impact. Many of the examples we noted above showed how the "master status" aspect of deviantized roles lends them a unique potential for such role primacy. The ex-prostitute who reported that, "It's as if—you did it once, you become it"; the strippers whose "respectable" activities and, most likely, self-concepts gradually receded into the background; the mental retardates who had to cope with the devastating impact of being judged incompetent—persons like these who experience deviantizing responses almost always face a constriction of the range of options open to them. The field study involving hypothetical employment applicants indicates but one of the very practical restrictions on opportunity that the person defined and treated as a deviator is likely to encounter. Because it is the overall or "essential" character of such persons that has become tainted, they face the probability of obstacles in almost all domains of ordinary existence—getting and keeping jobs, finding a satisfactory place to live, forming social and sexual relationships, and so on.

Again, this impact will occur in varying degrees, depending partly on the preexisting resources of particular individuals. Nonetheless, serious imputations of deviantness will almost always carry the likelihood of some appreciable narrowing of options. A good way of thinking about this is in terms of *denial of "role distance"* (Lofland, 1966, p. 170). Deviantized persons find themselves less and less able to step back from the tainted role, precisely because they are allowed fewer and fewer options. As Lofland notes, this occurs most flagrantly in "total institutions" such as prisons and mental hospitals (see Adaptation Seven, below; also Goffman, 1961), where the entire daily existence is centered around the new and demeaning inmate role. Yet something very much like this frequently happens in the outside world as well, often building up to a very high degree of role restriction indeed. Here, too, imputed deviantness seems to follow wherever the individual goes. Scott, for example, notes "the fact that most encounters involving the blind and the sighted are defined as charitable" (Scott, 1969, p. 36). From this it follows that, whatever else blinded persons are attempting to accomplish, they are almost always forced into playing some standard version of "the blindness role."

We have seen, too, that past as well as present deviation is difficult to cast aside. Frank Tannenbaum's discussion of the "dramatization of evil" made the point nicely with respect to the delinquent or criminal. Once the individual has been so stigmatized, "the community expects him to live up to his reputation, and will not credit him if he does not live up to it" (Tannenbaum, 1938, p. 477). Here again, through retrospective interpretation, reactors tend to "see" only those bits of evidence that are consistent with the imputed deviantness. Numerous studies have documented the extreme difficulties encountered by former mental patients, treated drug addicts, and ex-convicts in convincing other people they are "no longer like that"—a prerequisite to "making it" on "the outside." Thus the belief that, say, "once an addict, always an addict"—which some addicts themselves may have come to believe—can easily become self-confirming. Marsh Ray, writing of drug addicts who have undergone institutional withdrawal treatment, refers to such a person's " 'running struggle' with his problems of social identity" on return to the community. The ex-addict who is successful in this struggle, "relates to new groups of people, participates in their experience, and to some extent begins to evaluate the conduct of his former associates (and perhaps his own when he was an addict) in terms of the values of the new group" (Ray, 1961, p. 136). This is not at all easy to do, given the general and persisting reactions people in the community at large have to perceived deviators. (The possibilities for such "re-labeling" *within* and through treatment programs are considered in Chapter 6). From her careful ethnographic study of skid row alcoholics, Jacqueline Wiseman concluded bitingly that, apart from the few who somehow manage to "reclaim a lost existence," there are "three major ways off Skid Row: (1) become a live-in servant for an institution (or, once in a while, for a professional woman); (2) go into alcoholic rehabilitation as a profession; (3) die" (Wiseman, 1970, p. 237).

Further Amplification

Feeding back into as well as going beyond the engulfment of particular individuals in deviant roles, is a broader amplification and secondary expansion of deviance situations or social problems. One of the advantages of using the term "role engulfment" to describe the impact of deviantizing on individuals is that then the concept "secondary deviation" can be used in a more inclusive sense, to cover both that impact and the broader aspects of community- or society-level expansion.

Through their general influence on public attitudes and also through the role they may play in relation to specific deviance-and-control cycles, the mass media may significantly contribute to deviance amplification. The media would seem to be in a pivotal position with respect to undermining and rebutting or, on the other hand, promoting and reinforcing many of the widely held stereotypes and misconceptions regarding deviance issues. All too often, at least until recently, media content has served to reinforce false beliefs and short-sighted attitudes. Typically, an issue of great public concern has been whether crime depictions on television, for example, would cause people to become "criminals." But an equally important issue, though one much less discussed, is this potential impact of the media on defining and reacting to deviation of various kinds.

Noting research on "popular conceptions of mental health" (Nunnally,

1961) in which extensive stereotyping was found in media content, Thomas Scheff has suggested that cross-pressures probably shape public attitudes and beliefs in this area: "the opinions of experts, as expressed in mental-health campaigns and 'serious' mass media programming, pulling public opinion away from stereotypes, but with the more frequent and visible mass media productions reinforcing the traditional stereotypes" (Scheff, 1966, p. 70). Most flagrantly, as Scheff and others have pointed out, the media create distorted impressions through the common practice of linking persons' records of past deviation with their involvements in current incidents. References to "ex-mental patient" in reports on violent crimes are frequent, even though the actual incidence of such crimes among former mental patients is lower than among the general population. As Scheff points out, a news item like the following is most improbable: "Mrs. Ralph Jones, an ex-mental patient, was elected president of the Fairview Home and Garden Society at their meeting last Thursday" (Scheff, 1966, p. 72). Through this mechanism of *selective reference*—a version of the aforementioned retrospective interpretation—false beliefs are engendered, both about the general adjustment of former mental patients and about a supposed link between mental illness and violent crime. References in crime reporting to "an ex-convict" or "a former convict released on parole" carry the same kind of distorting potential; this practice "hides" the fact that overall parolees do not have very high rates of involvement in serious crimes. A similar kind of reinforcement of popular conceptions was the long-standing practice in news reporting, now largely abandoned, of placing the phrase "a Negro" after the name of black criminal suspects while not similarly designating race when the suspect was white.

This news account (p. 248) suggests the potential for a kind of "double" deviance-amplification involving the media. The police behavior depicted in the programming is, to begin with, a kind of secondary deviation—improper or criminal acts by law-enforcers that have been prompted by efforts to root out the "primary" criminality. This development does occur frequently in actual police work (see the section on "victimless crimes," pp. 450–457). When illegal police behavior is then presented with apparent approval on TV, additional amplification of deviance may occur. Public attitudes that could further reinforce or encourage such police illegality itself may develop or be strengthened. At the same time, such attitudes may add general fuel to the "war on crime" mentality which, paradoxically, often leads to more crime as well as to more crime "control."

A British study (Armstrong and Wilson, 1973) has pointed up how the media can contribute to the expansion of deviance in a specific situation. In the late 1960s, substantial newspaper and television coverage was devoted to the "problem" of juvenile gangs in the Easterhouse section of Glasgow. Ironically, the coverage—which the authors of the study found to convey highly questionable images of youths in the area—was in part due to the publicity attending announcement of a new "helping" project to be conducted there. Research showed, though, that members of the public "accepted the content of media portrayal,

NEWS SPOT
Police Illegality on TV

(May 1977). As a result of research in which they monitored television crime dramas during more than a two-year period, legal studies professors Stephen Arons and Ethan Katsh have warned about the depiction of police illegality in such programs. Asserting that unconstitutional and illegal behavior by police officers is frequently presented with approval, if not glorified, Arons and Katsh charged that the result could well be public acceptance of such police illegality in real-life contexts. In the course of monitoring TV crime shows broadcast between the fall of 1974 and spring of 1976, they found, for example, that in 15 randomly selected prime-time programs televised during one week, there were 43 separate scenes "in which serious questions could be raised about the propriety of the police action." They judged 21 of these to involve "clear constitutional violations," 15 others to involve police brutality or harassment, and the final 7 to be "cases in which there was no mention of a citizen's constitutional rights." Commenting that television crime programs seemed to project an image "that is alien to the Constitution," the researchers noted further that exposure to such programming might represent the average citizen's main source of information about police work. The challenge for television, they concluded, is "how to give sane, constitutional values access to the TV crime scene."

(*Source:* Based on news article in *The New York Times,* May 31, 1977, p. 59.)

and even enlarged on it." Residents of the area themselves "felt threatened by such media messages" and started a campaign to defend the area's good reputation. Overall, however, the area became an "object of curiosity" and came to be seen generally as "a severe delinquent area." "But more importantly, publicity began to sensitize authorities to the possibilities of 'trouble' there." As a result, there was "widening of police definitions of 'delinquent behaviour,'" which in turn had a marked effect "by colouring youth's attitudes towards the police, by causing more of them to be officially labelled delinquent, and by effecting behavioural changes in the peer group." As Armstrong and Wilson properly noted, in the ongoing struggle over alternative public views of the area, "The Easterhouse youth were the group with *least power* of all to present their definitions, and conceivably the group for whom the consequences of the reputation were greatest." Over a period of time, the actual consequences included exclusion and withdrawal from various conventional activities and the experiencing of a generalized stigma simply because of living in the area. The authors concluded that, "the events surrounding the emergence of the reputation of Easterhouse youth brought about *objective* changes in the day-to-day conditions of interaction of these boys. The reputation, whilst emerging *independently* of any shift in youth behaviour, created conditions whereby amplification could occur" (Armstrong and Wilson, 1973, pp. 86–88).

As this example shows, the implementation of public policy itself frequently has deviance-amplifying consequences. Indeed, social control agencies (see Chapter 6) "produce" deviance through their processing activities. The deviation they deal with at any given time, furthermore, is often amplified in the future as the individuals they have processed find legitimate opportunities closed to them and experience other indications of persisting stigma. By documenting self-confirming elements of societal reaction, recent "labeling" and "law-in-action" analyses have lent much support to Lemert's idea that social control might often cause deviance rather than vice versa. The Easterhouse study underlines the fact that as community dimensions of the perceived problem expand, the role engulfment of particular persons seen as deviators or potential deviators is likely to increase simultaneously. Both kinds of deviance-amplification are joined in a common process and typically display a more or less shared sequence. Figure 4.3 illustrates the way in which public policy efforts—in this case, those relating to public intoxication—can contribute to a deviance-amplification "cycle" of initial behavior, definition and reaction, subsequent behavior, redefinition and further reaction, and so on.

The expansion here is at two levels: on the one, affecting public consciousness of a general social problem and, on the other, reinforcing the meaning category that designates a specific "type" of offending person (the "drunk," the "bum") both within the public at large and among the "offenders" themselves. To *fully* know one is "a drunk," perhaps, a person must have gone through *some* such cyclical process. For the chronic public drunk, it is typical to experience such processing repeatedly. Hence the common reference to the "revolving door" treatment accorded impecunious alcoholics. As Jacqueline Wiseman states, "Although the chronic drunkenness offender makes many trips through drunk court, it is not too surprising that he never becomes completely accustomed to the way he is treated there. The mass sentencing, the arbitrariness of the judge, the extraneous factors that seem to go into sentencing decisions, all these shock and embitter him" (Wiseman, 1970, p. 100). Along with the aforementioned restrictions on opportunity, the frequent but abortive efforts at "drying out" and the generally debilitating and demoralizing conditions of life on skid row, these legal processes contribute to a very substantial reinforcement and intensification of personal deviantness as well as of the broader dimensions of the drunkenness problem (Wiseman, 1970, p. 100; see also Blumberg, *et al.*, 1973; President's Commission on Law Enforcement and Administration of Justice, 1967a; and Adaptation Nine).

Drug Policies: A Major Example

Amplification of deviance situations becomes even more striking when, as in the case of narcotics control efforts, it is not merely certain public behavior but the very possession and use of a desired substance that is legally proscribed.

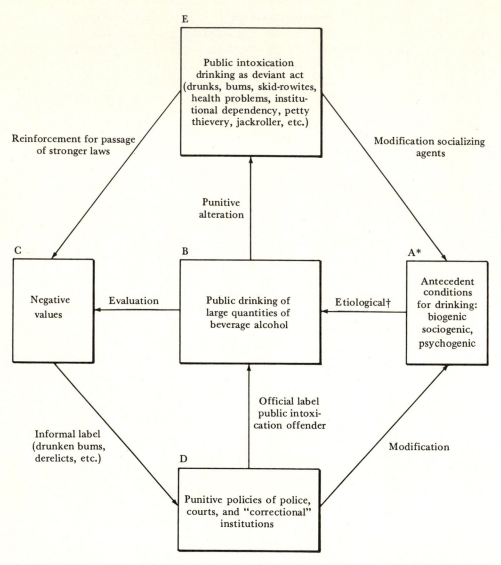

* Letters indicate theoretical sequence of events.

† Arrows indicate theoretical direction of influence.

Figure 4.3. Model of the deviancy reinforcement cycle for public intoxication. *Source: David J. Pittman, "Public Intoxication and the Alcoholic Offender in American Society," in President's Commission on Law Enforcement and Administration of Justice, Task Force Report: Drunkenness. Washington, D.C.: U.S. Government Printing Office, 1967, p. 10.*

Commenting on police efforts to control marihuana use in the Notting Hill district of London, Jock Young has nicely depicted major aspects of the self-propelling deviation-reaction sequence:

1. Intensive police action serves to increase the organization and cohesion of the drug-taking community . . . heightening their consciousness of themselves as a group with definite interests over and against those of the wider society. . . .

2. A rise in police action increases the necessity for the drug-taker to segregate himself. . . .

3. The further the drug-taker evolves deviant norms, the less chance there is of his re-entering the wider society. . . .

4. As police concern with drug-taking increases, drug-taking becomes more and more a secret activity. . . . Drug-taking and trafficking thus move from being peripheral activities . . . to become a central activity of great symbolic importance. . . .

5. The price of marihuana rises, the gains to be made from selling marihuana become larger and the professional pusher begins to emerge as police activity increases. . . . The criminal underworld becomes more interested in the drug market. . . .

6. The marihuana user becomes increasingly secretive and suspicious of those around him. . . .

7. As police activity increases, the marihuana user and the heroin addict begin to feel some identity as joint victims of police persecution. . . . The general social feeling against all drugs creates a stricter control of the supply of heroin [under Britain's legal-prescription-for-addicts policy] to the addict. . . .

8. As the mass media fan public indignation over marihuana use, pressure on the police increases . . . the police will act with greater vigilance and arrest more marihuana offenders . . . statistics for marihuana offenders soar . . . [and, as public alarm grows] We have entered what I term a fantasy crime wave, which does not necessarily involve at any time an actual increase in the number of marihuana smokers . . . (Young, 1971, pp. 45–51).

Many writers have noted a similar process of amplification—only on a larger scale and with more extensive adverse consequence—in connection with American efforts to control heroin addiction through restrictive criminal laws. Most disinterested observers agree that major aspects of the American heroin situation reflect substantial secondary elaboration of the problem; that is, they are in the main directly attributable neither to the factors that "cause" people to take such drugs in the first place nor to any necessary effects produced through using the drugs. Rather, they are fostered and reinforced by the very policies that aim at limiting, if not eliminating, the drug-taking (see Lindesmith, 1947; Schur, 1962; Schur, 1965; Lindesmith, 1965; President's Commission on Law Enforcement and Administration of Justice, 1967b; Goode, 1972; Brecher, *et al.,* 1972; Wald, *et al.,* 1972). When we consider the more general issue of "victimless crimes" in Chapter 7), we will be exploring further a number of standard ways in which restrictive laws aimed at proscribing a variety of consensual transactions tend to amplify rather than reduce deviance. Prostitution, abortion, homosexuality, gambling, and pornography are other major examples of this kind of situation. However, we should note now, at least some key aspects of amplification such as that seen in the case of drugs.

Without question, the most significant secondary elements in this situation are the illicit drug traffic and crimes by addicts to support their habit. American drug policies, under which possession and use of heroin have been strongly banned by law, have promoted and reinforced a supply-and-demand cycle that provides powerful economic incentives that support black-market operations. Because the banned drugs are widely and strongly desired, their provision becomes so profitable that ways of making them available are always found; and police efforts to curb this traffic meet with little success. As Herbert Packer, a law professor, wisely pointed out, the restrictive law establishes a "crime tariff": "Regardless of what we think we are trying to do when we make it illegal to traffic in commodities for which there is an inelastic demand, the effect is to secure a kind of monopoly profit to the entrepreneur who is willing to break the law" (Packer, 1968, p. 279). Far from deterring suppliers, enforcement efforts have for the most part only increased the risks of black-market operations—the costs of which have been borne by the "consumer" through higher prices, which represent higher profits for the illicit trafficker. As drug consultants to the Ford Foundation pointed out not long ago, "The illegality of heroin is, of course, the sole reason for its high cost in this country. In England, the pharmacy cost of heroin is $.04 per grain (60 mg.), or $.00067 per mg. In the United States, the recent street price is $30–$90 per grain, or $.50–$1.50 per mg., depending on the time and place of sale and the quantity and quality of the drug" (Wald, *et al.,* 1972, p. 28).

Most students of the American drug scene likewise assert that a great deal of the theft and prostitution that exists in our large cities is attributable to the efforts of addicts to finance their habits. The weight of the available evidence supports this claim (see, for example, Brecher, *et al.,* 1972; Wald, *et al.,* 1972), although come commentators persist (see discussion in Wilson, *et al.,* 1972; Wilson, 1975) in disputing the addiction-leads-to-crime interpretations. They cite findings indicating prior criminality on the part of many persons who become addicts and insist also that a greater proportion of the money-producing crimes is committed by nonaddicts. Recent research has thrown into some question, too, the previously assumed invariability of long-term users developing the complete dependence on heroin that would necessarily generate a habit requiring large amounts of money. One study (McAuliffe and Gordon, 1974) suggested a distinction between "weekender" and "hardcore" types of heroin users; another (Gould, *et al.,* 1974) referred to the possibility of being a "chipper." Against these possibilities, however, must be placed the undoubted fact that for those many impecunious Americans who *do* become fully addicted—and *regardless* of what their prior law-abiding or law-violating record may have been—crime almost certainly becomes an economic necessity. Thus, the research report that mentioned "chippers," went on to note:

> Being a dope fiend involves a lot of money. Here in Riverdale a bag costs $6, a nickel bag costs $10, and a half load goes for anywhere from $45 to $60. While there aren't many dope fiends in Riverdale shooting more than a half load a day, that is still a lot of money to come up with on a regular basis. There are some people who earn almost all their dope money legitimately, usually by running something like a leather goods store, or working for the university. But there aren't too many jobs around that provide the kind of money, freedom, and spare time that a dope fiend needs. And, let's face it, if a guy really wanted to make it in the business world, he probably wouldn't be into heroin. So most dope fiends have to hustle for their money (Gould, *et al.,* 1974, pp. 48–49).

The fact that doctor-addicts in our country (see Winick, 1961) and British addicts who obtain heroin legally hardly ever commit such money-generating offenses underscores the fact that it is the financial pressure generated by illegality that largely propels this criminal behavior.

What all this means for specific individuals who become addicted will, of course, vary somewhat depending upon their particular circumstances. The general tendency seems clear. Except for a small proportion with great financial resources, people who become heavily addicted will of necessity be forced into secondary crime to obtain funds with which to buy drugs, will become heavily immersed in an underworld-related drug distributing system and associated drug subculture, and will run high risks of arrest and incarceration. As a result, their lives will come to revolve almost entirely around buying, selling, and using drugs; this would not necessarily be the case were the drugs legally available. In short, by treating addicts as criminals these policies have forced them to become criminals. (As we will see later on, laws of this type also tend to generate a good deal of secondary deviation of various kinds on the part of the police.)

Awareness of this secondary elaboration of our overall drug situation lies behind the strong interest many American observers have evinced in the contrasting British heroin policies (see Schur, 1962; Lindesmith, 1965; Scull, 1972). While the British have long maintained statutory controls over possession and distribution of drugs, treatment of addiction has always been considered a medical matter. This has meant that addicted persons can obtain drugs legally by medical prescription and free or at nominal cost under the National Health Service. For many years under this system the British drug situation remained benign. Beginning in the early 1960s, British authorities began to express concern about a possible increase in addiction. As a consequence, official policy on prescribing for addicts was tightened somewhat—thenceforth addicts would only be able to obtain their drugs at government-designated treatment centers. Because the medically oriented approach in Britain has occasioned much controversy over the years in the United States, there was considerable publicity here at that time suggesting a "failure of the British system." Many objective observers believe such an assessment involved great exaggeration. Even during the period of heightened official concern, the dimensions of the heroin problem in Britain remained extremely modest by American standards. Thus, by the late 1960s, when the tightened system might already itself have had an apparent amplifying effect (for example, by producing higher statistics through better reporting), the government was estimating a total of fewer than 3000 addicts to heroin and other opiate-type drugs for the country as a whole (Scull, 1972, p. 294). More important still, authoritative accounts make clear that no significant amount of addict-crime and no substantial illicit traffic in opiates have emerged under the British approach (Scull, 1972, pp. 282–314; May, 1972).

Although we must recognize the difficulties in comparing the impacts of these contrasting drug policies—after all, the two countries are far from identical socioculturally, and their drug "problems" differ too—many American commentators continue to believe that the medically oriented approach has helped Britain keep its addiction situation within reasonable limits. By enabling addicts to obtain their drugs legally, it has undercut the economic incentives that support a black market in drugs and has all but eliminated the addict's need to commit crimes to support the habit. Between 1912 and 1925 American addicts were somewhat similarly able to receive low-cost drugs through clinics set up in over 40 cities. For a variety of reasons, including some instances of blatant mismanagement, the clinics were shut down by the government. Although most observers view that specific experiment as having proved unsatisfactory, the broader implications of the American clinic experience are not really clear. Although its failure has often been asserted by opponents of drug-law reform, including American narcotics officials, objective evidence suggests that it did not constitute any kind of "fair test" of medical prescription-for-addicts in general (Lindesmith, 1965, ch. 5).

When various proposals have been advanced more recently in the United States to undertake an experimental test of the British approach, the aim has been to see whether in this country, too, the secondary aspects of the drug scene might not thereby be greatly reduced. Invariably, these proposals have met with great opposition, particularly on the ground that legal prescription of drugs to addicts constitutes "giving up" the fight to "cure" addiction. However, advocates of the British approach have never implied that the scheme could eliminate addiction. Instead, they have focused on the possibilities for reducing the secondary social harms currently associated with it. Addicts, they insist, get their drugs now—illegally. A medical approach would prevent their "criminalization," and placing drug provision in a medical rather than underworld context might also increase the eventual prospects for long-term individual cures. They also assert the inevitable failure of the currently existing law-enforcement approach to drug problems (see the section on "victimless crimes" in Chapter 7), a "vested interest" in which, some have suggested (Lindesmith, 1965), has led various narcotics officials to oppose changes in our drug policies.

A similar concern with reducing secondary deviation has provided the main impetus for the recent American development of methadone maintenance programs. Under this scheme, addict-patients are first hospitalized and withdrawn from heroin; then they are switched over to the milder addictive drug methadone, which can be administered orally in an orange juice solution. Once they are "stabilized" on a proper dosage, they should experience neither craving for heroin nor any adverse effects from the methadone—provided its use is continued. Administration of the drug can be on an outpatient basis, eventually with the patient obtaining, say, a week's supply for daily home administration. As a consequence of methadone maintenance, many addicts have been quite successful in leading otherwise normal lives—working satisfactorily, functioning reasonably well in ordinary life situations, and avoiding involvement in crime (see discussion in DeLong, 1972). Although numerous objections have been made to these programs and they have often suffered administrative and other setbacks, their potential for reducing addict-crime seems particularly significant. Figure 4.4, taken from one of the more careful evaluation studies of methadone maintenance, indicates the significant overall decline in arrest rates that can occur when addicts avail themselves of such treatment. Not all studies have produced such "positive" findings. (For a more negative assessment, see Kleinman, Lukoff, and Kail, 1977.) And, admittedly, methadone programs are limited to volunteer patients who may be relatively good prospects for avoiding criminal involvement. Furthermore, as the parenthetical figures at the bottom of the page, which indicate the absolute numbers of patients still under evaluation at successive time periods, make clear, such programs experience substantial attrition over a number of years. But these same figures also point up an encouraging fact: For those addicts who *do* stick with such a program, there may be a continuing and dramatic decline in the risk of arrest.

Critics of "Secondary Deviation"

Recently, certain sociologists—as part of a more general evaluation and critique of the labeling perspective—have criticized the distinction between primary and secondary deviation (see discussion of these criticisms in Suchar, 1978, pp. 224–232). In doing so, these critics have not been much concerned with the kinds of broad amplification and secondary expansion of deviance situations that we have just been examining. This seems a significant oversight, since at least one important value of focusing on secondary aspects of deviation lies in highlighting this overall amplification of deviance problems. However, the main point the critics have been raising refers to something else—whether, in studying the individual deviator's role engulfment, labeling analysts may have exag-

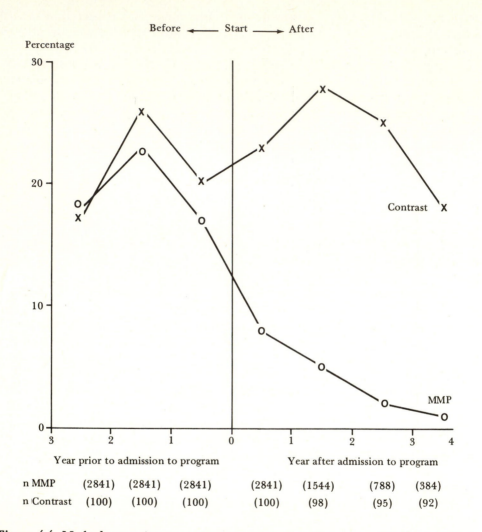

Figure 4.4. Methadone maintenance treatment program—Percentage distribution of arrests for 2841 men in methadone maintenance program, 3 months or longer as of March 31, 1970, and contrast group by months of observation. *Source:* Frances Rowe Gearing, "Successes and Failures in Methadone Maintenance Treatment of Heroin Addiction in New York City," in *Proceedings,* Third National Conference on Methadone Treatment. National Institutes of Mental Health. Washington, D.C.: U.S. Government Printing Office, 1971, p. 12.

gerated or asserted without adequate basis the importance of secondary elements. This argument is, essentially, twofold: On the one hand, these critics note, it is possible for "deviant careers" to develop without any official "labeling" of the individuals concerned. At the same time, they assert in a second strand of the argument, that when labeling does occur, it *does not always increase or amplify* the deviation. As a consequence, they claim, labeling is "neither a necessary nor a sufficient condition" for the presence of deviant identity or career (see Davis, 1972, p. 461; Davis, 1975, pp. 186–187; and Mankoff, 1971).

If the point of these arguments is simply to demonstrate that it is difficult to sort out for analytic purposes the primary and secondary aspects of deviance, they would be useful, though they would not necessarily contradict any claim to the contrary by those who adopt a labeling perspective. In fact, it seems to be the critics who wish to separate these elements, in order to show that the supposed secondary ones are *less* important than the primary ones. It may be questioned whether this effort really makes much sense or, indeed, whether— given the "building-up" and reciprocally interacting process that shapes deviance outcomes—it is at all possible.

We can see this better by looking at some specific examples. Two of the leading critics, Mankoff and Davis, both cite studies showing that individual deviation can clearly persist even in the absence of any formal labeling. Among the major examples given are marihuana use—noting particularly the study by one of the labeling approach's main theorists, Howard Becker (Adaptation Five, in this chapter); homosexuality, the persisting occurrence of which does not for the most part seem to be "accounted for" by negative labeling; and the physician-addict, who avoids official labeling but nonetheless persists in his or her drug-taking. Mankoff, arguing further that most deviation (which he considers "achieved," as opposed to the "ascribed" deviation of physical disabilities) requires a deviating act, emphasized the possibility that career deviance may often be due to "the *continued* effects" of whatever caused the initial rule-violating rather than to the impact of any secondary elaboration (Mankoff, 1971, p. 212).

As you by now may have gathered, such arguments incorporate a very narrow conception of labeling and evidence little attention to the important distinction between the occurrence of behavior and its characterization. What do we really mean when we speak of a "deviant" identity or career? Mankoff, for example, wants to hold open the possibility that sometimes "deviant behavior" persists because of "a positive attachment to rule-breaking." This reflects a commendable desire to depict certain types of perceived deviators (bohemians, counter-culturists, the politically disenchanted, etc.) as "freely espousing career deviance as a positive alternative to career conformity" (Mankoff, 1971, p. 212). No doubt it is true that such behaviors as marihuana use, homosexuality, radical politics, and so on, are persisted in regardless of whether individual offenders are officially identified and reacted against. But does that mean that deviant careers and identities are free of secondary elements and that they are explained fully by reference to primary "causes" or free choices? It does not.

After all, it is deviantness—a specific complex of meaning qualities—that makes a career or identity "deviant," and, unless we can somehow accept the notion that such meanings inhere in the behaviors or the individuals themselves, then we have to recognize that *all* the deviantness is secondary. Thus, some of *the broader kinds of labeling*—collective characterizations of the sort Becker had in mind when he noted that "social groups create deviance by making the rules" —*must always be a factor* in deviant careers and self-conceptions. To put it simply, one may freely choose to be a marihuana smoker or a homosexual, but that is not the same as freely choosing to be "a deviant." It is uncommon for people to seek deviantness as the type of meaning they would like to have widely attached to their behavior. Acts subject to deviantizing *may be caused* by a variety of factors *or freely chosen; deviantness is almost always imposed on behavior from without.*

The argument against the secondary deviation concept falters because it rests on an exclusive preoccupation with the presence or absence of the behavior itself along with a heavy focus on the reasons for the behavior's occurrence. In other words, these critics are insisting, to take just one example, that people do not become homosexuals or persist in homosexuality *because of* labeling. The "becoming" and "persisting" aspects of this argument should be considered separately. As to the former, the critics are really arguing a point that is largely irrelevant to how we should evaluate the merits of the secondary deviation concept, for the users of that concept themselves would attribute the becoming mostly to a variety of primary causal factors. Indeed, that is precisely the other side of or the complementing theme in the primary-secondary distinction. The issue of the behavior's persistence is more complicated. Some labeling analysts do at times seem to be saying that persistence in deviation is due to official negative reactions, emphasizing their impact on self-conceptions, the narrowing of available options, and so on. If and when the argument is that persisting deviation is *only, always,* or *completely* due to that impact, the critics are right to dispute the claim. However, few labeling-oriented statements have actually been that extreme.

At any rate, explaining the mere fact of persistence, exploring the "why" of it, represents at most but one of the concerns of any reasonably broad definitional-processual perspective. In such a perspective, an even more important focal point for our interpretation must be the deviantness itself. Exploring the deviantness invariably takes us beyond the causes of any behavior's presence or persistence. *Whatever* those causes may have been, the kinds of and degrees of deviantness attached to the behavior are going to make a difference. Even when they recognize this possibility, the critics insist that we must be able to specify precisely *how much* of a difference the reaction has made in any deviance situation or outcome we happen to be studying. Again, the urge to quantify and neatly categorize lies behind such insistence. And, again, it may be questioned whether the kind of specification the critics demand is really possible. We have seen how perceived and reacted-against deviators—subject to varying circumstances, including individual capacities for offsetting stigma—often come to incorporate other persons' definitions of their behavior into their own outlooks.

Yet we know this occurs—or, more accurately, emerges—through subtle interactive and perceptual processes over a period of time. It hardly seems conceivable that we could easily and neatly sort out and quantify the constituent elements in this emergence. The critics would like to see "proof"—say, that "80 percent of homosexual self-concepts are 'secondary' in origin, 20 percent 'primary.'" Given the building-up aspect, the action-reaction-counterreaction process of identity development and change, the hope for any such "findings" seems forlorn indeed. No matter how ingenious our research methods aimed at sorting out the contributing factors in this process might be, whatever "separation" we achieved would be largely an artifact of our techniques and distinctions. The intermixed and continuously changing elements, as they affect actual deviators, cannot be pinned down in such a simplistic manner.

The other major strand of the argument against secondary deviation— to the effect that negative labeling doesn't always increase or amplify deviance— rests similarly on a demand for quantification that can have only limited value. Here, the critics have a slightly easier time of it, because by and large they argue "on their own ground." They pose the issue as one involving specific occurrences —strictly speaking, recurrences—rather than the inevitably less clear-cut self-concept aspects of deviance situations. Thus, they assert that the punishment and "correction" of criminal offenders (Tittle, 1975; also Hirschi, 1975), the institutionalization of mental patients (Gove, 1970; Gove, 1975); and certain treatment programs for alcoholics (Trice and Roman, 1970; Robins, 1975) may actually render subsequent deviation *less* likely, rather than have deviance-amplifying consequences. As the critics themselves realize, the problems of careful evaluation of treatment and correctional programs are extremely complex. (See discussion in Chapters 6 and 7.) They include the difficulties in following up individuals released from the programs, in deciding how long a follow-up evaluation is necessary to determine "success" or "failure," and in determining the specific criteria for designating such outcomes. There is, for example, much dispute as to *how high* a rate of "relapse," recidivism (recurrence of officially recorded crime), or recommitment to a treatment institution is necessary for us to say there has been failure. Or, to turn this around, *how low* a rate must be for us to conclude that the program overall is a success.

With respect to these matters, the critics of labeling analysis again may provide a healthy corrective to 'extremist" claims regarding the impact of formally imposed stigma and processing. However, there are actually very few analysts who claim that formal negative labeling must always lead to amplified deviance or that that is the *only* kind of effect such labeling can have. Extremism aside, the critics' focus on specific officially recorded recurrences of deviation limits the value of their observations. Not only are we required to assume that the recorded relapses include or are representative of all actual relapses, but no account whatsoever is taken of the persisting stigma and difficulty that probably, in some manner and degree, plague most once-processed deviators *even* when they are able to avoid subsequent "official" trouble. There is little doubt that the life of the released mental patient, as compared to that of a person never having undergone such hospitalization, will usually continue to be significantly touched by that experience. The ex-convict encounters serious problems even if he or she manages to stay "clean." The point, quite simply, is that studying the officially recorded recurrences is not adequate for an understanding of all the kinds of secondary deviation that may evolve. Only a concept such as *degrees of deviantness* will permit us to take account of the full range of possibilities.

Self-Labeling?

We have just seen that at least some of the critics of secondary deviation return to what appears to be a kind of recurrent stumbling block for the labeling perspective—Becker's early category of the "secret deviant." Davis and Mankoff, particularly, support their argument for the nonnecessity of labeling in deviant careers at least partly with the studies of "hidden" rule-violators. One way of talking about such concealed offenders that has recently developed is in terms of their having labeled themselves, rather than their having been labeled by others (see discussion in Hawkins and Tiedeman, 1975, pp. 253–260). A leading statement of this view has been presented by Judith Lorber, who asserts:

> Hidden deviance implies that even though his social group assumes his innocence, the deviant either sees himself as doing wrong according to his own reference group or, condoning his own behavior, he realizes that others will condemn his actions according to their standards. In either case, to avoid the consequences he feels will occur if his deviance comes out into the open (is socially labeled), he pretends to be conforming to the standards of the group in a position to condemn him for what he is doing secretly. In short, in response to his self-label of his behavior as apt to incur sanctioning, he acts in such a way as to achieve a social label of conformity. Like any other social actor who attempts to influence the response of others to him, *he puts on a performance* (Lorber, 1967, p. 303).

Carol Warren and John Johnson, in a phenomenologically oriented critique of what they see as the labeling approach to homosexuality, develop a somewhat similar point in using the concept of *"symbolically labeled* deviance." The elaboration of homosexuality and self-conscious homosexual identity results, they argue, not from acts of official labeling, but rather from "having an identity infused with the cognizance of its public opprobrium" (Warren and Johnson, 1972, p. 77).

These discussions are perfectly consistent with the definitional orientation to interpreting deviance, provided we be very clear as to their real import. How are we to describe the situation of people who realize that "others will condemn" them, who are aware of the "public opprobrium" attaching to their behavior? Saying or implying that they label themselves deviant would not seem accurate. More properly, we might say that *they recognize that other people may label them* and they act accordingly. Concealment is secondary in the sense that it is not something directly implied by or necessarily associated with the behavior or condition that is imbued with deviantness. On the contrary, it is prompted by the potentially damaging social reactions. Even if these deviators are not "accepting" other people's definitions of their behavior, they are responding to them and being affected by them.

Caution must also be exercised in interpreting certain situations in which, instead of practicing concealment, deviators disclose or even, perhaps, positively affirm the existence of the deviation. Levitin has suggested that people with temporary physical handicaps often may call attention to their disability, but her reference to this as avowing deviance seems questionable. In fact, her discussion goes on to show that what such people are really avowing is the "temporariness," not the disability (Levitin, 1975, pp. 552–553). Even when the disability is voluntarily disclosed, we have to realize this is not the same as "avowing" deviantness. When there are some secondary gains to be wrought from disclosing a disvalued condition—as in the case of "the sick role" implying a release from certain duties—the avowing is undertaken precisely because it implies an outcome of *less* deviantness, not more. In a sense, the same is true of situations in which a person deviates as a result of conflicting group pressures or loyalties. Citing the example of Japanese-Americans who renounced their U.S. citizenship in relocation centers during World War II, Ralph Turner has suggested that individuals sometimes find "identification with a deviant role" to be the lesser of two evils and may therefore consciously incur negative labeling (Turner, 1972). Yet what is really happening here is that by courting negative labeling in one context, a person is positively labeled in another. Describing this as **deviance avowal** or "self-identification with a deviant role" remains accurate only as long as these terms do not divert us from the truly two-sided effect of the deviation. Once again, at the risk of repetition, people rarely choose to have themselves devalued. On balance, they usually seek positive evaluations—at least by the others who for them "count." They may avow or affirm an act, a condition, or even a disvalued status, but affirming that one is a certain kind of person is not labeling oneself "a deviant." Most *deviantness is ascribed, not "achieved."*

REFERENCES

Altman, Dennis
1973. *Homosexual: Oppression and Liberation.* New York: Avon Books.

Armstrong, Gail and Mary Wilson
1973. "City Politics and Deviancy Amplification," in Ian Taylor and Laurie Taylor, eds., *Politics and Deviance.* Baltimore: Penguin Books, Inc. Pp. 61–89.

Beck, Bernard
1967. "Welfare as a Moral Category," *Social Problems,* 14(Winter), 258–277.

Becker, Howard S.
1963. *Outsiders*. New York: The Free Press.
1973. "Labelling Theory Reconsidered," in *Outsiders, rev. ed.* New York: The Free Press.

Berger, Peter L.
1963. *Invitation to Sociology*. Garden City, N.Y.: Doubleday & Company, Inc.

Black, Donald J. and Albert J. Reiss, Jr.
1970. "Police Control of Juveniles," *American Sociological Review,* 35(February), 63–77.

Blumberg, Leonard, *et al.*
1973. *Skid Row and Its Alternatives*. Philadelphia: Temple University Press.

Brecher, Edward M., *et al.*
1972. *Licit and Illicit Drugs*. Boston: Little, Brown and Company.

Bryan, James H.
1965. "Apprenticeships in Prostitution," *Social Problems,* 12(Winter), 287–297.

Cogswell, Betty E.
1968. "Self-Socialization: Readjustment of Paraplegics in the Community," *Journal of Rehabilitation,* May–June, 11–13, 35.

Cohen, Albert K.
1965. "Sociology of the Deviant Act: Anomie Theory and Beyond," *American Sociological Review,* 30(February), 5–14.
1966. *Deviance and Control*. Englewood Cliffs, N.J.: Prentice-Hall, Inc.

Cressey, Donald R.
1953. *Other People's Money*. Glencoe, Ill.: The Free Press.

Dank, Barry M.
1971. "Coming Out in the Gay World," *Psychiatry,* 34(May), 180–197.

Davis, Fred
1963. *Passage Through Crisis: Polio Victims and Their Families*. Indianapolis: The Bobbs-Merrill Co., Inc.
1970. "Focus on the Flower Children: Why All of Us May Be Hippies Someday," in Jack D. Douglas, ed., *Observations of Deviance*. New York: Random House, Inc., Pp. 327–340.

Davis, Nanette J.
1972. "Labeling Theory in Deviance Research: A Critique and Evaluation," *The Sociological Quarterly,* 13(Fall), 447–474.
1975. *Sociological Constructions of Deviance*. Dubuque, Iowa: William C. Brown Company.

DeLong, James V.
1972. "Treatment and Rehabilitation," in Patricia M. Wald, *et al., Dealing with Drug Abuse: A Report to the Ford Foundation*. New York: Praeger, Publishers, Inc. Pp. 173–254.

Douglas, Jack D.
1967. *The Social Meanings of Suicide*. Princeton: Princeton University Press.
1970. "Deviance and Respectability: The Social Construction of Moral Meanings," in Jack D. Douglas, ed., *Deviance and Respectability*. New York: Basic Books, Inc., Pp. 3–30.

Douglas, Jack D. and John M. Johnson, eds.
1977. *Official Deviance*. Philadelphia: J. B. Lippincott Company.

Edgerton, Robert B.
1967. *The Cloak of Competence: Stigma in the Lives of the Mentally Retarded*. Berkeley: University of California Press.

Freidson, Eliot
1965. "Disability as Social Deviance," in Marvin B. Sussman, ed., *Sociology and Rehabilitation*. Washington: American Sociological Association. Pp. 71–99.

Gibbs, Jack P.
1966. "Conceptions of Deviant Behavior: The Old and the New," *Pacific Sociological Review,* 9(Spring), 9–14.

Glaser, Daniel
1971. *Social Deviance*. Chicago: Markham Publishing Co.

Goffman, Erving
1961. *Asylums*. Garden City, N.Y.: Doubleday & Company, Inc.
1963. *Stigma*. Englewood Cliffs, N.J.: Prentice-Hall, Inc.

Goode, Erich
1972. *Drugs in American Society*. New York: Alfred A. Knopf, Inc.

Gould, Leroy, *et al.*
1974. *Connections: Notes from the Heroin World*. New Haven: Yale University Press.

Gove, Walter R.
1970. "Societal Reaction as an Explanation of Mental Illness: An Evaluation," *American Sociological Review,* 35(October), 873–884.
1975. "Labelling and Mental Illness," in Walter R. Gove, ed., *The Labelling of Deviance*. New York: Sage-Wiley. Pp. 35–81.

Grier, William H. and Price Cobbs
1968. *Black Rage*. New York: Basic Books, Inc.

Halperin, Morton H., *et al.*
1976. *The Lawless State*. New York: Penguin Books, Inc.

Hawkins, Richard and Gary Tiedeman
1975. *The Creation of Deviance*. Columbus, Ohio: Charles E. Merrill Publishing Co.

Heyl, Barbara Sherman
1977. "The Madam as Teacher: The Training of House Prostitutes," *Social Problems,* 24 (June), 545–555.

Hirschi, Travis
1975. "Labeling Theory and Juvenile Delinquency," in Gove, ed., *op. cit.,* pp. 181–203.

Hoffman, Martin
1969. *The Gay World*. New York: Bantam Books, Inc.

Horan, Patrick M. and Patricia Lee Austin
1974. "The Social Bases of Welfare Stigma," *Social Problems,* 21(June), 648–657.

Hughes, Everett C.
1945. "Dilemmas and Contradictions of Status," *American Journal of Sociology,* 50(March), 353–359.

James, Jennifer
1977. "Prostitutes and Prostitution," in Edward Sagarin and Fred Montanino, eds., *Deviants: Voluntary Actors in a Hostile World,* Morristown, N.J.: General Learning Press. Pp. 368–423.

James, Jennifer, *et al.*
1975. *The Politics of Prostitution.* Seattle: Social Research Associates.

Kardiner, Abram and Lionel Ovesey
1951, 1962. *The Mark of Oppression.* Cleveland: Meridian Books.

Kleinman, Paula Holzman, Irving F. Lukoff, and Barbara Lynn Kail
1977. "The Magic Fix: A Critical Analysis of Methadone Maintenance Treatment," *Social Problems,* 25(December), 208–214.

Kriegel, Leonard
1969, 1971. "Uncle Tom and Tiny Tim: Some Reflections on the Cripple as Negro," *American Scholar,* 38(Summer 1969), 412–430; as reprinted in Edward Sagarin, ed., *The Other Minorities.* Waltham, Mass.: Ginn & Company.

Lee, Nancy Howell
1969. *The Search for an Abortionist.* Chicago: University of Chicago Press.

Lemert, Edwin M.
1951. *Social Pathology.* New York: McGraw-Hill Book Company.
1967. *Human Deviance, Social Problems, and Social Control.* Englewood Cliffs, N.J.: Prentice-Hall, Inc.

Levitin, Teresa E.
1975. "Deviants as Active Participants in the Labeling Process: The Visibly Handicapped," *Social Problems,* 22(April), 548–557.

Lindesmith, Alfred R.
1947. *Opiate Addiction.* Bloomington, Ind.: Principia Press; slightly revised as *Addiction and Opiates.* 1968. Chicago: Aldine Publishing Company.
1965. *The Addict and the Law.* Bloomington: Indiana University Press.

Lippmann, Walter
1922. *Public Opinion.* New York: Macmillan, Inc.

Lofland, John
1966. *Deviance and Identity.* Englewood Cliffs, N.J.: Prentice-Hall, Inc.

Lorber, Judith
1967. "Deviance as Performance: The Case of Illness," *Social Problems,* 14(Winter), 302–310.

Mankoff, Milton
1971. "Societal Reaction and Career Deviance: A Critical Analysis," *The Sociological Quarterly,* 12(Spring), 204–218.

Matza, David and Henry Miller
1976. "Poverty and Proletariat," in Robert K. Merton and Robert Nisbet, eds., *Contemporary Social Problems, 4th ed.* New York: Harcourt Brace Jovanovich. Pp. 641–673.

May, Edgar
1972. "Narcotics Addiction and Control in Great Britain," in Patricia M. Wald, *et al., op. cit.,* pp. 345–394.

McAuliffe, William E. and Robert A. Gordon
1974. "A Test of Lindesmith's Theory of Addiction," *American Journal of Sociology,* 79 (January), 795–840.

McHugh, Peter
1970. "A Common-Sense Conception of Deviance," in Jack D. Douglas, ed., *op. cit.,* pp. 61–88.

Millett, Kate, *et al.*
1973. *The Prostitution Papers.* New York: Avon Books.

Nunnally, J. C., Jr.
1961. *Popular Conceptions of Mental Health.* New York: Holt, Rinehart and Winston.

Packer, Herbert L.
1968. *The Limits of the Criminal Sanction.* Stanford, Calif.: Stanford University Press.

Phillips, Derek L.
1963. "Rejection: A Possible Consequence of Seeking Help for Mental Disorders," *American Sociological Review,* 28(December), 963–972.

Piliavin, Irving and Scott Briar
1964. "Police Encounters with Juveniles," *American Journal of Sociology,* 70(September), 206–214.

Polsky, Ned
1967. *Hustlers, Beats, and Others.* Chicago: Aldine Publishing Company.

President's Commission on Law Enforcement and Administration of Justice
1967a. *Task Force Report: Drunkenness.* Washington, D.C.: U.S. Government Printing Office.
1967b. *Task Force Report: Narcotics and Dangerous Drugs.* Washington, D.C.: U.S. Government Printing Office.

Ray, Marsh B.
1961. "The Cycle of Abstinence and Relapse Among Heroin Addicts," *Social Problems,* 9(Fall), 132–140.

Reiss, Albert J., Jr.
1971. *The Police and the Public.* New Haven: Yale University Press.

Robins, Lee N.
1975. "Alcoholism and Labelling Theory," in Gove, ed., *op. cit.,* pp. 21–33.

Rubington, Earl and Martin S. Weinberg, eds.
1973. *Deviance: The Interactionist Perspective, 2nd ed.* New York: Macmillan, Inc.
1978. *Deviance: The Interactionist Perspective, 3rd ed.* New York: Macmillan, Inc.

Ryan, William
1972. *Blaming the Victim.* New York: Vintage Books.

Sagarin, Edward
1975. *Deviants and Deviance.* New York: Praeger Publishers, Inc.

Sagarin, Edward and Fred Montanino, eds.
1977. *Deviants: Voluntary Actors in a Hostile World.* Morristown, N.J.: General Learning Press.

Scheff, Thomas J.
1966. *Being Mentally Ill.* Chicago: Aldine Publishing Company.

Schur, Edwin M.
1962. *Narcotic Addiction in Britain and America.* Bloomington: Indiana University Press.
1965. *Crimes Without Victims.* Englewood Cliffs, N.J.: Prentice-Hall, Inc.
1971. *Labeling Deviant Behavior.* New York: Harper & Row, Publishers.

Schwartz, Richard D. and Jerome Skolnick
1962. "Two Studies of Legal Stigma," *Social Problems,* 10(Fall), 133–142.

Scott, Robert A.
1969. *The Making of Blind Men.* New York: Russell Sage Foundation.

Scull, Andrew
1972. "Social Control and the Amplification of Deviance," in Robert A. Scott and Jack D. Douglas, eds., *Theoretical Perspectives on Deviance.* New York: Basic Books, Inc. Pp. 282–314.

Simmons, Jerry L.
1969. *Deviants.* San Francisco: The Glendessary Press.

Skipper, James K., Jr., and Charles H. McGaghy
1970. "Stripteasers: The Anatomy and Career Contingencies of a Deviant Occupation," *Social Problems,* 17(Winter), 391–405.

Snyder, Mark and Seymour W. Uranowitz
1978. "Reconstructing the Past: Some Cognitive Consequences of Person Perception," *Journal of Personality and Social Psychology,* 36(January), 941–950.

Suchar, Charles S.
1978. *Social Deviance: Perspectives and Prospects.* New York: Holt, Rinehart and Winston.

Sudnow, David
1965. "Normal Crimes: Sociological Features of the Penal Code in a Public Defender Office," *Social Problems,* 12(Winter), 255–276.

Tannenbaum, Frank
1938. *Crime and the Community.* Boston: Ginn & Company.

Tittle, Charles R.
1975. "Labelling and Crime: An Empirical Evaluation," in Gove, ed., *op. cit.,* pp. 157–179.

Trice, Harrison M. and Paul M. Roman
1970. "Delabeling, Relabeling, and Alcoholics Anonymous," *Social Problems,* 17(Spring), 538–546.

Truzzi, Marcello
1971. "Lilliputians in Gulliver's Land: The Social Role of the Dwarf," in Sagarin, ed., "The Other Minorities," *op. cit.,* pp. 183–204.

Turner, Ralph H.

1953. "The Quest for Universals in Sociological Research," *American Sociological Review,* 18(December), 604–611.

1972. "Deviance Avowal as Neutralization of Commitment," *Social Problems,* 19(Winter), 308–321.

Wald, Patricia M., *et al.*

1972. *Dealing with Drug Abuse: A Report to the Ford Foundation.* New York: Praeger Publishers, Inc.

Warren, Carol A. B. and John M. Johnson

1972. "A Critique of Labeling Theory from the Phenomenological Perspective," in Scott and Douglas, eds., *op. cit.,* pp. 62–92.

Wilkins, Leslie

1964. *Social Deviance.* Englewood Cliffs, N.J.: Prentice-Hall, Inc.

Wilson, James Q.

1975. *Thinking About Crime.* New York: Basic Books, Inc.

Wilson, James Q., *et al.*

1972. "The Problem of Heroin," *The Public Interest,* Fall.

Winick, Charles

1961. "Physician Narcotic Addicts," *Social Problems,* 9(Fall), 174–186.

Wiseman, Jacqueline P.

1970. *Stations of the Lost: The Treatment of Skid Row Alcoholics.* Englewood Cliffs, N.J.: Prentice-Hall, Inc.

Yablonsky, Lewis

1968. *The Hippie Trip.* New York: Pegasus.

Young, Jock

1971. "The Role of the Police as Amplifiers of Deviancy," in Stanley Cohen, ed., *Images of Deviance.* New York: Penguin Books, Inc. Pp. 27–61.

REVIEW OF KEY TERMS

amplification of deviance. The secondary expansion of deviance situations as a result of societal reaction, including efforts at "social control." Self-fulfilling or snowballing processes that may be set in motion and reinforced by various factors such as media content, restrictive legislation, police drives, etc.

analytic induction. A research method aiming at "universal" causal explanation (applying to all cases of the phenomenon to be explained), in which a working hypothesis is continuously revised to take account of "negative cases." Its strength lies in its ability to describe a common process rather than to predict; it is utilized in several major deviance studies.

deviance avowal. Positive affirmation by the individual of behavior or a condition that others imbue with deviantness. However, affirming the act, condition, or status should be distinguished from desiring deviantness, which rarely occurs. (See also **self-label.**)

deviant careers. The persistence in deviation over time. Also the continuous development and reshaping over a period of time and in response to the reactions of others of a person's behavior and, particularly, self-conceptions.

identification (or selection). Being perceived as a deviator or selected out of a pool of potential "offenders" for deviance-processing. Identification is a necessary condition for being directly reacted to as a deviator and, therefore, is a key element in acquiring deviantness.

retrospective interpretation. The rereading of a person's "essential character" that typically follows from their having been identified as a deviator. Case histories and news accounts indicate one key function of this process—to provide a consistent biography for the perceived deviator and to thus substantiate current social reaction.

role engulfment. The process by which reacted-against deviators—owing to self-incorporation of other people's definitions and narrowing of options—increasingly come to be limited to and involved with a "deviant role." Lemert used the similar term *role primacy*.

secret deviant. Becker's original term for the rule-violator who has not been perceived as such by other people or publicly. Interpretation of this situation is a great bone of contention in academic disputes regarding labeling theory. The existence of people in this position, however, is not in doubt.

self-label. A term used by critics of the labeling perspective to indicate that "deviant careers" and "identities" may be significantly shaped by the actor's own outlooks and choices, as well as by the responses of others (but see cautionary comment under **deviance avowal**).

social distance scale. Research (questionnaire, interview) device consisting of questions posed to determine what degrees of "social distance" (limits on intimacy or even acquaintanceship) respondents hypothetically would maintain between themselves and designated types of people. It is useful as a rough indicator of degrees of deviantness attaching to various behaviors or conditions.

tolerance limits. A term useful in designating the point at which deviation will be reacted to strongly and similar, therefore, to the concept of "moral boundaries." These limits can be exhibited by individuals or collectivities and can vary according to the type of behavior, the extent of same, the type of person doing the reacting, the type of person seen to deviate, and so on. They typically vary over time and from place to place. Sometimes such limits are determinable only by studying actual responses; at other times, there are reasonably good indicators of them (laws, high degree of consensus in attitudes, etc.).

typification. A term used particularly by phenomenologically oriented sociologists to designate the routine "typing" or categorizing of individuals or cases evident at various levels in societal response to deviation. Such categorizing is seen particularly in organizational studies of deviance-processing.

visibility. The extent to which one's person, behavior, or condition is readily observable by or apparent to others. Since this may include conditions not observed visually, Goffman suggested the term "evidentness" as being more inclusive. It is a key factor in determining the likelihood that a deviator will encounter stigmatizing social reactions—a risk that underlies efforts at partial or substantial concealment of certain deviations.

PROJECT 4
Determining Degrees of Deviantness

Introductory Comment

Although some deviance researchers have tried to establish patterns of deviance-defining simply by asking respondents to indicate what behaviors they considered to be "deviant," this approach has decided limitations. Actual use of that term, after all, was not what Becker had in mind when he referred to behavior that people "so label." Rather, he meant to suggest a certain *quality of response*—the meanings and associated reactions that constitute "deviantness." Furthermore, as we have seen, deviantness can be attached to a given behavior or condition, or individual, in varying degrees. Therefore, attitude studies in this area ought preferably to be geared to determining the *degree* of deviantness imputed in connection with any one type of behavior or condition or the *relative degrees* of deviantness attached when a set of problematic behaviors or conditions is to be evaluated. Of course, findings about such attitudes can only tell us about respondents' *hypothetical* reactions. How they would actually behave in real-life situations could be very different. We have seen, too, that there are many sources of variation in probable response quite apart from the type of behavior or condition that is being encountered. Nonetheless, it should be at least suggestive to explore the apparent levels of overall deviantness people impute, even hypothetically, when asked to evaluate behaviors and conditions that commonly elicit disapproval or that are viewed as threatening.

Since several substantively different kinds of reaction (moral disapproval, distaste, fear, etc.) can enter into deviantness, efforts to "measure" it should, insofar as possible, employ methods that somehow will "cut across" or incorporate these not fully comparable themes. One method that may approximate this is to ask respondents to rank a variety of behaviors or conditions so that we can see which disturb them the most or which they believe call for the most severe reactions. Another method is the "social distance scale" discussed above, which seeks to put the research subjects in specific hypothetical situations to which they must (hypothetically) respond.

Assignment

(NOTE: this exercise can be done on either an individual or group basis, but, given the desirability of as large a "sample" of respondents as possible, a class project would probably be preferable. The class might work together in making up the questionnaire or interview schedule, which could then be administered either to other classes, perhaps on arrangements made by your instructor, or in some kind of house-to-house survey in the area, with individual students serving as interviewers.)

     1. *Compose a list* of 10–15 behaviors or conditions that you believe are subject to some considerable degree of disapproval, distaste, and avoidance, or other "deviantizing" reactions. Be sure to include categories that you think vary in degrees of deviantness and also to keep in mind the full range of types of perceived deviations—acts, conditions, beliefs, life-styles, and so on. Arrange the list in some "random" order, perhaps alphabetically.

     2. Next to the items on the list *provide spaces for four rank orderings* by the respondent. For example:

Armed Robbery	_____	_____	_____	_____
Lesbianism	_____	_____	_____	_____
Political Corruption	_____	_____	_____	_____
Psychosis	_____	_____	_____	_____

Respondents can then be asked to rank the 10 or 15 items in the following four ways: (1) In the first column, place the figure 1 next to the item they *personally* find the "most disturbing, upsetting, or fearsome" and rank the others in descending order down to the least "disturbing," etc. (2) In the second column, provide a similar ranking to indicate how "disturbing, upsetting, or fearsome" the various items are to *most people*. (3) In the third column, respondents could give their *personal* ranking as to the items' "seriousness as a social problem about which something should be done." (4) In the fourth column, they could indicate what they considered to be *most people's* ranking on that same "social problem" dimension.

     3. After the questionnaire has been administered, it should be relatively easy to compute *mean* (average) *ranking* scores for the various items on each of the kinds of ranking. If the items are then reordered according to the respondents' ranking of them, that should provide some rough indication of the relative degrees of deviantness respondents attach to them and the relative degrees of deviantness respondents believe people generally attach to them.

     It will be interesting to see whether respondents' own reactions and those they project on to "most people" are similar. It should also be interesting to observe the relation between respondents' ranking on "disturbing, upsetting, or fearsome" and their ranking as to the seriousness of the item as a "social problem." Another interesting comparison would be provided if, before administering the questionnaire outside the class, student-researchers themselves attempted their own rankings, which could then be looked at along with those of the respondents.

     4. Depending on time considerations and on how much effort the class wishes to devote to the project, any number of *modifications* which would render the study more sophisticated could be made. The questionnaire might include a *social distance scale* relating to each item (see the studies by Phillips and Simmons, cited in this chapter, or any standard textbook on research methods). Thus, respondents would indicate in each case how much restriction on intimacy they would place between themselves and the various kinds of perceived deviators.

If, short of that approach, something more than the simple ranking suggested earlier is desired, there are various ways in which respondents could be asked to indicate *how strongly* they feel about *each* item rather than simply rank the set. Your instructor could help you develop these elaborations as well as suggest various "face items" (social background data, etc.) and general attitude questions that you might wish to include in the overall questionnaire. These additions would provide further possibilities for breakdowns of the findings, comparisons, possible cross-tabulations, or even the use of various statistical tests of the significance of the findings should you wish to develop the study in these ways. But even the simple ranking effort posed at the outset—especially if undertaken with a decent-sized sample—could provide a lot of material for interpretation and class discussion.

Implications

The danger in such an exercise lies in thinking of the findings as reflecting response patterns that are fixed and uniform. Not only does the generalizability of such findings depend on the size and nature (broad representativeness) of the sample of respondents, but the difference between professed attitudes and real behavior must not be forgotten. It is only by studying people's behavior in actual situations that we can know, really, what the "operative" attitudes and norms are. On the other hand, an exercise of this sort may very roughly indicate the relative risks of "acquiring deviantness" that persons run, *all other things being equal,* when they engage in or display the behaviors in question.

PROLOGUE 5

*Our images of self are facilitated and restrained by the
expectations of others; we are sensitive to the expectations
of those who are most significant to us. But our selection
of significant others is limited by our positions in the varied
institutions of which we are members. Within these institutional limits, however, we will generally turn toward
those whom we believe will confirm the desired image we
would have of our self. And, if others' expectations and
images of us are contrary to our desired image, we will
try to reject them, and seek only confirmation among more
congenial others.*
—Hans Gerth and C. Wright Mills, *Character and
Social Structure*

*While structures of social relations are, of course, profoundly
influenced by common values, these structures have a significance of their own, which is ignored if concern is exclusively with the underlying values and norms. Exchange
transactions and power relations, in particular, constitute
social forces that must be investigated in their own right....*
—Peter M. Blau, *Exchange and Power in Social Life*

The recently emphasized interactionist view of social relations brings to the fore-
front of interpretation *subjective meanings of action* and also highlights the
elements of *contingency* and *emergence* in social process. It implies a very complex conception of the human being as a social actor. If people are subject to the
not fully predictable reactions of others, they nonetheless have a hand in eliciting
those reactions through their own behavior and through the expectations and
images they project. This is, in a way, an interactional counterpart of the relation between the individual and dominant social institutions and values; the
individual is constrained by those aspects of the sociocultural order yet, at the
same time, helps to shape them. In neither case is the individual a completely
passive object, played on by forces completely beyond his or her control. On the
other hand, a person's placement in some aspects of the institutionalized social
order (most notably, the stratification system) greatly affects one's capacity to
control his or her own fate in and through interaction. People are free to choose,

to act, to assert their own identities, but some people are a good deal freer than others.

Much debate in the deviance field has centered around the issue of whether recent perspectives may have exaggerated the passivity of the morally disvalued and stigmatized individual. The potential for such an exaggeration is almost certainly present in such perspectives, with their heavy emphasis on ascribed deviantness, unforeseen contingencies, and the like. These outlooks were an important corrective to traditional notions that deviators *simply* and *automatically* "brought upon themselves" negative evaluations and responses. Yet it is well to keep in mind that the offending individual's behavior *does* play some part in generating most deviance situations and, furthermore, that it *continues* to play a part after disvaluation becomes likely or actually occurs. In this chapter, we will be concerned with this latter point, more specifically with the techniques by which stigmatizable or stigmatized individuals can themselves avoid, counter, or otherwise deal with such responses (see Focal Point Two, Sec. B(2) of the Paradigm, in the Appendix). Even perceived deviators continue to try to "negotiate" their situations and identities. Resourcefulness (in two senses—that of making shrewd and effective use of available techniques and that of having basic resources of social power at one's command) is a crucial determinant of how well they succeed.

CH.5
AVOIDING STIGMA

INTRODUCTION

Not every person who is subject to deviantizing feels the impact of stigma with equal force. Since most people court the favorable evaluations of at least "those who count," it is not surprising that deviators routinely engage in various efforts at stigma-avoidance. While there are many techniques that may be employed for such a purpose, most of them fall into three major categories: attempts to conceal the deviation, efforts to neutralize or lessen the stigma, and, where circumstances allow, individual or collective actions designed to directly confront or repudiate the stigma. Variants on these general lines of defense may be adapted to the particularities of specific deviance situations, and they may be employed singly or sometimes in combination. Several factors help to determine just which techniques an individual will use and how successful they are likely to be.

Clearly, the type of deviation itself is one of these factors. For example, high visibility or evidentness of a given act or condition will severely limit the possibilities for concealment, and individuals in such situations will have to try to reduce stigma by other means. Another highly relevant factor consists of the tolerance limits—for the specific deviation and also for that deviation when displayed by this particular type of person—of individuals and groups with whom the deviator must regularly or significantly deal. What the deviation is and who reacts to it thus combine to influence both the individual's initial likelihood of being stigmatized—held "accountable" (see Scott and Lyman, 1968)—and the preferred choices among various means of defense. As the following comment indicates, even those persons for whom concealment of the deviation is virtually impossible will invariably have *some* means of ameliorating the stigma:

Salience of stigma varies, however, with type of social other and type of social setting, with the paraplegic definition and projection of self as worthy or demeaned, and with the paraplegic's skill in managing others' definitions of him. Thus, paraplegics may reduce the stigmatizing effects of disability in the following three ways: (1) by limiting social encounters to social others and social settings where they feel stigma is less salient; (2) by projecting a definition of self as worthy, which tends to counter negative definitions by social others; and (3) by becoming skilled in eliciting positive definitions of self from others (Cogswell, 1967, pp. 20–21).

Implicit in this statement is the importance of the deviating individual's having certain kinds of resources at his or her command. We have seen that deviance situations develop around responses to perceived threat. This "threat" may take many forms. The same is true of reactions to it. Regardless of these specifics, deviance outcomes will always hinge on the answers to the following questions: "Who can, with relative impunity, 'threaten' whom?" and, to turn this around the other way, "Who can, with relative effectiveness, stigmatize and disvalue whom?" Essentially, these are issues of personal and social power. As Becker has emphasized, "people are in fact always *forcing* their rules on others, applying them more or less against the will and without the consent of those others" (Becker, 1963, p. 17). If we define "rules" broadly enough, Becker's statement applies to all of the varied kinds of deviance situations we have been considering throughout this book, and, as Table 5.1 shows, the power factor is also at work at several different "levels," affecting not only outcomes in personal interaction and organizational "processing," but also the formation and application of collective definitions at the societal level. At each of these levels, the higher the individual's or group's power resources, the more likely they will be, all other things equal, to achieve favored outcomes.

It is perhaps in the shaping of society-level outcomes (see further discussion in Chapter 7) that the "political and economic power" which Becker also mentions most clearly comes into play. From the standpoint of an individual who faces direct stigmatizing—either informally or through the action of social control agencies—additional dimensions of power may be relevant. What personal and social resources will prove to be, in a given context, most "salient"—that is, effective in providing ammunition that will help in the defense against stigma—will vary considerably from situation to situation. By and large, it is no doubt true that, as Becker suggests, at least many of the formal rules in our society are in effect imposed by adults against youths, whites against blacks, men against women. Yet recall the example of the corporate executive whose high socioeconomic status may help him or her avoid the stigma of "white-collar criminality" but not that attaching to, say, homosexuality or alcoholism. When the executive faces imputations of this latter sort, high socioeconomic position may no longer offer full protection. The individual is still, basically, caught up in a conflict situation in which power will determine the outcome. But other, more "personalized" kinds of resources may become increasingly salient for such pur-

Table 5.1 Relation Between Salient Resources and Deviance Outcomes

	INTERPERSONAL REACTIONS	ORGANIZATIONAL PROCESSING	COLLECTIVE RULE-MAKING
High resources (of individual or group)	High ability to resist imputations of deviant identity *or* to "manage" *desired* deviant roles successfully	High resistance to processing efforts Low rates of "official" deviance	Dominant social perception of individual or group norms as "conformist" High ability to impose rules
Low resources (of individual or group)	Low ability to resist imputations of deviant identity *or* to manage *desired* deviant roles successfully	Low resistance to processing efforts High rates of "official" deviance	Dominant social perception of individual or group norms as "deviant" Low ability to impose rules

Source: Edwin M. Schur, *Labeling Deviant Behavio*r. New York: Harper & Row, 1971, p. 150.

poses. While general social prestige and economic wherewithal are almost always helpful, sometimes a kind of "social psychological" power resource, such as the individual's preexisting self-esteem (itself often tied up, however, with socioeconomic standing), may become especially crucial.

We can also see in Table 5.1 that having high **salient resources** implies in several different ways being in a favored position with respect to achieving desired outcomes. A point noted there under "collective rule-making" but equally applicable at the other levels is that those with the most power are in the best position to impose rules or to stigmatize others. This is, of course, simply the other side of the coin in situations where those with the least power are most susceptible to deviantizing. Returning to the matter of defense, relevant power can sometimes help one to avoid initial identification as a deviator; at other times, it will enable one to avoid or reduce stigma even after being so identified. In yet other situations, it will influence the outcome in the course of official "processing." Finally, such power will be significant in allowing an individual to achieve acknowledgement *in* a "deviant role" when, as is sometimes the case, that is a desired outcome.

Failure to appreciate this last possibility has sometimes given rise to a misunderstanding of the power interpretation that Becker and others have developed. Thus, Walter Gove and Patrick Howell, in line with the former's general critique of "labeling" approaches to mental illness, have written:

> According to this perspective, the greater the individual's social and economic resources, the greater the likelihood that he will be able to deal successfully with others and the less the likelihood that he will be channelled into a deviant role. With regard to mental illness, this means that persons with resources will be more likely to avoid psychiatric treatment, particularly in a mental hospital, and that if they are hospitalized, they will have been able to delay their hospitalization (Gove and Howell, 1974, p. 86).

This interpretation fails to grasp the core of the labeling analyst's general thesis about power and deviance situations, which is simply that the more relevant power you have, the more likely you will be to achieve the outcomes you desire—*whatever* they may be. Thus, for the people who *want* to undergo psychiatric treatment or even to go to a mental hospital, high resources will facilitate their efforts. Findings Gove and Howell present, which purport to show that persons high in socioeconomic status as well as those who are married display no special success in "avoiding" psychiatric treatment, would be interesting *if* they were limited to *compulsory* hospitalization and treatment. For a variety of not very convincing reasons, these authors do not distinguish between voluntary and involuntary patients. At least insofar as voluntary submissions to treatment are concerned, such findings can hardly be taken to refute the "power" interpretation. On the contrary, they are quite consistent with it. At any rate, we must keep in mind that the sociologist's use of standard "resources" (even the extremely important one of socioeconomic status) in this categorical way to "test" the power thesis has serious limitations, for, even though such resources are bound to play a significant role, they may, as we have just seen, not be the only ones to do so.

NEGOTIATING DEVIANCE OUTCOMES

A deviance outcome can be conceived of both as a concrete state of affairs and as a "definition of the situation." When a particular way of defining the situation gains ascendancy, even if its dominance is only temporary, participants must in many respects accommodate their behavior and outlooks to it. Since people do not always share common definitions—since they do not always make similar evaluations or agree as to what states of affairs are to be desired—it is understandable that they must constantly be striving to have situations defined in the ways that they prefer. Much of our everyday interaction in all areas of social life can be construed as a running struggle—sometimes overtly combative, sometimes extremely mild—over alternative definitions of routinely encountered situations. When "transformations of identity" (Strauss, 1962) are at stake, such struggles become especially consequential. Being subject to definition as a deviator implies ramifications that can vitally affect an individual's life patterns and overall sense of self. Understandably, then, people do what they can to avoid such an outcome or, when it cannot be fully avoided, to soften the negative impact it has on them personally.

One useful way of thinking about these efforts is in terms of **negotiation.** If we give that concept its broadest meaning, then it is clear that we spend a great deal of our time "negotiating" various definitions of situations. Sometimes this process occurs quite explicitly, as when we systematically and self-consciously go about the business of striking bargains. In other instances, there occurs what might be called "implicit negotiation." This more subtle type of bargaining undercurrent seems to be at work, with or without our fully conscious realization, in the continuous interaction through which our personal identities emerge and are sustained or altered. Central to this process is the way in which our "presentation of self" (Goffman, 1959; see also Strauss, 1959) can result in our eliciting, or failing to elicit, desired responses from those other people whose reactions are in one way or another important to us.

Negotiation implies exchange. In developing exchange theories, sociologists and others (economists, mathematicians, etc.) have stressed the fact that a person's bargaining position depends crucially on the "benefits" he or she can offer as an inducement for other people's "compliance," that is, in order to achieve the desired response (Blau, 1964). What kind of benefit the deviator can provide in exchange for lessened stigmatization will vary a great deal depending on the situation. In cases of graft, political corruption, and some kinds of corporate crime, there may be a quite blatant "exchange" of monetary and other favors for noninterference. Professional criminals and those who earn their livings through one or another type of illicit trafficking (black-market) activity, have long used the "fix" to achieve, in a similar way, police protection or acquiescence. Sometimes a withholding of threatened violence may be offered in exchange for the ignoring of ongoing deviation. Frequently, the deviator who already has come under official processing has a bargaining resource in the administrative convenience for the organization or control agent of being able to expedite the handling of at least part of what is potentially an overwhelming caseload. This is one central factor (another is the "benefit" for a prosecutor in having a high conviction rate) affecting the explicit exchanges that constitute plea bargaining in our criminal courts (to which we will return very shortly).

In less structured situations, the deviator may not have any such tangible benefits to offer for bargaining purposes. Yet, as our discussion of "salient resources" has implied, even then the individual may not be totally powerless. Such relatively subtle factors as the desire to maintain an ongoing relationship of some sort, the desire to feel one is doing the fair or decent thing, and the wish not to appear in any kind of "bad light" will at times lead reactors to relax or even abstain from deviantizing responses. Sometimes, however, the nature of the deviation itself may come close to wiping out all prospects for reciprocity. Noting the blind person's extremely low capacity "to perform socially valued favors," Scott has commented:

The blind person is, therefore, by virtue of his dependency, the subordinate in a power relationship. As a rule, none of the alternatives available to subordinates in power relationships are open to him. He cannot forego the service required, since performing important activities of daily life depends on the cooperation of sighted persons. It is unlikely that he will turn elsewhere, partly because he cannot always do that on his own and partly because his situation will be unlikely to change greatly if he does. Finally, he cannot very well rely on force to have favors done for him. He is, therefore, backed into a position of compliance (Scott, 1969, p. 36).

Blinded persons who are lucky enough to have a preexisting reservoir of monetary resources, community standing, professional influence, or even a large amount of outstanding "credit" in good will or for past favors to others may, however, be able to use these resources to offset this likelihood of extreme dependency.

One of the key contributions of a labeling focus on deviance has been to show how being treated as a deviator is itself likely to result in a narrowing of one's "negotiating" options and resources in subsequently encountered situations. Once tainted with deviantness, a person, by that very fact, will usually have "less to bargain with" in the future. This is, of course, just another way of talking about the process of role engulfment. In particular, the concept of **denial of role distance** is extremely apt with respect to a branded deviator's subsequent efforts to negotiate a favorable identity and desired outcomes. In such efforts, the personal resources an individual might otherwise have brought to bear are likely to be overshadowed by the stigma, or, to put this another way, the stigma has become a key element in the position from which the person must bargain. Assessments by other people regarding what such a person "has to offer" now typically reflect a factor extraneous to basic personal attributes, capacities, and demonstrated or potential performance. This is a major consequence of "having a record," whether it be for a criminal offense, as a result of mental hospitalization, through having been dependent on "welfare," or whatever.

Though we know that past stigma will often have such a powerful and long-term carry-over effect, probably the most severe experiencing of role-distance denial occurs in more circumscribed and time-bounded contexts. The "status-degradation ceremony"—at least when it works out to the individual's detriment, as in conviction for a serious crime or commitment to a mental hospital—involves high intensification of this kind of role engulfment. Even more striking is the inmate's experience within such a "total institution" as a prison or mental hospital. Many studies have shown that inmates and custodians in these institutions do negotiate certain of the conditions of life there (Sykes, 1958; Goffman, 1961). But precisely because the routine patterns in such institutions center almost entirely around the inmate status of the people confined within them, such persons can never really disregard or step away from that status and its implications. Indeed re-socialization (informal as well as formal) to the "inmate role," is usually necessary if one is to manage even reasonably well in such a setting (Goffman, 1961). Notwithstanding the many informal day-to-day bargains that may be struck in such a context, the inmate's "essential character" is to some extent established and, at least for the time being, largely beyond his or her own control. As Adaptation Seven dramatically indicates, under such circumstances one's basic identity (at least for purposes of interacting within that context) may have been rendered nonnegotiable.

ADAPTATION SEVEN
Pseudopatients*

In 1973 there appeared in the prestigious journal *Science* (published by the American Association for the Advancement of Science) a most startling research report. When D. L. Rosenhan, professor of psychology and law at Stanford University, had placed "pseudopatients" (persons not known to be suffering from any mental disorders) in a variety of mental hospitals, they remained undetected; they were persistently treated as "insane" by medical staff; aspects of their normal behavior were viewed as "symptoms"; and, despite their own secret knowledge of their sanity, they found themselves "caught up in and fighting the process of depersonalization." Findings from Rosenhan's study illustrate a number of key points emphasized in this text. Imprecision of and lack of consensus on deviance definitions (in this instance, definitions of mental illness), the demoralizing impact of becoming an "inmate," the influence of relative power positions on relations between definers and the defined, the process of retrospective interpretation, and the severe difficulty involved in trying to shed "deviantness" once it has been assigned—all of these factors were present and, in fact, interwoven in the situation he created. Above all, the very fact that he could create "deviants" in this way raises grave questions for those who persist in seeing deviance as being intrinsic to particular individuals.

Among the eight pseudopatients in this ingenious experiment were three psychologists, a pediatrician, a psychology graduate student, a housewife, and a painter. Using pseudonyms and, in some cases, disguising their real occupations, they managed in the course of the research to gain admission to twelve different hospitals. This was achieved by going to the admissions offices and complaining of "hearing voices" (which were described as saying "empty," "hollow," and "thud," if the research collaborator was pressed for more detail). Apart from the changes in names and occupations and the reporting of the hallucinations, those seeking admission provided details of their actual life histories. Once they had been admitted to the psychiatric ward, they ceased all simulation of symptoms and, insofar as possible, adopted their normal ways of behaving (except that they kept written notes on their observations, first secretly then openly). If staff asked them how they felt, they said they felt fine and were no longer experiencing hallucinations. Since they had been instructed (by Rosenhan) that they would have to convince the staff they were "sane" in order to be released, there was a special incentive to act normally and to cooperate with doctors and other staff members.

Of the twelve admissions, eleven were with a recorded diagnosis of

---

* *Source:* Summary and interpretation of D. L. Rosenhan, "On Being Sane in Insane Places," *Science*, 179, no. 4070 (January 19, 1973), 250–258. Direct quotations reprinted by permission.

"schizophrenia" and one of "manic-depressive psychosis." Hospitalized for periods ranging from seven to fifty-two days (an average of nineteen days), the pseudo-patients eventually were discharged on grounds of their psychoses being "in remission." As Rosenhan suggests, "the evidence is strong that, once labeled schizophrenic, the pseudopatient was stuck with that label. If the pseudopatient was to be discharged, he must naturally be 'in remission'; but he was not sane, nor, in the institution's view, had he ever been sane." Highlighting the possibility that medical staff "saw" insanity even when it wasn't there was the fact that other (real) *patients* frequently recognized the collaborators' normality. Rosenhan's feeling that he had uncovered a strong expectation effect in diagnosis (psychiatrists finding illness when they expected to find it) was reinforced through a related experiment he undertook in which the expectation was reversed. In one hospital to which *no* pseudopatient was in fact admitted, he informed staff that such admissions were going to be attempted. Staff members involved with admissions over a three-month period were asked to rate (on a ten-point scale) each of 193 admittees as to the likelihood of their being pseudopatients. "Forty-one patients were alleged, with high confidence, to be pseudopatients by at least one member of the staff. Twenty-three were considered suspect by at least one psychiatrist. Nineteen were suspected by one psychiatrist *and* one other staff member."

Once the actual pseudopatients (in the major experiment) had been diagnosed," the process of retrospective interpretation occurred with a vengeance. As Rosenhan puts it, "Once a person is designated abnormal, all of his other behaviors and characteristics are colored by that label. Indeed, that label is so powerful that many of the pseudopatients' normal behaviors were overlooked entirely or profoundly misinterpreted." He cites, for example, the "translation" into pathological symptoms of one pseudopatient's reported life history. Although the details conveyed included "nothing especially pathological" and simply some typical changes in interpersonal relationships, the case record referred to "considerable ambivalence in close relationships," "attempts to control emotionality," and the like. Rosenhan concluded that the psychiatrists unintentionally distorted the facts, interpreting them in a way that would be consistent with familiar psychodynamic theories of schizophrenia:

It is true that the pseudopatient's relationships with his parents changed over time, but in the ordinary context that would hardly be remarkable—indeed, it might very well be expected. Clearly, the meaning ascribed to his verbalizations (that is, ambivalence, affective instability) was determined by the diagnosis: schizophrenia. An entirely different meaning would have been ascribed if it were known that the man was "normal."

Similarly, the aforementioned note-taking by the pseudopatients was seen as a symptom of underlying disturbance. " 'Patient engages in writing behavior' was the daily nursing comment on one of the pseudopatients who was never questioned about his writing." If pseudopatients reacted strongly to incidents involving mistreatment by staff, such reactions too were viewed as symptomatic.

Since interpretations of this sort are regularly inscribed in the hospital's written records, they reinforce both the diagnosis and an expectation of continuing psychopathology. As Rosenhan comments, "A psychiatric label has a life and an influence of its own. . . . When a sufficient amount of time has passed, during which the patient has done nothing bizarre, he is considered to be in remission and available for discharge. But the label endures beyond discharge, with the unconfirmed expectation that he will behave as a schizophrenic again."

The diagnostic labels also greatly affected the nature of pseudopatient-staff interaction. Rosenhan suggests that, although they would no doubt deny it, many mental health professionals probably exhibit "an exquisite ambivalence" in their relations with psychiatric patients. They are not totally free of the negative attitudes and avoidance tendencies that often characterize reactions to the "mentally ill." In a way, the very structure of the mental hospital may reinforce these tendencies, for there tend to be a strong segregation of staff and patients and also a hierarchical organization of the staff, according to which, "Those with the most power have least to do with patients, and those with the least power are most involved with them." In four of the hospitals, Rosenhan had the pseudopatients approach staff members with routine and courteously presented requests for information. The overwhelmingly predominant types of reactions revealed:

> . . . the degree to which staff avoided continuing contacts that patients had initiated. By far, their most common response consisted of either a brief response to the question, offered while they were 'on the move' and with head averted, or no response at all.
>
> The encounter frequently took the following bizarre form: (pseudopatient) "Pardon me, Dr. X. Could you tell me when I am eligible for grounds privileges?" (physician) "Good morning, Dave. How are you today?" (Moves off without waiting for a response.)

This pattern was in sharp contrast to data Rosenhan obtained at Stanford University, where, without exception, inquiries made of supposedly busy faculty members walking on the campus were met with direct and helpful responses. (Even at the University hospital, inquiries made of doctors by persons not there identified as patients produced a higher degree of cooperative response than that obtained by the hospitalized pseudopatients.)

Between the avoidance tendencies they experienced and other (unpleasant, sometimes even brutal) aspects of institutional life, the pseudopatients (it should perhaps be mentioned that Rosenhan himself was among their number) developed a strong awareness of their powerlessness. Lack of direct response and the substantial absence of freedom of movement or personal privacy produced a "depersonalization" at times so severe "that pseudopatients had the sense that they were invisible, or at least unworthy of account." Many of these feelings, according to Rosenhan, can be attributed to the nature of the hospital settings themselves. The total institution type of environment, as discussed by Goffman and exemplified here, may generate many consequences that "seem undoubtedly counter-therapeutic." One inference he draws is that if we can "refrain from sending the distressed to insane places, our impressions of them are less likely to be distorted." To that extent, nonjudgmental and community-based treatment programs may have special merit. High priority, too, should be given to increasing "the sensitivity of mental health workers and researchers to the *Catch 22* position of psychiatric patients." Overall, Rosenhan and his collaborators found most staff members to be sincere and strongly committed to treatment efforts. "Their perceptions and behaviors were controlled by the situation, rather than being motivated by a malicious disposition."

Analysis of deviance-processing short of institutional commitment has frequently revealed the importance of explicit or implicit negotiation. Without doubt the most commonly cited example, at least of explicit bargaining, has been the aforementioned plea bargaining in the criminal courts—long cited as a key feature of our justice system by specialists in criminology. As we are going to see further (in the next chapter), this kind of negotiation closely reflects the organizational context within which the processes of criminal justice operate (see Newman, 1956; Sudnow, 1965; Skolnick, 1966; Blumberg, 1967; Downie, 1972; Rosett and Cressey, 1976). Largely as a consequence of plea bargaining, approximately 90 percent of criminal cases in this country never go to full trial (see discussion in Reid, 1976, pp. 263–270). There are various specific kinds of agreements that are reached, all of which involve concessions of some sort being granted in exchange for a plea of guilty (often to a "lesser included offense"). The prosecution may, for example, present the charges in such a way as to ensure reduction in sentencing; there may be an outright agreement to leniency in sentencing; or prosecutors may agree not to pursue some charges at all if defendants plead guilty to others.

Actually, this kind of bargaining perhaps might better be called "pseudo-negotiation." The defendants themselves frequently play little part in the process, and it is far from clear that their interests will be forcefully represented. As several studies have shown, contrary to the supposed clash of "the adversary system," this bargaining often takes the form of a cooperative venture between the ostensibly "opposing" attorneys. It works primarily to further their common interests and those of the "system," rather than the defendant's. Abraham Blumberg, himself an experienced lawyer as well as a sociologist, notes:

> An accused and his kin, as well as others outside the court community, are unable to comprehend the nature and dimensions of the close relations between the lawyer "regular" and his former colleagues in the prosecutor's office. Their continuing colleague-ship is based on real professional and organizational needs of a quid pro quo, which

goes beyond the limits of an accommodation one might ordinarily expect in a seemingly adversary relationship. Indeed, adversary features are for the most part muted and exist in their attenuated form largely for external consumption Blumberg, 1967, p. 66; see also Sudnow, 1965).

These cooperative mechanisms enable prosecutors to maintain high conviction rates, help the system to deal with enormous overload of the court calendars, and facilitate ongoing personal relations among the various participants in the court system. Although widely criticized for bypassing the requirements of due process of law (Downie, 1972; also Packer, 1968), there is considerable indication that the system cannot easily be eliminated. One major study recently concluded:

> For financial reasons, if for no others, adoption of a no-plea-agreement system surely would stimulate some abbreviated form of trial or other simple procedure for the disposition of cases that are not seriously contested. The likely net effect of the proposed reform, then, would be merely a change of the subject of negotiations from the guilty plea to negotiation about the disposition to be made if the defendant agrees to an abbreviated trial rather than demanding his right to a full one. From the perspective of either the defendant or the community, the change will not be significant (Rosett and Cressey, 1976).

A study by Aaron Cicourel of factors affecting the disposition of cases in the less formalized juvenile justice system has highlighted a subtle process of implicit bargaining that may occur in the interviewing and early screening of juveniles by probation officers. According to Cicourel, delinquency researchers have typically failed to recognize this kind of negotiation because they failed to probe beneath the superficial information in the written reports such screening efforts produce. Only by directly observing the interaction, as Cicourel himself did, could the researchers see how "physical appearance of the juveniles, their facial expressions, affectual communication, and body motion are all integral features of the action scene," and recognize the "hints, direct accusations, moral arguments, denials, defamation of character, threats, presumed or imputed lying, and the like, that invariably arise in the course of the exchange" (Cicourel, 1968, pp. 122, 130). Particularly central to this bargaining, Cicourel found, was the question of imputing "guilt" or "disturbance." He noted:

> . . . a juvenile who is "appealing and attractive" and who "wants very much to be liked and relates in a friendly manner to all around her," is a prime candidate for clinical interpretations as opposed to criminal imputations. Finding "problems" in the home is not difficult. . . . The transformation of the juvenile into a sick object permits all concerned to suspend the criminal imputations of her acts, even though the penal code sections are quoted each time the police report theft or burglary (Cicourel, 1968, p. 132).

Psychiatric diagnosis is another mode of deviance-defining that the concept of negotiation may help us to interpret. In examining the Yarrow study of husband-wife interaction preceding mental hospitalization, we saw that a continuously shifting sequence of assessments and reassessments seemed to occur in those situations. Were we to explore such a sequence with an eye to the participants' differential power resources, we might readily interpret what happened—and what could have happened had the resources been distributed differently—in terms of a kind of implicit negotiation process. An example of much more explicit negotiation is provided by Edgerton as part of his findings about recognition of mental illness in East African societies. He relates the case of a 16-year-old boy among the Hehe in Tanzania (Edgerton, 1969, pp. 59–61). Brought to a native doctor who "specialized" in mental disturbances, the boy, who was "entirely out of touch with reality," was at first diagnosed as incurably psychotic, and his condition was determined to be "probably inherited rather than being caused by witchcraft or the will of god." Although such a diagnosis, produced through elaborate ritual, ordinarily carried great authority, numerous entreaties by the boy's father—including an offer "to pay the doctor well if he could identify the witch and the malevolent witchcraft being used, cure the boy, and then punish the witch"—caused the doctor, after further ritual, to reverse his position. Subsequently the doctor told Edgerton that, in fact, the initial diagnosis had been correct:

> He insisted that he changed his diagnosis not because of the money involved, but because it was so important to the family that he do so . . . "it is very important to them that their boy not be psychotic. Do you think I have no heart?"
>
> . . . The parents and relatives were determined to resist any label for the boy that would jeopardize his—and thus their—economic future. Although the Hehe doctor rarely changed his diagnoses, in this case he did so despite the fact that he actually never doubted the accuracy of his original label. It is impossible in this context to do more than hint at the complexity of the involvements in this case, but its negotiated character is obvious (Edgerton, 1969, p. 61).

Drawing on writings of the English psychoanalyst Michael Balint, Thomas Scheff has suggested that a very subtle, largely un-self-conscious type of negotiation may be present even in cases where individuals have come voluntarily for private psychiatric treatment. Here, the bargaining may not center around the issue of whether the person has a problem that requires treatment, but rather around a determination of the *kind* of problem that the patient presents. Both the doctor and the patient, according to Scheff, are likely to have ideas regarding which "nature of the problem" interpretations are most acceptable to them. Initial psychiatric interviews may involve some subtle bargaining over this kind of "definition of the situation." However, as Scheff points out, all other things being equal, the therapist has an enormous advantage in any such bargaining: "his definition is more important than the client's in determining the final outcome of the negotiation, principally because he is well trained, secure, and self-confident in his role in the transaction, whereas the client is untutored, anxious, and uncertain about his role" (Scheff, 1968, p. 6).

The example of suicide determinations suggests that a person need not be present or even available for his or her character to be negotiated. We have already encountered Douglas' suggestion that many suicide researchers have failed to appreciate how such determinations may represent outcomes of inter-action. It is easy to see how such interaction, between personally concerned others and those functionaries authorized to issue official "cause of death" designations, can include a subtle form of bargaining. Arguing that there probably are socially patterned differences (particularly between social classes) in the likelihood of attempting to conceal suicide as well as in the ability and willingness "to manipu-late information-giving phenomena" in such a way as to produce desired cause-of-death determinations, Douglas suggests that the following general proposition may apply: "the more integrated the deceased individual is into his local com-munity and with the officials, the more the doctors, coroners, or other officials responsible for deciding what the cause of death is will be favorably influenced, consciously or subconsciously, by the preferences of the deceased and his sig-nificant others" (Douglas, 1967, pp. 210–211, 213).

Although the situations discussed in this section may offer some of the more striking illustrations of negotiating deviance outcomes, it should by now be evident that *some* aspects of *most* deviance situations are "negotiated," at least if we give that term the very broadest possible meaning. In fact, one can interpret virtually all of the efforts people characteristically make to avoid being imbued with deviantness as attempts to negotiate, manage, or control personal and social identity. Thus, the common techniques of concealment, neutralization, and con-frontation, to which we now turn, represent endeavors by persons who face nega-tion and stigma to avoid or withstand deviantizing forces, drawing on whatever salient resources they have at their command.

CONCEALMENT

Passing and Self-Segregation

We have seen that different types of deviation will vary greatly in degree of visibility or evidentness; the obvious corollary of this is that, likewise, there is variation in the possibilities for concealment. Clearly, acts committed in relative privacy are concealed from other people with greater ease than those that occur in broad public view. Conditions that are immediately and "externally" evident to others, such as being a dwarf or a cripple, are extremely hard to conceal. Those that are more "internal"—for example, hemophelia or, perhaps, some forms of mental retardation—may, under some circumstances at least, be more readily kept hidden. Deviating life-styles, unless they are ecologically and socially circum-scribed, will usually be difficult to hide. Perhaps most concealable among the general categories of deviation are disvalued belief systems and personal orienta-tions. Since beliefs do not have to lead to any actions, individuals can "keep them to themselves." However, this may well be unsatisfactory to the deviating believer, since often—particularly in the case of political beliefs—being able to openly profess what one believes will be strongly desired if not considered essential.

Personal orientations can also, at least theoretically, be kept completely hidden from other people. It is not absolutely necessary, for example, to act on or even tell anyone about your basic sexual orientation in order to have one. In his research on "coming out," Dank found that approximately 20 percent of the acknowledged homosexuals he interviewed had come to the conclusion they had that basic orientation prior to ever engaging in homosexual acts (Dank, 1971, p. 188). We also know that, similarly, there are many persons who view themselves as heterosexual yet who have not engaged in any actual heterosexual relations. Presumably if one's sexual orientation is a stigmatized one, it would be possible to *choose* simply not to act on it for purposes of self-protection, yet most persons would find the resulting situation highly undesirable. As a consequence, concealment of deviating sexuality is usually only partial concealment. The deviator tries to pattern his or her existence in such a way that the orientation can be acted upon, but with a minimum of resulting stigma and other negative social consequences (see the discussion by Delph, 1978).

There is a substantial sociological literature dealing with the partial concealment efforts of homosexuals (recent findings are presented in Bell and Weinberg, 1978, pp. 62–68). Because, contrary to popular misconception, their orientation need not be readily apparent on the basis of external appearance, homosexuals maintain considerable control in determining who shall know about it. How particular individuals exercise this control will depend on their complex assessments of personal priorities and resources in a number of areas. These include: the importance to them of unquestioned acceptance or even approval in various social circles and positions, the extent to which their self-acceptance and pride depend on their being in all circumstances open and aboveboard (what is now often called "up-front"), the likely impact of varying kinds of disclosure on their financial security and general life prospects, their estimates regarding likely reactions to disclosure on the part of key individuals with whom they must deal in a number of domains, the extent of their social-psychological resources ("ego-strength," etc.) and support from others that would help them withstand any stigmatizing consequences of disclosure, and their assessments of the risk of arrest or other law-enforcement interference that might be entailed in different aspects of disclosure.

Of course, we know there are homosexuals who make little or no attempt at concealment and also that patterns in this area are currently undergoing considerable change (see Chapter 7). Yet, in all probability, it remains true in this country that "there are very few who do not feel, at least in part, the need to live a double life" (Altman, 1973, p. 41). In a major survey of homosexuals' problems and adaptations, 30 percent of the more than 1000 respondents reported that they tried to conceal their homosexuality from *all* heterosexuals; another 38 percent said they tried to conceal it from most heterosexuals. On the other hand, about

20 percent claimed that they hid their orientation from only a few or no hetero-sexuals (Weinberg and Williams, 1975b, pp. 139–140). Agreement is not complete regarding the psychological impact of this **passing** on the individuals who engage in it. Many professional observers see it as likely to further reinforce the low self-esteem, or even self-hatred, which many homosexuals have developed and which the passing itself may in part reflect. Various commentators, including some who are themselves homosexual, have also cited the strong anxiety that may be generated by continuous fear of disclosure. On the other hand, Goffman, in his more general discussion of the "management of spoiled identity," suggests that close study of passers of various kinds might well reveal "that this anxiety is not always found and that here our folk conceptions of human nature can be seriously misleading" (Goffman, 1963, p. 87). Whatever the precise anxiety and guilt levels may be, it is difficult to believe that concealment can often be prac-ticed without some detrimental psychological consequences or at least without the experiencing of a great deal of unpleasantness. For most people, pretending to be what they are not will, in all likelihood, exact some kind of toll. In his pioneering autobiographical account, Donald Webster Cory noted an incident in which he had felt compelled to smile at a "queer joke." He felt he had "de-based my character by giving tacit consent and even approval to the abuse of which I felt I was personally the victim" (Cory, 1960, p. 11). Constant dissembling only heightens the difficulty of taking such incidents in stride. "A person cannot live in an atmosphere of universal rejection, of widespread pretense, of a society that outlaws and banishes his activities and desires, of a social world that jokes and sneers at every turn, without a fundamental influence on his personality" (Cory, 1960, p. 12).

The phenomenon of passing illustrates once again the amplifying effects of stigma, for passing ensures that the deviator will be continuously preoccupied with, "engulfed" by, the deviation. Thus passing reflects and, at the same time, strongly reinforces the "role primacy" that deviance situations so commonly exhibit. Indeed, concealment by homosexuals shows this in especially virulent form because it guarantees that the deviation becomes a key reference point for the deviator *even* in those areas and situations in which it should be *least* rele-vant. One such area is that of work. A great many homosexuals expend consider-able effort to keep separate their domains of work and leisure. In the Weinberg and Williams survey cited earlier, respondents were asked, "Would there be problems at work if people found out [that you were homosexual]?" They answered as follows (Weinberg and Williams, 1975b, p. 138):

No	21.9%
Yes, but only to a very small degree	21.7
Yes, to some degree	22.1
Yes, very much so	32.2
Most people I work with already know	2.2

Although, on balance, lesbians may encounter somewhat less severe social and legal pressures than do male homosexuals, for them, too, caution frequently dictates concealment at work. Two writers who are also acknowledged lesbians state:

> There are still far many more in the closet than out. Professional women who have been able to declare themselves openly, like Phyllis, have unique jobs with foundations or institutions outside of the system, where emphasis is on people and their contributions, not on labels. But these opportunities are, of course, very rare. Some offices are more sophisticated and ready to accept gay people openly. And we've heard of a few Lesbians who have been able to survive being the butt of jokes in industrial plants. But such openness, at least at this stage of the game, is still somewhat hazardous (Martin and Lyon, 1972, p. 126; see also Simon and Gagnon, 1967; and Simpson, 1977).

The attempt to compartmentalize work and leisure is closely tied up with the hierarchical patterning of occupational opportunities for homosexuals. In their early study of "secret" and "overt" homosexuals, Leznoff and Westley found that the extent to which homosexuality was tolerated in various occupations became a major factor in the modes of adaptation particular individuals chose. Furthermore, the more prestigious the occupation, the greater the overall tendency was not to tolerate openness. "The overt homosexual tends to fit into an occupation of low status rank; the secret homosexual into an occupation with a relatively high status rank" (Leznoff and Westley, 1956, p. 260). More recently, Laud Humphreys has commented: "My research indicates that a disproportionately high number of male homosexuals find employment as hospital orderlies and technicians, travelling salesmen, retail sales clerks, short order cooks, and waiters. I doubt that gay men gravitate to these jobs because they enjoy changing bed linens, washing dishes, waiting tables, or stocking merchandise. The greater probability is that these are the only positions open to discreditable individuals" (Humphreys, 1972, p. 34).

If efforts at concealment produce a tendency to segregate work and leisure, that is not their only consequence. They also significantly influence the substance and structuring of activities and facilitating institutions within the domain of leisure itself. The desire to maintain personal anonymity is at least one factor accounting for the frequenting by many homosexuals of various specialized settings that facilitate making contacts for quick and impersonal sex. In his study of "tearooms"—public restrooms used for such purposes—Humphreys suggested that transitory contacts of this sort may reflect the more general appeal in our society of opportunities for anonymous, impersonal, and uncommitted sexual activity (Humphrey, 1970, 1975; see also discussion in Chapter 8). However that may be, the special concern of homosexuals to preserve their anonymity is no doubt a major determinant of much tearoom-frequenting. Noting that 54 percent of his research subjects were married men living with their wives, Humphreys commented that, "I see no reason to dispute the claim of a number of tearoom respondents that their preference for a form of concerted action that is fast and impersonal is largely predicated on a desire to protect their family relationships"

(Humphreys, 1970, 1975, p. 105). As the same writer pointed out, persons with relatively low occupational autonomy will similarly feel special pressures to preserve their anonymity. We should note, incidentally, another general point of some importance highlighted by Humphreys' findings: A person need not be fully or continuously committed to a deviating orientation in order to experience stigma and take steps to avoid it. In this instance, what might be considered "part-time" homosexual activity carries the potential to seriously discredit people, even though their "dominant" orientation may be heterosexual.

Heightening, if not directly creating, the concern about being openly discredited is the added pressure that results from the legal proscription of homosexual acts (see Schur, 1965; also discussion of "victimless crimes," pp. 450–457). Commenting on an early analysis of the relative unenforceability of such laws (Schur, 1965), Humphreys has cautioned us to realize that, nonetheless, "the average homosexual has ample cause to fear arrest" (Humphreys, 1972, p. 19). This claim is well borne out in the Weinberg-Williams survey, where 24.6 percent of the respondents reported they had at some time been arrested on a charge relating to their homosexuality (Weinberg and Williams, 1975b, p. 140). Concern with possible legal interference as well as with remaining relatively anonymous even to those with whom one has sexual contacts helps to explain at least part of the appeal of other relatively segregated settings such as gay bars and gay baths. No doubt, these serve additional functions; they can be congenial gathering sites as well as "back places, where persons of the individual's kind stand exposed and find they need not try to conceal their stigma, nor be overly concerned with cooperatively trying to disattend it" (Goffman, 1963, p. 81). However, the relative safety, through control over personal disclosure, is a major advantage of such segregation. In a recent analysis of gay baths—"licensed men's health clubs that provide a setting for impersonal homosexual sex"—it was emphasized that while such settings did not provide absolute protection and anonymity, they did afford these in high degree. To maximize such safety, many precautions were taken, ranging from location in inconspicuous settings to screening of potential customers.

One national chain of baths requires that each member bath must be operated as a private membership club. This gives some safeguard against police intrusion on the grounds of invasion of privacy. For baths in this chain, other rules that limit the possibility of legitimate intrusion by authorities include compliance with health and safety regulations, the actual existence of a steam room or sauna to give the semblance of a health club, keeping an orderly place, and prohibiting drug use. In one bath, a sign notes that police have received complaints about bath patrons' parking illegally on residential streets and concludes, "Please do not let parking endanger the _____ Baths" (Weinberg and Williams, 1975a, p. 128).

Interpretations of the segregative tendencies that are central to homosexual life in America today are bound to vary. It was suggested earlier that these patterns may reflect the combined impact of voluntary or self-segregation and of restrictions and tensions produced by negative societal reactions. As social change in this area accelerates, the thesis of Hoffman cited above—that social stigma creates a deep psychological inability to form meaningfully intimate relationships—may become less widely applicable. In a similar way, the characteristic settings for homosexual contacts and socializing may either change or take on new meaning.

At present, however, it continues to be largely true that a kind of "ghetto" situation prevails, perhaps partly through free choice, but without question also as a defensive adaptation. One writer has stated, "It is a ghetto, rather than a free territory, because it is still theirs. Straight cops patrol us, straight legislators make our laws, straight employers keep us in line, straight money exploits us" (Wittman, 1972, p. 157). At an extreme, as we noted earlier in considering the persisting relevance of the Chicago ecological work, geographical concentration of gay-oriented establishments and living places can result in a ghetto that is actual as well as symbolic. However much those with a deviating orientation may at times want to be together with "their own kind," such close segregation is bound to become oppressive and limiting.

Edgerton has used the term "passing" to describe certain efforts by formerly hospitalized mental retardates to manage their day-to-day existence in the outside community (Edgerton, 1967, pp. 144–168). In these instances, there are two somewhat related aspects to the concealment. Retardates try to avoid precise and full disclosure of their prior hospitalization, that is, of their "record" or personal history of deviance-processing. At the same time, they are continuously involved in attempts to hide current incapacity. As Edgerton succinctly puts it, they do this by trying to develop a "cloak of competence" that will divert attention from the many difficulties they experience in accomplishing various routine actions and in managing general social interaction.

The people Edgerton studied used various ingenious techniques to prevent other people from knowing they had spent much of their lives in a hospital. Because "the ex-patient lacks the ordinary souvenirs of a normal past," many of them engaged in a continuous "search for memorabilia," ranging from collections of china cups to purported athletic trophies; "one married woman had a photograph album filled with photos of assorted relatives, friends, and family—and not a single photograph in the album was legitimate" (Edgerton, 1967, p. 156). Similarly, in efforts that combined a shielding of the past with a covering of current difficulty, some of Edgerton's subjects displayed substantial libraries of unread books and large quantities of presumably accumulated but actually falsified mail. When someone did learn of their past hospitalization, they relied on a variety of "tales" to explain why they had "really" been in a hospital, which included treatment for "nerves," alcoholism, or various types of physical illness, and some claimed improper commitment at the hands of spiteful relatives. Another set of tales had to be constructed to explain the "eugenic" sterilization most of the patients had undergone while hospitalized; this posed special problems for women, who had a noticeable scar from the operation.

Concealment of continuing incapacities was equally difficult. Verbal de-

ficiencies were dealt with by "saying as little as possible when they are in public."
Characteristic reading difficulties were managed through various cover stories:

> . . . the ex-patients have developed serviceable excuses for most contingencies.
> For example, one woman was twice observed to excuse her inability to read labels in
> a market by saying that she had been drinking and couldn't focus her eyes very well.
> But one excuse is almost universally valid, and the ex-patients use it often. When the
> challenge to read cannot be avoided, the retardate simply fumbles about for an instant,
> then says that he's forgotten his glasses and can't see the words in question. The obliging
> normal usually can be depended on both to accept the excuse and to read aloud what-
> ever is needed (Edgerton, 1967, p. 164).

Numbers posed special problems for these retardates. Difficulty in telling time
was overcome largely by having alarm clocks set by others. Yet many of the retardates, even those who could not tell time, wore watches:

> It helps greatly, in asking for the time, to be able to look at one's watch and
> ruefully remark that it has stopped running. As one man, who wears a long-inoperative
> watch put it: "I ask 'em, 'Is it nine yet?' and I say that my old watch stopped, and some-
> body always tells me how close it is to the time when I got to be someplace. If I don't
> have that old watch of mine on, people just act like I'm some kind of bum and walk
> away" (Edgerton, 1967, p. 166).

Counting problems posed even greater obstacles in the area of dealing with
money. Few of Edgerton's subjects could count money well, and most experienced serious job-related and other difficulties as a result. This was an area, then,
in which they were particularly dependent on others (the aforementioned "benefactors") for direct help in managing their lives.

Quite different in nature, but equally intriguing for students of deviance, are the versions of "passing" engaged in by transvestites and transsexuals.
In neither of these cases does the passing primarily consist of concealing deviation. Nonetheless, both crucially involve at some stage a person's efforts to be
viewed by others, that is, to "pass," as occupying a sex-role or gender-status in
which they might not otherwise be cast. **Transvestites** are individuals who at times
cross-dress; they put on clothing and other accoutrements of the opposite sex
and attempt to present themselves in that guise. As one knowledgeable observer
has pointed out, the transgression in such cases consists merely in sex inappropriate behavior or, more accurately, appearance, for this is a kind of visual deviation: "The heterosexual transvestite only dresses. He does not steal, smoke dope,
rape children, or beat his wife. Yet he is judged totally on how he looks when
dressed . . ." (Feinbloom, 1977, p. 252). The male cross-dressers Feinbloom
defined themselves basically as men with a highly compartmentalized "female
corner" to their personalities, and most of them claimed to be exclusively heterosexual as far as overt sexual behavior was concerned. Their wives often knew
about the cross-dressing, some even tolerating it at home. Usually the complete
"dressing" was limited to informal gatherings of a transvestite club to which
they belonged. They described the dressing as more of an "art form" than a

kind of sexual fetishism and, indeed, were careful to exclude those whose motives were predominantly sexual. Transvestites are "expected to dress from head to toe":

> Were a member to wear bra and panties only, he would be excluded from the meeting. Proper attire suggests proper motives. . . . Bra and panty fetishists are carefully excluded as deviant exhibitionists, as autoerotic in goal, as more deviant than the group can tolerate. If a transvestite is at a lingerie phase but has a future in full dressing, the group may be more accepting and will aid in the completion (Feinbloom, 1977, p. 118).

In the process of dressing, the deviation itself consists of passing. Successfully passing as a woman—for instance, when dressing goes beyond the confines of a club or home—is a thrilling achievement for the transvestite. It would also clearly be responded to by most other people as a deviation. As a result, the transvestite typically will have to engage in the more usual kind of passing as well, that is, partial concealment of the cross-dressing itself. The men described in Feinbloom's book were "visually perfect examples of 'compartmentalized' deviance. For the most part, their cross-dressing is carefully delimited in time and place and hidden from the rest of their lives. Their appearances, occupations, avocations, etc., outside of dressing, are strictly masculine" (Feinbloom, 1977, p. 126).

It appears also from Feinbloom's data that the compartmentalizing may have "internal" aspects as well. Her subjects displayed generally conservative political and social outlooks and "traditional male attitudes toward women." Furthermore, they showed little tolerance for "deviance." Thus, one of them stated:

> I can't really warm up to homosexuals. Once I told my father the priest had tried to proposition me. My father blew his top and really got that priest in trouble. I felt bad after. But still have trouble with the idea. As long as they leave me alone, I'll let them be. But if my kid ever said,"I'm gay, Daddy," I think I'd die. I still think of homosexuals as fags, queers, and fruits (Feinbloom, 1977, p. 105).

The transsexual's situation is quite different. In the early days of sex-change operations, such surgery was largely restricted to cases of children born with hermaphroditic conditions (partial development of genitals of both sexes) and other similar anomalies. It was found that if the surgical sex "assignment" were made early enough and wisely enough and if significant others treated the child in the ways considered normal for the assigned sex, then in all behavioral and psychological respects, the child would develop as and continue to be a person "of" that sex. More recently, adults who have had no such physiological anomalies have been increasingly drawn to these sex-change operations. These have been persons who perceived their anatomy and their gender identity (sense of maleness or femaleness) as being inconsistent, that is, biological men who deeply felt that their "real nature" was female or biological women whose sense of core identity was male. Nowadays, the term **transsexual** usually refers to adults with this kind of "cross-gender identification" (Feinbloom, 1977, p. 148), including those who do not intend to undergo actual sex-change, those who are merely considering it, and those who have already taken that step.

In what respects can we say that transsexuals pass? This question is rather tricky, and to answer it we need to consider different "stages" in transsexualism. Of the person who simply "feels" the cross-gender identification but does nothing to "adopt" or "establish" it, we might indeed say that they believe themselves to be *involuntarily* passing for whichever sex their biological appearance seems to indicate. In other words, their anatomy is passing them off as that which they are convinced they are not. At the same time, since this very conviction would, if openly expressed, elicit deviantizing responses, the transsexual in even this "covert" situation will probably conceal from others this deep feeling and, to that extent, consciously pass as "normal."

When transsexuals move beyond merely feeling this cross-gender identification and take steps of various kinds and degrees toward the possibility of an eventually complete sex-reassignment, they find themselves in new situations that may require additional types of passing. Under hormone treatment, they may over time bring about substantial changes in their secondary sexual characteristics. They will, then, begin to develop some of the appearance of the desired (to them "real") gender. Particularly if they expect to take the final step of sex-change surgery (replacement of the present genitals with "constructed" ones appropriate to the opposite sex), they will want to test out in more and more situations how it really feels to be reacted to as being of the desired gender. This is bound to require various kinds of passing and compartmentalizing. Jan Morris (formerly James Morris) writes:

> . . . my worst miseries were over now, and my preoccupations were, so to speak, largely logistical. I had to remember in which role I was known in any given circumstance. As I divided my life more absolutely between the sexes, there were many places in which I could not appear as a man, and vice versa. There were families who knew me only as a male, or only as a female, or as both—or some people at a dinner table might know the truth about me, but not others—or I might be a member of one society in this sex, of another in that (Morris, 1975, p. 131).

With the actual sex-change surgery, one presumably makes a full commitment to a complete sex-reassignment. One now will present oneself only and always as a woman, if one has been a man, or vice versa. Acceptance of this may be precarious, and various accounts indicate the need not only for support from other people but also for new "credentials" (identity cards, driver's license, legal change of name, new passport, etc.) that will help certify the change. Psychologically, too, the individual has to shake off the lingering aspects of self-conception that were associated with the old anatomy.

Since sex-change is such a profound step, difficulties and setbacks of one sort or another seem almost inevitable. Given the stigma that no doubt attaches to undertaking the step, even the transsexual who has a completely new gender

NEWS SPOT
Tennis and Transsexuals

(August 1976–September 1977). During the 1976–1977 tennis season, considerable public attention was focused on Dr. Renee Richards, a player whose qualifying credentials had been challenged by tournament officials and questioned by some women players. Dr. Richards is a transsexual. A 42-year-old ophthalmologist, she had been known, prior to a 1975 sex-change operation, as Richard Raskin and, as such, had recently been ranked third in the East and thirteenth in the nation in the men's 35-year-old and over division. For Richards, more than a year's efforts to establish her right to play in women's tournaments finally paid off when a judge ruled in August 1977 that officials of the U.S. Open tennis championships could not bar her from participation solely on the ground of chromosome tests for sex-determination. For many Americans, the extensive news and television coverage of Richards at the important Forest Hills tournament (where she lost in the opening round to Wimbledon winner Virginia Wade) may well have represented their first close and knowing observation of a self-disclosed transsexual.

Dr. Richards first encountered difficulty when she was admitted to a 1976 tourney in New Jersey. Twenty-five women players withdrew, protesting that she had an unfair muscular advantage and should not be allowed to compete as a female. From that point on and until the 1977 court ruling, she faced almost continuous obstacles in her attempts to be accepted as a woman tennis player. In the process, she became something of a cause celèbre, and her situation prompted considerable media discussion of transsexuality. Letters to editors appeared in national newspapers—some lauding her stand and insisting that her decision to acknowledge herself as a woman ought be acceded to by tennis officials. Other correspondents worried over the confusion her entry to tournaments would cause; one even voiced a fear that women's sports might now be "taken over by a giant race of surgically created women." A letter from an anonymous transsexual was printed in which the writer noted the fact that almost all media coverage was using the designation "she"—"already a big advance over a few years ago."

Richards herself, who at the outset had described her efforts as posing "a human rights issue," seemed to be surprised by all the publicity. Looking back on her long ordeal from the vantage point of Forest Hills, where she actually experienced the greatest direct media exposure, she described her distress over being stared at as though she were "a monkey in a glass cage." Reporters quoted her as saying that while the whole experience had been extremely hard on her from a "personal" standpoint, "from a social standpoint it's been worth it." Most news analysts seem agreed that Richards had, in fact, effectively raised important issues regarding the rights of transsexuals and that in the process she had more generally heightened public awareness of a largely unfamiliar condition. Having accomplished that, Renee Richards seems hopeful that now perhaps she can be viewed by tennis fans as just a player and nothing more.

(*Source:* Based on articles and correspondence in *The New York Times,* August 31, 1976, p. 32; September 5, 1976, sec. 5, p. 2; August 2, 1977, p. 35; August 17, 1977, p. B7; September 2, 1977, p. A15.)

identity may well pass to the extent of concealing the old one. Though some writers seem to use the term "passing" for the person's efforts to gain complete acceptance in the new gender-role, that application of the term seems somewhat questionable. At least from the transsexual's own viewpoint, at that advanced stage there is in that sense no passing; on the contrary, such people feel that finally they are free and able to be what "they really are" and "have been all along." Whatever psychiatrists may make of their inner feelings and motivation, there is little question but that such individuals, when they disclose their real situation, will encounter serious social difficulties at the present time. That sex-change occurs in the face of such obstacles is testimony to the strength of the identification that prompts it.

Disavowal and Denial

When persons subject to stigma cannot conceal their deviation, they frequently engage in efforts that have been termed **disavowal** and **denial.** These concepts have been used in a number of different ways, but basically they highlight the attempt to convince others (disavowal) and oneself (denial) that the deviation is not really an impediment to normal existence. The two processes are obviously interrelated, since the self-concepts a person is able to maintain will depend on the images of himself or herself that other people will accept and reinforce (and, probably to a lesser extent, vice versa).

The clearest examples of disavowal and denial involve the efforts of physically disabled persons to achieve some degree of ordinariness in their everyday interaction. Since their deviation is typically both evident *and* heavily defined by others as extraordinary and impeding, this is not at all an easy thing to do. Because of its "master status" quality, the deviation dominates the other person's reactions:

I get suspicious when somebody says, "Let's go for a uh, ah [imitates confused and halting speech] push with me down the hall," or something like that. This to me is suspicious because it means that they're aware, really aware, that there's a wheelchair here, and that this is probably uppermost with them. . . . A lot of people in trying to show you that they don't care that you're in a chair will do crazy things. Oh, there's one person I know who constantly kicks my chair, as if to say "I don't care that you're in a wheelchair. I don't even know that it's there." But that is just an indication that he *really* knows it's there (Davis, 1961, p. 123).

. . . several blind people have told me that when they use public transportation, fellow passengers will occasionally put money into their hands. When this occurs, a blind man cannot very well give a public lecture on the truth about blindness; in fact, to do anything but acquiesce and accept the gift will leave him open to charges of ingratitude and bitterness (Scott, 1969, p. 23).

In the case of transitory contacts, the person with a serious and highly evident physical handicap probably cannot really anticipate being treated by many people as acceptably ordinary. Even in the case of continuing relationships, as Davis has suggested, several stages of interaction must be gone through before the other person can be expected to regularly "normalize" the handicap. It will usually take considerable time to overcome "the interactional barrier that lies between narrow fictional acceptance and more spontaneous forms of relatedness" (Davis, 1961, pp. 128–129). This is "a redefinitional process"—a redefining of the condition and the relationship; in many respects, it is likewise "a process of identification." The nonhandicapped person gradually is "cued into a larger repertoire of appropriate responses," and interaction is increasingly eased as the "stifling burden of unspoken awareness" is reduced. Paradoxically, as Davis goes on to note, this eventual normalizing of the handicap must again be transcended so that a final, "normal, but" stage in the relationship can be achieved. This involves the problem of "sustaining the normalized definition in the face of the many small amendments and qualifications that must frequently be made to it." In other words, the handicapped person cannot in the last analysis perform and be treated in *just* the same ways as would a nonhandicapped person. The insistence on "equal and normal status" must somehow be integrated with "minor waivers of the same claim" (Davis, 1961, p. 130).

In his research on polio victims and their families, Davis noted the "fatal flaw" of normalization or disavowal—"the fact that others are frequently unable or unwilling to go along with it." No doubt this is a major reason why another strategy, *disassociation* (insulating oneself from "contacts, situations, and involvements" in which disavowal is difficult), also has strong appeal (Davis, 1963, pp. 148–163). Disassociation, or avoidance, when adopted by the handicapped, is really very similar to the self-segregation of the homosexual or other deviator who practices partial concealment. Here, perhaps, the technique is less one of compartmentalizing different established parts of one's life than of avoiding the intolerable "compartments" (intimidating situations, social circles, etc.) as much as possible.

One form this may take, in cases of suddenly imposed stigmatizing disability, is avoidance of old acquaintances. Thus, Cogswell reports that, "Paraplegics and pretrauma friends alike find it difficult to maintain their pretrauma friendships. Friends are attached to definitions of the paraplegic as he once was and have difficulty relating to him as the new person whom disability requires and allows him to be. Paraplegics find it difficult to try out and develop a new identity before an audience who knew them before injury" (Cogswell, 1967, p. 21). A common finding is that the person newly stigmatized in this way will (have to) turn for friendship to those who, in other respects, are of lower social status. Davis' polio victims experienced a "gradual, socially coerced process of downward mobility in the 'normal' peer group" (Davis, 1963, p. 147), and, similarly, Cogswell has reported:

By choosing friends of lower status, paraplegics are able to balance the negative definitions of disability against some negative characteristic of other. In these relationships where both participants have a social handicap, paraplegics find failure less threatening and feel freer to experiment with new behavior and new definitions of self. If in relationships with others of lower status paraplegics become successful in projecting themselves as persons of worth and become skilled in eliciting this definition, they proceed to more difficult social relationships, eventually forming successful relationships with new others of equal status (Cogswell, 1967, p. 21).

Avoidance techniques enable the handicapped to head off the characteristic avoidance *of them* by others. In the process, they serve important functions for potential reactors as well as deviators. Avoidance has much the same effect that Goffman perceptively describes in his general comments regarding our conceptions of a "good adjustment" on the part of the stigmatized individual: "it means that normals will not have to admit to themselves how limited their tactfulness and tolerance is; and it means that normals can remain relatively uncontaminated by intimate contact with the stigmatized, relatively unthreatened in their identity beliefs" (Goffman, 1963, p. 121). It is a crucial reflection of their dependent power position that in relation to so-called "normals," stigmatized persons should be expected to "try to help them and the social situation by conscious efforts to reduce tension" (Goffman, 1963, p. 116) in this and other ways.

As already suggested, denial (convincing oneself that the perceived deviation need not be a basis for disvaluation or an impediment) is heavily dependent on successful disavowal (convincing others). Denial efforts represent the person's defense or counterattack against the aforementioned likelihood of lowered self-esteem, even self-hatred, that may follow from direct deviantizing. Hardly ever can the individual deny the very fact of being perceived by others as a deviator. In a sense, something like this may happen when a person "suppresses" or "represses" self-awareness of a deviantized orientation—such as homosexual preference for example. More typically, perceived deviators attempt to deny to themselves as well as to others that the deviation *is* their "essential character," or, to put it another way, they try to deny the inevitability of its "role primacy." They hope to establish and maintain their own sense of their personal worth *notwithstanding* the deviation. To do this does in a way mean denying a certain "reality"—namely the deviantness-laden definition of the situation that other people invariably tend to impose. Looking back on her fat childhood, one writer has stated: "I started to develop two coping or protective devices which became quite elaborate later. For one thing, I started to try to establish my worth in areas not related to physical attributes, while at the same time avoiding activities involving my body. The other mechanism was an active fantasy world where I was always the center of attention. These techniques were, I suppose, attempts to deny my situation to myself if not to others" (Anonymous, 1974, p. 71).

Much as in the case of disavowal, denial efforts, too, may come up against the "normal, but" problem. This is particularly true with respect to physical handicaps as defined within a context of efforts at rehabilitation. From a "therapeutic" standpoint, too adamant a denial of deviation may impede rehabilitative progress. Thus there may be a paradoxical need for the person to accept the stigmatized label, though not all of the deviantness attaching to it, in order to confront it. Cogswell notes that, "Initial identification with the disabled role is tenuous and negative. . . . the physician must explain several times before paraplegics cognitively accept the label of disability. . . . paraplegics vacillated between identification with the normal and disabled roles. . . . Over time paraplegics shifted to a disabled perspective which allowed them to see the advantages of rehabilitation . . ." (Cogswell, 1967, p. 18; see also Levitin, 1975). As we will see below, certain kinds of voluntary treatment programs in a variety of substantive areas center their schemes precisely around this kind of "positive" acceptance of the deviation.

The discussion in this section has really only begun to indicate what efforts at disavowal and denial may involve. In a sense, it is probably more accurate to conceive of these concepts as referring to desired *outcomes* rather than specific techniques. They indicate a sought-after definition of the situation, one in which the centrality of the deviation and the deviantness attached to the individual are lessened. As we have seen, the very nature of the deviance-defining process implies that people trying to achieve these outcomes will encounter severe difficulties in doing so. Certain kinds of standard resources (high socioeconomic status, psychological stability, etc.) will probably be of some help. A variety of specific conditions and techniques that facilitate "neutralizing" stigma (which are discussed next) can also be conceived of as resources. Their availability or nonavailability will significantly influence the outcomes of stigma-avoidance efforts, including the extent to which attempts at disavowal and denial can succeed.

NEUTRALIZING STIGMA

Accounts

Marvin Scott and Stanford Lyman have emphasized the special importance for the sociology of deviance of what they have called **accounts**—"linguistic forms that are offered for untoward action," typically excuses and justifications of various kinds (Scott and Lyman, 1968). Certainly, when stigma attaches to acts seen as voluntary, but, in a sense, even when the deviation is a condition for which they are not, strictly speaking, considered "responsible," perceived deviators are being held accountable. In some way or other and whether it is thought to be within or beyond their control, they are held not to be giving a good enough "account of themselves." Even the physically disabled are *treated* as if there were something "inexcusable" about their condition, although those who treat them that way would rarely admit to harboring any such conception. If this tendency underlies most deviantizing, then it should follow that if you can provide an acceptable account, you will reduce the likelihood of being severely stigmatized. Here again, we see the very close link between successfully conveying desired images to other people and being able to incorporate them in one's own self-conceptions. When people offer rationales or rationalizations for possibly problematic behavior, they are trying to ease their situation in two ways: by convincing other people and by convincing themselves.

The reader will recall Sutherland's references to "motives, drives, rationalizations, and attitudes" as comprising some of the important learned elements contributing to criminality. Taking this formulation as a point of departure, Gresham Sykes and David Matza, in an early journal article, developed the important idea **of techniques of neutralization** (Sykes and Matza, 1957). Their argument, intended primarily as a contribution to theories about juvenile delinquency, was that delinquents often employ rationalizations that are very much like the technical "defenses" or "exceptions" to criminal liability provided in our system of criminal law. Furthermore, they claimed, it might well be the case that such rationalizations "precede deviant behavior and make deviant behavior possible." They cited the following major neutralizing techniques: *denial of responsibility* (in effect, that the offender couldn't "help it"), *denial of injury* (no real harm done), *denial of the victim* (who deserved it), *condemnation of the condemners* (as spiteful, hypocritical, etc.), and *appeal to higher loyalties* (claim that one acted out of group loyalty, etc.). Sykes and Matza, as part of a critique of conventional subculture theories, inferred from the delinquents' use of these neutralizing techniques that they at least partially accepted the dominant values according to which they were being condemned. Yet it does not seem logically necessary that one "agree" with other people's negative characterizations in order to employ such devices. Even where no guilt or shame were consciously felt, one might well offer justifying rationales in the hope of lessening what could be, nonetheless, very real stigmatizing pressures.

Various examples of stigma-neutralizing accounts can be found in the literature on deviance. Since operative (as opposed to professed) values and norms in the area of business-related honesty and fraud tend to be ambiguous in our society, it is not surprising that rationalizations are readily available and widely used to justify white-collar crime. As we have already seen, corporate offenders are quick to justify legal infractions on the ground that they were only practicing "business as usual." Similarly, Cressey, in his major study of embezzlement, found trust-violators' "vocabularies of adjustment" to be a major factor leading to such offenses. He found that the rationalizations were present "before the criminal act took place," rather than simply constituting an after-the-fact attempt at justification. Cressey concluded that, "The rationalization is his motivation, and it not only makes his behavior intelligible to others, but it makes it intelligible to *himself*." Furthermore, these rationalizations reflected "contacts with cultural ideologies which themselves are contradictory to the theme that honesty is expected in all situations of trust" (Cressey, 1953, pp. 94, 94–95, 99). A few brief excerpts from Cressey's interviews with convicted embezzlers will convey a sense of the substance of these "accounts":

> In all instances where I collected for clients I made remittances in part. Frequently I would use part of the deposits and collections because I knew I could always replace the necessary funds. The money used wasn't mine, but I had money or some source of money to cover it. That was wrong, but it is not criminal. . . . This was highly

unethical but not illegal because there was no criminal intent . . . I was borrowing the money—stealing is stigmatized with criminal intent, but my method wasn't.

In the real estate business you have to paint a pretty picture in order to sell the property. We did a little juggling and moving around, but everyone in the real estate business has to do that. We didn't do anything that they all don't do.

Some fellows have the intention to embezzle to use the money for a good time, others use it for working capital. The last isn't embezzlement. (All quoted in Cressey, 1953, pp. 103–104, 104–105, 112.)

In a rather different area, that of stigmatized sexual activity—again, a domain in which cultural values tend to be confused or ambivalent—Bryan's field interviews with call girls revealed standard rationalizing ideologies that helped them to neutralize stigma and maintain their self-respect. (Note the rather interesting similarity between these formulations and Davis' classic theory of the "functions" of prostitution cited in Chapter 2.)

We girls see, like I guess you call them perverts of some sort, you know, little freaky people and if they didn't have girls to come to like us that are able to handle them and make it a nice thing, there would be so many rapes and . . . nutty people really. . . .

I could say that a prostitute has held more marriages together as part of their profession than any divorce counselor. . . .

I don't regret doing it because I feel I help people. A lot of men that come over to see me don't come for sex. They come over for companionship, someone to talk to. . . . a lot of them have problems. (All quoted in Bryan, 1966, p. 443.)

As the recent women's movement has helped to make clear, in a society in which women generally have been subordinated and exploited, there is also available a clear rationale for considering prostitutes as victims rather than offenders (see James, *et al.,* 1975; also Adaptation Eleven, "Broadsides and Manifestoes").

Stigma implies the possibility, indeed, the likelihood of shame. An important function of justifying rationales or rationalizations is to neutralize shame by redefining the activity in such a way as to reduce the shamefulness. To some extent this involves offering accounts and undertaking associated efforts aimed at altering the dominant conceptions of what the activity *is*. Polsky brings the point out well in his discussion of pornography:

. . . the stigma attached to pornography is lessened when pornography is tied to some other socially valued end, such as art or science. One important result is this: when the "situation" being defined by society is a naturalistic depiction of sex, the most real consequence of a definition that labels it something other than pornographic is to increase its pornographic use in the society by reducing the inhibitions on acquiring it. This is obvious from the libraries of countless souls who avidly buy highly erotic works that society labels "art" or "literature" or "science" or "scholarship," but who take care not to buy "real" pornography (Polsky, 1967, p. 199).

As this example begins to suggest, accounts sometimes go beyond the "linguistic forms" that Scott and Lyman emphasized. Shame-reducing and other rationalizations often involve manipulation of various symbols and situations in addition to and as a basis for actual verbalizations. Goffman has written about the strategy of concealing or obliterating "signs that have come to be stigma symbols" (Goffman, 1963, pp. 92–94). Although he had in mind primarily "identifiers" and other signs of deviation that have been directly attached to the individual and which must be shed or hidden (for example, the addict's needle marks), the notion of stigma symbols can be applied to situations as well as individuals. Donald Ball's description of an illegal abortion clinic illustrates this possibility. Closely studying one such establishment (in a California-Mexico border town), he found that the clinic employed a complex set of "presentational strategies" that provided a "rhetoric of legitimation," and which included manipulation of "verbal but also . . . visual symbols such as objects, gestures, emblems, etc." (Ball, 1967, p. 296). The physical layout and furnishings of the clinic, the clothing and demeanor of the staff, and the display of medical paraphernalia were all calculated to create an aura of respectability and legitimate surgical care. For both patrons and staff, Ball concluded, these impression-management techniques—the creation of what Goffman has termed a "front" (Goffman, 1959), pp. 22–30)—facilitated "a minimization of the threat to identity which is built into their illicit transaction" (Ball, 1967, p. 301).

Readers may recall that the manipulation of stigma and respectability symbols was noted earlier (though not discussed in exactly those terms) when we considered some of the "passing" techniques cited in Edgerton's study of mental retardates (fictitious mail and unread books, cover stories for sterilization scars, etc.). In many respects, the seemingly diverse techniques of concealment, disavowal and denial, avoidance, rationalization, and "front"—whether utilized together or separately—all display a common goal: stigma-reduction or, to put this in other terms already suggested, giving a good "account" of oneself. Also facilitating efforts to achieve this goal may be certain cultural forms and organized supports, which are reviewed in the remaining sections of this chapter. It should be apparent, too, that the prior comments regarding "negotiation" are likewise extremely pertinent with respect to the matter of accounts. The negotiation of basic identities is, by the same token, a negotiation of accounts. It makes little difference which terminology we employ. What is at stake is clear: The participants in the situations are trying to achieve outcomes favorable to themselves. For those subject to stigma, these will be ones in which the centrality or primacy of the deviation is kept to a minimum.

Our earlier discussion of "responsibility" should also be brought to mind by the notion of accounts. The two ideas often do bear a special relation to each other, even if sometimes "involuntary" deviators are treated as though their conditions could not be excused. It is no doubt true that, in many instances, being able to effectively present oneself as not responsible will lessen one's moral accountability. However, as we saw in considering the question of physical disabilities, this is an area in which the concept of degrees of deviantness is particularly helpful. In effect, it is often not a case of being held either fully accountable or not at all. There are probably types and degrees of accountability and types and degrees of acceptability, to various audiences, with respect to the justifying accounts that people offer.

Nonetheless, the voluntary-involuntary issue is one that often comes to the fore in the negotiation of accounts. We saw this in connection with Cicourel's study of subtle bargaining between delinquent youths and probation officers. And we noted also the considerable appeal that biological explanations, which may render the condition involuntary and the individual less accountable morally, have for some homosexuals. Similarly, Feinbloom found that heterosexual transvestites often cited biological need as a way of denying responsibility. One of her respondents is quoted as follows: "Perhaps it's all hormonal. I don't know—so many people say that it's all in the blood. Maybe I inherited it. It's part of me—comes and goes—might as well live with it" (Feinbloom, 1977, p. 95). We will return in later sections to some policy issues involving personal responsibility. For the moment, we should simply note that determining responsibility is an extremely complex matter, one that often poses difficult questions for decision-makers in a variety of social, medical, and legal contexts (see the general discussion in Aubert and Messinger, 1958; also Stoll, 1968).

Alternative Norms

Sometimes there develop around a problematic activity special norms that greatly facilitate the participants' efforts to give good accounts of themselves. Again, some of the perspectives noted earlier alert us to the importance of this element. We have seen that what is stigmatized in some contexts may often be acceptable in others. Cultures, and also subcultures, exhibit considerable normative variability; and sometimes even more narrowly circumscribed situations may generate and be governed by distinctive outlooks and "rules." In his notion of an oppositional subculture, Cohen showed how the specific content of alternative norms could help allay status anxiety and sustain favorable self-conceptions among those unable to meet the dominant standards. The implicit accounts offered by Cohen's delinquent boys were as much directed toward themselves as toward others.

A good deal of our discussion of learned elements in deviation also indicated the central role of what might be called "normative deviating." As Becker's interpretation of marihuana smoking showed, the supportive function of special norms, as in the delinquency case, will probably be most evident where the deviation is part of a rather broad subcultural pattern (see the next section of this chapter). However, there are also instances in which alternative norms help to reduce stigma even in the absence of a generalized subculture. Indeed, this is suggested by the just-concluded discussion of rationalizing accounts. We can see from the abortion clinic example and from Polsky's comments on pornography that implicit accounts may often evolve around or even rely upon special sets of norms. In both of these cases, there are distinctive "rules" as to *how the activity should be engaged in* if the participants are to maintain favorable self-images.

The apparent norms governing customer behavior in pornographic bookstores provide an illustration of a situational system of stigma-reducing rules. An intensive observational study of two pornography stores revealed standard ways of behaving in such a setting. On entering, customers often acted as though they came into the store by mistake:

. . . one afternoon at Store B a very well-dressed and respectable looking gentleman about fifty-five came in. He immediately looked at John, and without so much as a glance at anything else in the store asked if the store carried chewing gum. John said no. The man nodded an acknowledgment and very slowly began to look around at the store. As soon as John looked away, he slowly moved off toward the magazines. He stayed in the store for about a half hour (McKinstry, 1974, p. 37).

Other observed customer norms included silence; maintenance of physical separation; not looking at the other patrons; "not showing any facial expressions, particularly expressions of pleasure;" and, for those customers deciding to make a purchase, special ways of approaching the sales counter (making "distracting comments," etc.) aimed at diverting attention from the substance of the transaction. The author of this study suggested that customers had been "socialized into the norms of the adult store even before stepping inside the door. Hence the store is able to maintain its semi-respectable appearance over time even though its incumbents are constantly changing, and the borderline deviant can maintain his privacy without which he cannot gain the satisfaction he desires" (McKinstry, 1974, p. 40).

A more explicit, more fully developed, and more subculture-related system of alternative norms has been described by Albert Reiss in his analysis of delinquent youths who engage in homosexual acts for money (Reiss, 1961). The youths he studied, who were "also delinquent in many other respects," were able to view "getting a queer" as "an acceptable substitute for other delinquent earnings or activity" and to engage in this behavior without defining themselves as either "hustlers" (male prostitutes) or homosexuals. This was possible, Reiss found, because of a complex pattern of peer-group understandings and support and was facilitated through socialization of the youths to a set of quite specific norms governing these sexual transactions. Under this normative system, the encounter was defined as a way of making money rather than as a sexual relationship. Around this theme clustered a number of more specific expectations: that the youth would not actively seek sexual gratification; that the transaction would be strictly limited to mouth-genital fellation; that both participants "should remain affectively neutral during the transaction" so as to underline that the encounter is strictly a business deal; that violence would not be used "so long as the relationship conforms to the shared set of expectations between queers and peers" (Reiss, 1961, pp. 112–116). According to Reiss, these boys had been socialized into appropriate definitions of "peer-queer relations" in advance —they "know all this *before* they have any contact with a fellator." Violence or threatened violence represented a kind of backup device, resorted to when the customer's behavior violated the youths' expectations. Usually the normative system itself was strong enough to sustain the boys' sense of their own masculinity:

So long as he [the delinquent youth] conforms to these expectations, *his "significant others" will not define him as homosexual;* and this is perhaps the most crucial factor in his own self-definition. The peers define one as homosexual not on the basis of homosexual *behavior* as such, but on the basis of participation in the homosexual *role,* the "queer" role. The reactions of the larger society, in defining the *behavior* as homosexual is unimportant in their own self-definition. What is important to them is the reactions of their peers to violation of peer group norms which define roles on the peer-queer transaction (Reiss, 1961, p. 119).

A final example of "situated" alternative norms, which again reflects some influence of a broader subculture and, in this instance, which is further enhanced by a distinct ideological element is nudism. Adaptation Eight shows how special norms to which nudist camp participants are socialized help to neutralize stigma for the unclothed and even to generate stigma in connection with behavior which outside the camps would be considered "conventional."

ADAPTATION EIGHT
Making Nudism Normal*

Nudism, by definition, involves a significant departure (even if only in degree) from a widespread expectation in conventional American society that the body ordinarily will be clothed in public. For "social nudists," who wish at least on occasion to "violate" this rule, the nudist camp provides a partially protected site for interaction with like-minded others. Sociologist Martin Weinberg, who studied such camps through participant observation, interviews, and mailed questionnaires, found that members were able to construct there a "situated morality." Through careful "strategies" and their own special system of norms and sanctions, the nudists were able to provide each other with valuable group support and to neutralize or discount the negative imputations their behavior often elicits from clothed people. Noting that one major "strategy" involved taking precautions in admitting persons to the camps, Weinberg went on to discuss the rules governing interaction within the camps.

Norms regarding patterns of interpersonal behavior are the second element of the strategy to maintain the organization's system of moral meanings. These norms are as follows.

No Staring

This rule controls overt signs of overinvolvement. In the words of a publisher of a nudist magazine, "They all look up to the heavens and never look below." Such maintained inattention is most exaggerated among women, who show no recognition that the male body is unclothed. Women also recount how they expect men to look at them when they are nude, only to find that no one communicates any awareness when they finally do get up the courage to undress. As one woman states, "I got so mad because my husband wanted me to undress in front of other men that I just pulled my clothes right off thinking everyone would look at me." She was amazed (and appeared somewhat disappointed) when no one did.

The following statement illustrates the constraints that result:

[Q: Have you ever observed or heard about anyone starting at one's body while at camp?] I've heard stories, particularly about men that stare. Since I heard these stories, I

---

* *Source:* excerpted from Martin S. Weinberg, "The Nudist Management of Respectability: Strategy for, and Consequences of, the Construction of a Situated Morality," in Jack D. Douglas, ed., *Deviance and Respectability*. New York: Basic Books, 1970. Excerpts reprinted with permission, introductory and concluding comments are the present's author's—not in the original.

tried not to, and even done away with my sunglasses after someone said, half-joking, that I hide behind sunglasses to stare. Toward the end of the summer I stopped wearing sunglasses. And you know what, it was a child who told me this.

[Q: Would you stare . . . ?] Probably not, cause you can get in trouble and get thrown out. If I thought I could stare unobserved I might. They might not throw you out, but it wouldn't do you any good. [Q] The girl might tell others and they might not want to talk to me. . . . [Q] They disapprove by not talking to you, ignoring you, etc.

[Someone who stares] wouldn't belong there. [Q] If he does that, he is just going to camp to see the opposite sex. [Q] He is just coming to stare. [Q] You go there to swim and relax.

I try very hard to look at them from the jaw up—even more than you would normally.

No Sex Talk

Sex talk, or telling "dirty jokes," is uncommon in camp. The owner of a large camp in the Midwest stated: "It is usually expected that members of a nudist camp will not talk about sex, politics, or religion." Or, as one single male explained, "It is taboo to make sexual remarks here." During my field work, it was rare to hear "sexual" joking such as one hears at most other types of resort. Interview respondents who mentioned that they had talked about sex qualified this by explaining that such talk was restricted to close friends, was of a "scientific nature," or, if a joke, was a "cute sort."

Asked what they would think of someone who breached this rule, respondents indicated that such behavior would cast doubt on the situated morality of the nudist camp:

One would expect to hear less of that at camp than at other places. [Q: Why is that?] Because you expect that the members are screened in their *attitude for nudism*—and this isn't one who prefers sexual jokes.

I've never heard anyone swear or tell a dirty joke out there.

No. Not at camp. You're not supposed to. You bend over backwards not to.

They probably don't belong there. They're there to see what they can find to observe. [Q: What do you mean?] Well, their mind isn't on being a nudist, but to see so and so nude.

No Body Contact

Although the extent to which this is enforced varies among camps, there is at least some degree of informal enforcement in every camp. Nudists mention how they are particularly careful not to brush against anyone or have any body contact, because of how it might be interpreted. The following quotations illustrate the interpersonal precautions that are taken:

I stay clear of the opposite sex. They're so sensitive, they imagine things.

People don't get too close to you. Even when they talk. They sit close to you, but they don't get close enough to touch you.

We have a minimum of contact. There are more restrictions [at a nudist camp]. [Q] Just a feeling I had. I would openly show my affection more readily some place else.

One respondent defined this taboo as simply common-sense knowledge:

Suppose one had a desire to knock one off or feel his wife; modesty or a sense of protocol prohibits you from doing this.

And when asked to conceptualize a breach of this rule, typical of the response was:

They are in the wrong place. [Q: How is that?] That's not part of nudism. [Q: Could you tell me some more about that?] I think they are there for some sort of sex thrill. They are certainly not there to enjoy the sun.

If any photographs are taken for publication in a nudist magazine, the subjects are also usually allowed to have only limited body contact. One female nudist explained: "We don't want anyone to think we're immoral." Outsiders' interpretations of nude body contact are made in the framework of a constructed morality that would cast doubt on the characteristics set forth as the nudist way of life.

A correlate of the body contact taboo is a prohibtion of dancing in the nude. Nudists cite this as a separate rule. This rule is often talked about by members in a way that indicates organizational strain—where the rule itself makes evident that a strategy is in operation to sustain their situated morality. The following remark notes this: "This reflects a contradiction in our beliefs. But it's self-protection. One incident and we'd be closed."

No Alcoholic Beverages in American Camps

This rule guards against breakdowns in inhibition that could lead to "aggressive-erotic" signs. Even respondents who admitted that they had "snuck a beer" before going to bed went on to say that they fully favor the rule:

Yes. We have [drunk at camp]. We keep a can of beer in the refrigerator since we're out of the main area. We're not young people or carousers. . . . I still most generally approve of it as a camp rule and would disapprove of anyone going to extremes. [Q] For common-sense reasons. People who overindulge lose their inhibitions, and there is no denying that the atmosphere of a nudist camp makes one bend over backwards to keep people who are so inclined from going beyond the bounds of propriety.

Anyone who drinks in camp is jeopardizing their membership and they shouldn't. Anyone who drinks in camp could get reckless. [Q: How is that?] Well, when guys and girls drink, they're a lot bolder—they might get fresh with someone else's girl. That's why it isn't permitted, I guess.

Rules Regarding Photography

Photography in a nudist camp is organizationally controlled. Unless the person is an official photographer (that is, photographing for nudist magazines), the photographer's moral perspective is sometimes suspect. One photographer's remark that led to his being so typed was, "Do you think you could open your legs a little more?"

Aside from a general restriction on the use of cameras, when cameras are allowed, it is expected that no picture will be taken without the subject's permission. Members especially tend to blame the misuse of cameras on single men. As one nudist said: "You always see the singles poppin' around out of nowhere snappin' pictures." In general, control is maintained, and any infractions that exist are not blatant or obvious. Any overindulgence in taking photographs communicates an overinvolvement in the nude state of the subjects and casts doubt on the denied connection between nudity and sexuality.

Photographers dressed only in camera and light exposure meters, I don't like them. I think they only go out for pictures. Their motives should be questioned.

The official photographers taking pictures for nudist magazines recognize the signs that strain the situated morality that characterizes nudist camps. The following comment was made by an official photographer: "I never let a girl look straight at the camera. It looks too suggestive. I always have her look off to the side."

A nudist model showed the writer a pin-up magazine to point out how a model could make a nude picture "sexy"—through the use of various stagings, props, and expressions—and, in contrast, how the nudist model eliminates these techniques to make her pictures "natural." Although it may be questionable that a nudist model completely eliminates a sexual perspective for the nonnudist, the respondent discussed how a model attempts to do this:

It depends on the way you look. Your eyes and your smile can make you look sexy. The way they're looking at you. Here, she's on a bed. It wouldn't be sexy if she were on a beach with kids running around. They always have some clothes on, too. See how she's "looking" sexy? Like an "oh dear!" look. A different look can change the whole picture.

Now here's a decent pose. . . . Outdoors makes it "nature." Here she's giving you "the eye" or is undressing. It's cheesecake. It depends on the expression on her face. Having nature behind it makes it better. Don't smile like "come on honey!" It's that look and the lace thing she has on . . . Like when you half-close your eyes, like "oh baby," a Marilyn Monroe look. Art is when you don't look like you're hiding it half-way.

The element of trust plays a particularly strong role in socializing women to the nudist perspective. Consider this in the following statements made by another model for nudist magazines. She and her husband had been indoctrinated in the nudist way of life by friends. At the time of the interview, however, the couple had not yet been to camp, although they had posed indoors for nudist magazines.

[Three months ago, before I was married] I never knew a man had any pubic hairs. I was shocked when I was married. . . . I wouldn't think of getting undressed in front of my husband. I wouldn't make love with a light on, or in the daytime.

After she had been married for three months, she posed for national nudist magazines:

None of the pictures are sexually seductive. [Q] The pose, the look; you can have a pose that's completely nothing, till you get a look that's not too hard to do. [Q: How do you do that?] I've never tried. By putting on a certain air about a person; a picture that couldn't be submitted to a nudist magazine—using [the nudist photographer's] language. . . . [Q: Will your parents see your pictures in the magazine?] Possibly. I don't really care . . . My mother might take it all right. But they've been married twenty years and she's never seen my dad undressed.

No Accentuation of the Body

Accentuation of the body is suspect as being incongruent with the situated morality of the camp. Thus, a woman who had shaved her pubic area was labeled "disgusting" by other members. There was a similar reaction to women who blatantly sat in an "unladylike" manner:

I'd think she was inviting remarks. [Q] I don't know. It seems strange to think of it. It's strange you ask it. Out there, they're not unconscious about their posture. Most women there are very circumspect even though in the nude.

For a girl [sitting with your legs open] is just not feminine or ladylike. The hair doesn't always cover it. [Q] Men get away with so many things. But, it would look dirty for a girl; like she was waiting for something. When I'm in a secluded area I've spread my legs to sun, but I keep an eye open and if anyone came I'd close my legs and sit up a while. It's just not ladylike.

You can lay on your back or side, or with your knees under your chin. But not with your legs spread apart. It would look to other people like you're there for other reasons. [Q: What reasons?] . . . To stare and get an eyeful. . . . Not to enjoy the sun and people.

No Unnatural Attempts at Covering the Body

"Unnatural attempts" at concealment are ridiculed, since they call into question the element of the situated morality that there is no shame in exposing any area of the human body. If such behavior occurs early in one's nudist career, it is usually responded to with more compassion, as a situation where the person has not yet assimilated the new morality.

It is the decoding of the behavior, however, rather than the behavior per se, that determines the way in which the concealment is considered:

If they're cold or sunburned, it's understandable. If it's because they don't agree with the philosophy, they don't belong there.

I would feel their motives for becoming nudists were not well founded. That they were not true nudists, not idealistic enough.

Communal Toilets

Communal toilets are also sometimes part of the strategy to sustain the special moral reality of the nudist camp. Not all camps have communal toilets, but the large camp where I did most of my field work did have such a facility, which was marked, "Little Girls Room and Little Boys Too." Although the stalls had three-quarter-length doors, this combined facility still helped to provide an element of consistency; that is, if you are not ashamed of any part of your body or any of its natural functions, men and women do not need separate toilets. Thus, even the physical ecology of the nudist camp was designed with respect to the strategy for sustaining situated moral meanings. For some, however, communal toilets were going too far:

I think they should be separated. For myself it's all right. But there are varied opinions; and for the satisfaction of all, I think they should separate them. There are niceties of life we often like to maintain, and for some people this is embarrassing. . . . [Q] You know, in a bowel movement it always isn't silent.

> *In the remainder of his research report, Weinberg discussed breakdowns in the camps' "situated morality" and the problems nudists encountered in dealing with "clothed society." Despite occasional lapses, the nudist camp presents an illuminating example of the conversion of what is more often seen as "deviance" to "normality" or "conformity." That such a thing can be accomplished is a fascinating demonstration of the "social construction of reality."*

The Role of Subculture

When there is a full-fledged subculture either built up around the deviation or incorporating it as a key element, the prospects for stigma-avoidance may be greatly enhanced. Cohen, it will be recalled, saw subcultures emerging when there were "in effective interaction with one another, . . . a number of actors with similar problems of adjustment" (Cohen, 1955, p. 59). We know that in a broad sense all deviators have similar adjustment problems—how to cope with the prospect of stigma and disvaluation. Yet not all types of deviation give rise to or derive support from any distinctive subculture. This is so because the extent to which the individuals involved will be "in effective interaction with one another" will vary a good deal, depending largely on the nature of the problematic behavior or condition.

Goffman has suggested that the term "social deviants" should be applied only to deviators "who come together into a subcommunity or milieu" and that their situations ought constitute the core subject matter for any distinctive sociology of deviance (Goffman, 1963, p. 143). For our purposes, however, this would be unduly restrictive, since it could detract from attention to the many behaviors and conditions which are not part of a subculture yet which are imbued with deviantness. Both categories display the common element of deviantizing reaction; individuals in both situations will seek to avoid stigma, even though their problems and prospects are somewhat different. A crucial determinant of subcultural development would seem to be "the need for continuous contact with other like individuals" in order to carry out or display the deviation (Schur, 1965, p. 173). There is, for example, relatively little need of any supportive subculture in connection with certain isolated acts that may be perceived as deviation, such as abortion or suicide. It is true that the initial motivation for such behaviors can be thought of as arising out of the subcultures in which individuals have been socialized. As we saw earlier, even "acts of passion"—such as violence between spouses—are in some respects "learned" in and reflective of a specific sociocultural context; although, by the same token, such acts often tend to be recurring rather than isolated ones. And in the case of illicit abortion, we also noted, involvement with other persons who can provide information and leads may be necessary. Beyond that, however, no real subculture of abortion-seekers develops.

Similarly, a person does not need "continuous contact with other like individuals" in order to "have" a stigmatized disability or a condition treated as mental illness. As to the latter, again there may well be subcultural factors involved in initial "causation." Interactional approaches to psychopathology, including family-centered theories of schizophrenia, suggest this. Similarly Lemert, in an intriguing study of cases of paranoia arising within organizational settings, found that the characteristic feelings of persecution often did have *some* real basis in the person's relations with other workers (Lemert, 1962). Our earlier consideration of interaction leading to mental hospitalization again suggests a kind of subcultural interpretation. As we will see, too (in Chapter 6) there are instances in which, for persons with physical disabilities as well as for mental patients, certain treatment settings ("total institutions," "sheltered workshop" programs, and, perhaps, particularly some "therapeutic communities") can take on a subculturelike, encompassing, way-of-life quality.

However, the more fully elaborated subcultures usually evolve around continuing activities that require or at least characteristically involve the regular and long-term participation of other people. These may include: group-based criminality, whether by "professional thieves" or delinquent gangs; those forms of "deviant consumption and selling" that are often engaged in on a repeated basis—as in the "drug scene" or prostitution; basic personal orientations—such as homosexuality and, perhaps, in cases of extreme involvement, political or religious orientation; and other stigmatized behaviors that constitute generalized life-styles (really, by definition, "subcultures")—such as "skid row" patterns or bohemianism ("hippies," the youthful "counterculture," etc.).

Before examining more fully a few specific examples, it may be useful to note briefly some general "functions" that many of these subcultures serve. Most subcultures seem, to some degree or other, to be of continuing value to the participants in the following three spheres:

1. **General facilitation, learning, and sociability.** The subculture provides whatever forms of practical assistance are needed in order to carry out the activity. This will include access to necessary settings, arrangements, and "supplies" (where relevant). As we have already seen, it may also include important forms of learning, of key definitions and outlooks, as well as of specific techniques. The individual is helped to redefine the behavior in ways that permit more favorable and less disturbing self-concepts. We saw this in Becker's marihuana study. It was brought out even more dramatically by the same author in another study of changes in typical reactions to LSD hallucinations over time. During the early years of LSD use, the resulting hallucinations were very disturbing to the individuals experiencing them, and there were many related "psychotic episodes." As Becker sensitively noted, when more users gained experience with the drug and helped novices to anticipate and react to the resulting sensations, disturbing reactions became much less frequent. LSD-users "learned" that hallucinations were "normal," that they were not "going crazy." A socializing and supportive subculture had helped to "produce" a new kind of response (Becker, 1967).

In much the same way, homosexual subculture facilitates a redefinition that enables individuals to acknowledge to themselves having such an orientation:

> The meaning of the category must be changed because the subject has learned the negative stereotype of the homosexual held by most heterosexuals, and he knows that he is no queer, pervert, dirty old man, and so on . . . He differentiates himself from the homosexual image that straight society has presented to him. Direct or indirect contact with the gay subculture provides the subject with information about homosexuals that will challenge the "straight" image of the homosexual (Dank, 1971, p. 189).

The sociability functions of subcultures are rather obvious; much deviation involves congenial group participation. This is patently true of most deviating sexual activities since, ordinarily, at least two people will be involved, and other stigmatized behaviors that theoretically could be engaged in alone rarely are. The best example is marihuana use, which characteristically occurs in groups and really *is* a form of congenial socializing (see Goode, 1970; Johnson, 1973; also Adaptation Five, above).

2. **Defensive adaptation, status-provision, and morale-enhancement.** Particularly where legal reactions are anticipated or where considerable concealment is desired, various aspects of the subculture will, at least in part, represent patterns of **defensive adaptation**. There are times when the goal and direct function of protection and defense will be readily apparent. If call girls, for example, employ elaborate codes during telephone conversations, the aim of avoiding de-

tection and police interference is obvious. However, since frequently the defensive and the more "positive" functions appear or operate together (see the examples developed later in this section), it is not always easy to establish which particular patterns are "essentially" defensive in nature. Carefully controlled comparison studies of the same behaviors as they occur under contrasting social and legal reactions are necessary in order to resolve such issues. In the absence of such comparative evidence, we can nonetheless conclude that defensiveness is at least *one* important function served by many of the subcultural patterns. The same can be said of status-provision and morale-enchantment, which again might or might not still be "needed" even under less oppressive conditions. Such functions, as well as sociability ones, are regularly served by subcultural opportunities for regularly coming together with one's "own" and with "the wise"—knowledgeable and tolerant nondeviators (Goffman, 1963, pp. 19–31). Especially when concealment is being practiced elsewhere, an important relaxation is provided from the strain of constantly being "on" (Messinger, *et al.,* 1962).

3. **Internal social control.** As the Weinberg nudism study pointed up, groups of deviators typically have their own rules and regulations. To recall a point much emphasized in the beginning of this book, such a social control system is inevitable because some form of "deviance" is bound to occur as in any group or society. Even if the norms are not highly formalized, some approved and disapproved patterns will emerge. Where a group is itself deviantized from without, the maintenance of internal control becomes particularly important. It reduces internal distractions and fractionalizing, and enhances individual morale as well as collective solidarity. Groups of people subject to stigma under the dominant values and norms have enough to worry about without "fighting among themselves." Furthermore, internal deviations by some members of the group—for example, failure to abide by an important "defensive" norm—could result in direct and serious damage to other members as well as to the general standing of the group as a whole.

In practice, the various subcultural functions mentioned above often go unstated, largely taken for granted by the participants, and usually several different functions are served by major features or patterns of the subculture. An interesting example of this combination-of-functions tendency is provided in Earl Rubington's study of "bottle gangs" (Rubington, 1973). Bottle gangs are the small groups of indigent street drinkers that form for the purpose of cooperatively buying and sharing a bottle, usually of cheap wine. Rubington found that there was a standard bottle-gang cycle of six stages: salutation, negotiation (pooling the funds), procurement, consumption, affirmation (complimenting the leader, etc.), and dispersal. For each stage, there were tacit rules that functioned to facilitate carrying out the central task safely and with optimal congeniality. Vigilance was necessary; at the same time, the group had to work together in good faith.

Rubington also found, however, that this social control system was far from foolproof. There were many breaches of the rules (e.g., purchaser failing to return with the bottle or with a full bottle), and the supporting sanctions were not always too clear. Though internal social control efforts were aimed at avoiding police interference, they also served a more general symbolic function by providing "an illusory sense of a social order replete with definite rules and sanctions." In that respect, they were closely tied to the provision of some kind of status for men who by dominant standards were outcasts:

> . . . as all become more deeply involved in a drinking-centered existence, statuses and roles, beliefs and norms coalesce around this axis of life. In the process, the usual urban complexities change in meaning and shrink in scope. Now obvious social failures can sustain a life which is to be understood in terms of deviant social drinking with all of its rewards and punishments. Obtaining and maintaining a supply of drinks in accordance with a set of rules provides a schedule, a calendar, a routine, and a morality all its own. The net effect of this life-style is to deny failure in the pursuit of drink in company (Rubington, 1973, p. 342).

Status and congeniality are presumably also factors in the subcultural life of drug addicts, but given the severe legal pressures that addicts must confront and the urgency of their demand for drugs, this subculture has been dominated by concern for protective adaptation and practical facilitation of drug buying and selling (Schur, 1965, pp. 138–145; Waldorf, 1973; Gould, *et al.*, 1974). We have already noted, in considering the general process of deviance-amplification, how stringent drug policies may have helped push addicts into increased subcultural involvement. Facing continuous danger of law-enforcement interference, both drug users and sellers rely on subcultural contacts for protection. As one researcher notes, the safest procedure for sellers is "to avoid completely selling anything to strangers, who are often undercover police, and to sell only to users who are known and can be trusted not to be informers. Relationships in the dope fiend culture allow the seller to know those who buy from him and, therefore, help protect him against arrest (Waldorf, 1973, p. 22). At the same time, this protective and facilitative side to the subculture tends to merge with a more "positive" function of providing an accepting and acceptable milieu:

> The thing about the streets which makes them so attractive is that they are always there and always open. They belong to dope fiends just the way dormitories belong to college kids. . . . Unless he is very special, a dope fiend off the streets is like a fish out of water: he can't make connections to get dope, hustling is difficult without the various services the streets offer, it is difficult to conceal himself in a world he doesn't belong in, and (maybe most important) he can never feel comfortable and relaxed in the straight world (Gould, *et al.*, 1974, p. 45).

As our discussion of concealment suggested, homosexual subculture also is characterized by a mixture of caution and sheer sociability. Recognition of the prevalent desire for anonymity and for avoiding arrest should not obscure the fact that the subculture does provide significant opportunities to meet and mingle in a relatively relaxed congenial fashion. In the process, both individual morale and group solidarity—perhaps even a positive and shared "feeling of socio-psychological unity" (Hooker, 1967, p. 171)—are likely to be enhanced. Gay bars are not *just* sexual marketplaces; they are also important centers of sociability (see Hoffman, 1969, p. 56). Invariably, however, even the recreational side of organized gay life comes to be tinged by the negative social and legal pressures. As one researcher has commented, "The gay community exists within leisure time, since the contexts of stigma and secrecy prevent its extension into work time" (Warren, 1974, p. 18).

Earlier we encountered Hoffman's assertion that social stigmatization has bred homosexual "promiscuity," a point he has expanded on in claiming that a more generalized "sex fetishization" characterizes much of gay communal life (Hoffman, 1969, pp. 59–61, 188–190). Homosexual activist Dennis Altman has made a somewhat similar characterization of the gay world: "far from being a genuine community, providing a full and satisfying sense of identity for homosexuals, it consists predominantly of a number of places that facilitate making contacts with other homosexuals." At best, according to Altman, it can be seen as a "pseudo-community" (Altman, 1973, p. 41). These interpretations help to suggest the characteristic combination of "positive" and "negative" consequences often generated through the involvement of deviators in specialized subcultures. They highlight what might be called *the paradox of subculture:* That in the very process of providing a context for coping with stigma, the subculture will for many purposes tend to *heighten* the "primacy" of the stigmatized deviation and also to *increase* the gulf between deviators and "conformists." To put this another way, one that quickly enables us to see parallels in other social realms, segregation is bound to have limiting as well as protecting effects. Thus, Waldorf has suggested that the drug-addict subculture "reinforces the addict's alienation from society, defines him as a criminal to the larger 'respectable' society, and impedes his ability to overcome his addiction" (Waldorf, 1973, p. 22). Even where the pressures and consequences are not that severe, intensive subcultural involvement can be at least as restricting as it can be liberating. Altman's comment is extremely germane: "Most homosexuals, given a fully accepting society, would, I suspect, eschew constant gay company; one has interests that extend beyond sexual orientation" (Altman, 1973, p. 64).

PATTERNS OF ADJUSTMENT

How successful any given individual will be in avoiding stigma depends on a number of factors. In negotiating deviance outcomes, having salient resources is, as we have seen, what counts most. Yet we have also seen that the term "resources" must be interpreted broadly and that which kinds of resources will be most "salient" is bound to vary according to the type of deviation and from situation to situation. Furthermore, the general availability of particular "solutions" or socially-supported patterns of adjustment will also vary according to circumstances. Thus a combination of individual and collective or socially institutionalized factors works to shape modes of adjusting to stigma. Not even the more highly patterned of these elements provide a good basis for "predicting" the outcome in any given case. Particularly insofar as the individual's adjustment is bound up with what other specific individuals, or groups, or organizations may do, we have to recognize that *unforeseeable contingencies* can play a very important role.

To know how any one person facing stigma is going to fare, we would need, in addition to an inventory of preexisting personal resources, a wide range of information that is usually unavailable in advance (since it may only become evident through emerging interaction sequences). Among the relevant factors would be the specific tolerance levels and patterns of formal and informal reaction the person is likely to encounter, the modes of interpersonal or collective support they may be able to draw upon, and the institutionalized adaptations potentially available to people in their situation. Despite this considerable unpredictability of individual outcomes, certain common patterns of adjustment are evident. As much of the above commentary should have made clear, few such adjustments are "total" or "permanent." These "outcomes" emerge through ongoing interaction and are continuously shifting or undergoing some modification in the course of development over time. With these caveats in mind, however, at least five major adjustment patterns can be identified: (1) *capitulating* to stigma; (2) *accommodating* to stigma; (3) *capitalizing* on stigma; (4) *normalizing* the (otherwise-stigmatized) deviation; and (5) *politicizing* the deviation.

Capitulating

So far we have reviewed several kinds of individual techniques for avoiding stigma, concentrating primarily on "defensive" efforts. In Chapter 7 we will be noting some additional possibilities that arise through organized social and political action. Short of becoming involved in or benefiting from such collective efforts, there is a range of possible outcomes or adaptations that vary in degrees of "positiveness" or "favorableness." **Capitulation** is the least favorable of these outcomes. When personal stigma-reducing techniques "fail" and broader "solutions" are unavailable or go unrecognized or unused, the individual capitulates to the stigma. This can occur in several different ways.

Some forms of capitulating in the face of stigma are very dramatic. For example, destitute drug addicts or chronic petty offenders who hang themselves in prison cells may represent an extreme in succumbing to harsh and continuous stigmatizing pressures, including imprisonment itself. Obviously, at the same time, they often are succumbing to their other life conditions, which are likely to be uniformly deplorable, but that only illustrates their lack of offsetting resources which might have enabled them to resist capitulation. In a very broad sense, social stigma and associated reactions and policies generate and reinforce some of the conditions in which other types of perceived deviators sometimes meet their deaths. Thus deviantizing may well have indirectly contributed to such final outcomes as the addict's death by overdose, the homosexual's murder at the hands of a "straight" hustler, the skid-row alcoholic's ultimate demise, even the political radical's death in a shoot-out with the police.

These situations are, of course, far from typical, and, furthermore, it would be rather simplistic and extreme to view them simply as being "due to" negative labeling and accompanying reactions. A much more common type of capitulating will involve the role-engulfment and other deviance-amplifying processes cited earlier, which can without question engender a good deal of demoralization and degradation, even when physical health, let alone life, is preserved. At a theoretical extreme, such role engulfment could result in the individual's viewing himself or herself as "nothing but" such and such a type of deviator and in acting accordingly. In fact, such a theoretical extreme is hardly ever reached since, notwithstanding the notion of the full "secondary deviant" in Lemert's writings, people simply do not and cannot spend all their time "deviating." Even a lifelong inmate of a mental institution, who is also subject to severe delusions, will act perfectly "normal" at times, even by outside standards.

As we have seen, however, there are many degrees of engulfment that can be thought of as involving considerable capitulation to stigma. To the extent self-doubt and self-disvaluation set in, the individual can be said to be capitulating. Sometimes capitulation may take the rather special and interesting form of intentional noninvolvement in an existing subculture of like individuals or even (where possible) of consciously "foregoing" the deviation:

> Unfortunately for the Lesbian, she is stereotyped as primarily a sexual being. This stereotype often turns a quiet life into one of quiet desperation and brings about a turning away from sex and/or involvement with other Lesbians simply because such noninvolvement seems the only "safe" way to survive in a hostile society. It is ironic (but consistent with America's confused view of sex) that a large number of people whom society would castigate for sexual variation, i.e., Lesbians, actually don't engage in sex at all, or do so very rarely (Martin and Lyon, 1972, p. 99).

It seems clear that "giving in" to stigmatization takes various forms and occurs in varying degrees. People succumb to stigma when and to the extent that their active efforts to confront it fail. They succumb to the extent they are unable or unwilling to make such efforts. In some instances—for example, the "skid row" way of life—the capitulation comes close to being complete. More often it is partial or episodic. When that is so, the line between capitulation and accommodation is hazy.

Accommodating

Most persons who have experienced stigma or who face that prospect, nonetheless "manage somehow" much of the time. Depending on the degree of deviantness involved, it may often be true that they are not able to manage easily or extremely well. Still, they make various less than satisfactory accommodations, usually relinquishing a certain amount of their freedom of choice and action in order to make life tolerable. The implicit bargain they strike with the dominant social forces is essentially as follows: They will, up to a point, acquiesce in their own disvaluation and reduce the visibility or extent of various claims they might otherwise make; in exchange for which, negative definitions of them and reactions to them will be moderated, and they will be left relatively free of interference, at least within designated social spheres, settings, and limits.

It should by now be apparent that some type of compartmentalizing lies at the core of most of these accommodations. The phenomenon of "passing" represents a standard type of accommodating adjustment. In exchange for not "contaminating" or threatening some people or situations, for not "rocking the boat" too much, the deviator is spared certain indignities and difficulties. Often this compartmentalizing may be relatively easy to manage—for some people, keeping separate their worlds of work and leisure or maintaining two distinct acquaintanceship or friendship circles may not pose insurmountable problems. Under certain circumstances, however, compartmentalizing can become almost impossible. Thus one study (done in Belgium) of homosexuals who were also partners in heterosexual marriages found that *none* of the "modes of adjustment" they adopted ("Platonic marriage," "innovative marriage," a double standard, etc.) was truly successful in the sense of providing both mutual freedom of action and marital happiness (Ross, 1971).

Another major type of accommodation involves the partial accepting or **playing** of a socially approved **deviant role.** This is the kind of accommodation that most physically disabled persons are forced into, at least some of the time. It represents the other side of the difficulties such persons experience in disavowing their deviations, which we noted earlier. Approved deviant roles are not so much specific positions (occupations, etc.) as they are generalized ways of behaving that conform to dominant expectations regarding a given type of deviator. Acting out other people's stereotypes lies at the heart of this mode of adjustment. As Scott's analysis has shown in the case of blind persons, the expectations tend to include docility, dependency and helplessness, melancholy, gratitude (to helpers), and even a special "spirituality." When blind people act in these ways, they can be said to be playing "the blindness role" (Scott, 1969). Scott's example, cited earlier, of blind persons who have money forced on them by charitable others on occasions when they use public transportation indicates how difficult it is to totally ignore these dominant expectations. Leonard Kriegel similarly describes an incident during the period when he was undergoing rehabilitative therapy for polio in which a well-meaning drugstore counterman felt free to suggest to him that he should take up an easy occupation, so as to earn a living without having to work too hard. Kriegel comments that, "My inability to tell that man to mind his own business was an act of spiritual acquiescence. Had I told him where to get off, I would have undoubtedly been guilty of an unpardonable sin in his eyes. But I would have moved an inch forward toward personal emancipation. Cripples, though, simply do not address normals in such a way" (Kriegel, 1969, 1971, p. 182).

To the extent that acquiescing in the stereotypical expectations remains strictly situational and expedient, the impact on self-conceptions may not be too severe. This is, of course, a matter of degree; few individuals are likely to remain completely unaffected by having to behave in this way. As Scott notes, some blind people (he terms them "true believers") "come to concur in the verdict" the sighted have reached about them. When this happens and the stereotypes are in fact adopted as part of the blind person's self-concepts, the individual may be close to thinking and acting in "nothing, but" terms. At some point, then, when they must be relied on continuously and become central to a person's overall life pattern, accommodating adaptations uneasily shade over into capitulation. On the other hand, when the individual can maximize the expediency element by playing out the accepted role with a high degree of deliberateness, accommodating adjustment can start to take one in the opposite direction toward a more "positive" capitalizing on the stigma.

Capitalizing

There are several ways in which stigmatized persons can "turn around" their situation so that perceived deviation works to their benefit. We have already noted one form of this adaptation in the "secondary gains" (relief from certain duties, expectations, etc.) attaching to "the sick role." At least those deviators who are not consciously reacted to as morally blameworthy may, under certain circumstances, be able to "use" their deviation to obtain various types or forbearance or even preference. The more dramatic types of **capitalizing** involve using the deviation for monetary profit (Scott's example of the blind beggar, mentioned earlier) or even converting it into a full-time occupation (see Goffman, 1963, pp. 26–28). Scott defines "the 'professional' blind" in a very broad way, including all those people "whose lives are almost entirely organized within some part of the blindness system" Scott, 1969, p. 87). But even in a narrower "occupational" sense, many people end up making their deviation into a job or profession.

In earlier days, such possibilities tended to be more limited, and, given their nature, they could hardly be often viewed as a very positive kind of capitalizing. A rather extreme example of this sort of ambiguous capitalizing would be the option of exhibiting one's deviation for profit, as in the cases of deformed people in circus "sideshows." Perhaps only slightly less "minstrelizing" is the situation of "midgets" whose most clear-cut employment opportunities may still be as performers in circuses and elsewhere. The current more extensive and more favorable opportunities to capitalize occupationally have risen as a consequence of the growth of social action organizations and treatment or rehabilitation programs in which deviators or ex-deviators play significant roles. In the former category, the occupational opportunities may not yet be extremely widespread, but, for at least some people, there is already the distinct possibility of full-time respectable employment as a "gay rights activist," a "lobbyist for the handicapped," an "organizer of prostitutes," and the like.

In the area of treatment and rehabilitation, the possibilities may be even more considerable. As we will see, ideologies and practices regarding what might be called "participatory treatment" have generated a great many programs and organizations in which ex-deviators become the crucial "change agents" for current deviators or in which current deviators work to help and "treat" each other. The possibilities for such "therapeutic careers" among the deviating already range across many substantive areas, including crime and delinquency, alcoholism, drug addiction, mental illness, sexual deviations, obesity, and even suicide (prevention or counseling of attempters). A related point to which we will return but which should be at least noted here is that in these programs one often sees another sense in which people may be able to capitalize on the deviation. Many of them consciously employ a very heavy focus on, even an affirmation of, the stigmatized deviation as a therapeutic device. When such emphasis works, participants will have capitalized on stigma, by initially emphasizing it in order eventually to reduce it.

Normalizing

We have touched on a good many aspects of this adjustment pattern in our earlier discussion. Although sometimes other people, particularly relatives or friends, may try to normalize an individual's deviation—this was true of the wives in the Yarrow study and also of the parents of the polio victims in the Fred Davis study—by and large, the goal of **normalization** (or disavowal) becomes paramount primarily for deviators themselves. Probably the most noteworthy fact about normalization as an adjustment "outcome" is the extreme difficulty deviators have in achieving it. Many of the stigma-reducing techniques we have already reviewed represent attempts to normalize. Usually, because of the tenacious primacy of deviantness, they fall far short of the ultimate goal, which is to render the deviation irrelevant for most purposes and in most situations.

Under complete normalization, other people would pay attention to the deviation no more than might be physically necessary. It would no longer be the orienting point of their reactions to the person, who indeed would then be viewed less as an instance of a category and more as a distinct individual. Obviously, there are differences among particular deviations as to the extent to which this dis-attending is possible (recall the "normal, but" problem involved in some disabilities). Nonetheless, when it can be maximized, the deviator will have achieved a high point in stigma-reduction, and, given the intimate connection between treatment by others and self-conceptions, such people ought to be in an optimal position to dis-attend the deviation themselves.

We might say that when normalizing is effective, other people "adjust to the deviation" at least as much as the deviator does. Theoretically, at an end point in this process, nobody need adjust at all, because in many respects it is as though the deviation were not there. At any rate, normalization implies complete human status for the deviator and the absence of stigma-related restrictions on leading a relatively independent and full existence. Under such conditions, there should be little need to compartmentalize or to make other significant types of accommodation; nor should it be necessary to capitalize on one's stigma. We know that most adaptations are not this "successful" from the strenuous efforts to normalize that most deviators must continuously engage in and also from the frequency with which such people become enmeshed in or "settle for" the more accommodative patterns. Indeed, normalization as an outcome and "deviance," as that concept is developed in this book, are close to being logical opposites. When normalizing is *fully* successful, then deviance no longer really exists.

Politicizing

We have seen that in reflecting a society's general power structure and the more specific conflicts over the nature and imposition of rules, all deviance issues are "political." But there is a narrower sense in which deviators themselves can consciously seek to "politicize" deviations, to alter existing deviance definitions, reactions, and policies. Clearly, this kind of effort tends to be collective rather than individual; furthermore, it is likely to both reflect and become part of still broader currents of sociocultural change. Some of these aspects will be discussed in Chapter 7.

However, politicizing also has important implications for individual self-conceptions and adjustment that should be mentioned here. To the extent the person is able to view his or her "problem" as being a public and political issue rather than a personal "failing," "deficiency," or "offense," prospects for favorable self-concepts and improved morale are going to be greatly heightened. Humphreys, referring to a process of "stigma conversion," has commented:

> In converting his stigma, the oppressed person does not merely exchange his social marginality for political marginality, although that is one interpretation the socially dominant segments of society would like to place upon the process. Rather, he emerges from a stigmatized cocoon as a transformed creature, one characterized by the spreading of political wings. At some point in the process, the politicized "deviant" gains a new identity, an heroic self-image as crusader in a political cause (Humphreys, 1972, p. 142).

How many such persons actually develop "heroic" self-images may be questioned, but involvement in organized politicizing with one's fellow deviators is almost bound to enhance self-respect and afford a new sense of purpose. The individual gains not only a more acceptable way of defining the deviation, but also an added sense of group solidarity, the satisfaction afforded through actively striving for desired social change, and a positive anticipation of improved life conditions and prospects. The payoff from politicizing, then, is personal as well as social, and it can be considerable.

It may be something of a moot point which adjustment better or more fully enables the individual to avoid stigma—normalizing or politicizing. At first glance, politicizing seems the more "militant" or "positive" of the two patterns. The individual can be proudly assertive, rather than simply "asking for" tolerance or even acceptance. However, though it usually aims at an ultimate normalization (except when some goal of "separatism" is envisioned), politicizing may have one short-term disadvantage: Even as it seeks to legitimate the deviation, such effort necessarily gives great primacy to it. To be militant is to represent the deviation, as it were, and this can invite reinforcement of other people's "nothing, but" preconceptions. In the long run, of course, successful politicizing implies the elimination of such problems. At any rate, there is little evidence that either complete normalization or complete politicization as an overall outcome will pertain with respect to major deviance issues in this country within the foreseeable future. In the meantime, individuals facing stigma will no doubt rely on both modes of adjustment in order to register personal and social gains whenever and wherever possible.

REFERENCES

Altman, Dennis
1973. *Homosexual: Oppression and Liberation.* New York: Avon Books.

Anonymous
1974. "Losing: An Attempt at Stigma Neutralization," in Jerry Jacobs, ed., *Deviance: Field Studies and Self-Disclosures.* Palo Alto, Calif.: National Press Books. Pp. 69–82.

Aubert, Vilhelm and Sheldon L. Messinger
1958. "The Criminal and the Sick," *Inquiry,* 1, 137–160.

Ball, Donald W.
1967. "An Abortion Clinic Ethnography," *Social Problems,* 14(Winter), 293–301.

Becker, Howard S.
1963. *Outsiders.* New York: The Free Press.

1967. "History, Culture, and Subjective Experience: An Exploration of the Social Basis of Drug-Induced Experiences," *Journal of Health and Social Behavior,* 8(September), 163–176.

Bell, Alan P. and Martin S. Weinberg
1978. *Homosexualities: A Study of Diversity Among Men and Women.* New York: Simon and Schuster.

Blau, Peter M.
1964. *Exchange and Power in Social Life.* New York: John Wiley & Sons, Inc.

Blumberg, Abraham S.
1967. *Criminal Justice.* New York: Quadrangle/The New York Times Book Co.

Bryan, James H.
1966. "Occupational Ideologies and Individual Attitudes of Call Girls," *Social Problems,* 13(Spring), 441–450.

Cicourel, Aaron, V.
1968. *The Social Organization of Juvenile Justice.* New York: John Wiley & Sons, Inc.

Cogswell, Betty E.
1967. "Rehabilitation of the Paraplegic: Processes of Socialization," *Sociological Inquiry,* 37(Winter), 11–26.

Cohen, Albert K.
1955. *Delinquent Boys: The Culture of the Gang.* Glencoe, Ill.: The Free Press.

Cory, Donald W.
1960. *The Homosexual in America: A Subjective Approach.* New York: Castle Books.

Cressey, Donald R.
1953. *Other People's Money.* Glencoe, Ill.: The Free Press.

Dank, Barry M.
1971. "Coming Out in the Gay World," *Psychiatry,* 34(May), 180–197.

Davis, Fred
1961. "Deviance Disavowal: The Management of Strained Interaction by the Visibly Handicapped," *Social Problems,* 9(Fall), 120–132.
1963. *Passage Through Crisis: Polio Victims and Their Families.* Indianapolis: The Bobbs-Merrill Co., Inc.

Delph, Edward William
1978. *The Silent Community: Public Homosexual Encounters.* Beverly Hills, Calif.: Sage Publications, Inc.

Downie, Leonard, Jr.
1972. *Justice Denied.* New York: Penguin Books, Inc.

Douglas, Jack D.
1967. *The Social Meanings of Suicide.* Princeton: Princeton University Press.

Edgerton, Robert B.
1967. *The Cloak of Competence: Stigma in the Lives of the Mentally Retarded.* Berkeley: University of California Press.
1969. "On the 'Recognition' of Mental Illness," in Stanley C. Plog and Robert B. Edger-

ton, eds., *Changing Perspectives in Mental Illness*. New York: Holt, Rinehart and Winston, Inc. Pp. 49–72.

Feinbloom, Deborah Heller
1977. *Transvestites and Transsexuals*. New York: Delta Books.

Goffman, Erving
1959. *The Presentation of Self in Everyday Life*. Garden City, New York: Doubleday & Company, Inc.
1961. *Asylums*. Garden City, New York: Doubleday   Company, Inc.
1963. *Stigma: Notes on the Management of Spoiled Identity*. Englewood Cliffs, N.J.: Prentice-Hall, Inc.

Goode, Erich
1970. *The Marijuana Smokers*. New York: Basic Books, Inc.

Gove, Walter R. and Patrick Howell
1974. "Individual Resources and Mental Hospitalization," *American Sociological Review,* 39(February), 86–100.

Gould, Leroy, *et al.*
1974. *Connections: Notes from the Heroin World*. New Haven: Yale University Press.

Hoffman, Martin
1969. *The Gay World*. New York: Bantam Books, Inc.

Hooker, Evelyn
1967. "The Homosexual Community," in John A. Gagnon and William Simon, eds., *Sexual Deviance*. New York: Harper & Row, Publishers. Pp. 167–184.

Humphreys, Laud
1972. *Out of the Closets*. Englewood Cliffs, N.J.: Prentice-Hall, Inc.
(1970), 1975. *Tearoom Trade: Impersonal Sex in Public Places, rev. ed.,* Chicago: Aldine Publishing Company.

James, Jennifer, *et al.*
1975. *The Politics of Prostitution*. Seattle: Social Research Associates.

Johnson, Bruce D.
1973. *Marihuana Users and Drug Subcultures*. New York: John Wiley & Sons, Inc.

Kriegel, Leonard
1969, 1971. "Uncle Tom and Tiny Tim: Some Reflections on the Cripple as Negro," *American Scholar,* 38(Summer 1969), 412–430; as reprinted in Edward Sagarin, ed., *The Other Minorities*. Waltham, Mass.: Ginn & Co. Pp. 165–183.

Lemert, Edwin M.
1962. "Paranoia and the Dynamics of Exclusion," *Sociometry,* 25(March), 2–25.

Levitin, Teresa E.
1975. "Deviants as Active Participants in the Labeling Process: The Visibly Handicapped," *Social Problems,* 22(April), 548–557.

Leznoff, Maurice and William A. Westley
1956. "The Homosexual Community," *Social Problems,* 3(April), 257–263.

Martin, Del and Phyllis Lyon
1972. *Lesbian/Woman*. New York: Bantam Books, Inc.

McKinstry, William C.
1974. "The Pulp Voyeur: A Peek at Pornography in Public Places," in Jacobs, ed., *op. cit.,* pp. 30–40.

Messinger, Sheldon L., *et al.*
1962. "Life as Theater: Some Notes on the Dramaturgic Approach to Social Reality," *Sociometry,* 25, 98–110.

Morris, Jan
1975. *Conundrum.* New York: Signet Books.

Newman, Donald J.
1956. "Pleading Guilty for Considerations: A Study of Bargain Justice," *Journal of Criminal Law, Criminology and Police Science,* 46(March–April), 780–790.

Packer, Herbert L.
1968. *The Limits of the Criminal Sanction.* Stanford: Stanford University Press.

Polsky, Ned
1967. *Hustlers, Beats, and Others.* Chicago: Aldine Publishing Company.

Reid, Sue Titus
1976. *Crime and Criminology.* Hinsdale, Ill.: The Dryden Press, Inc.

Reiss, Albert J., Jr.
1961. "The Social Integration of Queers and Peers," *Social Problems,* 9(Fall), 102–120.

Rosett, Arthur and Donald R. Cressey
1976. *Justice by Consent: Plea Bargains in the American Courthouse.* Philadelphia: J. B. Lippincott Company.

Ross, H. Laurence
1971. "Modes of Adjustment of Married Homosexuals," *Social Problems,* 18(Winter), 385–393.

Rubington, Earl
1973. "Variations in Bottle Gang Controls," in Earl Rubington and Martin Weinberg, eds., *Deviance: The Interactionist Perspective, 2nd ed.,* New York: MacMillan, Inc. Pp. 338–347.

Scheff, Thomas J.
1968. "Negotiating Reality: Notes on Power in the Assessment of Responsibility," *Social Problems,* 16(Summer), 3–17.

Schur, Edwin M.
1965. *Crimes Without Victims.* Englewood Cliffs, N.J.: Prentice-Hall, Inc.

Scott, Martin B. and Stanford M. Lyman
1968. "Accounts," *American Sociological Review,* 33(February), 46–62.

Scott, Robert A.
1969. *The Making of Blind Men.* New York: Russell Sage Foundation.

Simon, William and John H. Gagnon
1967. "The Lesbians—A Preliminary Overview," in John H. Gagnon and William Simon, eds., *Sexual Deviance.* New York: Harper & Row, Publishers. Pp. 247–282.

Simpson, Ruth
1977. *From the Closet to the Courts.* New York: Penguin Books, Inc.

Skolnick, Jerome H.
1966. *Justice Without Trial.* New York: John Wiley & Sons, Inc.

Stoll, Clarice S.
1968. "Images of Man and Social Control," *Social Forces,* 47(December), 119–127.

Strauss, Anselm
1959. *Mirrors and Masks.* Glencoe, Ill.: The Free Press.
1962. "Transformations of Identity," in Arnold M. Rose, ed., *Human Behavior and Social Processes: An Interactionist Approach.* Boston: Houghton Mifflin Company. Pp. 63–85.

Sudnow, David
1965. "Normal Crimes: Sociological Features of the Penal Code in a Public Defender Office," *Social Problems,* 12(Winter), 255–276.

Sykes, Gresham M.
1958. *Society of Captives.* Princeton: Princeton University Press.

Sykes, Gresham M. and David Matza
1957. "Techniques of Neutralization: A Theory of Delinquency," *American Sociological Review,* 22(December), 664–670.

Waldorf, Dan
1973. *Careers in Dope.* Englewood Cliffs, N.J.: Prentice-Hall, Inc.

Warren, Carol A. B.
1974. *Identity and Community in the Gay World.* New York: John Wiley & Sons, Inc.

Weinberg, Martin S. and Colin J. Williams
1975a. "Gay Baths and the Social Organization of Impersonal Sex," *Social Problems,* 23 (December), 124–136.
1975b. *Male Homosexuals: Their Problems and Adaptations.* New York: Penguin Books, Inc.

Wittman, Carl
1972. "Refugees from Amerika: A Gay Manifesto," in Joseph A. McCaffrey, ed., *The Homosexual Dialectic.* Englewood Cliffs, N.J.: Prentice-Hall, Inc. Pp. 157–171.

REVIEW OF KEY TERMS

accommodation. Any compromise pattern of adaptation in which the person facing stigma accepts a degree of disvaluation and restriction in exchange for some freedom from interference, that is, within accepted limits. Partial concealment represents such an adjustment; so, too, may **playing a "deviant role"** (see below).

accounts. The term used by Scott and Lyman for excuses and justifications offered in support of "untoward action." It is an important concept for the interpretation of deviance situations, in that accounts can help significantly to neutralize stigma. They can be verbal, or they can involve other manipulation of "stigma symbols." Acceptability of accounts will vary, depending on the persons offering them, the audience for them, and a variety of other circumstances.

defensive adaptation. An important function served by aspects of subcultures that develop around deviations. They provide protection (including anonymity), facilitation, and support in the face of negative social and legal reactions. In line with the general controversy over "secondary deviation," it is difficult to determine which aspects of subculture are generated by the need for defensive adaptation and which are more intrinsic (primary) and "positive." In practice, most aspects of subculture serve several different functions simultaneously.

denial. Efforts by individuals subject to stigma to convince themselves that their deviations are not serious impediments to normal existence or deserving of stigma. The success of such efforts is heavily dependent on success in convincing other people, that is, **disavowal** (see below).

deviant role, playing a. Acquiescing in or acting out other people's stereotyped expectations regarding a particular type of deviator. In cases of visible physical handicap, it is extremely difficult to avoid this completely. It is a standard type of accommodation to stigma which, when extreme, can amount to substantial "role engulfment" and, in effect, represent **capitulation.** On the other hand, when carried out deliberately, it can sometimes provide opportunities for **capitalizing** on the deviation.

disavowal. Efforts by deviators to get other people to "normalize" the deviation. The degree of success achieved will strongly affect the deviator's self-concepts as well as opportunities. The "master status" quality in deviantness works against disavowal efforts. See also **denial.**

negotiation. Explicit or implicit bargaining that is an important element in the process out of which deviance outcomes emerges. It reflects the power and conflict aspects of deviance situations as well as the diversity of individual and group values, norms, and interests. See also **salient resources.**

neutralization, techniques of. The term used by Sykes and Matza in their analysis of excuses and justifications employed by juvenile delinquents. They are devices for rationalizing deviation so as to reduce stigma. See also **accounts.**

normalization. Defining and treating a problematic behavior or condition as though it were "normal." Dis-attending or not reacting in terms of a deviation. Although sometimes desired and sought by other people, it is, more significantly, an "outcome" desired by the deviator. See also **denial** and **disavowal.**

passing. Presenting yourself as what you "are not." Typically, this consists of concealment of the stigmatized condition in certain situations and social circles and usually involves compartmentalizing one's existence—"leading two lives."

role distance, denial of. The condition under which the deviator cannot "step away" from the disvalued status and role because of extreme "role engulfment" or "primacy," perhaps at a maximum in the "total institution."

salient resources. Those sources of power most helpful in negotiating desired outcomes in deviance situations. Which resources will be most salient will vary depending upon the circumstances, including the type of deviation. "Standard" resources (economic standing, general social prestige, etc.) will usually be relevant but not necessarily determinative. See also **negotiation.**

transvestite. A person who on some occasions likes to cross-dress (wear clothing appropriate to the opposite sex and engage in aspects of a corresponding "presentation of self"). Transvestites may be predominantly heterosexual in their overt sexual relations.

transsexual. A person who experiences a profound "cross-gender identification," in which the anatomical-biological gender is felt to be "incorrect." Such identification can but need not lead to intentional alteration of bodily characteristics through hormone treatment and/or reconstitutive surgery. Sexual preference for other members of the (original) "biological" sex is not viewed by transsexuals as being "homosexual," since they do not conceive of that sex as their "real" one.

PROJECT 5
Scripting an Interaction

Introductory Comment

Interpreting social interaction is not an easy thing to do. If all of us encounter difficulty in dealing with other people—partly because we do not know what their real motivations and intentions are or what their subsequent actions are likely to be—we can expect sociologists to face even greater problems when they try to interpret interaction in which they themselves are not direct participants. Being removed from the situation is supposed to make the researcher more "objective," but at the same time it implies that the underpinnings of the interaction can all too easily remain unexperienced and unobserved. Sociologists typically try to transcend this difficulty in two ways: either by actually immersing themselves in the interaction they want to study ("participant observation") or by drawing inferences from the corpus of data and understanding developed through past research of various kinds conducted by themselves and others. There is, in other words, considerable existing knowledge—indirect as well as direct—that we can draw on in trying to figure out what is "really going on" in a given situation.

The mechanisms, processes, and tendencies discussed in the past two chapters (and also earlier in the book) have come to light through such ongoing investigations. They represent standard features underlying or reflected in the interaction sequences through which deviantness is imposed and resisted. Not all of the specific possibilities will be present in every problematic situation, but we can expect almost always to find illustrations of the more central or general aspects. Thus, most actual situations will exhibit such features as emergence and unpredictability (a reciprocal interplay of response and counterresponse), elements of at least latent conflict and implicit negotiation, typing and identification and attempts by the potential deviator to avoid same, the tendency toward retrospective interpretation and the associated risk for the deviator of amplification or engulfment. Now, of course, one would have to follow a course of interaction over quite a bit of time in order to see its development and apparent outcome. On the other hand, even in short-term or transitory situations and interactions, signs of disvaluation (avoidance, "put downs," indications of "typing") often are evident, as are some of the perceived deviator's efforts to counter these reactions or adapt to them.

Although constructing an imaginary or hypothetical interaction in a way removes us even further than conventional research does from real interaction itself, like the early analysis of literary depictions, it, too, can be an extremely useful exercise. The present project should help students to draw on key concepts and themes developed in this section of the text, to show how they might be relevant to interpreting even the early states of what might become "deviance situations."

Assignment

Select *one* of the following hypothetical situations:

1. A former drug addict being interviewed for a teaching job by the principal of a school

2. Several persons' street encounters with a "bowery bum"

3. The interaction between a "blind beggar" and the occupants of a subway car from whom he tries to beg

4. Sexual harassment of a woman pedestrian by bystander males

5. A covert male homosexual being interviewed for membership in an exclusive (heterosexual) social club

6. Interaction between various pedestrians and a "panhandler"

7. Interaction between streetwalkers on the "beat," police officers on patrol, and male and female pedestrians

8. Interaction between an audience of passersby and a religious cult spokesperson making an ideological presentation in a public park

Write the script (as though for use in a play or film) of such an interaction in as much hypothetical detail as possible. Use your own judgment as to the extent and nature of the interaction and other specifics of the situation. Include in your script not only verbal statements by the participants in the interaction, but also (parenthetically, as "stage directions") locations and movements, postures and gestures, looks, tones and intensities displayed, unspoken thoughts, and any other relevant nonverbal aspects of the situation (including clothing and general appearance, "props," etc.).

Suggestions

Although the script is to be hypothetical—the account and detailed description of an interaction that you have made up—at least a few of the situations lisited could in fact be rather easily "researched" beforehand through field observation. This is not a requirement of the exercise, but obviously seeing what actually happens in some instances of the kind of situation you intend to depict could be very helpful in indicating points to include in your script, including ones you might otherwise overlook.

Here are a few specific questions you might have in mind when you start organizing your ideas for the scriptwriting itself:

1. How conscious of any "deviantness" in the situation do you want your characters to be and in what ways would you depict this?

2. What kind of balance will you want to show as existing between the influence of actions, appearances, verbalizations, etc.?

3. Who seems to affect whom, in what ways and degrees, and why?

4. Is there a discernible overall pattern that characterizes the developing situation—such as "escalation" in some direction, apparently "even" or "balancing-out" contributions to the interaction, or "harmonious" or "chaotic" interaction?

5. How predictable do you think the patterns you depict would be, and why? To what extent are the actions and statements of your participants not as much predictable in advance as they are heavily dependent on the preceding ones of the other people in the situation?

6. What seem to be the underlying sentiments of the participants?

7. Do the participants (any, or all of them) seem to enjoy the interaction itself? Are they antagonized by it? Or do they find it very unpleasant? Why?

8. How important do the interaction and its outcome seem to be to the various participants? In what respects, and why?

9. Which has the stronger influence on the developing situation you depict, the type of "deviation" involved or the types of people participating in the interaction? How would you explain that?

Implications

Once you have completed your script, it should be revealing to go back over the last two chapters of the text and see which points developed there you made use of and which you did not employ. Why do you think this pattern regarding use of the text materials resulted? By chance, or was there a logic to your choice of aspects to emphasize? Hopefully, the latter. If so, thinking about it a bit should help you to see more generally in what kinds of situations which of the concepts and themes become most appropriate. It would also be interesting, once the scripts are completed, for them to be "presented" (either read, or "acted") in class for evaluation and criticism by the whole group.

PART 3

BEYOND THE INTERPERSONAL LEVEL

PROLOGUE 6

Bureaucratization offers above all the optimum possibility for carrying through the principle of specializing administrative functions according to purely objective considerations. Individual performances are allocated to functionaries who have specialized training and who by constant practice learn more and more. The "objective" discharge of business primarily means a discharge of business according to calculable rules and "without regard for persons."
—Max Weber, *The Theory of Social and Economic Organization*

Two traditional areas of sociological research and interpretation have been occupations and professions, and complex organizations. Studies and concepts in these "subfields" of the discipline have represented something of a middle-range focus, since the direct subject matter tends to fall somewhere in between the broadest study of societal structures and forces on the one hand, and the microscopic analysis of interaction process and individual social psychology on the other. Indeed, to explore occupational roles and organizational factors is, in a sense, to focus on some key aspects of the ordering and mediating of the relation between the individual and the larger social system. Often the impact of the larger social forces on individuals is felt through the structuring and work of occupations and organizations, while, at the same time, the ongoing activity and interaction of individuals within such contexts feeds back into the overall structure of the society.

Increased examination, within the sociology of deviance, of relevant occupational roles and organizations has been an important recent development. Though many different interpretations have been developed in both of these other subfields, there is a core of basic concepts and perspectives that proves extremely helpful in considering the processing of deviance. (Note the questions listed under Focal Point Three of the Paradigm, in the Appendix.) The recent shift in attention, from an exclusive preoccupation with "deviance" to a greater concern for "control," inevitably meant that such concepts and perspectives would be drawn upon. There are both officials and other occupations that regularly "deal with" deviance. And much of the "processing" of deviators takes place within the context of one or another type of formal organization. Control agents and agencies, then, become a central topic for the modern sociology of deviance. A good deal can be learned by studying them in their own right and also for the added light they throw on deviance situations and "careers."

CH.6

AGENTS
OF CONTROL

INTRODUCTION

The likelihood and extent of an individual's acquiring deviantness are crucially influenced by the responses and actions of other people. This is the central reason why "deviant careers" are highly unpredictable. However much we may know about the offending individual—including background, current behavior, and personal resources—we can never completely predict who will be directly reacting to the deviation, in what contexts, or in what manner. When it is said that mental patients, or criminal offenders, or persons with physical disabilities "suffer from contingencies," the importance of these reactions by other people is highlighted. As we have seen, this element of unpredictability or "emergence" makes it difficult to construct neat theories about deviance causation. For the potentially stigmatized people themselves, however, these uncertain aspects of their life situations are understandably of much more than theoretical interest.

Although deviantizing processes can occur in rather private and informal small-group settings—as when one participant in everyday interaction ascribes deviantness to another—much of the social task of "doing something about" commonly perceived deviance situations rests with a variety of socially designated or acknowledged agents and agencies of "social control." In line with the recent sociological emphasis on actual processes and real consequences, as opposed to mere expressions of intent, and also with the general conception of deviance situations now widely adopted in the field, we should give "control" as well as "deviance" a broad interpretation. There now exists a wide range of socially institutionalized positions and organizations geared to doing something about problematic behaviors and individuals, whether it be through prevention, assistance, rehabilitation, rule enforcement, treatment, or correction. From this perspective, psychiatrists as well as police officers, rehabilitation specialists as well as judges, mental hospital attendants as well as prison guards can be viewed as **agents of control.** The people in these positions all exert a kind of control over identified deviators, regardless of what else they believe they are doing or of the additional functions we may agree they are serving. Among the uncertain elements facing those subject to stigma, one of the most important centers around the likelihood of direct contacts with such control agents.

Some critics have suggested that in focusing on the deviator's being "publicly caught and labeled," recent analysts have unwisely neglected the broader social structures that generate deviation and the society-wide policy preferences that shape deviance issues. While there may be some truth to this argument, it would be equally unwise to try to restrict deviance analysis to a single level. However important what goes on at the collective level may be (see Chapter 7), from an interactionist standpoint these direct contacts with reacting agents and agencies are also of vital significance. They have special impact on the "processed" individuals and on the overall deviance situations in a number of different ways.

To begin with, the institutionalization of control clearly affects the power element that is so crucial in shaping deviance outcomes. Officially designated or socially sanctioned control agents act with the stamp of public authority or at least collective approval, and frequently their efforts are backed up by the threat or exercise of official state power. They are often viewed as being disinterested specialists working "in the public interest," whereas suspected or identified deviators are thought of as pursuing no interests but their own, which, by definition, already tend to be seen as socially offensive. It stands to reason that individuals who undergo deviance-processing, by whichever particular types of control agents, rarely stand "on an even footing" for purposes of negotiating their identities and life-chances. We noted above the relatively unfavorable power position of the patient in psychotherapy and the defendant who plea bargains in criminal court. The same kind of vulnerability is experienced by the pedestrian questioned by a police officer, the student designated a "troublemaker" by teachers or school officials, the blind or otherwise-disabled person who may be heavily dependent on the personnel of "helping" agencies. This is by no means to suggest that control agents are always free to or invariably do impose harsh sanctions. Rather, the point is simply that to a high degree they are in a special position to decide what, if anything, will happen.

The destinies of individuals subject to deviance-processing are, then, going to be significantly shaped by the decisions and actions of these other designated persons, who, because they, too, are human beings and social actors, are not motivated *merely* by the public interest or by accepted professional objectives. Control agents are people who not only have their own personal backgrounds, needs, and problems, but who also are subject to complex occupational demands, specific working conditions that influence their behavior and outlooks, and a variety of pressures and constraints that emanate from colleagues and the general public. Furthermore, most of the social control activity of individual agents is carried out as part of the ongoing work of some larger organization. Often this organizational context itself becomes a crucial determinant not only of what particular control agents may do but, in a more general sense, of the central features and overall patterns of deviance-processing.

Through such organizations there occurs what Rubington and Weinberg have described as a bureaucratization of deviance: "deviants come under the regulation of hierarchy, specialization, impersonality, and systematic formal rules." In such a bureaucratic context, the same writers note, "What the deviant may experience as a unique personal crisis . . . is usually merely organizational routine for the agent and the agency" (Rubington and Weinberg, 1978, pp. 160, 159). Organizational goals, caseloads, work routines, and internal staff interaction patterns, as well as ongoing relationships with other agencies and additional out-side forces (including sources of funding and other needed support), all may have a part in determining what happens to processed deviators. For control agents in such a setting, who are likely to become preoccupied with "getting a job done" and maintaining "a working system," deviance-processing, as that very term suggests, often comes to be seen primarily as a kind of managerial problem. As a consequence, heavy reliance is placed on the typing mechanisms we noted earlier. Cases are "typified" through quick classification into standardized categories that elicit routine responses. The individuals dealt with by the organization are reacted to as instances of those "normal" types, and disposition of their cases (i.e., decisions about what will happen to them) are made accordingly. The likelihood of this happening is heightened still further when, as so often occurs, work overload compels the organization to employ "assembly-line" methods.

The "output" of such people-processing organizations represents a "production of deviance." Control agencies turn out "deviants," and, as a result, they help to determine the nature and extent of broad social problem situations. Currie's witchcraft study (Adaptation Four), showed us how the structuring of social control activity can have this type of broad societal impact. On a more immediate level, the impact of any one specific control agency will similarly reflect its particular organizational structures, needs, and problems. The organization tends to develop "a life of its own," which greatly influences deviance-processing. Sometimes this influence becomes so strong that it overshadows or displaces the goals (enforcement, justice administration, treatment, correction, etc.) for which the organization was established in the first place. As an extreme organizational rigidity sets in, there is strong resistance to change, and deviance workers develop **vested interests** in particular policies and programs. Let us now look a bit more closely at some aspects of the control agent's role and of the organizational context that often shapes it.

AN AMBIGUOUS ROLE

Dirty Work

Everett Hughes has pointed out that in all societies "good people" shield themselves from a full awareness of certain kinds of **dirty work** that is done partly in their name (Hughes, 1962). Special occupational roles are established to handle these unpleasant tasks which the general citizenry in one sense takes for granted yet in another refuses to openly acknowledge. In many respects, people who regularly deal with deviance are engaged in dirty work of this sort. They must accept the chore of doing something about people commonly perceived as socially unacceptable. They are expected to introduce control where it has been notable by its absence. Above all, perhaps, they are supposed to contain and regulate the offending elements, shielding other people from contamination by them. Occupational roles that are geared to these goals often involve tasks that are in a way themselves contaminating—work which is extremely distasteful, potentially harmful to others, sometimes dangerous to oneself, or which requires continuous contact with the socially tainted.

Social control agents frequently must take part in character-staining processes ("status-degradation ceremonies"). Their work often requires them to impose deprivations of liberty, including incarceration, and other hardships on the offending individuals. In effect, if not by intention, their actions may do psychological or even physical violence to these persons. At an extreme, the deviance-processer produces actual death—as in the cases of the executioner, or the police or correctional officer who must kill someone "in the line of duty." In some instances, this violence by control agents may be collective and extremely devastating:

> Forty-three citizens of New York State died at Attica Correctional Facility between September 9 and 13, 1971. Thirty-nine of that number were killed and more than 80 others were wounded by gunfire during the 15 minutes it took the State Police to retake the prison on September 13. With the exception of Indian massacres in the late 19th century, the State Police assault which ended the four-day prison uprising was the bloodiest one-day encounter between Americans since the Civil War (New York State Special Commission on Attica, 1972, xi).

Involvement of the police in collective violence becomes likely, too, when a central part of their control function involves the subduing of "civil disorders" (urban, often racial, riots) and the containment of collective political demonstrations (see National Advisory Commission on Civil Disorders, 1968; Connery, ed., 1969; National Commission on the Causes and Prevention of Violence, 1968; Silver, 1967).

Certainly these extreme actions do not represent the core of everyday run-of-the-mill work done by most agents of control. However, other kinds of distasteful and fearful activities are routine features of the job for those who deal with society's undesirables. This is particularly true for police officers, given not only the threat to others of subsequent legal processing that their intervention implies but also the possibility of their immediate use of violent force. As Egon Bittner has noted, "the police are nothing else than a mechanism for the distribution of situationally justified force in society" (Bittner, 1970, p. 39). Even if in particular situations such force may retrospectively be deemed "justified," the general potential for and threat of violence in police work is something that most people, the police themselves included, cannot accept with complete equanimity. From the police standpoint, of course, the danger of violent force being used against *them* is also a central factor influencing their outlooks and behavior. Thus, Jerome Skolnick has described continuous concern about the "symbolic assailant" as a key feature of police culture. He comments that, "The element of danger is so integral to the policeman's work that explicit recognition [of it] might induce emotional barriers to work performance" (Skolnick, 1966, 1975, p. 47; also Rubinstein, 1974, ch. 7).

Because of the sanctions they can employ and because in various other respects the police constitute "visible reminders of the seamy and recalcitrant portions of human behavior" (Clark, 1975, p. 243), both public attitudes toward them and their own self-images reflect a great deal of ambivalence (see also discussion in Manning, 1977, especially ch. 4). Numerous studies have indicated feelings of social isolation, defensiveness, and impaired self-esteem experienced by many police officers. Though there are additional contributing factors—including other working conditions, remuneration levels, and so on—the moral ambiguity surrounding their social control role seems to be a major reason why the police frequently consider themselves to be disvalued, contaminated, stigmatized. In Clark's study of police isolation (based on data drawn in three Illinois cities), respondents were asked if being a policeman made any difference in their friendships with other people. Forty percent replied affirmatively and 35 percent added that it also affected their immediate family's dealings with the general public (Clark, 1975, p. 252). Similarly, Skolnick's research in "Westville" (a West Coast city of about 400,000) included asking 282 policemen how they rated the prestige that police work receives from others. Seventy percent ranked it fair or poor, 29 percent as being "good," and only 2 percent said it was "excellent." Skolnick's interviews also disclosed specific incidents respondents had experienced in which their identity as police officers had greatly hampered everyday social interaction (at parties with friends, for example). One policeman told Skolnick, "I try to put my police work into the background, and try not to let people know I'm a policeman. Once you do, you can't have normal relations with them" (Skolnick, 1966, 1975, pp. 50, 51).

The public image problems of the police, which also must affect self-conceptions somewhat, are understandably increased when—in a way that lends support to the intergroup conflict interpretation of deviance and social control—

predominantly white police patrol predominantly black neighborhoods. James Baldwin's often-quoted statement makes the point forcefully:

> Their very presence is an insult, and it would be, even if they spent their entire day feeding gumdrops to children. They represent the force of the white world, and that world's real intentions are, simply, for that world's criminal profit and ease, to keep the black man corraled up here [Harlem], in his place. The badge, the gun in the holster, and the swinging club make vivid what will happen should his rebellion become overt (Baldwin, 1961, pp. 650–666).

Under the circumstances, it may be surprising that reported public attitudes toward the police are as favorable as they are (see President's Commission on Law Enforcement and Administration of Justice, 1967); at the same time, it is easy to see why the police themselves regularly anticipate negative response and sometimes even overestimate the amount of hostility they evoke (Crawford, 1975).

Certain specific enforcement demands make it all the more likely that the police will risk contamination through the substantive nature of their work. As we will see, in considering "victimless crimes" (pp. 450–457), pressure on the police to apply these unpopular and relatively unenforceable laws forces reliance on highly distasteful investigative practices (the "News Spot" on p. 343 provides, for the moment, but one example) and also encourages police corruption (see The Knapp Commission Report on Police Corruption, 1972). Efforts by the police to control political dissidents likewise lead to routine use of agents provocateur (decoys) and informers—techniques that have an ambiguous standing, moral as well as constitutional (see Marx, 1974).

Being routinely called upon to perform a variety of "social service" and "peacekeeping" functions (see Banton, 1964; Cumming, et al., 1965; Wilson, 1968b; Reiss, 1971; Manning, 1977, ch. 4)—to intervene in family altercations and barroom brawls, to deal with derelicts (see Adaptation Nine, in this chapter) and other social outcasts, and so on—may only serve to increase further the police officer's vulnerability to job-related contamination. This suggests a more general point of some importance. It is not simply the potential for overt violence that relegates control agents to the domain of dirty work. Thus, a variety of social "helpers" besides the police may experience a similar taint. At least to an extent, this quality attaches to some psychiatric work. Robert Emerson and Melvin Pollner studied psychiatric emergency teams (PET) working out of a community mental health clinic in Southern California that made crisis-intervention field trips in response to emergency calls to the clinic. They found that members of these teams themselves designated certain routine tasks as involving "shit work." Such work occurred in situations where team members not only felt they couldn't do anything *for* "clients," but also recognized the necessity of doing something *to* them (cooperating in their restraint, removal, or hospitalization, etc.). That such activity threatened to discredit the team members was indicated by the manner in which they used the "shit work" characterization itself. According to

NEWS SPOT
Prostitution Tactics Rejected

(December 1976). The Manhattan District Attorney's office in New York City has declined to use a controversial type of evidence in prosecuting prostitutes that was offered to it by a special mayor's task force appointed to assist in midtown "clean-up" efforts. To use the rejected evidence, private investigators hired by the task force to elicit the necessary sexual acts or overtures would have provided the incriminating testimony. A recent obstacle to the long-time use of plainclothes "decoys" has been that prostitutes now will rarely even talk about sex until a "customer" has undressed; yet, under a New York City police regulation, officers cannot disrobe while on duty. In rejecting the proffered testimony of private decoys, an assistant district attorney described the practice of using private investigators to perform sexual acts in order to get evidence as "offensive" to high law enforcement standards and said he would be unwilling to present such a case to a grand jury, whom it would "repel and disgust." For his part, the task force director termed such rejection "ridiculous," a missed opportunity to enforce the law.

(*Source:* Based on a news article in *The New York Times,* December 2, 1976, p. 47.)

Emerson and Pollner, it was "a way in which workers economically expressed to observers (such as colleagues or ourselves) that the task at hand should not be taken to exemplify the nature of either the work or the worker" (Emerson and Pollner, 1976, p. 252).

In such psychiatric emergency work and, similarly, in suicide-prevention efforts and in some general psychotherapy, no doubt an important part of the control agent's contamination results from the ever-present possibility of the patient's self-harm or even self-destruction. This possibility imposes great strain, consciousness of responsibility, uncertainty, and potential guilt on the worker. That there is a stigma attaching to certain persons who must routinely deal with death has been shown by David Sudnow in his research on the treatment of the dying in hospitals. Particularly telling were his observations concerning the morgue attendant who felt "trapped" in his occupational role and who made various ingenious efforts to disavow it. Indeed, at least implicit in Sudnow's discussion is an argument to the effect that death itself represents a form of deviance. If that is so, then any continuous association with it is bound to be discrediting (Sudnow, 1967, especially pp. 51–60).

Quite apart from the prospect of suicide or the client's harming other people, the need for the psychiatrist to participate in incarceration efforts or proceedings frequently lends a dirty work quality to the occupational role. This requirement, along with other institutional demands made upon psychiatrists may place a considerable strain on the reinforcing of favorable self-concepts

through professional ideologies that emphasize public service. Referring to control agents who actually work in mental hospitals, Goffman has stated, "Each
time the mental hospital functions as a holding station, within a network of
such stations, for dealing with public charges, the service model is disaffirmed.
All of these facts of patient recruitment are part of what staff must overlook,
rationalize, gloss over about their place of service" (Goffman, 1961, p. 354). In
other social service-oriented fields as well, the recent "unmasking of euphemism"
(discussed in Chapter 7) is making it more and more difficult for control agents
to ignore the fact that they are doing things *to* their clients—exercising "control"
over them—in the very process of trying to help them. For example, in the
benevolently inspired field of juvenile justice, workers' confidence that their aims
of helping kids in trouble and serving the public are being met is far from complete. Thus, one survey of attitudes among staff members of the California Youth
Authority found that a solid majority of the respondents advocated, among other
things, "a strong effort to divert more youth from the justice-correctional system—
because of its potential for harm" (Knight, 1972, x).

Multiple Mandates

Also contributing to the ambiguity of social control agents' roles is the
multiplicity of goals they are often expected to pursue or implement. As already
noted, the police are a striking example of this, for they are expected to "handle"
anything and everything—to be wide-ranging social workers, friendly neighborhood guides and information-conveyors, as well as law enforcers and crime controllers. Many observers have commented on this, suggesting that neither by
background and training nor in terms of available time and resources are the
police in a good position to succeed in all these diverse functions. Nonetheless,
it is not uncommon for the police to be blamed when there are public signs of
failure in one of these realms.

Typically, the diverging and sometimes contradictory demands placed on
individual control agents reflect the multiple goals confronting the control organizations of which they are a part. These organizations (as we will see further
in just a moment) put pressure on their workers to meet the public expectations
which they confront. Thus, if people expect "correctional" and "treatment" institutions to provide at one and the same time secure custody and meaningful
rehabilitation, it is not surprising that individual workers in such institutions
often find themselves engaged in a complicated juggling act with respect to these
not always compatible functions. In one study of a residential juvenile institution
that underwent a dramatic change, with the sudden introduction of a new and
more treatment-oriented administration and program—"cottage parents" found
themselves expected to perform in unfamiliar and undesired ways, combining
some involvement in the therapeutic program with their traditional and more

custodial tasks. They responded not only with signs of irritation and rebellion, but also with patterns of "withdrawal" and even psychosomatic symptoms (Weber, 1961). Similarly, control agents involved in the work of the juvenile court must regularly cope with the multiple demands placed on that agency. As a consultant to the President's crime commission noted, "The court is expected simultaneously to preserve the institution of law, to enhance the legitimate interests of its clients, especially those of children, and to serve the welfare of the community while protecting public order" (Vinter, 1967, p. 85; see also Lemert, 1971; Schur, 1973).

Although we may not often think of schoolteachers and educational administrators as being social control agents, in fact, they often exercise a mixture of educational and control functions. When they are expected to spot potential "troublemakers," to recognize "minimal brain dysfunction," to utilize various psychological and behavioral "screening" devices, to recommend medication for unruly students, to participate in segregating difficult children, or to contribute information to student dossiers that later may be put to questionable use, they must go well beyond their ordinary teaching role. Besides the obvious questions of competence and legitimacy that such practices pose, it seems clear that they involve the teacher in implementing "a spreading ideology of 'early intervention' and 'treatment' in which the language and, often, the techniques of medicine are used extensively to serve the purposes of social control." The teacher is asked to cooperate in imposing "increasingly narrow limits on [what will be accepted as] tolerable behavior." To the extent such use of teachers represents a significant societal trend, it could well "serve the purpose of legitimizing and enlarging the power of institutions over individuals" (Schrag and Divoky, 1976, pp. 12, 14, 16). Similarly, a study of the role of high school guidance counselors has pointed up the control function as it appears at the secondary education level:

> The classification of students differentiates those who are and are not "having trouble." The evaluation of student performance and the classification it produces has more than nominal significance for the future educational, occupational, and life careers of students. In a bureaucratically organized school such as Lakeshore High, the classification of students routinely initiates organizational actions that may progressively define and limit the development of such careers (Cicourel and Kitsuse, 1963, p. 75).

As Cicourel and Kitsuse discovered, such classification often incorporates the counselors' clinically oriented search for "deeper" explanations of academic and situational difficulties. At the same time, they noted, this categorizing and imputing process is in large measure a response to pressures on both the students and the schools from parents eager to see their own ambitions for their children fulfilled.

In certain kinds of situations, the psychiatric role may be similarly compounded and confounded by a mixture of therapeutic and control functions. As we noted in Chapter 2, the broad social control potential of psychiatry rests in part on the casual extension and application of mental illness conceptions to any number of socially problematic behaviors or conditions. From that standpoint alone, it is apparent that psychiatrists, when viewed collectively and in terms of their general role in defining and dealing with deviance situations, are very important agents of control in modern societies. There is, as we have also seen, an argument advanced by some critics—most notably the psychiatric mavericks Thomas Szasz and R. D. Laing—to the effect that social control is *intrinsic* to much psychiatric practice. Such critics insist that psychiatric diagnoses and treatment almost always incorporate elements of control. Diagnoses reflect underlying value premises that help determine which problematic acts or conditions are seen as "disturbance." Treatment involves doing something *to* patients as well as *for* them. Psychiatrists often must implicitly "take sides" in situations of interpersonal conflict, even if they "habitually conceal and mystify their partisanship behind a cloak of therapeutic neutrality, never admitting to being either the patient's ally or his adversary" (Szasz, 1970, p. 71; see also Schur, 1966).

This line of criticism has, in particular, been leveled against various legally institutionalized uses of psychiatry, such as the central participation of psychiatrists in involuntary mental hospitalization court proceedings and in psychiatric testimony regarding competency to stand trial or in relation to "insanity as a defense" in criminal cases (see Szasz, 1963; Szasz, 1965; also Torrey, 1975). At an extreme, it has been claimed that these uses of psychiatry in the legal system represent a general and dangerous trend toward government control over the individual, perhaps even heralding the onset of "psychiatric fascism" or "the therapeutic state." However one may feel about these charges and accompanying ones to the effect that such extensive recourse to psychiatry is undermining "personal responsibility," there is little doubt that, potentially, psychiatry provides a powerful tool for governments willing and able to use it as a central means of official control. The recent practice in the Soviet Union of using mental hospitalization as a device for dealing with political dissidents (see Bloch and Reddaway, 1977) vividly illustrates such potential.

Apart from the broad control impact of major uses of psychiatry, there are various specific instances in which particular psychiatrists are forced to deal with multiple and sometimes conflicting role demands. Some of the legal situations just noted may be like this: The psychiatrist assessing a defendant's "responsibility" at the time of a crime, for example, is supposed to strictly apply legal criteria that neither conform with standard psychiatric concepts nor permit the tentativeness that most cautious diagnosticians would wish to express (see Goldstein, 1967). More intense problems arise, however, when the dual expectations are built into or threaten to compromise the integrity of the psychiatrist's full-time occupational position. An extreme example of this may be the military psychiatrist:

The private psychiatrist is traditionally a "free professional" who offers his talents and expertise on a fee-for-service basis. The central feature of this relationship is one of free choice and trust. The military psychiatrist and his patient are both employees of the same system. They each have bureaucratic commitments irrespective of personal predilections. . . .

Within the military context, the psychiatrist becomes an agent of the bureaucracy. The patient becomes a referral whom the psychiatrist sees in his capacity as an agent of the establishment, not as the patient's agent. Therefore, when problems of conflicting interests arise, the psychiatrist may be placed in a quandary. What is best for the patient may be the opposite of what is best for the system (Daniels, 1972, pp. 154–155).

Specific dilemmas of the military psychiatrist usually center around command influence of various kinds—pressure to keep men in combat, inadequacy or absence of privileged communication, official conceptions regarding appropriate treatment. Although exercising considerable discretion and, hence, wielding much direct power, the military psychiatrist is also subject to the chain of command and must obey lawful orders. At the heart of the dilemmas in this psychiatric position, therefore, is the hierarchical and highly authoritarian nature of the work organization, which is, in effect, a counterpart of what we find at the societal level in the case of Soviet control through psychiatry. Indeed, as earlier American analyses suggested, the demands of officialdom have long posed serious role conflicts for all physicians in the Soviet Union (Field, 1957).

Another setting in which the psychiatrist may confront multiple and confusing role requirements is that of the educational organization, perhaps, particularly the college or university (Szasz, 1970; Halleck, 1972; but see also discussion in Kahne and Schwartz, 1978). Possible uses of psychiatry and associated schemes in the lower schools have already been noted. At the college level, there are the dilemma-producing possibilities for defining student activism and other forms of troublesomeness as psychiatric problems and, above all, the moral quandaries that surround preserving the confidentiality of voluntary student-patient disclosures. Once again, there is the danger of a kind of "command" influence, since the psychiatrist is employed—full-time or part-time—by the college or university and may be put under considerable pressure to share privileged information with academic administrators. As Seymour Halleck has commented, there may also be considerable initiation of referrals by teachers or administrators:

Whenever I confronted the professors and deans about the propriety of their referrals, they usually insisted that they only wanted reassurance that it was safe to allow the disturbed student to continue in school. Some maintained that the primary reason for referring a student was to ensure that he would receive help. For the most part, the professors and deans were sincere . . . but I suspect that in a few instances they were trying to use me to provide a convenient medical rationalization for weeding out troublemakers. During the past decade, I have tried to persuade administrators . . . that involuntary examination of disturbed students is, except in rare instances, an improper use of psychiatry (Halleck, 1972, p. 142).

Resulting Role Strain

Early in this text we considered the relevance of role conflict in generating deviation, and we also have encountered much evidence of the strains on an individual that being cast into a deviant role can produce. By now it should be apparent that role conflict and role strain very much affect those on the control side of deviance situations as well. The characteristic combination of being forced to handle dirty work and also being subjected to divergent and sometimes unreasonable expectations and demands, including some important organizational ones to which we will turn shortly, often produces tension, uncertainty, poor morale, low self-esteem, and even hostility. This is not to suggest that most social control agents are as badly off as the people they control. They do have considerable power and authority in the immediate processing situation. Their disvaluation, when it occurs, is nowhere near as severe, and often there are factors that serve to counterbalance what negative impact it might have. At the very least, however, the strains of such work are likely to generate some degree of disillusionment, abandonment of high ideals, reduced concern for the client, a routinizing managerial approach to doing the job. At the worst, control agents may become arbitrary, capricious, or discriminatory in carrying out deviance-processing duties; alternatively, they may succumb to job-related temptations to deviate in other ways—dealing brutally with clients, accepting favors in exchange for noninterference, and the like.

Control agents probably can be thought of as comprising a stratification system of sorts. Relative standing in this hierarchical order will influence the likelihood of agents themselves deviating and also of their strongly experiencing the demoralizing impact of multiple and conflicting role demands. Everett Hughes' thesis about dirty work is part of a broader formulation concerning the **moral division of labor** (see Hughes, 1971). According to this conception, the degree of involvement in dirty work is roughly correlated with position in the stratified occupational order. It is in part because those in the lower echelons of the job system handle such undesirable tasks that persons at the upper levels can maintain a high degree of behavioral conformity and moral integrity. In a major study of occupational deviance (Carlin, 1966), Jerome Carlin investigated the conformity and deviation of lawyers with respect to the legal profession's established canons of ethics (the organized bar's "internal" system of ethical rules). The large sample of New York lawyers Carlin interviewed was highly stratified, with differential prestige and reward positively correlated with variations in the size of law firms (large firm lawyers tended to be at the "top" of the stratification order, individual practitioners at the bottom). Asked how they had behaved or would behave in a variety of situations of ethical conflict, most large firm lawyers turned out to be high conformers (to the canons of ethics), while the likelihood of deviating increased as one went down the occupational ladder. Among a variety of factors accounting for this, the typically unstable clientele and precarious financial position of "solo practitioners" and others low in the prestige hierarchy stood out as especially significant. Also important was the fact that lawyers at the different levels characteristically experienced different kinds of court and agency contacts; the organizational milieux in which the lower-level lawyers regularly operated (e.g., lower criminal courts) tended to exhibit a general atmosphere that was further conducive to deviation.

Most likely something akin to this moral division of labor can also be found among the various kinds of social control agents. In some instances, the potential for disvaluation because of having to engage in dirty work will be offset by other security-providing and morale-enhancing aspects of the job. Thus, the financial remuneration and considerable prestige enjoyed by most psychiatrists and high court judges may well serve to largely insulate them from the stigma attached to deviance-processing. Much as in the Carlin study, there is a hierarchy of social control tasks, in which the degree of dirtiness or extent of direct and continuing contamination correlates inversely with prestige and probable morale. Those who must directly and regularly "dirty their hands" in dealing with distasteful problems—prison guards and mental hospital attendants, psychiatric emergency teams, ordinary police officers, some criminal defense lawyers—are likely to be near the bottom of this stratified system. Police and hospital administrators, lower court judges, public prosecutors and public defenders, and various types of rehabilitative personnel may be in somewhat better protected positions.

We can see, in this probable stratification of control agents, a "replaying" of a number of themes emphasized earlier in this text. The relation between the conformity of some control agents and the deviation of others is similar, in a way, to the reciprocal nature of conformity-deviation at the societal level emphasized in discussions of boundary-maintenance. In both instances conformity is seen almost to *depend upon* deviation, in the sense that we could not recognize or maintain the former without the latter. Also paralleling the interpretations developed above is the implicit negotiation of status and identity by control agents. Because they must engage in dirty work, many agents of control face the possibility of stigma. The precise nature of their jobs (just as the precise nature of the deviation for deviators) has great bearing on the types and degrees of stigma potential in their work situations. Beyond that, however, and again as in the case of perceived deviators, a variety of personal and social resources become salient for purposes of avoiding stigma and maintaining favorable self-conceptions. Although, as we have seen, control agents are likely to hold a kind of situational power, in that they tend to have the upper hand in their direct encounters with persons undergoing deviance-processing, their overall social power may not always be great. This matter of overall power, too, significantly influences the ways in which control agents go about their work. A final parallel worth noting is that agents of control may sometimes use the same devices deviators employ in order to neutralize disvaluation. The police officer who tries not to let people know his job is, after all, attempting to pass as "normal." Likewise, the aforementioned use of "shit work" characterizations by the PET members themselves represents an offered "account" or, more accurately, to use a similar concept developed by other authors (Hewitt and Stokes, 1975), a "disclaimer." When control agents employ such disclaimers, they are insisting that, despite the occasional need to undertake dirty work, they are not really, or basically, "like that."

SELECTIVE INTERVENTION

Discretion

An understanding of these elements of ambiguity in the control agent's role provides some of the relevant background for exploring the ways in which deviators may be treated. Another major key to the nature of deviance-processing is the phenomenon of **discretion**—the freedom or authority to make decisions and to choose from among various possible processing actions. Discretion is one way of describing the leeway in reacting to problematic behavior that most individuals have in situations of informal interaction. For example, we could say that what happened to the erratically behaving husbands in the Yarrow study was partly subject to the discretion exercised by the wives. They were relatively free to respond in various ways, ranging from efforts at total normalization to taking steps that would lead directly to their spouses' hospitalization. More generally, the perceptual and other social-psychological mechanisms that we have seen involved in imputing deviantness, for a wide range of behaviors and conditions, often come into play without any formal rules or even strong pressures compelling the reactions. Responders choose to or have learned to react in those ways, but, at least in theory, they are relatively "free" not to. In fact, such responses— as our consideration of tolerance limits and threat suggests—are far from automatic or uniform.

One consequence of this informal discretion to react is that the ways in which it is exercised help to determine which instances of perceived deviation will come to the attention of the more formal agents of control in the first place. This is true even in regards to behavior in violation of the law. Citing findings from national "victimization" studies conducted during the 1960s (in which respondents were asked about criminal offenses ever committed against them and in which high proportions of nonreporting to the police were indicated), Albert Reiss has insisted that the "discretionary decisions of citizens" play a major role in determining the nature of police activity (Reiss, 1971, pp. 65–88). Furthermore, Reiss suggests, far from being free to act in any way they want, police, in making decisions when crimes do come to their attention, often are highly dependent on citizens—for example, in providing the information needed to establish "probable cause" as the basis for an arrest (Reiss, 1971, p. 79). At any rate, it seems evident that, for a variety of reasons, the specific instances of deviation (of various kinds) that come to the initial attention of formal control agents comprise some kind of "selection" from among the larger pool of potential cases. Nor is there any particular reason to believe that the individuals thus selected out will always be fully representative of all those who might have been so selected.

Though control agents may be more constrained than laypersons to react to deviation in specified ways, since they often are supposed to apply applicable rules and are subject to organizational guidelines, nonetheless they, too, invariably have considerable leeway in deciding how to respond. A point mentioned earlier should be reiterated in this connection. A key option in many situations may be to take *no* direct action. Particularly in the context of ongoing control efforts "in the field," such as routine police patrolling, a variety of considerations may dictate such nonintervention—incapacity to handle all instances of deviation encountered, uncertainty about the evidentiary basis for taking other actions, an anticipation of lack of support for taking them, or simply a general conclusion that to intervene would produce more harm than good. In connection with this last reason, the need to maintain a working relationship of rapport in the community may take on special importance.

Certain kinds of problems that control agents routinely encounter may especially lend themselves to decisions not to intervene. Egon Bittner's research (conducted in California) showed, for example, that police officers were usually quite reluctant to directly exercise the fairly broad authority granted them under state law to initiate a person's mental hospitalization when deemed necessary for that person's own protection or the protection of others (Bittner, 1967). Of the many instances in which this intervention might have been possible, only if the situation fell into at least one of five categories, Bittner found, would such action be likely. These were: (1) indication of a suicide attempt (current or past), (2) distortion of normal physical appearance ("injuries of unknown origin, seizures, urinary incontinence, odd posturing, nudity, extreme dirtiness, and so on") as an accompaniment to other indications of psychological disorder, (3) a high degree of apparently unpacifiable agitation, (4) severe disorientation or creation of a public nuisance, (5) requests from "instrumentally-related persons" (teachers, employers, landlords, etc.) who were usually assumed to have exhausted other procedures, whereas "similar requests, in quite similar circumstances, made by family members, friends, roommates, or neighbors are usually not honored" (Bittner, 1967, pp. 283–285). In a wide range of cases, the officers Bittner studied were able to rely on various kinds of "psychiatric first aid" in order to restore control, rather than having to initiate emergency hospitalization.

When the context in which social control decisions are made takes on the features of a relatively stable and more or less circumscribed subculture, the likelihood of routine and informal handling of many incidents becomes even greater. Adaptation Nine illustrates this, drawing on another aspect of Bittner's extensive police research.

ADAPTATION NINE
Peace Keeping on Skid-Row*

As one might expect, the "skid-row" areas found in most large American cities have, over the years, been of considerable interest to sociologists. A distinctive feature of modern urban life and a good example of a "deviant subculture," skid-row also illustrates nicely the regularized interaction between deviators and agents of "social control." From the standpoint of skid-row inhabitants, if that word can be applied to the area's rather transient population, dealing with a variety of official and unofficial controllers and "helpers" is a central aspect of everyday existence. From the standpoint of the police, too, skid-row is a problem of management. Through a cumulation of experience there, informal as well as formal ways of managing emerge. It is partly as a consequence of these interaction patterns that the skid-row situation takes shape, that what outsiders may view as "deviant" is in a sense rendered more "normal."

Sociologist Egon Bittner studied these patterns through eleven weeks of field research in skid-row and skid-row-like districts, augmented by approximately one-hundred interviews with police officers. Noting that skid-row represents but one of many situations in which the police function centers around "peace keeping," Bittner examined the policing of skid-row as an accomplishment of "practical skill." In using this terminology, he had in mind patterns of daily practice that the policemen themselves viewed as "proper and efficient." From this standpoint, he was not concerned with providing any objective evaluation of efficiency or a moral evaluation of desirability. Instead, he deliberately confined his analysis to "a description of what police patrolmen consider to be the reality of their work circumstances, what they do, and what they feel they must do to do a good job."

Most police work on skid-row does not involve an actual making of arrests. As a consequence, the officer has even fewer formalized criteria or guidelines to assist him than he does in some other work situations. The only evident societal mandate in this case seems to call for "containment" of the area and its occupants. How this is to be achieved is left to the police. Bittner found that, "the prevailing method of carrying out the task is to assign patrolmen to the area on a fairly permanent basis and allow them to work out their own ways of running things." His research also disclosed that patrolmen assigned to such districts tend to develop quite uniform conceptions of the nature of life on skid-row and the relevant characteristics of its occupants. It is on the basis of such conceptions that a regularized way of policing comes about.

* *Source:* A Summary and interpretation of Egon Bittner, "The Police on Skid-Row: A Study of Peace Keeping," *American Sociological Review*, 32 (Oct. 1967), 699–715. Direct quotations used with permission.

One of the central features of skid-row life is the "overall atmosphere of fortuitousness." Interaction and outlooks tend to be focused on the "occasion of the moment;" relatively little concern is displayed for the contributing background or possible future consequences of presently experienced situations. The skid-row resident, therefore has little sense of personal control over events or of predictability in the behavior of others. Under these circumstances:

> . . . irresponsibility takes an *objectified* form on skid-row. The places the residents occupy, the social relations they entertain, and the activities that engage them are not meaningfully connected over time. Thus, for example, address, occupation, marital status, etc., matter much less on skid-row than in any other part of society. . . . Of course, everybody's life contains some sequential incongruities, but in the life of a skid-row inhabitant every moment is an accident. That a man has no "address" in the future that could be in some way inferred from where he is and what he does makes him a person of *radically reduced visibility*. If he disappears from sight and one wishes to locate him, it is virtually impossible to systematize the search. . . .

A related aspect of this transient and uncommitted way of life that colors police practice is the constant danger of predatory action, including violence. Yet in this regard the police are not working so much to protect the outside society, as to keep the peace on skid-row itself. Bittner found them to be involved in the "protection of putative predators from one another," a task demanded by the fact that "everyday life on skid-row is viewed as an open field for reciprocal exploitation."

In order to cope with this difficult situation, the policemen Bittner studied adopted an approach that incorporated three major elements: a "richly particularized knowledge of people and places" in the area, a reduction in the importance given to "strict culpability" as a ground for decision-making, and a gearing of such decisions to the exigencies of immediately confronted situations. As to the first, the patrolman on skid-row was found to have:

> . . . an immensely detailed factual knowledge of his beat. He knows, and knows a great deal about, a large number of residents. He is likely to know every person who manages or works in the local bars, hotels, shops, stores, and missions. Moreover, he probably knows every public and private place inside and out. Finally, he ordinarily remembers countless events of the past which he can recount by citing names, dates and places with remarkable precision.

This kind of detailed knowledge is continuously reinforced through new observations and frequent "exchanges of small talk" with a wide range of individuals in the area. Bittner found such exchanges to be remarkably casual in nature:

> Not only does the officer himself avoid all terms of deference and respect, but he does not seem to expect or demand them. For example, a patrolman said to a man radiating an alcoholic glow in the street, "You've got enough of a heat on now; I'll give you ten minutes to get your ass off the street!" Without stopping, the man answered, "Oh, why don't you go and piss in your own pot!" The officer's only response was "All right, in ten minutes you're either in bed or on your way to the can."

As Bittner perceptively noted, this apparent conversational license is actually part and parcel of an implicit and mutually understood bargain governing police-resident interaction. In exchange for allowing such informality, the patrolman routinely feels free to intrude (by asking questions on the street, freely entering premises, etc.) into the private lives of residents to an extent that would under other circumstances immediately be viewed as infringing on their civil liberties. The resident who refuses to permit this intrusion (for example, by refusing to answer questions or by challenging the right to ask them) significantly increases the chance of being arrested on a minor charge (almost always present as a possibility). There is, however, an additional aspect of reciprocation in this apparent invasion of privacy; frequently, it is linked to the officer's ability to provide valuable help—something he does over and over again and in many small ways (mediating and cooling off altercations, directing individuals to lodging, food sources, or medical services, etc.).

A similar informality reigns with respect to determining (or paying attention to) technical violations of law. On skid-row, Bittner found, "patrolmen often make decisions based on reasons that the law probably does not recognize as valid." As already noted, their efforts are less devoted to strictly enforcing the laws than to the general function of keeping the peace; law is seen primarily as a "resource" to assist them in this task. This can work in several ways. The officer can and, in fact, must continually overlook technical violations that might have led to arrest. On the other hand he can easily, and frequently will, "find" a violation when it seems necessary to the accomplishment of peace keeping. In none of this decision-making is technical guilt the major criterion. Furthermore, in many of the situations routinely confronted by the patrolman, the issue of culpability is ambiguous:

For example, an officer was called to help in settling a violent dispute in a hotel room. The object of the quarrel was a supposedly stolen pair of trousers. As the story unfolded in the conflicting versions of the participants, it was not possible to decide who was the complainant and who was alleged to be the thief, nor did it come to light who occupied the room in which the fracas took place, or whether the trousers were taken from the room or to the room. Though the officer did ask some questions, it seemed, and was confirmed in later conversation, that he was there not to solve the puzzle of the missing trousers but to keep the situation from getting out of hand. In the end, the exhausted participants dispersed, and this was the conclusion of the case. The patrolman maintained that no one could unravel mysteries of this sort because "these people take things from each other so often that no one could tell what 'belongs' to whom." In fact, he suggested, the terms owning, stealing, and swindling, in their strict sense, do not really belong on skid-row, and all efforts to distribute guilt and innocence according to some rational formula of justice are doomed to failure.

Asked whether informal methods did not often (that is, when arrests do result) violate both good police practice and the residents' civil liberties, the officers Bittner interviewed emphasized the quickly grasped sense of probable trouble they had developed through experience in the area. Recognizing that some of their actions might not be fully justifiable under ordinary legal standards, they believed that the goals of protecting residents and preventing the spread of trouble demanded this kind of *"ad hoc* decision-making." Bittner found that the general rule seemed to be to intervene in the most economical way: "the person whose presence is most likely to perpetuate the troublesome development [will] be removed." The aim of breaking up situations of potential trouble also means that where a person happens to be when encountering the police may be a crucial factor in determining what happens:

> . . . it matters not only whether a man is found in a conspicuous place or not, but also how far away he is from his domicile. The further away he is, the less likely it is that he will make it to his room, and the more likely the arrest. Sometimes drunk arrests are made mainly because the police van is available. In one case a patrolman summoned the van to pick up an arrested man. As the van was pulling away from the curb the officer stopped the driver because he sighted another drunk stumbling across the street. The second man protested saying that he "wasn't even half drunk yet." The patrolman's response was, "OK, I'll owe you half a drunk." In sum, the basic routine of keeping the peace on skid-row involves a process of matching the resources of control with situational exigencies. The overall objective is to reduce the total amount of risk in the area.

In both of the situations just discussed—apprehending the mentally ill and policing skid-row—officers in the field must rely heavily on their own best judgments as to how to deal with commonly encountered situations. This is true of all police work in the field. Building up through experience a stock of knowledge regarding the characteristics of the community and its inhabitants helps to provide a basis for everyday decision-making. Much of the needed information can only be obtained "on the job," rather than conveyed in the formal training of the police academy. It emerges and cumulates, sometimes in a none too systematic form. "The patrolman's knowledge of people develops haphazardly. He is constantly recording bits of information about people he meets which he uses in making judgments about them if he encounters them again. He remembers places where he has had trouble or where trusted colleagues have met resistance" (Rubinstein, 1974, p. 186).

It may be worth emphasizing that police on patrol cannot avoid almost constant decision-making. They continuously confront situations that *might* be treated as "cases" and about which some choice *must* be made (if we recognize that choosing *not* to take action is itself a choice, an exercise of discretion). They cannot possibly intervene actively in all of these multitudinous situations. Nor do the laws on the books make it fully clear how and when they should act. While they cannot ignore these laws or the professed goals of the criminal justice system, they must at the same time develop their own set of working goals and priorities (see Manning, 1977, ch. 8). And they must do this in the context of a continuing relation to the community and also with an awareness of the ever-present potential for danger to themselves.

Precisely because of this need to exercise personal judgment and to work out a set of viable responses, which often must be implemented on the spot, without hesitation, police regularly engage in "typification" of the sort noted earlier. Typing or categorizing both situations and individuals is understandably relied on as a means of sifting through an overwhelming body of observations and impressions to gain a sense of predictable patterns and some confidence in reacting to them. As the aforementioned Briar and Piliavin study of police encounters with juveniles showed, superficial appearance often provides major clues used in typifying persons. To some extent (the "buzzer system" seemed to imply this) such superficiality may be almost inherent in the deviantizing process, by whomever employed. For overworked police officers, it may seem the only meaningful way of systematizing their experience and impressions. Furthermore, in many situations the combination of a sense of immediacy and personal threat heightens recourse to typification:

> The policeman, because his work requires him to be occupied continually with potential violence, develops a perceptual shorthand to identify certain kinds of people as symbolic assailants, that is, as persons who use gesture, language, and attire that the policeman has come to recognize as a prelude to violence. This does not mean that the violence by the symbolic assailant is necessarily predictable. On the contrary, the policeman responds to the vague indication of danger suggested by appearance (Skolnick, 1966, 1975, p. 45).

As the accompanying news article points up, fear of violence is certainly not the only circumstance generating police typifications. In this instance, the difficulty of obtaining evidence in drug-violation cases puts pressure on law-enforcers to employ such practices.

While we are devoting special attention to the police in this section, the reader should realize that the basic point about exercising discretion has a more general applicability. In many respects, the police officer represents a prototype of what we might call "front-line" workers in deviance-processing. The police often are the first link between informal reactions to deviation by "significant others" in the lay community and the formal organizational processing of a deviator. Their activity, then, constitutes a key phase of what often may become a rather extended screening and reacting sequence. There are other control agents who commonly exercise this front-line, in-the-field, position; examples would include truant officers, community mental health "outreach" personnel, suicide-prevention workers, some probation officers, and perhaps the recently mentioned psychiatric emergency teams. Undoubtedly they all exercise some similar kinds of early-stage discretion. Yet because the "jurisdiction" of the police extends so broadly over an enormous range of situations that may lead to deviance-

NEWS SPOT
Long-Haired Drivers Stopped

(October 1977). The U.S. Supreme Court dealt a blow to defenders of freedom of appearance when it refused (in a 7–2 split decision) to reconsider a ruling by the Court of Appeals for the Third Circuit upholding the right of New Jersey state police to stop long-haired drivers on the state's highways and search their cars for illicit drugs. Although terming the policy "insensitive" and "indifferent" to the rights of travelers, the Appeals Court felt unable to intervene because of earlier rulings holding that injunctions against civil-rights violations would not be issued unless there was evidence of "a plan or scheme to suppress constitutional rights." The case originally arose in 1970 when thirty-seven plaintiffs charged in Federal District court that the state police had violated their constitutional rights by arbitrarily and unreasonably stopping and searching their cars—solely on the basis of their personal appearance. At trial, the judge denied them a general injunction against the practice but did award some of them damages for violations of their civil rights. The plaintiffs then carried their cases to the higher courts in hopes of obtaining the broader remedy. A variety of delays—including those caused by the death of two district court judges during trial—led to the unusually long time-lag in the case reaching the Supreme Court.

(*Source:* Based on a news article in *The New York Times,* November 1, 1977, p. 76.)

processing—including virtually all of those dealt with by these other control agents and potentially covering every substantive type of perceived deviation—the discretionary role of the police is of paramount importance. This is also the reason why the bulk of the research literature on discretion in the field has focused on police practice.

The Deviance Funnel

Even within the formal system of administering justice, however, police work represents *only* one stage. At virtually every subsequent stage as well, key social control role occupants exercise similar discretion as to "what happens next." Prosecutors, as we have seen, have considerably leeway to influence the disposition of cases through plea bargaining; but many cases never even get that far, for the prosecutor also has wide discretion not to prosecute at all.

Under pressure to keep the judge's case calendar as light as possible, the prosecutor drops charges against defendants wholesale before the cases can reach the judge. These decisions, made by a young assistant prosecutor, usually overworked and inexperienced, are often based on a quick glance at police reports of arrests. Summarily, he tosses out cases that seem too "weak;" cases involving charges, such as a husband's beating his wife, that seem too tawdry for the court to consider; those involving, as defendants, neat-looking, middle-class people who seem "respectable" and not likely to get into trouble again (Downie, 1972, p. 30).

The further processing of cases that continue in the courts invariably rests on a variety of additional discretionary judgments.

Where there is a full jury trial, the jurors—though supposedly restricted to "finding the facts" and applying the principles of law on which the judge instructs them—in fact, often shape outcomes according to their generalized sense of justice, their "gut feelings," or even their personal prejudices (see Frank, 1949; Schur, 1958; but also Kalven and Zeisel, 1966). At any rate, they must make difficult and uncertain choices, assisted insofar as possible by evidence presented at the trial, in their reconstruction of past events. Where the trial is before a judge, he, too, has considerable leeway to reach various dispositions. Without question, the most notable exercise of discretion by judges has been in sentencing convicted offenders (see Hogarth, 1971; Frankel, 1972; Gaylin, 1974; and von Hirsch, 1976). Ostensibly as a means of "individualizing" justice in order to implement ideals of rehabilitation, judges have often had great latitude in trying to mete out the appropriate sentence for any one individual. As we will see below, the enormous sentencing disparities that have resulted recently have caused much alarm, and, as a result, there has been growing interest in sentencing guidelines that would encourage greater uniformity. Likewise, in order to place limits on the currently extensive discretion of correctional officials and parole boards in deciding what happens to convicted offenders after sentencing, some specialists now favor greater use of determinate sentences (fixed by statute) and, perhaps, even a complete abolition of parole (conditional release).

As we might well expect and as the quoted statement about discretion not to prosecute implies, typifications of various kinds (partly depending on the nature of the deviations being processed) underlie these several exercisings of discretion, just as they influence decision-making by the police. If any kind of orderly decision-making is to occur, cases presented for decision must somehow be sorted out into meaningful categories. There are sometimes certain obvious criteria that may be used, usually along with others, in classification—for example, in sentencing, seriousness of the offense, "prior criminal record," and the like. However, it seems clear that in addition a broader "type of person" categorizing frequently exerts strong influence. In his close study of one juvenile court, Robert Emerson concluded that central to the court's work was "a process of inquiry into the youth's *moral character*." He noted further:

> Court staff distinguish three general kinds of juvenile moral character. First, a youth may be *normal*, i.e., basically like most children, acting for basically normal and conventional reasons, despite some delinquent behavior. Second, a youth may be regarded as a *hard-core* or *criminal-like* delinquent, maliciously or hostilely motivated, consciously pursuing illegal ends. Third, a youth may be *disturbed*, driven to acting in senseless and irrational ways by obscure motives or inner compulsions.

For the juvenile court these categories of moral character provide institutionally relevant means for "explaining" or "accounting for" the patterns of behavior that led to the identification of "trouble." To explain such behavior by fitting the individual case into one of these categories both suggests and justifies particular court actions to deal with it (Emerson, 1969, p. 91).

Emerson depicts a complex process of negotiation in which some eventual balance is struck between evidence and arguments constituting character "denunciations" and those constituting "pitches" for the child, or, in other words, favorable data. This involves "constructing a biography that locates the delinquent and his offense . . ." Major inputs include the child's delinquency history (if any) and "the reports made of his family situation" (Emerson, 1969, pp. 101–132).

   Sentencing practices of the judge in drunk court provide another good example of typification. Wiseman has reported that judges processing individuals on public drunkenness charges sort them out implicitly into the following categories: "overindulgent social drinker," "chronic drunken bum," and "sick alcoholic." If a person falls into the first category and seems to be "a wayward, but basically solid citizen," suspended sentence and a warning may suffice. If the judge, however, concludes that the defendant falls into the second category, then probably "he must be dried out for his own good, since he is a menace to himself and society." In all of this reasoning, Wiseman notes, the judge's decision-making is complicated by awareness of the third definition—alcoholism as an illness—according to which jail may be seen as an inappropriate response to the drunk's behavior. At any rate, the basic sentencing process is one in which "the men are objectified into social types for easy classification." Social position (of which "dress is an all-important clue"), general physical appearance, and past drunkenness record, all significantly influence this classification and the resulting dispositions (Wiseman, 1970, pp. 86–94).

   It should be realized that in some substantive areas of the law (delinquency and public drunkenness being two prime examples), social typification has, in effect, been virtually required because of dominant conceptions favoring "individualized" administration of justice (a matter discussed further in the next chapter). As more generally in the matter of criminal sentencing, the idea has been to deal with "the whole person" who comes before the court and to reach a disposition that is appropriate for each such person. It is easy to see that when the basic mechanism for doing this becomes a "type of person" classification, stigma relating to past deviation or present socioeconomic circumstances is likely to be reinforced or amplified. Thus, the conditions of the individual's history and present biography that a judge or other control agent considers in order to determine whether the person is or is not a good "risk" or "prospect," become self-fulfilling. This implies not only the likelihood of further disadvantage for the already-disadvantaged, but also, by the same token, that the best prospects for favorable treatment lie with those who already have enjoyed relative benefit.

   Since there usually is a sequence of specific stages in formal deviance-processing at each of which discretionary choices are made about the individuals passing through (usually through typifications), we can recognize a kind of **funneling** process at work. Rubington and Weinberg have something like this in mind when they write of "the deviance corridor" (Rubington and Weinberg, 1978, pp. 271–272); Goffman, referring partly, however, to informal as well as formal reactions in the "prepatient phase," comments on a "betrayal funnel" in the processing of mental patients (Goffman, 1961, pp. 140–141). The funnel metaphor is particularly helpful, because it graphically suggests the sifting out process through which a large number of potential cases at the outset is reduced, through actions taken at successive stages, to a very much smaller number reaching the final stage. This is the process that criminologists sometimes describe as **case mortality.** Thus, in the administration of criminal justice, not all of the criminal offenses that are committed become "known to the police;" not all of those that do result in an arrest; not all arrests lead to trials; not all trials lead to convictions; not all convictions lead to imprisonment. At each stage, some cases "drop out" of the processing system, while others continue on.

Rosett and Cressey have recently presented some overall statistics indicating this funnel effect:

> . . . more than two out of three adult felony arrests are disposed of or are lost somewhere in the system before formal charges are filed in any felony trial court. At the point of arraignment, less than one-third of the persons arrested for felonies still face felony charges. About 85 percent of those who face felony court charges will be convicted of some offense, but only 10 percent will be tried before a judge or jury. In California, over 40 percent of the persons arraigned on a serious felony charge plead guilty to a misdemeanor only, and many more plead guilty to a lesser felony.
>
> The selective process continues when sentence is pronounced. Only 13 percent of those convicted in California's felony courts are sent to state prisons. Another 41 percent are sentenced to serve time in a county jail. Seventy percent of those convicted are placed on probation, either directly or after a short jail sentence (Rosett and Cressey, 1976, pp. 33–34).

Blumberg, examining the disposition of all felony arrests in Kings County (Brooklyn), New York, during the years 1960–1962, had earlier documented this sifting-out process, which he termed "the sieve effect." He emphasized, however, that as far as an individual's being completely dropped out of the system is concerned, the sieve effect progressively diminishes. Whereas "initially its escape holes are somewhat broad and coarse," at subsequent stages, higher proportions of the remaining cases are retained within the system, and, finally, at the level of actual court trial in felony cases (as seen also in the figures Rosett and Cressey cite), "the process almost freezes, and only infrequently from then on can the accused free himself from the procedural engine in which he is enmeshed" (Blumberg, 1967, pp. 50–51).

The juvenile justice flowchart, presented in Figure 6.1, shows the structuring of such funnel effects in one specific type of court and agency system. Comparable flowcharts no doubt could be used to depict funneling sequences in

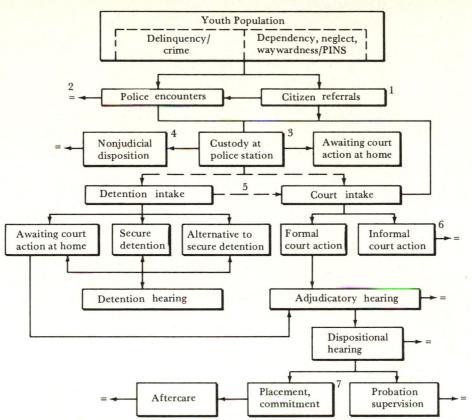

1. Citizen referrals include referrals of cases from parents, schools, welfare agencies—even occasionally children themselves.
2. This symbol (=) indicates a point at which the juvenile leaves the system as depicted here. Youth may avail themselves of services, counseling, or other arrangements on the recommendation of individuals in the system. However, formal control over the youth has ceased.
3. This point includes the options of station adjustment, referral to community services, or return home. Police screening decisions are made by the police juvenile unit in communities whose police departments have established such units. Police juvenile policies typically delineate cases appropriate for station adjustment or court referral. Presumably, serious or repeated offenders are routed directly to the juvenile court.
4. Youth Services Bureaus exist in an increasing number of communities but are still the exception rather than the rule. Where they or other appropriate resources are unavailable, a greater proportion of juvenile cases are probably routed directly to the juvenile court by the police (or other community agencies) for the intake screening and decision as to further action.
5. Detention and court intake processes are related. One concerns the pre-judicial arrangement for custody and care of the child, whereas the other concerns the judicial process surrounding the child's case.
6. Informal court action can include the youth's and parents' consent to (informal) supervision or the use of community services and must be agreed to by parents and child.
7. Placement or commitment can cover a wide range of dispositions, from training schools and other correctional facilities to psychiatric institutions, foster family homes, hostels, relatives' homes, and so on.

Figure 6.1. A schematic view of the juvenile justice system. *Source:* Margaret K. Rosenheim, ed., *Pursuing Justice for the Child.* Chicago: University of Chicago Press, 1976, xi; reproduced with permission.

a variety of other substantive areas of deviance-processing. Looking at such a flowchart helps make clear that the various exercises of discretion in deviance-processing are not *merely* the result of case overloading or of the capriciousness of particular control agents. Such factors may influence the nature of the specific decisions reached, but the need to make such decisions at each of the stages in the sequence is *built into the processing system itself.* This is particularly so in an area such as that of juvenile justice (see pp. 461–469), in which there has been a philosophy emphasizing alternative processing options and an institution-alizing of various possibilities for "diversion" of children from ordinary court processing.

Being aware of the funneling or case mortality phenomenon forces us to recognize the enormous extent to which the actions of other people (in this case, formal control agents) shape individual deviance careers. That deviance outcomes are subject to "contingencies" beyond the offending person's control is highlighted when we focus on processing sequences, the necessary exercise of discretion at various stages, and the multiplicity of decision-makers any one individual may confront. Because of the inevitable need to choose from among various processing options, the control agent's action is rarely automatic or predetermined by official decree. Indeed, as we saw in the last chapter, in specific instances such responses often emerge through and are influenced by direct or subtle sequences of interaction with the individuals being processed. For all these reasons, sociologists increasingly feel that studying the control agent's role as it exists "on paper" or is revealed statistically will not suffice. Realization of the prevalence of funneling and typification has been greatly enhanced by the recent preference for direct field studies of deviance-processing "in action," and, as that realization has grown, the conviction that such field investigations are indeed necessary has been further reinforced.

Another significant value of recognizing the funneling phenomenon is that doing so underscores a sense of the limitations of official statistics. We saw, in the early part of this book, that the re-thinking of theories about deviance causation has reflected a growing disenchantment with the methodologies lying behind such data. Research findings that demonstrated the existence of consid-erable case mortality and a disillusionment regarding the value of "matched sample" comparison studies of supposed deviants and nondeviants have tended to go hand in hand. Some quite early inquiries, in which respondents drawn from the general population were asked whether they had ever engaged in various behaviors that might have led to criminal liability, showed tremendous discrep-ancies between the social distribution of such "actual" offenses and that reflected in the recorded crime and delinquency statistics. Thus, one study found that college student respondents had committed a great many offenses for which they might have been brought before the juvenile court, yet, unlike the nonstudents with whom they were compared, practically none of them had been officially dealt with in this way (Porterfield, 1946). Given the successive stages in criminal processing at which cases dropped out of the system, criminologists began to conclude that the "further away" statistics were from the "actual" offenses, the greater the problems of representativeness. Prison statistics were seen to be more faulty—as an indicator of the true social characteristics of offenders, for example—than conviction statistics, conviction statistics less adequate than arrest statistics, and so on. It was also recognized, as in several early delinquency studies, that a great many cases never got into the formal processing system at all because they were handled informally in the schools or by private welfare agencies (see for example, Robison, 1936).

Since the early revelations along these lines, a great deal of research effort has gone into trying to systematically determine the extent and social distribution of such "hidden" deviance. (For discussion and many specific citations, see Schur, 1973, pp. 155–160; Reid, 1976, pp. 5–78; also Hirschi, 1975; and Tittle, 1975). In particular, more sophisticated "self-reported behavior" studies have been undertaken. The results of these and other investigations bearing on the issue of "true" deviance remain somewhat inconclusive. Most observers are now agreed that much potential crime and delinquency remains officially unrecorded and that the overall distribution of such behaviors within our society is considerably wider than official statistics might suggest. Yet interpretations continue to vary as to how much systematic bias these discrepancies entail. Some analysts insist that whereas much middle-class crime and delinquency remains hidden, the same is true of working-class offenses and that the official data are not significantly unrepresentative with respect to the most serious types of "street" crime. We have seen, similarly, that a debate continues regarding the mentally hospitalized, with such writers as Gove insisting that despite all typification, negotiation, and labeling, it is the most seriously ill who are most likely to end up in institutions. On the other hand, as we noted in Chapter 2, categoric differences in deviance "rates" (whether by race, social class, sex, or whatever) do inevitably reflect patterned variations in ways of defining and reacting as well as possible variations in the actual incidence of problematic behaviors. We have also considered the crucial role of power resources in affecting individual negotiation. Although none of this would *have* to imply substantial systematic bias, relatively few contemporary deviance analysts would assert that official rate figures are completely free of processing-induced distortion.

An intriguing and perhaps somewhat radical conception of the meaning of official statistics—one which, depending on how it is interpreted, can be seen either to eliminate or to evade the problem of assessing the discrepancy between "actual" and recorded deviance—has been suggested by Kitsuse and Cicourel (Kitsuse and Cicourel, 1963). They argue that official statistics should be considered an object of investigation to be explained in their own right. Our primary interest should not be in what they might tell us about the causation of deviance, but rather in exploring the causation of the rates themselves. From this standpoint, the essence of control agency activity is not really reacting "to" deviance, but rather engaging in a **rate-producing process**. Adopting a radical version of the social constructionist outlook mentioned earlier, these authors insist that, in effect, those rates are what deviance really is. Viewing the selection and processing of identified deviators against the background of some supposedly larger pool of "real" ones may only serve to obscure the definitional-reactional process *through which* deviance comes about. "To reject these statistics as 'unreliable' because they fail to record the 'actual' rate of deviant behavior assumes that certain behavior is always deviant independent of social actions which define it as deviant" (Kitsuse and Cicourel, p. 136; see also Rains, 1975). Direct study of the work of control agencies, including explanation of their organizational "output" (cases processed, statistics recorded, etc.) is, then, among the most meaningful and straightforward ways to study the "causes" of deviance.

THE ORGANIZATIONAL CONTEXT

Kitsuse and Cicourel have thus suggested one statistical sense in which it can be said that organizations produce deviance. This is also the import of the funneling process itself, and we should realize that Kitsuse and Cicourel are not denying the existence of typification and selective processing of cases; rather, their criticism has to do with describing the nonselected instances as deviance. (In much the same way, this text has stressed the distinction between mere occurrence of a behavior and the assignment of deviantness.) However, organizations also produce deviance in yet another sense by providing the specific contexts within which particular instances of processing occur and particular outcomes are reached. Individuals who undergo deviance-processing, after all, do not confront the "agencies of control" in the abstract; on the contrary, they are thrust into specific organizational milieux. And, by the same token, the control agents who react to them do this reacting within the framework of a particular organization's ongoing operations. What the organization is like—what it is trying to accomplish, how it is structured formally and informally, and the pressures and problems it encounters—significantly determines what happens within it. Hence, the aforementioned reference to the "bureaucratization of deviance."

An increased use of organizational analysis in interpreting deviance is part of the "decompartmentalization" of the field cited at the beginning of this book. Sociologists of deviance have been bringing into their studies concepts and perspectives developed in the sociology of complex organizations, and, at the same time, students of organizations have shown growing interest in "people-processing" agencies. As we have seen, until recently deviance research and theorizing were heavily preoccupied with the individual deviator; as a consequence, interpretations of deviance were unlikely to build directly on work in the organizational field. What exploration of organizational factors did occur was largely restricted to two specific spheres. One was the closed or **total institution—**

particularly prisons and mental hospitals—and, in this connection, great stress was placed on the development in such settings of informal social organization, usually referred to as "inmate subculture." The other, mentioned earlier, was perhaps more implicit than explicit—some sociologists showed how "deviance and control" arose within organizations (informal norms and sanctions among workers, etc.).

As the major emphasis in sociological deviance studies came to be placed on processes of interaction rather than on norms and their functions, as such, the significance of organizations was seen in a new light. For one thing, under the process focus—with its implicit stress on processing sequences—a wider range of control agencies and more complex interorganizational processing "systems" were investigated. This expansion was tied to the growing preference for field studies, which now were undertaken not only in residential control institutions, but also in a wide variety of organizational contexts, such as courts, police departments—including patrol activities—probation departments, community mental health programs, etc. Even the view of general work organizations as a milieu in which job-related or other deviance might arise received new kinds of interactionist interpretation. Lemert's aforementioned analysis of paranoia (Lemert, 1962) suggested that being paranoid was not simply a "static condition," but one that developed over time and through interaction with others in the work situation. Often the people who ended up diagnosably paranoid had, in fact, correctly perceived that co-workers had been isolating, excluding, or manipulating them, even if they developed distorted (exaggerated and conspiratorial) impressions of the nature and extent of these activities. More recently, Goffman has presented an interpretation of deviance-defining in organizations that tries to steer some kind of middle course between "labeling" notions and certain "functionalist" ones (deviance as personal dysfunctioning, incapacity, etc.). In this view, deviantness is assigned for behavior that, in effect, is interactionally dysfunctional within a particular setting:

> Mental symptoms, then, are neither something in themselves nor whatever is so labeled; mental symptoms are acts by an individual which openly proclaim to others that he must have assumptions about himself which the relevant bit of social organization can neither allow him nor do much about.
> It follows that if the patient persists in his symptomatic behavior, then he must create organizational havoc and havoc in the minds of members (Goffman, 1972, p. 356).

Perhaps the most significant development in organizational analysis of deviance, however, has been the increasingly intensive exploration of the structure and workings of deviance-processing organizations themselves as "producers of deviance." Two main themes have been developed in this body of work: the organization's internal and external "relationships," and the organization's "needs" (as seen in work pressures, organizational goals and interests, and the development of entrenched ideologies).

Internal and External Relations

Organizational analysts commonly divide internal relations into three basic categories: client-client, staff-client, staff-staff. The first two received attention in traditional deviance studies. Analysis of inmate subculture was, of course, an exploration of client-client relations. The frequently evolving accommodations between custodial staff and this subculture (e.g., between prison guards and prisoners) provided a major focal point for examining staff-client relations. Since closed treatment and correctional institutions were the organizations most often studied, it was also to be expected that the characteristic conflicts and strains between "custodial" and "treatment" staff members working together in such settings would be the key theme in analyzing intrastaff interaction.

Research along all of these lines does continue today, and the findings remain useful for interpreting certain kinds of deviance-processing. In correctional institutions, the treatment-custody conflict point continues to have very strong pertinence. The following statements by staff members (in juvenile institutions), representing the two sides of this uneasy alliance, mirror the comments we noted earlier about the strain on any one control agent of confronting multiple mandates. Weber quotes a psychologist's remarks about nonprofessional colleagues:

> It seems that many of the cottage parents have worked out rather simple schemes for dealing with behavior problems. It apparently makes them more comfortable, even though it may be harmful to the boys. It's difficult to approach them about these things because you are apt to break down whatever relationship you have.

And the nonprofessionals were discomfited by what they saw as the unrealistic "book learning" approach of the specialists:

> It's fine and easy for you people working up in the administration building to come at eight o'clock, leave at five, and have a half-day off on Saturday, but we cottage parents are with the boys all the time. If we aren't, one of our helpers is.

> That guy who calls himself a psychologist is so busy studying what he calls psychopathology and working in therapy that he doesn't know the rest of the world the kid lives in. The way he is going about things, it doesn't look like he's going to have much chance to learn about it (quoted in Weber, 1969, pp. 429, 430).

Recent work on deviance has extended analysis of staff-staff relations and problems beyond this particular issue, in the process of examining a wider range of deviance-processing settings.

As we noted very briefly in the introduction to this chapter, control agents usually do their work in a context structured and influenced by some organization. Whatever the specific type of agency that is involved, the way in which it is organized—both formally and informally—will greatly affect how they go about their work and, thus, eventually what happens to processed deviators. Control organizations and processing systems may vary greatly as to the degree and substance of formal structuring. The military-bureaucratic organization of police forces—with their strict chain of command, military-type discipline, and the like—probably represents an extreme in formal lines of authority and accountability. According to one close observer, however, "The effort to inspire loyalty and a sense of duty in policemen by military discipline has never worked well, although every department uses the initial training period to instill some kind of fear into the recruits and maintains a bulky book of regulations employed to threaten, punish, and dismiss the recalcitrant, the lazy, and the untrustworthy" (Rubinstein, 1974, p. 13). This failure to exercise absolute control reflects the uncontrollable nature of the exigencies of police work "in the field," the officer's public as well as organizational mandate and accountability, and the inevitable compromise of formal authority through evolving informal working relationships between subordinates and supervisors. (Rubinstein provides a particularly good observation-based discussion of this last development.)

At the same time, the preoccupation of many police workers with aspects of the organization's internal structure probably does remain high and influence their work in various ways. One paradoxical consequence may be a loosening of control over some areas of police work. Thus Bittner suggests that, "one who is judged to be a good officer in terms of internal, military-bureaucratic codes will not even be questioned about his conduct outside of it. The message is quite plain: the development of resolutely careful work methods in the community may be nice, but it gets you nowhere!" (Bittner, 1970, p. 55). On the other hand, "it is far from unusual that officers decide whether to make an arrest or not on the basis of their desire to live within departmental regulation rather than on the merits of the case at hand" (Bittner, 1970, p. 56). Since "arrest quotas" (Rubinstein, 1974, pp. 44–54) and favorable "clearance rates" (cases disposed of, by arrest or otherwise; see Skolnick, 1966, 1975, ch. 8) are standard aspects of police work, responsiveness to department pressures does shape the officer's overall pattern of activity, even if militarylike structures cannot by themselves dictate precisely how, when, and where the arrests will be made. Comparative research on different types of police departments indicates further the complex impact of organization on activity. In a study by Wilson, a more highly "professionalized" department (bureaucratized, with high specialization, strict accountability, etc.) also had higher arrest rates for juveniles than did a more loosely structured "fraternal" department (Wilson, 1968a). While bureaucratization may reduce the individual officer's discretion in the field, this usually means, among other things, less freedom for informal handling of minor misbehaviors.

Whatever the degree of bureaucratization in a deviance-processing agency, each control agent occupies a specific position within the formal organizational structure. This implies some spelling out of the agent's "jurisdiction" and some degree of control over that person's exercise of discretion. Even more important, it places the agent within a network of relations within the organization, the nature of which significantly structures and influences the job. In order to really understand a control agent's work and, hence, also its consequences, study of his or her **role-set**—the set of other established positions in the organization with whose occupants regular job-related interaction is necessary—is very important. To fully understand the place of the judge in a criminal court, the judge's relations with colleagues on the bench, prosecutors, defense attorneys, and other court staff must be considered. Likewise, the example of the psychiatrists and cottage parents in a juvenile institution noted above provides another example of the need for control agents regularly to work with other role-incumbents in an organizational setting.

These internal relationships are usually in some degree hierarchically structured, and how a particular role fits into such an ordering of the various organizational positions significantly affects those occupying it. In his study of a juvenile court, Emerson found that the chief judge exercised a wide-ranging authority over various aspects of the organization's work. This authority not only included operating rules and procedures for the court, but also extended to hiring, organizing and overseeing court staff, and establishing general policies that court-associated probation officers were expected to implement. The judge also controlled the balance between legal formality (procedural safeguards, etc.) and informal "individualizing" in the juvenile hearings themselves. In this structure, the probation officer, appointed by the chief judge, occupied an ambiguous position:

> On the one hand, he performs the routine chores which keep the court operation going. His court work provides his occupational identification and elicits a great deal of commitment on his part. On the other hand, the probation officer has low professional status within the court itself, relative to both judges and clinic personnel. Furthermore, he is the organizational subordinate of the judges; probation officers hold their jobs at least partially at the discretion of the chief judge, who may dismiss an officer for "cause" subject to review by the Probation Board, and who also directs and evaluates their work. However, the officer's practical knowledge and experience tend to offset this low professional and hierarchical standing (Emerson, 1969, pp. 16–17).

As the references here to "routine chores" and "practical knowledge and experience" begin to indicate, the formally specified role structure of a control agency invariably is mediated through emerging patterns of informal working relations. This is so to such a degree that often one cannot easily distinguish between the formal and informal structuring of interaction. However, assuming such a distinction to be possible, one would probably have to conclude that the informal patterns have even greater importance than do the formal ones. No "table of organization" can fully prescribe how the ongoing work of the agency will be done or how incumbents of the various interrelated roles will interact with each other. We have seen, particularly in connection with plea bargaining, the tendency for informal cooperative patterns within the organization to emerge over time and on the basis of collective experience. Underlying this development are the need to "get the job done" in as expeditious and smooth-running a manner as possible and the fact that the various deviance workers must maintain continuing, on-the-job relationships (and, hence, must also "get along with each other," at least to a reasonable extent). These needs extend across the processing of specific cases and transcend the formal designations of particular work roles and objectives.

That this is so was best illustrated by the already cited cooperation between prosecutors and public defenders (studied by Sudnow, Blumberg, and others) who, if their formal "job descriptions" were fully adhered to, would be adversaries much more than collaborators. The extent to which the opposite occurs is well depicted by Sudnow:

> . . . the district attorney, and the county which employs them both, can rely on the P.D. not to attempt to morally degrade police officers in cross examination; not to impeach the state's witnesses by trickery; not to attempt an exposition of the entrapment methods of narcotics agents; not to condemn the community for the "racial prejudice that produces our criminals" (the phrase used by a private attorney during closing argument); not to challenge the prosecution of "these women who are trying to raise a family without a husband" (the statement of another private attorney during closing argument on a welfare fraud case); in sum, not to make an issue of the moral character of the administrative machinery of the local courts, the community or the police. He will not cause any serious trouble for the routine motion of the court conviction process (Sudnow, 1965, p. 273).

Although the fact that the public defender is employed by the county suggests an element of official "cooptation" here, the working accommodations that develop go beyond what any such governmental control or influence might imply. They are present in most private organizations as well as in public ones. Deviance workers who participate in a joint processing endeavor, who must develop and promptly implement shared routines, who must deal with each other as human beings daily over long periods of time, and who face common job pressures and sometimes joint accountability inevitably develop a kind of "we" feeling. They come to form a kind of "processing community." Their relationship becomes one of colleagues, co-workers in a regularized enterprise.

The external relations of social control organizations are at least as important as the internal ones. An agency's "outside" relationships often are exceedingly complex. The organization most often is enmeshed in an interorganizational network, aspects of which must constantly be taken into account in the course of doing its own work. It would be a mistake, furthermore, to assume that such complexity exists only in the largest, most heterogeneous metropolitan areas. In one study of a youth services agency in "a cornbelt county" of only 105,000 population, it was noted that the county's main urban center was served by eight agencies "whose primary function is dealing with pre-adults" and an additional twelve having "a major interest" in such people (Berry, 1975). Sometimes outside agencies are in competition with the organization for clients or for public support and fundings. At other times, a control organization will have to work directly with various outside agencies on a continuing basis, their efforts combining as parts of a yet broader deviance-processing "system." Particularly when this happens, problems of jurisdiction, authority, and organizational coordination can easily arise.

For one broad domain of deviance-processing, such a situation has been depicted as follows:

> . . . in the field of delinquency control, there is no clear authority channel for the resolution of disagreements. Police systems operate largely on the local and municipal level, probation and the courts operate on a district or county level, and correctional facilities operate on the state level. When psychiatric services are made available, they are typically organized through state mental health units, although their actual services may occur at the level of the district court. The point is simply that there is no single centralized agency that operates throughout the process. Providing that each group remains within legal bounds, none has the right to tell the other how to do their work (Wheeler, *et al.,* 1968, p. 33).

This is, of course, a description of juvenile justice processing systems in general. In specific instances, and much as in the case of an organization's internal relations, the complexities and difficulties that appear "on paper" frequently will be moderated in the course of time and experience by informal working arrangements. Mutual dependence and the need to maintain enduring occupational relationships are, again, key factors in this development. Actually, all kinds of unexpected factors may facilitate or impede cooperation. For example, in Emerson's juvenile court study, the good working relations between that court's probation officers and the local police department reflected, in part, "a common lower-middle class Irish background, as well as a tendency for probation officers to be upwardly mobile policemen (two of the court's probation officers came from police backgrounds). It also reflects a common nonprofessional status in a field increasingly preempted by professionals" (Emerson, 1969, p. 47).

Social control organizations must not only take into account outside agencies that work directly in their area of substantive concern, they must also accommodate their work to a variety of other external agencies, pressures, and "forces." The precise nature of these outside influences will vary somewhat from situation to situation; however, direct sources of funding and more general support as seen through "public opinion" and "good community relations" will almost always be two key orienting themes in this regard. In addition, there will usually be some significant relationship to or concern for the legislative, judicial, and law-enforcement systems; the local political and party system; and the local media of mass communication. Depending on a control agency's specific focus, any number of private organizations, groups, and "lobbies" can come into the picture—be they educational, religious, philanthropic, or "political" in nature.

Figure 6.2 presents a hypothetical depiction of some of the more significant external relationships with which a local multipurpose agency for the handicapped would probably have to contend. As can be seen there, the broad range

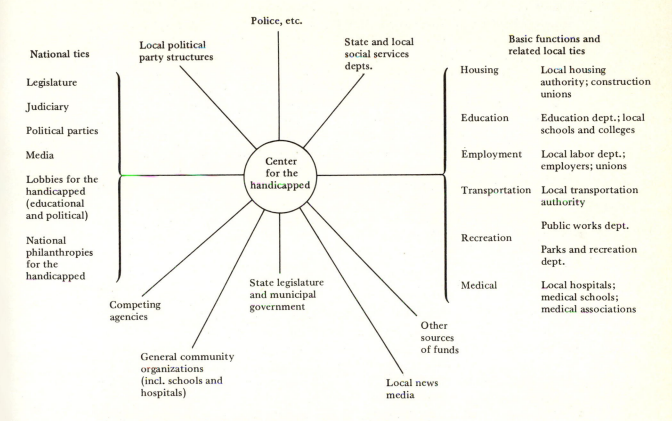

Figure 6.2. External relations of a center for the handicapped.

of likely outside agencies and forces reflects *multiple levels* of authority and influence—local, ranging from municipal through county to state (though these are not differentiated in the chart), and national—and also the *multiple functions* of the organization itself as reflected in the various substantive spheres of social life its services touch on. Through efforts to serve its clients' needs in such diverse areas as medical rehabilitation, housing, education, employment, transportation, and recreation, the agency will be influenced by and will want to exert influence on a very large number of outside organizations and public authorities. Among these external units locally will be some with which it may have to deal frequently on a continuing basis, including perhaps the local social service department, the police, and local hospitals and schools. At various levels, the agency's work will also bear some relation to sources of funding, influence on and control by government (legislative, judicial, administrative, political party structures, etc.), and the nature of public opinion. Although some of these forces may, at the national level, seem quite removed from the day-to-day operations of a given local agency, they can have a strong influence on its work. Ultimately, it is through what goes on at this broader societal level that an organization's overall mandate, jurisdiction, support, and operating conditions will be determined.

Displacement of Goals

The foregoing discussion has already revealed the gist of the goal-displacement process. One of the most significant ramifications of both internal and external organizational relations, for example, is that the problems they pose and the adaptive patterns to which they give rise often become major preoccupations of the workers. As Merton has emphasized more generally, under such conditions, bureaucratic means often are transformed into ends in themselves:

> Discipline, readily interpreted as conformance with regulations, whatever the situation, is seen not as a measure designed for specific purposes but becomes an immediate value in the life-organization of the bureaucrat. This emphasis, resulting from the displacement of the original goals, develops into rigidities and an inability to adjust readily. Formalism, even ritualism, ensues with an unchallenged insistence upon punctilious adherence to formalized procedures. This may be exaggerated to the point where primary concern with conformity to the rules interferes with the achievement of the purposes of the organization, in which case we have the familiar phenomenon of technicism or red tape of the official (Merton, 1957, p. 199).

Organizational theorist Amitai Etzioni gives as an illustration of this tendency the social worker who rigidly applies agency policy despite a personal judgment in a given situation that an exception may be called for. As he puts it, "The policy [his specific example is one of allowing children, however disturbed, to remain in home situations] becomes the prevailing criterion for decision, and the worker bends the clients' needs to fit the policy" (Etzioni, 1964, p. 12).

One of the major reasons why informal working arrangements emerge within formal bureaucratic structures is that workers need to have ways of circumventing such organizational inflexibility. As we have seen, the everyday operations of social control agencies to a considerable extent reflect this development of informal modes of adaptation. Some of these adaptations are, at least in part, worked out by individual deviance workers "in the field" (certain of the police practices we have noted, while not totally unique to particular officers, may be of this type). Even more often, perhaps, the adaptive patterns are collective in nature, reflecting the situation of a number of workers who must get together and cooperate in order to manage the standard tasks involved in a specific job of deviance-processing. Frequently the informal patterns and the officially prescribed ones blend into each other in complex ways. Through evolving practice, the formal structures bend and the stated rules are relaxed in order to enhance work performance and worker morale.

Such relaxations and accommodations do not, however, eliminate the problem of **goal displacement.** If anything, these informal working arrangements may be even more likely than formal policies and rules to become ends in themselves, supplanting the original purposes of the organization. In both cases, what seems not uncommon is that *sustaining the organization itself and managing the work situation* begin to take precedence over the substance of the organization's work. Who the agency is dealing with and also what its supposed substantive objectives are recede into the background. When this happens, the *real criteria* applied in dealing with cases may be ones of expediency, efficiency, and worker or organizational self-interest. Control agents' regular use of typification, the cooperative behavior as co-workers of functionaries who ostensibly should oppose each other (e.g., prosecutors and public defenders), and the tempering of agency policies in order to maintain adequate funding and good "community relations," are only some of the common patterns that reflect use of such criteria.

One way or another, the significance of this for the perceived deviators who face processing is clear: What happens to them may very well depend upon other factors besides the problems they allegedly pose and the possible underlying problems they have. Because they are typically processed as instances of predetermined categories, the facts and "merits" of individual cases are most unlikely to receive full and careful attention. A good, if perhaps extreme, illustration of this is found in Thomas Scheff's report on an observational study (conducted in a midwestern state) of court procedures for the screening of involuntary mental hospitalization cases:

> . . . in court B, we observed twenty-two judicial hearings, all of which were conducted perfunctorily and with lightning rapidity. (The mean time of these hearings was 1.6 minutes.) The judge asked each patient two or three routine questions: "How do you feel?" "How are you being treated?" "Would you cooperate with the doctors if they think you should stay awhile?" *Whatever* the patient's answer, however, the judge immediately ended the hearing, managing in this way to average less than two minutes per patient (Scheff, 1966, pp. 135–136).

In discussing these procedures with the judges and other court officials, the researchers learned that "although the statutes give the court the responsibility for the decision to confine or release persons alleged to be mentally ill, they would rarely if ever take the responsibility for releasing a mental patient without a medical recommendation to that effect" (Scheff, 1966, pp. 138–139). Accordingly, they followed up their observation of court hearings by intensive study of the work of court-appointed psychiatrists and other physicians who examined "patients" for this purpose. The researchers were able to directly observe 26 of the screening interviews:

> Interviews ranged in length from five minutes to 17 minutes, with the mean time being 10.2 minutes. . . . All of the examiners seemed quite hurried. One psychiatrist, after stating in an interview (before we observed his examinations) that he usually took about thirty minutes, stated:

It's not remunerative. I'm taking a hell of a cut. I can't spend 45 minutes with a patient. I don't have the time, it doesn't pay.

In the eight examinations that we observed, this physician actually spent, 8, 10, 5, 8, 8, 7, 17, and 11 minutes with the patients, or an average of 9.2 minutes (Scheff, 1966, p. 144).

Evaluating in a more substantive way the screening examinations they had observed, the researchers concluded that in many cases it was questionable whether the statutory bases for hospitalization were present, even though the examiner made an unqualified recommendation that the person be hospitalized. This almost invariable recommendation, Scheff concluded, stemmed from an apparent strong presumption of illness, use of which was highly expedient for the examiners. Since they only received a flat fee ($10 per examination), undertaking the kind of thorough documentation that might support a convincing recommendation of release simply did not pay.

Ideologies and Vested Interests

A control organization's "own needs" may not only lead to specific patterns of expediency in implementing processing mechanisms of this sort, but may also more broadly influence its policies and programs. Adaptation Ten, based on Scott's study of blindness agencies, suggests the close relation that may exist between such organizational imperatives as funding and public support, on the one hand, and the substance of rehabilitation ideologies and agency programs on the other hand. It is the interplay between such elements that in large measure determines what happens to the organization's clients.

ADAPTATION TEN
Blindness Agencies*

Persons who have a physical disability such as blindness are not usually considered wrongdoers who are to be held "responsible" for their condition. Nonetheless, as we have seen, they often elicit from other people responses that, in effect, mark them as "deviant." These reactions of others may, in varying degree and depending upon all the circumstances, deeply affect disabled persons' self-conceptions and behavior and limit the practical opportunities open to them. It was this sort of impact that sociologist Robert A. Scott had in mind when he titled the book based on his extensive field research on blindness organizations, *The Making of Blind Men*. Such organizations, Scott succinctly noted, "teach people who have difficulty seeing how to behave like blind people."

Behind this seemingly paradoxical or quizzical statement lay Scott's recognition that a disability such as blindness is not just an organic condition, but also a learned social role. Indeed, it is a role learned, if not played, by all members of our society insofar as they assimilate early in life various beliefs about, attitudes toward, and expectations of blind people. Since misleading preconceptions about the blind are widespread, and given the position of dependence from which the blind person invariably confronts situations of human interaction, the blindness role tends to place one, all other things being equal, among the relatively powerless in the society. Yet precisely because of the stigmatizing and limiting preconceptions, the person with a serious visual handicap often will be forced to accommodate to the role, notwithstanding a desire to adopt other outlooks and patterns of behavior.

Scott found that the prevailing ways of identifying blind people actually apply the blindness label to a broad and diversified population encompassing a wide range of degrees of visual impairment. Stating that "the currently accepted administrative definition of blindness is a crude and imprecise method of categorizing people who have severe loss of vision," he went on to note that in fact most people who are labeled and treated as "blind" have at least "some measurable visual acuity." This fact underlines the sociological importance of the process of learning the blindness role: "The strength of this socialization process is suggested by the fact that people who can see come to behave as though they cannot and that from so heterogeneous a population such homogeneity is eventually created."

Surveying the many organizations and facilities that make up "the blindness system," Scott discovered that no overall policy or plan guided their activities.

* *Source:* A summary and interpretation of Robert A. Scott, *The Making of Blind Men*. New York: Russell Sage Foundation, 1969, chs. 5–8. Direct quotations used with permission.

Rather, they comprised "an aggregate of bureaucratic entities that share a common interest in the problems of blindness, but whose activities are not coordinated and integrated to any meaningful degree." Furthermore, their services were suitable for and made available to only a "small, highly selected portion of the blind population." At least 60 percent of all the organizations' resources were earmarked for services to children and non-aged adults. Such important categories as multiply-handicapped children and the elderly blind received relatively little attention from these agencies.

For those individuals who did become clients of blindness agencies, Scott found there was strong pressure both to consider themselves as totally "blind" (notwithstanding possible residual vision) and to adopt the views about blindness held by agency workers. If a client wished to progress in an agency's program, it was necessary to accept and reinforce the clinician's conception of his or her problems and prospects. Alert clients, Scott noted, were therefore quick to develop the requisite "insights." Because the agency workers have such a strong hand in defining and shaping efforts to deal with blindness problems, their beliefs and outlooks about the condition take on an overriding significance. Scott analyzed two major approaches to blindness that may be adopted by agency workers (he interviewed approximately 100) and that can significantly shape the work of blindness organizations. One he termed restorative, the other accommodative. The restorative approach aims at maximizing the blind person's capacities for independence and is grounded in the assumption that most blind people can be enabled to lead a reasonably normal life. It seeks to identify and restore the several kinds of losses associated with blindness. Thus, efforts are made to develop the other senses to make up for the loss of sight; the person is trained in everyday skills and the use of mechanical devices to restore the sense of "psychological security" and assisted to meet the attitudes that sighted people are likely to adopt toward him. Loss of mobility is combatted through training in use of a long cane or guide dog; communication loss through braille. A wide variety of specific techniques may be used. "The goal of this process is to reintegrate the components of the restored personality into an effectively functioning whole." Whichever techniques are used, it is the goals and outlooks of the workers that most distinguish this approach. The focus on fulfilling the individual—insofar as possible—is likely, according to Scott, to have "a profound impact" on the client's self-image.

If the restorative approach is morale-enchancing and option-maximizing, the accommodative approach is likely to have contrasting effects. In agencies adopting the latter, blindness is seen as posing almost insurmountable obstacles to leading an independent existence. Those blind persons who are able to do so are considered exceptional, rather than taken as models on which to base general programs for the blind. Scott found many specific manifestations of this view. For example:

The physical environment in such agencies is often contrived specifically to suit certain limitations inherent in blindness. In some agencies, for example, the elevators have tape recorders that report the floor at which the elevator is stopping and the direction in which it is going, and panels of braille numbers for each floor as well. Other agencies have mounted over their front doors special bells that ring at regular intervals to indicate to blind people that they are approaching the building. Many agencies maintain fleets of cars to pick up clients at their homes and bring them to the agency for services. In the cafeterias of many agencies, special precautions are taken to serve only food that blind people can eat without awkwardness. In one agency cafeteria, for example, the food is cut before it is served, and only spoons are provided.

According to Scott, the implicit assumption underlying the work of the accommodative agencies is that "most of their clients will end up organizing their lives around the agency." For such a limited purpose, the approach trains them well. But the other side of this is that since the entire socialization process has been geared to such highly limited functioning, it almost ensures an inability to function adequately in the larger community. Although Scott did not claim to present any systematic data on the outcomes produced through the different approaches, he stated his belief that the "independent blind" probably comprise the smallest subgroup in the blindness population. This particular outcome seems almost totally unlikely under an accommodative program.

An important finding in Scott's research was that although most blindness organizations give some lip service to the restorative approach, their actual practice seems to follow the accommodative model. He attributed this not only to staff outlooks, but also to economic, manpower, and community pressures confronting the agencies. While most blindness organizations have managed to attain generous financial support from the community, this economic security has depended upon their adopting outlooks and practices consistent with dominant community sentiments. According to Scott, the perceived needs of the sighted public at large, rather than the needs of blind people themselves, have been allowed to shape the policies of blindness agencies. Central to these perceived needs is the isolation of blind people, so that the sighted can avoid contact with them. This avoidance tendency follows from the stereotypes about and fear of blindness, and the uneasiness and guilt sighted people experience in interaction with the blind. Public support of the agencies is closely tied to their facilitating this avoidance:

> Blind persons are strongly encouraged to seek assistance at blindness agencies, but there is covert, yet stubborn, resistance in the community to any genuine movement of blind people from the agency back into the mainstream of community life. . . . the agency for the blind that genuinely stresses the reintegration of its clients may have difficulty raising enough money to keep its doors open. This sequestering of the blind from the community not only minimizes the occasions for contact between the sighted and the blind, but also decreases the visibility of the problem. The blindness agency

that is able to contain blind people and to control their access to the community de-
creases awareness of the problem within the community.

Thus, it is the most accommodative of the agencies that have been most successful
in maintaining financial support. Interestingly, Scott noted, both sighted people
and blindness workers feel guilty about this outcome and, to assuage this guilt,
require continuous expressions of approval and gratitude by the clients. "Perhaps
the most insidious consequence of the vicious cycle," he commented, "is that the
blind who have been victimized by this arrangement are ultimately required to
give the public assurances that captivity is their genuine desire."

The pressure to maintain an accommodative strategy is heightened by
the fact that there is a relatively large number of agencies competing for clients.
Once an agency gets a client, it doesn't want to lose him or her. Furthermore, at
least some of the blindness workers develop a "vested interest" in such strategies.
The financial standing of their agencies and, hence, their own job security, may
depend upon maintaining the accommodative pattern.

All of these factors come together to shape Scott's conclusion that the
accommodative approach to blindness:

. . . contains many of the features of an ideology. This term, which is borrowed
from studies of political conflict, implies that some of the beliefs that blindness workers
hold about what blind people need or want are bound up with their vested interests
and those of the agencies that employ them. "Needs" of blind people are shaped, molded,
and even invented ex post facto to explain why service programs exist. These needs are
not "discovered" by independent scientific inquiry; rather, they are the needs that
blind people must have if they are to fit into and be served by programs that have arisen
for other reasons.

Although the development of social control policies and programs partly
reflects the pressures and interrelationships confronted by the agencies that deal
with a particular "problem," worker commitment to those policies and programs
often becomes so entrenched that they begin to take on an independent force of
their own. When this happens, the underlying belief systems do more than provide theories and rationales for dealing with deviance problems in particular
ways. They take on the character of self-perpetuating ideologies that mask the
vested interests of workers and agencies in the maintenance and reinforcement of
those approaches and institutions from which they derive benefit. These ideologies may even become the basis for concerted public efforts by the organizations
themselves to shape outlooks and deviance-processing arrangements in the directions they favor. Under these circumstances, social control agents and agencies
can indeed play the role of "moral entrepreneur" (see Chapter 7), openly or
covertly striving to influence collective definitions on deviance issues.

To speak of vested interest (a built-in personal and especially economic
stake in a particular state of affairs) is not to cast aspersions on what are usually

sincere personal convictions as to how best to deal with deviance problems. From a sociological standpoint, the objective consequences of deviance-processing schemes and systems are at least as important as the conscious motives of individuals, favoring or opposing them. Furthermore, few sociologists would go so far as to say that vested interest provides a *complete* explanation of deviance situations. Clearly, more is involved in these situations than what is suggested by such truisms as that psychiatrists "need" patients and prison guards "owe their jobs to" the presence of prisoners. Nonetheless, it is an important fact of life that deviance is big business, that many organizations as well as individuals do derive their living from it (see Hawkins and Tiedeman, 1975, ch. 6). As we saw in Chapter 3, Karl Marx himself recognized the irony of crime as an economically productive source of work, for criminals and also for those who provide services for them or who work "against" them. (Indeed, he went on to note that, in the most general sense, even professors who write about crime and publish their theories as a "commodity" on the market, indirectly derive benefit from it!) Two illustrations of broadly expanding economic interest in society-wide deviance policies and trends are suggested in the following statements:

Since the end of the Great Society in 1968, "learning disabilities" has become a bonanza in an otherwise depressed and barren territory, a source of funds from state and federal agencies which have been cutting back in other areas of educational support, a fertile field for prospective or unemployed teachers "where you know there'll be a job," and a means of attracting students to schools of education facing diminishing enrollments. In the process it has become the foundation of a new and thriving industry of private schools, diagnostic centers, clinics, ranches, summer camps and remedial projects, and of the materials and literature which these employ to work their cures (Schrag and Divoky, 1976, p. 69).

About 860 prison facilities are either under construction or in planning stages. . . . Prison experts estimate that the new projects will cost some $5 billion—a sum that means business for contractors, architects, and equipment producers, who have been hard hit by the decline in school and public housing projects in recent years (Luxemberg, 1977).

For the most part, these very broad economic interconnections have only a subtle and indirect influence on priorities and decisions concerning deviance issues. Sometimes, however, the connections are more explicit and the influence more direct. A further finding in Scott's blindness study, for example, was that many workers in blindness agencies had developed their expertise almost entirely through years of work experience and had little in the way of relevant formal credentials. With the growth of professionalism in the blindness field, such untrained workers have low job mobility; their status and security have become heavily dependent upon "the continued functioning of the agency with which they are identified" (Scott, 1969, pp. 101–103).

One much-discussed example of the role of control agencies as active campaigners for policy measures that support their own interests has been that of the Federal Bureau of Narcotics in relation to the passage and early enforcement of the Marihuana Tax Act (one of the most important early antinarcotics laws) during the 1930s. Following up Becker's suggestion that the Bureau had "furnished most of the enterprise that produced" this legislation (Becker, 1963, p. 138), Donald Dickson stressed the organizational imperatives lying behind the Bureau's action. Bureaucratic considerations, he argued, were more important than moralistic ones in activating this particular "moral crusade." Examining both the work of the agency and its lobbying efforts over a 30-year period, Dickson concluded that, "Faced with a steadily decreasing budget, the Bureau responded as any organization so threatened might react; it tried to appear more necessary, and it tried to increase its scope of operations (Dickson, 1968, p. 155). Although this interpretation of the origin of the marihuana law recently has been challenged by other researchers (Galliher and Walker, 1977; and see Musto, 1973) who claim to demonstrate that, in fact, the Bureau did not play such an activist role in that instance, the entrepreneurial activity of the same agency in the complementary area of heroin control policies has been heavily documented (King, 1953; Schur, 1962; Lindesmith, 1965).

The above statement by Dickson suggests some points of persisting general importance, whatever conclusion we might reach regarding the historical support for his specific argument about the marihuana legislation. As his reference to an "organization so threatened" indicates, the significance of the element of perceived threat in shaping deviance situations (much emphasized earlier in this book) is great with respect to social control workers and agencies, as well as to other individuals and social units. (We will return to both the question of threat and to collective efforts to respond to threat in the next chapter.) His comments about an agency trying to appear more necessary and expanding its scope of operations also have wide applicability. As Dickson emphasized in his article, public control agencies may have some special resources of legitimation, power, and publicity that facilitate their influence on policy-making. At the same time, however, they are especially dependent upon public support and funding through the legislature. Characteristically this leads to a kind of "numbers game." The organization alternates between producing statistics that purport to show the alarming extent or growth of the relevant deviance "problem" (and, hence, how "necessary" the agency's work is), and ones that indicate steady reductions in the problem (thus, demonstrating how well the agency is doing its job). We see here, of course, yet another ground for questioning official "data." In a way, expanding its scope of operations serves the organization in both respects. Such expansion creates the "alarming" statistics, but it also provides the agency with increased opportunities for demonstrating its worth.

It might be noted that the self-interested urge to expand operations is not by any means limited to public bureaucracies or even to control agencies (public and private) that incorporate or provide large numbers of paid jobs. The processing or assisting of deviators provides the overarching *raison d'etre* for all control organizations. Thus, even some of the organizations that make widespread use of ex-deviator volunteers (discussed further in this chapter under the heading "Participatory Treatment") demonstrate this tendency toward problem-expansion, "creating" deviance as they "react" to it. A recent student of Alcoholics Anonymous, discussing member activity geared to the "twelfth step" in the A.A. credo ("Having had a spiritual awakening as the result of these steps, we tried to carry this message to alcoholics, and to practice these principles in all our affairs."—A.A. World Services, 1953), has stated:

> Converting new members and believers to A.A. philosophy is called, accordingly, "Twelfth step work." Here A.A. senior members form the core of an unpaid army of volunteers who make house calls, hold workshops, speak before high school students, PTA meetings, visit alcohol treatment centers, jails, mental institutions, medical societies—you name it . . . the size and scope of this anti-alcohol movement is phenomenal. Perhaps not since the temperance movement has such an anti-alcohol lobby come together. Because of A.A.'s broad definition of alcoholism (anyone who has trouble with alcohol) and their recommended treatment (total abstinence), one could say that it certainly resembles a "neotemperance" movement itself (Boscarino, 1977, p. 179).

That such activity is not simply educational in nature is evident in the same researcher's findings regarding the growing A.A.-generated and reinforced tendency for industry to set up alcohol referral programs for employees. He found that many of the counselors in such programs "go out and actively 'search' for such cases. For example, one counselor who worked in a civil service agency that gave a large number of sick-days off during the year, said that he would go out to branch offices and look through attendance records. If he found an individual was taking too many 'long weekends,' as he put it, he would call the individual into his office and begin to interrogate the "suspect.' " Examining other bases for referral used in these programs, which also frequently involved active efforts to find cases, Boscarino concluded that, "The moral here seems to be that if one looks hard enough, one will always find enough alcoholics to justify the existence of these 'treatment' programs" (Boscarino, 1977, p. 104).

TREATMENT AS CONTROL

No attempt will be made in this book to survey the wide-ranging fields of "corrections"and "treatment." These topics are dealt with extensively in separate courses on criminology and penology, sociology of medicine, sociology of mental illness, sociology of rehabilitation, and the like. The burgeoning literature of relevant research and theory has been reviewed in numerous specialized texts, readers, and summaries of the work in those fields. (For representative readings, theoretical overviews, and extensive citations see for *corrections:* Cressey, ed., 1961; Hazelrigg, ed., 1969; Johnston, Savitz, and Wolfgang, eds., 1970; Reid, 1976, pp. 468–717; and for *treatment:* Mechanic, 1968; Mechanic, 1969; Freidson, 1970;

Freidson and Lorber, eds., 1972; Clinard, 1974, pp. 570–624; Clausen, 1976). Here and in parts of the next chapter we will be touching only on a number of findings, ideas, and developments in these areas that have special relevance for a general interpretation of deviance.

Although we have by now reviewed most of the basic "ingredients" of the deviantizing process, some note must be taken of the special qualities that attach to that process in certain treatment contexts. Entry into a treatment or correctional institution or program is, after all, one of the more fateful steps in the "careers" of many identified deviators. Such institutions and programs are, likewise, among the most important of the organizational contexts within which deviance-processing occurs and control agents work. We have already noted in passing some of the controversy over whether treatment "works" or "backfires." This is a matter to which we will return in Chapter 7, in considering some recent trends in the treatment-corrections fields. In the present section, our main focus will be on certain "control" elements in selected treatment contexts. Two contrasting settings for treatment will be briefly considered—the "total" institution and the much more open and "participatory" context developed in several group-oriented treatment programs. These two categories have special importance for several reasons. In a sense, they represent the opposing *extremes on a continuum* of types of treatment context, ranging from those in which the control aspect is central to those in which it is minimal. Second, studying these polar types underscores the *importance of the organization* in providing a milieu that influences control efforts and that specifies the nature of deviator-control agent relations. And finally, interpretation of these two extreme contexts has produced ideas of *special theoretical significance* for our comprehensive understanding of deviance.

The Total Institution

Erving Goffman's book *Asylums* (1961), already cited in this text several times, was a landmark work that has enormously influenced the sociology of deviance. Based largely on a year of observational field work at St. Elizabeth's Hospital (a federal mental institution) in Washington, D.C., *Asylums* brought together many insightful comments on the inmate's situation, staff members' problems, and the overall hospital milieu to produce a comprehensive and incisive interpretation of what goes on in that particular kind of institutional context. Part of Goffman's contribution lay in *recognizing that it is a general type* of context—to at least some extent, the mental hospital displays certain key features in common with prisons, concentration camps and prisoner-of-war camps, military compounds, and, in some respects, even such places as boarding schools and monastaries (see also the recent discussion by Foucault, 1977). All of these institutions are places of "residence and work where a large number of like-situated individuals, cut off from the wider society for an appreciable period of time, together lead an enclosed, formally administered round of life" (Goffman, 1961, xiii). Another reason why the book has been so influential is that Goffman in a way combined the virtues of "traditional" sociology (including concern for structure, function, organization, etc.) with those of the more processual "natural history" perspective. Thus, he could develop a sequential analysis of the inmate's "moral career" which related the individual's changing self-conceptions to various elements of organizational structure and routine. Although the book was not particularly about deviance *per se,* it made a vital contribution—along with the work of Lemert, Becker, Kitsuse, Erikson, and others—to the growth of a labeling or interactionist perspective in the deviance field.

Among the major themes that Goffman developed in *Asylums* were the following:

1. The *all-enveloping round of life* in such institutions and the sharp separation between this life and that of the outside world.

2. The ritual *mortification* of entering inmates.

3. Enforced *dispossession of former identities* and a *"reassembly of the self"* to meet the requirements of the inmate role.

4. The high probability of *stigmatizing* consequences.

5. The resulting likelihood that mental hospitals and, perhaps, other kinds of total institutions were, *on balance, not accomplishing what they set out to do.*

As Goffman perceptively noted, in such institutions the spheres of sleep, work, and, to the extent it can persist, play are no longer separated the way they are on the outside. On the contrary, "all aspects of life are conducted in the same place, and under the same single authority" (Goffman, 1961, p. 6). Furthermore, each inmate is treated not as an individual person, but rather as one occupant of the standard inmate role or, we might say, as "nothing but" an inmate. Collectively, inmates must adhere to a closely scheduled existence imposed by the officials in charge. In order to dramatically mark the inmate's divorce from life on the outside and to establish the staff's authority and "distance" from those who are incarcerated, entering inmates are routinely subjected to a process of ritual mortification or "identity-stripping." This usually includes being stripped of one's possessions, normal appearance (clothing, hairstyle, etc.), one's privacy (often marked by a literal "stripping" of the new inmate), indeed, of everything that constitutes what Goffman calls the person's "identity kit." In this process, basic "territories of the self" are violated in ways that cannot always be reversed or remedied. Gradually, the person must adapt to this new inmate status and identity; most inmates begin to "learn the ropes," to "do their time," even to "work the system" for their relative short-term advantage.

Although recognizing that the consequences of all this are not absolutely uniform, Goffman emphasized the demeaning, defacing, dis-culturating impact. He depicted the patient's "moral career" (including prepatient, inpatient, and ex-patient phases) as one long status-degradation ceremony, from the effects of which it became most unlikely the person could ever fully recover. As far as what happens in the hospital itself is concerned, we encountered vivid illustration of key aspects of this degradation of the self in Adaptation Seven, the Rosenhan "pseudopatient" study. We saw in action there a process Goffman treated as central to identity-stripping and reconstituting—retrospective interpretation. We also noted that even the mock-patients experienced strong feelings of depersonalization and frustration at being reacted to by doctors and other staff as "nothing but" patients, indeed, as something akin to nonpersons. This treatment is tied to a mechanism referred to earlier, "role distance denial" (Lofland, 1969, pp. 170–171), which tends to be maximal in such total institutions. Officially prescribed arrangements, routines, and socially defined modes of interaction, between staff and inmates and between inmates themselves, leave little or no room for "preserves" of the self that would allow the person to avoid total engulfment in the institutionally designated role ("patient," "prisoner," etc.).

The **total institution,** then, constitutes a prototype of one extreme in the relation between organizational context and deviance-processing. The organizational arrangements dominate almost all aspects of the work being done in such an institution. In addition, the control component is at a maximum, whatever may be the official statements regarding the institution's work (Wright, 1975; Foucault, 1977). Less clear is the extent in the long run of the carry-over or deviance-amplifying effects of such work. The thrust of Goffman's argument is simply that when one has been an inmate in such an institution, one has experienced long-term and consistent imputations of a high degree of deviantness. It follows that some unusual resources, or unusual good luck, will be needed in order to shake off the esteem-lowering and prospect-diminishing ramifications of having been treated in that way. The ex-inmate must try to make up for many lost opportunities and to relearn old ways and unlearn new ways, not only of acting but also of thinking—about self as well as others. In addition, there is the undoubted taint of now having "a record" that in some degree continues to follow one around. Lofland refers to "place imputation," noting that morally tinged imputations are made with respect to territories and places as well as to people. "Imputations to places imply some conception of an appropriate (even if immoral) clientele felt typically to inhabit or to frequent them" (Lofland, 1969, p. 168). Knowledge that a person has been in a total institution is likely to activate imputations of that sort. If one has been there, then one *is* "that kind of person."

As we have already noted in a more general vein, there is little question but that some individuals do successfully disavow, neutralize, or combat such stigma. Goffman's analysis in no way implies that to do this is impossible, only that it is extremely difficult and that when it does occur, we can assume that some kinds of favorable resources and/or circumstances came into play. The interpretation offered in *Asylums* does not even require us to conclude that all of the forces and pressures *within* the total institution must work only in disvaluing and debilitating directions. Presumably certain rehabilitative efforts can produce some "restitutive" effects (see Gove, 1975, pp. 57–67), and, likewise, in some institutions the overall impact of "negative labeling" on self-esteem may be unclear or less than pervasive (see Tittle, 1972). What Goffman's work suggests is only that the total institution is a system containing many significant built-in obstacles to achieving overall outcomes "favorable" to the individual. Despite all of the aforementioned debate about precise *degrees* of success or failure, the overwhelming bulk of available evidence provides no reason to dispute that general contention.

At any rate, it is noteworthy that Goffman's work, as well as influencing the thinking of academic social scientists, has had a considerable impact in the public policy realm. It helped alert many institutional administrators and others involved in committing persons to such institutions to some significant unintended and undesired consequences of their work. It has also had an influence in promoting a recent general trend toward "decarceration" (to which we will return in the next chapter), in which increased interest has been shown in finding alternative, in-the-community approaches to social control. Notwithstanding this trend, however, Goffman's work remains important for the critical interpretation it provides of a still much-utilized type of control organization. Our society continues to "warehouse" numerous types of perceived deviators, ranging from convicted criminals to drug addicts to the implicitly disvalued aged, in total institution settings. As the reports summarized in the accompanying "news spot" indicate, the conditions under which at least some of these inmates (prisoners) are living continue to be extremely harsh ones, hardly likely to facilitate "rehabilitation."

Participatory Treatment

A strikingly different organizational context, and a contrasting balance between control and treatment elements, is found in a variety of voluntary rehabilitation programs run by ex-deviators themselves. Perhaps the classic example is Alcoholics Anonymous—a somewhat religiously tinged fellowship of self-designated former alcoholics (see Lemert, 1951, pp. 367–369; Maxwell, 1967; Sagarin, 1969, ch. 2; Trice and Roman, 1970; Clinard, 1974, pp. 486–492). A vital orienting point of the A.A. program is permanent abstinence. Alcoholics are viewed as having an allergylike basic predisposition to the condition, with which conventionally therapeutic "cures" cannot contend. Thus, the only way to deal with one's alcoholism is to stay away from drink entirely. Any evidence indicating that former alcoholics can undertake occasional social drinking with no serious mishaps meets with strong resistance from A.A., including the argument that such

NEWS SPOT
Recent Prison Conditions Condemned

(1976–1977). Statistics published at the beginning of 1977 showed that the number of people incarcerated in state and federal prisons had risen to a record level of 283,268—an increase of 13 percent over the prison population recorded the previous January. At the same time, surveys and investigations during the year repeatedly disclosed dissatisfaction, even on the part of correctional officials, concerning a wide variety of prison conditions. Surveyed by the nonprofit Correctional Information Service, prison administrators in 40 states reported that their prisons were overcrowded. Early in the year, Federal Judge Frank Johnson issued a much-publicized ruling in Alabama declaring that state's prison system to be plagued with "massive constitutional infirmities." He ordered state authorities to put into effect a minimum set of constitutional standards, which he delineated in 44 guidelines (each with various subdivisions) covering such basic matters as adequate living space, decent meals, reduction in guard-inmate racial disparity, meaningful jobs and needed educaton and training, adequate medical treatment, recreational opportunities, and regular visits.

In July of 1976, a New York State Commission of Correction investigating team sent to the Attica prison found conditions there to be "as bad, perhaps worse" than just before the inmate rebellion in 1971 that resulted in 43 deaths. The director of the investigating team reported that the prison was still badly overcrowded, that there had been recent inmate charges of "systematic brutality," and that tensions were extremely high. Describing the prison as a "combat situation," he asserted that, "The environment is so physical, so potentially dangerous, the power of both the inmates and the guards is so awesome, that it can go off at any time. Both sides have the power of death in their hands." Various incidents and public hearings have likewise focused attention on deplorable conditions in New York City's prisons. Early in May of 1977 the city's advisory, citizen Board of Correction proposed new minimum living standards for those institutions. According to one account, "If adopted, the recommendatons by the watchdog agency would significantly alter every aspect of daily prison life."

The proposal, however, at once provoked negative reaction in the city's Correction Department, which predicted many problems and lack of budgetary realism. The Department's Commissioner asserted that such changes would "cost many, many millions of dollars" and would create administrative confusion. Although the advisory board's proposals were well-intended, the Commissioner stated, "Standards must be promulgated that are responsive not only to the needs of inmates but must also take into account the ability of the taxpayers to pay and the department to administer." The new proposals, it appeared further, conflicted in some ways with an earlier set of standards called for the previous year by yet a third group—a state "watchdog" unit. At any rate, and regardless of which agency's views and proposals have exerted the most influence, there was little indication by the end of 1977 that conditions in New York City prisons had been greatly improved, and, indeed, there was little or no public disagreement about that fact.

Source: Based on news articles in *The New York Times,* January 14, 1976, p. 1; July 21, 1976, p. 1; February 18, 1977; May 5, 1977, p. B2.

persons were never really "alcoholics" (see discussion in Sagarin, 1969, pp. 48–53). Some years ago, Lemert succinctly characterized the organization as follows:

> Viewed objectively by the sociologist, the Alcoholics Anonymous organization is a sect integrated through missionizing activity. It redefines the self and role of the alcoholic as that of an ex-alcoholic, or as that of a special kind of biological person who can under no circumstances drink alcoholic liquors without wanting to drink himself into intoxication. Open confession of past alcoholic and other transgressions or "wrongs" is relied upon as a technique to bring about the unemotional acceptance of the socially castigated self (Lemert, 1951, p. 367).

Although the core of the A.A. program is the chapter meeting at which several members will speak, declaring that they are alcoholics and telling their "stories," also important is the mechanism of sponsorship of novices by established members and mutual assistance (to weather crises, etc.), and, as already mentioned, there is in addition an extensive educational and, in effect, proselytizing effort. While the organization's "treatment" ideology is a rather rigid one (the necessity or validity of which has often been thrown into question), it should be recognized that voluntary acceptance of it as a basic operating premise is a key to A.A.'s relative success. (Measuring this success is, as one might expect, difficult, and it is rendered all the more complicated by persisting uncertainty as to how given individuals might have fared under other approaches. However, there is general agreement that a good many one-time alcoholics have for long periods managed to remain abstinent within the A.A. program.) One specialist on the sociology of drinking problems, Harrison Trice, suggests several ways in which A.A. "works" for its members:

> Prominent among the reasons is A.A.'s effect on self-concepts. Thus through "Twelfth Step" work the A.A. member continues to see himself as he used to be. At the same time membership promotes an abstaining, acceptable image of the self. In addition, his role permits him to recapture a respectable social position in the community: A.A. is truly a "way back."
> Another important reason why A.A. works, once affiliation takes place, is that it sets up a network of social controls, for example, an "in-group" atmosphere that serves as a potent sobriety guide. Furthermore, the primary group flavor of A.A., a *gemeinschaft* [community] in a secular, anomic society, gives a member an opportunity to satisfy his need for warmth, reassurance, and dependency (Trice, 1966, p. 100).

The nature of the social control network to which Trice refers is, of course, in sharp contrast to the context of control in the total institution. Members assume "control" over each other and over themselves; there are no official "overseers" imposing an inescapable and all-enveloping authority and prescribed regime. Despite the fact that A.A. work does come to occupy much of the time of at least some of its members, no rigid enforced separation between the organization and life "outside" is present.

Recently, Alcoholics Anonymous has been of special interest to several deviance theorists who have seen it as possibly representing an exception to labeling interpretations. What they have focused on specifically is the mechanism through which members declare *themselves* to be *permanent* "alcoholics." Along with A.A.'s other self-control oriented activities and ideologies, this procedure has been referred to as "deviance avowal" (Turner, 1972) and as "delabeling" or "relabeling" (Trice and Roman, 1970). In this vein, one can go on to argue that, contrary to a central labeling thesis, the application of "negative labels" in this context appears to have predominantly deviance-reducing effects rather than deviance-amplifying ones. Turner's discussion of "avowal" may be particularly interesting, for it highlights the undoubted fact that central to A.A.'s effectiveness is the member's public insistence "that he is not like over people, that he is an alcoholic in the full sense of the term. . . . Furthermore, he must accept alcoholism as a role that cannot be put on and taken off to suit the occasion, but as a role that is deeply imbedded in his person" (Turner, 1972, pp. 315–316).

Such affirmation does indeed seem very much like the "nothing but" characterizations more often used to disvalue individuals. At first glance, it appears that the "avower" himself or herself is proclaiming the very same "once an alcoholic, always an alcoholic" theme that is so often used by stigmatizers. This is, to be sure, an intriguing way for a person to deal with imputed deviantness, and clearly it is one that poses interesting theoretical issues. Once the *context and real meaning* of the affirmation are considered, however, it becomes questionable whether this procedure amounts to avowing "deviance" or using a "negative label" to produce positive consequences. To claim that that is what happens in A.A. is to interpret the concepts of "label" and "labeling" in a narrow literal sense that does not do full justice to the meaning qualities that pertain to this kind of situation.

Trice and Roman's "relabeling" thesis helps us to recognize this. As they note, a key to A.A.'s success seems to be "the effective contrivance of a repentent role." This role becomes "a social vehicle whereby, through contrite and remorseful public expressions, substantiated by visibly reformed behavior in conformity to the norms of the community, a former deviant can enter a new role which is quite acceptable to society" (Trice and Roman, 1970, pp. 542, 544). What A.A. members are doing, it seems, is not so much self-labeling themselves as "deviants," as it is re-labeling themselves. Within the A.A. context and given the way in which it is used, the self-proclamation of alcoholism does not really amount to a negative label. Indeed, although members keep saying they "are" alcoholics, the essence, for all practical purposes, of what they are affirming (except for the entering novice) is that they "were" alcoholics and are such no longer. Thus, they are indeed entering or affirming "a new role" (as Trice and Roman put it), and it is for *this* that they receive group support and approval. By the same token and despite the ideology of permanent alcoholism, they are in no way declaring themselves to be "nothing but" alcoholics. On the contrary, members' stories at meetings frequently emphasize the success and respectability they have been able to achieve since joining the organization. In short, the self-declarations are not ones to which, in the A.A. context, negative evaluations attach. Indeed, insofar as members affirm that they are successful ex-alcoholics, even within the society at large they are using a self-label that may be imbued with only slight deviantness.

Laslett and Warren have similarly challenged labeling theorists to explain comparable mechanisms that their research showed to be working successfully in a voluntary weight-control organization (Laslett and Warren, 1975). According to their interpretation, this organization used "intensive stigmatization" of members to promote "the normalization of deviant behavior" (in this case, obesity):

> Members are told that the world is dichotomized into two types of people with reference to food and weight: the fat, and the "civilians" (the slender). The stigmatized identity of fat person is permanent. It cannot be erased by weight loss, although it can be shifted from a visible stigma to an invisible one—from discrediting to discreditable. For the fat person who has become thin, weight loss is always potentially reversible and is an ever-dangerous invisible stigma which threatens the individual. . . . The continual awareness of an essential fat identity, whether visible (in pounds and fat) or invisible, acts as a warning device against the type of eating behavior promoting the discredited fat state (Laslett and Warren, 1975, p. 72).

Again, it is not entirely clear how one should interpret this treatment process. Normalization is not exactly what is happening, for efforts are being made to change the person's eating behavior and not simply to reinterpret it in a more favorable way. While the lecturers at this group's meetings did charge members with being "essentially" fat, the primary aim was to get them to take action to become thin. The process seems to have been similar to that which we noted earlier in connection with the rehabilitation of individuals who have physical disabilities. In that case, facing up to the existence of the disability may be seen as a prerequisite to rehabilitative efforts. Here, too, an initial admission of fatness seems to have been emphasized as a requirement for "doing something about it." Both instances underscore the fact that since stigma inheres in the reactions of others, the deviator's simply ignoring it will not cause it to go away.

Other key aspects of this organization's program were the pattern of group support and the characteristics of the "change agents" (in this instance, lecturers at the regular group meetings). As Laslett and Warren pointed out, "All the lecturers and other organizational personnel are fat persons turned thin-on-the-outside; they provide a vital symbol of identification for persons who believe that 'no one ever loses weight and keeps it off'" (Laslett and Warren, 1975, pp. 77–78). This common experience of members and "staff" is *the* central feature of all the **participatory treatment** schemes. Instead of confronting official control agents (a situation that invariably generates "them" and "us" outlooks), members voluntarily become "control" and "change" agents for one another. In most such programs, both oppressive control and formal organizational structuring are thereby kept to a minimum.

Perhaps the most influential model for participatory treatment has been the somewhat different version first developed by Synanon (Volkman and Cressey, 1963; Yablonsky, 1965). In its original form, this voluntary and residential program, which became the prototype for a wide variety of **therapeutic community** approaches to treating addiction and other self-recognized problems, emphasized communal life and work in a drug-free environment. Synanon was founded by a former A.A. member and, pursuant to that organization's lead utilized former addicts as treatment agents. Established members helped new members undergo withdrawal from drugs (abruptly, but in a context of strong interpersonal support). On a continuing basis, all members participated collectively in group efforts to keep individuals and the entire environment drug-free and committed to antidrug values. A central feature of the Synanon-type program has been the harshly candid group discussions (called "small s synanons"), in which members dissect and criticize each other's behavior and attitudes with such forcefulness that the technique has also been referred to as "attack therapy." In addition, Synanon houses and many of their more recent counterparts have maintained a system of graded work roles, in which members gradually take on positions of increased responsibility. Most of these programs have run their own small businesses, often with considerable success.

Sociological analyses have noted the careful structuring within such programs of conditions that seem to facilitate the individual's return to socially acceptable outlooks and behavior patterns. As Volkman and Cressey have shown, in many respects Synanon accomplishes a kind of reverse (law-abidingness oriented) "differential association," in which the context and conditions of rehabilitation directly counter the general processes that Sutherland believed were crime-producing. Alienation from old patterns and values and assimilation into new ones are aided by common purpose, group cohesion, persistent indoctrination, provision within the new group of significant status opportunities, and, particularly, by the technique of using former "offenders" as the key change agents (Volkman and Cressey, 1963). To some extent, all of this becomes possible because the "therapeutic community" type of program retains some of the features of the total institution. Synanon-type programs usually have combined residence and work aspects, thus maintaining considerable control over the member's entire "round of life." Often the member's entire existence has come to be built around the program to such an extent that critics have cited its failure to "graduate" members to the outside world, sometimes describing Synanon as a "protective" rather than truly "therapeutic" community. These organizations usually have a very strict system of rules governing member conduct—again, somewhat reminiscent of the total institution, even though here they are enforced collectively rather than from "above."

The combination of residential control, provision of a new way for the members to organize their lives, along with consistent group support and the development of new affective bonds makes for a context in which "status-elevation" (to undo the earlier status-degradation) and return to "normal" identity often become possible (see Lofland, 1969, pp. 209–295). The somewhat controversial group-session technique around which much of the program is built has no doubt played an important part in the organization's relatively successful social control efforts. Although they are sometimes criticized for employing harsh attacks on the individual's "self" (including much name-calling, which critics claim could backfire psychologically), the ultimate effect of even these sessions seems, for the most part, to be self-esteem building and morale enhancing. The technique used reflects the more general development of group therapy methods, partly in response to growing disillusionment regarding the prospects for using conventional one-to-one psychotherapy in treating social deviators. More specifically, it builds on "guided group interaction" approaches, involving democratically-run, common-problem oriented group discussions developed in early experiments in treating juvenile delinquents (McKorkle, *et al.*, 1958; Empey and Rabow, 1961). Some version of this group technique is now used in most therapeutic community programs. As a recent research report on one such drug-treatment effort has noted, when it works effectively, it does so by generating a "stigmatizing self-appraisal [that] can gradually serve to bring about a disaffection or dissociation from the identity and way of life on the street" (Vallas, *et al.*, 1977, p. 23).

Wide adoption of the therapeutic community concept reflects these relatively favorable stigma-reversing features. Many conventional total institutions, such as closed mental hospitals, have—following early experiments to design and implement a comparable "milieu therapy" approach— been moving at least some parts of their programs in this direction. New therapeutic communities are continuously being developed, applying these methods to the rehabilitation of various types of deviators (see, for example, Hampden-Turner, 1977). Although proponents of some of these programs, which have often reflected the influence of strongly charismatic founders or leaders, sometimes make excessive claims and become almost messianic in their proselytizing, there is little doubt that the approach does represent a major challenge to the conventional control-agent model of deviance "rehabilitation." Writing of Synanon some years ago, one of its major sociologist-advocates Lewis Yablonsky asserted:

> This may be a new therapeutic revolution. It is to be expected that professionals, especially the conservative wing, will increasingly attempt to put this "uprising" down. Among other reasons, their fear may be related to a financial threat. This fear (already registered by some professionals) is, of course, absurd, since the increasing complexity of our world and social problems demands increased help from all quarters—professional therapists included. The only fall professionals may take by the ascendancy of the people's therapy role is one in status (Yablonsky, 1965, p. 401).

Repeated conflict among proponents of different approaches, at least evident in the field of drug-addiction treatment, suggests that part of Yablonsky's prediction was accurate. At the same time, the steady growth of therapeutic community programs indicates that early concern (which he expressed in the same book) that the approach might effectively be squelched by threatened professionals, appears to have been unfounded.

REFERENCES

A.A. World Services
1953. *This Is A.A.* New York: A.A. World Services.

Baldwin, James
1961. *Nobody Knows My Name.* New York: The Dial Press.

Banton, Michael
1964. *The Policeman in the Community.* London: Tavistock.

Becker, Howard S.
1963. *Outsiders.* New York: The Free Press.

Berry, J. J.
1975. "Deviant Categories and Organizational Typing of Delinquents," in F. James Davis and Richard Stivers, eds., *The Collective Definition of Deviance.* New York: The Free Press. Pp. 350–359.

Bittner, Egon
1967. "Police Discretion in Emergency Apprehension of Mentally Ill Persons," *Social Problems,* 14(Winter), 278–292.
1970. *The Functions of the Police in Modern Society.* National Institute of Mental Health, Center for Studies of Crime and Delinquency, Washington: U.S. Government Printing Office.

Bloch, Sidney and Peter Reddaway
1977. *Psychiatric Terror.* New York: Basic Books, Inc.

Blumberg, Abraham S.
1967. *Criminal Justice.* Chicago: Quadrangle/The New York Times Book Co.

Boscarino, Joseph
1977. *Alcohol Career Patterns in Alcoholics Anonymous.* Unpublished Ph.D. Dissertation, Dept. of Sociology, New York University.

Carlin, Jerome
1966. *Lawyers' Ethics.* New York: Russell Sage Foundation.

Cicourel, Aaron V. and John I. Kitsuse
1963. *The Educational Decision-Makers.* Indianapolis: The Bobbs-Merrill Co., Inc.

Clark, John P.
1975. "Isolation of the Police: A Comparison of the British and American Situations," as reprinted in Richard L. Henshel and Robert A. Silverman, eds., *Perception in Criminology.* New York: Columbia University Press. Pp. 241–262.

Clausen, John A.
1976. "Mental Disorders," in Robert K. Merton and Robert Nisbet, eds., *Contemporary Social Problems, 4th ed.* New York: Harcourt Brace Jovanovich. Pp. 105–139.

Clinard, Marshall B.
1974. *Sociology of Deviant Behavior, 4th ed.* New York: Holt, Rinehart and Winston, Inc.

Connery, Robert H., ed.
1969. *Urban Riots,* New York: Vintage Books.

Crawford, Thomas J.
1975. "Police Overperception of Ghetto Hostility," in Henshel and Silverman, eds., *op. cit.*, pp. 263–271.

Cressey, Donald R., ed.
1961. *The Prison: Studies in Institutional Organization and Change.* New York: Holt, Rinehart and Winston, Inc.

Cumming, Elaine, *et al.*
1965. "Policeman as Philosopher, Guide and Friend," *Social Problems,* 12(Winter), 276–286.

Daniels, Arlene K.
1972. "Military Psychiatry: The Emergence of a Subspeciality," in Eliot Freidson and Judith Lorber, eds., *Medical Men and Their Work.* Chicago/New York: Aldine/Atherton. Pp. 145–162.

Dickson, Donald T.
1968. "Bureaucracy and Morality: An Organizational Perspective on a Moral Crusade," *Social Problems,* 16(Fall), 143–156.

Downie, Leonard, Jr.
1972. *Justice Denied.* Baltimore: Penguin Books, Inc.

Emerson, Robert M.
1969. *Judging Delinquents: Context and Process in Juvenile Court.* Chicago: Aldine Publishing Company.

Emerson, Robert M. and Melvin Pollner
1976. "Dirty Work Designations: Their Features and Consequences in a Psychiatric Setting," *Social Problems,* 23(February), 243–254.

Empey, LaMar T. and Jerome Rabow
1961. "The Provo Experiment in Delinquency Rehabilitation," *American Sociological Review,* 26(October), 679–695.

Etzioni, Amitai
1964. *Modern Organizations.* Englewood Cliffs, N.J.: Prentice-Hall, Inc.

Field, Mark G.
1957. *Doctor and Patient in Soviet Russia.* Cambridge: Harvard University Press.

Foucault, Michel
1977. *Discipline and Punish.* New York: Pantheon Books.

Frank, Jerome
1949. *Courts on Trial.* Princeton: Princeton University Press.

Frankel, Marvin E.
1972. *Criminal Sentences.* New York: Hill and Wang.

Freidson, Eliot
1970. *Profession of Medicine.* New York: Dodd, Mead & Company.

Freidson, Eliot and Judith Lorber, eds.
1972. *Medical Men and Their Work.* Chicago/New York: Aldine/Atherton.

Galliher, John F. and Allynn Walker
1977. "The Puzzle of the Social Origins of the Marihuana Tax Act of 1937," *Social Problems,* 24(February), 367–376.

Gaylin, Willard
1974. *Partial Justice.* New York: Alfred R. Knopf, Inc.

Goffman, Erving
1961. *Asylums.* Garden City, N.Y.: Doubleday & Company Inc.
1972. *Relations in Public.* New York: Harper Colophon Books.

Goldstein, Abraham S.
1967. *The Insanity Defense.* New Haven: Yale University Press.

Gove, Walter R.
1975. "Labelling and Mental Illness: A Critique," in Walter R. Gove, ed., *The Labelling of Deviance.* New York: Sage-Wiley. Pp. 35–81.

Halleck, Seymour L.
1972. *The Politics of Therapy.* New York: Harper & Row, Publishers.

Hampden-Turner, Charles
1977. *Sane Asylum: Inside the Delancy Street Foundation.* New York: William C. Morrow & Co., Inc.

Hawkins, Richard and Gary Tiedeman
1975. *The Creation of Deviance.* Columbus, Ohio: Charles E. Merrill Publishing Co.

Hazelrigg, Lawrence, ed.
1969. *Prison Within Society: A Reader in Penology.* Garden City, N.Y.: Doubleday & Company, Inc.

Hewitt, John P. and Randall Stokes
1975. "Disclaimers," *American Sociological Review,* 40(February), 1–11.

Hirschi, Travis
1975. "Labelling Theory and Juvenile Delinquency: An Assessment of the Evidence," in Gove, ed., *op. cit.,* pp. 181–203.

Hogarth, John
1971. *Sentencing as a Human Process.* Toronto: University of Toronto Press.

Hughes, Everett C.
1962. "Good People and Dirty Work," *Social Problems,* 10(Summer), 3–11.
1971. *The Sociological Eye: Selected Papers.* Chicago: Aldine Publishing Company.

Johnston, Norman, Leonard Savitz, and Marvin E. Wolfgang, eds.
1970. *The Sociology of Punishment and Correction.* 2d. ed. New York: John Wiley and Sons, Inc.

Kahne, Merton J. and Charlotte Green Schwartz
1978. "Negotiating Trouble: The Social Construction and Management of Trouble in a College Psychiatric Context," *Social Problems,* 25(June), 461–475.

Kalven, Harry, Jr. and Hans Zeisel
1966. *The American Jury.* Boston: Little, Brown and Company.

King, Rufus G.
1953. "The Narcotics Bureau and the Harrison Act: Jailing the Healers and the Sick," *Yale Law Journal,* 62(April), 736–749.

Kitsuse, John I. and Aaron V. Cicourel
1963. "A Note on the Use of Official Statistics," *Social Problems,* 11(Fall), 131–139.

The Knapp Commission on Police Corruption
1972. *Report.* New York: George Braziller, Inc.

Knight, Doug
1972. *Delinquency Causes and Remedies: The Working Assumptions of California Youth Authority Staff.* Sacramento: California Youth Authority.

Laslett, Barbara and Carol A. B. Warren
1975. "Losing Weight: The Organizational Promotion of Behavior Change," *Social Problems,* 23(October), 69–80.

Lemert, Edwin M.
1951. *Social Pathology.* New York: McGraw-Hill, Inc.
1962. "Paranoia and the Dynamics of Exclusion," *Sociometry,* 25(March), 2–25.
1971. *Instead of Court: Diversion in Juvenile Justice.* National Institute of Mental Health, Center for Studies of Crime and Delinquency. Washington: U.S. Government Printing Office.

Lindesmith, Alfred R.
1965. *The Addict and the Law.* Bloomington: Indiana University Press.

Lofland, John
1969. *Deviance and Identity.* Englewood Cliffs, N.J.: Prentice-Hall, Inc.

Luxenberg, Stan
1977. "Crime Pays—A Prison Boom," the New York *Times,* July 17, Sec. 3, p. 1.

Manning, Peter K.
1977. *Police Work: The Social Organization of Policing.* Cambridge, Mass.: The MIT Press.

Marx, Gary T.
1974. "Thoughts on a Neglected Category of Social Movement Participant: The Agent Provocateur and the Informant," *American Journal of Sociology,* 80(September), 402–442.

Maxwell, Milton A.
1967. "Alcoholics Anonymous: An Interpretation," in David J. Pittman, ed., *Alcoholism.* New York: Harper & Row, Publishers. Pp. 211–222.

McCorkle, Lloyd W., Albert Elias, and F. Lovell Bixby
1958. *The Highfields Story.* New York: Holt, Rinehart and Winston.

Mechanic, David
1968. *Medical Sociology.* New York: The Free Press.
1969. *Mental Health and Social Policy.* Englewood Cliffs, N.J.: Prentice-Hall, Inc.

Merton, Robert K.
1957. *Social Theory and Social Structure, rev. ed.,* Glencoe, Ill.: The Free Press.

Musto, David
1973. *The American Disease: Origins of Narcotic Control.* New Haven: Yale University Press.

National Advisory Commission on Civil Disorders
1968. *Report.* New York: Bantam Books, Inc.

National Commission on the Causes and Prevention of Violence
1968. *Rights in Conflict (the Walker Report).* New York: Bantam Books, Inc.

New York State Special Commission on Attica
1972. *Attica: The Official Report.* New York: Bantam Books, Inc.

Porterfield, Austin L.
1946. *Youth in Trouble.* Ft. Worth, Texas: Leo Potishman Foundation.

President's Commission on Law Enforcement and Administration of Justice
1967. *Task Force Report: Crime and Its Impact—An Assessment.* Washington: U.S. Government Printing Office.

Rains, Prudence
1975. "Imputations of Deviance: A Retrospective Essay on the Labeling Perspective," *Social Problems,* 23(October), 1–11.

Reid, Sue Titus
1976. *Crime and Criminology.* Hinsdale, Ill.: The Dryden Press, Inc.

Reiss, Albert J., Jr.
1971. *The Police and the Public.* New Haven: Yale University Press.

Robison, Sophia M.
1936. *Can Delinquency Be Measured?* New York: Columbia University Press.

Rosett, Arthur and Donald R. Cressey
1976. *Justice By Consent: Plea Bargains in the American Courthouse.* Philadelphia: J. B. Lippincott Company.

Rubington, Earl and Martin S. Weinberg, eds.
1978. *Deviance: The Interactionist Perspective, 3rd ed.* New York: Macmillan, Inc.

Rubinstein, Jonathan
1974. *City Police.* New York: Ballantine Books, Inc.

Sagarin, Edward
1969. *Odd Man In: Societies of Deviants in America.* Chicago: Quadrangle/The New York Times Book Co.

Scheff, Thomas J.
1966. *Being Mentally Ill.* Chicago: Aldine Publishing Co.

Schrag, Peter and Diane Divoky
1976. *The Myth of the Hyperactive Child—and Other Means of Child Control.* New York: Dell Publishing Co., Inc.

Schur, Edwin M.
1958. "Scientific Method and the Criminal Trial Decision," *Social Research,* 25(Summer), 173–190.
1962. *Narcotic Addiction in Britain and America.* Bloomington: Indiana University Press.

1966. "Psychiatrists Under Attack: The Rebellious Dr. Szasz," *The Atlantic* (June), 72–76.

1973. *Radical Nonintervention: Rethinking the Delinquency Problem.* Englewood Cliffs, N.J.: Prentice-Hall, Inc.

Scott, Robert A.
1969. *The Making of Blind Men.* New York: Russell Sage Foundation.

Silver, Allan
1967. "The Demand for Order in Civil Society," in David J. Bordua, ed., *The Police: Six Sociological Essays.* New York: John Wiley & Sons, Inc. Pp. 1–24.

Skolnick, Jerome H.
1966, 1975. *Justice Without Trial, 2nd ed.,* New York: John Wiley & Sons, Inc.

Sudnow, David
1965. "Normal Crimes: Sociological Features of the Penal Code in a Public Defender Office," *Social Problems,* 12(Winter), 255–276.

1967. *Passing On: The Social Organization of Dying.* Englewood Cliffs, N.J.: Prentice-Hall, Inc.

Szasz, Thomas S.
1963. *Law, Liberty and Psychiatry.* New York: Macmillan, Inc.

1965. *Psychiatric Justice.* New York: Macmillan, Inc.

1970. *Ideology and Insanity.* Garden City, N.Y.: Doubleday & Company, Inc.

Tittle, Charles R.
1972. "Institutional Living and Self-Esteem," *Social Problems,* 20(Summer), 65–77.

1975. "Labelling and Crime: An Empirical Evaluation," in Gove, ed., *op. cit.,* pp. 157–179.

Torrey, E. Fuller
1975. *The Death of Psychiatry.* New York: Penguin Books, Inc.

Trice, Harrison M.
1966. *Alcoholism in America.* New York: McGraw-Hill Book Co.

Trice, Harrison M. and Paul M. Roman
1970. "Delabeling, Relabeling, and Alcoholics Anonymous," *Social Problems,* 17(Spring), 538–546.

Turner, Ralph H.
1972. "Deviance Avowal as Neutralization of Commitment," *Social Problems,* 19(Winter), 308–321.

Vallas, Steven P., *et al.*
1977. *Passage Through Treatment: Identity Transformation in a Therapeutic Community.* Newark: Rutgers, the State University, mimeo, 35 pp.

Vinter, Robert D.
1967. "The Juvenile Court as an Institution," in *President's Commission on Law Enforcement and Administration of Justice, Task Force Report: Juvenile Delinquency and Youth Crime.* Washington: U.S. Government Printing Office. Pp. 84–90.

Volkman, Rita and Donald R. Cressey
1963. "Differential Association and the Rehabilitation of Drug Addicts," *American Journal of Sociology,* 69(September), 129–142.

von Hirsch, Andrew
1976. *Doing Justice: The Choice of Punishments* (Report of the Committee for the Study of Incarceration). New York: Hill & Wang.

Weber, George H.
1961. "Emotional and Defensive Reactions of Cottage Parents," in Donald R. Cressey, ed., *The Prison: Studies in Institutional Organization and Change*. New York: Holt, Rinehart and Winston. Pp. 189–228.
1969. "Conflicts Between Professional and Nonprofessional Personnel in Institutional Delinquency Treatment," in Lawrence Hazelrigg, ed., *op. cit.*, pp. 426–454.

Wheeler, Stanton, *et al.*
1968. "Agents of Delinquency Control: A Comparative Analysis," in Stanton Wheeler, ed., *Controlling Delinquents*. New York: John Wiley & Co., Inc.

Wilson, James Q.
1968a. "The Police and the Delinquent in Two Cities," in Wheeler, ed., *op. cit.*, pp. 9–30.
1968b. *Varieties of Police Behavior*. Cambridge: Harvard University Press.

Wiseman, Jacqueline P.
1970. *Stations of the Lost: The Treatment of Skid Row Alcoholics*. Englewood Cliffs, N.J.: Prentice-Hall, Inc.

Wright, Erik, Olin
1975. *The Politics of Punishment*. New York: Harper Torchbooks.

Yablonsky, Lewis
1965. *The Tunnel Back: Synanon*. New York: Macmillan, Inc.

REVIEW OF KEY TERMS

agent of control. Any person whose official or occupational position involves regular participation in deviance-processing or otherwise "dealing with" deviance problems. Included in this category are "treatment" and "rehabilitation" personnel as well as law-enforcers and justice-administrators.

case mortality. Selective retention of "cases" by a deviance-processing system, through decisions at each stage as to which cases will be passed on to subsequent stages and which cases diverted or "dropped." See also, **discretion** and **funneling.**

dirty work. Undesirable tasks that a group or society relegates to people in special (usually low-ranked) occupational roles. It is a term applicable to the role-behavior of many agents of social control. See also, **moral division of labor.**

discretion. The freedom to make choices between alternative courses of action. Some discretion is exercised by almost all agents of social control, at whatever stage in deviance-processing. It includes the freedom to take *no* formal action.

funneling. Another term useful in describing case mortality. It highlights the "dropping out" of cases at various stages, with a much smaller number of cases "coming out" of the funnel than was "fed in."

goal displacement. The process in which an organization's own formal rules, "needs," and problems come to take precedence over the substance of the work being done. It is a standard feature of bureaucracy and is extremely common in deviance-processing organizations and systems.

moral division of labor. A concept applied by Everett Hughes to the relation between the stratification of occupational roles and the allocation of "dirty work." It highlights the dependence of upper echelons' "morality" on the existence of special lower-echelon roles to handle "dirty work."

participatory treatment. Self-help treatment and rehabilitation schemes in which deviators or ex-deviators themselves serve as key "control" and "change" agents and which usually involve group (therapy or discussion) sessions. The **therapeutic community** is one major example.

rate-producing process. One way of conceptualizing the major function of deviance-processing organizations, emphasized by Kitsuse and Cicourel. The production of "cases" and deviance statistics through the processing activity itself.

role-set. The network of other role-occupants with which the occupant of a given role must regularly interact in an organizational context. In deviance-processing, the control agent's role-set is seen as an extremely important influence on the agent's behavior and outlooks.

self-reported behavior studies. A technique developed for overcoming sampling difficulties in early statistical-comparison studies of deviance that consists of drawing "deviant" and "nondeviant" samples directly from the general population, instead of from officially processed populations, by asking respondents about problematic behaviors they have ever engaged in.

therapeutic community. A treatment scheme that combines features of **participatory treatment** with some aspects of the **total institution.** A democratically based voluntary program in a residential context. Synanon is the prototype for this kind of organization.

total institution. Goffman's influential term for traditional residential correctional and treatment institutions (e.g., prisons and mental hospitals); whose characteristics include all-enveloping "round of life," separation from the outside world, and strict routine officially prescribed and enforced by separate control or treatment staff. Their common processes and effects include "mortification" and "depersonalization."

vested interest. A built-in "stake in" various outcomes (usually an "economic" stake) which can develop among control agents and agencies, with respect to deviance policies and programs.

PROJECT 6
Observing in a Courtroom

Introductory Comment

Although it is possible to study control agencies indirectly through questionnaires, interviews, and an examination of written materials (such as formal "tables of organization," flowcharts, and various statistics relating to the agency's work), such investigations will almost always fail to produce a full and compelling picture of the agency's routine operations. One of the main ingredients that such indirect methods tend to miss is *interaction*—within the staff, between the agency and outside organizations and forces, and between staff and "clients" in the course of the people-processing itself. If the element of interaction is not grasped, the likelihood is that a rather static picture of the organization's work will emerge. On-the-job problems and "solutions," reciprocal pressures and influences, and cumulating effects—in short *process*, will not be fully appreciated.

Clearly the best way to grasp the ongoing work of an organization is through intensive, long-term *observation*—along with use of the other methods mentioned above. It is unlikely, for purposes of your deviance course, that such an approach will be feasible; but it may be, in place of a long paper or as another kind of major course assignment. If so, it may be possible for your instructor to "place" you as an observer in one of a wide variety of local control treatment and rehabilitation agencies. Often such organizations are happy to have volunteer helpers, and this can provide the entrée you would need.

Usually, however, such placement and long-term observational study is too tall an order to be manageable along with other course work, particularly in a one-semester course. The following short-term and very simple and straightforward exercise may be "the next best thing." Since most courtrooms are open to the public, no problem of initial or continuing access is involved; people are usually free to come and go there more or less as they wish, so it will be possible to vary the length and precise nature of the observations according to your own or the course's requirements.

Assignment

Sit in on (for whatever length of time the instructor and class decides upon) and *observe as carefully as you can* the proceedings in a criminal court or some other court proceeding that involves any type of deviance-processing (for example, some "civil commitment" proceedings may take place in civil, rather than criminal, court). Write a paper *describing thoroughly what you observed* and *explaining* how the apparent features and processes you saw are of *socio-*

logical significance. Which of the features and processes discussed in the text seem to have been in evidence? What implications would you draw regarding the general nature of the kind of proceeding you observed, assuming that what you saw was "representative?"

The class can decide which *kinds* of court proceedings would be appropriate, what *stages* of deviance-processing might be observed, and whether a student-observer ought to observe repeated *instances of one stage or* instead follow *a single case through various stages.*

Key Questions

Among the questions you might have in mind as you conduct your observations are the following:

1. What seem to be the general patterns of communication among the participants? Who talks to whom, about what, and when? Do they seem to understand each other? Indeed, can they even hear each other?

2. In what ways does the authority of the judge seem to color the proceedings? Does the formality of the court setting and proceedings seem to have a significant influence on how the participants behave? In what respects, and with what apparent consequences?

3. To what extent, insofar as it becomes apparent at various stages, does a presumption of the defendant's innocence or guilt seem in evidence? Do you see indications of a status-degradation ceremony at work? If so, what are they? How "deviantized" does the defendant seem to be in the eyes of the other participants and his or her own?

4. If a jury is involved in what you are observing, what do you make of its role? Do the jurors seem to understand what is going on? Do they seem to be taking their formal role seriously?

5. What is the behavior of the lawyers in the case like? Does the proceeding have the quality of a real adversarial conflict, or do they seem to be cooperating with each other in a common task?

6. Are there any signs of "negotiation" occurring or having occurred?

7. Are there witnesses involved in the proceeding? If so, what does their role seem to be, and what do the other participants seem to make of the evidence they offer?

8. Does the proceeding show any signs of "assembly-line justice?" Explain.

9. Do you observe any indications of "external" relationships or influences—the court's dealings with any outside agencies (police, other government offices, schools or health departments, etc.) or forces? What are they, and how do you explain their significance?

Implications

Obviously there are many other questions you might explore. Needless to say, short-run observations in a single setting or case do not provide much of a basis for generalizing about the administration of justice. However, they may give you at least a partial sense of the way in which organizational context can shape deviance-processing. Many details of the setting, of the way the proceeding is formally arranged, and of the participants' behavior, should help give you a more immediate "feel for" one processing milieu than you could obtain through just reading about it. At the same time, the exercise may cause some of the concepts discussed in the text to "ring true" in a way that words alone cannot always convey.

PROLOGUE 7

Crime brings together upright consciences and concentrates them.
— Emile Durkheim, *The Division of Labor in Society*

The ideas of the ruling class are, in every age, the ruling ideas: i.e., the class which is the dominant material force in society is at the same time its dominant intellectual force.
— Karl Marx, *The German Ideology*

Interactionist approaches to deviance have sometimes been criticized as being too heavily preoccupied with individual social psychology. To the extent that labeling analysts have undertaken research mainly on deviant careers and the social-psychological dynamics of interaction between reactors and deviators, they may have invited such criticism. However, as we saw earlier in this text, a definitional-processual perspective—if broadly conceived—does not necessarily imply such a limited focus. On the contrary, once we have defined certain general reaction processes as the distinguishing feature of deviance situations, then we are almost inevitably drawn to interpreting such responses and the forces generating them at various levels of the social order. While broad conceptions concerning deviantness are in a sense built up out of a multitude of small-scale interactions, these collective characterizations in turn exert their own reciprocal influence, helping to determine the likely course of interaction in specific situations.

At the level of collective definition and reaction (see topics under Focal Point One of the Paradigm, in Appendix), we find many of the same basic features that are present in the direct relations between individual deviators and reactors. Meaning and process are here, too, the keys to interpreting deviance. Just as deviance outcomes emerge through direct interaction, so also do they evolve sequentially at the societal level. It follows that negotiation, conflict, and the resources that influence conflict outcomes, are major considerations at this collective level as well. Similarly, adopting this broader societal focus highlights the elements of sociocultural diversity and social change that may sometimes be obscured when we microscopically examine individual moral careers.

Attending to these more macrosociological facets of deviance situations underscores most forcefully that such situations are basically political in nature.

403

Large segments of the population (social categories) and sometimes organized social groups are directly concerned with and affected by deviance outcomes at this broader level. These collective interests often result in overt efforts to influence society-level conceptions and related public policies. As the statements from Durkheim and Marx suggest, there are different ways in which such broad conceptions and policies can be interpreted. We have seen that the general process of deviantizing can serve certain "functions" for the social system as a whole. Yet it also seems clear that particular patterns of imputing deviantness are decidedly more "functional" for some people, categories, and groups than for others. Whichever facet one chooses to emphasize, we know that deviantness characterizations and associated responses do not just appear out of the blue. They have their own specific histories, and they continue to undergo change, even as they exert their own influence on the course of events.

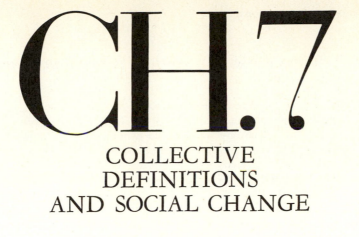

CH. 7
COLLECTIVE DEFINITIONS AND SOCIAL CHANGE

INTRODUCTION

It has been common for several decades to remark, in introductory sociology courses and elsewhere, that American society is undergoing "rapid social change." Urbanization, bureaucratization, and secularization are typically cited as major forces reshaping our lives and culture. Though some sociologists may have gone overboard in trying to apply these notions indiscriminately to explain anything and everything, few observers would deny that to a considerable extent American values and institutions are indeed in a state of flux. As our earlier discussion indicated, until recently such conditions were of interest to the sociologist of deviance primarily for their possible role in "causing" acts of deviation. Sociocultural pressures of one sort or another were seen to generate problematic behavior, to push particular individuals into deviating. As contemporary interpreters of deviance are beginning to recognize, however, the greater significance of these broad sociocultural developments may actually lie elsewhere—namely, in *their bearing on the meaning and uses of deviantness* in our society. In short, such underlying forces are as much causes of deviance *definitions* as they are causes of deviation.

Perhaps as part of the much-emphasized secularization of our society (the decline of the "sacred," whether religious or simply traditional in form), absolutist perspectives on deviance command much less acceptance than before, and specific imputations of deviantness frequently evoke direct challenge. Although, clearly, it is not possible to generalize about the entire citizenry, it seems fair to say that, overall, Americans have tended to become more self-conscious in their awareness of and response to deviance issues. Attitudes and policies on such issues are increasingly seen as being open to considered choice, rather than as simply being self-evident. This general outlook is described as follows by sociologist Jack Douglas:

> Only by coming to understand better which particular kinds of activities have bearings on the general welfare, and which do not, and by seeking to control only those that do have such public effects, are we likely to avoid polarizing important segments of our society and turning them into the "enemies of society." Only by *deabsolutizing* all social rules except those necessary for the construction of an "optimal" social order are we likely to avoid violent disorder as our society becomes more international, changeable, open, complex, and pluralistic (Douglas, 1971, p. 322).

Contributing to the growth of this outlook, however, has been an increasingly open discontent over the effects of past and present "polarizing" of precisely the sort Douglas appears to condemn. We can expect such polarizing to continue, even as it changes in detail, for we are certainly very far away from any complete "deabsolutizing" of values and norms. By the same token, we have to recognize that the prospects for a full consensus regarding what would be involved in "construction of an 'optimal' social order" are not great. Nor is there any clear agreement as to who could provide the specifications of such an order or the criteria according to which this might be done. It seems most unlikely that sociological judgment would be widely accepted in this regard, nor is any other purported source of societal guidance likely to receive uniform support.

Under these circumstances a continuing *politicizing* of deviance issues should be expected. The increasingly self-conscious approach to these matters is not totally disinterested. A rejection of absolutism may involve some greater tolerance for diversity in a "pluralistic" society, and, at the same time, generate repudiation of dominant norms by those whose interests and goals they impede. Part and parcel of the growing openness with respect to deviance is the emergence of group consciousness among stigmatized persons and their supporters. A hardening of opposition to change among those whose beliefs and interests favor the status quo is a likely corollary of this development. This sort of crystallization of opposing outlooks and interests in the deviance field in many respects mirrors the social ferment that recently has surrounded a variety of other social movements in our society—the civil rights movement, the antiwar movement, the "counterculture" of youth, the contemporary women's movement. Gains registered in these other contexts have provided encouragement to those who seek change in deviance-related outlooks and policies, and such movements have also provided models for collective organization. They may furthermore have helped presently defined deviators to more easily see themselves in a new light—as oppressed minorities and forerunners of "social change." This possibility has been suggested by one perceptive commentator on the "counterculture," who noted that, "a subculture of youth that looked at first like a deviant group [has] turned out to be a vanguard" (Flacks, 1971, pp. 17–18; see also Roszak, 1969).

At any rate, the persisting public ferment over deviance matters in our society seems both to constitute "living proof" of the collective dynamics of deviance situations and to afford excellent "natural laboratory" (current, real-life) conditions for researching and interpreting them. Probably it is not surprising that, under these conditions, sociologists are increasingly alert to the collective dimensions and broadly political aspects of deviance. There is a growing concern analytically to examine both stability and change in deviance-defining and to "place" such processes in a context that includes cultural setting, historical forces, the clash of opposing group interests and values, as well as evolving sequences of specific events.

THREAT, BOUNDARIES, AND CHANGE

The Limits of Consensus

This text has given very strong emphasis to elements of diversity, variability, and unpredictability in defining deviance and reacting to it. It is necessary also to acknowledge, without "retreating" significantly from that general position, that collective characterizations of deviance are not totally haphazard. Important, though limited, elements of consensus do underlie some frequently encountered perceptions of behaviors as being problematic or offensive. For example, several important studies have shown this to be the case with respect to public attitudes in this country regarding major crimes. Thorsten Sellin and Marvin Wolfgang conducted research in Philadelphia during the early 1960s, in which samples of judges, police, and college students were asked to rate the "seriousness" of various criminal offenses on an eleven-point scale (Sellin and Wolfgang, 1964). They found considerable agreement on this seriousness-ranking of crimes. More recently, and with a more representative sample (a "block quota" sampling of Baltimore households), Peter Rossi and associates came up with similar findings, utilizing in their research a nine-point "seriousness" classification. In the Rossi study, based on interviews conducted in 1972, the survey data showed, "considerable agreement on the ordering of crime seriousness among subgroups of the sample defined by cross classifying race, sex and educational attainment" (Rossi, et al., 1974, p. 233). The researchers concluded, therefore, that there were basic norms of crime-seriousness that "are quite widely distributed among blacks and whites, males and females, high and low socio-economic levels, and among levels of educational attainment" (Rossi, et al., 1974, p. 237). As would be anticipated, crimes against persons (particularly murder) received significantly higher seriousness ratings than property crimes not involving a threat of violence. Public "disturbance" offenses received low ratings, as did white-collar crimes and "victimless" crimes (homosexuality, pornography, etc.). Offenses against police officers were regarded as being especially serious, and, interestingly, crimes committed by strangers tended to be viewed as more serious than those in which the victim was known to the offender. On the basis of such research findings, a committee of experts on punishment recently concluded that "people from widely different walks of life can make common-sense judgments on the comparative gravity of offenses and come to fairly similar conclusions" (von Hirsch, 1976, p. 79).

There are also available some data on the basis of which one might extend this kind of assertion beyond the United States. Thus, Graeme Newman has done research on comparative perceptions of some prototypical forms of deviance, employing selected samples from six different countries (Newman, 1976). Table 7.1 shows some of his general findings, indicating considerable agreement across national boundaries concerning the general choice of sanctions (using the rough categories of "treatment," "punishment," and "nothing"). When he examined respondents' expressed preferences regarding more specific types and degrees of sanctioning (within the "punishment" and "treatment" classifications), Newman did find evidence of considerably more cross-national diversity (Newman, 1976, pp. 144–147). Even with respect to the more general perceptions of the various acts, Newman was careful to note that the degree of consensus across countries, regarding extent of overall disapproval, varied considerably for several major groupings of offenses. The highest consensus on disapproval was, predictably, for "traditional crimes." With respect to these Newman goes so far as to state, "One might argue that these crimes have *always* been disapproved of. They are therefore not relative to particular periods or places . . . one hesitates to say it, but they are, functionally speaking, *absolute* standards" (Newman, 1976, pp. 285–286).

Considerably less agreement existed on disapproving such borderline offenses as homosexuality, abortion, and drug taking. "The principles of normative relativism may more easily apply to this class of acts, which appears to be susceptible to the campaigning of interest groups and where persons' moral evaluations of them are strongly affected by the norms of particular societal groups or cultures" (Newman, 1976, p. 286). The least consensus across countries existed with respect to the highly ambiguous act (or "act by omission") of not helping a person in distress. Newman's overall conclusion is, for the most part, a moderate one:

> While there appears to be a basic invariance in the structure of deviance perception across cultures, and in the classifications of deviant action, there is also a very broad diversity in particular aspects of perception. This applies especially to respondents' preferences for the types [i.e., specific means and severities] of social control. Such diversity may be seen as clearly explained by the facts of the particular culture (Newman, 1976, p. 297).

However, the basis for his further assertion that the diversity he did find "should not be confused with cultural or any kind of moral relativism" is obscure. Nor is it at all clear, as Rossi and his coresearchers imply, that findings from crime-ranking studies such as their's seriously undermine conflict interpretations of deviance.

Table 7.1 The Preferred Societal Sanctions* (Percentages)

ACT AND SANCTION	INDIA (N = 497)	INDO-NESIA (N = 500)	IRAN (N = 475)	ITALY (SARDINIA) (N = 200)	U.S.A. (N = 169)	YUGO-SLAVIA (N = 500)
Robbery						
Treatment	6.2	0.8	5.4	7.0	16.8	0.6
Punishment	85.6	89.6	87.0	92.0	79.6	94.8
Nothing	8.0	5.2	7.6	4.0	0.0	1.8
Incest						
Treatment	29.3	12.4	17.2	41.0	62.7	41.4
Punishment	45.7	55.0	82.3	62.5	12.4	50.8
Nothing	24.9	25.4	2.8	4.5	16.0	2.2
Appropriation						
Treatment	2.0	0.4	4.4	4.0	6.0	0.0
Punishment	93.1	87.4	82.1	91.0	85.7	90.2
Nothing	4.9	7.6	13.6	4.5	1.8	2.0
Homosexuality						
Treatment	26.9	14.4	26.8	65.5	33.7	58.8
Punishment	20.2	21.6	60.9	22.5	5.9	17.4
Nothing	52.9	57.6	12.3	9.5	60.4	13.0
Abortion						
Treatment	5.6	6.4	13.5	15.0	14.9	1.0
Punishment	9.2	43.8	48.4	32.0	4.0	11.2
Nothing	85.1	45.2	38.1	52.5	77.5	80.8
Taking drugs						
Treatment	23.0	19.8	68.9	63.0	78.1	68.4
Punishment	21.4	25.4	15.8	4.0	15.4	18.2
Nothing	55.8	48.0	15.1	15.0	1.2	5.6
Factory pollution						
Treatment	3.0	2.6	1.1	2.0	1.2	0.2
Punishment	82.3	46.8	78.2	62.5	87.0	76.2
Nothing	14.7	42.2	20.8	26.5	6.5	14.8
Public protest						
Treatment	1.6	3.6	5.3	1.5	3.0	0.2
Punishment	19.2	10.6	22.6	7.5	5.3	21.2
Nothing	79.4	73.2	71.9	85.5	91.7	60.4
Not helping						
Treatment	5.4	2.4	7.1	2.5	11.6	0.2
Punishment	15.2	8.4	22.6	59.0	14.7	42.6
Nothing	77.3	84.0	70.1	38.0	56.2	55.4

Source: Graeme Newman, *Comparative Deviance: Perception and Law in Six Cultures.* New York: Elsevier, 1976, pp. 142–143; reproduced with permission.

* "Treatment" = Choice of probation, mental hospital, other treatment.
  "Punishment" = Choice of prison, fines, corporal or capital punishment, other punishment.
  "Nothing" = Choice of "nothing" or "warning only."

Notwithstanding the apparent degree of broad consensus revealed in these domestic and cross-national inquiries, there are at least several major reasons for adhering to the relativistic, conflict-and-contingency-oriented, emergent, patterned-variation outlooks developed earlier in this book. They include the following:

1. At best, these studies tell us about the respondents' *professed attitudes and hypothetical preferences.* Yet, as we have seen, what counts much more in affecting deviance-defining processes and determining deviance-situation outcomes is people's actual behavior. Social-psychological research, particularly in the area of minority-group relations, indicates that there can be a large gap between a person's statements of attitude and actual behavior. For example, many individuals whose answers to hypothetical questions would suggest they are unprejudiced may, when confronted with the need to act in a real-life situation, discriminate against minority-group members. Just six weeks before the 1977 referendum on a homosexual-rights ordinance in the Miami, Florida, area (discussed further below), an opinion poll taken in Miami showed that 68 percent of the respondents believed homosexuals should be protected from discrimination (Ross, 1977). Yet, as we will see shortly, the ordinance prohibiting such discrimination was overturned by a more than two-to-one vote. Thus, either attitudes changed rapidly or, more likely, a substantial gap between attitude and voting behavior was revealed. We can particularly expect such discrepancies (and rapid shifts) in the borderline deviance areas where public opinion is most uncertain and unsteady. With respect to some "traditional crimes" (for example, murder or armed robbery), professed attitudes and actual responses may be more likely to coincide.

2. Similarly, apparent consensus on seriousness-rankings and statements about broad policy preferences *mask all the elements of systematic variation in* the *identification and selection* of particular individuals as "offenders" within the various offense categories. The characteristics and problems of control agents, organizational needs and exigencies, and standard typification and funneling processes all work to produce specific results that are not predictable from or necessarily consistent with the generalities of agreement indicated in these "consensus" findings. Likewise, *variations in* the availability and use of *individual resources to avoid or neutralize* stigmatizing processes also intervene as significant factors contributing to deviance outcomes.

3. These studies *do not cover all deviantized behaviors and conditions.* Generally speaking, such surveys of attitudes have been preoccupied with criminal offenses and penalities. It is true that Newman tried to adopt a broader deviance framework. Yet it is significant that the further he got away from the standard criminal categories, the less consensus he found.

4. Invariably, the consensus research and findings are *static* in nature. This is without any question their biggest shortcoming. At best, they reveal the state of opinion at a given time. Except perhaps with respect to a few of the most "universal" crimes (homicide, theft, etc.—and even in those instances we know there are many variations in specific interpretation and application of proscriptions), Newman's statement that certain behaviors "have always been disapproved of" seems rash. At the very least, there are a great many more sometimes-deviantized behaviors and conditions for which this claim would definitely *not* hold true than for which it would. As we saw in Chapter 2, changes over time (both short-run and long-run) that affect deviance situations can include shifting patterns of behavior, changes in relevant general values and attitudes, changes in overall characterizations of deviance and in more specific reactions and policies, and changes in the resources committed to efforts at social control. We have seen examples of "new" types of perceived deviance coming to the fore and of a reduction in the deviantness attaching to other behaviors and conditions. Sometimes these changes are quite dramatic. A recent example is "group sex." Under developing ideologies of sexual liberation and freedom to experiment, advocates of such activity have sought a relabeling of behavior which not long ago would have been widely condemned as "orgies" as now constituting "swinging," which they consider to be something akin to an "alternative life-style" (See Walshok, 1971; Stephenson, 1973). In New York City, their success has been sufficiently great that currently several nightclublike establishments ("on-premises swing clubs") offer admission-paying patrons the opportunity to engage in an evening of varied sexual acts with like-minded individuals, under semipublic conditions of relative anonymity and no personal "involvement" (Smith and Harlib, 1977). So far, these clubs appear not to be encountering substantial legal interference. In part, this may reflect the fact that "swinging" is a predominantly heterosexual activity; or the owners may be effectively maintaining their "private club" claim, a subterfuge that offers some protection to gay baths and other homosexual gathering places as well.

At the opposite end of the sexual-behavior continuum and illustrating the deviantizing side that often may accompany a "liberalization," is the trend toward disvaluation of chastity. As one writer has perceptively commented, virgins and other sexually abstinent persons are more and more stigmatized in the course of the alleged increase in sexual tolerance. "It is they who are now being solemnly assured that they are, indeed, sick; they are, indeed, unnatural; that they urgently need some course of therapy that will bring them into line with the rest of the community before they can hope to lead lives of happiness and fulfillment" (Morgan, 1977). In the face of such popular labels as "frigid" or "sexually unresponsive," those who can take sex or leave it begin themselves to become convinced that something is wrong with them. While expressing general approval of the new sexual tolerance, Morgan went on to urge that it be applied at "both ends of the spectrum." It might then become possible (as often nowadays it is not) "that a young girl could go to a party and reply to a sexual over-

ture as casually as she might respond to the offer of a cigarette: 'No, thanks—
I don't,' and expect to have her statement accepted with as little comment"
(Morgan, 1977).

No one would deny that there are *some* elements of *relative* consensus
and stability in any society's *overall* "deviance picture." However, to allow superficial appearances of uniformity and continuity to dominate one's entire understanding of deviance-defining is to miss out completely on all of the important
fluctuations over time, and variability within any one time period, that most
deviance situations regularly exhibit. Unfortunately, those who emphasize the
consensus theme give implicit support to absolutist and essentially "conservative" outlooks. In line with the "either-or" thinking discussed earlier, they leave
the impression that some behaviors are "really deviant." Yet, as we have seen,
interpretations geared to this kind of all-or-nothing categorization may be considerably less meaningful than ones that take account of *degrees of deviantness.*
It is vital to realize that such degrees of deviantness attach to specific behaviors
and conditions and, especially, to particular types of individuals *within,* or notwithstanding, any broader domains of agreement that may exist.

Furthermore, we must keep in mind that any current indicator of consensus (e.g., wide agreement on disapproval of a given "offense") has an identifiable "background," and can itself be interpreted in terms of its "causes." In
fact, such apparent agreement typically represents the current and tentative outcome of a long history of sociocultural developments—one that frequently will
have included significant clashes of value and interest. Similarly, surface consensus often reflects a balancing of currently opposed forces and, thus, may
obscure significant though covert elements of social conflict in even the present-
day situation.

It is not easy, then, to settle the consensus-conflict issue that confounds
many interpreters of the patterns we do find in deviantizing. If no patterns existed,
we would be hard put to interpret deviance at all—from whatever perspective
we chose to adopt. The recently emphasized outlooks tend to see the patterns
primarily as ones of process and definition. Yet clearly there is *some* substantive
patterning as well, or, in other words, there are discernible "types of behaviors"
that elicit deviantizing response as well as types of individuals. Interpreting these
substantive commonalities is difficult, because they can be seen as reflecting either
consensus or *dominance.* For example, survey data that show widespread agreement in our society regarding a low "seriousness" evaluation of white-collar
crimes can be taken either to indicate citizen consensus on this issue or, alternatively, to show the power-based dominance of business interests in American life.
In a sense, rather than one of these views being "true" and the other "false,"
they are differing and probably irreconcilable interpretations of the same factual
situation. It is unlikely that one could expect to settle easily and conclusively the
question of which-causes-which, of whether corporate power primarily reflects
or, alternatively, determines "public opinion."

Recent interpretations of deviance lean toward greater emphasis on the dominance theme or at least indicate an unwillingness to accept a static surface depiction of any deviance situation at face value. Sociologists increasingly want to explore the process through which any present agreement on given norms came into being. Likewise, they seek to determine whether the surface indicators of consensus actually reflect a basic underlying agreement or, instead, cover over an uneasy "truce" in an ongoing conflict. They are beginning to explore the social histories of specific society-wide deviance situations and to try to develop on the basis of such studies a better understanding of the "natural history" of deviance situations in general.

Boundary Shifts

We have noted in early sections of this book that **perceived threat** is a major factor activating efforts to deviantize. As many of the examples we have considered make clear, the substance of what it is that is found threatening can be almost infinitely variable. This is so at the collective level, just as for particular individuals. As one extreme (actual occurrence of truly horrendous acts), people may feel that their very integrity would be threatened by a failure to actively express their moral outrage. At the other extreme (as in common reactions to blindness and other severe physical disabilities), threat may arise out of little more than the feelings of uncomfortableness and, perhaps, guilt that "normal" people experience in the presence of those who have evident handicaps. In between these extremes we find a multitude of types of directly felt threat which may involve fear (of potential violence, for example), insecurities of various kinds (as in homophobia, individual or collective), envy (thought by many to activate much stigmatizing of youths by their elders, condemnation of the sexually free by the straightlaced, etc.), and challenge to a wide variety of strongly held values (such as the challenge to the values of hard work and honesty posed by some "theft," the challenge that extreme alcohol or drug use raises against the value of sobriety, and the like).

Particularly insofar as perception of and response to threat at the collective level are concerned, these examples represent only the more direct and clearly definable types. Collectivities—groups and societies, subgroups and social categories within societies—also experience threat in more subtle and complex ways. Concern over the unit's survival and persisting distinctiveness is one of the more important of these sources of threat. Preservation of a group or category's relative status or standing within a wider social system, which can involve both prestige and power aspects, is another. Joseph Gusfield had in mind this kind of indirect threat when he described certain social movements concerned with deviance-defining as "symbolic crusades." In his sociohistorical studies of the Women's Christian Temperance Union and its antialcohol activities from the 1820s into the present century, Gusfield found the issues surrounding alcohol use and, for a time, its prohibition to be symbolic ones centering on "status politics." Drinking and antidrinking activities and outlooks symbolized a broader clash between "cultures" in American society—with the once-dominant native, rural, Protestant segment coming under the challenge from the growing immigrant, urban, and non-Protestant segments.

Ratification of the Eighteenth Amendment in 1919 and passage of various implementing statutes had, according to Gusfield, important symbolic meaning:

> What Prohibition symbolized was the superior power and prestige of the old middle class in American society. The threat of decline in that position had made explicit actions of government necessary to defend it. Legislation did this in two ways. It demonstrated the power of the old middle class by showing that they could mobilize sufficient political strength to bring it about and it gave dominance to the character and style of old middle-class life in contrast to that of the urban lower and middle classes (Gusfield, 1966, p. 122).

Subsequent repeal of the Eighteenth Amendment carried a similarly symbolic but contrasting message:

> . . . it meant the repudiation of old middle-class virtues and end of rural, Protestant dominance. This is what was at issue in the clash between the Wets and the Drys. Victory had bolstered the prestige of the old middle classes. Defeat meant decline. Temperance norms were now officially illegitimate and rejected as socially valid ways of behaving (Gusfield, 1966, p. 126).

More generally, Gusfield has called attention to the fact that "deviance designations have histories," that they tend to become symbols of general cultural attitudes and, hence, often generate conflict between supporting and opposing groups and segments of a society (see Gusfield, 1967).

A study of two different antipornography campaigns (one in the north Midwest, and one in the Southwest) reached the similar conclusion that they "were symbolic more than utilitarian." The authors of this research found that public demonstration in support of a particular life-style and set of values was, in these instances, more important to the participants than was achieving effective measures to eliminate the pornography "problem" (Zurcher, *et al.*, 1971). We can expect that, in one form or another, symbolic status aspects will be present in most controversies over deviance-defining. This follows directly from the conception of deviance we have been developing throughout this text, with its key emphasis on processes of disvaluation. If deviance situations always involve some people trying to disvalue others, then by the same token they always pose issues of "status." Albert Cohen has suggested that what is basically at issue in deviance-defining is the public evaluation of identities, collective as well as individual:

> Members of a collectivity have a stake in the collective identity, or corporate self, because it is one of the components of their own identities. They bear its name and, to some extent, whatever taint or aura attaches to that name. It is a source to them

of pride or shame. We should expect, then, that the rules by which men in collectivities judge one another will demand behavior that supports the collectivity's claims to distinction . . ." (Cohen, 1974, p. 14).

The threat that activates deviantizing—that provokes reinforcement of "moral boundaries" or signals an exceeding of "tolerance limits"—is, it should be emphasized, *perceived* threat. It need *not* be a real or objective threat. Whether the threat be material and imminent or greatly exaggerated such perception can trigger deviance-defining and associated reactions. Since this perception is the key to how such situations evolve, we can see that the "causes" of boundary-maintaining actions and shifts in boundaries really lie more with the reactors themselves (viewed collectively) than with the deviators. This fact has led one sociologist to state that, "Deviance can be thought of as a product of the movement of moral boundaries rather than as a product of the movement of actors across those boundaries" (Lauderdale, 1976, p. 661).

Lauderdale conducted an ingenious experiment to test various propositions about threat and boundaries under small-group "laboratory" conditions. Subjects were asked to engage in a social work evaluation of the case histories of various juvenile delinquents and to recommend appropriate correctional treatment for them. One supposed subject who was actually a confederate of the researcher (the "deviant") consistently adopted an extreme position during the group's evaluation discussions. To some of the sessions (there were 40 different groups) Lauderdale introduced an additional factor of "outside threat"—an observer of the group discussions (ostensibly a criminal justice expert) commented to Lauderdale within the hearing of the group members that "this group should probably not continue." At the end of the meeting, group members were told it might become necessary to reduce the group size and were asked to rank other members in terms of their own preference for serving with them again. While the "deviant" (the confederate-extremist) received considerably lower preference ratings than did other members overall, this difference was much greater (i.e., rejection was much stronger) in the "threat" situation.

Similar results were obtained when members were separately asked in an interview whether there were any people in the group with whom they particularly did not want to work. Thirty percent rejected the "deviant" in the threat condition, as opposed to only 10 percent rejection where no threat had been imposed (Lauderdale, 1976, pp. 664–667). While these were just some of Lauderdale's findings, they are especially significant ones. They show that deviantizing (boundary-maintenance efforts) can occur or change *independent* of any actual change in the deviation. In all the groups, the deviator's problematic or offending behavior was essentially the same. The only thing that varied was the "external" threat. Although Lauderdale was exploring the impact of outside threat on reactions to "internal" (within-the-group-itself) deviation, the overall thrust of these findings seems applicable to deviance situations generally. It is change in the perception of threat, regardless of whether there has been change in the extent of deviation *per se,* that provokes these rejecting responses.

Just how "imaginary" can the threat be and still produce such results? As the earlier comments about inherent status implications in deviantizing suggest, when such responses occur, there will almost always have been *some* grounds for perceiving threat. To extend this point a bit, social changes never occur "for no reason at all." Even in the Lauderdale experiment we saw an "explanation" of the response—namely, a kind of mistake in perception, since the subjects there were "duped" into feeling threatened. There are always reasons, then, for people acting to impute deviantness. Sometimes the reason may be a "mistake," sometimes irrational fear. More usually, the reason is found in sociocultural conditions or forces. Yet these reasons sometimes may have little to do with the purported deviation itself. We saw this in Currie's witchcraft study, which showed how the "creation" of witches varied according to sociocultural context and the nature of the sociolegal control systems.

Another side to this perplexing relation between purported deviation and the collective "response to it," concerns the overall *volume* of perceived or processed deviance in a society at any given time. We noted earlier a point developed by Kai Erikson—that the volume of deviance may reflect the extent of processing efforts or the size of the social control apparatus itself. Deviance-production, we might say, depends on deviance-"finding." Erikson suggested this as part of a broader claim that, "social groups are likely to experience a relatively stable 'quota' of deviation . . ." (Erikson, 1966, p. 163). He found a fairly constant offender rate" in Puritan Massachusetts (during the period 1651–1680) and concluded that several apparent "crime waves" in that period represented fluctuations and "displacements" within such an overall "quota." Walter Connor questioned this notion of constant volume in his analysis of the Soviet political purges of the late 1930s (Connor, 1972b). Noting that these purges seemed to represent a virtual "epidemic" of deviance, Connor asserted that under totalitarian conditions (a highly "repressive" control system, drawing on Currie's distinction between that type and the more "restrained" type) "elasticity" in the volume of deviance rather than the "constancy" Erikson had described seemed to be present. Under these special circumstances, there seemed to be hardly any limits on the "creation" and processing of supposed deviants. Connor pointed out that certain specific control arrangements—such as containing the "offenders" in remote camps rather than in prisons and using them for forced labor—facilitated the expansion of control limits without an incurring of excessive cost.

"Discovering" Deviance

In a very broad sense, deviance is *always* collectively "created" because deviance-defining requires initially some characterization and categorization of types of behaviors and appropriate responses. In other words, there must be the *idea* of "witchcraft" and its implications before "witches" can be identified and processed. With the rise of "social construction of reality" and other definitional perspectives, sociologists have become interested in researching this element of the "discovery" of particular deviance categories. Presumably, the rise of every such category might be documented in terms of the sociocultural, historical, and political context in which it occurred. The origins and functions of the idea of "mental illness" is an example of this background conceptualizing that has generated a good deal of recent interest among sociologists and also in other disciplines. Thus, the French historian and critic Michel Foucault has perceptively traced the development of ideas of "madness" in Europe from the Middle Ages to the age of modern psychoanalysis (Foucault, 1967). Psychiatrist Thomas Szasz has treated the same general development in a more ideologically tinged way, adopting as his title *The Manufacture of Madness* and claiming to show close analogies between the "mental health movement" (which he condemns) and the Inquisition (Szasz, 1970b). Social historian David Rothman has investigated the growth of the "asylum" (mental hospitals, prisons, almshouses) in the United States during the 1820s and after. His analysis highlighted a mixture of collective anxiety and reformist optimism:

> The response in the Jacksonian period to the deviant and the dependent was first and foremost a vigorous attempt to promote the stability of the society at a time when traditional ideas and practices appeared outmoded, constricted, and ineffective. The almshouse and the orphan asylum, the penitentiary, and the reformatory, and the insane asylum all represented an effort to insure the cohesion of the community in new and changing circumstances. Legislators, philanthropists, and local officials, as well as students of poverty, crime, and insanity were convinced that the nation faced unprecedented dangers and unprecedented opportunities. The asylum, they believed, could restore a necessary social balance to the new republic, and at the same time eliminate long-standing problems. At once nervous and enthusiastic, distressed and optimistic, they set about constructing and arranging the institutions (Rothman, 1971, xviii).

More recently, yet another interpreter has emphasized parallels between lunacy reform movements in America and Britain, in proposing that "growth of the capitalist market system and . . . its impact on economic and social relationships" triggered the rise of the asylum (Scull, 1977b).

Another, already cited, instance of the creation of a new deviance conception is "hyperkinesis" (also known as minimal brain dysfunction, hyperactive syndrome, etc.). Pointing to a variety of *"social factors* that set the context for the emergence of [this] new diagnostic category," Peter Conrad has linked its development to a broader trend toward "medicalization," "individualization," and "depoliticization" of problematic behavior. "By defining the overactive, restless and disruptive child as hyperkinetic we ignore the meaning of behavior in the context of the social system. If we focused our analysis on the school system we might see the child's behavior as symptomatic of some 'disorder' in the school and classroom situation, rather than symptomatic of an individual neurological disorder" (Conrad, 1975, p. 20; see also Schrag and Divoky, 1976).

The growth of other deviance classifications involving children as both offenders and victims have similarly been investigated. In his sociohistorical exploration of the American juvenile court movement, Anthony Platt emphasized that prior to the passage of the first juvenile court legislation (Illinois, in 1899) "delinquency" did not exist. This was not to say that kids didn't get into trouble, often serious trouble, but rather that these statutes embodied new conceptions of youthful trouble, provided new ways of identifying and classifying it, and new court and court-related procedures for dealing with it. Hence Platt's subtitle, "The Invention of Delinquency." As Platt pointed out, this movement not only embodied humanitarian concern for youth:

> It brought within the gambit of governmental control a set of youthful activities that had been previously ignored or handled informally. It was not by accident that the behavior selected for penalizing by the child savers—drinking, begging, roaming the streets, frequenting dance-halls and movies, fighting, sexuality, staying out late at night, and incorrigibility—was primarily attributable to children of lower-class migrant and immigrant families (Platt, 1969, p. 139).

In a later section of this chapter, we will return to some persisting implications of this particular processing system. One of the very important contributions of Platt's study has been to show that this change in collective deviance-defining had as much to do with the reformers as with the "problem." Examining the special role of a group of middle-class feminist welfare reformers, he found even that, "The child savers were aware that their championship of social outsiders such as immigrants, the poor, and children, was not wholly motivated by disinterested ideals of justice and equality. Philanthropic work filled a void in their own lives, a void which was created by the decline of traditional religion, increased leisure and boredom, the rise of public education, and the breakdown of communal life in impersonal, crowded cities" (Platt, 1969, p. 77).

With respect to yet another child-related area, a sociologist recently has written of "the discovery of child abuse." According to Stephen Pfohl, the passage of special laws against this offense in all 50 state legislatures during a 16-year period beginning in 1962 was "not attributable to any escalation of abuse itself." Rather, various developments in the profession of medicine, including the growing influence of pediatric radiology as a subspecialty and the fact that abuse provided a field for mutually beneficial alliance between pediatrics and psychiatry, may have been key determinants of this change (Pfohl, 1977). As these several examples should indicate, the "invention of deviance" thesis can be useful in studying almost any specific type of deviantizing.

Very likely this particular "social construction of reality" aspect of deviance situations comes across most clearly with respect to legal categories. There, because the technical offense is so literally "created" through legislation, it is hard to ignore the specific context within which it was legislated. Thus such crimes as "corporate price-fixing," "sexual harassment," "illegal wiretapping," "improper prescribing of barbiturates," "advertising fraud," and political "conflict of interest," all have a rather evident time- and context-bound quality. To fully understand any one of them, we would have to explore the context and developing events out of which it arose. But this is true also of disvaluation categories that do not come to be directly embodied in formal laws. Some examples would be the loosely used designations of "commie" and "pinko," "speed freak" and other such drug-related classifications, "hippie" (to the extent that was a deviantizing label), and, more recently (at least in some circles), "white racist" and "male chauvanist pig."

Even long-standing and widely adopted deviance classifications have their special histories and reflect aspects of the context out of which they emerged. The aforementioned studies of the history of "madness" point up the possibilities for research along these lines. Another good illustration was provided by William Chambliss' sociohistorical investigation of the law of vagrancy. Tracing this offense back to an English statute of 1349, Chambliss concluded that the "prime-mover" for such legislation had been the Black Death, which had just before then devastated England, in particular, decimating the labor force. The new laws were calculated to force workers to accept employment even at low wages in order to bolster the position of employers, which had already been threatened by other social changes in the preceding period. Subsequent shifts in the vagrancy statutes attended the growth of commercialism. The laws came to be directed primarily against people who preyed on merchants transporting goods, and, hence, their focus changed from worker control to the control of more "criminal" types. Later, in the United States, their use to cover a broad range of criminals and undesirables persisted (Chambliss, 1964; see also, Chambliss, 1976). More recently, the writer Susan Brownmiller has made an important contribution to our understanding of the offense of rape, in large part by examining it in broad sociocultural and historical perspective. With respect to early legal conceptualizations in this area she asserts:

The ancient patriarchs who came together to write their early covenants had used the rape of women to forge their own male power—how then could they see rape as a crime of man against woman? Women were wholly owned subsidiaries and not independent beings. Rape could not be envisioned as a matter of female consent or refusal; nor could a definition acceptable to males be based on a male-female understanding of a female's right to her bodily integrity. Rape entered the law through the back door, as it were, as a property crime of man against man. Woman, of course, was viewed as the property (Brownmiller, 1976, p. 8).

Comparative research discloses that not only the emerging classifications of stigmatizable behavior, but also the major rationales for stigmatizing deeply reveal the stamp of the particular sociohistorical and political contexts. Connor's research on deviance-defining in the Soviet Union clearly illustrates this contextual influence. Because of Marxist ideology, which traditionally has treated most deviance as an artifact of the capitalist system, the Soviet authorities have been hard put to explain and respond to the very clear persistence in their country of a variety of problematic behavior patterns (including adult crime, delinquency, and alcoholism). On the one hand, Marxist doctrine emphasizes the socioeconomic determinism of most behavior; on the other hand, the state authorities cannot very easily admit to their social and economic system having "caused" these persisting deviations. As Connor shows, they have tried to avoid this dilemma by attributing the problems to the alleged malfunctioning of basically sound institutions such as the family, the school, the factory, the youth organization. With respect to delinquency, for example, they propose prevention by improving the effectiveness of such specific institutions. This approach incorporates "a denial that there are delinquency-provoking factors inherent in Soviet Society" and, at the same time, a denial that the delinquent is some "special type of person." By focusing on improving the workings of the "infrastructure," Soviet policy "maintains ideological acceptability while admitting, as a practical matter, that the performances of concrete institutions of control and socialization both can be and are frequently flawed" (Connor, 1972a, p. 94).

Similarly context-revealing rationales for deviance-defining have been noted in postrevolutionary Cuba. Martin Loney, studying the persisting use there of strong public sanctions against "loafing," political dissidence, and even homosexuality, ties these to the needs of the Cuban political economy and the authorities' conviction that they must maintain revolutionary vigilance and a "monopoly on cultural symbolism" (which is believed threatened by alternative "life-styles"). The recent Cuban experience, then, reflects both the need to maintain revolutionary commitment and, at the same time, the fact that revolution alone is not sufficient to produce a problem-free society; as a consequence, "progressive" and "reactionary" tendencies continue "uneasily to coexist" in such a setting (Loney, 1973). Needless to say, these two examples should not be taken to imply that collective deviance characterizations and responses reflect sociopolitical context only under revolutionary or totalitarian regimes. As we noted before—particularly in considering the failure to strongly deviantize white-collar and corporate crimes—and as various writers have strongly emphasized (see, for example, Chambliss and Mankoff, 1976), the dominant conceptions and responses in our own country equally illustrate the same general thesis, in that they reflect the structure and priorities of a system geared to advanced "monopoly capitalism."

For all of the reasons suggested in the material we have just reviewed, sociologists now seek to place instances and categories of deviance-defining in an historical context. There are at least two levels on which this sociohistorical research and interpretation can proceed. One is the *level of broad historical developments and overall "functions"* of a particular type of deviance-defining for the society or for subgroups. At the other level, we can examine *the sequences*

of more specific events and the efforts by various individuals or groups to influence these events that immediately surround a particular change in imputing
deviantness. Clearly, the short-term and long-term "histories" tend to meld into
one another. As we noted earlier, the concrete developments at any given time
must reflect the broader forces; yet, it is also true that the broader history is
"made up of" many such more specific events.

At the intersection of these two levels may be the "boundary crisis," some
possible causes of which we have just been considering. Threat, uneasiness, uncertainty, and a felt need to clarify, reaffirm, or redefine existing conditions and
outlooks—and, in the process, "moral boundaries"—seem to be the underlying
determinants of these crises. Of the several specific "crime waves" occurring in the
Massachusetts Bay colony during the seventeenth century, Erikson has noted that,
"each followed a period of unsettling historical change, during which the boundaries which set the New England way apart as a special kind of ethic threatened
to become more obscure" (Erikson, 1966, p. 70). With respect more specifically to
one of the concrete crises that arose—that posed by the unorthodox religious
beliefs of Anne Hutchinson and her followers—Erikson has written:

> The settlers were experiencing a shift in ideological focus, a change in com-
> munity boundaries, but they had no vocabulary to explain to themselves or anyone else
> what the nature of these changes were. The purpose of the trial was to invent that
> language, to find a name for the nameless offense which Mrs. Hutchinson had committed.
> All in all, Anne Hutchinson and her band of followers were guilty of something called
> "Hutchinsonianism," no more and no less, and one of the main outcomes of the trial
> was to declare in no uncertain terms that people who acted in this fashion had tres-
> passed the revised boundaries of the New England Way (Erikson, 1966, p. 102).

Moral Crusades

The translation of broadly experienced trends into specific "crises" or
other deviance-related events does not just happen automatically. As Becker has
put it, deviance "is always the result of enterprise. Before any act can be viewed
as deviant, and before any class of people can be labeled and treated as outsiders
for committing the act, someone must have made the rule which defines the act
as deviant" (Becker, 1963, p. 162). Particularly with respect to deviance situations
that incorporate legal enactments, a full sociological interpretation requires some
attention to the sequence of specific events through which the passage of legislation evolved or the growth of an enforcement practice or policy emerged.

An early example of this kind of analysis was Sutherland's exploration
of the "sexual psychopath" laws which were enacted in many American states
during the 1930s and 1940s and which typically provided for indefinite confinement in a mental hospital, applying the amorphous psychopathy label to individuals committing a highly varying range of sexual "offenses." Sutherland
found that characteristically there were three major stages leading up to the

passage of such legislation: (1) the arousal of much fear in the local community as a result of a number of serious sex crimes; (2) a stage of "agitated activity of the community" resulting from this fear, in which people became familiar with the dangers and felt a consequent need for some control action; and (3) the appointment of a committee to marshall the facts and to make recommendations. Even when there was substantial terror within a community, Sutherland asserted, if such a committee was not formed, the likelihood of a sex psychopath law resulting was much lower than when this happened (Sutherland, 1950).

Pamela Roby's close examination of one legal enactment—a revision of New York State's prostitution law during the mid-1960s—points up the value of directly studying testimony and debate at legislative hearings, the substance of commission proceedings, relevant contemporaneous events and public statements, and other such highly specific yet potentially very influential elements in particular deviance situations (Roby, 1969). She found that a small number of strongly interested individuals and organizations used legislative hearings and commission deliberations (during the course of a "five phase" sequence of developments) to exert major influence on the eventual outcome in that instance.

In their recent reformulation of the aforementioned, group-conflict oriented "natural history of social problems" analysis, Spector and Kitsuse have sought to generalize broadly about the typical "stages" found in the emergence and development of collective characterizations of situations as being problematic. Although not specifically framed in deviance terms, their delineation of stages is nonetheless highly pertinent for our purposes here. They suggest the following characteristic stages:

Stage 1: Group(s) attempt to assert the existence of some condition, define it as offensive, harmful or otherwise undesirable, publicize their assertions, stimulate controversy, and create a public or political issue over the matter.

Stage 2: Recognition of the legitimacy of these group(s) by some official organization, agency, or institution. This may lead to an official investigation, proposals for reform, and the establishment of an agency to respond to those claims and demands.

Stage 3: Reemergence of claims and demands by the original group(s); or by others, expressing dissatisfaction with the established procedures for dealing with the imputed conditions, the bureaucratic handling of complaints, the failure to generate a condition of trust and confidence in the procedures and the lack of sympathy for the complaints.

Stage 4: Rejection by complainant group(s) of the agency's or institution's response, or lack of response to their claims and demands, and the development of activities to create alternative, parallel, or counter-institutions as responses to the established procedures (Spector and Kitsuse, 1977, p. 142).

As these authors further note, crucial determinants of success in these "claims-making" efforts include the relative power of opposing groups and their ability to document their claims and generate a broader movement of social support. In his thorough research on one concerted change campaign, for reform of juvenile justice procedures in California, Lemert found that the following factors also were very important in generating effectiveness: a group's sound organization and strong commitment to clear-cut goals, its having access to key decision-makers, its ability to dramatically demonstrate the evils it seeks to overturn, and its ability to generate a belief among the opposition of its inevitable success in the struggle (Lemert, 1970, p. 157).

The term **moral crusade** is now widely used in deviance sociology to describe concerted and sometimes organized efforts to shape deviance policies. Becker used this term primarily for moralistic individuals and groups working to create new deviance categories, to label new groups of "outsiders." Similarly he employed the concept of **moral entrepreneur** (thereby highlighting the fact that some individuals develop a strong stake in moral crusading), distinguishing two basic types—rule-creators and rule-enforcers (Becker, 1963, chs. 7 and 8). Yet, as much of the foregoing discussion should have made clear, on most deviance issues we actually find an ongoing *two-sided struggle over competing collective definitions* of the situation. Although Becker adopted the term "crusader" because of its connotations of holy mission and rooting out evil, partisans and activists on *both* sides in any such struggle could be viewed as being similarly engaged in crusading of a sort. Both are engaged in "moral enterprise," which Becker describes as "the creation of a new fragment of the moral constitution of society, its code of right and wrong" (Becker, 1963, p. 145). The accompanying News Spots describes a specific confrontation that erupted as part of one ongoing moral struggle of this sort.

POLITICIZATION OF DEVIANCE

From Latent to Overt Conflict

By seeking the causes of deviance in the offending individual and by tending to assume general social agreement on norms, traditional approaches frequently diverted attention away from the conflict aspects of deviance situations. Lack of overt public conflict all too often was taken to indicate underlying consensus or harmony. Conflict theorists as well as those who have been developing other versions of a definitional perspective on deviance have persistently argued that this apparent consensus was illusory. They have insisted that latent conflict lay just beneath the surface, that an open clash of conflicting norms and values was prevented only by the overbearing power of dominant social forces and interests. Today, this once-latent conflict is becoming increasingly overt and, thus, impossible to ignore.

If the concept "moral crusade" usually has been applied to campaigns for the expansion of deviance definitions, the term "politicization of deviance" has implied the opposite—organized attempts to narrow or overturn such definitions, to "un-deviantize" existing deviance categories, and to combat collective

NEWS SPOT
Gay Rights in Miami

(January–November 1977). Gay rights as a public and political issue began to receive heavy national attention in late spring of 1977 as a result of publicity that attended the acrimonious controversy over a local ordinance and subsequent referendum in the Miami, Florida, area. The previous January, Dade County's commissioners had adopted a civil rights ordinance that guaranteed homosexuals equal rights in jobs, housing, and public accommodation. Although similar legislation had been passed in over 30 other cities across the nation, in this instance, the measure soon generated strong and organized opposition. Spearheading attempts to overturn the ordinance was singer Anita Bryant, who until then was perhaps best known for her nationwide television commercials for Florida orange juice. Under Bryant's leadership, a local group called Save Our Children was organized, and some 60,000 signatures were obtained (only 10,000 were needed) on a petition to place the ordinance before the public in a referendum vote.

Bryant, a devout Southern Baptist and mother of four school-age children, argued on religious grounds that homosexuality is immoral (she was widely quoted as branding it an "abomination" and conjuring up general visions of Sodom and Gomorrah) and claimed that the ordinance would result in homosexual proselytizing, possibly even molestation of children. "If homosexuality were the normal way," she stated, "God would have made Adam and Bruce." Bryant's "crusade," as even some sympathetic observers termed it, quickly led to a polarization of the local community (for example, Miami clerics divided sharply on the issue, with a small but rather influential group openly supporting the ordinance which, they asserted, was intended "neither to approve nor to condemn any one life style") and also produced a substantial influx of "outside" activists and organizers on both sides of the issue. Gay liberation groups in various parts of the country offered support; letters and contributions flowed in to Save Our Children headquarters; some gay activists mounted a boycott of orange juice as a way of denouncing Bryant; civil liberties and other specialists publicly charged Save Our Children with using false and manufactured issues to reinforce stereotyping and discrimination, citing in particular, a large body of evidence to the effect that child molestation is predominantly a heterosexual offense. Just before the referendum took place, two national gay leaders declared in *The New York Times* that, "Anita Bryant and her Save Our Children Inc. are doing the 20 million lesbians and gay men in America an enormous favor: They are focusing for the public the nature of the prejudice and discrimination we face."

In the referendum vote, which took place June 7, residents of the Miami area overturned the gay rights ordinance by a 202,319 to 89,562 vote. More than 40 percent of eligible voters had gone to the polls, an unusually large turnout for a local referendum. According to one analysis of the voting patterns, "In a county where 59 percent chose Jimmy Carter in November, where Democrats outnumber Republicans 4 to 1, and where a large Jewish population traditionally votes liberal, only 61 of 446 precincts voted to keep the antidiscrimination law." As a close student of the area's politics stated, "Obviously, homosexuality is still a very scary thing to many people here."

The Miami vote provoked large gay rights demonstrations in several American cities and led national gay activist leaders to proclaim they would expand and strengthen their efforts to alter public outlooks and policies. Meanwhile, Bryant and her organization, since reestablished on a national basis with the new title of Protect American Children (PAC), were planning to carry their antihomosexuality campaign to other parts of the country. There were reports that PAC had ties with the Conservative Caucus—a group bringing antigay forces together with those opposing abortion, the Equal Rights Amendment, and gun control. In a *New York Times* column that was in many ways favorable to her cause, conservative journalist William Safire wrote that, "The trouble with Miss Bryant's victory is that she now intends to treat the Miami landslide as a license to launch a vast national crusade. That means that the ringing answer given to the activists' demand for moral legitimacy might lash back into an invasion of their legitimate civil rights."

At the same time, increasing debate on and general media coverage of gay rights issues were occurring. National survey results published during July 1977 indicated a continuing ambivalence in the public's attitude. Fifty-six percent of the respondents said that homosexuals should have equal rights in job opportunities; yet they were evenly split on the question of whether homosexual relations between consenting adults should be legal. Sixty-five percent held that homosexuals should not be hired as elementary schoolteachers, and 54 percent would have similarly excluded them as clergy. As gay reformers were rededicating themselves to their cause, the news came in November that the Florida Citrus Commission, notwithstanding considerable public pressure, had extended Anita Bryant's contract to advertise orange juice through August 1979. The Commission issued a resolution supporting her right to state her views on any subject. Some civil libertarians expressed approval of this result, seeing the orange juice boycott as having posed disturbing free speech implications.

Already-angry gay activists may well have concluded from this move that public antihomosexuality was far from becoming a discredited stance. One chronicler of the gay movement predicted that Miami might well have been "the first explosion of the nation's next major struggle."

Source: Based on articles and columns in *The New York Times,* May 10, 1977, p. 18; May 31, 1977, p. 14; June 7, 1977, p. 35; June 8, 1977, p. 1; June 9, 1977, pp. 1, A21, D21; July 17, 1977, p. 34; July 19, 1977, p. 17; November 17, 1977, p. C2; *The Village Voice,* April 4, 1977, p. 11; June 20, 1977, p. 13; *The Nation,* November 19, 1977, p. 526.

---

disvaluation and stigmatization. Irving Horowitz and Martin Liebowitz have suggested that until recently a social welfare ideology, in which specialists recognized the "problems" of deviators for whom or about whom something had to be done, helped keep the underlying conflicts hidden. Under such an ideology, "decision-making concerning deviance has been one-sided. The superordinate parties who regulate deviance have developed measures of control, while the subordinate parties, the deviants themselves, have not entered the political arena" (Horowitz and Liebowitz, 1968, p. 282). This situation seems rapidly to be changing. Citing early deviance self-help organizations such as Synanon, Horowitz and Liebowitz noted the development of organized responses to collective repression. "A broad base for the political organization of deviants now exists, and demands for the legitimation of deviant behavior will increasingly be made" (Horowitz and Liebowitz, 1968, p. 283). As they went on to suggest, what may once have been a tenable distinction between "political marginality" on the one hand and "social deviance" on the other has been rendered largely obsolete. Particularly through civil rights and antiwar activities, the line between the two categories has become blurred. More and more, politically motivated individuals have felt it necessary to engage in acts that otherwise would be labeled "deviance" (e.g., urban rioting, bombings by revolutionary groups, etc.). At the same time, the fuzziness in the distinction has increased from the other side as well, as so-called "deviants" have increasingly been drawn to what ordinarily would be termed "political" action, organizing to influence policy, holding political demonstrations, engaging in lobbying, and even running their "own" candidates for office.

In a now-classic essay on reference-group theory, Robert Merton sought to distinguish between ordinary deviance and "nonconformity." The latter term would apply to those failures or refusals to conform in which there was a fairly clear commitment to or advocating of alternative norms (Merton, 1957, pp. 357–368). Merton appears primarily to have had in mind extreme contrasting types—career (perhaps "professional") criminals, on the one hand; avowedly political dissidents ("radicals," etc.) on the other. Yet with the growth of organized efforts to reshape a wide range of deviance definitions, the distinction—which these events in a way tend to undermine—should be considered in a broader context. Merton cited the following major grounds for distinguishing between the nonconformist and the criminal:

1. Whereas the criminal typically tries to hide his norm-violating, the nonconformist "announces his dissent."

2. Nonconformists openly challenge the legitimacy of the norms they violate (that is, the violation is actually a rejection), whereas, according to Merton, the "criminal" is likely to accept the basic legitimacy of such norms.

3. Nonconformists want to change the norms, whereas criminals only seek to avoid the sanctions for violating them. The nonconformist typically "appeals to a 'higher morality.' "

4. Most importantly, because of such moral claims, the nonconformist is, however reluctantly and subconsciously, assumed to depart from prevailing norms for wholly or largely disinterested purposes; the criminal is assumed to deviate from the norms in order to serve his own interests (Merton, 1957, pp. 360–361).

As this last point suggests, the greatest significance of Merton's distinction lies in the contrasting evaluations elicited by the two types. In fact, we might even conclude that these terms more accurately connote types of collective characterization than they do types of behavior. Merton himself emphasized this social response aspect:

The avowed nonconformist tends to be regarded with mingled feelings of hate, admiration, and love, even by those who still cling to the values and practices being put in question. Acting openly rather than secretively, and evidently aware that he invites severe sanctions by the group, the nonconformist tends to elicit some measure of respect, although this may be buried in thick layers of overt hostility and hatred among those who have a sense that their sentiments, their interests, and their status are threatened by the words and actions of the nonconformist (Merton, 1957, p. 366.).

In short, the nonconformist is not as much disvalued as the criminal although, as we have seen (and as Merton does acknowledge by referring to "overt hostility," etc.), political deviation itself can certainly provoke stigmatizing responses. Merton's distinction seems to incorporate some questionable assumptions regarding criminality (he treats "the criminal" as a single type), and it is not easily applied in considering such "involuntary" deviators as the physically disabled, who are neither held to be conscious norm-"violators" nor on the other hand "respected." Beyond those problems, however, the recent politicization of deviance throws the entire distinction into question. The line between the two types has become exceedingly blurry.

In effect, what has been happening is that more and more people who, before now, have been deviantized are asserting a claim to being treated as "nonconformists." Such people are insisting that their behaviors and conditions not be considered "social problems," but rather that they be recognized as "alternative life-styles" that should be included among legitimate "options" as "minority patterns" that have been unfairly and unwisely suppressed, or as private and free "choices" and individual "rights" that deserve legal protection. In other words, they are trying collectively to negotiate "political" rather than "deviance" definitions of their situations. When gay activists call for an end to oppression of homosexuals, when abortion reformers insist on woman's freedom to choose whether to bear a child, when the disabled demonstrate for governmental assistance and greater public support, they are all invoking broadly political terminology and seeking political solutions. They are offering, in a societal-level counterpart of a device we considered earlier in discussing individuals and stigma, alternative "accounts."

In the running struggles over conflicting collective definitions of once-stigmatized behaviors and conditions, relative social power significantly affects outcomes. As at the individual level, various kinds of resources may provide a basis for such power. Table 7.2 depicts a number of ways of characterizing certain collective conflict situations. There, size, organization, and political and economic power of the opposing groups, along with the degree of perceived threat experienced by the more powerful group are taken to be the main factors determining which type of definition will prevail. However, we should recognize that the nature, characteristics, and relative power of the groups themselves will usually represent only part of the overall deviance situation. General features and trends in a society during a given period, various other situational occurrences, and, perhaps, an overall atmosphere of general inertia or receptiveness to social change

Table 7.2 Conflict Situations: Dimensions of the Character and Relations of Parties in Conflict

RESULTING POPULAR DEFINITION OF THE CONFLICT SITUATION	SIZE AND ORGANIZATION OF PARTY FEARED	ECONOMIC AND POLITICAL POWER OF PARTY FEARED RELATIVE TO PARTY FEARING	DEGREE TO WHICH THE WELL-ORGANIZED OPPOSING LARGE MINORITY OR MAJORITY FEELS FEARFUL OR THREATENED
Deviance ("crime," etc.)	Individual or small, loosely organized groups	Almost none	Very high
Civil uprising or disorder	Small, loosely organized groups	Relatively low	Very high
Social movement	Sizeable organized minority	Relatively low	Mild
Civil war	Large, well-organized minority	Relatively high or almost equal	Very high
Mainstream party politics in the United States	Large, organized minority	About equal	Mild

Source: John Lofland, *Deviance and Identity* (Englewood Cliffs, N.J.: Prentice-Hall, 1969), p. 15; reproduced with permission.

may all contribute to specific deviance-defining developments. Thus, shifting responses to, say, abortion and homosexuality not only result from the power and activity of partisan groups, but they also reflect broader trends in values relating to sexual behavior and sex roles and, perhaps, general demographic trends as well. Another way of putting this is to say that there are always reasons why one group has more power than another; to understand the sources of such power, we must often look beyond the groups themselves.

Nonetheless, differential power remains extremely important. Implicit in Table 7.2 is the possibility—though for some sets of categories shown there it may not easily pertain—that a given set of facts could produce several different "resulting popular definitions of the conflict situation," depending upon the distribution and uses of power. It is in that sense that Merton's deviance-nonconformity distinction remains useful as pointing up two alternative types of characterization and, not so much, as we noted earlier, fixed types of behavior. However, for a group's preferred definitions to prevail, not only must the distribution of power and the sociocultural context be favorable, but the group's activities and implicit underlying motivation also must be consistent with the image it tries to convey. In discussing the significance of public reactions to recent racial disturbances, Ralph Turner developed this point by noting how such reactions affect both the course and the results of collective behavior.

To be viewed as legitimate protestors rather than criminals or wild-eyed revolutionaries, a group has to display appropriate characteristics:

> To be credible as protestors, troublemakers must seem to constitute a major part of a group whose grievances are already well documented, who are believed to be individually or collectively powerless to correct their grievances, and who show signs of moral virtue that render them "deserving." Any indication that only few participated or felt sympathy with the disturbances predisposes observers to see the activities as deviance or as revolutionary activity by a small cadre of agitators (Turner, 1969, p. 818).

Furthermore, if the desired response is to be attained, the group must have been ordinarily law-abiding, and the protest must seem more or less spontaneous and unmotivated by personal gain. Turner also analyzed various other features of such situations, including likely patterns of differential response to these disturbances: "groups who see themselves as even more disadvantaged than the protestors are least likely to grant their claim. Viewed from below, disturbances are most easily comprehended as power plays or as deviance" (Turner, 1969, pp. 819–820). In gearing his analysis to urban racial disturbances, with their characteristic elements of "rioting," "looting," and the like, Turner focused on an especially charged type of situation, one in which group "image" may take on particularly heightened significance. Yet it seems likely that a comparable process of public perception vitally shapes conflicts over all kinds of deviance-defining. Indeed, we see illustrated at this collective level yet another version of the "labeling" and "social construction of reality" theses. Here, too, the processes of perception and meaning attribution, and the patterns of associated response, determine, in many important respects, what "is."

Liberation Movements

In a book on "societies of deviants in America," published ten years ago, Edward Sagarin recorded the formation of self-help organizations among alcoholics, drug addicts, gamblers, illegitimate children, homosexuals, transvestites and transsexuals, convicts and ex-convicts, fat people, dwarfs, and ex-mental patients (Sagarin, 1969). Many of these groups were modeled after the early leader in this kind of venture, Alcoholics Anonymous, as can be seen in such titles as Narcotics Anonymous, Fatties Anonymous, and Illegitimates Anonymous. At that time, most of the organizations aimed at providing the stigmatized individual with group support, mutual aid, and often their special versions of therapy. Thus, they were oriented primarily to adjustment, if not to cure. For the most part, the focus remained on the individual members, on helping them to overcome their deviation or the obstacles it presented, to manage better in a predominantly hostile world. A great deal of emphasis was placed on the value of getting together with similarly stigmatized people in a nonthreatening atmosphere. Recognition of common experience and mutual discussion of ways of adapting would enhance member morale. Many of these groups also offered various kind of practical assistance and served as informal clearinghouses for needed information and contacts.

As part of the more recent politicization of deviance, a new kind of organization has emerged—sometimes directly out of these self-help forerunners, sometimes alongside them and now continuing to co-exist with them. The newer groups tend to be more overtly political in orientation. They are not so much concerned with members' immediate problems and personal adaptations as they are with influencing public attitudes and public policies. They seek to overturn institutionalized oppression, rather than to improve individual adjustment. This recognition of systematic oppression, of categorical discrimination, is perhaps the key to the political intent of these groups. Such organizations are fostering a new consciousness, an awareness that the "problem" resides not in the members but, rather, in the disvaluating responses of others. In a sense, this shift in perspective among the stigmatized themselves is similar to what has often occurred through "consciousness-raising" group sessions in the recent women's movement. Although some of these groups have a rather strong "therapy" aspect, the crucial focus of the discussions has been problems the women have experienced *as women*. As a consequence, group members come to recognize the institutional sources of what previously seemed like individual shortcomings or "symptoms" of personal maladjustment. One writer states that, "Consciousness raising is one of the most political acts in which women can engage. In CR, women learn what economics, politics, and sociology mean on the most direct level: as they affect their lives" (Dreifus, 1973, p. 6).

The new outlooks and collective efforts among deviantized people also clearly reveal important parallels to and some influence from the civil rights movement (see Howard, 1974). A growing unwillingness to accept stigmatization without protest, the emergence and organized fostering of a new self-esteem (for example, "gay pride," an obvious parallel to earlier "black pride" concepts), and increasingly direct action to confront and change repressive policies and practices, all mirror development of collective confidence and militancy in the black movement. Indeed, a theme often developed in the recent politicizing of deviance is that of the oppressed minority. At the beginning of this text we noted some of the parallels between minority-group status and deviance, and the subsequent discussion of deviantizing has developed some of those points more fully. Table 7.3 summarizes major elements common to both minority and deviance situations. As can be seen there, these fall into two broad categories. One includes basic features and consequences of the stigmatizing process itself. The other reflects similarity in the techniques now being used to overcome oppression. We might say that the features in category A have given rise to the efforts listed in category B and also have provided the basis for militant deviators to assert and make

Table 7.3 Similarities Between Deviance and Minority Situations

A. DEVIANTIZING AND ITS CONSEQUENCES	B. COLLECTIVE EFFORTS TO ALTER DEVIANTIZING
Stereotypes and misconceptions	Repudiation of stereotypes and general public reeducation
Master status trait; role primacy—the person seen in terms of the category	Redefining the "problem" as resting with the oppressors—e.g., "racism," "sexism," "homophobia," "agism," etc.
General disvaluation; less than "full" status as a person	Re-"labeling" the deviantized category—e.g., "blacks" (not Negroes), "gays," "little people," use of "Ms.," etc.
Avoidance and/or segregative tendencies on the part of others	
Restricted opportunities	Collective organization for support and social action
Possibility of "role engulfment"	Direct political action—lobbying, demonstrating, electioneering, etc.
Likelihood of lowered self-esteem	
Possible need to engage in defensive adaptations—self-segregation, disavowal, denial, neutralization, etc.	Ameliorative legislation—equal opportunity statutes, civil rights commissions, etc.
	"Test cases" in the courts

public use of the minority-group analogy. As both Merton's discussion of nonconformity and Turner's analysis of the perception of protest show, asserting a claim to political status and having it accepted are two different things. At present, public response in this country to the minority-group analogy remains uncertain. Members of the more "traditional" racial and ethnic minorities—often in conflict among themselves regarding the relative merits of their respective needs and claims—no doubt find it difficult to accept these "other minorities" (Sagarin, ed., 1971) as being equally deserving of recognition and corrective action.

A claim to minority status is, however, only one of various tacks that deviance liberation organizations can take. While activists might wish ultimately to see a dramatic shift in public attitudes establishing wide credibility of their claims to having been oppressed, their more immediate priority involves changes in specific policies and practices, in institutionalized arrangements that perpetuate stigma and disadvantage. Just as enforcement of civil rights legislation can reduce discrimination against blacks even when the underlying attitudes of would-be discriminators have not always changed, so, too, can oppression in these other areas be reduced even in the absence of wholesale alteration of current perceptions. At the same time, as various studies of interracial contacts suggest, increased breakdown of the institutionalized barriers to contact and communication can gradually lead to increased mutual tolerance as stereotypes and other misconceptions crumble.

A major current illustration of strong collective efforts to undo systematic oppression against presumed deviators is the gay liberation movement. This movement grew out of the so-called "homophile" organizations (such as the

Mattachine Society), which formerly represented the only source of collective support and assistance for homosexuals (see Sagarin, 1969, ch. 4). Through those early groups, some sense of pride in homosexual identity and rejection of the prevailing disvaluations and "diagnoses" began to develop. While the glimmerings of a new militancy may have been present earlier, there has been a very dramatic eruption and expansion of homosexual organizing and activism since the late 1960s. (The militant gay movement is often said to have come into being during the summer of 1969 through an incident in New York City involving direct confrontation between homosexuals and the police.) The recent organizations have, among other things, lobbied for repeal of antihomosexuality criminal laws and passage of civil rights protection for gay people, organized important public demonstrations in support of gay rights, publicized the opinions and votes of political candidates on homosexuality-related issues, generated electoral candidates from the gay community itself, urged bloc voting by homosexuals, and brought test cases in the courts to challenge antigay discrimination. They have also monitored and criticized the mass media, organized speakers bureaus in a widespread public reeducation effort, and have even helped bring about the establishment of gay churches and other specialized gay organizations.

As studies of the gay liberation movement reveal (Humphreys, 1972; Altman, 1973), it is actually made up of a large variety of not very well-coordinated organizations that differ considerably as to major objectives and preferred strategies. This is not surprising since the movement holds appeal for homosexuals (and some heterosexual allies) of all ages, socioeconomic backgrounds, education levels, occupations and professions, and political orientations. What one finds now, then, is a wide range of groups varying both in degrees of militancy and in major ideological focus. There are organizations made up of avowedly political activitists. Some of these are totally preoccupied with the homosexual's own cause; others see themselves as being in the vanguard of some broader "radical" change in American life. There are still other groups that are less concerned with political action (though they will support it) and more with furthering the gay "life-style" and gay pride. And all kinds of combinations of these different themes are represented as well. Some of the organizations bring together male homosexual and lesbian activists, and others are more "separatist." Overall, however, what is indisputable is an enormous growth in visibility, open declaration of demands and voicing of protests, and recourse to direct public confrontation. Even if the movement is somewhat fragmented, the composite impact has been considerable. As such, it demands to be taken seriously, by sympathizers and opponents alike.

The same kind of spread of militancy has occurred in a good many other deviance-related areas as well. Physically handicapped people are coming to view themselves as constituting an oppressed minority and are acting accordingly. "Using some of the tactics that worked for blacks, including angry and ironic slogans such as 'You gave us your dimes, now we want our rights,' thousands of disabled are picketing, filing suits and lobbying for the equal protection promised but never received under the Fourteenth Amendment" (Schultz, 1977). In April of 1977 a coalition of groups representing 36 million handicapped Americans staged a sit-in at the office of the Secretary of Health, Education and Welfare in Washington, D.C., demanding implementation of a federal law prohibiting discrimination against the handicapped that had been passed four years earlier. Several weeks later, the Secretary signed the implementing regulations, which will widely affect employment practices, the design and construction of buildings, and various practices at schools, colleges, and hospitals that receive federal support (see *The New York Times*, April 11, 1977, p. 12; April 29, 1977, p. 1).

Influence from the women's liberation movement has helped bring about much of the recent collective militancy regarding several specific deviance issues, such as abortion, rape, and prostitution. The rapid acceleration (beginning in the mid-1960s) of efforts to repeal restrictive abortion laws is especially noteworthy. While a potential impetus to change existed earlier in the experience of women who had undergone dangerous illegal abortions and in critiques of the repressive laws by medical and legal specialists (see Calderone, ed., 1958; Schur, 1965; Lader, 1966; also "Victimless Crimes," below), the prospects for even moderate reform did not seem very strong. With the growth of the women's movement and the recognition of abortion as a major women's issue, rapid and thoroughgoing legal change suddenly became a real possibility. Rallies were held, protest coalitions formed, and test cases brought into the courts (Lader, 1973). The result was dramatic—repeal of legal restrictions on abortion in several states, including New York, and more moderate reform in others, and a decision by the U.S. Supreme Court in January 1973 that ruled unconstitutional any legal restrictions on abortion during the first three months of pregnancy (except that the operation be performed by a licensed physician) (see Sarvis and Rodman, 1974, ch. 4). The continuing and highly fluctuating debate and course of developments since then, which at the time of this writing includes a heated controversy regarding federal funds for indigent women who seek abortions, only serves to reinforce the conclusion that policy in this deviance area has become a highly politicized matter.

The growth of black militancy and of general political protest during the 1960s have contributed directly to heightened liberation efforts in yet another sphere of deviance-defining by helping to radicalize prisoners and ex-prisoners (Wright, 1975). In her survey of American prisons, writer Jessica Mitford noted that the opening wedge for current militancy was forged by Black Muslims in the early sixties when, despite attempted repression by the authorities, they won important court decisions allowing them to practice their religion within the institutions. Since then a great expansion in prisoner militancy has occurred:

> Radical and revolutionary ideologies are seeping into the prisons. Whereas formerly convicts tended to regard themselves as unfortunates whose accident of birth at the bottom of the heap was largely responsible for their plight, today many are questioning the validity of the heap. Increasing numbers of prisoners are beginning to look

upon the whole criminal justice system, with the penitentiary at the end of it, as an instrument of class and race oppression (Mitford, 1973, p. 232).

The influx of new radically oriented types of prisoners, the contacts with them that have been maintained by certain outside militant organizations, and the opposition-reinforcing impact of events such as the aforementioned Attica killings, all serve to strengthen the developing pattern of militancy. A related development (seen in one of the documents reproduced in Adaptation Eleven) is the growth of prison unions. Such organizations are now at work in more than ten states, despite persisting opposition from local corrections officials (Reid, 1976, pp. 545–547).

As these comments have indicated, a number of major trends in organizing for social change in American life have come together as precursors of and models for the politicizing of deviance issues. We can see the same kinds of influences at work in the closely analogous efforts of older people to combat disvaluation and discrimination (see the Gray Panther material in Adaptation Eleven). One recent discussion of the elderly as a political force noted:

> On the national level, the elderly demonstrated their growing power this fall [1977] by promoting legislation that bans mandatory retirement before age 70 in most cases. They are also winning the battle to liberalize limits on how much a recipient of Social Security is allowed to earn without losing any benefits.
> In state legislatures, vigorous lobbying by older people has produced a vast array of legislation on issues ranging from the sale of generic drugs to reduced rates on income and property taxes. Given this political power, the elderly are also capturing a growing share of Government outlays for social services (Roberts, 1977, p. 26).

In the rhetoric they employ, their organizational "style" (which attempts to maintain what sixties radicals called "participatory democracy"), and their commitment to a broad set of radical social goals for American society, the Gray Panthers have clearly drawn on the examples provided by earlier liberation movements. While the organization (which began developing in 1970) at first consisted only of older people and had a relatively narrow focus on problems of the aging, both the membership and the organization's goals have since been considerably broadened. The group now incorporates young persons as well as old and, as the statement in Adaptation Eleven shows, is dedicated to eradicating not only "agism," but also sexism, racism, and even "militarism and extreme nationalism." There has also been a substantial expansion of the organization's activities, which now include many projects at both the local and national levels, a proliferation of "local networks" in many parts of the country, national conferences, extensive lobbying, and cooperation with other sympathetic reform groups (Earley and Kuhn, 1974). The organization's wide-ranging policy platform probably helps explain its growing influence in co-existence with or, sometimes, "competition" with other less militant organizations for the elderly, such as National Association of Retired Persons and Concerned Seniors for Better Government. The fact that one in ten Americans is now over 65 years of age obviously helps to ensure a broad potential "constituency" for the various groups working in this area.

This last point suggests a more general issue regarding organized efforts to politicize deviance issues. As Lofland's chart (Table 7.2) on the different ways of characterizing conflict situations indicates, the size and influence (power) of reform (and also antireform) groups are key factors in determining their effectiveness. The broader and more heterogeneous the support that an activist organization can enlist, the more likely it is going to have a significant impact on public policy. The sheer size of the aging, female, and male homosexual segments of the population (estimates often place one in ten American males in this category) implies a good deal of potential influence on certain deviance issues. However, as we already noted in connection with the gay liberation movement, this very broadness and inclusiveness of the stigmatized category can also mean a good deal of factionalism, since *within* the potential constituency are many crosscutting social and political groupings. Some of the general confusion and divisiveness within the current "women's movement" in our society illustrates this problem. Racial and social class differences, differences in commitment to feminism and/or radicalism, and differences in sexual orientation (lesbians/heterosexuals) have all served to limit development of unified "women's" positions on various deviance issues. Potentially, the power is there, and a good many such issues can be seen to fall under the "women's issue" umbrella. Thus, the International Tribunal on Crimes Against Women, convened in Brussels in March 1976 (and one resolution from which is included in Adaptation Eleven), discussed, among other things, abortion, prostitution, rape, persecution of lesbians, "woman battering," "sexual objectification" of women, and "economic crimes" against women (Russell and Van de Ven, 1976). In order for maximum collective power to be marshalled on such issues, the various bases for factionalism within the broader movement would have to be moderated or overcome in some fashion.

Similar types of factionalism emerge in most antideviantizing movements. Some reference already has been made to the uneasy alliance of various gay groups and segments; in that instance, special problems have centered around the partially differing commitments of lesbian and male subgroups, and also the division between political radicals and what some in the movement term "the gay establishment." It should also be noted that many of the *organizational features and tendencies* we considered earlier with respect to social control agencies can also influence the work of liberation organizations. Complex internal and external relationships, routinization, displacement of goals, and even the growth of entrenched ideologies and vested interests can all undermine activist commitment and unity. Finally, some efforts may falter for lack of a sizeable and diversified power base to begin with, which may be a factor that somewhat limits rapid success in efforts to de-stigmatize prisoners and prostitutes. Maximal conditions for exerting influence seem to include a large unfactionalized constituency, general social receptiveness to the group's position (the aforementioned sociocultural context and trends), and ability to enlist support from influential groups and individuals that are not themselves directly affected by the policies at issue. This is what seems to have happened with respect to marihuana law reform (see below)—not only has there been the enormous growth in use of the drug cited earlier and an associated shift in public attitudes, in addition, the organized change efforts, spearheaded by the National Organization for the Reform of Marihuana Laws (NORML), have been greatly assisted by support from prominent figures and major groups in the medical, legal, and social science professions.

A variety of factors, then, will determine whether a deviance reform organization will be able to develop a strong "liberation" focus and whether it can lay claim to constituting a real "social movement." In both respects, success is likely to be measured in degrees. If there are many obstacles present within any one such effort to politicize a deviance issue, it follows that the prospects for all such efforts to come together as a single coherent overall "deviance liberation movement" are probably slim. Sagarin, writing of the early deviance self-help organizations, saw them as constituting some new type of social movement (Sagarin, 1969). And we have seen that, without doubt, they represent a broad trend of increasing politicization. But, it remains true that the various organizations, campaigns, and specific "movements" tend to have at the very least different priorities. On some matters they will work together; on others their efforts may go off in different directions. They all favor liberation, but they do not always define that goal the same way; nor are they in complete agreement as to who most needs liberation and to what ends. Nonetheless, and unified or not, collective organizing to combat particular types of deviantizing is having, on a composite basis, a profound impact in contemporary American society. Adaptation Eleven presents a variety of statements that help to convey the spirit of the new militancy.

ADAPTATION ELEVEN
Broadsides and Manifestoes

Best known among recent "deviance liberation movements" is the gay rights movement discussed in the text. Efforts to politicize deviance issues actually extend into a variety of substantive areas, focus on a great many specific patterns and policies, and range from single incidents and lone crusades to national or even international organizing. The statements included in this adaptation indicate some of this diversity. They reflect the growing political consciousness and action of people presently incarcerated, formerly incarcerated, harassed and intermittently prosecuted, or subject to socioeconomic discrimination and indignity. Inclusion of the Gray Panther material points up the analogy developed in the text between deviance-defining and other types of stigmatizing and collective discrimination. As that organization's statements show, part of what has happened to older people in our society is that they, too, have, in effect, been deviantized.

PRISONERS*

FOLSOM MANIFESTO—Demands from Folsom (Cal.) Prison's 19-day strike of 1970, also used in the Attica rebellion:

1. *We demand* the constitutional rights of legal representation at the time of all Adult Authority hearings, and the protection from the procedures of the Adult Authority whereby they permit no procedural safeguards such as an attorney for cross examination of witnesses, witnesses in behalf of the parolee, at parole revocation hearings.

2. *We demand* a change in medical staff and medical policy and procedure. The Folsom Prison Hospital is totally inadequate, understaffed, prejudicial in the treatment of inmates. There are numerous "mistakes" made many times, improper and erroneous medication is given by untrained personnel. . . .

3. *We demand* adequate visiting conditions and facilities for the inmates and families of Folsom prisoners. The visiting facilities at this prison are such as to preclude adequate visiting, for the inmates are permitted two hours, two times per month to visit with families and friends, which of course has to be divided between these people. We ask for additional officers to man the visiting room five days per week, so that everyone may have at least four hours visiting per month. . . .

4. *We demand* that each man presently held in the Adjustment Center be given a written notice . . . explaining the exact reason for his placement in the severely restrictive confines of the Adjustment Center.

5. *We demand* an immediate end to indeterminate Adjustment Center

terms to be replaced by fixed terms with the length of time served being termi-
nated by good conduct and according to the nature of the charges, for which
men are presently being warehoused indefinitely without explanation.

6. *We demand* an end to the segregation of prisoners from the Mainline
population because of their political beliefs. Some of the men in the Adjustment
Center are confined there solely for political reasons and their segregation from
other inmates is indefinite.

7. *We demand* an end to political persecution, racial persecution, and
the denial of prisoners to subscribe to political papers, books or any other educational and current media chronicals [sic] that are forwarded through the United
States Mail.

8. *We demand* an end to the persecution and punishment of prisoners
who practice the constitutional right of peaceful dissent. Prisoners at Folsom and
San Quentin Prisons according to the California State Penal Code cannot be
compelled to work as these two prisons were built for the purpose of housing
prisoners and there is no mention as to the prisoners being required to work
on prison jobs in order to remain on the Mainline and/or be considered for
release. Many prisoners believe their labor power is being exploited in order
for the State to increase its economic power and continue to expand its correctional industries which are million dollar complexes, yet do not develop working
skills acceptable for employment in the outside society, and which do not pay
the prisoner more than the maximum sixteen cents per hour wage. Most prisoners
never make more than six or eight cents per hour. Prisoners who refuse to work
for the two to sixteen cent pay rate, or who strike, are punished and segregated
without the access to the privileges shared by those who work, this is class legislation, class division, and creates class hostilities within the prison.

9. *We demand* an end to the tear-gassing of prisoners who are locked
in their cells, such action led to the death of Willie Powell in Soledad Prison in
1968 and of Fred Billinslea on February 25th, 1970 at the San Quentin Prison.
It is cruel and unnecessary.

10. *We demand* the passing of a minimum and maximum term bill which
calls for an end to indeterminate sentences whereby a man can be warehoused
indefinitely, rehabilitated or not. That all prisoners have the right to be paroled
after serving their minimum term instead of the cruel and unusual punishment
of being confined beyond his minimum eligibility for parole, and never knowing
the reason for the extention [sic] of time, nor when his time is completed. The
maximum term bill eliminates indefinite life time imprisonment where it is
unnecessary and cruel. . . . if a man cannot be rehabilitated after a maximum of
ten years of constructive programs, etc., then he belongs in a mental hygine [sic]
center, not a prison. . . .

11. *We demand* that industries be allowed to enter the institutions and
employ inmates to work eight hours a day and fit into the category of workers
for scale wages. The working conditions in prisons do not develop working incen-

tives parallel to the money jobs in the outside society, and a paroled prisoner faces many contradictions on the job that adds to his difficulty to adjust. . . .

12. *We demand* that inmates be allowed to form or join Labor Unions.

13. *We demand* that inmates be granted the right to support their own families. . . . Men working on scale wages could support themselves and their families while in prison.

14. *We demand* that correctional officers be prosecuted as a matter of law for shooting inmates, around inmates, or any act of cruel and unusual punishment where it is not a matter of life and death.

15. *We demand* that all institutions who use inmate labor be made to conform with the state and federal minimum wage laws.

16. *We demand* an end to trials being held on the premises of San Quentin Prison, or any other prison without the jury as stated in the U.S. Constitution as being picked from . . . the peers of the accused; that being in this case, other prisoners as the selected jurors.

17. *We demand* an end to the escalating practice of physical brutality being perpetrated upon the inmates of California State Prisons at San Quentin, Folsom, and Soledad Prison in particular.

18. *We demand* appointment of three lawyers from the California Bar Association for full-time positions to provide legal assistance for inmates seeking post-conviction relief, and to act as liaison between the Administration and inmates for bringing inmate complaints to the attention of the Administration.

19. *We demand* update of industry working conditions to standards as provided for under California law.

20. *We demand* establishment of inmate workers insurance plan to provide compensation for work-related accidents.

21. *We demand* establishment of unionized vocational training program comparable to that of the Federal Prison System which provides for union instructors, union pay scale, and union membership upon completion of the vocational training course.

22. *We demand* annual accounting of Inmate Welfare Fund and formulation of inmate committee to give inmates a voice as to how such funds are used.

23. *We demand* that the Adult Authority Board appointed by the Governor be eradicated and replaced by a parole board elected by popular vote of the people. In a world where many crimes are punished by indeterminate sentences, where authority acts within secrecy and within vast discretion and gives heavy weight to accusations by prison employees against inmates, inmates feel trapped unless they are willing to abandon their desire to be independent men.

24. *We strongly demand* that the State and Prison Authorities conform to recommendation #1 of the "Soledad Caucus Report," to wit, "That the State Legislature create a full-time salaried board of overseers for the State Prisons. The board would be responsible for evaluating allegations made by inmates, their families, friends, and lawyers against employees charged with acting inhu-

manely, illegally or unreasonably. The board should include people nominated by a psychological or psychiatric association, by the State Bar Association or by the Public Defenders Association, and by groups of concerned, involved, laymen."

25. *We demand* that prison authorities conform to the conditional requirements and needs as described in the recent released manifesto from the Folsom Adjustment Center.

26. *We demand* an immediate end to the agitation of race relations by the prison administrations of this state.

27. *We demand* that the California Prison furnish Folsom Prison with the services of Ethnic Counselors for the needed special services of Brown and Black population of this prison.

28. *We demand* an end to the discrimination in the judgement and quota of parole for Black and Brown People.

29. *We demand* that all prisoners be present at the time that their cells and property are being searched by the correctional officers of state prisons.

BILL OF RIGHTS—Distributed by the Prisoner's Union along with this manifesto is a "Bill of Rights of the Convicted Class." The Preamble reads as follows: "We the people of the convicted class, locked in a cycle of poverty, failure, discrimination and servitude; do hereby declare, before the world, our situation to be unjust and inhuman. Basic human rights are systematically withheld from our class. We have been historically stereotyped as less than human, while in reality, we possess the same needs, ambitions and dignity indigenous to all humans. Our class has been unconstitutionally denied equal treatment under the law. We are the first to be accused and the last to be recognized. [There follow general articles and specific sections covering such matters as legal representation, medical care, voluntary employment and job training, and qualifications of correctional personnel—"as the foundation upon which we shall be liberated".]

* Source: Distributed by the Prisoner's Union, San Francisco; reprinted here by permission.

FORMER MENTAL PATIENTS*

Statement, Mental Patients' Liberation Project

We, of the Mental Patients' Liberation Project, are former mental patients. We've all been labeled schizophrenic, manic-depressive, psychotic, and neurotic—labels that have degraded us, made us feel inferior. Now we're beginning to get together—beginning to see that these labels are not true but have been thrown at us because we have refused to conform—refused to adjust to a society where to be normal is to be an unquestioning robot, without emotion and creativity. As ex-mental patients we know what it's like to be locked up in mental institutions for this refusal; we know what it's like to be treated as an object—to be made to feel less of a person than "normal" people on the outside. We've all felt the boredom, the regimentation, the inhumane physical and psychological abuses of institutional life—life on the inside. We are now beginning to realize that we are no longer alone in these feelings—that we are all brothers and sisters. Now for the first time we're beginning to fight for ourselves—fight for our personal liberty. We, of the Mental Patients' Liberation Project, want to work to change the conditions we have experienced. We have drawn up a Bill of Rights for Mental Patients—rights that we unquestioningly should have but rights that have been refused to us. Because these rights are not now legally ours we are now going to fight to make them a reality.

MENTAL PATIENTS' BILL OF RIGHTS. We are ex-mental patients. We have been subjected to brutalization in mental hospitals and by the psychiatric profession. In almost every state of the union, a mental patient has fewer *de facto* rights than a murderer condemned to die or to life imprisonment. As human beings, you are entitled to basic human rights that are taken for granted by the general population. You are entitled to protection and recourse to the law. The purpose of the Mental Patients' Liberation Project is to help those who are still institutionalized. This Bill of Rights was prepared by those at the first meeting of the MPLP held on June 13, 1971 at the Washington Square Methodist Church [in New York City]. If you know someone in a mental hospital, give him/her a copy of these rights. If you are in a hospital and need legal help, try to find someone to call the Dolphin Center.

1. You are a human being and are entitled to be treated as such with as much decency and respect as is accorded any other human being.

2. You are an American citizen and are entitled to every right established by the Declaration of Independence and guaranteed by the Constitution of the United States of America.

3. You have the right to the integrity of your own mind and the integrity of your own body.

4. Treatment and medication can be administered only with your consent, you have the right to demand to know all relevant information regarding said treatment and/or medication.

5. You have the right to have access to your own legal and medical counsel.

6. You have the right to refuse to work in a mental hospital and/or to choose what work you shall do and you have the right to receive the minimum wage for such work as is set by the state labor laws.

7. You have the right to decent medical attention when you feel you need it just as any other human being has that right.

8. You have the right to uncensored communication by phone, letter, and in person with whomever you wish and at any time you wish.

9. You have the right not to be treated like a criminal; not to be locked up against your will; not to be committed involuntarily; not to be fingerprinted or "mugged" (photographed).

10. You have the right to decent living conditions. You're paying for it and the taxpayers are paying for it.

11. You have the right to retain your own personal property. No one has the right to confiscate what is legally yours, no matter what reason is given. That is commonly known as theft.

12. You have the right to bring grievance against those who have mistreated you and the right to counsel and a court hearing. You are entitled to protection by the law against retaliation.

13. You have the right to refuse to be a guinea pig for experimental drugs and treatments and to refuse to be used as learning material for students. You have the right to demand reimbursement if you are so used.

14. You have the right not to have your character questioned or defamed.

15. You have the right to request an alternative to legal commitment or incarceration in a mental hospital.

The Mental Patients' Liberation Project plans to set up neighborhood crisis centers as alternatives to incarceration and voluntary and involuntary commitments to hospitals. We plan to set up a legal aid society for those whose rights are taken away and/or abused. Although our immediate aim is to help those currently in hospitals, we are also interested in helping those who are suffering from job discriminaiton, discriminatory school admissions policies and discrimination and abuse at the hands of the psychiatric profession. [There follows telephone number and address at which, at the time of this writing, the Project was no longer located.]

* *Source: The Radical Therapist,* 2, 4 (December 1971), as reprinted in Phil Brown, ed., *Radical Psychology.* New York: Harper & Row, Publishers, 1973, pp. 521–524; reprinted here by permission.

PROSTITUTES*

BACKGROUND STATEMENT OF COYOTE (from organization's press kit):

COYOTE   October 29, 1976
P.O. Box 26345
San Francisco, CA 94126
(415) 957-1610   IMMEDIATE RELEASE

BACKGROUND

COYOTE: *Call Off Your Old Tired Ethics*

FOUNDED: Mother's Day, 1973

CHAIR MADAM: Margo St. James

MEMBERSHIP: Working membership 850, mailing constituency of 10,000. A coalition of prostitutes, ex-prostitutes and friends of prosstitutes.

STATUS: Nonprofit; office manager/bookkeeper receives a stipend for coordinating volunteers, mail and office procedures ($200 per month).

DUES PER ANNUM: $3 Student Senior Citizens, $5 General, $25 Contributing, $50 Participating, and $100 Sustaining.

PRIMARY GOAL: To initiate and cooperate with legislators on a State and National level that will remove prostitution from the criminal code and from any governmental control. Making prostitution legal is NOT Coyote's stand because it would still involve and enable the government to license and to regulate what a woman does with her body.

ORGANIZATIONAL GOALS: Recommending adequate counsel, arranging for bail, helping prostitutes fill out arrest forms, educating prostitutes to their rights, including their rights to plead not guilty and demand a jury trial; developing a bail fund for prostitutes who so plea and working for their release on their own recognizance; assist with pre-trial diversion if such a program exists. In addition to challenging requirements that prostitutes be subject to VD quarantines, provide for emergency housing for women immediately out of jail, providing child care for women while they are in jail, providing emergency help for the battered prostitute and helping develop job opportunities for women who wish to leave the profession.

MEANS OF SUPPORT: Membership dues, fund raising events (Hooker's Ball), speakers bureau, tapes, books, Coyote Tee shirts, buttons and printed materials.

PUBLICATION: Coyote Growls dedicated to exposing and eliminating current laws against prostitution and other non-crime crimes.

---

* *Source: Press Kit,* distributed by Coyote, San Francisco; reprinted here by permission.

[Supplementary statement by Margo St. James: "Coyote became a political concept and inspired support groups for hookers around the globe. *Coyote Howls,* a quarterly published by Margo St. James, evolved as the voice of the exploited and oppressed prostitutes of America. A National Task Force on Prostitution was launched in 1978 in conjunction with a call for hookers to 'turn in their antis' (ERA legislators) to the nearest NOW, and a request was made to VISTA to fund reformed hookers who were doing peer counseling and crisis center work. Prostitution has been accepted by the women's movement and will be on the NOW agenda (nationally) in October." *Source:* personal correspondence with the author, July 1978.]

AN INTERNATIONAL RESOLUTION*

Be it resolved that sexual acts in private between consenting adults shall be outside the purview of the criminal laws, that commercial sexual activities be recognized as a service business, not as a criminal act, and that it be treated as such, that women be as free to walk and converse on the streets as men. All laws that discriminate against such activity by statute or by enforcement shall be eliminated, that women who choose to be prostitutes do so of their own free will after the age of consent and that no coercion by anyone be tolerated.

That prostitution be recognized as dependent on a repressive sexist socialization that can eventually be changed. Women and men who are free from sexual stereotypes and economic discrimination will be free from commercial sexual exchange.

* *Source:* Diana E. H. Russell and Nicole Van de Ven, eds. Proceedings of the International Tribunal on *Crimes Against Women.* (Millbrae, Calif.: Les Femmes, 1976), p. 196.

THE HANDICAPPED*

What Is Disabled in Action (DIA)?

An organization consisting primarily of—and directed by—people with disabilities dedicated to improving their legal, social and economic condition so they may achieve complete integration into society. A "disability" is defined as a physical or mental impairment which substantially limits one or more major life activities. DIA is a non-profit, tax-exempt organization.

What Are DIA's Specific Areas of Concern?

Abolishing discrimination against people with disabilities in such areas as:

Education
Employment
Housing
Public Accommodations
Transportation

Combating paternalistic attitudes toward disabled people by public and private agencies and institutions.

Eliminating the social ostracism that separates disabled people from the mainstream of society.

How Does DIA Seek to Accomplish Its Goals?

By working for passage of laws that would affirm the rights of people with disabilities. Among legislation that DIA has supported are the Special Vehicle Identification permit law—the Merola bill—and the 1974 Flynn-Koppel law aimed at combating discrimination against disabled people in housing, employment and public accommodation.

By educating government officials, leaders of established institutions and the general public about disability and disabled people.

By public demonstration, when such action is necessary to call attention to matters of deep concern to people with disabilities. DIA organized the protest against the 1976 United Cerebral Palsy (UCP) telethon and joined with other groups during the gas crisis demonstration in 1974.

By monitoring the activities of those agencies which administer programs for disabled people. Among such agencies are the N.Y. State Office of Vocational Rehabilitation (OVR) and the U.S. Social Security Administration (SSA) which distributes Supplemental Security Income (SSI) and Social Security Disability Benefits (SSDB).

By testifying at public hearings on issues of concern to DIA.

How Is DIA Organized?

Membership in DIA is open to all persons, whether or not disabled.

DIA is governed by the Board of Directors—composed of eleven DIA members and elected annually by the general membership—and by an executive board consisting of the President, two Vice Presidents, a Secretary and a Treasurer, all of whom are elected by the Board of Directors.

Membership entitles you to attend all DIA meetings, receive its newsletter and other publications, and participate in its wide-ranging activities.

Members may also join one or more of the following DIA committees:

> Legislative
> Social Welfare
> Newsletter
> Consciousness-raising
> Membership
> Fund-raising
> Public Relations

How Do I Become a Member of DIA or Obtain Information?

If you will complete and mail the attached questionnaire, one of our members will contact you. Please print all information.

* *Source:* Mailing distributed by Disabled in Action, Metropolitan New York Area, n.d.; reprinted with permission.

OLDER PEOPLE*

Revised Gray Panther Goals

1. To develop a new and positive self-awareness in our culture which can regard the total life span as a continuing process in maturity and fulfillment.

2. To strive for new options for life styles for older and younger people that will challenge the present paternalism in our institutions and culture and to help eliminate the poverty and powerlessness in which most older and younger people are forced to live, and to change society's destructive attitudes about aging.

3. To make responsible use of our freedom to bring about social change, to develop a list of priorities among social issues, and to struggle non-violently for social change that will bring greater human freedom, justice, dignity and peace.

4. To build a new power base in our society uniting presently disenfranchised and oppressed groups, realizing the common qualities and concerns of age and youth and working in coalition with other movements with similar goals and principles.

5. To reinforce and support each other in our quest for liberation and to celebrate our shared humanity.

Distinctive Characteristics

The Gray Panthers consider themselves distinctive in the following ways:

1. We attack agism by viewing aging as a total life process in which the individual develops from birth to death. Therefore, we are concerned about the needs of all age groups.

2. We are a movement of older and younger persons.

3. We have a flexible structure as opposed to a bureaucratic organization: a network with multiple leadership and with no formal membership or dues.

4. We accept and work with cultural, racial, ethnic, and religious diver-

sity both within the movement and in society; we look for options rather than conformity.

5. We have a strong sense of militancy. Our concern is not only for study, education and services, but for effective non-violent action with an awareness of timing and urgency.

6. We advocate a radical approach to social change by attacking those forces such as materialism, paternalism, militarism and extreme nationalism which corrupt our institutions, attitudes and values.

Major Concerns

PREAMBLE: Like racism and sexism, agism is a destructive force which permeates our social institutions. In all of our efforts to solve societal problems, our primary goal will be to attack any manifestation of agism as well as racism and sexism.

Priorities for guiding us in planning resources, advocacy and information. Adopted by the national steering committee, March 9, 1975.

• Advocating participatory democracy and concern for all residents in institutional settings and participants in educational institutions, social service programs, and other social institutions.

• Adequate governmental support of mass transportation systems with minimal or no cost to consumers.

• Enactment of a universal, national health care program which will be administered through a public corporation rather than commercial insurance companies.

• Abolition of arbitrary and compulsory retirement and age discrimination in employment. Adequate job training and new career possibilities.

• Systematic approach toward the abolition of poverty with such measures as adequate universal guaranteed income, radical tax reform, guaranteed employment opportunities, and adoption of national compulsory standards for private pension systems and adequate supervision of the standards.

• Renewed effort by the government and industry to encourage and support a national program of housing with a thorough cultural mix of all age groups, income levels and racial background.

• Immediate effort to obtain general amnesty for all resisters and deserters in the Southeast Asian war. Redirection of monies poured into military programs and equipment into efforts to solve problems which concern people in their daily living.

• Reform of our educational system to include programs and opportunities for people of all age groups at minimal cost to participants.

PRIMARY GRAY PANTHER ISSUE: Health care delivery with emphasis on preventive health care (including home care) and alternatives to institutional care.

* *Source: The Gray Panther Network,* 1, (July 1974); reprinted with permission.

THE TREND TOWARD DECRIMINALIZATION

Some recent politicization campaigns have drawn encouragement and strength from a related general trend in sociolegal thinking—the growing belief that formal criminal sanctions should be leveled against only the most serious offenses. Legal philosophers down through the ages have debated the proper use of the criminal law, and many have stressed that there may be situations in which little can be accomplished by applying legal sanctions. There is some early sociological analysis along these lines, too, as in the work of William Graham Sumner, who stressed the resistance of entrenched norms ("the mores") to sudden change by law or otherwise (Sumner, 1906, 1960). Sutherland expressed concern about this same point in his writings on crime, noting that, "When the mores are adequate, laws are unnecessary; when the mores are inadequate, the laws are ineffective" (Sutherland and Cressey, 1966, p. 11). Another sociologist has used the term "patterned evasion of norms" for situations in which deviation from expressed rules is so widespread that formal control is impotent and a strong ambivalence about the behavior and the prohibition prevails (Williams, 1960, ch. X).

Generally speaking, however, until recently sociological analyses of deviance gave little attention to the substantive criminal law. As one eminent criminologist stated over 30 years ago: "We have made considerable efforts to discover what sort of person the offender is and why he has broken the law, and we rack our brains to find out what to do with him. . . . Hardly ever do we pause for a moment to examine critically the contents of that very law the existence of which alone makes it possible for the individual to offend against it" (Mannheim, 1946, p. 1). During the past two decades, a conjuncture of developments in legal thought and sociological analysis has produced renewed interest in this matter. Without question, a major influence on this course of events was the Wolfenden Report (named after the Committee's chairman), issued in Britain in 1957 by a governmental Committee on Homosexual Offences and Prostitution. Although best known for its recommendation that homosexual acts between consenting adults in private should no longer be considered a criminal offense (a change later enacted by Parliament), at least as important was the general stance the Committee adopted regarding the uses of criminal sanctions. It took the position that the criminal law is intended to preserve public order and decency, to protect the citizenry from offensive and injurious behavior, and to guard against exploitation and corruption, particularly of those who might have some special vulnerability. Beyond carrying out those purposes, however, it should not intrude into the private lives of citizens. Furthermore, the Committee stated, "Unless a deliberate attempt is to be made by society, acting through the agency of the law, to equate the sphere of crime with that of sin, there must remain a realm of private morality and immorality which is, in brief and crude terms, not the law's business. To say this is not to condone or encourage private immorality" (Committee on Homosexual Offences and Prostitution, 1957, pp. 9–10, 24).

The Wolfenden Report sparked a heated debate among legal scholars which continues to the present day. One eminent British jurist, Patrick Devlin, vigorously opposed the Committee's arguments, asserting that "the criminal law as we know it is based upon moral principle. In a number of crimes its function is simply to enforce a moral principle and nothing else." Furthermore, Devlin insisted, "The suppression of vice is as much the law's business as the suppression of subversive activities; it is no more possible to define a sphere of private morality than it is to define one of private subversive activity" (Devlin, 1965, pp. 7, 13–14). On the other hand, the renowned British legal philosopher H. L. A. Hart defended the Committee's stand. His tightly reasoned philosophical argument, closely following John Stuart Mill's writings on liberty, led him to the conclusion that immorality as such ought not be a crime. Noting the considerable human suffering that laws against private homosexuality had caused, Hart held that legal proscription produced no social gain sufficient to justify the interference with individual freedom that it entailed (Hart, 1963).

In the time since these early statements, it appears that, on balance, the Wolfenden-Hart "side" in the controversy has been winning out over the Devlin position, both in academic treatments of these issues and in terms of real-world events (legislation, judicial rulings, etc.). Increasingly, legal and other scholars have been asserting that, as Herbert Packer put it, "the criminal sanction, inflicting as it does a unique combination of stigma and loss of liberty, should be resorted to only sparingly in a society that regards itself as free and open" (Packer, 1968, pp. 249–250; see also Allen, 1964; Morris and Hawkins, 1970; and Kittrie, 1971). It should be apparent that the recently emphasized labeling and definitional perspectives in the sociology of deviance complement this legal view. Labeling-oriented studies of deviant careers and of control processes have highlighted the possibly undesirable, though unintended, consequences of "criminalizing." Definitional and "social constructionist" orientations underline the sense in which crime and crime problems are "created" through criminal legislation. A plausible policy implication of these recent approaches is that we should not attach negative, particularly official, labels to people any more than necessary. In the wake of these legal and sociological currents of thought, there has emerged what might be called a "minimalist" model of the criminal law (see Packer, 1968; Morris and Hawkins, 1970). An important aspect of this approach has to do with where the burden of argument and evidence is seen to lie. Many commentators now believe, in line with the arguments of the Wolfen-den Committee and H. L. A. Hart, that a heavy *burden of justification* always rests on *those who would limit individual freedom through the criminal law* (even where they simply support long-standing legislation). Thus, the presumption should be that recourse to criminal sanctions is an undesirable last-ditch effort at "social control." It is the supporters of such sanctions, rather than the opponents, who bear the heaviest burden to "prove" their case. This kind of reasoning has led an American Friends Service Committee study group to conclude that reliance on the criminal law is only justified when all of the following conditions are met:

1. there is compelling social need to require compliance with a particular norm;
2. the law and its administration can be applied equally, so that all are weighed with the same scales and so that the human costs of enforcement are spread among the largest feasible number of offenders.
3. there is no less costly method of obtaining compliance; and
4. there is some substantial basis for assuming that the imposition of punishment will produce greater benefit for society than simply doing nothing (American Friends Service Committee, 1971, p. 66; see also Packer, 1968, ch. 16).

Victimless Crimes

Considerable evidence has been adduced in recent years suggesting that there is a range of borderline "offenses" traditionally covered by the criminal law and with respect to which such criteria as were just cited cannot be met. A concept that has proved useful in describing at least some of these situations is that of "crimes without victims" (see Schur, 1965; Morris and Hawkins, 1970; Geis, 1972; Schur and Bedau, 1974; also Duster, 1970; Kittrie, 1971). The notion of **victimless crime** has been used in a number of different ways, some of which have provoked endless public controversy. Often, for example, the term is taken primarily to imply "lack of harm to others." Though many would insist that a wide range of supposed offenses are of that nature, the problem with using literal "absence of victimization" as the hallmark of this category is that there is a striking lack of consensus regarding specific applications of such a test. People may disagree strongly as to the presence or absence of a victim, especially in nonviolent "consensual" crimes. Thus, some would argue that the prostitute is a victim (of social conditions, of her pimp, or of exploitation by men), that the illegal drug-user is a victim of the drug, that the fetus is a "victim" of abortion. There is no easy way to reconcile the diverse moral judgments regarding victimization in such instances, and, indeed, the fact that criminal legislation has existed in such areas strongly suggests that at one time dominant segments of society found some kind of victimization (even if only with "society as the victim") to exist in these situations. In that very broad sense, there would never be *any* victimless crime. Another approach to these borderline offenses in which the focus is on improper "legislating of private morality" is equally problematic. On the one hand, all crime laws impose some "morality." Yet, how are we to determine what morality is "private," in order to know that its legislation was improper? Here again, the invariable intrusion of value judgments and priorities prevents consensus and confounds attempts to apply such a criterion.

There is a third sense, however, in which certain crimes are victimless, one which, from a sociological standpoint, can be much more useful. Some "offenses" consist of *willing exchanges of strongly desired (though legally proscribed)* goods or services. The crucial point about these situations is that, *regardless of* whatever victimization judgments outside observers might make, the participants do not see themselves as being directly victimized by the illicit transaction. As a consequence, nobody directly involved in the situation is likely to initiate enforcement of the law by complaining to the police. In the ordinary course of events, the drug-user does not wish to complain about the pusher's illegal drug-selling; the illicit gambler does not feel victimized by the bookie who facilitated his or her betting. In other words, these are characteristically "complainantless crimes." A large array of substantively varying offenses display this consensual transaction feature, with its typical absence of a complaining "victim." The category includes illicit drug use, consenting illicit sexual behavior (including homosexuality and prostitution), sale of pornography, and gambling and abortion (where illegal).

Clearly, these offenses differ from one another a great deal in certain respects. However, there are some very important objective consequences that almost always seem to follow from attempts to control by criminal law illicit exchanges of this sort. To begin with, laws of this type are *singularly unenforceable*. Because of the lack of a complainant, evidence needed for prosecution is extremely hard to come by. Because of the widespread demand for the proscribed goods and services, enforcement efforts are confounded by the persistent and ingenious development of illicit supply techniques and channels. Because of public ambivalence regarding the laws, enforcement officers attempt to apply them in an atmosphere of extremely uncertain support. This attempt, for the most part, is frustrated not only by the consensual nature of the transactions but also by the fact that frequently they occur in private—a combination of conditions that serves to maximize enforcement difficulty (see Duster, 1970, pp. 23–28).

Under these unpromising circumstances, enforcement authorities generally settle for a policy of routine harassment, periodic "crackdown," and "containment" of the most publicly visible aspects of the offending behavior. Enforcement policy becomes essentially geared to *regulating the problem,* with many enforcers openly admitting the impossibility of eliminating it. Applicable to all victimless crimes is the pessimistic kind of conclusion the President's Crime Commission reached with respect to laws against gambling: "People have been arrested, prosecuted, and convicted, but the prohibited conduct has flourished. The law may operate in some measure to diminish demand, but it is clear that criminal enforcement does not begin to control the problem" (President's Commission on Law Enforcement and Administration of Justice, 1967a, p. 100). Although there is sometimes a public clamor to "do something about" one or another of these offenses and legislatures occasionally respond by trying to stiffen the laws, this "get tough" approach rarely seems effective, at least in the long run. The news item summarized here provides a recent major illustration of this characteristic ineffectiveness.

The argument for decriminalizing victimless crimes does not, however, rest only on their unenforceability. These laws are not merely ineffective. Many informed observers have concluded, on the basis of all of the available evidence regarding their operation, that *the laws on balance do more harm than good.* Beyond their inevitable failure to curb the proscribed behaviors, they have produced unintended consequences that *have, overall, increased the amount of social*

NEWS SPOT
Harsh Drug Law Deemed Failure

(June 1977). In 1973 the New York legislature enacted the country's harshest antinarcotics law (popularly called "the Rockefeller drug law"), raising most penalties for sale and possession of illicit drugs and providing long mandatory minimum sentences for the more serious offenses with the possibility of life sentences in some cases. A careful evaluation of experience to date under this law, made for the Committee on Drug Law Evaluation (established by the Association of the Bar of the City of New York and the independent Drug Abuse Council and supported by large government and private grants) has indicated that, despite the possibility of stiff sentences, neither drug use itself nor drug-related crime has been effectively reduced. According to the Committee, the state spent $76 million implementing the law between the time of its passage and June 1976. In New York City alone, 31 new judges were appointed to deal with drug cases. Nonetheless, the Committee reported, "Police, courts, and prosecutors alike saw the law as a new drain on resources, which in their view were already inadequate."

Among highlights revealed in the report were the following: that heroin use was as widespread in New York City several years after the law had been passed as it had been before; that money-producing crimes commonly attributed to addicts increased despite the law; that the actual risk of imprisonment for some serious offenders decreased, notwithstanding the possibilities created through the statutes; that the risk of arrest did not actually increase and, therefore, "drug traffickers were not likely to see the new law as a serious threat." The major conclusion reached by the Committee was that neither stiff penalites nor special resources could by themselves be expected to produce effective control. Rather, "the efficiency, morale and capacity of the criminal justice system is even more of a factor in determining whether the law is effectively implemented." At any rate, the Committee emphasized, passing a new law is not enough.

Source: Based on an article in *The New York Times,* June 22, 1977, p. 1.

harm associated with the problems they aim to control. Such largely "secondary" consequences can be conveniently discussed as *"costs of criminalizing"* (Schur, in Schur and Bedau, 1974, pp. 11–37). Some of these costs have been suggested or implied at one point or another earlier in this text. However, it should be useful to gather these points together in this section, in order to appreciate fully their composite significance for our understanding of this general type of crime situation. Major costs of criminalizing in these areas can be placed in four categories: enforcement costs, other economic costs, "secondary crime" costs, and costs entailing corruption and disrespect for law.

1. **Enforcement costs.** Attempts to enforce victimless crime laws dissipate very limited social control resources (of personnel, time, and energy as well as money) that otherwise might be devoted to more serious crime situations. Thus, Morris and Hawkins have stated, "we must strip off the moralistic excrescences of our criminal justice system so that it may concentrate on the essential. The prime function of the criminal law is to protect our persons and our property; these purposes are now engulfed in a mass of other distracting, inefficiently performed, legislative duties" (Morris and Hawkins, 1970, p. 2). Victimless crime laws are unusually costly to enforce, precisely because of the absence of citizen complainants, which means that police must rely a great deal more on their own resources in order to garner evidence needed to support a prosecution. Since most experts agree that at present the entire criminal justice system—up to and including the courts—is greatly overburdened, many now question the current allocations of resources to the victimless crime areas.

Enforcement efforts in these areas are not only costly; they also raise serious ethical and constitutional issues. In the absence of direct complainants, the need to drum up evidence of such offenses pushes the police (as mentioned earlier in the discussion of "dirty work") into reliance on highly questionable investigative practices. Informers and decoys, long-term clandestine surveillance, wiretapping and other "bugging," and surprise ("no-knock") raids—these are the common means of investigating victimless crimes. A leading student of the police has noted that, "Without a network of informers—usually civilians, sometimes police—narcotics police cannot operate" (Skolnick, 1975, p. 120; see also Lindesmith, 1965, ch. 2). The use of decoys in seeking to incriminate prostitutes was mentioned in an earlier section. Similar techniques and also hidden surveillance are widely used in efforts to apply antihomosexuality laws (see Weinberg and Williams, 1975). Likewise, where abortion has been illegal, complicated surveillance techniques and elaborate "raid" procedures have been necessary in order to build a case against an illicit practitioner (Schur, 1965, pp. 35–38). Enforcement of antigambling legislation has always involved heavy reliance on wiretapping and other questionable information-gathering procedures.

It is significant that most major decisions of the U.S. Supreme Court concerned with the propriety of enforcement techniques (i.e., dealing with questions of compulsory self-incrimination, illegal search and seizure, invasion of right to privacy) have been in cases that arose out of police attempts to administer victimless crime laws. That not even these extreme and highly unsavory (often improper) techniques produce significant enforcement success except in isolated instances or short-term crackdown "drives" is more evidence of the inherent unenforceability of these statutes. What they do produce is police conduct that is unseemly, sometimes crime-supporting (as when addict-informers are paid for their information), and, when pushed too far, "illegal"; extensive invasions of individual privacy; and cynicism on all sides regarding the police role.

2. Economic costs. The major economic consequence of these laws was noted earlier in this book—the creation and reinforcement of a "supply-demand" cycle along the lines indicated by Packer's concept of "the crime tariff." Illegality provides strong economic incentives for illicit trafficking in the proscribed goods and services, for taking the risks involved in being part of such a black market. It is this illegality and the attendant risk for the illicit operators that, given per-sisting strong demand, pushes up prices and profits. As we saw in the case of drugs, most disinterested observers are convinced that such a profitable illicit enterprise could not easily prevail in competition with legal provision at cost of the currently illegal goods or services. In situations where it is difficult to impose even slight restriction on the availability of whatever is desired (for ex-ample, in victimless sexual offenses), the economic cycle does not necessarily become a major central feature of the "problem." But where the goods wanted are or become reasonably scarce (e.g., heroin) or where the services desired involve special skills (abortion) or complex organization (large-scale gambling), the stage is set for a thriving illicit market.

Such highly profitable enterprises understandably attract organized crime. As the President's Crime Commission pointed out, organized criminal groups, "participate in any illegal activity that offers maximum profit at minimum risk of law-enforcement interference. They offer goods and services that millions of Americans desire even though declared illegal by their legislature" (President's Commission on Law Enforcement and Administration of Justice, 1967c, p. 2). Noting that gambling is believed to provide the largest revenues for organized crime, Packer commented: "The combination of illegality and the need for organization produces a classic operation of the crime tariff. These monopoly profits then become available to sustain the activities of the criminal organiza-tion on a wide variety of fronts, including the penetration of legitimate and quasi-legitimate economic markets" (Packer, 1968, p. 350).

Another, more indirect type of economic "cost" of criminalizing—also alluded to in previous discussion—is the sharpening of socioeconomic class dif-ferences, both with respect to obtaining the desired goods or services and also with respect to the likelihood of encountering interference from law enforcers. Where the offense involves a direct economic transaction, these laws work to the heightened disadvantage of poor people. This is most dramatically clear in the heroin and abortion situations, but, to some extent, it may be true in other victimless crime areas as well. We have already seen how, when heroin is illegal, ability to pay becomes a key determinant of the addict's situation. Under this system, an addict who is well-to-do fares very differently indeed from one who is not; drug-users who do not have the financial wherewithal to support an expensive habit almost invariably are driven to money-producing crimes on that account. The same kind of differential is present when abortion is illegal. Affluent women can afford to pay for competent and safe termination of their pregnancies, while poor women run serious risks of injury or even death at the hands of unskilled and often unscrupulous practitioners. This kind of discrepancy ought not exist under a legal abortion system, though current restrictions on federally assisted abortions for poor women do imply its partial perpetuation.

Under victimless crime laws, similar differentials work their way into enforcement practice. As already noted, police focus on the most publicly visible and seemingly most offensive manifestations of the proscribed behavior. Faced with an untenable and overwhelming enforcement task in areas where both the statutory provisions and the immediate situations afford wide discretion in deciding which particular instances will be selected-out for treatment as "offenses," the police necessarily establish working priorities. Here again, we see operating indirectly the role of differential power resources in shaping individual deviant careers, for the better-off deviators have a much stronger chance of shielding themselves from police interference. In the case of drug-law enforcement, for example, the main thrust of policing activity has been felt by the poverty-stricken "street addicts," who frequently are driven to "pushing" as well as other money-producing crime to finance their habit. Both the more fortunately situated drug-users (physician-addicts, college students, etc.) and the remote (and usually not-addicted) drug distributors have usually maintained relative immunity from interference. Similarly, enforcement activity is routinely directed against streetwalkers rather than the relatively more affluent "call girls," against "numbers" operators rather than upper-class gamblers. Some of this selectivity very likely follows along racial as well as social-class lines. At any rate, the characteristic choice of enforcement targets—one that, from the police standpoint, makes a lot of sense in terms of apparent "seriousness" and enforcement ease—frequently serves to reinforce patterns of preexisting discrimination or differential opportunity. In short, what often happens under victimless crime laws is that those deviators whom many observers would see as already having been most victimized socially are selected out for further victimization through the law.

3. "Secondary crime" costs. There is little need to belabor this point here, since we have considered it quite a bit in earlier sections of this book. Recent perspectives on deviance bring out the several important ways in which these laws create or increase crime and criminal "careers." To begin with, they under-

line the sense in which the criminal statutes by definition make "criminals" of persons who would not otherwise be so designated. The precise extent of adverse consequences flowing from this fact alone may not be absolutely clear, but there is considerable agreement that some deviance-amplification harmful to the individuals involved is almost inevitable. The policy of labeling as criminals "otherwise" respectable and law-abiding people has been especially condemned in such areas as marihuana use (where it has been felt to promote antisocial outlooks), abortion (where it has produced postabortal guilt, not so typically found in less repressive legal situations), and homosexuality (where it is widely held responsible for impairing the self-esteem of a great many Americans).

Often the amplifying consequences go considerably beyond that, and we have noted at some length the most significant example of this expansion as seen in the case of secondary crime by addicts to finance drug-purchasing. These laws also produce secondary crime in another sense, by creating or supporting a wide range of illegal occupations connected with the illicit practices and markets. Such ancillary roles include virtually all people involved in the provision of the banned goods or services as well as others who benefit from their illegality —from the professional heroin-trafficker to the pimp, from the landlords of premises used for prostitution to manufacturers and sellers of pornography, from those who operate illegal gambling establishments to people who devote themselves to robbing or blackmailing homosexuals. And when the intolerable pressures confronting enforcement officials in these areas drive them into practices that are against the law, that is yet another secondary crime cost of criminalization policies.

4. **Police corruption and public disrespect for the law.** Several key features of these enforcement situations set the stage for widely acknowledged tendencies toward police corruption (see Knapp Commission Report, 1972; Sherman, ed., 1974; also Rubinstein, 1974, ch. 9). Among these features are the characteristic latitude afforded the police in identifying specific offenses and offenders, their recognition of the highly ambivalent public attitudes in these areas, their awareness of the enormous profits that are circulating in connection with the banned transactions, the routine eagerness of illicit operatives to offer them financial incentives to "look the other way," the realization that most potential offenses would not be proceeded against anyway, and the general atmosphere of seediness and hypocrisy that surrounds the entire enforcement effort with respect to victimless crimes.

Illegal gambling has been the offense in connection with which the most extensive evidence of large-scale graft has been revealed, although payoffs by narcotics distributors, persons providing premises for prostitution or for the gathering of homosexuals, as well as those running call girl and illegal abortion businesses have also been quite common. With respect to gambling, the Knapp Commission on police corruption in New York City reported: "The collection of tribute by police from gamblers has traditionally been extremely well organized and has persisted in virtually unchanged form for years despite periodic scandals, departmental reorganizations, massive transfers in and out of the units involved, and the folding of some gambling operations and the establishment of new ones" (Knapp Commission Report, 1972, p. 71). The Commission also noted that many police officers, aware that the public likes to place bets, consider gambling payoffs "clean" graft. For their part, professional gamblers tend to treat such payoffs as a "necessary business expense" comparable to the legitimate businessman's purchase of insurance (Knapp Commission Report, 1972, p. 73).

Although the public's outlook on enforcement corruption has usually been heavily oriented to weeding out the "bad apples" in a given police department, most specialists are convinced that the basic sources of the problem lie much deeper than that (see Sherman, ed., 1974, pp. 1–39). Notwithstanding the undoubted fact that some officers are a good deal more corruptible than others and that some—for example, those who directly and on their own inititiative "shakedown" homosexuals or illegal operatives of various kinds—need little or no inducement to be on "the take," there is little doubt that victimless crime laws themselves establish situations that are highly conducive to police deviation. The Knapp Commission also received extensive testimony indicating that, at least in ghetto areas of New York, there was widespread public knowledge of police corruption, particularly in connection with gambling and narcotics enforcement, and a consequent high degree of cynicism regarding police integrity. Since people living in these situations already have many other reasons to question the ways in which "justice" is administered, this knowledge could well serve to heighten general disrespect for the entire legal system. To cite a rather different set of circumstances in which victimless crime laws may generate disrespect for the law, various commentators have noted the adverse impact on the outlooks of college students and other middle-class marihuana users toward a system that brands them as criminals. Likewise, the evident hypocrisy in administering prostitution laws against the prostitutes themselves, yet rarely against the customers, anti-abortion statutes which clearly discriminate against the poor, and antihomo-sexuality laws which place a premium on gay individuals staying "in the closet," hardly encourages positive feelings about the nature and uses of our legal system.

A Continuing Controversy

Because little evidence has been forthcoming to indicate effectiveness in curbing the proscribed exchanges—evidence that might offset the documentation of these several costs—policymakers as well as academicians increasingly have looked with favor on the idea of **decriminalization** (for discussion of various policy alternatives see Skolnick and Dombrink, 1978). Some of the most dramatic shifts in policy have been with respect to marihuana use and abortion. Increases in both the use of marihuana and in favorable public attitudes toward its use were cited earlier. These developments have reflected or been accompanied by significant legal analyses favorable to decriminalization (for example, Kaplan, 1971), medical evidence showing that the psychological and physiological dangers of occasional use had been exaggerated (see Grinspoon, 1971), sociological demonstrations that few marihuana smokers go on to become opiate addicts (Goode, 1969; 1970), and the much-publicized report of a National Commission that recommended decriminalizing possession of small amounts of the drug for personal use (National Commission on Marihuana and Drug Abuse, 1972). At the time of this writing, one report notes that ten states, including California and New York, have decriminalized possession of small amounts of marihuana, at least to the extent of substituting citations and fines (ranging from $100 to $250) for the previously employed jail sentences (Chase, 1977).

We have already noted the relative success of the abortion decriminalization campaign as a result of which legal abortions are now available in various states, including New York, subject however to limitations on financial assistance from the federal government that currently are generating a great deal of controversy in Congress and in public debate. Beginning with Illinois (in 1962), a small number of states have removed from their criminal laws private consensual homosexual acts between adults (see Weinberg and Williams, 1974, pp. 35–38). [As this text goes into print, the ongoing struggle over gay rights continues to generate specific political controversies in various localities which tend to exhibit highly fluctuating outcomes. For example, whereas the 1977 vote overturning a gay rights ordinance in Miami was widely viewed as a major setback for gay liberation, the November 1978 repudiation by the California electorate of an initiative that would have permitted the firing of homosexual public school teachers in that state represented a considerable victory. Despite some occasional indications nationally of an "anti-gay backlash," the overall trend still seems to be in the direction of decriminalization and further expansion of the rights of homosexuals.] State-run lotteries, off-track betting, and currently expanding casino gambling all represent measures of legalization in that area. Proposals have been made for decriminalizing prostitution (see discussion in Vorenberg, 1977), and various cities have put into effect or have considered "adult zones" in which pornography and other sex-related establishments would be relatively free from interference. One of the proscriptions that appears most resistant to decriminalization is that against heroin use. Although proposals are advanced from time to time for limited and controlled experimental studies to determine what the effects of heroin decriminalization would be, even these modest proposals have been routinely rejected.

Needless to say, many specific arguments pro and con decriminalization have been advanced with respect to each of these substantive areas of the criminal law. It is not possible to consider all of those arguments in this brief discussion. Some of the more general issues that cut across the particular offense categories do, however, merit brief comment. To begin with, it must be recognized that while the overall trend is definitely in the direction indicated so far, the entire matter of victimless crime and decriminalization remains a topic of extensive and heated controversy. In some circles there is a strong feeling that the mere fact of a law being on the statute books ought to carry great authority. People who feel this way do not accept the aforementioned idea that the burden of justification lies with those who would utilize criminal sanctions as a means of control. On the contrary, they would insist that an overwhelming case for abolition must be made out by anyone who would seek to overturn long-standing laws. At an extreme, there are those among whom the very idea of decriminalization in any area immediately produces visions of a flood of "horrible consequences" (a nation of dope fiends, total demise of the family system, etc.) that they suppose would automatically follow in its wake. Despite the lack of any significant evidence to substantiate such prognostications, as mentioned in the beginning of the book feelings run high in many of these areas and sometimes popular preconceptions receive support through strongly adhered-to traditional religious pronouncements.

There is no doubt that moral issues—in some cases, very difficult moral dilemmas—are involved in the debate over victimless crime policies. However, opponents of decriminalization have sometimes misleadingly presented themselves as being the sole protectors of "morality" in these matters. Yet being "moralistic" is not the only way of being "moral." This point has sometimes been obscured in the heat of the debate, with the case for decriminalization being depicted as grounded in other than moral considerations. In actuality, parties on both sides of the controversy are equally committed to moral decisions and solutions. It is with respect to the choice of methods to reach these and the weighing of substantive policy alternatives that they are more likely to differ. The emerging policy position sketched out earlier, according to which criminal prohibitions should be justified by showing, in effect, that they are necessary and are likely to produce more good than harm, is itself a kind of moral position. Some commentators might consider this kind of weighing of empirical evidence regarding social benefits and harms as being, literally ,"unprincipled" from a moral standpoint (see the discussion by Bedau, in Schur and Bedau, 1974). Yet, despite the attempts of philosophers (for example, Rawls, 1971; Dworkin, 1977) to delineate basic and overarching principles of justice, it is not at all clear that anyone has provided, or can provide, a coherent and agreed-upon set of "objective" moral principles that will definitely dispose of all the specific and complex moral decisions found in the victimless crime areas. Thus, a commitment to maximizing individual freedom or even human life does not easily provide a solution in situations where different rights to freedom or life may conflict (e.g., the freedom or life of the mother "versus" that of the fetus in some abortion situations, assuming we accept the notion that the fetus has "rights").

It seems likely that different moral judgments will continue to be made in matters of this sort. At the same time, it is also likely that some public policy will be in force, reflecting the dominance of one sort of judgment over another and having very real consequences for the human beings affected by the laws in question. Under such circumstances, fateful policy decisions are always being made and will continue to be made whether or not there is general agreement as to the substance of morality and the means of determining it. Advocates of decriminalization insist only that it is socially, even morally, shortsighted to try to reach these decisions without weighing all the available evidence regarding the actual operation and consequences of the laws in question. They maintain that the *morality* (or immorality) *of these laws* is one of the major moral issues at stake in this debate. Opponents of decriminalization sometimes are almost totally preoccupied with the morality of the proscribed behaviors considered in the abstract. Yet, many observers would now argue, following the Wolfenden Committee's lead, that those evaluations do not by themselves provide an adequate basis for determining whether or not criminalization is warranted.

One might well believe, for example, that "drug addiction is immoral" or at least highly undesirable and, nonetheless, also conclude that on balance and in actual operation restrictive narcotics laws make a bad situation worse rather than better. If the basic concern is to develop policies that work to minimize the overall social harm associated with a given problem, then using the criminal law merely to express moral disapproval when the actual result of such use will be an exacerbation of the disapproved conditions readily becomes counterproductive. Furthermore, and this is another point that is sometimes obscured in the heat of debate, the realistic choice facing policymakers and, indirectly, the electorate that mandates their actions is usually not one of either "allowing" or "not allowing" the offending behavior. Opponents of decriminalization sometimes insist that "we cannot allow" such and such a deviating activity, glossing over the fact that such activity will in fact persist if not thrive under criminalization as well as decriminalization. To cite a major example, despite the strong feelings and moral dilemmas relating to abortion, large numbers of women will take actions to terminate their pregnancies whether this behavior is legal or not. The real policy choice is not between "legalizing" the practice and "refusing to permit it." It is between enabling women to have safe and competent pregnancy terminations or driving them to dangerous attempts at self-induced abortion or the almost equally serious risks involved at the hands of many illegal practitioners.

Critics of decriminalization tend to emphasize the undoubted limits of what it can accomplish. The author of one recent text has stated that, "Decriminalization has many attractive features, but it does not solve the basic behavioral problem that is involved unless it is one that requires no other solution than legalization" (Sagarin, 1975, p. 390). Yet it should be realized that advocates of decriminalization themselves realize it is no panacea. They advance such proposals with an eye to accomplishing specific and limited improvements, and the value of these proposed policy changes should be assessed in terms of their ability to achieve those limited goals. The basic idea behind decriminalization is, quite simply, *reducing the amplification or secondary expansion of various deviance problems*. Taking steps in this direction *in no way precludes* continuing *efforts to cope with* what some would insist are *more "basic causes" of the problems*. One could still work at creating socioeconomic and other conditions that reduce drug-taking, improving contraception so as to reduce the need for abortion, creating healthier sexual outlooks and relationships that might cut the demand for pornography or prostitution, and so on. Nor would decriminalization in any way prevent therapeutic efforts for individuals who are seriously troubled by their behavior or situation. However, experience with various efforts to impose such "therapy" by law is not at all encouraging. Enforced treatment may well be a contradiction in terms (see Kittrie, 1971).

Just how effective decriminalization will be in reducing secondary aspects of deviance problems and in what specific ways will vary a good deal depending on the nature of the situation. It is clear that the probable impact is linked to the extent of important secondary dimensions of the problems. Thus, decriminalization can produce the greatest changes in those deviance situations that feature the most substantial secondary amplification, such as those surrounding drug addiction and abortion. In other areas, the impact—particularly in the short-run—is likely to be less dramatic. For example, there is little evidence to suggest that the basic situation of a homosexual in Illinois or in the other states that have decriminalized private consensual homosexuality has appreciably changed for the better. Acts engaged in in private were rarely a basis for criminal prosecution even before the change in the laws. But it is equally noteworthy that none of the frequently prophesied "horrible consequences" of decriminalization have occurred there either (nor, for that matter, in the many foreign countries that have similar legislation).

Even if the change in such a deviance situation is only slight, in the absence of undesired side-effects any such reduction in intimidation, pressure, and stigma may be seen as beneficial. Those who might argue that certain deviations may "deserve to be stigmatized" should, in any case, keep in mind that decriminalization does not amount to destigmatization. Only the added stigma of criminality is thereby reduced; not all stigma and its consequences. This may be seen as a major limitation by those favoring the abolition of stigma and a "saving grace" for those who believe a given type of stigmatization is warranted.

Juvenile Justice

A similar trend is evident in the area of juvenile justice. The special legal apparatus for the processing of "delinquents" has come under serious challenge, and there is a strong tendency toward removing the less serious juvenile offenses from the jurisdiction of the juvenile court (see Lemert, 1970; Schur, 1973; Rosenheim, ed., 1976; Sarri and Hasenfeld, eds., 1976). As we have already seen, "delinquency" is a technical legal designation, in effect created through the passage of special juvenile court legislation. Delinquency is, then, best defined as behavior that is prohibited by such delinquency laws, and, notwithstanding much cross-jurisdictional variability in detail, the range of behaviors proscribed through such statutes has been incredibly broad. This was succinctly indicated by the President's Crime Commission:

> In addition to behavior that would be criminal on the part of an adult, delinquency includes behavior illegal only for a child: Conduct uniquely children's—truancy, incorrigibility—and conduct tolerated for adults but objectionable for children—smoking, drink, using vulgar language, violating curfew laws, hanging around in bars or with felons or gamblers.

> The provisions on which intervention in this category of cases is based are typically vague and all-encompassing: Growing up in idleness and crime, engaging in immoral conduct, in danger of leading an immoral life. Especially when administered with the informality characteristic of the court's procedures, they establish the judge as arbiter not only of the behavior but also of the morals of every child (and to an extent the parents of every child) appearing before him (President's Commission on Law Enforcement and Administration of Justice, 1967b).

In recent years there has been a mounting attack on these vague and all-embracing provisions, which extend far beyond serious criminality to include what Margaret Rosenheim properly calls "juvenile nuisances" (Rosenheim, 1976). These acts, which would not be criminal if committed by an adult, are also sometimes described as "status offenses," in that it is the status of being a juvenile itself that lies at the heart of the proscription. Some writers also view them as constituting a type of "victimless" crime, using a "no harm to others" rather than a "consensual transaction" definition of that term. (Various of the transactional victimless offenses, it might be noted, likewise have "status offense" features. Thus, in a way, though not literally, it is the status of being a drug addict or of being a homosexual that has been legislated against.)

Criticism of the "overreach" of the juvenile court was first voiced by legal analysts who (as we will see in a moment) were also much concerned about the procedures used in administering this legislation. More recently, wide agreement has developed among lawyers, social scientists, and practitioners directly involved in the juvenile justice system that the standard system for processing delinquency was badly in need of reform. Some reforms have now been instituted (see below), and there is much current discussion regarding the future direction of the juvenile justice system. In order to understand this ferment, a brief indication of the major points emphasized by the early legal critics should prove helpful. There have been four interrelated aspects of the traditional juvenile court system, which both provided its distinctive stamp and, at the same time, generated serious criticism and eventually partial repudiation.

1. "Individualized justice." There have already been references at several points in this text to the commendable-sounding but exceedingly vague notion

of "individualizing" justice. In the area of delinquency, this term expressed the hope that a specialized court could make dispositions that would meet the particular needs of each child coming before it, whatever those needs might be (see Allen, 1964; Platt, 1969; Lemert, 1970). This broad needs-serving or problem-solving approach was, of course, closely linked to the nebulous and far-reaching statutory definitions of delinquency. As for its implementation, optimally there would be made an exhaustive exploration by court-associated probation officers or other staff of the youth's general character, social and psychological condition and current situation, and overall life prospects. In the traditional juvenile court approach, this kind of rather loosely structured investigation to a considerable extent superseded the usual criminal law requirement for adults of determining guilt or innocence with respect to the commission of a closely specified criminal act. The intention behind this procedure was to maintain flexibility and to search out all relevant problems. But legal critics suggested quite early on that, particularly when viewed together with the vague statutory provisions, such a system might well abridge the basic principle of "rule of law." That principle often is summarized in two maxims, neither of which seemed adequately sustained in the juvenile court: no punishment without crime, and no crime without law.

2. **Informal procedure.** Closely tied to the goal of individualized justice was the desire for informal and supposedly "nonadversary" court procedures. Reformers believed that the combative atmosphere and legalistic formality of the ordinary criminal trial would have traumatizing effects on the child and, in addition, would inhibit the free-flowing social investigation they thought necessary if correct dispositions were to be made. Therefore, in addition to relaxing the ordinary requirements of specificity and proof, the juvenile court typically bypassed strict rules of evidence as well as the child's right to adequate legal representation. The rationale for the latter was that the court itself "represented" the children coming before it, who therefore needed no special representation of their own. This idea derived from the court's groundings in the early legal doctrine of *parens patriae,* under which the state was held to have ultimate responsibility for the welfare of children—a responsibility it might be required to exercise directly, when that which had been delegated to the child's parents proved inadequate. Not surprisingly, loose evidentiary rules and absence of counsel were objected to by legal specialists on the ground that the child was being unconstitutionally deprived of basic procedural safeguards. Indeed, Platt has suggested that the juvenile court movement might be considered " 'anti-legal' in the sense that it encouraged minimum procedural formality and maximum dependency on extra-legal resources." The role model for the juvenile court, he noted, was not the lawyer, but the doctor-counselor. " 'Judicial therapists' were expected to establish a one-to-one relationship with 'delinquents' in the same way that a country doctor might give his time and attention to a favorite patient" (Platt, 1969, pp. 141, 142.)

3. New terminology. A third key feature of the system, also linked to the reformism and notions of protectiveness that permeated it, was the creation of a special terminology relating to children's offenses and the court's procedures. The child would be "adjudicated" a "delinquent," rather than being "convicted" as a "criminal." Similarly, the proceeding was not to involve action by the state "versus" a "defendant," but rather (in line with the *parens patriae* philosophy) was undertaken "on behalf of" or "in the best interests of" the child. Disposition was not to be described as "sentencing" and was not to be viewed as "punishment." Instead of being sent to "prison," the child would be committed to the care of a "training school." All of these changes were, again, extremely well-intended. Reformers really believed that they were acting, and that a court could act, in the child's best interests. They wanted to erase the stigma of a criminal record and also to eradicate earlier practices of placing juveniles in the same jails and prisons as hardened adult offenders. However, legal critics and, later, others were not long in questioning whether this surface renaming of things really amounted to substantive change. Legal scholar Francis Allen made this point forcefully when he wrote:

> It is important . . . to recognize that when, in an authoritative setting, we attempt to do something *for* a child "because of what he is and needs," we are also doing something to him. The semantics of "socialized justice" [often used as a synonym for "individualized justice"] are a trap for the unwary. Whatever one's motivations, however elevated one's objectives, if the measures taken result in the compulsory loss of the child's liberty, the involuntary separation of a child from his family, or even the supervision of a child's activities by a probation worker, the impact on the affected individuals is essentially a punitive one. Good intentions and a flexible vocabulary do not alter this reality. . . . We shall escape much confusion here if we are willing to give candid recognition to the fact that the business of the juvenile court inevitably consists, to a considerable degree, in dispensing punishment (Allen, 1964, p. 18).

This statement represented an opening wedge in what later became a broader interdisciplinary "unmasking of euphemism" (Schur, 1973, pp. 126–130) in a variety of deviance-processing areas and contexts (see Gaylin, *et al.*, 1978). As the focus on direct study of processing systems in operation grew, it became quite clear that official designations and descriptions often belied the actual consequences. As emphasized throughout this text, the real gist of the labeling approach is on how people are defined and treated; how they are literally "called" is only one (sometimes important) aspect of this process.

4. Indeterminate commitment. A similar unmasking of euphemism has occurred with respect to the fourth major feature of the traditional juvenile court system—indeterminate commitment to a correctional institution or potential commitment up to a specified age. Such indeterminacy represented an effort to orient the court's activity to the reformers' hopefulness regarding the rehabilitation of troubled youths. It followed directly from the ideal of individualized justice and also from the concept that the court was not so much punishing the child for committing a specific criminal act as it was dealing in a more general way with the child's overall problems and needs. If individual solutions were to be found, the early thinking went, then the rehabilitation specialists at the institution would be the ones to determine when the child was ready for return to life in the community. Such a scheme also seemed to have the advantage of providing the possibility of quite short commitment if longer rehabilitation did not prove necessary. There is little indication, however, that that option was ever much used, and the catch to this treatment "flexibility" was that it also afforded the prospect of very long commitment (as actually tended to happen) in many cases. In fact, early critics of indeterminacy pointed out that, in the name of individualized justice and rehabilitation, a child could often be committed to a juvenile institution for a longer period of time than would have been possible under the more strictly drawn criminal statutes had he or she engaged in precisely the same behavior as an adult. Gradually the criticism of indeterminacy came also to reflect growing disenchantment regarding the prospects of rehabilitation efforts themselves. If rehabilitation rarely seemed to work, then submitting children to it on a longer-than-for-adults basis seemed especially unjust.

Developing sociological perspectives and findings from empirical research complemented and reinforced these legal criticisms. As we have seen, the sociological work highlighted elements of discretion in the selection and processing of juveniles, organizational features or problems that might displace "the best interests of the child," and the difficulties control agents and agencies face in trying to perform effectively a multitude of different functions. Above all, labeling interpretations and studies pointed up the possible dangers of early stigmatization and the snowballing and self-reinforcing patterns of amplification that seemed central to many, if not most, deviant careers. Tannenbaum's aforementioned early "dramatization of evil" analysis dealt, of course, directly with delinquency and became an important forerunner of what eventually became the most influential thinking about the processing of delinquents. More recently, Matza's theory of "drift" and his discussion of the possible delinquency-reinforcing effects of the traditional juvenile court system (both of which were cited earlier) have had an especially strong influence on thinking in this area. In addition, a host of specific findings (also reviewed in the foregoing chapters) regarding police encounters with juveniles, problems of the juvenile court, and so on, have contributed to the developing concern about whether the juvenile justice system operated fairly and with real effectiveness.

The various legal criticisms, very likely with some support from these strands of social science thinking, led to a major U.S. Supreme Court decision in 1967, holding that children in juvenile court proceedings must be afforded most of the usual constitutional safeguards, including right to counsel, opportunity to confront witnesses, and the protection against self-incrimination. The Court noted that "however euphemistic the title, a 'receiving home' or an 'industrial school' for juveniles is a place of confinement in which the child is incarcerated. . . . Under our Constitution, the condition of being a boy does not justify a kangaroo court" (In re: Gault, 1967). The full implications and consequences of this decision are not yet clear (Schultz and Cohen, 1976), although there seems little doubt that more attention will now be paid in most juvenile courts throughout the country to systematizing procedures and providing at least minimal safeguards.

More generally, the new thinking about juvenile justice has prompted a broad trend in delinquency policies which has been termed **radical nonintervention** (Schur, 1973).   This outlook carries a number of related policy implications. The main policy thrust has to do with limiting the jurisdiction of the juvenile court to the most serious cases. Even the President's Crime Commission, made up of moderate "public figures," made a recommendation along these lines: "in view of the serious stigma and the uncertain gain accompanying official action, serious consideration should be given complete elimination from the court's jurisdiction of conduct illegal only for a child" (President's Commission on Law Enforcement and Administration of Justice, 1967b, p. 27). Rosenheim has aptly referred to such a policy as involving the "normalization of juvenile nuisances." Noting that minors who are neither seriously criminal nor severely disturbed, "probably comprise the majority of all children dealt with under juvenile justice auspices in most communities," she suggests that delinquency policy has suffered from excessive **problemization** (Rosenheim, 1976, p. 180). As she points out, this is a tendency that more generally affects all of the "helping" professions in a range of substantive areas. Normalizing is the undoing of such overreach by the helpers: "If we think about the situation of juvenile nuisances as essentially 'normal,' new policies and programs are likely to augment, if not replace, the traditional models. 'Normalizing' assumes that much juvenile misconduct is minor, albeit annoying or troubling, and rarely persistent or deeply alarming" (Rosenheim, 1976, p. 185).

With respect to these areas of borderline offending behavior, many states are now in the process of moving to develop various forms of community-based "nonjudicial handling," to adopt a phrase used by the Crime Commission. This trend is usually referred to as **diversion**—a category that includes a variety of specific programs of guidance and supervision, often centered in newly formed "youth service bureaus" (Lemert, 1971; Nejelski, 1976). Even with respect to these new diversion schemes, Rosenheim suggests a need for greater "normalizing" flexibility. She calls for less reliance on formal "diagnosis" and treatment of the individual, which could be a holdover from earlier approaches, and greater emphasis on a kind of social "first aid" as well as greater attention to the clients' own definitions of their troubles—as opposed to the helpers' definitions (Rosenheim, 1976, pp. 188–191). A variety of policy developments reflecting the nonintervention outlook complements the diversion emphasis: the setting up in some states of new "noncriminal" categories such as PINS, MINS, or CHINS (persons, minors, or children in need of supervision) for the channeling of youths into the less-stigmatizing procedures (Schultz and Cohen, 1976); growing criticism of juvenile pretrial detention facilities and practices (P. Wald, 1976); a new scrutiny of practices relating to court intervention on behalf of "neglected" children (M. Wald, 1976); increased concern for and control over possible invasions of privacy and dangers of stigmatizing through access to juvenile "records" (Lister, 1976; and, in general, new approaches to individual "treatment" in community settings (see below).

As regards the more serious incidents of criminality that would remain within the court's jurisdiction under policies of this sort, it is now generally agreed that, insofar as possible, there should be (as the Crime Commission urged) "procedures designed to assure fair and reliable determinations"—including, presumably, a clear finding that the youth did in fact commit a criminal act. With respect to the final dispositions in such cases, the course of future public policy is not entirely clear. The dominant trend would seem to be in the direction of maximizing predictability, consistency, and fairness—precisely those qualities that Matza emphasized were so evidently lacking in the traditional juvenile court outcomes. In line with a more general trend toward a "justice" focus (discussed in the next section), a preference seems to be developing for dispositions (perhaps now even openly acknowledged to be "penalties") commensurate with the seriousness of the offense committed, rather than ones based on some broad conclusion about the youth's "problems and needs." Partly this reflects a strong disenchantment with the earlier practice of interdeterminate commitment. Although some specialists continue to assert the value of rehabilitation efforts, there is now little support for allowing the entire disposition process to rest on that uncertain goal. It may be noted that the move toward fixed penalties for serious offenses implies that, on balance, the recent trend will not necessarily have been toward a "soft" policy. The key new theme is fairness rather than either sympathy on the one hand, or toughness on the other.

Table 7.4 is designed to suggest apparent interrelationships between policy tendencies in the juvenile justice field and the course of delinquency theorizing and research which we examined in Chapter 3. The categories presented there were developed for the purpose of organizing a great many complex and overlapping tendencies, theories, and practices. They are not meant to imply absolutely clear-cut and mutually exclusive approaches to delinquency. Nor are all the possible outlooks included (for example, one might add a "get tough" perspective). On the contrary, they are merely meant to be suggestive; they may prove helpful in analyzing a variety of specific developments in the field. (See various references to them in Rosenheim, ed., 1976.) For our more general purposes in interpreting deviance situations and problems, the table may be of interest because of the parallel developments in "theory" and "practice" that it tentatively indicates. Such parallels are noteworthy, because observers frequently

Table 7.4 Reactions to Delinquency

	INDIVIDUAL TREATMENT	LIBERAL REFORM	RADICAL NONINTER-VENTION
Basic Assumptions	Differentness of offenders; delinquency a symptom; psychosocial determinism	Delinquency concentrated in lower class; individual constrained—particularly by subcultural pressures; social determinism	Delinquency widespread throughout society; basic role of contingencies; neo-antideterminism
Favored Methodologies	Clinical; comparison of matched samples	Analysis of rate variations; ecological analysis; study of subcultures	Self-reports; observation; legal analysis
Focal Point for Research	The individual	Social class; local community	Interaction between the individual and the legal system (and other agencies of reaction)
Representative Causal Perspectives	Psychodynamic theories; family-oriented theories	Anomie theories; cultural transmission; opportunity theory	Labeling analysis; drift and situational theories
Prevention	Identification of "predelinquents"; probation and counselling	Street gang work; community programs; piecemeal socioeconomic reform	Deemphasis on singling out specific individuals; radical sociocultural change
Treatment	Therapy; training schools	Community programs; improving conditions in institutions	Voluntary treatment
Juvenile Court	"Individualized justice"; rehabilitative ideal	Better training and caseloads; more attention to social factors	Narrow scope of juvenile court jurisdiction; increased formalization

Source: Edwin M. Schur, *Radical Nonintervention: Rethinking the Delinquency Problem* (Englewood Cliffs, N.J.: Prentice-Hall, 1973), p. 20.

imply that little or no relation exists between "ivory tower" academic outlooks on a topic and what is going on in "the real world." In this instance, although the precise lines and sequences of influence are not clear, there does seem to be a considerable and generally consistent "clustering" tendency with respect to theory, research, and a variety of policy measures. Certain policy efforts tend to "go along with" certain outlooks and studies, both reflecting broad ways of thinking about delinquency and key assumptions regarding it. There seems little doubt that sociological thinking has exerted *some* influence over the course of practical events in this area, although there may well have been reciprocal influence in the other direction.

Another implication of the table is that the different "clusters" of outlook-practice can be placed roughly along a political spectrum, with particular positions ranging from "conservative" to "radical" in their overall tone and appeal. Again, the dividing lines between the three categories certainly are not hard and fast, and the placement within one or another of some of the specific theories and policies may be debated. But it is important to recognize that public deviance policies do have broad political significance, and, if sociological outlooks influence them, then they do also. This is a matter to which we will return briefly in the next chapter. A final point to consider is whether some similarly organized parallels might be found to exist with respect to theory and policy in specific deviance-related areas other than delinquency. It seems likely that a comparable positioning of various outlooks in a variety of substantive spheres of deviance-defining could be shown to exist, even if debate will continue regarding which positions are "conservative" (and why) and which ones progressive or even "radical."

Some Related Trends

Closely related to the developments regarding victimless crimes and juvenile justice has been a movement toward **decarceration** or **deinstitutionalization,** as it is also called (Scull, 1977a; Vinter, *et al.,* 1975). A major influence in this regard has been the aforementioned analysis of the "total institution" developed by Goffman and others. At an extreme, decarceration would imply the complete abolition of such highly-restrictive "closed" institutions, including adult and juvenile correctional institutions and mental hospitals. However, such extreme proposals have received little support, and it does not seem likely that anything approximating that situation will be achieved in the foreseeable future. There have been some striking experiments in deinstitutionalizing, perhaps the most notable being the effort in Massachusetts to almost completely replace a system of large institutions for delinquents with one of smaller community-based residential and nonresidential treatment programs (Miller and Ohlin, 1976). But by and large, the decarceration tendency has been reflected more modestly in efforts to limit the use of custodial institutions, in particular, by removing specific individuals and categories of people felt to be inappropriately incarcerated and by developing alternative programs of treatment in the community (Lerman, 1975; Scull, 1977a). A recent national survey of juvenile corrections noted that the trend toward decarceration was still very far from being a dominant one:

Deinstitutionalization rates for the forty-eight reporting states indicated that only four states assigned as many youth to community as to institutional settings, that thirty-six states had rates of less than 25%, and that the average national rate was only 17.7%. . . . [although] Inclusion of foster care in our measures increased the number of states with a deinstitutionalization rate 50% or higher from four to ten, with four states instead of one attaining a rate of 70% or above (Vinter, *et al.,* 1975, p. 73).

Nonetheless, strong interest in the idea of alternatives to incarceration has been an important development in recent years. Contributing to it has been not only the critique of dehumanizing and deviance-amplifying consequences of the total institution, but also the recognition that such places are being extensively and questionably used to detain or "warehouse" a wide range of society's "undesirables" (Scull, 1977a; also Goldfarb, 1976). Efforts by civil liberties organizations to force recognition of the legal rights of inmates, particularly mental patients (to hearings, appeals, etc., and to not be kept institutionalized without proper cause), have also been instrumental in pressing state agencies to reduce incarcerated populations. The enormous cost of keeping people in these institutions has often been a not always openly acknowledged factor as well. Finally, and perhaps most importantly, there has been a steadily growing disenchantment regarding the effectiveness of various rehabilitation efforts. As we have noted, there continues to be debate regarding the consequences of treatment that can be but is not always actually provided in mental hospitals. In the field of corrections, particularly juvenile corrections, efforts have been made to diversify and modernize programs (Street, Vinter and Perrow, 1966), but most evaluation research on residential institutions remains far from encouraging regarding the results (for example, Vinter, ed., 1976). With respect even to community-based and closely individualized treatment alternatives, despite some claims of success (see, for example, Warren, 1970), general assessments by sociologists remain negative or at least fail to report substantial evidence of demonstrated beneficial results (Lerman, 1975; Scull, 1977a). The leading evaluation of correctional rehabilitation efforts, which covered *both* institutional and noninstitutional programs, has concluded that "no clear pattern" exists to indicate the efficacy of "any particular method of treatment" (Martinson, 1974; also Lipton, Martinson, and Wilks, 1975; and see Greenberg, 1977).

"Community approaches," however, continue to be fashionable and to receive special support, so much so that such evaluators as Lerman and Scull see them as facilitating a major and, to them, questionable extension and expansion of the country's social control apparatus. A similar critique has been made with respect to the movement toward "community mental health" (prevention-oriented psychiatric outreach programs), which some observers see as carrying an almost unlimited potential for broadening the definition of mental illness and applying it coercively to ever-widening categories of "troubled" or troublesome individuals (Leifer, 1966; Szasz, 1970a; but see Caplan, 1966; also Lehman, 1976). Yet again and notwithstanding such criticism, the establishment and growth of federally funded community mental health centers throughout the nation has made this a very significant development in psychiatry and one which in recent years has received much public approbation as being "progressive." The related growth of a conviction that conventional one-to-one office psychotherapy may be inappropriate in dealing with a variety of problematic behaviors and conditions reinforces the likelihood that such community-based approaches will continue to flourish and influence a variety of deviance situations.

The aforementioned disenchantment regarding rehabilitation has been one underlying factor in another important recent trend, this one in the criminal justice system, toward what may be called a **justice model** (Morris, 1974; von Hirsch, 1976). Advocates of this approach emphasize the inequities that have resulted from extreme rehabilitation-oriented discretion and individualizing in the processing and treatment of criminal offenders. They conclude, on the basis of the available evidence, that such disparities have occurred to no good effect. As one study group has asserted:

> The basic meaning of "law," it seems to us, is holding all responsible to the same rule. This basic principle has been lost in recent decades as the focus of the criminal system shifted from the act to the individual, giving rise to the practice of varying criminal sanctions according to individual characteristics. Since there is no sound scientific or moral basis for doing this, we recommend strongly a return to the principle of uniform application of penal sanctions (American Friends Service Committee, 1971, p. 151).

Recent proponents of this approach, despairing of "the rehabilitative ideal" and showing some greater interest in the possible deterrent effects of criminal sanctions, which currently are attracting heightened research attention (Zimring and Hawkins, 1973; Gibbs, 1975, and Newman, 1978, ch. 11), have also called for a candid acknowledgement that such sanctions impose *punishment*. Considering that punishment may indeed sometimes be necessary, they argue for policies geared to a principle of "just deserts" or "proportionality." As the Committee for the Study of Incarceration has put it, *"Severity of punishment should be commensurate with the seriousness of the wrong.* Only grave wrongs merit severe penalities; minor misdeeds deserve lenient punishments. Disproportionate penalties are undeserved—severe sanctions for minor wrongs or vice versa" (von Hirsch, 1976, p. 66; italics in the original). Under such an approach penalties would be fixed rather than indeterminate, though there might be some special bases for possible variation in unusual cases. Despite the undoubted lack of complete consensus in the matter, considerable agreement might be reached (as per the ranking studies mentioned earlier) on ordering offenses as to degrees of seriousness. If there were such a system of fixed penalties, discretion as to sentencing and also length of incarceration would be severely restricted and the now-resulting disparities much reduced. Currently there are proposals and considerable support at the federal governmental level for criminal justice revision along these lines, including the eventual abolition of early release of prisoners on parole (Clymer, 1977).

The new interest in punishment has, for some commentators, phased over into a general reassertion of philosophies that emphasize the value of holding specific individuals responsible for their wrongdoing (van den Haag, 1975; Wilson, 1975). Critics who have seen in such statements a virtual enthusiasm for punishing, assert that their authors represent a broad "neoconservative" political stance as regards a wide range of social problems and policies (Schur, 1974; Curtis, 1976; Silver, 1976; but see Wilson, 1976; van den Haag, 1976). Among the premises underlying this stance appear to be many of the notions about the "extraordinariness" of deviation and the "differentness" of deviators that we considered early in this text. Critics have charged these writers with a lack of concern regarding socioeconomic deprivation and other injustices perpetuated in our society, but it is indisputable that their writings have, to some extent, struck a responsive chord with a public that is often confused and frightened about crime problems. It remains to be seen whether a new willingness to openly punish people, along with other tendencies toward coercive control—such as the variety of behavior-modification (forced conditioning) techniques now often resorted to in "treating" various problematic conditions (see Geiser, 1976)—will produce a really significant trend we might term a "deviantizing backlash." Thus far, these restrictive-repressive tendencies have, on balance, been overshadowed by the more flexible outlooks and "undeviantizing" trends that we have considered in this chapter.

REFERENCES

Allen, Francis A.
1964. *The Borderland of Criminal Justice*. Chicago: University of Chicago Press.

Altman, Dennis
1973. *Homosexual: Oppression and Liberation*. New York: Avon Books.

American Friends Service Committee
1971. *Struggle for Justice: A Report on Crime and Punishment in America*. New York: Hill & Wang.

Becker, Howard S.
1963. *Outsiders*. New York: The Free Press.

Brownmiller, Susan
1976. *Against Our Will*. New York: Bantam Books, Inc.

Calderone, Mary Steichen, ed.
1958. *Abortion in the United States*. New York: Paul B. Hoeber, Inc.

Caplan, Gerald
1966. "Some Comments on 'Community Psychiatry and Social Power,'" *Social Problems*, 14(Summer), 23–25.

Chambliss, William J.
1964. "A Sociological Analysis of the Law of Vagrancy," *Social Problems*, 12(Summer), 67–77.

1976. "The State and Criminal Law," in William J. Chambliss and Milton Mankoff, eds., *Whose Law, What Order?* New York: John Wiley & Sons, Inc. Pp. 66–106.

Chase, Marilyn
1977. "Marijuana Smoking in Public Increases as Penalties Drop," the New York *Times,* November 28, p. 18.

Clymer, Adam
1977. "Fixed Prison Terms Gain Favor as Doubts on Parole Rise in U.S.," the New York *Times,* October 16, pp. 1, 26.

Cohen, Albert K.
1974. *The Elasticity of Evil: Changes in the Social Definition of Deviance.* Oxford: Basil Blackwell (for the Oxford University Penal Research Unit).

Committee on Homosexual Offences and Prostitution
1957. *Report.* Home Office, Cmnd. 247. London: Her Majesty's Stationery Office.

Connor, Walter D.
1972a. *Deviance in Soviet Society.* New York: Columbia University Press.
1972b. "The Manufacture of Deviance: The Case of the Soviet Purges, 1936–1938," *American Sociological Review,* 37(August), 403–413.

Conrad, Peter
1975. "The Discovery of Hyperkinesis: Notes on the Medicalization of Deviant Behavior," *Social Problems,* 23(October), 12–21.

Curtis, Lynn A.
1976. "The Conservative New Criminology," *Society,* 14(March/April), 8, 14–15.

Devlin, Patrick
1965. *The Enforcement of Morals.* London: Oxford University Press.

Douglas, Jack D.
1971. *American Social Order: Social Rules in a Pluralistic Society.* New York: The Free Press.

Dreifus, Claudia
1973. *Woman's Fate: Raps from a Feminist Consciousness-Raising Group.* New York: Bantam Books, Inc.

Duster, Troy
1970. *The Legislation of Morality.* New York: The Free Press.

Dworkin, Ronald
1977. *Taking Rights Seriously.* Cambridge, Mass.: Harvard University Press.

Earley, Stanley and Maggie Kuhn
1974. "Gray Panther History." Philadelphia: Gray Panthers, 11 pp. mimeo.

Erikson, Kai T.
1966. *Wayward Puritans.* New York: John Wiley & Sons, Inc.

Flacks, Richard
1971. *Youth and Social Change.* Chicago: Markham Publishing Company.

Foucault, Michel
1967. *Madness and Civilization.* trans. by Howard. New York: Mentor Books.

Gaylin, Willard, *et al.*
1978. *Doing Good: The Limits of Benevolence.* New York: Pantheon Books.

Geis, Gilbert
1972. *Not the Law's Business?* National Institute of Mental Health, Center for Studies of Crime and Delinquency. Washington, D.C.: U.S. Government Printing Office.

Geiser, Robert L.
1976. *Behavior Mod and the Managed Society.* Boston: Beacon Press, Inc.

Gibbs, Jack P.
1975. *Crime, Punishment, and Deterrence.* New York: Elsevier.

Goldfarb, Ronald
1976. *Jails: The Ultimate Ghetto.* Garden City, N.Y.: Doubleday & Company, Inc.

Goode, Erich
1969. "Multiple Drug Use Among Marijuana Smokers," *Social Problems,* 17(Summer), 48–64.
1970. *The Marijuana Smokers.* New York: Basic Books, Inc.

Greenberg, David F.
1977. "The Correctional Effects of Corrections: A Survey of Evaluations," in Greenberg, ed. *Corrections and Punishment.* Beverly Hills, Calif., Sage Publications.

Grinspoon, Lester
1971. *Marihuana Reconsidered.* Cambridge: Harvard University Press.

Gusfield, Joseph
1966. *Symbolic Crusade.* Urbana, Ill.: University of Illinois Press.
1967. "Moral Passage: The Symbolic Process in Public Designations of Deviance," *Social Problems,* 15(Fall), 175–188.

Hart, H. L. A.
1963. *Law, Liberty and Morality.* Stanford: Stanford University Press.

Horowitz, Irving Louis and Martin Liebowitz
1968. "Social Deviance and Political Marginality: Toward a Redefinition of the Relation Between Sociology and Politics," *Social Problems,* 15(Winter), 280–296.

Howard, John R.
1974. *The Cutting Edge: Social Movements and Social Change in America.* Philadelphia: J. B. Lippincott Company.

Humphreys, Laud
1972. *Out of the Closets: The Sociology of Homosexual Liberation.* Englewood Cliffs, N.J.: Prentice-Hall, Inc.

In re: Gault
1967. 387 U.S. 1.

Kaplan, John
1971. *Marijuana—The New Prohibition.* New York: Pocket Books.

Kittrie, Nicholas N.
1971. *The Right to Be Different: Deviance and Enforced Therapy.* Baltimore: The Johns Hopkins University Press.

The Knapp Commission Report on Police Corruption
1972. New York: George Braziller.

Lader, Lawrence
1966. *Abortion*. Indianapolis: The Bobbs-Merrill Co., Inc.
1973. *Abortion II: Making the Revolution*. Boston: Beacon Press, Inc.

Lauderdale, Pat
1976. "Deviance and Moral Boundaries," *American Sociological Review,* 41(August), 660–676.

Lehman, Edward W. and Ethna
1976. "Psychiatrists and Community Mental Health," *Journal of Health and Social Behavior,* 17(December), 364–375.

Leifer, Ronald
1966. "Community Psychiatry and Social Power," *Social Problems,* 14(Summer), 16–22.

Lemert, Edwin M.
1970. *Social Action and Legal Change: Revolution Within the Juvenile Court*. Chicago: Aldine Publishing Company.
1971. *Instead of Court: Diversion in Juvenile Justice*. National Institute of Mental Health, Center for Studies of Crime and Delinquency. Washington, D.C.: U.S. Government Printing Office.

Lerman, Paul
1975. *Community Treatment and Social Control*. Chicago: University of Chicago Press.

Lindesmith, Alfred R.
1965. *The Addict and the Law*. Bloomington, Ind.: Indiana University Press.

Lipton, Douglas, Robert Martinson and Judith Wilks
1975. *The Effectiveness of Correctional Treatment*. New York: Praeger Publishers, Inc.

Lister, Charles E.
1976. "Privacy, Recordkeeping, and Juvenile Justice," in Margaret K. Rosenheim, ed., *Pursuing Justice for the Child*. Chicago: University of Chicago Press. Pp. 205–222.

Loney, Martin
1973. "Social Control in Cuba," in Ian Taylor and Laurie Taylor, eds., *Politics and Deviance*. New York: Penguin Books, Inc. Pp. 42–60.

Mannheim, Hermann
1946. *Criminal Justice and Social Reconstruction*. New York: Oxford University Press.

Martinson, Robert
1974. "What Works?—Questions and Answers about Prison Reform," *The Public Interest,* (Spring), 22–54.

Merton, Robert K.
1957. *Social Theory and Social Structure. rev. ed.* Glencoe, Ill.: The Free Press.

Miller, Jerome and Lloyd E. Ohlin
1976. "The New Corrections: The Case of Massachusetts," in Rosenheim, ed., *op. cit.,* pp. 154–175.

Mitford, Jessica
1973. *Kind and Usual Punishment: The Prison Business*. New York: Alfred A. Knopf, Inc.

Morgan, Elaine
1977. "In Defense of Virgins," *The New York Times,* November 25, p. A35.

Morris, Norval
1974. *The Future of Imprisonment.* Chicago: University of Chicago Press.

Morris, Noval and Gordon Hawkins
1970. *The Honest Politician's Guide to Crime Control.* Chicago: University of Chicago Press.

National Commission on Marihuana and Drug Abuse
1972. *Marihuana—A Signal of Misunderstanding.* New York: Signet Books.

Nejelski, Paul
1976. "Diversion: Unleashing the Hound of Heaven?" in Rosenheim, ed., *op. cit.,* pp. 94–118.

Newman, Graeme
1976. *Comparative Deviance.* New York: Elsevier.
1978. *The Punishment Response.* Philadelphia: J. B. Lippincott Company.

Packer, Herbert L.
1968. *The Limits of the Criminal Sanction.* Stanford: Stanford University Press.

Pfohl, Stephen J.
1977. "The 'Discovery' of Child Abuse," *Social Problems,* 24(February), 310–323.

Platt, Anthony M.
1969. *The Child Savers: The Invention of Delinquency.* Chicago: University of Chicago Press.

President's Commission on Law Enforcement and Administration of Justice
1967a. *Task Force Report: The Courts.* Washington, D.C.: Government Printing Office.
1967b. *Task Force Report: Juvenile Delinquency and Youth Crime.* Washington, D.C.: U.S. Government Printing Office.
1967c. *Task Force Report: Organized Crime.* Washington, D.C.: U.S. Government Printing Office.

Rawls, John
1971. *A Theory of Justice.* Cambridge: Harvard University Press.

Reid, Sue Titus
1976. *Crime and Criminology.* Hinsdale, Ill.: The Dryden Press.

Roberts, Steven V.
1977. " 'Gray Power' Surging in Politics," *The New York Times,* November 28, pp. 1, 26.

Roby, Pamela A.
1969. "Politics and Criminal Law: Revision of the New York State Penal Law on Prostitution," *Social Problems,* 17(Summer), 83–109.

Rosenheim, Margaret K.
1976. "Notes on Helping: Normalizing Juvenile Nuisances," *The Social Service Review,* 50(June), 177–193.

Ross, Ken
1977. "Gay Rights: The Coming Struggle," *The Nation,* November 19, pp. 426–430.

Rossi, Peter, *et al.*
1974. "The Seriousness of Crimes: Normative Structure and Individual Differences," *American Sociological Review,* 39(April), 224–237.

Roszak, Theodore
1969. *The Making of a Counter Culture.* Garden City, N.Y.: Doubleday & Company, Inc.

Rothman, David J.
1971. *The Discovery of the Asylum.* Boston: Little, Brown and Company.

Rubinstein, Jonathan
1974. *City Police.* New York: Ballantine Books, Inc.

Russell, Diana E. H. and Nicole Van de Ven, eds.
1976. *Crimes Against Women: Proceedings of the International Tribunal.* Millbrae, Calif.: Les Femmes.

Sagarin, Edward
1969. *Odd Man In: Societies of Deviants in America.* New York: Quadrangle/The New York Times Book Co.
1975. *Deviants and Deviance.* New York: Praeger Publishers, Inc.

Sagarin, Edward, ed.
1971. *The Other Minorities.* Waltham, Mass.: Ginn & Company.

Sarri, Rosemary and Yeheskel Hasenfeld, eds.
1976. *Brought to Justice: Juveniles, the Courts, and the Law.* National Assessment of Juvenile Corrections. Ann Arbor: University of Michigan.

Sarvis, Betty and Hyman Rodman
1974. *The Abortion Controversy, 2nd ed.* New York: Columbia University Press.

Schrag, Peter and Diane Divoky
1976. *The Myth of the Hyperactive Child—and Other Means of Child Control.* New York: Dell Publishing Co., Inc.

Schultz, J. Lawrence and Fred Cohen
1976. "Isolationism in Juvenile Court Jurisprudence," in Rosenheim, ed., *op. cit.,* pp. 20–42.

Schultz, Terri
1977. "The Handicapped, A Minority Demanding its Rights," *The New York Times,* February 13, p. 8E.

Schur, Edwin M.
1965. *Crimes Without Victims.* Englewood Cliffs, N.J.: Prentice-Hall, Inc.
1973. *Radical Nonintervention: Rethinking the Delinquency Problem.* Englewood Cliffs, N.J.: Prentice-Hall, Inc.
1974. "Crime and the New Conservatives," in Irving Howe, ed., *The New Conservatives.* New York: Quadrangle/The New York Times Book Co., pp. 228–242.

Schur, Edwin M. and Hugo Adam Bedau
1974. *Victimless Crimes: Two Sides of a Controversy.* Englewood Cliffs, N.J.: Prentice-Hall, Inc.

Scull, Andrew T.
1977a. *Decarceration.* Englewood Cliffs, N.J.: Prentice-Hall, Inc.

1977b. "Madness and Segregative Control: The Rise of the Insane Asylum," *Social Problems,* 24(February), 337–351.

Sellin, Thorsten and Marvin E. Wolfgang
1964. *The Measurement of Delinquency.* New York: John Wiley & Sons, Inc.

Sherman, Lawrence, ed.
1974. *Police Corruption: A Sociological Perspective.* Garden City, N.Y.: Doubleday & Company, Inc.

Silver, Isidore
1976. "Crime and Conventional Wisdom," *Society,* 14(March/April), 9, 15–19.

Skolnick, Jerome H.
1975. *Justice Without Trial, 2nd ed.* New York: John Wiley & Sons, Inc.

Skolnick, Jerome H. and John Dombrink
1978. "The Legalization of Deviance," *Criminology,* 16(August), 193–208.

Smith, Howard and Leslie Harlib
1977. "Scenes," *The Village Voice,* November 21, p. 16.

Spector, Malcolm and John I. Kitsuse
1977. *Constructing Social Problems.* Menlo Park, Calif.: Cummings Publishing Co.

Stephenson, Richard M.
1973. "Involvement in Deviance: An Example and Some Theoretical Implications," *Social Problems,* 21(Fall), 173–190.

Street, David, Robert D. Vinter, and Charles Perrow
1966. *Organization for Treatment.* New York: The Free Press.

Sumner, William Grahan
1906, 1960. *Folkways.* New York: Mentor Books.

Sutherland, Edwin H.
1950. "The Diffusion of Sexual Psychopath Laws," *American Journal of Sociology,* 56 (September), 142–148.

Sutherland, Edwin H. and Donald R. Cressey
1966. *Principles of Criminology, 7th ed.* Philadelphia: J. B. Lippincott Company.

Szasz, Thomas S.
1970a. *Ideology and Insanity.* Garden City, N.Y.: Doubleday & Company, Inc.
1970b. *The Manufacture of Madness.* New York: Harper & Row, Publishers.

Turner, Ralph H.
1969. "The Public Perception of Protest," *American Sociological Review,* 34(December), 815–831.

Van den Haag, Ernest
1975. *Punishing Criminals.* New York: Basic Books, Inc.
1976. "Crime, Punishment and Deterrence," *Society,* 14(March/April), 11, 21–23.

Vinter, Robert D., *et al.*
1975. *Juvenile Corrections in the States: Residential Programs and Deinstitutionalization.* National Assessment of Juvenile Corrections. Ann Arbor: University of Michigan.

Vinter, Robert D., ed.
1976. *Time Out: A National Study of Juvenile Correctional Programs.* National Assessment of Juvenile Corrections. Ann Arbor: University of Michigan.

von Hirsch, Andrew
1976. *Doing Justice: The Choice of Punishments.* New York: Hill & Wang.

Vorenberg, Elizabeth and James
1977. " 'The Biggest Pimp of All': Prostitution and Some Facts of Life," *The Atlantic,* January, pp. 27–38.

Wald, Michael S.
1976. "State Intervention on Behalf of 'Neglected' Children: A Search for Realistic Standards," in Rosenheim, ed., *op. cit.,* pp. 241–278.

Wald, Patricia M.
1976. "Pretrial Detention for Juveniles," *ibid.,* pp. 119–137.

Walshok, Mary Lindenstein
1971. "The Emergence of Middle-Class Deviant Subculture: The Case of Swingers," *Social Problems,* 18(Spring), 488–495.

Warren, Marguerite Q.
1970. "The Community Treatment Project," in Norman Johnston, Leonard Savitz, and Marvin Wolfgang, eds., *The Sociology of Punishment and Correction, 2nd ed.* New York: Wiley & Sons, Inc. Pp. 671–683.

Weinberg, Martin S. and Colin J. Williams
1975. *Male Homosexuals: Their Problems and Adaptations.* New York: Penguin Books, Inc.

Williams, Robin
1960. *American Society: A Sociological Interpretation, 2nd ed.* New York: Alfred A. Knopf, Inc.

Wilson, James Q.
1975. *Thinking About Crime.* New York: Basic Books, Inc.
1976. "Thinking About *Thinking About Crime,*" *Society,* 14(March/April), 10, 19–21.

Wright, Erik Olin
1975. *The Politics of Punishment.* New York: Harper & Row, Publishers.

Zimring, Franklin E. and Gordon J. Hawkins
1973. *Deterrence.* Chicago: University of Chicago Press.

Zurcher, Louis A., Jr., *et al.*
1971. "The Anti-Pornography Campaign: A Symbolic Crusade," *Social Problems,* 19(Fall), 217–238.

REVIEW OF KEY TERMS

decarceration. The trend favoring alternatives to placement of individuals in closed treatment and correctional institutions that is based in part on the critique of "total institutions" (by Goffman and others) and on the lack of positive evidence for rehabilitation.

It reflects a growing preference for "community treatment" programs. Decarceration also is sometimes called **deinstitutionalization.**

decriminalization. The trend toward removing borderline "offenses" from the substantive criminal law. In such efforts, the aim is to reduce secondary expansion of the problematic situation. There is continuing controversy over the merits of this trend. See also **victimless crimes.**

diversion. Schemes for the nonjudicial handling of "delinquent" juveniles. It is a major theme in recent thinking about juvenile justice that is closely related to the trend toward removing "nuisance" or "status" offenses from the formal jurisdiction of the juvenile court.

justice model. A recently recommended approach to criminal justice, especially punishment, emphasizing the principle of "just deserts." It reflects a preference for fixed criminal penalties ordered according to seriousness of offense and aims at reducing inequities produced through extreme discretion and "individualizing."

moral crusade. An organized campaign, sometimes attaining the force of a general social movement, aimed at influencing deviance definitions and policies. Usually the term is applied to campaigns that seek to expand such definitions or, in other words, to impose deviance.

moral entrepreneur. The term used by Becker in referring to individuals who take major roles in initiating moral crusades. It suggests the possibility that individuals involved may sometimes have an economic stake in the outcome.

perceived threat. A condition that activates moral crusades and influences various shifts in moral boundaries. As Lauderdeale's experiment showed, threat may provoke deviantizing reaction independent of any actual change in objective deviation. The substance of perceived threat can vary greatly, the crucial factor being the perception, not the nature and extent of "actual" threat.

problemization. The term used by Rosenheim in referring to official overreaction to "juvenile nuisances," which she suggests should instead be "normalized." As she points out, it is a general tendency with respect to the "helping" professions which could, therefore, be relevant in interpreting a variety of deviance situations.

radical nonintervention. Recent tendencies in juvenile justice policy that reflect a growing reluctance to interfere in children's lives. A major aspect of this move toward reform is removal of "noncriminal" delinquency from the jurisdiction of the juvenile court. It is a trend reflecting concern about early stigmatization and also legal-social criticism of the juvenile court laws and procedures.

victimless crimes. "Offenses" that involve the willing exchange of strongly demanded though illegal goods or services, characterized by absence of a complaining victim to initiate enforcement activity. They, therefore, could also be called "complainantless crimes." Other meanings have focused on the absence of harm and interference with private morality. Sociological critiques emphasize enforcement, economic, and social consequences (deviance-amplification) of legislating in these borderline areas.

PROJECT 7
Case Study in the Politics of Deviance

Introductory Comment

It is good to keep in mind that deviance situations involve actual occurrences, live human beings, and often public and collective controversy. These are the conditions, after all, that have generated the sociologist's concepts and theories about deviance. Perhaps even more than in other subfields of sociology, the world of current affairs and policy making and the world of academic research and theorizing continuously interact. As we have seen, the very subject matter of deviance sociology is, virtually by definition, political in the broadest sense of that term. Even informal deviantizing among interacting individuals could be said to be political in nature (involving power, conflict, etc.), but the best examples of the politics of deviance develop out of specific controversies regarding public policies. The following exercise allows an in-depth look at one such controversy.

Assignment

Select any issue relating to governmental policy in an area of deviance-defining or processing (of any sort, substantively), about which there has been extensive recent public discussion or controversy, either nationally or locally. (A look at almost any day's newspaper should give you some initial ideas regarding issues you might wish to examine.)

In the library, *read* available materials (newspaper accounts, magazine articles, any relevant books, etc.) detailing the development of the controversy and its resolution to date. Read these materials with special attention to: participants on various "sides" of the controversy, and more general sources of support; arguments and techniques used to advance the various positions; any apparent sequence in the course the controversy has taken (stages, etc.); and apparent determinants of any tentative "outcomes" that were reached (legislation passed or defeated, other policy measures adopted or overturned, etc.).

Construct a chart which depicts the organizations, groups, or forces in conflict over the issue and which shows the major activities they engaged in, arguments they used, and sources of support and specific events they benefited from in the course of the controversy. Be prepared also to *present in class a brief report on the chronology of the controversy*, telling at least roughly what happened, when, and, to the extent you have ideas about it, why. What is your estimate as to any direction the controversy (if it remains brewing) may take in the future? Explain.

Suggestions

In evaluating the forces on various sides of the issue and their arguments and activities, it may be useful to be alert to the following matters:

1. Any apparent socioeconomic, racial, ethnic, religious, and "political" (in the narrower political-party sense) breakdowns among the competing forces.

2. Contemporaneous events that may have influenced the course of the controversy.

3. Any broadly symbolic meaning the issue may have had for participants on either side or for the public generally.

4. The size and organization of the competing forces.

5. The role of entrenched ideologies and vested interests, if any.

6. The existence of any key "moral entrepreneurs," if so, how did they influence the course of events, and what do you think accounts for that influence?

7. The way in which the controversy related to broader social trends and outlooks.

Implications

Your case study will be most useful to you if you now look back over the discussion in the preceding chapter and try to assess the relevance to the situation you examined of the various concepts and perspectives considered there. Again, one should not expect every item to be equally pertinent to your particular case study. Furthermore, it may be that your study gives you some reason to challenge, modify, or even rework one or another of the ideas in the text. If so, try to work out in your own mind at least the form that such a reworking might take. One of the purposes behind doing case studies, of course, is to produce new insights and to allow for a continuous checking and revision of concepts and theories. At the same time, you will no doubt realize that a single case study is only that; it cannot produce statistical generalizations about any broad class of situations or problems. Very likely its main value lies in the intense focus that is directed toward a single course of events. You should come away from such an exercise with a heightened appreciation of the role of conflict elements and sequential aspects as seen closely in at least one specific deviance situation.

PART 4

THE IMPLICATIONS OF STUDYING DEVIANCE

PROLOGUE 8

To have values or not to have values: the question is always with us. When sociologists undertake to study problems that have relevance to the world we live in, they find themselves caught in a cross-fire. Some urge them not to take sides, to be neutral and do research that is technically correct and value free. Others tell them their work is shallow and useless if it does not express a deep commitment to a value position.
—Howard S. Becker, "Whose Side Are We On?"

I also had to learn that the field worker cannot afford to think only of learning to live with others in the field. He has to continue living with himself. If the participant observer finds himself engaging in behavior that he has learned to think of as immoral, then he is likely to begin to wonder what sort of person he is after all. Unless the field worker can carry with him a reasonably consistent picture of himself he is likely to run into difficulties.
—William Foote Whyte, *Street Corner Society*

In recent times, sociologists have become increasingly self-conscious appraisers of their own research and theorizing operations. The basic premise of value-free inquiry has come under strong challenge. Many commentators, including influential persons within the discipline itself, argue that sociological inquiry is always affected to some extent by the value priorities of the investigator—if only through the choice of research topics in the first place. Nor is it possible, they insist, to avoid the fact that sociological theories and studies are put to use in the real world and, hence, carry inevitable moral implications of various sorts. Newly emphasized subfields within sociology—such as the sociology of knowledge, the sociology of science, and the aforementioned "ethnomethodology"—have focused attention on both the sources and ramifications of sociological thinking and study methods. Critiques by "radical sociologists" have added fuel to the demand for heightened self-awareness on the part of the student of society.

At the same time, social researchers have pushed their inquiries into domains of behavior that earlier seemed to defy investigation. To do this, they mastered various field research techniques that intensified their immersion in the very substance of what it was they were studying. These new research situations

485

and approaches, in turn, have increased the social and moral complexity of the sociological enterprise itself. Particularly in the area of deviance sociology, the need to openly confront this complexity is urgent. Issues relating to the responsibilities of sociologists—to themselves, to the people they study, and to the society at large—immediately come to the fore. Evasion of such issues in the name of "pure science" can only serve in the long run to compromise both the "purity" and the "science" that the researcher-theorist seeks to achieve.

CH.8
DEVIANCE SOCIOLOGY
AND THE PUBLIC GOOD:
THREE DILEMMAS

THE RESEARCH DILEMMA

The aim of this book has been to present, illustrate, and evaluate those sociological perspectives that should prove most valuable in the interpretation of deviance. We have also noted some of the associated trends in research methodology and, particularly in the previous chapter, a few specific deviance-related developments in the sphere of public policy. In order to round out our consideration of the emerging state of the field, at least a brief assessment of the general implications of studying deviance is necessary. It is relatively easy to spin out ideas and formulate theories, yet it is important to recognize that ideas have consequences—including, sometimes, unintended ones. Research, too, has a real-world impact. In a broad sense, it can indirectly influence public outlooks and social policy; at a more immediate level, it may have very direct consequences for the people who have been studied. What the sociologist says or does, then, may not always have earth-shaking consequences, but it is likely to "make a difference." Recognizing this forces the sociologist of deviance to confront at least three major moral dilemmas. The first relates to research methods themselves, the second to the sociologist's participation in policy formation, and the third centers around the "labeling" implications of studying particular forms of "deviance."

There is no way to study deviance that does not entail adopting some sort of moral stance regarding the research subjects. Those methods that seem furthest removed from direct interference in people's lives, statistical surveys and the like, tend to maintain the subjects' anonymity at the cost of ignoring their individual humanness. These techniques treat the individual as but an instance of a category, even if this is done with the best of intentions and for respectable sociological reasons (as a basis for statistical generalization and comparison). Not only are we kept from "knowing" the specific respondents in any comprehensive self-revealed way, but a single dimension or aspect of their lives (in this instance, usually some perceived deviation) is singled out as the basis for the restricted knowledge we do attain. As we have seen, it has been in part a realization of the sociological shortcomings of such approaches, if not their moral implications, that has drawn investigators toward more in-depth methods.

Furthermore, in an era of "data banks" (centralized archives for the storage of statistical data and other kinds of information) and computerized data "retrieval," it is no longer always clear even that the statistical approaches do preserve the individual respondent's anonymity. This was pointed up in a recently publicized controversy regarding a public health study which, whether it happened to involve sociologists or not, provides a good example of the potential for abridging confidentiality that may arise in many kinds of deviance-related research. The study (conducted in New York State) aimed at determining whether women who have had abortions, in comparison with those who have not, have higher rates of subsequent miscarriage and other pregnancy and childbirth complications. Computerized government records (those for abortionees based on fetal death reports that doctors must file on all abortion patients; those for the "control" group drawn from official birth records) provided the samples to be compared through follow-up of their later childbearing and medical histories. In efforts to track down some of the individual subjects, researchers sent their names to other agencies such as the State Department of Motor Vehicles. The subjects themselves were never notified of the study, because the researchers believed that "informed consent" would not be necessary. It only came to public light when two state legislatures got hold of a progress report on the research which included the names of 28 women. Critics quickly referred to the study (which involved 48,000 New York women) as a "massive invasion of privacy," and the state health commissioner, whose department had facilitated the research, promised an investigation (*The New York Times,* May 15, 1977, p. E4).

What is especially insidious, of course, about practices of this sort is the way in which names of and information about respondents can become available, at least to subsequent researchers, without the respondents being at all aware of what is going on. When the research activity is more direct and known-about by the people being studied, however, there is still no complete assurance that anonymity will be preserved even if the intention to preserve it is present. Thus, many field studies of small communities have been plagued by the problem of how to report findings and still maintain confidentiality; and there are some famous controversies that have arisen out of such investigations. Once the communities in question become identifiable to readers of published reports on the research, and others not directly involved in the research, it is virtually impossible, for example, to keep anonymous the key individuals within those settings (e.g., the mayor, chairman of the board of education, or whatever). Similar problems could arise in situated deviance studies, just as they have repeatedly in studies of "community power structure" and other investigations of local community life.

As we saw earlier, much recent research on deviance has utilized the techniques of in-depth observation, including "participant observation." The focus is on understanding the actors' own "subjective meanings of action," on studying people and behaviors in their "natural settings," and on a close and nonjudgmental experiencing of the relevant "situated morality." An important model for such work has been that developed in cultural anthropology, and, indeed, many of these newer deviance studies are designated "ethnographic" by the researchers themselves. Great effort is made in such research for the investigator to set aside preconceptions, including the commonplace notions about the basic "differentness" of deviators that we considered earlier. Needless to say, participant observation poses significant difficulties and dilemmas of its own (McCall and Simmons, 1969; Douglas, ed., 1972). Not the least of these has to do with the situational immersion or involvement that permits an investigator to appreciate the "ordinariness" of deviation. The researcher who makes this effort always runs the risk of overinvolvement. This can easily produce distortions just as misleading as those that stem from underinvolvement when using more remote and quantitative techniques. Whereas researcher detachment usually compels a heavy reliance on uncertain inference, overinvolvement can at times cause one to lose a sense of perspective and to abdicate completely the attempt at reasonably objective interpretation.

But overinvolvement does not only undermine disinterested research. It can also have effects on the researcher which are unexpected and undesired. A classic discussion of such possibilities has been presented by William Foote Whyte in the enlarged version of his early study *Street Corner Society*. As Whyte relates, "hanging around" with the streetcorner youths he wanted to study gradually became his major research method. Engaging in the group's everyday activities proved to be the best way to get a real feel for the structure and patterns of their social existence. Whyte became concerned about his own involvement, however, when on one occasion it carried him along to voting twice in an election—a common practice in the district. Noting that the risk of arrest was only one troubling aspect of this behavior, he has written:

When I discovered that I was a repeater, I found my conscience giving me serious trouble. This was not like the picture of myself that I had been trying to build up. I could not laugh it off simply as a necessary part of the field work. I knew that it was not necessary; at the point where I began to repeat, I could have refused. . . . I had to learn that, in order to be accepted by the people in a district, you do not have to do everything just as they do it (Whyte, 1955, pp. 316–317).

More commonly, involvement does not push researchers themselves into deviation, but by definition (in deviance studies) it causes them to directly observe or at least know about deviation, sometimes including serious crimes. The rights and obligations of the sociologist in this kind of "guilty knowledge" situation are far from clear. Most researchers will make some effort to "draw the line," as Polsky has put it, regarding their own involvement with serious criminality, refusing to engage in it, to assist in the commission of crimes, or to encourage them. They may, indeed, intentionally limit even their observations and direct knowledge. Thus, Polsky, discussing his experience in studying professional criminals, has noted that, "although I am willing to be told about anything and everything, and to witness many kinds of illegal acts, when necessary I make it clear that there are some such acts I prefer not to witness. (With two exceptions I have had this preference respected.) To the extent that I am unwilling to witness such acts, my personal moral code of course compromises my scientific role—but not, I think, irreparably" (Polsky, 1967, p. 133). It may be possible, by placing limits on observation or knowledge, to avoid some of the most difficult dilemmas. Rapport and mutual trust between researcher and subjects are necessary if the latter are to act normally (unaffected by the presence of the investigator) and speak candidly. Yet such a relationship can be severely strained or threatened through the researcher's "guilty knowledge"—to cite an extreme example, through advanced knowledge that a homicide is to be committed. Relatively few sociologists in such a situation would completely disclaim any obligation to "report" such information or at least to try somehow to avert the act.

Adding to the moral quandary in situations of this sort is the researcher's uncertain and highly precarious legal situation. Unlike members of the "established" professions (Carlin, 1966; Freidson, 1970), social scientists are not yet definitely accorded a legal privilege for the protection of confidential disclosures. In some instances, it will not be possible for researchers to protect themselves and their subjects at the same time. They must decide either to violate confidentiality or run the risk that they may be prosecuted as an accessory to crime, for contempt of court, or on various other grounds. Two leading students of this question have written:

. . . social scientists must directly confront the uncomfortable problem of their obligation, on the one hand, to aid the state in the detection and prosecution of crime and their obligation on the other hand to protect their subjects. One distinction might be that the researcher would not be obligated to reveal crimes which were the subjects of his research. For example, a researcher studying homosexual behavior would not be expected to report each of his subjects when they violated a statute concerning homosexuals, but he would be obligated to give evidence concerning a murder about which he inadvertently gained knowledge during his research (Nejelski and Finsterbusch, 1973).

However, this distinction is merely a suggestion for one direction in which the law regarding these matters might develop; as it now stands, the researcher does not even have this kind of protection. Clearly, the nature of the "offense" will have a considerable bearing on how morally compelling the dilemma seems to the social scientist in any given instance. But by the same token, the distinction just mentioned (between crimes one is studying and those one is not) would be more or less tenable morally and legally depending upon the circumstances. For the researcher investigating, say, the professional "hit man" (hired killer), there would be no easy way out of the dilemma.

If moral uncertainty sometimes surrounds an openly acknowledged relationship between researcher and subject, the situation is even more complicated when researchers do not disclose their real identities or purposes. Many of the most strenuous moral dilemmas that have arisen in the course of research on deviance are ultimately attributable to the investigators' concern about the difficult matter of achieving initial "access" to the data. In many traditional studies, the subjects themselves had little opportunity to grant or withhold such access. For example, there sometimes was a tendency to treat the literally "captive" population of incarcerated prisoners, processed "delinquents," or hospitalized mental patients as "fair game" for research purposes. These people (and, to a lesser degree, even the students in a classroom presented with a questionnaire to fill out) were rarely in any position to refuse cooperation. They could be observed and questioned almost at will, much as the physically sick patient in a teaching hospital is routinely "shown" to troupes of medical students making their rounds. Indeed, this easy access was but one more sign of the disvaluation and depersonalization built into deviantness and, unfortunately, in some such cases, capitalized on even by the sociologist. Nowadays there is much concern that people (whatever their status) ought in most circumstances only be studied with their free consent.

Despite this new sensitivity to the rights of the individual research subject, a new version of the "access" problem has arisen. There are many deviance situations in which sociologists may feel that informed consent to undertake a study would not be forthcoming. Although Polsky argues that researchers may have exaggerated the difficulties of obtaining direct access to deviators, the elements of shame and discreditability and the pressures for concealment in the stigmatized person's situation are, as we have seen, very real indeed. Under the circumstances, and given the likelihood of suspicion regarding the investigator's motives and trustworthiness, it is not unreasonable to believe that preliminary research requests often might be denied. Because of this belief (and also on the assumption that an undisclosed researcher will be more likely to obtain observations that are free from "contamination" on account of the research situation itself), sociologists of deviance have frequently employed a variety of "disguised participant observation" techniques. In this approach, the true identity of the participant-observer is kept hidden, and access is achieved by presenting and managing a "cover" (sometimes that of being simply an ordinary member of the group that is under scrutiny).

As one sociologist highly supportive of field research has stated, "there has been considerable argument, both among sociologists and those outside the field, over the whole issue of *secret research*. Two fundamental questions are involved in this issue: (1) the question of *effectiveness*—Which provides the more reliable evidence, secret or nonsecret involvement? and (2) the question of *morality*—Is secret research immoral and, if so, should it therefore be rejected by sociologists?" (Douglas, ed., 1972, p. 5, italics in original). Douglas goes on to suggest that these questions have not really been explored systematically. Acknowledging a potential danger that secret research could encourage "moral blindness and a willingness to *use* people," Douglas went on to urge that sociologists "guard against such abuse by recognizing it as a danger and instituting measures against it" (Douglas, ed., 1972, p. 8). Presumably such measures include meaningful efforts to protect the anonymity of the individual subjects and to see to it that the findings of the research are not used against the interests of those individuals. It is questionable, however, whether complete protection of this sort can often be provided. Some writers have argued that whenever there is any potential for harm to the subjects, methods of this sort are extremely difficult to justify (Erikson, 1967 and see also the recent discussion by Bok, 1978, ch. 12). On the other hand, many field researchers continue to insist that only the disguised investigator can achieve the full access and understanding that permit the unique contribution of in-depth field observation methods.

Many of these questions relating to hidden observation erupted into a considerable controversy ignited by Laud Humphreys' study of homosexual contacts in public restrooms (Humphreys, 1970, 1975), which was referred to briefly in an earlier chapter. Obviously, studying a covert and highly discreditable behavior of this sort is not an easy matter. At the outset, Humphreys determined that a totally detached and formal scientific stance, in which his identity as a researcher was fully acknowledged to his subjects, would not be tenable. He concluded that in order to really appreciate the situation of homosexuals, "I had to enter the subculture as would any newcomer and to make contact with respondents under the guise of being any other gay guy" (Humphreys, 1970, 1975, p. 24). During the early phase of his study, Humphreys went around to various gay bars and other gatherings in the local gay community, making general observations and inquiries. Although this involved his "passing as deviant," it was not this particular use of disguised research, but what he did later, that caused all the furor.

Having identified certain specific restrooms as the ones in which transient homosexual encounters regularly took place (they are known as "tearooms" in the gay community), Humphreys had to figure out how to study what went on there. Paradoxically, the participants' need for secrecy suggested a method. "The very fear and suspicion encountered in the restrooms produces a participant role, the sexuality of which is optional. This is the role of the lookout ('watchqueen' in the argot), a man who is situated at the door or windows from which he may observe the means of access to the restroom. When someone approaches he coughs. He nods when the coast is clear or if he recognizes an entering party as a regular" (Humphreys, 1970, 1975, p. 27). Humphreys assumed such a role, thus gaining direct access to the restroom. Since some of the men who play this role appear to do so because they enjoy watching the sexual activity, he could avoid participating and yet not arouse suspicion. Through this approach, Humphreys was able to make highly systematic observations of a large number of homosexual encounters ("some 200 acts of fellatio") and to describe the practices and patterns in great detail. When reported through his subsequent publications, this technique gave rise to much criticism. Several commentators viewed his method with evident distaste and either condemned this "spying" as an unethical invasion of the participants' privacy or charged Humphreys with a scientifically improper participation in, or abetting of, criminal acts.

A third procedure generated even more controversy. Still hoping for information as to who his subjects were and what had brought them there, Humphreys gradually was able to talk with some of the participants outside the restroom setting and even to disclose his research purpose. Twelve of these eventually became willing interview respondents. Seeking additional interviews, Humphreys employed the extremely unorthodox procedure of noting down the license plate numbers of participants' cars and, on that basis, tracing their names and addresses and some other information about them. About a year later, when he was asked to work on a different research project—a general health survey of men in the same local community—Humphreys made use of these new data. He managed to add his identified participants to the "sample" for the community study, which was exploring not only various aspects of social background, but also attitudes and sexual relationships that would be relevant for his own study. According to Humphreys' first account of this method, his subjects were in no way threatened by it:

> My master list was kept in a safe deposit box. Each interview card, kept under lock and key, was destroyed with completion of the schedule. No names or other identifying tags were allowed to appear on the questionnaires. Although I recognized each of the men interviewed from observation of them in the tearooms, there was no indication that they remembered me. I was careful to change my appearance, dress, and automobile from the days when I had passed as deviant. I also allowed at least a year's time to lapse between the original sampling procedure and the interviews (Humphreys, 1970, 1975, p. 42).

Later, however, when excerpts from Humphreys' book *Tearoom Trade* appeared in a national magazine, it became clear that some commentators took a very different view of the matter. Journalist Nicholas von Hoffman derided the study as a highly objectionable invasion of privacy, noting that the information Humphreys collected could have been used for blackmail, extortion, or as a basis for criminal prosecution. Neither good intentions nor indications that the information obtained might be socially useful would suffice to convince Hoffman that secret research in such an area could be justified. Sociologists Irving Louis Horowitz and Lee Rainwater (the latter a graduate school mentor of Humphreys) defended his work, stressing the value of social inquiry into controversial and hidden behaviors. They argued that the potential for good through such research outweighed any potential for harm through subsequent misuse of the data (see Humphreys, 1970, 1975, pp. 177–190). Since this first clash of views concerning Humphreys' work, various writers on research ethics and research methods have reviewed the issues posed by it, emphasizing the delicate problem of balancing the individual's right to privacy and the public's "right to know."

Humphreys has performed a service by reprinting many of these discussions in an enlarged edition of his book, where he has also offered a response to his critics. Continuing to insist that the disguised observation techniques had been justified, he now, however, expressed greater concern than before regarding the legal problems. When he began his investigation, the possibility of legal action against himself had not even occurred to him. In addition to reassessing that possibility, he had come to have second thoughts regarding his license-plate tracing scheme. "I now think my reasoning was faulty and that my respondents were placed in greater danger than seemed plausible at the time." Nonetheless, he stated: "I remain proud of the work done. I often wish other sociologists would give more attention to some of my substantive findings that I believe provide an increment of understanding of social behavior in our society" (Humphreys, 1970, 1975, pp. 230, 231).

These substantive findings may indeed have been very useful in contributing to a more accurate understanding of homosexual behavior in our society. Humphreys' research suggested that this type of sexual encounter may be quite widespread and not confined to exclusive homosexuals (as mentioned earlier in this book, many of his respondents appeared to be happily married men). He also documented both the fear of disclosure and routine police harassment that continuously plague the homosexual community. He sharply challenged the necessity and desirability of the existing repressive policies toward homosexuals. However, against these possible benefits must be weighed the risks that were incurred through the methods Humphreys adopted, even while having in mind that alternative methods might not have been readily available. Opinions will continue to differ as to whether these techniques were or are ethically justifiable and professionally acceptable. Yet the more general discussion that Humphreys' study provoked has been extremely valuable in its own right. It has alerted researchers and all students of the social sciences to major dilemmas and ramifications of research on socially and morally controversial topics.

THE POLICY DILEMMA

Should the sociologist become involved in the policymaking process and, if so, how? Some aspects of this question were briefly discussed in the opening chapter of this book. Although most sociologists remain committed to the general goal of conducting research in as disinterested and "value-free" a manner as possible, many would now insist that total "ethical neutrality" is an illusion. The researcher's unarticulated premises and value priorities affect the selection of research topics and the nature of interpretations. Furthermore, the findings and theories that sociologists produce are put "to use" by policymakers—with or without their originators' self-conscious participation or approval. Under these circumstances, many social scientists now recognize, it may be a misleading evasion of social and professional responsibility to completely disavow involvement in the policy process. Sociologists, in short, are involved—whether they like it or not.

By the same token, it may be unsatisfactory for the researcher to abjure involvement "until all the data are in." All the data will never be "in," since the social world is always changing and since new research is always being done. It is true that social research is a cumulative process in which findings and theories are always presented tentatively—subject to retesting, modification, even possible repudiation. On the other hand, as we have seen, policymaking on deviance issues cannot wait for any supposed "final" and conclusive evidence to arrive. It is necessarily an ongoing process and one which, to an extent, is always influenced by *some* underlying presuppositions regarding the relevant social patterns, factors, and forces. By providing the *best available evidence and interpretation*, sociologists can usefully contribute to this process. As we noted earlier, they should do this with an awareness on their part and also on the part of policymakers and the general public of the *inherent limitations* on such a contribution. But short of producing definitive "solutions" for all situations perceived as problematic, there is a great deal that the sociologist does have to offer.

The basic functions of documenting, demythologizing, and developing analytic and interpretive frameworks—all cited at the beginning of this text— offer vital inputs to policymaking. This is true in an indirect sense, as when the work of social scientists gradually influences "public opinion," which in turn comes to be reflected in specific policy measures. It is also true in a more direct sense, for policymakers and implementers themselves are affected by and even explicitly draw on social research and interpretation in connection with their practical work. Many of the studies cited throughout this book have been influential in one or another of these ways. Perhaps particularly in the "victimless crime" areas—in which public opinion has been ambivalent and public knowledge uneven and much affected by many false stereotypes—the sociology of deviance has had a major policy impact. A striking example has been the aforementioned dispelling of the misconception that marihuana use "leads to" heroin addiction. Although it is true that most heroin addicts had first used marihuana, a quite false reasoning is involved when one concludes, therefore, that using the milder intoxicant "causes" or "leads to" involvement with the physiologically addicting opiates. Careful statistical studies (e.g., Goode, 1969; O'Donnell, *et al.*, 1976) have definitively shown that, whereas most heroin users did use marihuana, only a small percentage of all marihuana users go on to heroin. As various commentators have pointed out, very high proportions of heroin addicts also first drank milk and smoked cigarettes; yet it would obviously be a false inference to suggest these early practices "led" them to heroin. The logic behind such reasoning would be the same, though in the case of the marihuana-progression argument the fallacy was less evident to the general public.

Similarly, many of the studies and specific findings regarding homosexuality that we have noted throughout this work have helped to dispel unwarranted fears and widespread misconceptions that we know have exerted an influence in the policy realm. Although the topic of abortion is not one on which sociologists have focused heavily in their research, even in this deviance area they have made some significant policy-relevant contributions. These have included analyses pointing up the already-emphasized unenforceability and dysfunctions of restrictive laws (Schur, 1965; 1968); the safety, at one time not widely realized, of early hospital abortions (Schur, 1965, 1968); the changing nature of public opinion on abortion issues; the relation of changing attitudes to the place of women socially and demographically in our society (Rossi, 1966); the social processes involved when women must seek illicit abortions (Ball, 1967; Lee, 1969); and the sociomoral complexity of the specific political controversy over abortion laws (Sarvis and Rodman, 1974). One could select almost any of the deviance issues discussed in this book with respect to which public policy questions have arisen and cite comparable policymaking contributions by sociologists.

Another controversial aspect of the deviance sociologist's relation to policy involves government-supported research and government-requested consultation. The moral dilemma here has to do with preserving critical independence despite the implicit power of governmental funding and prestigious advice-seeking to induce acquiescence in the status quo. The problem, to adopt terminology frequently used by radical critics, is to avoid *cooptation,* in effect, being "bought out" by the very government whose policies and practices the researcher should be engaged in evaluating. This danger has been cited especially in the area of criminal justice research and policymaking. Particularly in recent years and because of the combination of repressive national policies toward political deviation and a related stepping up of the technological side of our criminal justice (armaments, surveillance equipment, etc.), priorities in government-funded crime programs—and even research—have been much criticized. Referring to the existence of a "criminal justice-industrial complex," Richard Quinney argues that, "Criminal justice, in all its aspects, is becoming one of the last remaining capital-investment industries" (Quinney, 1977, p. 118). In discussing major priorities for government funding through the Law Enforcement Assistance Administration, he goes on to write:

Especially under the direction of LEAA, a multimillion-dollar market in domestic control has been established for hundreds of industries and research institutes. LEAA has contracted industries and institutes, directly or indirectly through state agencies, to develop and manufacture a wide range of weapons and technical devices for use in the criminal justice system. A technology and an industry created for scientific warfare abroad is now being applied to social control at home. Moreover, a field of research and development in criminal justice has emerged, putting control on a scientific basis as well as making a profitable industry. Under the sponsorship of LEAA, with lucrative contracts, private corporations, research institutes, and universities are gaining profits from the new system of criminal justice (Quinney, 1977, pp. 120–121).

While this critique in part concerns research in engineering, electronics, and the physical sciences, the argument is also made that funding priorities for the social sciences may have pushed crime researchers in unsavory directions (Quinney, 1974, pp. 32–43; see also Silver, ed., 1974). Even if they have not all personally been drawn into research on "counter-insurgency" techniques, better organization of riot control forces, new modes of surveillance, or ways of pacifying prisoners, the question has been raised whether social researchers should be indebted to or even accept support from a government that is stressing these activities. Political opinions on such matters will, of course, vary considerably. Furthermore, in many instances government funding agencies may in fact allow researchers full freedom to investigate and criticize where they see fit and may also support a wide range of types of research including many that social scientists would widely view as socially beneficial.

At any rate, caution should be exercised lest this general line of argument be glibly expanded and applied wholesale to the broader, more inclusive field of deviance research and interpretation. As part of an influential critique of the "labeling" approach (other aspects of which are discussed in the next section), Alvin Gouldner has taxed recent deviance analysts with adopting a "sociology of the underdog" perspective that leads them to focus only on the relations between deviators and local or middle-level control agents; major policies and practices at the level of national officials and agencies which "control access to large supplies of research funds" are left relatively free from scrutiny (Gouldner, 1968, pp. 108–110). The suggestion that the newer outlooks have a special payoff in funding and prestige because they do not challenge dominant policies nationally does not seem much warranted. For one thing, labeling-oriented researchers, in fact, have not shied away from critiques at the national level—the aforementioned studies highly critical of the federal Narcotics Bureau represent but one important example of this. Furthermore, the implication that recent researchers have jumped on some "labeling" bandwagon because of the funding opportunities does not hold up. In fact, the kinds of intense observational research that this perspective nurtures are not too likely to be heavily funded by the government. No systematic evidence on this issue has been collected, but there is reason to believe it would show that major labeling analysts have been relatively little "beholden" to funding agencies. Finally, assessments will vary as to the overall implications and uses of the bulk of labeling-oriented research. If its most direct focus has not been on the centralized (national) sources and agents of repression, many observers would nonetheless conclude that its general thrust has been strongly critical of repressive policies and practices.

Providing consulting services at the request of the government poses many of the same problems presented by engaging in government-funded research. Again, it is unlikely that there is one overwhelming pattern operating only and completely to support the status quo. A special kind of consultation that may pose significant cooptation problems involves the relation between sociologists and national commissions investigating specific deviance issues. It is often suggested, not merely in sarcasm, that when a government doesn't want to do or change anything, it appoints a commission! In recent years, we have seen national commissions on crime, violence, civil disorders, marihuana, and pornography and similar national inquiries into welfare, disability, mental illness, and the problems of juveniles. Critics of such efforts insist that despite important research done for such commissions and despite a good deal of enlightened discussion in their published papers, little has actually been accomplished by way of significantly altering the course of national policy.

Radical sociologists have pointed to the composition of these commissions as the underlying reason for their relative innocuousness. Typically, the members of these appointed bodies have been prominent political figures, leading lawyers and judges, and major business executives. Quinney has asserted that since such commissions are composed of "men of power," there is little likelihood they will "carry out a radical analysis" of our society's fundamental problems or suggest changes that would alter the established order. "Commissions provide the ruling class with one more means of protecting the existing order, which means securing domestic order—keeping the people of the underclass in their place, as colonials" (Quinney, 1974, p. 75). Sociologists usually have been in secondary roles when they have participated in the work of such commissions. Their contribution has centered around providing the background research, rather than making the basic policy decisions. Therefore, it has often been the case that the "consultant's papers" provided for commission guidance will have recommended one thing, and yet the commission itself in its final report will recommend something quite different (often, critics say, a "watered-down" version). Hence, the charge that the contributing sociologist has allowed himself or herself to be "coopted," to participate in an official "whitewash," to be "used" as an agent of the "establishment."

Actually, there has been some progression regarding the roles and influence of sociologists in these inquiries. Whereas at one time their services usually were contracted for in undertaking specific studies (and this continues), the trend more recently has been for social researchers also to be placed high on the commission's regular staff (with a sociologist, for example, as research director), and, in a few instances, sociologists have been included in the actual commission membership. As a consequence, it may be likely that sociological outlooks will more and more influence the deliberations and recommendations of these bodies. There also may have been a progression over time in the extent to which commissions have been prepared to challenge existing policies and programs. Some observers would conclude, as one writer on national commission recommendations in the field of juvenile justice has done, that in recent years certain commission proposals have been "relatively radical" (Tonry, 1976, p. 292). To the extent this has been so, it is presumably not the fault of such commissions if their suggestions have not always been acted upon; by the same token, it seems unfair to view the sociologists in question simply as having participated in a "whitewash." It may also remain to be seen whether these commissions will, in the long run, have produced no greater impact than the cirtics describe. The critique, in terms of direct short-run effectiveness, does seem justified. Yet, as we have seen, at least some deviance policies have been changing considerably in recent years, often in directions of which even radicals might approve. The published papers of these national commissions, with the heightened direct input from sociologists, have served to improve the general state of knowledge on deviance issues and, in many respects, may indirectly have helped to foster new progressive outlooks. While some of the interesting policy changes in recent times may have occurred despite the work of such bodies, others may be occurring partly through their influence and with their support.

THE "LABELING" DILEMMA

A third major dilemma in the deviance field is highlighted by the recently emphasized perspectives, even as they provide no easy means of averting it. If deviance is a matter of definition, a "social construction of reality," what, if any part, has sociology played in constructing it? Are sociologists to a degree responsible for "creating" that which they claim they have only been "studying?" When this labeling analysis is directed toward the work of deviance sociologists themselves, it is bound to make them feel somewhat uncomfortable. There seems little doubt that the term "deviance" itself is largely a sociological construct in much the same sense as are other basic concepts used in the social sciences. But if such constructs represent an admitted abstraction from reality, a categorizing for purposes of research and interpretation, it does not at all follow that sociology has completely or arbitrarily "created" the social patterns and processes that are being examined. The same problem arises in various other spheres of sociological inquiry. Thus, while sociology certainly bears heavy responsibility for producing the concept "social class," there is a highly meaningful social reality to which that term refers. Large bodies of empirical evidence show us that socioeconomic and prestige hierarchies, related differential life-styles, and stratified "life chances" do really exist and are extremely consequential. As the material in this text should have made clear, the same point is applicable in the deviance field. The social reaction processes through which deviantness designations are created, imputed, resisted, and changed are likewise very real and socially consequential.

To single them out as a focal point for sociological study is not simply to enact some whim of the sociologist. On the contrary, as we have seen, to do so may be to carry out a necessary and central part of the sociological enterprise.

However, even if we accept that claim, we may not have completely disposed of the deviance sociologist's own "labeling" dilemma. Precisely because deviance-designating is a matter of disvaluation of real individuals, qualms about calling attention to it, even under academic auspices, are likely to persist. Furthermore, a special version of the dilemma may be posed when sociology singles out *particular forms* of behavior or conditions as the substantive "subject matter" in the deviance field. To the extent they have done this, have sociologists unintentionally reinforced the *specific* current patterns of deviance-defining that they claim to be merely investigating? An argument to that effect has developed in which two interrelated assertions have been made. One is that sociologists are helping to enshrine and are even implicitly approving the existing deviance definitions by studying only those people who have been stigmatized, rather than the "real deviants." The other is that, in this process, the underlying social structures and forces that breed deviance in the first place (poverty, racism, sexism, "imperialism," "monopoly capitalism," etc.) are being ignored.

A major statement incorporating some of these themes has been made by Gouldner in his aforementioned critique of the "labeling" orientation. He was reacting particularly to an earlier paper by Becker (Becker, 1967), who had argued that deviance researchers should not be apologetic about pursuing their studies from the standpoint of the persons subordinated through deviantizing, since *some* orienting standpoint in research is always inevitable. Gouldner condemned Becker and other labeling analysts who had adopted an "underdog identification" for "inviting us to view the deviant as a passive nonentity who is responsible neither for his suffering nor its alleviation—who is more 'sinned against than sinning' " (Gouldner, 1968, p. 106). As mentioned earlier, Goulder criticized this underdog approach for its heavy focus on middle-level control agencies. "Insofar as this school of theory has a critical edge to it," he claimed, "this is directed at the caretaking institutions that produce the deviant's suffering" (Gouldner, 1968, p. 107). What the labeling approach amounted to, he contended, was "essentially a rejection of unenlightened middle class bigotry." Furthermore, taking the standpoint of the "underdogs" paradoxically implied seeing them "from the standpoint of respectable society and its dominant institutions," because it is that standpoint that deviators have incorporated into their own self-concepts and that causes them to see themselves as being in the underdog position" (Gouldner, 1968, p. 107). The price of adopting such orientations, Gouldner argued, "is an uncritical accommodation to the national elite and to the society's master institutions; and this is all to the bad" (Gouldner, 1968, p. 111).

This line of reasoning has been widely echoed among radical sociologists. In the more moderate critiques, the social-psychological emphasis in the labeling perspective (that we have seen, however, is merely one aspect of it) is criticized. Thus, Mankoff has asserted that such emphasis "may blind sociologists to macro-sociological analysis which traces social instability and career deviance to the very institutional arrangements—economic, political, cultural, that are supposed to maintain control" (Mankoff, 1971, pp. 214–215). Other writers have been rather more extreme in elaborating the Gouldner thesis. Dean Manders, in a Marxist critique of recent work on deviance, has referred to "bourgeois labelling theory" (Manders, 1975, p. 63). Alexander Liazos has found the implication of recent work to be that "the sociologist accepts current successful definitions of what is 'deviant' as the only ones worthy of his attention" (Liazos, 1972, p. 110). And Alex Thio has asserted that "labeling theory actually equates deviance with powerlessness. . . . This unavoidably implies that the powerless are necessarily deviants but the powerful not deviants at all!" (Thio, 1973, p. 5).

These statements not only adopt an unnecessarily limited view of the labeling outlooks, failing to recognize the collective-definition and the conflict aspects we have considered earlier in this book, but they also reveal an unfortunate misreading of the basic thrust and implications of a definitional-processual perspective. In addition, they point up once again the serious problems involved in continuing to use traditional terminology such as "deviants." As this text has emphasized, the entire point of the recently emerging outlooks has been to highlight and interpret the defining-reacting processes through which a certain kind of meaning (deviantness) is attached to individuals, behaviors, and conditions. From this standpoint, there is simply no such thing as a real, or necessary, "deviant." Deviance is *always* a social construction, and relative power is one of the major determinants of the "forms" it takes. The radical critics do serve an important function when they point to recent lack of interest in "alternative" deviance definitions. Yet, actually, as we have seen, the definitional framework does imply a dual focus on the powerless and the powerful. It is the latter's superior resources that largely account for the deviantizing of the former and *also* for their own immunity from deviantizing.

The chief emphasis of the recent perspectives is, to be sure, on processes of categorizing, disvaluing, and systematically oppressing. These are real processes having very evident impact in our society. To study them is hardly to approve of them—either in general, or as regards their specific current applications. On the contrary, since recent approaches tend to treat deviance as *being* a product or even a type of interpersonal and collective *oppression,* a major inference to be drawn from most of these studies is that deviantizing has produced much unnecessary and undesirable social harm. Regardless of any such conclusions, however, deviantizing is, in any case, a central part of the social world in which we live, and, as such, it merits sociological investigation. Such investigation should indeed include consideration of those who impose deviantizing as well as those

who personally experience it. But these two focal points for research and interpretation are not mutually exclusive; in fact, they are two sides of the same coin.
Studying the situation of particular categories of stigmatized persons in no way
implies "approval" of their stigmatization anymore than direct study of poor
people implies the researcher's approval of their poverty. If an investigator fails
to recognize and take account of the role of the powerful in creating these situations, the analysis is bound to be incomplete. On balance, there is little evidence
that recent students of deviance have fallen into such a trap.

　　At its core, the radical critique expresses a deeply felt concern that recent
work in the area of deviance may have diverted the attention of sociologists
away from some of the most pressing problems facing our type of society. In
essence, these critics are arguing that the problems of drug addicts, homosexuals,
and mental patients are not as important overall as such major institutionalized
problems as poverty, racism, sexism, distorted economic priorities, and the "warfare state." Many deviance specialists might well agree with this judgment. Yet
*all of these problems constitute legitimate, indeed, necessary topics for socio-
logical study.* Exploring deviantness—its meanings, functions, uses, and abuses—
focuses attention on some central and vital aspects of the complex and variegated
drama of human social life. There is every reason to believe that the new directions in deviance interpretation not only are helping us to view these aspects
with heightened awareness and understanding, but also may contribute usefully
to the development of a more humane society.

REFERENCES

Ball, Donald W.
1967. "An Abortion Clinic Ethnography," *Social Problems,* 14(Winter), 293–310.

Becker, Howard S.
1967. "Whose Side Are We On?" *Social Problems,* 14(Winter), 239–247.

Bok, Sissela
1978. *Lying: Moral Choice in Public and Private Life.* New York: Pantheon Books.

Carlin, Jerome
1966. *Lawyers' Ethics.* New York: Russell Sage Foundation.

Douglas, Jack D., ed.
1972. *Research on Deviance.* New York: Random House, Inc.

Erikson, Kai T.
1967. "A Note on Disguised Observation in Sociology," *Social Problems,* 14(Spring), 366–
373.

Freidson, Eliot
1970. *Profession of Medicine.* New York: Dodd, Mead & Company.

Goode, Erich
1969. "Multiple Drug Use Among Marijuana Smokers," *Social Problems,* 17(Summer), 48–64.

Gouldner, Alvin W.
1968. "The Sociologist as Partisan," *The American Sociologist,* May, 103–116.

Humphreys, Laud
1975. *Tearoom Trade.* Chicago: Aldine Publishing Company.

Lee, Nancy Howell
1969. *The Search for an Abortionist.* Chicago: University of Chicago Press.

Liazos, Alexander
1972. "The Poverty of the Sociology of Deviance: Nuts, Sluts, and Preverts," *Social Problems,* 20(Summer), 103–120.

Manders, Dean
1975. "Labelling Theory and Social Reality: A Marxist Critique," *The Insurgent Sociologist,* 6(Fall), 53–65.

Mankoff, Milton
1971. "Societal Reaction and Career Deviance: A Critical Analysis," *The Sociological Quarterly,* 12(Spring), 204–218.

McCall, George and Jerry Simmons
1969. *Issues in Participant Observation.* Reading, Mass.: Addison-Wesley Publishing Co., Inc.

Nejelski, Paul and Kurt Finsterbusch
1973. "The Prosecutor and the Researcher," *Social Problems,* 21(Summer), 3–21.

O'Donnell, John A., *et al.*
1976. *Young Men and Drugs—A Nationwide Survey.* Rockville, Md.: National Institute on Drug Abuse.

Polsky, Ned
1967. *Hustlers, Beats, and Others.* Chicago: Aldine Publishing Company.

Quinney, Richard
1974. *Critique of Legal Order.* Boston: Little, Brown and Company.
1977. *Class, State and Crime.* New York: David McKay Co., Inc.

Rossi, Alice S.
1966. "Abortion Laws and their Victims," *transaction,* Sept.–Oct.

Sarvis, Betty and Hyman Rodman
1974. *The Abortion Controversy, 2nd ed.* New York: Columbia University Press.

Schur, Edwin M.
1965. *Crime Without Victims.* Englewood Cliffs, N.J.: Prentice-Hall, Inc.
1968. "Abortion," *The Annals of the American Academy of Political and Social Science,* 376(March), 136–147.

Silver, Isidore, ed.
1974. *The Crime-Control Establishment.* Englewood Cliffs, N.J.: Prentice-Hall, Inc.

Thio, Alex
1973. "Class Bias in the Sociology of Deviance," *The American Sociologist,* 8(February), 1–12.

Tonry, Michael H.
1976. "Juvenile Justice and the National Crime Commissions," in Margaret Rosenheim, ed., *Pursuing Justice for the Child.* Chicago: University of Chicago Press. Pp. 281–298.

Whyte, William Foote
1955. *Street Corner Society.* Chicago: University of Chicago Press.

EPILOGUE:
Prospects for the Future

———

In this text, we have charted the course of development in deviance theory from an early reliance on notions of pathology and differentiation to more recent recognition of "ordinariness" and even basicness. An important related development has been the "decompartmentalizing" of the sociology of deviance itself, which has moved from a somewhat tangential or secondary position within its parent discipline to one of increasing centrality. In the process, there has been a greater interpenetration between various subfields and subject-matter areas of sociology. As a result, contributions from such fields as organizational sociology, the sociology of minority relations, and general social psychological theory have enriched the study of deviance situations.

The definitional and processual orientations that have dominated recent work in this field have helped to highlight the general nature and central role in social relations of the processes that shape deviance situations. Deviance sociology is seen no longer as consisting of disconnected studies of separate "social problems," but rather as a reasonably unified effort to produce theoretical formulations that apply across a wide range of substantively varied situations. The prospects are that this trend toward unification and centrality will continue. The fact that deviance is now widely seen to be a matter of definition does not mean that it can be "defined away," either through radical social change or through new formulations used by sociologists themselves. While the radical sociologist's vision of a society in which "the deviance sociologist would no longer be necessary" is an appealing one, as we have already noted, there is little reason to expect such conditions to arise soon or even to be realistically conceivable. On the contrary, comparative findings seem strongly to support the thesis that some deviantizing is virtually inevitable—whether the dominant forces attach deviantness to bank robbers or to bank presidents, to drug addicts or drug manufacturers, to radicals or counterrevolutionaries. Nor can new modes of theorizing in sociology itself be expected to afford some way of refuting or bypassing this apparent fact of social life.

The foregoing statements are not meant primarily as a dismal forecast. A reorienting of social priorities and a restructuring of our social institutions coupled with increased perceptiveness and tolerance for diversity can produce beneficial changes in many current deviance situations. Likewise, new research and reformulations in deviance theory can bring added data and insights to bear on our general understanding of deviance phenomena. It is the basic processes that will persist, as do all basic features of interaction and social structure. To recognize this is not to adopt a defeatist stance. Indeed, realism about and systematic interpretation of those features of social life that we would prefer not to encounter may well be a necessary step on the path to improving the human situation.

APPENDIX

A PARADIGM
FOR STUDYING
DEVIANCE SITUATIONS

─────────

INTRODUCTION

The purpose in presenting this Paradigm is to bring together in one place a statement of major focal points and topics for research to be attended in studying deviance. Such a listing should not only constitute a useful review tool for students in deviance courses, it should also serve as a helpful guide in connection with any more specific investigation of a deviance situation.

The Paradigm is built around four major focal points: The Collective Definitions, The Deviation, Deviance-Processing, and The (Resulting) "Social Problem." More specific research topics are indicated in the form of questions. These are questions that would call for investigation in a fully comprehensive analysis of almost any (perhaps every) substantive area or situation involving deviance-defining. It should be emphasized that this outline of focal points and research topics is in no way meant to constitute or even suggest a "theory of deviance." Although clearly influenced by "labeling" and other definition-processual ("interpretive") approaches, it draws at various points on other major perspectives as well. The aim is to indicate important "lines of analysis," rather than one integrated "system" of logically interrelated "propositions." The questions listed are not mutually exclusive; indeed, some appear in slightly different forms more than once, since similar analytic topics may arise despite the adoption of different initial points of departure. The Paradigm seeks to incorporate various levels of analysis—microsociological and macrosociological. Furthermore, it is not wedded to any particular research method. Methods of inquiry are not spe-

507

cifically referred to in the Paradigm; clearly, they will vary depending on the kinds of questions one is seeking to answer.

As some readers may recognize, a paradigm of this sort is quite different from the famous "Paradigm for Functional Analysis" presented by Robert Merton in *Social Theory and Social Structure*. Merton's effort constituted a guide for using one particular theoretical orientation (functional theory), and it contained "the minimum set of concepts" needed in undertaking that type of analysis (Merton, 1949, esp. pp. 49–55). The present "guide" is limited to one (admittedly very broad) substantive area—deviance—but it reflects the interests of diverse theoretical traditions and is closer to a "maximum" set of questions or topics than a minimum one. The intention here is to suggest the broad parameters of an "ideal" comprehensive framework for interpretation. Obviously, no single research project or analysis could be expected to explore adequately all or even a a large proportion of the relevant questions. Indeed, many worthwhile studies in specific areas might be limited to one or two of the research topics listed, each of which could, of course, be specified still further in terms of sudsidiary questions, special features of the particular situations investigated, research designs and strategies, and so on. At the same time, however, familiarity with a comprehensive framework of this kind should help any deviance analyst to orient specific investigations and to keep in mind the multidimensional multileveled nature of deviance situations.

REFERENCE

Merton, Robert K.
1949. *Social Theory and Social Structure*. Glencoe, Ill.: The Free Press.

A Paradigm
for Studying
Deviance Situations

FOCAL POINT ONE: THE COLLECTIVE DEFINITIONS

Section A. In this Particular Group or Society
(at the Present Time)

A1. *Nature and Distribution of the Collective Definitions*
 • Is there a coherent and clearly dominant collective definition (i.e., conceptualization and characterization) of behavior or condition X?
 • If so, what exactly is it, and how intensely is it held?
 • Are there other significant patterns of definition regarding behavior X held within the group or society? If so, what are they and how intensely are they held?
 • What is the social distribution of these several definitions (i.e., who holds which conceptions)?
 • What are the (types and) degrees of deviantness typically or potentially associated with X under the same characterizations?
 • Or, to put this another way, what are the tolerance limits for X exhibited in connection with the different definitions?
 • Do these collective tolerance levels for X vary systematically (e.g., depending on socioeconomic or other status of offending individuals, subtypes of the behavior or condition, other situational factors, etc.)?
 • What are the dominant and other significant rationales or rationalizations offered for the several patterns of imputing of deviantness in connection with X?

A2. *Groundings and Functions of the Collective Definitions*
 • What is the social distribution and accuracy of knowledge about behavior X and about individuals engaging in behavior X?
 • What is the nature of the dominant perceptual processes through which collective characterizations of X are made (e.g., to what extent based on direct experience, selective perception, rumor, etc.)?
 • Are there widely held stereotypes that are influential in determining characterizations of X? If so, how have they arisen and how have they been sustained?
 • What are the roles of informal socialization and formal education as they affect collective characterizations of X?
 • What part do the mass media play in this connection?

• Are there religious beliefs or other explicitly moral doctrines that influence the collective definitions of X? Are there political ideologies that influence such definitions?

• Are there scientific theories or findings that influence such definitions? In particular, what, if any, is the role of social science in this connection?

• To what extent and in what ways do collective definitions of X reflect dominant general value emphases within the group or society?

• To what extent and in what ways do they reflect the nature of institutionalized social roles within the group or society? To what extent and in what ways, the conflicting requirements of sets of institutionalized roles?

A3. *Social Conflict and Legal Institutionalization of the Collective Definitions*

• What is the relationship between the patterning and distribution of collective definitions of X and the general distribution of social power within the group or society?

• What relationship (direct, or indirect) is there between the collective definitions of X and the economic system of the group or society?

• To what extent and in what ways has X given rise to "political" issues or disputes within the group or society?

• What are the elements of "threat" that have helped activate collective imputations of deviantness in connection with X?

• Is there or has there recently been any running struggle explicitly relating to a choice between alternative (competing) collective definitions of X?

• If so, to what extent and in what ways has this struggle reflected or involved the competing (conflicting) interests (economic, political, symbolic, etc.) of specific groups or social categories?

• What factors have influenced the tentative, temporary "outcomes" of any such specific struggles?

• What "functions" do such outcomes and, more generally, the processes of characterizing X serve for the individuals who engage in such defining behavior?

• To what extent and in what ways have collective definitions of X been influenced by organized "moral crusades"? To what extent and in what ways by the activity of individual "moral entrepreneurs"?

• What functions do the processes of defining and reacting to X serve for the collectivity itself? In particular, to what extent and in what ways do these collective definitions and reactions appear to enhance social cohesion and strengthen the collective recognition of social "boundaries" (of group membership, between "deviance" and "conformity," etc.)?

• To what extent have the collective definitions of X been formally institutionalized through legal enactments or rulings?

• If there are laws "against" or relating to X, how are they administered?

• Do any such laws primarily reflect the other forces shaping collective definitions of X, or do they have a strong independent or reinforcing effect in their own right?

• What is the social distribution and accuracy of public knowledge regarding these laws, their administration, and their consequences?

Section B. Temporal and Comparative Aspects

• Has there been a discernible sequential patterning to recent changes in the collective definitions of X?

• In what ways have any such recent changes reflected (perhaps also influenced or reinforced) broader currents of social changes affecting the group or society?

• To what extent have these been value changes? changes in the general structure of power? economic or political changes? ideological changes?

• Taking a broader and longer historical view, what has been the overall course of development over time of collective conceptualizations and characterizations of X?

• What general historical forces have been most influential in shaping this course of development?

• To what extent, if at all, have patterns of change in the collective definition of X reflected specific contemporaneous events? To what extent specific "campaigns" aimed at influencing such definitions?

• To what extent and in what ways have historical fluctuations in the "volume" of X reflected changes in levels of perceived threat and in levels of social reaction, including allocation of "social control" resources?

• In what ways, if at all, do anthropological data and analysis aid our understanding of the collective definitions of behavior X? In particular, what do they reveal about elements of uniformity and variability in the conceptualization and characterization of X?

• Similarly, what do contemporary comparative data tell us about collective definitions of X? Are the same general conceptualizations and characterizations dominant in all modern societies? If not, what kinds of systematic variation exist and to what are such variations attributable?

• Are there comparative variations in the institutional groundings and supports for particular collective definitions of X (e.g., in socialization, religion, media, law, etc.)?

NOTE: In addition to the kinds of questions already listed under Section B, virtually any or all of the research topics included in Section A could also be examined in terms of comparative and historical data. The same is true of most items to be listed below (under Focal Points Two, Three, and Four), which will be worded, however, as they would be if they arose in connection with studies limited to a particular group or society.

FOCAL POINT TWO: THE DEVIATION

Section A. Occurrence of the Behavior
(or Condition)

A1. *Distribution and Etiology*

• What is the actual frequency of occurrence of behavior X in the general population?

• To what extent, if at all, does this vary from the official or other formal statistics regarding the frequency of X? How can one account for this variation?

• What is the actual social distribution among categories of the general population of instances of X?

• In what ways does this distribution vary from that indicated in the formal statistics? How can one account for this variation?

• What factors are influential in leading individuals to engage in or exhibit X?

• Does an understanding of X require an explanation in terms of "special" causes to a greater extent than some counterpart "conforming" behavior would?

• To what extent and in what ways, if any, apart from involvement in X itself, do individuals who engage in or exhibit X systematically differ from individuals who do not?

• To what extent, if at all, do instances of or involvement in X reflect the voluntary choices and acts of the individuals so involved?

A2. *Contextual Features*

• To what extent and in what ways is the occurrence of X a reflection of institutionalized roles and values in the group or society? To what extent and in what ways a reflection of characteristic role conflicts?

• What are the situational contexts and settings in which X typically occurs? Particularly, to what extent is X an individual phenomenon? To what extent is it a group phenomenon? Is any group aspect essential to the nature of X or incidental to it?

• What are the learned aspects of X? And what are the social processes through which these aspects are learned? In particular, is there a special "subculture" that facilitates such learning? Must the individual be "accepted" in same in order to engage in or exhibit X "properly"?

• To what extent and under what circumstances is X likely to be a discrete (unrepeated) act? a repeated act? a continuing activity or persisting condition?

• How much public visibility does X have? Does this vary significantly according to specific situational contexts?

Section B. Characterizations of the Behavior or Condition (Attachment of Deviantness)

B1. *Nature and Uses of Characterizations*
   • What meanings do the individuals who engage in or exhibit X attribute to their own behavior or condition?
   • Do these self-characterizations vary systematically according to X's visibility, degree or threat of negative sanctions, directly experienced reactions of others, etc.?
   • How are individuals who engage in or exhibit X or who are perceived as doing so typically defined and reacted to by others?
   • What systematic variations, if any, do these definitions and reactions disply? How can one account for any such variations?
   • In particular, what types and degrees of deviantness are assigned to such individuals and under what circumstances?
   • To what extent does the deviantness assigned in connection with X incorporate imputations of wrongdoing? of distastefulness? of incapacity?
   • In what ways and to what extent do stereotypes regarding X (or the individuals who engage in or exhibit X) enter into these reactions?
   • To what extent is the perception by others of individuals who engage in or exhibit X dominated by their awareness of the latter's involvement in X?
   • In what specific ways does such awareness produce "retrospective interpretations" (rereadings of the biographies and characters of such individuals)?
   • How likely is it that individuals who engage in or exhibit X will directly experience the reactions of others to it and to them? Which others, and what specific forms of reaction?
   • In particular, how likely is it that their involvement in X will be publicly revealed or bring them into contact with formal agents or agencies of "social control" (e.g., law enforcement, treatment, rehabilitative, etc.)?

B2. *Stigma and its Avoidance*
   • What feelings of stigmatization are typically experienced by individuals who engage in or exhibit X?
   • Are there systematic variations in the experiencing of such feelings and, if so, what accounts for them?
   • To what extent, in what ways, and with what likely degree of success do individuals consciously seek to conceal their involvement in X?
   • What are the characteristic strains and problems connected with any such efforts at concealment?
   • When the individuals do succeed in maintaining concealment, to what extent and in what ways are they nonetheless affected by their awareness of potential disclosure and the negative reactions that would then be likely?
   • What is the role of individual resources (socioeconomic, psychological,

other) in enabling individuals involved in X to shield themselves from and/or reduce the impact on them of stigmatizing reactions?

• To what extent does a special subculture provide morale-enhancing support and a means of collective adaptation for individuals who engage in or exhibit X?

• Which aspects of any such subculture are primarily "defensive" or "secondary" in nature (attributable to existing or potential reactions of others)? Which are more directly "intrinsic" to X itself?

• Are there "techniques of neutralization," collective ideologies, organized resistance efforts, or additional means by which individuals involved in X resist or disavow imputations or deviantness?

• Are there characteristic "careers in X" (standard sequences of developing involvements and self-conceptions)? If so, to what extent and in what respects are they self-imposed, and to what extent imposed through the reactions of others (i.e., which aspects of behavior and self-conceptions are "primary," which "secondary")?

• To what extent and under what circumstances is an individual who engages in or exhibits X likely to get "caught up" in such a career ("role engulfment")?

• How easy or difficult is it for individuals who have engaged in or exhibited X (or who have been inaccurately perceived as doing so) to "reverse" such a career or to "shed" the associated stigmatizing labels?

NOTE: Most of the items in this section are worded so as to refer to individuals who "engage in or exhibit" X. It should be kept in mind that usually *being perceived as* engaging in or exhibiting the behavior or condition (whether or not this perception is accurate) will suffice to activate the deviantizing conceptions and reactions.

FOCAL POINT THREE: DEVIANCE-PROCESSING

Section A. Nature and Extent of Deviance-Processing Mechanisms

A1. *Types and Distribution*

• Do social reactions to X occur primarily on an individual (informal) basis, or are there significant types of collective (and more formal) reaction?

• In particular, are there formal organizations ("agencies of social control") either especially concerned with X or "dealing with" it on a regular basis?

• If so, to what extent are these agencies public ("official")? To what extent private?

• To what extent are these agencies involved in "people-processing?" To what extent are they involved in other X-related program activities?

• Is there some set of interrelated organizations dealing with individuals who engage in or exhibit X such that we can speak of an X-processing "system?"

• What is the overall size and strength of such X-processing system? What factors determine same? What are the economic ramifications of such a system?

• In any such system, is there a regularized sequence of processing stages (either within one agency or involving several agencies)?

• If there are treatment, rehabilitation, or correctional institutions relating to X, to what extent are these institutions closed ("total institutions") and to what extent "open?"

A2. *Screening and Processing of "Cases"*

• What are the typical ways in which specific instances of X (or individuals believed to be involved in same) are first identified and brought to the attention of control agencies?

• In particular, is this initial screening "proactive" (made by control agents themselves) or "reactive" (brought about by referral to them from members of the general public)?

• To what extent is this initial screening "representative" of the overall frequency of X and its actual distribution in various categories of the general population?

• Where systematic collective or agency efforts are made to identify and select "cases" of X for "processing," what is the distribution of such efforts over time and from place to place? (continuous? periodic? cyclical? sporadic? evenly distributed? heavily concentrated? etc.).

• What factors account for any such distribution, and what are the apparent consequences of such distribution?

• What are the stated rationales for selection and processing efforts and practices? (protection of the public? protection of the X-involved individuals themselves? "early identification and treatment" of such individuals? etc.).

• What specific criteria of selection are used by those who implement the initial screening and later stages of X-processing?

• To what extent does "typification" (categorization according to limited and superficial cues) of cases and individuals occur?

• To what extent does "case mortality" (winnowing-out of cases at successive stages of processing) occur along systematically patterned lines, so that individuals in some social categories run greater "categoric risks" than do those in others of being passed along to subsequent processing stages?

• If this occurs, what accounts for it? In particular, to what extent, if at all, is it a consequence of processing "bias?" To what extent a reflection of actual patterned case differences?

• To what extent and in what ways does the availability or nonavailability of perceived alternative social control options (informal as well as formal) influence initial selection and "case mortality" processes relating to X?

• What is the substantive nature of the practices employed or administered in the X-processing system (including any correctional, treatment, or rehabilitation programs)?

• If aspects of X-processing involve the legal institutions, to what extent are formal legal safeguards guaranteed and general ideals of the legal system adhered to?

Section B. Organizational and Interorganizational Aspects

B1. *Organizational Goals, Internal Relationships, and Needs*

• To what extent do the practices and policies of the organization (or set of X-processing organizations) reflect a multiplicity of or uncertainty about possibly conflicting organizational goals?

• To what extent and in what ways do any such conflicts or uncertainties influence intrastaff relationships in X-processing organizations?

• What are the nature and implications of client-client and staff-client relationships within the organization? More particularly, in "total institutions," what is the extent and influence of "informal inmate subculture" and what are the informal understandings and accommodations between inmates and custodial personnel?

• How does the "life history" of any X-processing organization help to account for its current practices and policies? In particular, what have been the nature and impact of patterns of organizational stability and change?

• To what extent and in what ways, is X-processing influenced by a "displacement of goals," whereby the organization's own "needs" take precedence over stated aims relating to "dealing with" X?

• In particular, how does the organization's need to maintain a relatively smooth-working system influence the substance of its work?

• Are there dominant and other significant organizational ideologies regarding X, and, if so, what role do they play in shaping organizational programs and policies?

• To what extent, if at all, do the organizations have a "vested interest" (through concern with their own survival) in particular X-processing programs and policies? In what ways has this influenced their activities?

B2. *External Organizational Relationships*

• To what extent and in what ways is the work of the (any such) organization influenced by its ongoing relations with other social control agencies (i.e., by being part of a larger X-processing or broader deviance-processing system)?

• To what extent and in what ways is it affected by ongoing relations with any other kinds of local organizations, including political-party organizations and governmental agencies?

• What are the organization's major sources of funding (public or private) and general support, and what roles do these play in shaping its policies and practices?

• To what extent and in what ways does "public opinion" (particularly in the organization's immediate locale) influence its activities?

• In particular, how do dominant ideologies and understandings regarding X and its "treatment" affect the work of the organization?

• In what forms are X-processing organizations held "accountable" with respect to the substance of their work? What are the commonly applied criteria of "success"? Are there formal evaluations and, if so, of what sort, or are the grounds of accountability typically vague and impressionistic?

• To what extent and in what ways do specific incidents (e.g., released "mental patient" gets into subsequent trouble) affect public perceptions of the organization and its work?

• At the same time, how is reaction to such incidents determined by the continuously evolving general public perceptions regarding X and regarding the organization?

Section C. Role of the Control Agent

• Which specific types of control agents having standardized occupational roles are especially important in the processing of X?

• What are the typical socioeconomic and educational backgrounds of such control agents? How, if at all, may this affect relevant current attitudes and behavior patterns?

• More generally, what are the patterns of recruitment to this social control occupation? What formal occupational training do agents receive? What are the likely consequences or implications of these recruitment and training processes?

• What is the relative social standing and pecuniary reward pattern for this occupation? How do these affect the control agent's work?

• What is the typical nature of informal on-the-job socialization, and what are the implications of this experience in shaping attitude development and routine practices?

• In particular, to what extent, if at all, is the control agent's work made difficult by uncertainty and danger? public accountability? inadequate resources for doing the job? confused or contradictory mandates? absence of needed scientific findings or theories? unattainable social control goals? bureaucratic entanglements?

• In line with the last of these, to what extent is the control agent's work influenced by membership in a social control organization and by his or her specific position in the organization's hierarchical structure?

• Which are the members of the agent's typical "role-set," and how does interaction with them affect the agent's situation?

• To what extent do organizational ideologies influence the agent's work?

• Overall, what are the characteristic "role strains" (or role conflicts) experienced in connection with exercising the control agent's role? How are these strains reflected in the processing of X?

• To what extent is this social control occupation "professionalized" (seen as a profession by others as well as by the agents themselves), and what are the implications of this for the processing of X?

• Are control agents organized in specific professional associations or other similar occupational organizations, and of what significance are any such organizations?

• To what extent does the control agent have a vested economic interest in the continued existence of particular X-processing programs and practices? in specific social control organizations and systems? in particular ideologies regarding X or regarding "deviance" more generally? in the social definition of X, specifically, as "deviant"?

• To what extent and in what ways (direct or indirect) do any such interests influence the processing of X?

NOTE: Most, if not all, of the items relating to control organizations and control agents could be applied in connection with analysis pursued *either* within (or in terms of) a single X-processing organization *or* within a broader X-processing system (organizational network).

FOCAL POINT FOUR: THE (RESULTING) "SOCIAL PROBLEM"

• To what extent (which aspects, how consistently, and with what degree of intensity) and by whom is X viewed or reacted to as a general "social problem" about which "something should be done?"

• To what extent is there evident a "natural history" in the development of and changes in social characterizations of X as a social problem? What are the major "stages" in this course of development? And what has been their significance with respect to practices and policies relating to X?

• What are the typical purported "solutions" that are urged or attempted in relation to X as a social problem (e.g., punishment, treatment, reformation, etc.)? By whom and in what ways are these steps urged or attempted?

• Are there discernible conflicts over purported solutions, and what factors determine or influence the tentative, temporary "outcomes" of any such conflicts?

• To what extent and in what ways are there now "public policies" regarding X or individuals who engage in or exhibit X?

• To what extent and in what ways do any such public policies incorporate or reflect conceptions of X as illness? as wrongdoing? as deficiency, incapacity, or incompetence?

• To what extent and in what ways do any such policies accord authority for "dealing with" X (or individuals who engage in or exhibit X) to the medical profession? to treatment, rehabilitation, or other "helping" personnel? to the legal system (including law enforcement personnel)? to educational authorities? to other authoritative agencies or agents?

• To what extent and in what ways do such policies reflect an assignment of "personal responsibility" to individuals for engaging in or exhibiting X? To what extent do they assign some form of diminished responsibility and, in connection with a "rehabilitative ideal," substitute other parties to compulsorily act "on behalf of" the individuals in question?

• To what extent are the stated goals of extant policies: prevention and deterrence of X? treatment or rehabilitation of individuals who engage in X? punishment of such individuals or retribution for their actions?

• What are the typical sanctions imposed or "help" offered in the course of implementing such policies? What are the apparent consequences of same? To what extent and by what criteria are such consequences evaluated? What is the extent and accuracy of public knowledge of any such assessments?

• To what extent and in what ways have concepts of personal privacy and individual freedom influenced or entered significantly into public debates concerning public policies regarding X?

• Is there a vocal body of opinion to the effect that X is *not* a social "problem," that is, that nothing should be "done about it"? What are the distribution and apparent influence of such opinions?

• Overall, what are the *(reciprocal)* interrelationships between X as a "social problem" and public policies toward X? Which aspects of the overall problem situation are "primary" (attributable primarily to the nature of the behavior itself or the individuals engaged in it) and which aspects "secondary" (largely a consequence of the policies themselves)?

• To what extent do any groups or social categories have vested interests in the continuing characterization and treatment of X as a social problem? In what ways and with what consequences are those interests manifested as part of the overall X-problem situation?

NOTE: This section lists only a relatively small number of research topics or questions that may be highlighted when one adopts a "social problem" point of departure. It should be evident that, in a sense, any and all of the items in the previous sections would in some manner fit into such an analysis. To the extent a "social problem" exists, it is a kind of composite of (one might even say it is "produced" or "constituted" through) the three other facets of the deviance situation—the collective definition, the deviation, and the deviance-processing.

FINAL PROJECT
"Creating" a Form of Deviance

Introductory Comment

Deviance, it has been emphasized here, is a "social construction." Just what does this mean? As we have seen, one way of appreciating this aspect of deviance situations is to think of them as "outcomes" that have been produced or shaped by certain kinds of defining-reacting processes. Central to such situations are characterizations (of behaviors or conditions, and of individuals) that impute and affix "deviantness"; that disvalue and degrade, set apart, render alien, stigmatize. We have, throughout this book, examined a great many kinds of factors that may contribute to such outcomes. As a culminating exercise, one that requires drawing on most if not all the basic themes developed in this text, it may now be helpful for the student to actually try to "use" the "social construction" idea.

Part and parcel of that idea, as we have seen, is the assumption that *any* behavior or condition or type of individual is *potentially* subject to "deviantizing." In this connection, we have noted the possibility of considerable variations in meaning-attributions from place to place, over time, and so on. As we have also seen, deviance-defining processes are intimately tied up with (both reflecting and, in a way, constituting part of) social change. From this standpoint, shifts in the "construction" of deviance usually are part of a relatively gradual, unconsciously participated-in, uncertainly evolving process incorporating numerous changes within a society. At the same time, however, as also mentioned above, individuals and groups frequently do make conscious efforts to increase or decrease the deviantness typically associated with various kinds of behavior and conditions. Indeed, the social construction outlook even seems to imply that it may be *possible* to *intentionally* "create" deviance. Thus, if one were to push this notion to its logical extreme, one should hypothetically be able to "convert" conformity to deviance. Presumably, in democratic societies this does not often happen in such a blatant self-conscious way; however, thinking about what such a conversion process might entail or require helps us to appreciate more fully the changes in deviantness that do occur all the time in a more subtle manner. Of course, we should recall, too, when we consider the possibility of "conversion," the fallacy of either-or conceptions of deviance. Since it is usually more realistic to think in terms of degrees of deviantness, it probably makes more sense to frame a hypothetical deviance-creation exercise in terms of *increasing* or *decreasing* deviantness than to explore possibilities for more absolute intentional change between "present-or-absent" type categories.

Assignment

Select any form of behavior or condition that is not heavily subjected to deviance-defining in present-day society and explain in as much detail as possible all of the things that might be done in order to attach more deviantness to it.

As the comments above suggest, the more "startling" and extreme (but, in one sense, more revealing) form of this exercise would be to explore the "conversion" of a kind of behavior or condition that currently receives high overall approval in our society. If such behaviors can be "deviantized," then (we easily see) any can. Examples of subject matters for this version of the exercise would be having children, practicing personal cleanliness, going to church (note how this *has* been "deviantized" in the Soviet Union), being faithful to one's spouse, being extremely thin, being oriented to heterosexuality. In the more modest and "realistic" version of the project, the focus would be placed on increasing the degree of deviantness attaching to some behavior or condition already commonly viewed and treated as being somewhat problematic. For such purposes, appropriate examples might include the following: being a socialist, engaging in premarital cohabitation, eating a high cholesterol diet, practicing income tax "avoidance," smoking cigarettes (with respect to which we have already noted some recent change), being an avowed atheist, being left-handed, discriminating against people on the basis of sex (obviously undergoing considerable change at this time), being a "bully" (schoolchildren), engaging in "excessive daydreaming," reading pornographic books.

You can do either version of the project or both, depending on your own inclination or your instructor's or the class's decision. Again, the project can be done on either an individual or a group basis. It should fit nicely into a group discussion format, with the student "audience" appraising and amending the efforts of individual "presenters." Equally workable would be a "team" approach in which group discussion and preparation among sets of students collaborating on the various deviance-creation proposals precede the class presentations.

Guidelines

Keep in mind that you are only supposed to *propose* a plan for increasing deviance, to show *how* one would go about that. Do *not*, therefore, *undertake* such efforts yourself (e.g., by trying to stigmatize your thin acquaintances). You will have more than enough to do if you limit yourself to *figuring out all the things* that *might* be done or would have to be done to increase the deviantizing in question. The following suggestions may be helpful.

1. Assume you have unlimited funds and other relevant resources at your disposal in order to launch your deviantizing campaign. This will permit you to be ambitious in what you propose, to include efforts that might be "expensive," and it should make it easier for you to come up with the "optimal" program for deviantizing.

2. Remember to be comprehensive. There are many "levels" on which and areas in which you might take action aimed at increasing the overall deviantizing of the behavior or condition in our society. In particular, keep in mind that this may involve both "public" and "private" aspects. Presumably, you will want to alter public conceptions, possibly public policies, private attitudes and behaviors, and ultimately, perhaps, the self-conceptions of those engaging in or displaying the problematic behavior or condition. Do not hesitate to consider and trace out the implications of *all* the steps you might include. Use the Paradigm as a "guide." Though it is geared to the *study* of deviance situations, it should also serve to indicate key "pressure points" and "objectives" for any deviantizing campaign.

3. Be imaginative. There is no need to be bound by conventional thinking and currently prevailing patterns; indeed, the whole point of the exercise is to alter these. (For example, if there are current stereotypes about "fat" people, that is no reason why there might not be (created) such stereotypes about "thin" people.) Also, do not be inhibited by any feeling that somehow the various elements in your overall campaign must fit together neatly. All that is necessary is that they all work effectively toward your general goal of increasing deviantness.

4. To introduce a realistic note, your consideration of various steps to take should include an awareness of apparent obstacles that would have to be surmounted. This is the other side of the "being imaginative" point. (Thus, though you should not assume it would be impossible to have negative stereotypes about "thinnies," one of the problems you would nonetheless have to overcome in trying to disseminate them would be the various kinds of favorable views about thinness that currently prevail and such specific aspects of this as the association of thinness among women with "fashion models.") In a sense, of course, the entire deviantness-increasing project represents a battle to overcome such obstacles. Discussion of key impediments to the change you are attempting and decisions as to how they might best be dealt with represent important components of your proposal.

5. Again, be comprehensive in thinking about obstacles. They may range from prevailing prejudice to existing legislation, from ingrained habit to economic "vested interests." Indeed, potentially, every focal point for change is also a focal point of resistance to change.

Implications

The possibility that specific patterns of deviance can be intentionally "produced" or increased also suggests that they can be "eliminated" or decreased. Obviously, this should be encouraging to those who see much current deviance-defining as representing social oppression. But the most significant point highlighted by the exercise should be the "constructed" nature of all deviance situations. Examining the "building materials" used in such a construction process should help students to recognize not only that deviance-defining is subject to change, but also that, ultimately, we are all responsible for those definitions currently imposed. We maintain them either directly by providing one or another concerted type of support or indirectly by acquiescing in, rather than attempting to overturn the current state of affairs.

INDEXES

NAME INDEX

SUBJECT INDEX

80 81 82 9 8 7 6 5 4 3 2